LATIN AMERICAN POLITICS

ROBERT D. TOMASEK, a Professor of Political Science at the University of Kansas, is a specialist on Latin American politics who also has an interest in the new approaches to the study of underdeveloped politics. He received his B.A. from Grinnell College, studied at the School of Advanced International Studies of Johns Hopkins University, and received his M.A. and Ph.D. from the University of Michigan. Mr. Tomasek has traveled extensively throughout most of Latin America, and under a Doherty research grant spent a year in Chile studying its party system. He has contributed a chapter on Costa Rican politics to a current textbook, and has written articles which have appeared in the *Journal of Politics, Midwest Journal of Political Science, Political Science Quarterly, Combate, Orbis,* and the *Journal of Inter-American Studies.* His present research interests are on political parties of Latin America and the capabilities of the Organization of American States to settle disputes.

LATIN AMERICAN POLITICS

Studies of the Contemporary Scene

Edited by Robert D. Tomasek

Second edition revised and updated

Anchor Books
Doubleday & Company, Inc.
Garden City, New York
1970

Latin American Politics was originally published in an Anchor Books edition in 1966.

Revised Anchor Books edition: 1970

Library of Congress Catalog Card Number 77-111192

Printed in the United States of America

For Ruth

PREFACE TO THE FIRST EDITION

It is hoped that this book of readings will develop an interest in and lead to a better understanding of the politics of Latin America. The selections were chosen from books, professional journals, and the American Universities Field Staff reports. An attempt was made to choose a variety of approaches including the comparative, the behavioral, the historical analytical, the problem oriented, and the case study approach. The editor feels that all of these approaches can add to our knowledge of Latin America. Selections were also chosen for their readability and originality. Some have been important enough to revise the major thinking about an aspect of Latin American politics.

The emphasis has been placed on power groups, the political process, and the violent nature of Latin American politics. This is more relevant than describing constitutions and the structure of Latin American governments, since constitutional provisions are often ignored and decision making may occur in unexpected places. Latin American politics are essentially dynamic, involving a variety of actors such as dictators, the middle sectors, political parties, labor, and strong presidents in fluid combinations. This is the pattern also found in many other underdeveloped areas.

This book is divided between a topical approach and a country-by-country approach. Both approaches have utility. The topical approach provides the generalizations that are needed to see what is common throughout Latin America. The country-by-country approach illustrates the certain uniqueness of politics in separate countries. Many of the generalizations of the first selections can be checked against the specific political events discussed in the second part. Generalizations made in the two topical selections on the military, for example, can be tested in the selections dealing with the military in Mexico, Argentina, and Brazil. The country-by-country approach gives evidence of the great variety of politics in Latin America, and makes clear that many of the general political characteristics will have to be modified when applied to specific political events of separate countries. The political systems vary from those that are almost completely modern to those that are extremely backward. Almost all are in a state of change. This is what makes the study of Latin American politics so rich and exciting. There is much to choose from and a variety of ways to focus on the changing Latin American scene.

The editor wishes to thank all of the scholars and publishers who have given generous permission to reprint the selections chosen. Individual acknowledgments to authors have been listed with each selection.

Robert D. Tomasek

PREFACE TO THE SECOND EDITION

The basic format of the second edition of this book of readings has not changed considerably from the first. The book is still divided between a topical and country-by-country approach, still emphasizing power groups and the dynamics of the political scene within each state.

There has been one important change, however. Many selections have been dropped and new ones added. The selections deleted were those felt to be weaker in quality, or those that concentrated too closely on a specific election with the attendant problem of becoming out of date. In picking new selections I deliberately attempted to find materials that either focused on the conceptualization of political phenomena and/or demonstrated imagination and rigor in research methodology. The Latin American politics field badly needs conceptualizations; a good research design is exciting for both the professor and student and makes the acceptance of its findings much more likely. In 1969 there was a greater choice of materials than in 1965, when both editions were prepared. The editor still feels, however, that selections of high quality are especially difficult to find and that Latin American political study has far to go before it can rest on its laurels.

In many introductions to the selections, I have pointed out controversies among the specialists where controversy exists. Hopefully the reader will not interpret this as a weakness of the field. Controversy is the stuff of academic life and an indicator of a field in flux that is questioning old shibboleths that have stood too long unchallenged. The reader will notice an iconoclasm among some of the contributors that should be welcomed rather than deplored.

It might also be noted that the field is being enriched by the addition of new members. Some are represented in this book of readings. The editor wishes to thank these contributors and all of the other contributors, and their publishers, for permission to use selections from their work.

Robert D. Tomasek

CONTENTS

PART II
The Politics of Separate Countries

Part I

The Problems, Power Groups, Processes, and Forces Affecting Latin American Politics

A CONCEPTUALIZATION OF LATIN AMERICAN POLITICS

A conceptualization of politics in Latin America that gets at the essence of almost all of the many political systems is difficult. Yet Charles W. Anderson, Professor of Political Science at the University of Wisconsin, does this in an extremely perceptive manner. He points out that every political system has many power contenders desiring to gain influence in the government. These power contenders are often split internally, tend to ally in diverse ways with other power contenders, and each has certain power capabilities that it can utilize to make its demands made. Professor Anderson then points out that a demonstration of power and not the actual use of it is often sufficient for a power contender to be taken seriously. If a power contender is admitted to the channels of influence, however, he does this with the understanding that the old elites in government will not be displaced.

Thus Professor Anderson conceives of almost all of the Latin American political systems as museum pieces in that they consist of the old elites plus newly admitted power contenders in a strained and tentative way. With this conceptualization Professor Anderson points out that real change is almost impossible, but at the same time the status quo is hardly ever kept. The conceptualization enables one to look at elections in a different way, and also to rethink the significance of the Mexican and Cuban revolutions.

This conceptualization unfortunately has not been refined or utilized in a book about a specific country. Questions can be raised about whether it can apply to all of Latin America–an exception was made of Mexico and the conceptualization does not seem to fit the Dominican Republic previously under the Trujillo family. Finally, the conceptualization may be at such a highly theoretical level that it would fit the politics of a good portion of the underdeveloped world and not just Latin America. In fact, on reflection, perhaps the conceptualization is not really that different from what happens in most political systems in that inputs are directed toward the decision-making channels, new forces are gradually admitted and become less zealous as they partake of the perquisites of political power, and issues are compromised as they are processed through the political system.

*The Latin American Political System**

CHARLES W. ANDERSON

The problem of winning, consolidating, and maintaining political power is, of course, fundamental to the calculus of political prudence. Even in the most stable of political systems, assessment of the potential consequences of policy choice for future support is basic to the political craft. However, in Latin America, where few leaders can count on a guaranteed tenure in office to work out a strategy of governance, the weighing of potential effects of policy choices on political survival becomes a constant, day-to-day concern. Thus, in assessing the total rationality of development policy-making in Latin America, it becomes essential to devote some attention to the conditions under which political power is won and held in Latin America, and the characteristic ways in which Latin American statesmen cope with the problem of power.

The effort to state propositions about Latin American politics as a whole is immediately beset by certain objections and difficulties. Some of these, concerning the propriety of dealing with Latin American political life as a whole, have

* Reprinted from *Politics and Economic Change in Latin America,* by C. W. Anderson, Copyright © 1967, by Litton Educational Publishing, Inc., by permission of Van Nostrand Reinhold Company.

been discussed in the introduction. However other, perhaps more significant, reasons for skepticism have yet to be met.

Some may doubt the existence of that which could be called a political system in Latin America. Clearly, the political process in many Latin American nations does not correspond to constitutional norms or democratic "rules of the game." Latin American politics appears unstable, whimsical, chaotic. The prevalence of "crisis" makes it appear superficially that the political life of these nations is unpredictable and irregular, that the qualities of persistence and regularity of behavior that denote a social system do not exist. However, although the patterns are unfamiliar to the observer schooled in the processes of Western constitutional government, it would seem that there are certain relatively consistent patterns to the game of Latin American politics. The intervention of the military in politics, the technique of the *coup d'état,* the use of violence and terror as political instruments, insecurity of tenure for constitutionally established governments, are all phenomena that appear over and over again in the political history of the region. The rather rigorously applied conventions concerning political exile and asylum for the losers in power struggles hint at the existence of procedural customs and norms known to the participants.[1] As K. H. Silvert puts it:

> "Unpredictable" and "unstable" are the two adjectives most often applied to Latin American politics. The implications of both pejoratives are partially erroneous. First, to be "unstable" is not necessarily to be "unpredictable." As a matter of fact, one of the easiest things to predict is instability itself. And second, some types of revolutionary disturbance do not indicate instability. If the normal way of rotating the executive in a given country is by revolution, and there have been a hundred such changes in a century, then it is not facetious to remark that revolutions are a sign of stability—that events are marching along as they always have.[2]

[1] See, for example, Robert G. Caldwell, "Exile as an Institution," *Political Science Quarterly,* LVIII (June, 1942), pp. 239–262.

[2] Kalman H. Silvert, *The Conflict Society* (New Orleans: Hauser Press, 1961), p. 20.

Simply, our problem may not be that the notion of political system does not apply to Latin America, but that we have not yet understood the character of the system that exists. At best, we are now aware of the recurring patterns, and have described them, but we have not yet related these patterns to one another in a meaningful way.

The difficulty described above suggests another. There is a problem of the applicability of the models conventionally used by Western political scientists in alien environments. There is a temptation, in explaining Latin American politics, to mysteriously narrow one's eyes and suggest that one cannot know the deeper meaning of all this until one has "lived there," been somehow immersed in the culture of the area. This seems most undesirable. There is, after all, an obligation on the part of the political scientist interested in non-Western or semi-Western cultures to communicate with his professional colleagues, and the difficulties to effective communication are not really insurmountable. If one starts from the common ground rules and understandings of a social science discipline, one can move to modifications and recombinations of these ideas that should be satisfactory. At least, that will be the endeavor here, and despite temptations to begin afresh, an attempt will be made as the argument moves along to phrase ideas in terms of the approaches to politics which are common currency among Western political scientists.

Although we may all wish to adopt the same point of departure, there is no reason why we should all move together the rest of the way. Many of the conventional models of politics, if adopted inflexibly, provide unsatisfactory results if used in societies where their basic presuppositions do not apply. For example, many contemporary analyses of Latin American politics are based explicitly or implicitly on some variation of the "group process" technique. While Scott applied this technique with creditable results to Mexico,[3] its use in other countries or more generally applied to the region has simply not served to describe the political systems that exist. Either the role of Western-styled interest groups is magnified

[3] Robert Scott, *Mexican Government in Tradition* (Urbana: University of Illinois Press, 1959).

out of proportion to their role in the political process, or an effort is made to fit other factors that bear on politics into the interest group mold, thus encouraging the superficial perception of similarity in political process to the Western model where none in fact exists.[4] Of course, the identification and description of the prominent aggregations sharing common political interests and having an impact on politics is one commonsense point of departure for the discussion of Latin American politics. Like most other contemporary analyses of the subject, our discussion will use this as a prominent point of focus. But we cannot be satisfied by merely listing the more prominent of these "groups." We must go on to specify something of the pattern of their interaction, something of the system they describe, and in so doing, we shall be moving into relatively unexplored terrain.

Power Contenders and Power Capabilities in Latin American Politics

The first proposition that must be specified concerning politics in most Latin American nations is that there is imperfect consensus on the nature of the political regime. This in itself is not surprising, nor does it pose an unusual or difficult problem for political analysis, as witness the capacity of Western political science to cope with the problem of imperfect consensus in such nations as France. Nonetheless, the question of regime consensus, or "legitimacy," has attracted considerable attention in much current writing on the politics of the developing areas. Seymour Martin Lipset specifies political legitimacy as a critical variable in the process of political development.[5] Martin Needler has used the notion of legitimacy as a central concept in a discussion of political instability in Latin America.[6] However, to specify that

[4] See, for example, George Blanksten, "Political Groups in Latin America," *American Political Science Review*, LIII (March, 1959), pp. 106–127.

[5] Seymour Martin Lipset, "Some Social Requisites of Democracy: Economic Development and Political Legitimacy," *American Political Science Review*, LII (March, 1959), pp. 69–105.

[6] Martin Needler, "Putting Latin American Politics in Perspective," *Inter-American Economic Affairs*, XVI (Autumn, 1962), pp. 41–50.

a particular nation or region has failed to accept one set of institutions or processes as legitimate does not permit one to go much further until the sources and dimensions of that problem, and its particular impact on political life, have been designated and assessed.

To get to the heart of this matter in Latin America, one must shift perspective slightly from the usual development of the argument. Generally, discussions of legitimacy focus on the question of the acceptance of certain political institutions, or a certain locus of authority. In Latin America, however, the problem of legitimacy is very much a part of the political process itself, the way in which individuals and groups mobilize power within the society. For in Latin America, no particular techniques of mobilizing political power, no specific political resources, are deemed more appropriate to political activity than others. No specific sources of political power are legitimate for all contenders for power.

Of course, this is to some extent the case in every society, even those committed most strongly to one source of legitimate power. In the United States, whether we are disciples of C. Wright Mills or not, we recognize that possessors of certain power capabilities, control of legitimate force or economic wealth, for example, make or influence policy, despite the fact that democratic ideology prescribes the aggregation and mobilization of consent as the only legitimate means of structuring power relationships. However, in democratic society, the organization of consent according to prescribed norms is *generally* reinforced by possessors of other power capabilities, and in the long run, democratic processes serve as a sort of "court of last resort" in structuring power relationships. In contrast, in Latin America generally, democratic processes appear as an *alternative* to other means of mobilizing power. However, the point made should be clear, that in suggesting that no power capability is legitimate for all power contenders in Latin America, we are recognizing a difference of degree and not of kind, for the phenomenon applies to some extent in all political systems.

It will be noted that two new terms have been introduced into the discussion. This is not done out of any desire to create a new vocabulary, but to distinguish what is to be said from certain accepted uses of commonplace terms. Hence, a *contender for power* will be defined as any individual or group which seeks to have its demands implemented through state machinery, to control the allocation of values for the society through state machinery, or to make a specific source of power legitimate for the society through the exercise of a power capability. A *power capability* will be defined as a property of a group or individual that enables it to be politically influential, in other words, a political resource. Possession of a power capability is the price of admission to the political arena. Those who possess significant power capabilities will be "taken into account" when political decisions are made.[7]

Power contenders are also distinguished from power capabilities for another reason. Most conventional analysis of Latin American politics, by equating the two, assumes a unity of

[7] Examples of prominent power capabilities in Latin American politics would be:

Semi-legitimate control of armed forces (control of the military institutions and equipment of the nation).

Capacity to mobilize, organize, and aggregate consent.

Capacity to create non-institutionalized violence, terror, or civic disruption.

Traditional authority (control of land and labor force through the pattern of social relations involved in the *latifundia* system).

Control of natural resources, or economic institutions.

Skill at the manipulation and recombination of the abstractions, symbols, and processes involved in complex social organization (bureaucratic expertise).

Various power capabilities may appear, of course, in combination. For example, the power of the Catholic Church in Latin America must be defined as an alloy of traditional authority, ideology, capacity to aggregate consent, and in some instances, economic wealth.

A power contender then, is one who uses a power capability to attain certain specific objectives through political activity, in other words, a political actor. For example:

A military "clique," service, or unit.

A political party, interest group, or movement.

A group or association identified with a specific economic interest.

A community or region.

A family, class, or clique.

"interest" among the holders of a single power capability that is seldom the case.[8] By separating power contenders from power capabilities we avoid saying such things as "the military acts," or "the middle class supports," or "the urban mob or the terrorists are. . .". The use of such gross categories in all contemporary discussion of Latin American politics has led us to accept a rule of thumb theory which we all conventionally employ, but which is both imprecise and inaccurate. Hence, it seems more desirable to postulate a variety of power contenders using or competing for a similar power capability, and a political system that does not legitimate a single power capability, but includes a number of them.

At this point, it would be well to note that Latin American politics cannot be analyzed in terms of nationally self-contained systems. Certainly, foreign power contenders must be included in describing the patterns of alliance and conflict that make and unmake governments in the region. Again, we must distinguish the various power capabilities that serve as tickets of admission for these foreign contenders in the political process–economic assistance, military intervention, ideological influence, and so on. Considerable care must be taken in the units of analysis chosen to describe these foreign contenders. To discuss "United States influence" in Latin America is often most imprecise when the Department of State, the Agency for International Development, the military, and private firms may be pursuing quite diverse political objectives, in patterns of coalition that include distinct domestic sets of power contenders. Similarly, to use "Communist influence" as a single, undivided unit of analysis is to employ a most blunt and imprecise unit of analysis. In dealing with both foreign and domestic contenders for power, one must bear in mind the coalitional character of Latin American politics. The statement that the United States or the Soviet Union "controls" a certain government or movement certainly distorts an intricate arrangement of political forces in which

[8] See, as two examples among many, the "power factors" approach in Harold E. Davis, ed., *Government and Politics in Latin America* (New York: Ronald Press, 1958); and the "middle sector" approach in John J. Johnson, *Political Change in Latin America: The Emergence of the Middle Sectors* (Stanford, Calif.: Stanford University Press, 1958).

the foreign contender is one part of the political equation, but seldom plays an exclusive or totally definitive role.

If one insists on the grosser categories of analysis, one is easily driven to such simplistic logical inferences as, "He who controls the army, controls the government." However, control of the army is seldom secure in Latin America. Various contenders within the military establishment are competing for control of the power capability represented by armed force. In their strategy for gaining political power, such contenders may call into play others who have vastly different power capabilities. Thus, even in the more army-ridden states, politics is not irrelevant.

A more precise reflection of what is involved in the general Latin American political process involves not only the various factions within the military, but their relations to holders of various other power capabilities, parties, interest groups, urban mobs, student agitators, economic and bureaucratic elites—the entire spectrum of political forces operating in the society. For in discussing the role of the military in Latin American politics, one quickly comes to recognize that most military regimes are ended by military action, and that such struggles for power do not involve military action alone. Not so many years ago, many serious students of Latin American affairs predicted that as Latin American armies acquired more modern, lethal armaments, military totalitarianism would become more characteristic of the region, for the firepower that guerrillas and civilian mobs could amass would not be equal to tanks and jet bombers. That their prediction was faulty, for military totalitarianism has not greatly increased since the end of World War II in Latin America, would seem to have something to do with the fact that the prediction was based on a logical extension of a faulty initial premise concerning the relevant units of Latin American politics. For the military is not a rigidly united force in Latin America. Rather, military force is one power capability within the society, but control of that power capability is vigorously contested.

No one, of course, would want to hold that one set of propositions could account in detail for the diverse political circumstances of the twenty Latin American nations. Truly, there is no single political system in Latin America, and one is justified in saying that aggregation of consent is incrementally more important and legitimate as a power capability in Costa Rica or Uruguay, and use of military force more significant in Nicaragua or Paraguay. But to say simply that "Costa Rica is democratic" or "Nicaragua is controlled by the military" misses some significant points about the nature of power relationships in these nations. After all, Costa Rica has thrice had recourse to violent means of adjusting power relationships in the twentieth century, and the political strategy of the Somoza family and their heirs in Nicaragua involves a considerable component of manipulation of consent, the relations among economic elites, and other factors as well as sheer control of armed force.

The following set of propositions is not intended to apply only to the Latin American norm, and to exclude such deviant cases as Costa Rica and Paraguay. Rather, it would seem that they are of assistance in understanding the political dynamics of any Latin American nation, and can be adjusted to individual differences by the process of specifying that certain power capabilities are more effective or legitimate in structuring power relations in some countries than in others. (Thus, although we shall not perform the operation, one could construct a continuum for political classification of Latin American nations on the basis of the relative magnitude of effectiveness of various power capabilities in each.)

The Dynamics of Latin American Politics

The problem of Latin American politics, then, is that of finding some formula for creating agreement between power contenders whose power capabilities are neither comparable (as one measures the relative power of groups in democratic society by reference to votes cast) nor compatible. The political system of Latin America may be described as the pattern by which Latin American statesmen conventionally attempt to cope with this variety of political resources used in their societies, and the way in which holders of these diverse power capabilities characteristically interact one with another.

In restructuring our frame of reference to cope with this unfamiliar state of affairs, we might begin by suggesting that the techniques used in advanced Western nations as means of ratifying power relationships more frequently appear in Latin America as means of demonstrating a power capability. The significance of this can best be seen by examining three prominent techniques which we commonly assume are means of ratifying power relationships (that is, of structuring a regime or government) and reflect on where they fit in the Latin American political scheme of things. These would be election, revolution, and military dictatorship.

Elections are not definitive in many parts of Latin America. However, they are conscientiously and consistently held, and just as conscientiously and consistently annulled. Few Latin American nations can demonstrate an unbroken sequence of elected governments over any substantial period of time. In a sense, our real question is not that of why elections are ignored, but why they are held at all given their inconclusive character.

In Latin America, not all elites accept the constitutional norms of election as definitive. In fact, democratic election is really only relevant for those who possess certain specific skills and support, for those who have the capacity to aggregate consent through political parties and movements and the instruments of mass communication. Insofar as such contenders cannot be ignored by others involved in political life, election, which is the mechanism that tests and confirms their power capability, is part of the political process. But insofar as there are other contenders in the political arena, whose power is not dependent on this kind of popular support, or on popular support at all, elections are but a measure of power and not a means of determining who governs. As a strike may demonstrate the power capability of a labor union, or insurrection that of a military faction, so election tests and demonstrates the power capability of a political party.

Hence, the results of an election are tentative, pending responses by other power contenders. Whether the electorally successful group will be accommodated into the power structure or suppressed depends on subsequent negotiations[9] with

[9] These may actually occur as "negotiation" in the formal sense, but they are just as frequently inferences drawn from the statements and actions of the new contender's leaders.

other power contenders as well as prior perceptions of the threat posed by the movement.

Thus, for example, in Venezuela immediately after World War II, the existing government was overthrown in a military coup that involved the collaboration of a new political party, *Acción Democrática,* with certain dissatisfied elements of the armed forces. Shortly thereafter, the candidate of *Acción Democrática,* Rómulo Gallegos, was formally elected to the presidency. Inexperienced at the "inside" operation of the political system of Venezuela, the leaders of the party accepted the election as definitive, and launched a program which was perceived by the military and certain economic elites to threaten their position in the power structure. In 1948, the same military elements which had structured the situation that led to the election itself deposed Gallegos in a military coup. After ten years of harsh dictatorship, a wiser and more experienced *Acción Democrática* government returned to power, again in an election made possible by military collaboration. This time they were careful and consistent in their reassurances to other power contenders that their place in the political order would not be jeopardized. If one looks at the process of politics in Venezuela, as in many other Latin American nations, in this longer time span, rather than in terms of isolated incidents, what at first seems random and chaotic takes on pattern, a pattern in which election and constitutional procedure plays a part, but not an exclusive role in the structuring of power relations.

In terms of the rules of Latin American electoral activity, a party which is perceived by other power contenders to threaten their recognized place in the political system may be consistently suppressed, though it just as consistently is electorally successful, as in the tragic history of APRA of Peru, through the election of 1962. The resources devoted to such suppression may even be said to be a function of the extent of electorally demonstrated power, as in the case of *Peronismo* in Argentina. On the other hand, such moderately reformist parties as have come to power in Venezuela since 1958 and Colombia have, upon assuming power, been most explicit in their reassurances to other power contenders, and their accommodation to the power structure has not been recalled.

Not only the "tentative" election, but the "fixed" election can be explained as a demonstration of power capability rather than a technique of ratifying power relationships. While in the short run, the fixed election demonstrates the capacity of a government whose power is primarily based on other power capabilities to run a controlled election, suppress opposition, and mobilize the vote, these results are far from authoritative to those power contenders who by the nature of their power capabilities, must be committed to constitutional procedures. From their point of view, the results of a fixed election are subject to revision at the first opportunity. However, as in the case of the "tentative" election, such elections may be made more definitive by assurances that the government gives to these contenders who rely on some leeway for constitutional procedures to function, usually involving promises of a free electoral contest in a short period of time, after the situation is "stabilized."

Similarly, it is conventional to distinguish between "real" revolutions and "typical" revolutions in Latin America. Again, the "real" revolution, in the Western sense of the term, is a technique of ratifying power relationships, of structuring a new regime. In a "typical" revolution (El Salvador in 1948 and Costa Rica in the same year), the revolutionists did not through their action ratify a new power structure. Rather, they left the political system much as it had been before the "revolution" *although now they were included within it.* In short, they had demonstrated a power capability sufficient to be recognized by other contenders, and had subsequently been successful in their negotiations with other power contenders for the structuring of power relationships. (The "typical revolution" is thus also tentative until such satisfactory negotiations have been established, and this accounts in some important degree for the sequences of instability that have occurred in many Latin American countries, and for many of the revolutions that have failed, as in the case of Guatemala.)

Finally, we generally say that Latin American military dictatorship is to be distinguished from European military totalitarianism. With the possible exception of Perón, political intervention by the military in Latin America does not seem to have the effect of overhauling the power system of the society. Rather, under military governments in Latin America, holders of important power capabilities in the society are assured that their position in the society will not be endangered, and are permitted some participation in the political process. (Certainly, military governments may brutally restrict entrance of other new power contenders into the political arena, and in some nations they are supported by other power contenders for just this reason.) In general, the effect of military coup in Latin America is to add a new power contender to the "inner circle" of political elites, but one whose control is not exclusive or definitive.

The Demonstration of Power Capabilities

One may say that the most persistent political phenomenon in Latin America is the effort of contenders for power to demonstrate a power capability sufficient to be recognized by other power contenders, and that the political process consists of manipulation and negotiation among power contenders reciprocally recognizing each other's power capability.

It is apparent that it is often not necessary for a power contender actually to use a power capability, but merely to demonstrate possession of it. For example, in many Latin American nations the military has often proved to be exceedingly inept when actually called upon to use armed force in a combat situation. Thus, Porfirio Díaz's vaunted military power seemed to evaporate when challenged by Madero's ragtag forces in the Revolution of 1910. The fate of Batista's well-equipped Cuban army was similar in 1958. However, except in such "real revolutionary" situations, Latin American armies are seldom called upon to actually use armed force. In the conventional operation of the Latin American political system, it is usually only necessary for the military to demonstrate possession of the capacity of armed violence. In the strategy of the Latin American military coup, it is generally recognized, bloodshed is kept to a minimum, and such as takes place is usually coincidental. What is at issue is the demonstration and recognition of a *transfer* in the control of the power capability of armed force. This may be accomplished by an announcement of the shift of allegiance of certain critical garrisons, a show of armed force, and the declaration of martial law and a patrol adequate to prevent outbreaks by those who do not understand the manner in which the political system operates, or do not accept the system and consider this an appropriate moment for action. The fact that one of the primary targets in a military coup is control of a radio transmitter so that the insurgents can *inform* interested parties through a manifesto or proclamation that a change in control of power capability has taken place is a pointed demonstration of what is actually going on.

With reference to foreign power contenders, it might be noted that the demonstration, rather than use, of a power capability, is a long-established part of Latin American international affairs. Hence, gunboat diplomacy, "the showing of the flag" certainly pertains to this category of events, as do the subtleties of recognition policy.

Similarly, the "manifestation" or "demonstration" is a common political instrument in Latin America. Seldom is the power it implies actually used (as it was in the *Bogotazo* of 1948 when unrestrained mob violence virtually demolished the heart of the capital of Colombia); rather, the presence of the multitude assembled before the national palace is generally adequate for existing power contenders to recognize and seek to placate or accommodate the new power capability that has emerged in their midst.

Widespread use of manifestation also reflects the imperfections of representation in Latin American politics. Where democratic processes are not totally legitimate, and where institutional processes of representation do not effectively connect decision-makers with all major interests, manifestation substitutes for the more formal processes of structured access available in more fully democratic societies. Therefore, manifestation is frequently, though not exclusively, a technique used to demonstrate a power capability not previously recognized by established contenders. The sanction implicit in the presence of the assembled crowd may be violence, or it may be something far more subtle. This may be appreciated by examining another fascinating technique of demonstrating a power capability in urban Latin America, the general strike.

The *huelga de los brazos caídos,* or general strike, is a recognized part of the political process in Latin America. It was used with great effectiveness as part of a total strategy of deposing an incumbent regime in El Salvador in 1944, Costa Rica in 1948, the Dominican Republic in 1961, and in other nations as well. What is at issue in the general strike is the demonstration of a power capability inhering in the urban population which has not been effectively recognized by other power contenders. This power capability may be described as the disruptive effect of the withdrawal of a number of those specialized, systemic performances on which the complex interdependence of a modern urban community is based.

As a political weapon, the power capability demonstrated in the strike is that of an economic or social function whose performance is critical to the operation of the social order. Threat of nonperformance of a critical social or economic role, implicit or explicit, is a power capability that pertains to a wide variety of power contenders. Hence, the problem of flight capital, insofar as it reflects a vote of no confidence in the political regime, is the demonstration of a power capability in this sense, as is the threat or fact of disinvestment by foreign capitalists or entrepreneurs. Although such withdrawals of critical performances are not often designed directly as political strategies, at times they have been precisely such. For example, in 1962, when the reformist Rivera government in El Salvador enacted and enforced a quite thoroughgoing rural labor reform, the landholding elites of the nation threatened to cut down production of basic foodstuffs in retaliation and protest.

Even the use of noninstitutionalized violence and terror is often designed to show possession of a power capability rather than to use it directly for political ends. More true to the Latin American tradition in such matters than the political assassination or widespread destruction of property or life is the symbolic act of terrorism or violence. For example, the theft of an art collection in Caracas in 1962, the kidnapping and release unharmed of a United States officer, the hijacking of ships and aircraft, as components of a rather consistent strategy of the FALN terrorists in Venezuela, were designed to produce the largest dramatic appeal and embarrassment to the regime, without large-scale devastation of property. Although violence in Venezuela in the 1960–64 period often did degenerate into actual destruction of life and property, this seemed to have more to do with the inability of early terrorist leaders to control the forces they had unleashed than any strategic intent to create bloodshed and havoc.

I witnessed another instance of the symbolic use of violence and terror in Honduras in 1958. Certain political activists, demoralized by the electoral success of the Liberal party, attempted to show their continued presence and impact on the political process by engaging in sporadic bombings in the capital of Tegucigalpa. Yet the acts of violence were not directed against the leaders of the government or against critical urban facilities with the end of actual destruction. Rather, bombs were exploded in deserted soccer fields, or against the door of the post office in such a way as to create damage that would be witnessed by the maximum number of people, but did not actually interfere with the operation of that establishment.

While the Latin American political process is becoming more complex, and such acts of civic disruption and violence are growing more serious and threatening in intent (particularly with the emergence of guerrilla warfare as an increasingly prominent phenomenon) in the classic pattern of Latin American political life, such techniques of demonstrating a power capability seem generally accepted as appropriate to the political system. Thus, when such techniques as manifestation, strike, and even violence are used symbolically, that is, as the demonstration and not the use of a power capability, there would seem to be an *a priori* case that the appropriate response of government leaders should be conciliation and bargaining. However, when use of such techniques actually degenerates into important destruction of life or property, it seems more generally felt that the rules have been transgressed, and that the use of sanctions is called for. Brutal police suppression, with loss of life and widespread arrests, in the face of a student riot, even one that may have culminated in the burning of automobiles or the breaking of windows, may breed an ugly public mood. On the other hand, persistent agitation that acually disrupts the way of life of the society and is not dealt with firmly by constituted authority may lead quickly to agitation for a stronger, "no nonsense" government.

The line between "appropriate" and "inappropriate" demonstrations of the capacity to use violence is a fine one, most contingent on the way public opinion chooses to define a particular situation. However, it is clear that many Latin American governments can count the days to their downfall from some initial act of overstepping the bounds of what seems to be accepted as the legitimate use of force in the face of threats of civic disruption. Thus, many Latin American "revolutions" (Guatemala in 1944–45 will do as an example) have as part of their folklore a student demonstration or riot which was vigorously suppressed, and which served as a touchstone of increasing popular discontent against the regime, culminating in a military revolt.[10]

Thus, there is further evidence, which may be tested against a wide variety of situations, for the existence of a Latin American political system, not defined exclusively by constitutional norms, but generally understood by the contenders nonetheless. That manifestation, strike, and violence have so much to do with the day-to-day operation of the system is in part due to the imperfections of democratic procedures in Latin America, that most contenders for power do not have structured access to the representative system on the basis of an implicit assumption of their power capabilities, but are forced to demonstrate their power capabilities in extra-democratic ways. Yet, the existence of the system does not merely indicate that Latin America is waiting upon the time when democracy will be perfected, for the rules of the game themselves are part of

[10] The 1965 crisis in the Dominican Republic is an interesting though enigmatic case in point. Prior to the arming of civilians on Monday, April 26, the revolt was structured along classic lines, well within the rules of the Latin American coup. The resignation of Reid Cabral on April 25 was, in this sense, a recognition of the shift in the demonstrated power capabilities in the system. However, the determination of Wessin y Wessin to suppress the rebel movement, the outbreak of violence and civic anarchy in the subsequent week, were factors that transcended the normal terms of political transition. Whether United States intervention was or was not an appropriate reaction to the state of internal turmoil that existed by April 29 and 30 will be debated long and inconclusively for some time to come.

a political heritage which possesses its own legitimacy and persistence. To put this another way, it is still doubtful that young students with political aspirations, conscious of the lives of the national heroes that have gone before them, see themselves in their dreams of glory winning victories around the conference table rather than behind the barricades.

The Tentativeness of the Latin American Political Process

In understanding the day-to-day events of politics in Latin America, one must begin by postulating two distinct phases of the political process. In the first, contenders "outside" the coterie of elites which habitually take one another into account in planning their political strategies are seeking to demonstrate a power capability that will gain them access to the political process. The second phase may then be described as one of manipulation and negotiation among power contenders with reciprocally recognized power capabilities.

The terms on which such contenders negotiate for the structuring of power relationships varies from country to country and situation to situation. In some cases, recognized contenders seem generally to accept the procedures and norms of constitutional democracy as setting the conditions for their interaction. This characteristic of some Latin American political systems has often deceived outside observers. Thus, for many years, Colombia and Chile were honorifically described as "Latin American democracies," exceptions to the regional norm. Many were shocked when political events and subsequent "revisionist" research in these nations revealed acute inequalities of political influence and access. Today, we have a clearer picture of the operation of the political system in these nations. Parliamentary government in Chile and two-party competition in Colombia were not political processes that described the political system as a whole. Rather, the presence of democratic constitutional procedures in these countries seemed more to represent an agreement between certain established elites to treat each other in a civil fashion to restrain destructive conflict between them and to protect their established place in the political order. However, democratic procedures did not apply to all potential contenders in the political process.

The "two phase" process of politics may be seen in even the more democratic Latin American nations. As the literature of justification of the Costa Rican "revolution" of 1948 amply suggests,[11] what was in large measure at issue was the exclusion from the political process of a group of younger political aspirants by what they chose to call the "civil oligarchy." Although election was substantially accepted as definitive in the Costa Rican political process, the process of nomination was generally controlled by the "best families" to the exclusion of such younger activists as formed the backbone of the *Liberacíon Nacional* movement. To gain access to the political process, these activists resorted to military force. Once recognized by other power contenders through the exercise of this power capability, they were quite scrupulous about observing democratic procedures, voluntarily renouncing their military control in 1949 and graciously surrendering power after losing a free election in 1957.

The relationships among established contenders are not often so overt or structured as they are where democratic process regulates their interaction. In nations where democratic processes play a more peripheral role in the political system, structuring of power relations among established contenders is apt to be arrived at in a more informal manner. Generally, what occurs is that it is assumed that the interests of certain contenders will be customarily taken into account in policy decisions, and "understandings" with such contenders either actually or tacitly reached.

Seldom is this process fully conscious and deliberate. Often it does not consist of a formal situation of "negotiation" at all, but is rather implicit in the statements of a new government as it takes office, and carefully announces a policy format that accounts for the interests of all prominent elites, or as it delicately pursues a policy which takes account of dominant power contenders.

The character of the system is perhaps most strikingly illustrated in the "learning process" which Latin American re-

[11] Alberto Cañas, *Los 8 Años* (San José: Edit. Liberación Nacional, 1955).

formist movements undergo when they come to power. While "outside" the effective political arena, they build consent on the promise of radical and sweeping reforms. The power of the military will be reduced, large foreign economic interests will be nationalized, a thoroughgoing agrarian reform will be carried out. Having created and demonstrated a power capability on this basis, having assumed political power perhaps on the basis of an election, their attitude changes. They become proponents of "evolutionary change," of "gradual, reasonable, reforms," in which "all social forces must participate and contribute to the welfare of the nation." The army is confirmed in its perquisites. Economic policy becomes more moderate. Strong action contemplated against existing elites is modified or abandoned.

What is at issue is less political cynicism, or the difference between campaign oratory and actual statesmanship, than it is a process by which these newly accepted power contenders learn the conditions of their own rule. In some cases, this learning experience is quite overt and apparent in public pronouncements made before and after entering office. In others, such contenders learn only by hard experience, by being deposed, and subsequently readmitted to power as more docile contenders. Of the former type, Arturo Frondizi of Argentina is a prime example. A fire-eating reformer out of office, committed economic nationalist, and defender of the rights of labor, he became an economic moderate in office, once instructed in the economic "facts of life" of post-Perón Argentina, quite eager to accept the stabilization recommendations of the International Monetary Fund, to invite in foreign petroleum firms, to hold the line on labor wage increases. Of the later case, the *Acción Democrática* movement in Venezuela is revealing. Coming to power in 1945 on a program of reform, suggestions of action against both the military and foreign oil interests contributed to their replacement in 1948 by a harsh military government. The party returned to power in 1958, chastened and wiser, now seeking a "reasonable relationship" with the petroleum industry, and suggesting no diminution of the power of the army in national life.

The Latin American political system is "tentative." Unlike nations where constitutional provision and the legitimacy of election guarantees a specified life span for any government, in Latin America government is based on a flexible coalition among diverse power contenders which is subject to revision at any time if the terms under which the original government was formed are deemed violated. Revision occurs primarily when an existing holder of an important power capability feels threatened by action of government. Thus, in 1954, when the government of Jacobo Arbenz, the second consecutively elected government in recent Guatemalan history, attempted to carry out an extensive agrarian reform, dilute the army's power through creation of a "people's militia," and permitted overt Communist activity in collaboration with the government, it was overthrown by threatened holders of important power capabilities. Similarly, in Argentina, the government of Arturo Frondizi was deposed when Frondizi appeared prepared to permit *Peronista* electoral participation, adjudged a serious violation of previous "understandings" by important power contenders.

In each of these cases, and many more could be cited, the "understandings" between power contenders on which the government had been based were deemed to be violated by future actions. It was this breach of commitment that sanctioned the overthrow of the government, rather than any "understanding" concerning legitimate tenure for any government.

The Process of Change in the Latin American Political System

The Latin American political system, therefore, accounts for change and permits change, but only within a rather rigorous context. New contenders are admitted to the political arena of reciprocally recognizing elites in Latin America when they demonstrate a significant power capability, and when they provide assurances that they will not jeopardize the ability of any existing power contender to similarly participate in political activity. Thus, with the exception of "real revolutionary" situations, the normal rule of Latin American political change is that new power contenders may be added to the system, but old ones may not be eliminated.

It is this characteristic of the system that gives Latin American politics its distinctive flavor. While, in the history of the West, revolutionary experiences of secular change have sequentially eliminated various forms of power capability, contemporary Latin American politics is something of a "living museum," in which all the forms of political authority of the Western historic experience continue to exist and operate, interacting one with another in a pageant that seems to violate all the rules of sequence and change involved in our understanding of the growth of Western civilization. Politically pragmatic, democratic movements, devoted to the constitutional and welfare-state ideals of the mid-twentieth century, stand side by side with a traditional and virtually semi-feudal landed aristocracy. "Social technocrats" and economic planners of the most modern outlook confer and interact with an institutionalized Church which in some countries is favored with a political position not far removed from the "two swords" tradition of Medieval political thought. Military *caudillos* cast in a role set in the early nineteenth century, and little changed with the passage of time, confront an organized trade union movement, a growing middle class, a new entrepreneurial elite.

The rule that new power contenders will be admitted to the system only when they do not jeopardize the position of established contenders contributes to the tentativeness of the system in operation. Neither the accommodation of a new power contender (such as a reformist political party) nor its suppression is final. There is a marked reticence in the classic pattern of Latin American politics to define for all time who may and may not participate in the political process, illustrated by the rule that exile rather than purge is the appropriate way of coping with an antagonistic power contender. If a suppressed power contender can survive long years of banishment from the political forum, the chances are good that at some future date the patterns of coalition and alliance among established contenders will be revised in such a way that the contender will again be able to participate in political activity, to redemonstrate its power capability in an environment more hospitable to its admission to that inner circle of forces that reciprocally recognize each other's right to be part of the political system. The long and tragic history of the Peruvian

APRA party, suppressed and underground for long periods, yet recurrently admitted to the political arena by virtue of its capacity to demonstrate large-scale mass consent to its leadership and program, is illustrative.

New contenders are admitted to the political system when they fulfill two conditions in the eyes of existing power contenders. First, they must demonstrate possession of a power capability sufficient to pose a threat to existing contenders. Second, they must be perceived by other contenders as willing to abide by the rules of the game, to permit existing contenders to continue to exist and operate in the political system. If the first condition is not fulfilled, the power contender will be ignored, no matter what the merits of his case may be. (For example, a strike by a few hundred students over a penny increase in bus fares may bring on a full-scale governmental crisis and immediate concessions to the students, while a full-scale agrarian revolt in some remote province may merely be noted and deplored by decision-makers in the capital city. Given the urban bias of the Latin American political system, the former affects the conditions of power in the system, the latter does not.) If the second condition is not fulfilled, efforts will be made to suppress the new power contender.

The ability of established elites to suppress effectively a new power contender depends on a variety of circumstances. Some established contenders are not loathe to support a new contender to strengthen their bargaining position in the political process. Hence, in recent years, some military leaders in Latin America, reading the handwriting on the wall, have adopted a "reformist" or "democratic" posture, seeking alliances with mass movements or middle class parties. Increasingly, the Catholic Church is abandoning its old bases of political alliance, and throwing in its lot with the "modern" political forces. In addition, the basic style of the political process, which resembles a complex game of chess between political forces with reciprocally recognized power capabilities, implies a certain level of conflict and competition between the established power contenders. When such inner circle elites are in conflict or stalemate, a new contender may enter the process by the back door. For example, in 1945 in Peru, the APRA party, for years suppressed by dominant elites, was permitted to participate in an electoral contest. The election itself was in many respects the outcome of a deadlock between the established elites.

When disunity or deadlock among established contenders threatens to admit a potentially dangerous power contender to the political arena, military dictatorship is often the most satisfactory remedy to preserve the system intact. Without jeopardizing the status of existing contenders, the *caudillo* replaces bickering, conflict, and "politicking" among the dominant political participants with order, firmness, and suppression of the threatening new political force. That this is often the basis for military rule in Latin America is well evidenced by the enthusiasm and relief felt by established political groups when an Odría in Peru, or a Rojas Pinilla in Colombia comes to power to end a "crisis" of enmity and conflict between those elites which dominate the political system, and in which a threatening political force is bidding to come to power in the vacuum thus created. Yet, like that of other contenders, the rule of the military dictator is tentative, contingent on his ability to maintain the coalition of agreements and imputed objectives that brought him to power. Should he fail to maintain his power capability, or to obey the rules of the game that existing contenders are to be permitted to act politically according to the rules of negotiation and coalition, should he, in short, violate the implicit "understandings" that led to his acceptance, he too may be turned out. The fate of Idígoras Fuentes in Guatemala, of Perón in Argentina (particularly in his relations to the Church, the economic elites, and the military), and for that matter, of Odría and Rojas Pinilla, is illustrative.

It is inappropriate to view this classic political system of Latin America as entirely static. Often, we suggest that the normal course of Latin American politics is designed to reinforce the power of the oligarchy against the forces of change at work in the society. This is not entirely the case and, put this way, is somewhat deceptive. The rule of the system is, of course, that established elites will be permitted to continue to operate and to maintain many of their political and socioeconomic perquisites intact. But the rule of the system is also that new contenders, new holders of significant power capabilities will be able to partake in negotiation for a share of the resources and powers of the state if they do not jeopardize the right of established elites to act similarly. Hence, although the landowners, the Church, the military, continue as prominent political economic forces, the terms of their share in the perquisites which political involvement can offer has been adjusted by the accommodation into political life of a burgeoning middle class, new types of interest groups and political parties, a working class elite of skilled, organized, industrial laborers. It is true that these "new" forces have not achieved as great a share of the political economic resources of the society as have their counterparts in the advanced nations because of the requirements of the system that a substantial part of available resources must be allocated to the "older" contenders, the landowners, the military, and the like. However, it is in almost all Latin American nations quite untrue to suggest that these new contenders have been denied any share in political economic rewards at all, for the system has accommodated new power contenders, the system has changed. The conflict and crisis of contemporary Latin America is then more accurately described as one in which newer contenders feel that too large a share of social rewards are allocated to established contenders in fulfillment of the terms of the classic political system, rather than that the political system is one of complete rigidity and suppression, in which the emerging forces of change are unable to participate and derive benefit from political economic life at all. The peculiar character of Latin American political economic change, then, would seem to be best analyzed, not in terms of our conventional and oversimplified categories of "class warfare" and "resistance to change," but as product of the distinctive political system of the region, one that permits new power contenders to be added to the system, but is so designed that older political factors are not eliminated, one that is–if one can accept a most surprising use of the term–more "tolerant" as to the types of power capabilities that are relevant for political participation than are the political systems of the advanced Western nations.

Ironically then, Latin American politics are not characterized by "revolution" as we conventionally assume, but by the total absence of any historic revolution that could eliminate some power contenders from the political system, and legitimate certain types of power capabilities as exclusively appropriate in the mobilization of political power. The significance of the great democratic revolutions of the eighteenth century in Western Europe and North America, then, is seen as that of rejecting as legitimate power capabilities those based on the feudal control of groups of serfs and land, or sheer military power, or the divine right of monarchy in which Church and state mutually reinforced the other's claims to legitimacy. The significance of the great democratic revolutions was that they effectively eliminated all power contenders who could not, at some point, base their claim to power on the aggregation and mobilization of consent, electorally tested. Latin America never experienced this democratic revolution. Latin America never went through the process by which those whose skills and resources were appropriate to the mobilization and organization of consent (the middle class) became dominant in the society and could deny political participation to all those who could not base their claim to power on consent (which was only one of many possible in organizing power, and which did refer to the political resources available to only one part of the population). Latin America did not legitimate democracy, that is to say, it did not restrict political power to only those who could mobilize consent. In fact, Latin America, as a region, has not undergone a revolution that could legitimate any particular type of power capability. Hence, the power systems of divine right monarchy, military authority, feudal power, and constitutional democracy all exist side by side, none legitimate, none definitive, and the political system that has emerged is one in which all the political techniques that have been experienced by Western man continue as part of the system, and the system prescribes the rules for their interaction, and for the persistence of the system itself, by prescribing that none of these historic power capabilities may be eliminated entirely.

In saying this, we have implied a definition of revolution, which might be stated as follows: revolution occurs when some power contenders or some types of power capabilities are successfully eliminated from political participation. By this definition, some revolutions have occurred in Latin America, some political forces have chosen not to play according to the rules of the classic system just described, and have been successful in their endeavor.

Most students of Latin American politics agree that three regimes exist in modern Latin America that could properly be described as "revolutionary" in nature. These revolutions occurred in Mexico in 1910, Bolivia in 1952, and Cuba in 1959. Some note Guatemala from 1945 to 1954 as a revolutionary situation, and we will define it as a revolution that failed, or is temporarily in abeyance, perhaps going through a Thermidorian phase.

All three of these situations essentially fit our definition of revolution. In each, a large part of the thrust of revolutionary agitation was against foreign control of natural resources or economic institutions. It is to be noted that here the intent was to eliminate certain power contenders (the foreign owners) rather than the power capability (control of economic factors as a political resource). In two of the revolutionary situations, Cuba and Bolivia (the latter in relation to at least mineral resources) the objective was to add the power capability of economic control to other political resources of the revolutionary regime through the device of expropriation and nationalization. In Mexico, the economic power capability previously in the hands of foreign power contenders was eventually allocated both to the revolutionary regime (nationalization of some basic industries such as petroleum) and to a new private, but national, group of entrepreneurs (Mexicanization). In all three cases, a prime component of revolutionary ideology was "anti-imperialism" which we would define as the intent to eliminate external power contenders from participation in the political system, to "nationalize" the political process.

Agrarian reform in all three revolutions was designed to eliminate both the power contenders and the power capability represented by the semi-feudal control of land and labor through the institution of the *hacienda.* All three revolutions were to some extent successful in thus "modernizing" the political system (e.g., in eliminating an archaic power capability), but in all three, residual traces remained, and in each, there is some evidence that the power capability of traditional agrarian authority was in some areas merely transferred to the new administrator of the collective or state farm (Cuba) or the Agrarian or *Ejido* Bank (Mexico).

All three revolutions more or less successfully eliminated the traditional military as a prominent power contender. (However, only Costa Rica, which constitutionally abolished its army, can be said to have abolished the power capability of semi-legitimate control of armed force.) In Cuba, this power capability has been incorporated into the other political attributes of the regime through the device of the militia. In Mexico, the military remains as a power contender, though its capacity to use its power capability has been substantially, though always tentatively, reduced by the increasing legitimacy of other types of political resources.

In Mexico particularly, and to some extent in the other two nations, efforts were made, none completely successful, to eliminate the power capabilities of the Catholic Church. In these situations, as throughout Latin America, it is primarily the secular attributes of the Church (the *hacienda* power capability) that has successfully been reduced, while other power capabilities (ideology, capacity to aggregate consent) have remained more intractible.

The revolutionary mystique in Latin America insists that the classic system of politics can be transformed by the elimination of specific power contenders and power capabilities. The revolutionary experience in Latin America suggests that in some instances the characteristics of the older system re-emerge, though often in greatly revised form. Revolution may make a great difference in the course of Latin American political life, though generally, not all the difference expected by its perpetrators. Thus, the anti-imperialist strain in Cuban revolutionary thought culminated not in the elimination of the foreign power contender, but in the replacement of one set of foreign contenders (the United States interests, public and private) with an alternative set (the Soviet bloc). Similarly, the Bolivian revolution has been kept alive by giant infusions of United States aid, aid that has implied a prominent role for the United States in the decision-making processes of that nation. In Mexico, it is to be noted that foreign investors were eventually readmitted to the political economic system, though on terms that radically reduced their ability to use economic resources as a political capability.

The present political regime of Mexico, which Mexicans like to refer to as the "institutionalized revolution" is remarkably suggestive of the tenacity of the classic system of Latin American politics. Although the revolution of 1910 eliminated some power contenders, the eventual outcome of the revolutionary experience was the formation of a new set of elites, each recognizing, on the basis of demonstrated power capabilities, the right of the other to negotiate in the allocation of the resources available through the system. The interaction of the various sectors of the official party in Mexico–the *campesino,* popular, and labor sectors of the Party of the Institutionalized Revolution, or PRI–can only be described as manipulation and negotiation between mutually recognizing power contenders. The eventual inclusion of the new industrial and commercial elite of Mexico into the political system, though not into the official party, from which they are pointedly excluded, the reconciliation of the revolutionary regime with the Church, in contradiction to a basic theme of revolutionary ideology, reflects the capacity of the informal system to survive and reshape the formal structure of the Mexican revolutionary regime, just as the informal system survives and describes patterns of political interaction not anticipated in the formal, constitutional, democratic structures of other Latin American nations.

Change is accounted for in the classic system of Latin American politics, but at a pace that is too slow for some of the newer power contenders. For some, revolution, by eliminating some power contenders and power capabilities, promises to change the pace of change, to make the Latin American political system more compatible with those of advanced Western nations, which themselves eliminated certain archaic power capabilities through revolutionary techniques several centuries ago.

However, some Latin American elites see the possibility of increasing the pace of change without revolution, without the drastic elimination of power contenders from the system. The basic conflict between modern power contenders in Latin America concerns the relative merits of "evolutionary" or "revolutionary" change. For proponents of either method of accelerating the course of change, the conflict is with those who would preserve the "legitimacy" of the classic system of politics in Latin America.

The evolutionary route to accelerated change, embraced by such "democratic reformist" leaders as Rómulo Betancourt of Venezuela, José Figueres of Costa Rica, Fernando Belaúnde Terry of Peru, and many others, may be described as the quest to legitimate "democratic" power capabilities (those that rest ultimately on some form of aggregated consent) through the *conversion* of nondemocratic power capabilities into democratic ones. In other words, those whose power does not rest on consent will have their actions redirected through structural change of the system, their power capability converted and not destroyed. Hence, the military will be "professionalized," not eliminated from the political arena, but directed toward a role more appropriate to democratic states. The old *hacienda* owners will not be destroyed, but required to adopt modern means of production and modern forms of labor relations. Traditional authority, binding the patrón and peón, will gradually disappear to be replaced by bargaining between responsible employers and responsible representatives of organized labor. The effort, in short, is to revise the classic system in terms compatible with the classic system. Existing power contenders are assured that their position within the system will not be jeopardized, in fact, so the ideology of the evolutionary reformer goes, it will actually be enhanced. The power of the *latifundista,* for example, is on the wane, his economic importance diminishing. He can only preserve his power, and enhance it, by adopting more modern techniques of production and social and political interaction. Other democratic reformist leaders argue that such change is essential if the system is to remain the same, that the alternative to reformed performances by existing power contenders is their elimination through a revolutionary movement.

Their prime appeal is to something that can only be described as a notion of the "national interest," made vivid by the awakening of nationalism as a relevant and meaningful arena of reference and interaction for increasing numbers of publics in Latin America. Their vision and context of action is that of the interrelationship of the various sectors of the nation in development. Hence, labor unions must moderate irresponsible wage demands, for investment essential to national industrial development can only be achieved with moderate labor costs, and industrialization is vital if the goal of productivity, welfare, national greatness, and a higher level of industrial employment is to be achieved. However, industrialists must accept extensive programs of education, public health, and social welfare if a "modern" domestic market and pattern of consumption is to be achieved. Agrarian reform is essential if a level of agricultural productivity is to be achieved that will be sufficient to feed increasing urban populations, divorced from subsistence production of their own foodstuffs, if scarce foreign exchange earnings are not to be wasted on imported foodstuffs, if export agriculture that will provide the wherewithal for industrial expansion is to be increased.

The educational mission of statecraft implied by this approach has made a certain impact. For the modern sector, in some nations at least, the classes seem less antagonistic, the interests of industrialists and workers less contradictory, than they did some years ago. The prospects of the democratic reform approach may be seen by an examination of Betancourt's Venezuela, Rivera's El Salvador, Eduardo Frei's Chile. Its limitations are also apparent. The pace of change appears faster than that implied in the classic system, but for many, slower than that implied by revolutionary change, particularly that exemplified by the Cuban revolution. The economic shambles of Goulart's Brazil, the demise in frustration of Frondizi in Argentina, bring questions about the validity of the evolutionary approach in these nations. The collapse of Bosch's Dominican Republic and Villeda Morales' Honduras at the hands of the defenders of the "old order" frames the question clearly. The evolutionary style of reform may be undone either from the right or from the left.

Víctor Rául Haya de la Torre of Peru, the father of *Aprismo,* has said, "Latin America is not easy to govern." As this notion of the "system" of Latin American politics should make clear, the tasks of statecraft in this region are intricate, complex, and frustrating. Even the most skilled democratic political craftsman, a man of the stripe of Lyndon Johnson or Franklin Roosevelt might pale before the task at "creating agreement" among the diverse contenders and forces at work in the Latin American political milieu. In the classic or evolutionary styles of Latin American statesmanship, politics is supremely the art of the possible, the art of combining heterogeneous and incompatible power contenders and power capabilities together in some type of tentative coalition, one in which the various members feel no obligation to maintain the combination intact for any prescribed term of office. George Blanksten, in his *Perón's Argentina,* likens the task of the Latin American politician to that of the juggler, who must keep a large number of balls simultaneously in the air and is apt to be hit on the head by the one that he misses.

In view of the complexity and frustration of working within the system, it is no wonder that the apparent simplicity and malleability of revolution has an appeal in Latin America that itself adds to the complexity of government. But the attractions of the revolutionary alternative are often deceptive. Its simplicity is premised on the existence of a revolutionary situation, of a vivid and vital mass desire and capacity to start over again, on new terms, under new conditions, and that situation is exceptional rather than predictable. Certainly, there have been revolutions in Latin America, and there will be more, but there have been more insurgent movements that failed, that captured no following, that could not overcome and replace the going system.

Revolution requires exceptional leadership of a certain style to succeed, and those who have possessed it, the Maderos, Zapatas, Castros, and Bolívars and San Martíns, have entered the ranks of the vivid personal heroes of Latin American history. But there is another style of leadership which is relevant to the conduct of Latin American government, and there is no reason to believe that it is less available in this culture than that represented by the revolutionary politician in arms. The skills at the craft of politics, of working within the system to the end of transcending it, have been exemplified by men like Betancourt, Frondizi, Figueres, Lleras Camargo, López Mateos, and many others. They have their historic predecessors in such figures as Sarmiento and Júarez. Their skills and capabilities are not to be despised. In fact, set within the context of the system in which they have operated, and against the background of man's efforts to govern himself, they often appear as little short of incredible.

THE OLIGARCHY MUDDLE

In the past many Latin American specialists, and especially those desiring quick social reforms, have believed that narrow and conservative oligarchies ruled in most of Latin America and effectively prevented change. This viewpoint has been so pervasive that it has been taken for granted when elaborated upon in books and articles. Thus, although the viewpoint satisfies the emotional needs of the authors, it has hindered accurate research on Latin American politics for a long time.

In this selection James L. Payne, Professor of Political Science at the School of Advanced International Studies of Johns Hopkins University, systematically points out what a researcher would have to do to prove that some type of oligarchy controlled a Latin American political system. He covers all types of possible oligarchies, obtaining many of his ideas from research done on the question of power elites in the United States. Professor Payne, although not denying the possibility of oligarchies in Latin America, believes that the chances of finding any are extremely rare. Through his own research he shows that Colombia is not controlled by an oligarchy, contrary to what just about everybody believed before. In his book, *Labor and Politics in Peru,* he has also shown that no oligarchy exists to determine the outcome of labor issues in that country.

The Oligarchy Muddle

JAMES L. PAYNE*

An important task of the social scientist is the continual re-examination of his vocabulary. His purpose in such a re-examination should be the achievement of greater precision in meaning–that is, a more explicit statement of the real-world phenomena to which his terms apply. This research note is an attempt to stimulate the critical examination of the term "oligarchy" and related phrases identifying a ruling elite which have been used widely and repeatedly in discussions of Latin American political systems.

As presently used, the term "oligarchy" is highly ambiguous, referring to many different phenomena. Although many writers have been liberal in their allegations of oligarchy in Latin American countries, their claims are of little utility since it is seldom clear what they mean by the word. Even if we discern a vague outline of the meaning of "oligarchy" in some works, we still do not find explicit techniques for translating the concept into empirical form. And we do not find measurements or evidence. Furthermore, if we apply a few common meanings of "oligarchy" to a country where this phenomenon is held to exist, it is not at all clear that an oligarchy does obtain. In this discussion of the methodological problems involved in determining the existence of oligarchies, I shall use Colombia as a point of reference, since I have recently spent some time examining the politics of that country.[1] Colombia serves as a useful illustration because it is one of the Latin American countries to whose political system "oligar-

* This research note is a revision of a paper prepared for delivery at the 1967 Annual Meeting of the American Political Science Association. Reprinted from James L. Payne, "The Oligarchy Muddle," *World Politics* (April, 1968), pp. 439–453 by permission of publisher and author.

[1] For a more complete discussion of some of the data presented in this research note, the reader may refer to the work based on that research, *Patterns of Conflict in Colombia* (forthcoming 1968).

chy" is frequently applied by both local and North American writers.[2]

In customary usage, "oligarchy" has two components: it refers to (1) a group, which has (2) considerable "power." Each of these components has many possible referents. We might consider the following as oligarchic groups:

A. individuals of greatest prestige (suitably determined);
B. identified families;
C. individuals of greatest wealth (suitably determined);
D. employers (determined by size of firm or by number of workers, and so on);
E. landowners (determined by size of holding or by interest group membership, and so on);
F. the armed forces (or specified parts);
G. the Catholic church (or specified parts);
H. the holders of high political office at a given moment.

Each of these groups or any combination of these groups could constitute an oligarchy. I have given only a suggestive outline of each group's characteristic; an investigator would need to develop specific techniques to identify the particular group(s) making up his proposed oligarchy. He might select organized interest groups (employer organizations to identify employers, for example); he might use an opinion poll to determine the individuals with greatest prestige. "The Church" might be identified as the archbishop alone, or as all the bishops, or as all the clergy. The more specific the investigator makes the identification of his oligarchy, the easier it will be to prove or disprove claims about its power.

Further, an investigator would need to be alert to the matter of size in identifying the proposed oligarchy. He could not

[2] Two recent North American publications on Colombian politics in which assertions of oligarchy appear are Vernon L. Fluharty, *Dance of the Millions* (Pittsburgh 1957), and John D. Martz, *Colombia* (Chapel Hill 1962). Also see Robert H. Dix, "Colombia: A Two-Party System in Crisis," unpubl. Ph.D. diss., Harvard, 1962. Carlos Lleras Restrepo argues, against the tide to be sure, that local usage of "oligarchy" is simply political propaganda: "Here [in Colombia] all those who wish to practice demagoguery classify everyone else as oligarchs" (*Hacia la restauración democrática y el cambio social,* Vol. I [Bogotá 1963], 327).

select a group that numbered in the hundreds of thousands and then treat it as if it were a clique. For example, a loosely titled oligarchy of "landowners, merchants, and industrialists" in Colombia would, since it would include shopkeepers and small farmers, comprise several hundred thousand individuals. If the families of these people were also included, the investigator would have a proposed oligarchy of over one million: a massive, heterogeneous chunk of society. He could not, therefore, speak of it as a tiny aristocracy nor imply that it was tightly organized, united, self-conscious, or determined.

The investigator should also be sensitive to conditions of organization. Does the proposed oligarchy have a group life of a formal or informal nature? Are collective decisions taken? This matter is particularly important when an alliance of groups is claimed. Perhaps "alliance" means simply that two or more autonomous and independent groups are regularly found on the same side of an issue or series of issues. Perhaps the reference is to overlapping memberships, family ties, or monthly meetings. In any case, an explicit statement of the phenomenon to which "alliance" refers is necessary to avoid ambiguity.

The definition of "oligarchy" includes, in addition to the specified group(s), an attribution of power. For our purposes, we might examine four distinct power attributes that a group might have:

I. power as the extended tenure of political office;
II. power as the ability to prevail against other members of society on selected issues;
III. power as the ability to control opinion so that other members of society do not oppose the group's position;
IV. (an attribute that, as argued below, embodies a fallacy) power as a group's presumed ability to cause any state of affairs from which it benefits.

A complete definition of "oligarchy," then, includes both group(s) and power attribute(s), thus: "Type E-I oligarchy" would refer to the proposition that landowners (group E) occupy top governmental positions over a long period of time. We can easily see that the combinations and permutations of groups and attributes are very large, so that we are justified in saying that, when unqualified, "oligarchy" is a highly ambiguous term.

"Type B-II oligarchy," for example, says that a selected group of families defeats everyone else on selected issues; but this definition is different from that of a CDE-III oligarchy, in which identified groups of the wealthy, employers, and landowners control opinions so well that the rest of society does not oppose their position. And then a definition of G-IV oligarchy sees the Church "holding power" because that group is held to benefit from the existing state of affairs, while a definition of H-I oligarchy says that the same men in high political office have remained in these positions over a long period of time. It should be added, of course, that I have by no means exhausted the possibilities for either groups or power attributes; we deal here with only some of the more common meanings.

Moreover, when an investigator actually sets out to gather evidence for or against the existence of an oligarchy, it becomes clear that the phenomenon will be a matter of degree. It is not appropriate to say "there is" or "there is not" an oligarchy until the investigator has established some rather arbitrary dividing line on this or that index of measurement. He can then call cases falling clearly on one side of his line "oligarchy" and those on the other "not oligarchy." For the purposes of this research note, I shall consider conditions approximately similar to those in the United States "nonoligarchic," since those who apply "oligarchy" to Latin America typically suppose that they identify conditions dramatically different from those that prevail in the United States.

The investigator's selection of the type of oligarchy he wishes to examine is just the first step. Testing for each power attribute involves difficult problems of collecting and interpreting evidence.

Type I: Power as the extended tenure of political office. This conception of power has the advantage of being relatively simple to apply. The investigator selects his group and sees if all or some specified proportion of the identified political offices are held by members of this group over a period of time. A proposed H-I oligarchy is the easiest to test, since the group selected consists of the leading office-holders at a particular moment. The investigator need only see how many of these same persons are also in high offices several years thence.[3]

The evidence is strongly against the existence of an H-I oligarchy in Colombia at any time since 1830. Turnover in the various top political offices appears to be surprisingly high. At the presidential level, Rafael Núñez (president from 1880 to 1882 and from 1884 to 1893—the terms broken by the appointment of several designates) is the only man who remained in office more than five years continuously and whose total time in office exceeded seven years. On the congressional level, since 1923 (when the *Anales del Congreso* began keeping records of the members of Congress) about eighty percent of the national representatives and senators have been replaced at each election. In recent times, ministers and governors have usually lasted in office about one year. Inspection of the nineteenth-century pattern reveals approximately the same rate of turnover. This kind of evidence, then, would suggest that, for the offices mentioned, there has not been a Type H-I oligarchy in Colombia.

The Type I attribute may be applied to different groups (A, B, and so on) to form propositions about the social or economic backgrounds of high political officials. For example, the usage "Type AC-I oligarchy" proposes that the groups of the most wealthy and prestigious members of society occupy top political positions. As with other variants of Type I, this proposition would resolve itself into questions of degree, that is, the proportion of posts occupied by members of the proposed group. At a minimal level the investigator could define any representation in high office above the group's frequency in the population as a condition for Type I oligarchy. With such a definition then, apparently all countries would have Type I oligarchies of one kind or another. The overrepresentation of higher-status occupations and ethnic groups in

[3] H-I was the meaning given to "oligarchy" in the study of trade-union democracy by Seymour Martin Lipset, Martin A. Trow, and James S. Coleman, *Union Democracy* (Garden City 1962). The formulation of the "iron law of oligarchy" by Robert Michels in *Political Parties* is confused by the different meanings given to "oligarchy" in different places (Types I, II, and III).

American political leadership, for example, has been frequently shown.[4]

Of course, top office-holders, simply because they hold top offices, will automatically have considerable prestige and even wealth. To avoid circularity, the investigator would probably wish to consider the social origins of the office-holders and thus test for a modified AC-I oligarchy (ACm-I). The literature on Colombian politics and history offers sufficient evidence to cast doubt upon the existence of a high degree of ACm-I oligarchy in Colombia. In recent times, such men as Jorge Eliécer Gaitán, Gabriel Turbay, and Jorge Leyva, who all reached posts as high as cabinet minister, were men of humble backgrounds. Earlier, Marco Fidel Suárez, president from 1918 to 1921, was the illegitimate son of a laundress.[5] Luis A. Robles, a prominent Liberal leader in the late nineteenth century, was the dark-skinned son of an Indian and a Negro.[6] José María Rojas Garrido, president in 1867, was from a "poor and obscure" background;[7] Manuel Murillo Toro, president from 1864 to 1866 and from 1872 to 1874, was of a "modest family."[8] Juan José Flores, who consummated Ecuador's independence from Colombia and was twice president of Ecuador (1830–1834, 1839–1845), was of unknown parentage; one source reports his mother to have been a laundress,[9] another identifies his childhood as "poor and unprotected,"[10] and a third points out that he was illiterate until he reached manhood.[11]

[4] For a summary of these findings see Wendell Bell, Richard J. Hill, and Charles R. Wright, *Public Leadership* (San Francisco 1961).

[5] Fernando Guillén Martínez, *Raíz y futuro de la revolución* (Bogotá 1963), 155.

[6] Eduardo Rodríguez Piñeres, *Hechos y comentarios* (Bogotá 1956), 189.

[7] Gustavo Samper Bernal, *Breve historia constitucional y política de Colombia* (Bogotá 1957), 109. Also see Milton Puentes, *Historia del partido liberal colombiano,* 2nd ed. (Bogotá 1961), 249.

[8] Samper Bernal, 107. Also see Eduardo Rodríguez Piñeres, *El olimpo radical* (Bogotá 1950), 171, 195–96.

[9] A. J. Lemos Guzmán, *Obando,* 2nd ed. (Popayán 1959), 182.

[10] Oscar Efren Reyes, *Breve historia general del Ecuador*, Vol. II (Quito 1957), 510.

[11] Alfredo Pareja Diezcanseco, *Historia del Ecuador,* Vol. II (Quinto 1958), 14.

These cases are, of course, exceptional, but they do indicate, in much the same fashion as the Abraham Lincoln experience, that channels to high political office are at least open to those from low social backgrounds. A more complete picture of the social backgrounds of Colombian political leaders can be gained from a survey I made in 1965 of 130 political leaders.[12] Examination of the "father's occupation" responses showed that the bulk of the respondents had fathers in the medium-prestige, nonprofessional categories, particularly shopkeepers, small farmers, and white-collar workers. Six of the respondents gave their father's occupation as blue-collar worker. Approximately one-third of the respondents had fathers on the upper-prestige levels: lawyers, doctors, engineers, and large ranchers (see Table I). This evidence suggests that although there is certainly a degree of Am-I oligarchy in Colombia (using an occupational prestige measurement and taking this particular set of political leaders), it is not clear that the overrepresentation of individuals from higher-status backgrounds is greater there than in other countries, including the United States.

In concluding these observations about the Type I oligarchy I should add that when such an oligarchy is demonstrated (to the degree indicated by the investigator), this finding means nothing beyond what has been measured—that is, that the particular group does hold a given proportion of offices. Conclusions about "power" in other senses are unwarranted unless the investigator shows other propositions to be correct. A rich senator will not necessarily defend the rich; a president whose father was a farmer will not necessarily favor farm subsidies.

Type II: Power as the ability to prevail against other mem-

[12] These leaders were among the members of the departmental party executive committees in seven different departments (Cundinamarca, Tolima, Caldas, Valle, Cauca, Antioquia, and Atlántico) and big-city party executive committees (Bogotá, Ibagué, Pereira, Cali, Medellín, and Barranquilla). These executive committee members were, of course, the most prominent political leaders in the locality. I delivered and collected the questionnaires myself. For further details on the sample and sampling procedure, see Appendix I of my forthcoming *Patterns of Conflict in Colombia.*

bers of society on selected issues. This conception of power points toward the phenomenon of winning and losing openly fought political battles. What is meant by "Type II power" is the ability to defeat one's public opponents. This ability is measured by studying the decision-making process and not-

TABLE I. FATHER'S OCCUPATION OF COLOMBIAN UPPER LEADERSHIP SAMPLE

OCCUPATION STATUS RANK*	FATHER'S OCCUPATION	LIBERALS	CONSERVATIVES	TOTAL	PERCENT
2	Ambassador	1		1	1
3	Manufacturer	1		1	1
5	Architect		1	1	1
5	Doctor	2	2	4	3
5	Engineer	1	3	4	3
6	Lawyer	6	13	19	16
7	Rancher	2	1	3	2
7	Cattle-raiser	2	5	7	6
9	Merchant	16	19	35	29
10	Army officer		2	2	2
11	Journalist	1	2	3	2
11	Civil Servant	1	1	2	2
12	Accountant	1		1	1
14	Public employee	3	4	7	6
15	Schoolteacher	1	1	2	2
16	Small farmer	10	12	22	18
17	Carpenter (and other skilled blue-collar)	3	1	4	3
18	Laborer	2		2	2
	Totals, all known	53	67	120	100
	Unknown, no answer	7	3	10	
	Total, entire sample	60	70	130	

* This status rank of occupations was compiled from a survey conducted in 1965 among Bogotá university students from the universities of Los Andes, Externado de Colombia, and La Javeriana ($N = 75$). The students were given a questionnaire listing thirty-one occupations and asked to give a status rank (between 1 and 7) to each one. These scores were averaged and ranked to produce, when occupations that attained virtually similar scores were combined, eighteen status levels.

ing the outcomes of the contested areas of policy. Gathering evidence for a Type II oligarchy involves these steps:

1. identification of the proposed oligarchy;
2. selection of the issues to be examined (for this Type II formulation, an "issue" is a publicly expressed conflict);
3. observation that the proposed oligarchy has a unified (near-unified) position on these issues;
4. observation that all (most, many, some) of the other members of society take a position contrary to that of the proposed oligarchy;
5. examination of the actions taken by the proposed oligarchy and of the impact of these actions within the decision-making context;
6. evaluation of the outcomes as all (most, many) wins for the group.[13]

Parentheses indicate how these steps may be altered to identify different degrees of Type II oligarchy, from a strong conception to a rather mild one. But it does seem important that each of the steps be followed if winners and losers are to be identified. Obviously the investigator must have a certain clarity about the group that is supposed to be the oligarchy (step 1) to be able to determine whether it wins or not. And he must select issues (publicly expressed conflicts) upon which it is supposed to win (step 2). The requirement of group unity (step 3) is necessary because he cannot meaningfully speak of the entire group as winning or losing if the proposed oligarchs are opposing one another. The proposed oligarchy must have opponents (step 4) since there must be losers if there are to be winners. Ideally, the group should stand alone, opposed by everyone else, so that the investigator does not attribute a victory to the proposed oligarchy when in fact other, nonoligarchical participants who took the same

[13] In the discussion of Type II power I draw heavily upon Robert A. Dahl, *Who Governs?* (New Haven 1961); Dahl, "A Critique of the Ruling Elite Model," *American Political Science Review*, LII (June 1958), 463–69; and Nelson W. Polsby, *Community Power and Political Theory* (New Haven 1963). In my *Labor and Politics in Peru* (New Haven 1965), 272–77, I attempt a preliminary test for a Type D-II oligarchy in that country.

position caused the outcome. A certain amount of crossover, as well as degrees of apathy on either the oligarchy or non-oligarchy side, would have to be permitted in most real-world applications.

Further, the investigator must make an examination of the actions taken by the proposed oligarchy and the impact of these actions in the decision-making context (step 5). The understanding of Type II power concerns the causality of decisions; that is, the proposed Type II oligarchy must *do* something to determine the outcome of issues. It is not enough for the investigator to know that a group wanted *X* and that *X* resulted. He must show what actions the selected group took and how these actions affected or took advantage of the sanctions and incentives to which decision-makers respond. Finally, of course, he must evaluate outcomes of issues as wins or losses for the proposed oligarchy (step 6). This evaluation requires an estimate of which side got more of what it wanted.

A search for a Type II oligarchy in Colombia would involve extensive research and the presentation of detailed case-study information that is beyond the scope of this research note. However, certain preliminary observations can be made which would dim hopes for finding such an oligarchy in the grosser, more dramatic form. First, my impression is that most of the groups that are likely candidates for a Type II oligarchy—large employers, wealthy people, landowners, prestigious individuals—are, as groups, usually either apathetic or divided on important issues. For example, the major employer organization, ANDI (Asociación Nacional de Industrias), does not take any position on many issues. The Secretary-General of the Barranquilla Chamber of Commerce, which has about 4,000 members, identified a general problem of interest-group activity in politics in this way: "We try to stay out of the political issues. Suppose there's a case of corruption, for example. We can't say anything because that would be to attack the governor, or whoever it was. Then we would be accused of being partisan; and our membership would also divide."

Many likely candidates for the oligarchic groups suggested earlier (A, C, D, E) are active in different political parties or factions. These party groupings are heterogeneous with respect to wealth, prestige, and social background. Consequently, whenever particular factions happen to take different sides of an issue for purely strategic reasons—a very common occurrence—there will be conflict between members of that faction and members of the opposing factions, "membership" in prestige, wealth, or occupational groups notwithstanding.

A preliminary examination of the motivation of politicians casts further doubt upon propositions about high degrees of Type II oligarchy in Colombia. The overwhelming majority of politicians in Colombia are not seeking to defend any particular program, be it for or against upper-strata interests. They generally seek personal rewards, particularly status, and consequently are basically uninterested in governmental programs as such. Since elections are the major avenue to political office—and are meaningful—candidates tend to adopt "popular" positions to increase their opportunities for advancement. Once in office, the politicians apparently examine measures for their strategic content, asking whether it is in their private political interest to favor or oppose them. For example, if an office-holder is a member of an anti-presidential faction, then he will tend to oppose measures that might seem beneficial to the president's group. When such strategic considerations are unclear, then the participant is inclined to take the "popular" position (the one benefiting the lower strata) in keeping with his general vote-maximizing perspective.

The popular inclination of Colombian leaders is revealed in their attitudes toward certain programs that are directly or indirectly for the benefit of lower strata. In the survey of 130 leaders mentioned above, it was found that, regardless of party, they were overwhelmingly in favor of more government construction of housing; not one felt the government should do "less." They were moderately in favor of more governmental control of private industry and more legal protection of trade unions (see Table II).

Another indication of the popular orientation of Colombian leaders is the government's tendency toward deficit financing. Politicians are reluctant to approve tax increases, which are unpopular, but are anxious to spend more money on popular

TABLE II. RESPONSES OF TOP PARTY LEADERS TO POLICY QUESTIONS

"In housing construction do you believe the government should do . . . ?"

	LIBERALS	CONSERVATIVES
much more	50	54
more	10	12
the same as now	—	3
less	—	—
much less	—	—
no answer	—	1
Total	60	70

"Do you believe the government ought to control private industry . . . ?"

	LIBERALS	CONSERVATIVES
much more	16	20
more	20	21
the same as now	10	5
less	9	17
much less	2	5
no answer	3	2
Total	60	70

"In the legal protection of trade unions do you believe the government ought to do . . . ?"

	LIBERALS	CONSERVATIVES
much more	17	15
more	22	23
the same as now	18	18
less	2	11
much less	—	2
no answer	1	1
Total	60	70

items: public employment, schools, roads, housing, irrigation, subsidized buses, telephones, and railroads. Consequently the government seldom has a balanced budget and often runs staggering deficits. It is difficult to reconcile this demagogic fiscal policy with the notion that a small group of conservatives opposed to popular demands "controls" the national government.

Given the basic motivation of most politicians–to reach offices of greater prestige–it seems improbable that a small group could regularly and openly prevail against larger groups. Aspirants for office, in seeking to increase their electoral strength, would side with the most numerous group. Consequently, although there are undoubtedly variations in the ability of different groups to win on different issues in Colombia, it does not seem that a Type II oligarchy could exist in dramatic form.

Type III: Power as the ability to control opinion so that other members of society do not oppose the group's position. This power attribute is a highly sophisticated conception of control or domination. It recognizes that a group may act in such a manner as to prevent certain matters from becoming issues in the Type II sense of publicly expressed conflict. The distinction between the Type II and Type III power attributes might be illustrated by considering hypothetical worker-employer relationships in a company town.

Let us suppose that the workers engage regularly in annual strikes that are climaxed by a march to the owner's house and the presentation of a petition for wage increases. The owner rejects the wage demand, hires strikebreakers, and breaks the strike. He wins and the workers lose on the issue of wages. This pattern of worker-employer conflict would point to the possession of Type II power by the owner on the issue of wages.

But suppose that, in a second case, the employer takes action to prevent the public expression of conflict. He may discharge or murder potential leaders before they can organize a strike. He may, by establishing a system of informants, intimidate workers and thus prevent them from even discussing the subject of a strike. He may destroy channels of worker communication, both on and off the job, so that workers may not share and focus their grievances. Finally, through the control of various media—bulletin boards, loudspeakers, company newspaper, radio station—the employer may indoctrinate workers to the effect that strikes are immoral or unpatriotic. The result of these practices is that the workers do not engage in public conflicts with the employer and consequently wages are not an "issue" in the Type II sense. The occasional tourist would pronounce the workers "content."

The Type III power attribute is this phenomenon of action and influence at the pre-issue stages. It asks, What might a group be doing to prevent a certain subject from even becoming an issue? This question has become particularly relevant in view of modern totalitarian practices of intimidation and indoctrination, but it may be reasonably asked of any political system or subsystem.[14]

The search for a Type III oligarchy is complicated, in the first instance, because it takes as "issues" those questions on which there is little or no public disagreement. This point should be well understood: if there is public disagreement or conflict on an issue, then Type III power is *not* being exercised on that issue. If members of society are debating, proposing, and contesting certain matters—land reform, housing, price control—then we have instances of issue conflict, and the Type II approach must be used. The definition of a Type III oligarchy is precisely that the proposed group controls opinion so well that conflicts do not arise on the selected subject. Therefore, if a significant number of local participants are publicly protesting the position of "the oligarchy," *this alleged oligarchy cannot be of the Type III variety.*

Let us suppose, then, that the investigator does select a subject upon which he feels there should be protest in a society and he finds no such protest. He proposes that perhaps a specified group is responsible for the lack of protest, that this group has done something to prevent the "normal" emergence of conflict. For example, the investigator might decide

[14] The problem of "nonissue" power has been raised in the context of American municipal power studies by Peter Bachrach and Morton S. Baratz, "Two Faces of Power," *American Political Science Review,* LVI (December 1962), 947–52. See also Polsby, 95–97.

that Bolívar Square in Bogotá should be torn up and apartment houses built there. He suspects that there should be support for this idea and, finding none, further suspects that the storekeepers on the Square have controlled opinion so thoroughly that the rest of society is indoctrinated to believe that Bolívar Square is a good thing or is perhaps intimidated about saying anything negative. How can he test these suspicions?

In essence, the question seems rather simple. Since a group is proposed as having dominated attitudes and the expression of opinion on the matter, the investigator has to find out what the group has *done* toward this end. He must then estimate whether the group's activity accounts for the lack of protest. It is not enough to show, for example, that a man owns a newspaper to say that he is "dominating" opinion with it. He may be constrained by readership demand and profit considerations from including many of his private views in the content. People may not read the partisan content if it is there, selecting instead the bridge columns and sports pages. He may be so clumsy in including the partisan content that his readers see through the bias and discount his statements. And, of course, the impact of the newspaper must be evaluated in the total communication matrix: radio, television, personal observation, friends, scholarly books, speeches.

One approach to the Type III power phenomenon is an examination of the sanctions and rewards that discourage or encourage the expression of certain opinions. These sanctions, to have significance for the investigation of a particular oligarchic group, must be wielded by this group and not others in society. It is not enough to say that people are punished for expressing an opinion in a certain medium; it must be shown that the proposed oligarchy, either directly or indirectly (through laws, for example), is the group that applies the sanctions. The sanction-reward approach to opinion control might ultimately permit the construction of opinion deviation–sanction charts for different issues in different countries. Such charts might resemble contour maps giving the sanctions (if any) applied by the proposed oligarchy for the different degrees and forms of opinion deviation on the issues selected.

If there is a high degree of Type III oligarchy in Colombia, it is not immediately apparent. There seems to be considerable competition within the mass media (with the exception of television, which is a government monopoly). Communist literature is openly available, much more so than in the United States. Certain aspiring politicians (e.g., Alberto Ruiz Novoa, Alfonso López Michelsen, Gustavo Rojas Pinilla), who do not have the backing of large newspapers, vigorously and openly attack the *gran prensa* (large daily newspapers), and their remarks are broadcast by radio stations, inserted in their own irregular publications, and even reported in the same *gran prensa*.[15]

It seems clear that familiar totalitarian practices of opinion control are not practiced in Colombia; other possible applications of the Type III power conception remain to be defined and researched.

Type IV: Power as a group's presumed ability to cause any state of affairs from which it benefits. Identifying the two types of power just discussed–II and III–involves showing what a proposed oligarchy *has done* to obtain certain objectives. Such an identification does not purport to explain how or why inequalities or conditions exist except insofar as the specified group has done something to bring about or maintain these conditions. That is, we recognize the possibility that certain groups may be relatively well-off simply as a result of conditions, events, and attitudes beyond their control. There will be, of course, explanations for such states of affairs, but these explanations do not find the privileged group(s) to be the cause.

The Type IV oligarchy perspective implicitly rejects this possibility. It assumes that if a group benefits from a given condition then it must have done something to bring about or maintain the condition. Armed with this assumption, the

[15] One book published and sold in Colombia maintains that freedom of the press does not exist in Colombia. See Marco Tulio Rodríguez, *La gran prensa en Colombia* (Bogotá 1963). Indicative of the quality of this writer's arguments is his contention that freedom of the press does exist in the Soviet Union and Red China. He cites as evidence articles of the Soviet and Chinese constitutions that "guarantee" it (p. 83).

investigator may immediately attribute "power" to the favored group.

The Type IV conception is unacceptable because the basic assumption–that those who benefit (or are alleged to benefit), cause–is untenable. This assumption is the essence of what are commonly known as "devil theories": e.g., munitions manufacturers, because they are supposed to benefit from war, are held to cause war. Suppose, for example, we notice that it rains in Seattle. We speculate that taxi drivers make more money on rainy days. Therefore we propose that taxi drivers cause it to rain in Seattle. This conclusion will still be defective even if we are energetic in buttressing some empirical points: we can test the theory that taxi drivers do indeed benefit from rain; we can learn if they know they benefit from rain; we can find out if they actually favor rain. But it is still impossible to conclude that they cause rain since we do not show *what they do* to bring about rain and how these actions fit into existing knowledge about the phenomenon.

In addition to the basic fallacy of attributing causality where no causal relationship may exist, the loose usage of the Type IV perspective may generate spurious propositions about who benefits from a state of affairs. Such propositions have been advanced for Latin American countries in just this manner. Various groups–the wealthy, the Church, landowners, the army–have been identified as "oligarchs" on no more than the assumption that they benefit from a state of affairs: poverty, illiteracy, monoculture. Groups may, without meaningful evidence, be accused of benefiting when they do not benefit, of favoring when they oppose, and of causing when they do not cause. I can see little more in the Type IV oligarchy procedure than an irresponsible attempt to blame someone for Latin American backwardness.

In conclusion: (1) "Oligarchy" and related terms such as "elite rule" have many specific meanings. Therefore the investigator must state (or show through application) which meaning he gives to such terms if he uses them. (2) Each meaning of "oligarchy" must be cast in operational form so that evidence may be gathered to show the existence or nonexistence of the type(s) of oligarchy held to exist. (3) The appropriate evidence must be collected.

LATIN AMERICAN CULTURAL CHARACTERISTICS AND THEIR EFFECTS

In recent years writers on the underdeveloped areas have pointed out the significance of cultural characteristics for politics and social and economic developmental growth. In this selection, John P. Gillin, Dean of Social Sciences at the University of Pittsburgh, isolates six important cultural characteristics of Latin Americans and then discusses their political, economic, and social implications. A discussion of cultural characteristics inevitably raises questions that can be explored further. Little has been done, for example, in determining the variance of cultural characteristics from one Latin American country to another or of comparing them to cultural characteristics in other undeveloped areas. Also, one wonders if cultural characteristics in Latin America are as important as those in a country such as Burma in explaining particular political phenomena. Other factors may be of much more relevance.

*The Middle Segments and Their Values**

JOHN P. GILLIN

The values which are held in common and "taken for granted" by most members of the middle sectors in Latin America determine how they decide among alternatives offered by

* Reprinted from John P. Gillin, "Some Signposts for Policy," from *Social Change in Latin America Today* by Richard Adams, etc., (New York: Harper & Row, 1960), pp. 28–47 by permission of Council on Foreign Relations, Inc.

competing cultural and political systems of the outside world. They also serve to define a set of attitudes that distinguishes the Latin American middle strata from the middle classes of the United States and Western Europe. These controlling values may be grouped, for convenience, under several rubrics: personalism, kinship, hierarchy or stratification, materialism of a special kind, transcendentalism or interest in "spiritual values," the high worth of inner states and emotional expression, and fatalism. Two other values of the middle class have already been mentioned—"decency" in mode of life, and disdain for manual labor.

The controlling values of a culture perform many functions in a society. They provide a way of looking at the world and at people. They furnish those who hold them with a set of beliefs which explain, as it were, the structures and functions of what is perceived. They set out one or more approved goals toward which human effort ought to be channeled within that part of life with which each value is concerned.

Personalism, A Central Value

Both North Americans and Latin Americans place a high value on individuality and "the person." The use of similar words in English, Portuguese, and Spanish tends to conceal the profound differences between their actual meanings. To put the differences succinctly, the North American credo holds, at least ideally, to the notion of equality of opportunity. Each individual has inherently equal rights and supposedly each has an equal chance with every other. The culture places a heavy emphasis upon the external or social equality of persons. It implies that any claim to uniqueness must be proved by achievements of a socially approved type. In the United States the cultural definition of "the person" lays great emphasis upon the broad similarities among various social types. Individual differences, if disapproved, may lead to various types of social punishment; if approved, they may result in conferring "distinction" for greater than average achievement.

In Latin American culture the value emphases are quite different. Although most middle-status Latin Americans hold the Rights of Man in high verbal esteem, the underlying emphasis is upon the inherent uniqueness of each person. The individual is valued precisely because he is not exactly "like" anyone else. Each individual merits respect because of his unique inner worth, regardless of the social form it may take. This is the fundamental meaning of *respetar* (to respect), a word widely used in American Spanish to describe one's relations with others.

The inner essence of the person is usually spoken of as the "soul" or "spirit" (*alma, ánima, espíritu*), and Latin Americans are usually not at all loath to discuss this subject at length. This makes for misunderstanding on the part of North Americans, because in their current usage they usually feel uncomfortable in using words like "soul" or "spirit" when discussing living individuals, except perhaps in intimate discussions with priests or ministers of the Gospel.

The idea that each person merits respect for his inner worth and integrity does not hinder the complementary recognition of social position, of dignity of office, or of an established hierarchy of persons and "things." However, a Latin American, when first confronting an unfamiliar individual, typically "sees" in him a "soul" whose essence he must endeavor to understand and respect for what it is.

Each person has a certain endowment of dignity, honor, and valor which merits respect from others and which he must safeguard at all cost, even death. This is the value usually described as *dignidad de la persona,* literally, "dignity of the person." It refers, however, to inner dignity, rather than to social or other outward prestige. Originally, no doubt, the influence of the Catholic Church, with its strong emphasis upon the soul, contributed heavily to the definition of this value. As a part of the middle-strata culture, it has now lost any exclusively religious connotation and has become a secular guide to conduct.

The Ecuadorian writer, Benítes, explains in sociological terms the heavy emphasis upon the "soul." To the socially insecure Spaniards who conquered America, says Benítes, one's own person, one's soul, was the most tangible reality. "It was the *mystique* of a marginal class which wished to mark off its individuality. . . . *Dignidad* is the formulation of a marginal class insecure in its social position."[1] Another Ecuadorian writer, Pérez Guerrero, describes Latin Americans as "individualists," but in a manner different from North Americans. There is an "exaltation of the I, which does not perceive itself as a unit in the group, but as the whole group itself. Pride and *dignidad* are exaggerated, and the group serves as a pedestal for the self."[2] Essentially, the same is true of Mexicans, according to Iturriaga. "The Mexican," he states, "is not gregarious, but individualistic, and, as a consequence, he often lacks the spirit of collaboration. His unsociability and asperity unfit him to live with others without friction or to work creatively as a member of a team." These observations, quoted more or less at random among many statements by Latin Americans, carry a critical tone, but they reflect the awareness among middle-group writers of the value attached to the inner person.

The emphasis on personalism means that words or actions interpreted as insults to the individual's inner worth are highly explosive in their effects. They may evoke an intense emotional reaction, with verbal or physical violence, or else a sullen resentment, a refusal to cooperate, and a devious search for "revenge." For this reason perhaps, American Spanish and Portuguese idioms contain elaborately precautionary patterns of ceremonial politeness which are in constant use as a buffer between all but the closest of friends and kinsmen.

Various types of admired personalities are derived from the high value attached to "personalism." The *macho* (literally, "male") type is highly valued. The *macho* is expected to show sexual prowess, zest for action, including verbal "action," daring, and, above all, absolute self-confidence. He may express his inner convictions by resorting to physical force, as in the case of bandits and revolutionary military leaders, or he may do so verbally as a leading intellectual, lawyer, or politician. Not all *machos* are *caudillos* (leaders), but all *caudillos* must be *machos*. In politics, a man is not commonly elected

[1] Leopoldo Benítes Vinueza, *Ecuador: Drama y paradoja* (Mexico City: Fondo de Cultura Económica, 1950), pp. 52–54, 86.

[2] Alfredo Pérez Guerrero, *Ecuador* (Quito: Casa de la Cultura Ecuatoriana, 1948), p. 74.

or acclaimed to office because he represents the social, economic, and political positions of his followers, but because he embodies in his own personality those inner qualities that they feel in themselves and they would like to manifest, had they but the talent to do so, in their own actions.[3] Of course, some of the same charismatic qualities attach to leaders elsewhere. Yet, over the long run, in contrast to Latin America, North American followers or constituents seem to be more strongly motivated by rational or pragmatic judgments in choosing their leaders, when considered in prospect or on the basis of performance.

Traditionally, for the middle-status individual, only those with whom he feels an intimate, personal relationship are trustworthy. Personal friendship, plus a kinship relationship of some kind, is essential for "getting something done." The impersonal confidence which, say, a customer has toward a salesman of a large, established corporation in the United States is not yet a general feature of the middle-status pattern. This is one reason why the forms of democracy which exist throughout Latin America, borrowed in the first instance from the United States or the French Declaration of the Rights of Man, seem to have little effect on actual political behavior. Similarly, any "program," such as Point Four, requires the "personal touch" if it is to succeed. North American administrators and experts, regardless of their personal competence, will have little success in their dealings with the middle segments unless they are able to develop personal confidence and evoke *simpatía.*

It is notoriously difficult in Latin America to float large issues of stocks and bonds, only in part because of the scarcity of investment funds. Repeated studies have shown that many individuals and families with funds available for investment are loath to use them to buy "mere pieces of paper." Unless they know personally and understand the individuals involved, they lack confidence in them. The same attitude accounts for much of the political instability in Latin America. In the middle-status pattern of values, it is only natural for political

[3] Cf. René de Visme Williamson, *Culture and Policy: The United States and the Hispanic World* (Knoxville: University of Tennessee Press, 1949).

actions to be governed by personalistic considerations, rather than by adherence to "principles," party platforms, and similar abstractions. The reliance on persons is, of course, open to exploitation by politicians, who, by personalistic attacks upon the *dignidad* of their opponents, can block the kinds of compromise which in the United States and England are regarded as one of the mainstays of the democratic process.

The Strength of Family Ties

The personal intimacy that a middle-status Latin American requires in his social dealings with other individuals is bolstered by the persistent patterns of kinship. Generally speaking, he feels that members of his family or of a larger kin group understand his inner uniqueness and provide the sort of intimate contact that does not require him to "keep up his guard." Kin relationships traditionally include a wide range of persons related by blood or marriage. In addition, there are usually strong ties to the "ceremonial kin," through the *compadrazgo* (co-godparenthood). Even now, the middle-status family in Latin America tends to include a much wider circle of relatives than is at present common in the United States. The average person is often in fairly intimate contact with a large number of kinsmen of several generations and of various degrees of "remove" on "either side." The small immediate family, consisting only of husband, wife, and minor children, and isolated from most other kinsmen, is still an anomaly even in urban life.

Originally the family was patriarchal, with the father officially in absolute authority and with the mother and unmarried females restricted in their close contacts with males to their relatives and members of the clergy. During courtship, unmarried girls were always carefully chaperoned. Married men and boys carried on much of their social life outside the home, with groups of other men at bars or clubs, or with their mistresses or in houses of prostitution. Sons of the family were usually "spoiled" from a middle-class North American point of view. Married women, on the other hand, although restricted in their social and intellectual contacts, necessarily were trained to a role of responsibility, for they were the practical administrators of the household. This traditional pattern is breaking down among the more advanced and upward-mobile members of the middle segments, especially in the larger towns and cities.

One of the important trends is the emergence of women as significant figures in public life, a phenomenon so far confined almost entirely to the women of the middle groups. Yet, few "emancipated" women have cut themselves off from a large net of kinfolk, and kinship of all types is more highly valued by both sexes than among middle-class urbanites in the United States. Even in large cities, a person without kin, such as an abandoned orphan, is regarded as one of the most pitiable of human beings. And it is not mere politeness that customarily leads a Latin American to greet a friend, even on the street, with a stream of questions about the health and doings of wife, children, father, mother, and numerous other kindred. The inquirer is often genuinely interested in his friend's relatives as individuals. More important, he also sees his friend as part of a kin group and knows that his personal welfare and state of mind are influenced by those of his kinsmen.

The Importance of Hierarchy

For the Latin American, the universe, including human society, has traditionally been arranged in a series of strata, and the culture is still strongly influenced by the values which he attaches to hierarchy. The political, social, and religious structures of the colonial era were highly stratified. A rigid political structure, ultimately controlled from the Iberian peninsula, imposed upon the colonies a system of political ranks and powers. Most office-holders were sent out from the home country without consultation with the colonists. Although this system was more rigid in the Spanish domains than in Brazil, there also the local people had to "look upward" in the political sense. Even under the republics, political thinking and action were molded so strongly by this structure that some observers regard it even now as a controlling value.[4] The stratification of political power was rein-

[4] Blanksten sees the political system of Ecuador, as late as 1948, as "monarchy in republican dress"; George I. Blanksten, *Ecuador:*

forced by the traditional pattern of social class and caste. And while the church has always insisted upon the equality of all human souls before God, the heavenly scheme and the terrestrial ministry are alike arranged in explicitly hierarchical orders.

Under the weight of this tradition, it is not surprising that the typical middle-status individual sees most things on a scale ranging from "lower" to "higher." At first glance, this emphasis on hierarchy seems to contradict the value attached to personalism or inner uniqueness. But the distinctive worth of each individual has nothing to do with his social position or his recognized distinction; advancement in the hierarchy may come, although not necessarily so, as the result of fulfilling one's unique potentialities. In contrast with the United States' credo, Latin Americans do not believe that all men are born "equal." You cannot be equal to anyone else in your inner essence when, by definition, you and everyone else are "unique." It is also obvious that, from the point of view of social rank, everyone is not equal.

For at least the last hundred years the idea has been gaining ground that the ranks of the human hierarchies on this earth are "open," rather than preordained, and this is, of course, demonstrated above all by the emergence of the middle segments. The liberal revolutions and constitutions of the last quarter of the nineteenth century opened the doors of law and politics to increasing numbers of middle-status people and to the eventual appearance of the new upper class. And it is certainly true that the concept of equality of opportunity as a right of the citizen is spreading throughout Latin America.

Despite these trends, the controlling concept of hierarchy still explains much of the behavior of the middle groups. It is reflected, for example, in the strong sense of social position, in the pattern of "decency" of living standard, valued as much or more for symbolic than utilitarian values. A very important role is still played by the *patrón* system, or its modern variants, as a substitute for a more general sense of social responsibility. In Latin America the old aristocracy did not cultivate the

---

Constitutions and Caudillos (Berkeley: University of California Press, 1951), p. 169, and elsewhere.

patterns of *noblesse oblige*, as was the case in England, and perhaps one consequence has been the continuing absence of any real feeling of community responsibility. Although Rotary International and similar "service clubs" have been organized among upper-level middle-status businessmen in the larger cities, the notion of the "more fortunate" elements of society actually getting down to a man-to-man basis with the "more unfortunate" in order to help them is virtually unknown.

The *patrón* relationship was originally a reciprocal arrangement tying members of various social strata together, in terms not of social or economic equality, but of reciprocal obligations of an unequal sort. On a typical *hacienda* (plantation) or ranch, the owner was, and usually still is, *patrón* to his workers or tenants. They owe him a certain amount of work, variously calculated, in return for his supplying them with housing, tools, and perhaps individual plots of land. They also owe him a certain loyalty in disputes and other difficulties. In return he acts as their "protector" in brushes with the law and with higher authority. The custom by which *patrones* serve as godfathers to the children of their more faithful retainers sets up a solemn tie of ceremonial kinship, which in a way defines the whole enterprise as "one big family," although social equality is by no means implied. The *patrón*, nonetheless, is expected to take a personal interest in the welfare of his workers or tenants and their families. He knows them by their first names, attends them or sends them aid when they are ill, and contributes to their *fiestas*. Essentially the same sort of relationship has been traditional in handicraft shops, mines, and small factories. The *patrón* or "protector" idea permeates most sectors of the middle category.

Small *patrones* usually have *patrones* of their own—"bigger" and more powerful men upon whom they can rely and who serve them as protectors and as contacts in communicating with the higher political, social, or economic powers. A distributor of merchandise is often in a *patrón*-like relationship with his retail tradesmen, a manufacturer with his suppliers of raw materials, an employer of seasonal workers with his labor recruiters (*enganchadores*). In public service and political employment the system is especially strong. Every public employee tries to gain a "protector" in the higher levels of the administration simply as a form of job insurance, if not in the hope of promotion.

The armed forces, although organized hierarchically in Latin America as elsewhere, appear to constitute one of the few graded systems of social status in Latin American society in which the *patrón* relationship is relatively weak, possibly because the common soldiers are conscripted for a limited term of service and therefore are not in any continuing relationship with their superiors. However, career officers, whether commissioned or noncommissioned, usually try to develop *patrón* relationships with superiors.

Presidents of republics, whether dictatorial or democratic, are expected to play the *patrón* role toward their constituents. For this reason, they are usually available for several hours each week to any citizens, no matter how lowly their stations in life, who wish to see them in person.

Large business enterprises and large bureaucracies cannot preserve the personal relationship between the *patrón* and his clients. Nevertheless, the hierarchical outlook remains, and with it the expectation that someone or something "higher up" owes one certain obligations. As a consequence, the state has had to make some gestures toward filling this void, and it has moved to do so through developing labor codes, with appropriate machinery for supervising them, social security programs, free health and hospital services, public housing programs, and the like. Much of the leadership and all the administrative personnel for the development of the new "public *patrón*" system of welfare services have come from members of the middle groups.

In some quarters in the United States, there is a tendency to look upon these "welfare state" provisions in Latin American countries as dangerously "socialistic" innovations which may eventually lead to communism. On the contrary, I believe that they should be considered as responses to deep-seated values and as defenses against communism, provided they are honestly and efficiently administered. The danger of communism arises when a Latin American government merely pays lip service to the expectations of its people and fails to meet its need for protective services. It is noteworthy that much social legislation has been established under dictatorships that were opposed not only to communism, but also to democracy.

A Variant of Materialism

Many articulate Latin Americans like to say that their culture is essentially a spiritual one, and some of them derive an obvious satisfaction from contrasting this assumption with the "crassly materialistic" values they attribute to the United States. Yet even such critics, when in a frank and confidential mood, admit that they and their compatriots are not entirely uninterested in material things. The point is, I think, that materialism is seen and defined somewhat differently by them.

Perhaps the traditional Latin American variety can best be termed "tangible materialism." The pattern has been to trust and seek only those kinds of property "one can put one's hands on." Stocks and bonds, and other securities of corporations and companies not known "personally" to the investor, are mere pieces of paper; they are not tangible. Nor are copyrights, patents, royalty agreements, and similar "invisible" properties to be trusted. One apparent exception is lottery tickets, which many Latin Americans buy each week, but a lottery ticket is generally regarded not as "property" but as an investment in "fate."

Among all classes, land and buildings are regarded as the most tangible types of property. People of the middle class, however, do not work the land with their own hands. When one of them owns productive land, he has *peones* or tenants to do the labor. Furthermore, the ideal pattern is to have one or more servants to work about the house, as the wife and other members of the family are not supposed to stoop to domestic drudgery.

In some parts of society the controlling power of the values associated with tangible materialism is weakening. Still, its persistent strength explains some forms of behavior which differ widely from those now customary in the United States. It has usually been difficult, for example, to finance large undertakings by the widespread sale of securities. Savings and insurance plans are poorly developed, because of the distrust of smaller savers for impersonal pieces of paper and impersonal institutions. The disdain for manual work means that the market for labor-saving devices is proportionately much smaller among middle-class families than among similar groups in North America. It is usually cheaper and certainly more "respectable" to hire a maid, a cook, and a yard man than to buy the numerous gadgets that middle-class North American husbands and wives use in doing the household chores themselves. Credit is difficult to come by, and interest rates are high. A man who invests his money in a business enterprise may expect a return of 30 per cent or more a year and is reluctant to take risks.

This pattern has permitted foreigners or local people of foreign extraction to develop large areas of business more by default than by competition. Much of the alleged "Yankee economic imperialism," despite some mistakes and excesses, has simply represented a movement of outside enterprise into areas of economic vacuum. In almost every country some middle-status intellectuals have recognized the economic weaknesses of the present pattern and have sought to remedy them through governmental action and institutions. In the last twenty-five years many governments have endeavored to provide parts of the structural framework which have traditionally been provided by private enterprise in the United States: development corporations to encourage investment, with the government supplying much of the capital and taking most of the risk; government-financing of large industrial projects; small-loan banks of various types; government insurance plans; and so on. Again, some critics see these as moves toward "socialism" and the "welfare state," but until or unless basic patterns are changed they will probably continue to grow in importance.

Although middle-group people are sensitive about the degrading symbolic effects of "manual labor," it is a gross libel to call them lazy or indolent. They habitually expend enormous amounts of personal energy when engaged in something they consider valuable or interesting. On the other hand, working just for the sake of keeping busy is not regarded as necessarily a good thing, and temporary idleness is not regarded as in itself immoral.

Within the realm of materialistic values, the mere manipulation of things in order to explore their mechanical or functional potentialities is not an all-engrossing interest. Most Latin Americans of the middle class are not dominated by a "mechanistic world view," nor are they usually moved by an urge to undertake systematic, empirical investigations. There have been few outstanding contributions to science, either basic or applied, and little solving of everyday material problems to which industrially more advanced peoples have applied the common-sense ingenuity developed from their long familiarity with machines and physical forces. There is ample evidence that Latin Americans are able to achieve success in the mechanistic arts, but traditionally they have not been much interested in them.

The Weight of Transcendental Values

Of far more importance to most middle-status Latin Americans are what they often call spiritual or transcendental values—"the something beyond" (*lo algo más allá*). Just as, to them, an individual has an inner essence and a dignity that may not be immediately apparent, so the universe and human experience are believed to have a deeper, not always manifest, meaning. Not all people can express this pattern of values succinctly, but much of the cultural behavior does so obliquely. The cultural life of the middle groups has an aesthetic tone which middle-class North Americans of today do not often permit themselves. Northrop sees this as "aesthetic intuition."[5] And Iturriaga says, ". . . of the great cultural values–truth, goodness, justice, beauty, saintliness–the Mexican does not hesitate in his preference; beauty constitutes a force of gravity that attracts him. . . ." "Literary activity is of such vital importance to the lives of Latin Americans," writes Torres Ríoseco, "that it may be said to occupy a position similar to that of economic interest in the life of North America. . . ."[6] And in philosophy, says Sánchez Reulet, Latin Americans

[5] F. S. C. Northrop, *The Meeting of East and West* (New York: Macmillan, 1946), p. 23.

[6] Arturo Torres Ríoseco, *The Epic of Latin American Literature* (New York: Oxford University Press, 1956), p. 168.

"have a deep humanistic sense. They recognize the value of science and technology, but doubt that man can fulfill his destiny only by the road of science and technology. And in all this there is an exaltation of human creative energies, a constant insistence on the values of action and liberty."[7]

Nor are these views confined to professional "long-hairs" and "egg heads." In contrast to the tendency in the United States to regard the arts and philosophy as the exclusive province of ivory-tower specialists, among Latin American middle groups no one hesitates to pursue and display these interests. There it is not regarded as effeminate or eccentric to exhibit whatever talent one has. Even a businessman, before getting down to mundane matters, may display a verse he has written the night before or boast about his children's prowess in music. The middle-status reader expects his newspapers to inform him of philosophical questions and to offer him good literature and art criticism. Practically every large newspaper carries at least one page of literary material daily, whereas few of them have a financial page with complete stock quotations and other business news. Interest in the aesthetic aspects of architecture and city planning has always been strong in Latin America. Even small provincial towns take pride in beautifying at least the central plaza. Publicly supported band concerts, theaters, orchestras, opera and stage companies, and art museums are taken for granted as part of urban life.

Although undoubtedly there are psychological factors involved in this search for "the ultimate" and "something beyond," it is surely these values that in large measure make life worth living for many Latin Americans of middle status, and it is foolhardy for North Americans who wish to be friends with them to ignore or disparage this cultural strand. It must be kept in mind that in the field of practical politics and international relations prominent holders of political office, civil servants, and diplomatic representatives are often writers, philosophers, or poets of international renown. They receive such posts not only because of their prestige, but also because of a genuine belief that their success in aesthetic

[7] Aníbal Sánchez Reulet, ed., *La filosofía latinoamericana contemporánea* (Washington: Pan American Union, 1949), p. 19.

pursuits fits them for posts of national responsibility and leadership. It is obvious that for such men and women, and for the middle groups they usually represent, a purely pragmatic approach to problems does not necessarily constitute the most effective appeal.

The emphasis upon words, ideals, and elegance of expression has been condemned by some Latin American critics.[8] One of the causes of instability in political life, as they see it, is the tendency to feel that the job is finished when written expression has been given to ideals, through the composing of constitutions, party declarations, and statutes, while systematic, determined efforts to translate the verbalized ideals into reality often are wanting. Yet we must recognize that cultural idealism, even though occasionally naïve and falling short in adequate implementation, offers better prospects for progress than indifference or crass cynicism. In addition, it must not be forgotten that, along with the value they place on words and concepts, Latin Americans demonstrate a high degree of aptitude for logical thinking and clear statement.

Their consuming interest in ideas and sentiments also makes Latin Americans responsive to outside ideologies and emotional appeals. It is no accident that the slogans of the Four Freedoms, set forth in the Atlantic Charter, were eagerly accepted in Latin America, or that Marxist ideology has received careful study in many Latin American circles. Because of their admiration for a certain elegance in argumentation, Latin Americans are not slow to identify and ridicule inconsistencies and confusions which they perceive in U.S. propaganda. Nor is their enthusiasm aroused by what they often consider to be an undue emphasis on utilitarianism and pragmatism.

Emotion as Fulfillment of the Self

For Latin Americans, to be alive is to feel strongly, and when one feels an emotion one should express it. Such ex-

[8] For example, Carlos Octavio Bunge, *Nuestra América: Ensayo de psicología social* (6th ed.; Buenos Aires: Administración General, 1918). This author is still quoted frequently by Latin American writers on this and other matters.

pression is one of the openly approved values of the traditional culture. This deeply held value apparently is derived in part from the Iberian mother countries. It is difficult to find any parallel to it among the aboriginal peoples. As a rule the Indians are schooled to patterns that in public give the impression of passivity and taciturnity. Not so the average middle-status Latin American. He will usually speak his mind or, more properly, his feelings on almost any subject, given the slightest occasion. "The Spaniard," as Schurz puts it in sketching the Iberian background, "is a man of passion. . . . he may not do things according to reason or logic or cold calculation . . . but according to the light of intuition and the urge of strong feeling. He may even do something for no good reason at all, but only by the prompting of caprice. Then he will act under the blind impulse of *gana,* or the moving of the spirit."[9]

In Latin America many ordinary, "undistinguished" persons are among the most interesting conversationalists and impromptu storytellers in the world. Any mundane incident, such as a day's trip to the market, is often "milked" of all possible emotional content in the telling. And serious matters must customarily be expressed emotionally if they are to receive a positive response and interest. In politics the appeal to the emotions is, of course, ever present and frequently obscures other interests.

If all this is the positive aspect of the value attached to feeling, the negative facet is ennui or routine, which must be avoided or broken whenever possible. The most frequent expression of this urge is through the *fiestas* which occur at regular intervals throughout the year. The community *fiesta* serves as an occasion for renewing personal contacts and symbolizing social solidarity with a pleasant emotional overtone, in addition to being an escape from ennui. Laughter and *alegría* (happiness) are as important as the expression of more "serious" emotions. Latin Americans of most regions are particularly adept at the *chiste,* or joke, the play on words (*juego de palabras*), and the aphorism or proverb. In the exercise of this skill, sympathetic laughter and admiration

[9] William Lytle Schurz, *This New World: The Civilization of Latin America* (New York: Dutton, 1954), p. 82.

are the storyteller's sole rewards. Witticism is also used with devastating effect in politics and other public affairs. This can lead, however, to the emotionalizing of issues which in other cultures may be examined in their practical context. North Americans, in contrast, are often criticized for being dry and cold.

The Sense of Fatalism

Running through the other values which shape the outlook of the average member of the middle segments of Latin American society is the sense of fatalism. Perhaps it is less pervasive in Brazil than in the Spanish-speaking countries, but it is nowhere absent as an underlying factor in determining modes of behavior and attitudes. Its two general forms are those of heroic defiance and passive resignation. The first appears as a heightened expression of the value of personalism. Each person owes it to himself to strive, to mobilize and exert his inner resources, to live and die with *dignidad*. Yet, fate must ever be reckoned with and, for reasons beyond the control of man, it may often be unjust. As Unamuno expressed it in his classic statement, paraphrasing Sénancour: "And if it is nothingness that awaits us, let us so act that it will be an unjust fate."[10] This point of view has been accepted by many authors in Portuguese and Spanish America.

In the Spanish countries the bull fight (*corrida de toros*) is a dramatization of Man facing Death. The matador pits all his skill against the bull, which is Death incarnate. But he does it with finesse, with imperturbability, and with grace. If he is successful, Man has once more defied and conquered Death—for the time being. But in the next bull fate may show its hand, and the matador may fly through the air with his body ripped open, to fall a bloody, quivering mass on the sand. And fate can always win if, at "the moment of truth" when Man and Death face each other for the kill, the man's courage falters and he cringes, even in spirit. While the *corrida* is a dramatization of this theme staged before a great

[10] Miguel de Unamuno, *The Tragic Sense of Life*, tr. by J. E. Crawford Fitch (New York: Dover Publications, 1954), p. 263. (Original title, *Del sentimiento trágico de la vida,* 1912.)

crowd of spectators, many a Latin American thinks of less spectacular situations as a continuation of the same dramatic struggle with fate. He sees himself as "acting out" the heroic theme in his own small way. The sense of fatalism may be manifested in the seemingly fanatical defiance of danger by soldiers and revolutionary mobs, in an apparent willingness to endure hardships disproportionate to the goal at hand and to take risks beyond all rationality. The elaborate cult of death, funerals, and graveyards is a further expression of the value attached to fatalism.

The theme of resignation, within the deep-lying sense of fatalism, is expressed in both "happy" and "melancholy" customs. A cheerful aspect is shown in the universal hope for good luck, of which the lottery is perhaps the most ubiquitous form. Its less optimistic aspect is seen as the mood swings into *tristeza,* a sort of sweet sadness, to which people surrender with pleasure. A crowd will ask a brass band in the park to play *un triste*. Friends around the tables then start drinking earnestly in the hope of working into a mood of sadness, meanwhile having the time of their lives. Much popular music and the accompanying words are sad, and melancholy poems appear every day to please the public.

In public life, fatalistic resignation may lead to what Bunge, the Argentine sociologist and critic, called "creole indolence" (*la pereza criolla*), a tendency to shirk the seeking of constructive solutions to problems. In politics it has induced a general paralysis of action. In public health, one of the principal problems has been the ingrained belief that a certain amount of sickness and death is inevitable. It is "the will of God" or "fate."[11] As social mobility and the rewards of pragmatic ingenuity, combined with group action and the workability of democratic procedures, are demonstrated, the fatalistic complex will probably decline in importance.

From the viewpoint of social psychiatry, however, one advantage of the value associated with fatalism should perhaps be mentioned here. The sense of the blind power of fate is combined, for most members of the middle groups at least,

[11] George Foster, *A Cross Cultural Anthropological Analysis of a Technical Aid Program* (Washington: Smithsonian Institution, 1951; mimeographed), discusses this theme in several situations.

with the theme of striving, one of the values of "the person." An individual must strive to fulfill his inner potentialities as a unique person. If he fails, after having made "a good try," he is not torn by feelings of guilt, conscience, or inadequacy, which play a large part in the psychological aftereffects of failure in North American culture. For a Latin American who has "done his best," failure is due to the inscrutable ways of "fate" (or "the will of God"). It is not his personal "fault."

TYPES AND SIGNIFICANCE OF RECENT LATIN AMERICAN DICTATORS

Five dictators of importance in recent Latin American history have been Getúlio Vargas, Juan Perón, Manuel Odría, Rojas Pinilla, and Pérez Jiménez. In this selection, Tad Szulc, a *New York Times* correspondent, compares their similarities and differences. Mr. Szulc stresses that although all five attempted to ally with the working masses, they differed in their way of coming into power, their personal characteristics, their style of governing, their impact on society, their way of leaving office, and their later popularity. Mr. Szulc suggests that Manuel Odría might have been a benevolent dictator. This raises the question of what criteria one would stress in attempting to argue that such a dictator is possible.

*The Dictators**

TAD SZULC

Five great dictatorships overshadowed the history of South America in the last quarter of a century. Together they formed the main transition phase in the political, economic, and social development of the non-Anglo-Saxon portion of the hemisphere in the modern age. Chronologically staggered over twenty-five years but overlapping in most instances because their heaviest simultaneous concentration came in the late

* Reprinted from Tad Szulc, *Twilight of the Tyrants* (New York: Henry Holt & Co., 1959), Chapter 2 by permission of Holt, Rinehart & Winston, Inc. and Ashley Famous Agency, Inc. © 1959 by Tad Szulc.

1940's and lasted until the latter part of the 1950's, they influenced each other and helped to set the political tone for much of Latin America.

This discussion concerns itself with the dictatorships in Brazil, Argentina, Peru, Colombia, and Venezuela; the personalities of their chieftains; and the ultimate impact they had upon their societies—in the measure that it is possible to evaluate them with such a short perspective in time. These five dictatorships and dictators were singled out as subjects for examination because their histories are believed to offer the best insight into the process of basic transformations now occurring in Latin America.

The stories of Trujillo in the Dominican Republic, Somoza in Nicaragua, and Stroessner in Paraguay belong to an earlier dictatorial age, that of absolute domination or ownership of a country by a ruler who, for reasons of locally prevailing conditions, did not need to respond greatly to any of the undercurrents of thought sweeping the hemisphere at the present time. The Dominican Republic continues to be—as Nicaragua was until quite recently—the private estate of its dictator, and until new events occur it cannot be discussed in any other terms. But the death of the aging Trujillo, El Benefactor, which must come to him in a not too distant future even if it is from natural causes, could easily result in a political and social explosion akin to that in Venezuela at the passing of Gómez, the Tyrant of the Andes. Like Gómez, Trujillo, fearing possible rivals, did not allow the emergence of any strong personalities within his regime who could carry on after his death. His relatives seem as inept and ill-suited to dictatorial heritage as were Gómez' sons and brothers.

Paraguay, still stagnant and backward despite the stirrings of new economic activities and a slowly awakening political opposition, is in the hands of an army-backed civilian clique of the Colorado Party, which controls President Stroessner, rather than the other way round.

In terms of the transition that characterized the other South American dictatorships, the Paraguayan authoritarian experience is stationary at best, regressive at worst, even if the Stroessner regime did attract some industry and spread a bit of education. And if it were not for basic United States economic assistance, even these accomplishments would have loomed smaller. In April, 1959, giving in to growing external and internal pressures, Stroessner promised a series of political reforms designed to grant Paraguay at least a semblance of democratic government. The promises were received with natural skepticism, but even these verbal concessions indicated the dictator's uncertainty about his future.

The second Batista period in Cuba was of a hybrid nature, fitting somewhere in between traditional and modern dictatorships. It lacked ideological meaning even more than the Rojas Pinilla regime in Colombia, and, despite many up-to-date trappings, it was more suggestive of the doings of a Trujillo than of a Perón or Pérez Jiménez, who had political ideas of their own, lugubrious as they may have been. It was also distinguished for brutality.

Each of the five South American dictators discussed here has operated under different conditions, under different types of pressures, and in different ways. But one of the important things they had in common, and a revealing one in terms of historical trends in Latin America, was that all five, in varying degrees and in addition to the essential partnership with the military, reached out for alliances with the still politically amorphous working masses. By and large, these alliances were against the intelligentsia, the moderate and fast-growing middle classes, and the traditional elites of money and aristocracy.

In the end, however, this latter group supplied the decisive leadership in ousting the dictatorships and eventually massed behind them the majority of the people in the battles for freedom. In each case at least a large section of the underprivileged working classes turned against the dictators who had set out to woo them, as did the rulers' pampered military allies, who, when the chips were down, preferred to side with the rebelling populations.

Of the five great dictators, four are alive today and none of them has completely surrendered the hope of reconquering power. The fifth dictator has been dead since 1954, but his political influence continues to linger, like a voice from the Great Beyond, over his still-confused nation.

2

This man was Getúlio Dornelles Vargas, the only civilian in this dictatorial quintet, though he did acquire a home-town colonelcy in the course of one of the regional civil wars preceding the revolution that elevated him to power in Brazil. In order of time, Vargas, an outwardly cheerful, deceptively mild-looking man endowed with much erudition, great personal magnetism, immense toughness, and amazing political shrewdness, was the first of the remarkable modern South American dictators. In 1937, after seven years in office, he formally launched his *Estado Novo* (New State) regime as the Brazilian version of European fascism and corporativism, rich in studied demagoguery, political opportunism, and social appeal. He set himself up as the first contemporary "populist" president on the continent.

In point of personal and historical interest, Vargas towered over his more bombastic and superficial dictatorial colleagues of later days. While functioning as a dictator, he showed something akin to political brilliance. As a constitutional president, freely elected five years after his ouster from dictatorial power, he was a dismal failure, a tragic figure who finally chose suicide as the denouement of his long life. And from his deathbed he made the parting gesture of demagogic drama in the form of a political last will in which he proclaimed that he was giving his life to defend the working people from rapacious international interests.

Because he led Brazil, perhaps in erroneous fashion but always with conviction, through her greatest social revolution since the nineteenth century's abolishment of slavery and the change from empire to republic; because he was closely associated with the destinies of the largest and potentially the wealthiest of all the Latin-American nations for well over a quarter of a century; and because he was a man who commanded as much love as hate among his fellow citizens, Getúlio Vargas has left a deeper permanent mark on his country than any other modern dictator in his part of the world.

He is best remembered for revolutionizing political thinking in Brazil, fostering economic development, introducing social legislation, and instilling social consciousness into the masses that were being transformed from chattel-like farm hands and unskilled city workers into a fairly articulate rural and industrial proletariat. His policies and attitudes were paternalistic, his social legislation was so far ahead of the day that it often did more harm than good to the country as a whole, and in his dictatorial heyday he ruled with a constitution faithfully copied after European fascist charters.

Yet, as Latin-American dictatorships go, in spite of his secret police and his prisons and many attendant abuses and cruelties, Vargas' regime was not too oppressive. Benevolent was the word used for it by many observers of that era, and Vargas' official propaganda machine encouraged the impression.

Proceeding along a tortuous political line, adapting himself with enormous flexibility to the requirements of the moment, Vargas presided over the process of transforming Brazil from an economically feudal and almost completely agricultural nation into the dynamically expanding, partly industrialized country of today. Of course, this change was bound to come sooner or later, but Vargas, appearing on the scene at the historic moment, quickened it and directed the different forces at play into channels of his choosing. By centralizing all national controls in his hands and in the capital of Rio de Janeiro, he went far toward unifying Brazil politically and curbing the exaggeratedly autonomous powers of the twenty states forming the federal union.

Looking back at his period from the vantage point of many elapsed years, it is impossible to deny Vargas' many positive accomplishments—some of them fundamental for the development of Brazil—despite the central fact that he was a dictator and often a merciless one. This is a sympathetic judgment that cannot be applied to the other dictators, with the possible exception of General Manuel A. Odría of Peru.

Another fact setting Vargas apart from the other dictators was that he did not enrich himself in office—though most of his friends and relatives did in scandalous fashion and thereby set the stage for the final tragedy of his suicide. His personal life was quiet and unostentatious; he was a devoted husband and a good father. When Vargas died in 1954, he left behind a cash debt of about $40,000. His assets at his death were limited to the family ranch in the south of Brazil and an apartment in Rio de Janeiro. In sharp contrast, such dictators as Perón, Rojas Pinilla, Pérez Jiménez, and Batista amassed fortunes of millions of dollars during their tenures in power.

3

A dictatorship infinitely more outrageous and one almost completely barren of any of the positive aspects of the Vargas era in Brazil was the gift to Argentina of Juan Domingo Perón, army colonel turned politician. Perón rose to the presidency in 1946 through free elections, although some months earlier a mob-supported coup d'état had placed him in a commanding position to capture the votes of millions of workers who had fallen prey to his labor rabble-rousing. Like Vargas, but aping Mussolini's balcony-shouting techniques he had learned during his years in Italy, and which the Brazilian dictator never had to use, Perón presented himself and his wife Eva as the friends—the only friends—of the Argentine workingman. While he also controlled the army, Perón derived most of his power from the labor unions, whose leaders he made and unmade. Despite all abuses, the rank and file gave him their loyalty and support for a long time, perhaps mistaking the disruptive force he had handed them for the dignity and importance they had sought. And, damaging and distorting deeply Argentina's economy, he saw to it they were well off—no matter what was happening to the rest of the country. The loyalty of the Peronista workers did not end with Perón's overthrow in September, 1955. Greatly influencing from exile the political activities in Argentina, he issued instructions to vote for Arturo Frondizi in the February, 1958, elections that were obeyed by two million voters. But Frondizi turned his back on the Peronistas almost immediately after taking office, and the ex-dictator's followers became the worst thorn in his side, as they violently opposed his austere and courageous program of economic rehabilitation for Argentina.

Perón's strength stemmed chiefly from his appearance on

the national scene at the psychological moment when he could take advantage of a social explosion resulting from the disintegration of Argentina's cycle of rural semifeudalism. He passed on to the workers and their families the inebriating sensation that they, too, were running the country through something along the lines of a dictatorship of the proletariat, although Perón himself was never known to have used this expression. This approach, heavy on the social aspects of national life, explains why Perón and Vargas were the only ones among the five dictators to have retained a very substantial following for years after their exit from power.

But the decade of Perón's rule left Argentina, a once wealthy country, on the brink of economic ruin. Whereas Vargas had made a fairly serious attempt to find a new basis for the solution of Brazil's emerging social and economic problems, Perón's ideological contributions were his Justicialismo and Peronismo—two vague doctrines based almost exclusively on demagoguery, chauvinism, and mob rule in the streets by workers whipped into hysteria by his fascist methods. Vargas had never stooped that low in his dictatorial days, and, strangely, it took the return of democracy in Brazil to send him scurrying demagogically after the crowds.

A man of immense personal vanity that even defeat did not lessen, of highly objectionable morals that included a palace affair with a teen-age girl, and one of Latin America's leading exponents of corruption in public office, Juan Perón loomed as a tragic but probably unavoidable accident in Argentina's history.

4

If one would set out to make a case for an enlightened, benevolent dictatorship that has done a nation some good despite a denial of liberty, the eight years of the unspectacular regime of General of Division Manuel A. Odría in Peru could be singled out as the best modern example in Latin America. It cannot be put in the same class with the Vargas government because, while the Brazilian president led a social revolution along with his political experimentation, General Odría concentrated merely on sound administration, and, if anything, sociological transformation in the deep sense was arrested in Peru during his period. But important progress was made in improving the lot of the people through the development of the country's wealth, along with its social welfare and educational programs.

Odría assumed the presidential office in 1948 as the result of a military revolt designed to end the chaos into which Peru had been plunged by the attempts of a rabble-rousing political party, the APRA, to impose quick radical solutions for the country's deep-seated social problems. The age-old Andean problem of the destitute but stirring Indians—the problem that also is at the root of the revolutionary upheavals of neighboring Bolivia—was one of them. A disorderly and confused social revolution had been in progress in Peru when Odría stepped in at the head of his troops. The process of social ferment was then bottled up for eight years while the military regime successfully worked to restore peace and stability to Peru.

This done, General Odría took a step that became his main achievement and distinction: fulfilling an earlier promise, he allowed the holding of free elections in 1956. When the time came for the inauguration of Manuel Prado y Ugarteche, an old-line civilian politician and former president who emerged as his freely elected successor, Odría bowed out into the wings. Political democracy returned to Peru, and General Odría deserves his share of the credit for it. It was this unusual, and probably unprecedented, voluntary end of a military dictatorship that helped to make Odría and his period so worthy of note. It is an objective fact that he had been an efficient and successful administrator who, in eight years, led Peru from abysmal economic and political confusion to relative stability and a prosperous economy.

It may be reasonable to expect that the country's fundamental social problems will find a better and a less painful solution now that Peru stands on a sounder basis. APRA itself, mellower and more mature, has returned to the Peruvian scene as the mainstay of the Prado administration and is making a contribution to its endeavor to develop the country and its people. Political passions, red-hot in 1948, have died down in Peru to a surprising extent but, while deep differences remain among individuals as well as parties and new controversies emerge daily, the nation appears to be moving ahead in a more constructive and orderly fashion than ever before. And this time it is doing so within a free and democratic form of government.

As was to be the case later with Rojas Pinilla in Colombia and Pérez Jiménez in Venezuela, Odría's advent in Peru was greeted with much hope by the conservative classes, who saw in the military revolution a promise of the restoration of political peace and the consequent return of a favorable business and economic climate. This they found in the Odría regime, but they found also repression or denial of most of the freedoms. Thus, these influential but shortsighted people who were willing to go along with Bolívar's "able despotism" formula must share the blame for the initial strengthening of the dictatorship. But in time they learned their lesson and they showed it by helping to establish a public-opinion climate that must have played a key role in leading Odría to keep his word about restoring democracy to Peru.

With all that can be said in his favor, Odría was still a dictator, and in matters of freedom there evidently can be no rationalizations or compromise. He won an earlier election by imprisoning his opponent; he allowed no independent political parties to function in any real sense of the word; he tolerated no freedom of the press, except during the period immediately preceding the 1956 elections; he exiled many of his enemies and imprisoned others. Yet his rule was not characterized by the shocking police excesses of Perón's Argentina, Pérez Jiménez' Venezuela, or even Vargas' Brazil.

A colorless though forceful personality and a quiet, almost timid man, Odría evoked no strong emotions. He was neither hated nor loved. His leave-taking was not celebrated with wild demonstrations of joy, as took place at the fall of the dictators in Argentina, Colombia, Venezuela, and Cuba. Few missed him when he was gone. To the people of Peru, he was an accident of history, accepted while it lasted but forgotten almost immediately when Odría vanished from before the footlights.

5

In sharp contrast to the easygoing but efficient Odría in Peru, neighboring Colombia was run between 1953 and 1957 by an inept and vain military dictator, General Gustavo Rojas Pinilla. As commander in chief of the armed forces, Rojas Pinilla directed a coup d'état that threw out of office Dr. Laureano Gómez, a cantankerous right-wing dictator during whose presidential period the lingering civil war between the Conservatives and Liberals had reached bloody and alarming proportions. When democratic rule returned to Colombia late in 1958, the death toll for the decade of civil war stood near two hundred thousand. The country's population was under twelve million.

Rojas' coup was hailed throughout Colombia as an act of salvation. The general promised a government that would end the internecine strife and bring about the national unity needed to restore Colombia's traditional democracy and allow her to get back on a normal path of progress.

But the bright hopes did not last long. Rojas Pinilla, surrounded by a palace clique of rapacious relatives and friends, soon became a full-fledged dictator, imprisoning his critics, silencing the free press, and erecting a system of self-glorification, special privileges, and corruption. He participated in the latter with complete abandon and immense personal profit, and during his tenure in the presidency he became one of Colombia's biggest cattle owners.

Rojas flooded the country with his portrait in gala army and navy uniforms, with Caesarlike busts, and even with wrist watches bearing his picture on the face. With all this, Rojas Pinilla's performance in terms of being a successful dictator added up to total failure when compared to the records of his colleagues. Despite its opposition to him, the majority of Colombia's public opinion was willing to let him serve out his term ending in 1958, but Rojas, through a series of unnecessary and ill-advised measures, precipitated the 1957 revolt and his own fall. A member of Pérez Jiménez' dictatorial regime in Venezuela, a lethally efficient group, remarked once to this writer that "Rojas is downgrading and cheapening through his stupidities the whole institution of dictatorship." Yet the irony of it was that the Venezuelan dictator repeated some of the very same errors of Rojas and thereby brought doom upon himself.

Unlike Pérez Jiménez, General Rojas left very few important works as a monument to himself—a crucial dictatorial failing even if allowances are made for the fact that Colombia's resources and revenues were not comparable to Venezuela's. Finding a reasonably prosperous land despite years of civil war, Rojas turned it back to its people riddled with internal and external debts—and with precious little to show for them. He did not wreck Colombia's economy as efficiently as Perón did Argentina's—perhaps because he was not very efficient at anything and because he had only four years, against Perón's decade, in which to inflict the damage. To help eradicate all manifestations of independent political life in the nation—always a threat to a dictator—Rojas Pinilla came up with the slogan of "Motherland Above the Parties." Then he proceeded to build around himself a political faction called the Third Force that, in crude and pathetic imitation of Perón's Justicialismo, sought to draw support from organized labor and to do a considerable bit of glorification of the Supreme Chief. In further imitation of the Peróns, General Rojas' daughter Maria Eugenia took over Colombia's social assistance organization, but, having neither the looks, intelligence, nor personality of Evita, she did not extract from these activities important political dividends for her father.

Like Perón before him and Pérez Jiménez afterward, Rojas Pinilla collided with the powerful Roman Catholic Church, which had just launched its new liberal policy in Latin America and would not tolerate his awkward excursions into the realm of "populist" pseudo social experiments. In May, 1957, Rojas Pinilla, the man who was fully and tragically convinced until the last moment that he was truly beloved by his people, tumbled from power when all of Colombia rose in protest against his arrogant attempt to have his rubber-stamp National Constituent Assembly re-elect him a year ahead of time for another term in office. The democratic government that succeeded the post-Rojas Military Junta allowed him to return to Colombia late in 1958, and the deposed dictator, still dreaming of power, wasted no time in preparing a conspiracy. But so tiny was the support he commanded in the nation that the government had no difficulty breaking up the plot, even before it was actually staged, and arresting Rojas.

Politically, the Rojas Pinilla dictatorship stood for nothing in particular. Although it was conceived as a means of halting the civil war, actually hostilities increased under his rule, and acts of brutal retaliation by his troops, such as the massacre of the civilian population of the town of Chaparral in Tolima department, did nothing to establish peace. The regime was completely lacking in the kind of social content that had been offered as an excuse for Vargas or even Perón. It had tried to capitalize on political—and almost emotional—strife between two sections of the Colombian population, the Liberals and the Conservatives.

Such economic tensions as underlay the conflict were not of a scope to give Rojas Pinilla room or opportunity to contribute anything tangible—not even a sweepingly bad idea—in the social field. While Colombia has a terribly deep social problem in the enormous gulf between the wealthy minority and the utterly destitute rural and urban masses, the civil war was not fought over this issue in any fundamental way. With some exceptions, it was feudal-type civil warfare, but one that in all probability set the stage for new social conflicts already taking shape. Only now that a free government has been created and the old problems are seen in a new and urgent light is Colombia beginning to come to grips with her basic ills.

Thus, caught in a maelstrom he did not fully understand, Rojas was little more than a throwback to the old-fashioned Latin-American military man on horseback. But he, too, performed his historical function: the anti-Rojas revolution united the two warring parties as nothing else could have done. It stopped organized Liberal-Conservative warfare and it has finally put Colombia back on the democratic track after an upheaval-punctured lapse of eleven years. The proof of this new national maturity was the bipartisan support for Dr. Alberto Lleras Camargo in the presidential elections in the spring of 1958 and in the first phase of his administration.

6

The last and the most ludicrous of the South American dictators of mid-century was General of Division Marcos Pérez Jiménez of Venezuela. His was the most ruthless but also the most complex of these dictatorships. It was a bizarre mixture of rule by sheer brutal force and of striking social, economic, and political experimentation that reached all the way back to the beginnings of Venezuelan history, playing on a curious sense of national inferiority of the Venezuelans. Naming his regime the New National Ideal, Pérez Jiménez was, at least in his own eyes, a man with a mission. Like other contemporary Latin-American dictators, he took advantage of the great economic and social pressures in his country. But, deliberately, he ignored the political aspects of the historical transition of a nation that had long been starving while billions of dollars from oil-industry revenues were piling up in its coffers or were being misspent on schemes that were always grandiose but often totally unnecessary.

Pérez Jiménez had a Bolívarian obsession: while Bolívar, the Liberator, had been, nearly a hundred fifty years ago, the political emancipator of his native Venezuela and of much of South America, this intense self-conscious little General from the Andes aspired to the glory of being Venezuela's and, if possible, South America's economic "liberator." Surrounded by a weird cast of characters, some of them brilliant, if intellectually distorted, thinkers, Pérez Jiménez drew many of his basic policies and philosophical ideas from them. But it was his strength of purpose, his immense will power, and his outstanding qualities of cunning and intrigue that held together for nine years this system of total political aberration.

In a way Pérez Jiménez took up where Juan Vicente Gómez had left off at his death in 1935, when one of Latin America's longest personal dictatorships had come to an end after twenty-seven years. And the similarities between the two men were endless and striking. They shared modest beginnings in the Andean state of Tachíra, and both had Indian blood. They both had lust for power, for wealth, and for sensuous pleasure. Both smacked of the nouveau riche. They reacted in similar fashion to similar situations, they believed in oppression and suppression as basic instruments of power, and both of them made the prison and the torture chamber the grim symbol of their rule–along with achievements of economic development.

It was Gómez who started molding Venezuela into a modern state after nearly a century of civil wars and chaos, and who began to use the country's tremendous oil revenues for relatively constructive purposes. Pérez Jiménez turned the idea of economic development into a mania, particularly when this meant sweeping, spectacular projects with interesting photogenic possibilities and room for profitable financial arrangements for himself and for the members of his personal and official families.

The vast projects–hotels atop mountains, aerial trains, colossal bridges, long tunnels carved through mountains, spectacular highways, and industrial plants much too big for the country's needs–seemed to gladden the soul of this short, dull man born in the dwarfing immensity of the Andes. But where Gómez' approach to his task had been fairly primitive, Pérez Jiménez and his advisers embellished their regime with a *criollo* dialecticism. When he was ousted by the revolution, it became clear that his highly touted accomplishments were largely set off by the damage he left in his wake. Wealthy as Venezuela is, the dictator managed to contract a debt exceeding a half-billion dollars. His impressive highways linked the main cities but left untouched the interior of the country. So few schools were built and so few teachers trained during his decade that the illiteracy level in Venezuela rose instead of declined. Agriculture was sadly neglected. And while he claimed to have solved some of the social problems through the erection of vast housing projects in Caracas and other towns, he created a new social problem by encouraging unplanned and uncontrolled mass immigration from Europe that the country could not absorb smoothly.

Pérez Jiménez' dictatorship was the only modern government in the hemisphere candid enough to come out flatly and publicly against democracy and its bills of rights as an outmoded political system. Even Trujillo in the Dominican Republic has paid lip service to democracy. But the Venezuelan regime spoke only of social and economic democracy and of the conquest of "the physical environment." In the thinking of its leaders, the economic motive was the only one that mattered to men. As it was outspokenly anticommunist, one of the top ministers of the regime once took violent exception when this writer suggested that, essentially, there was little or no ideological difference between the New National Ideal and Marxism.

Borrowing helter-skelter from some of the latter-day ideas of the French Revolution and from Western European and American philosophers of the Industrial Revolution of the nineteenth century, the Venezuelan dictatorship set out to *despolitisar* (rid of politics) the entire nation so that an antiseptic atmosphere of concentration on economics could prevail. When *The New York Times* called the regime a technocracy and meant it disparagingly, official propaganda in Caracas picked it up as a compliment and quoted it in full-page advertisements in United States newspapers.

Pérez Jiménez and his crew capped their theories on the administration of a nation by displaying utter contempt and disregard for the people of Venezuela, their views or opinions. This, in turn, had the advantage of freeing Pérez Jiménez from the necessity of seeking through demagogic tricks the support of public opinion. As his physical appearance and oratorial gifts were particularly unsuited for any attempts at public spellbinding this was probably just as well. Such limited demagogic appeal as the government felt had to be exercised to justify before the nation what was being done to it was carried out through the medium of one or two annual radio-television speeches by the dictator, occasional addresses by one or another of his ministers, and official handouts that the newspapers were forced to publish. And that was another point of resemblance between Pérez Jiménez and Gómez: it is not believed that the old tyrant had ever delivered a coherent, full-fledged speech in public.

The assumption that the lethally efficient secret police, the prisons, the apparent prosperity, and the well-spread corruption were sufficient to control a nation led Pérez Jiménez to the conclusion that he could get away with anything and everything—only because he had got away with it since his first victorious military conspiracy of 1945. Consequently, on December 15, 1957, the regime held a "plebiscite" in which Venezuela was to decide upon the dictator's re-election for five more years. But this was where the assumption went so terribly wrong: within fifteen days of the "plebiscite" the very same people for whom Pérez Jiménez had felt such smug contempt rose in a bloody revolution that swept him out of office and Venezuela.

The political demise of Pérez Jiménez thus completed the cycle of the rise and fall of the great South American dictators of the modern period. Batista's fall in Cuba almost a year later extended to the Caribbean the mounting antidictatorial spirit of the Latin Americans as they broke into a new phase of political history.

THE MILITARY

The armed forces in most Latin American countries and in many underdeveloped areas have been the major power group in politics. In recent years scholars have turned away from berating the military for political interventions. They have been more interested in studying the causes for intervention, the socialization process of officers, the nature and effects of professionalization, the ability of the military to govern effectively, especially in carrying out social reforms and economic development, the relationship of the military to other power groups, the effects of interservice and intraservice disputes on military involvement in politics, and the ways—other than outright coups—the military can influence political decision making.

In the first selection, Edwin Lieuwen, Professor of History at the University of New Mexico, explains the numerous reasons for the resurgence of military intervention in Latin America in the 1930's and postwar period and then discusses the effectiveness of military rule. He is particularly interested in the past connections of many military leaders with social reform movements and the effects of internal squabbling, the inability to hire and work with competent civilian advisers, and their own loss of zeal on any good intentions the military may have had to modernize their countries socially and economically.

In the second selection, John J. Johnson, a Professor of History at Stanford University, is particularly concerned with the effects of professionalization and social background on the attitudes of the military. He describes the effects of professionalization on *junta* decision making, sensitivity of the officers to modernization, military isolation from and disdain for civilian concerns and politics, and the increasing ideological awareness of officers. The social background of the military has also been of great importance in the officers' ability to understand the complexity of corporate industry and technological development that goes along with modernization. Professor Johnson's elaboration of this point is skillfully developed as he describes the varied socialization patterns of military leaders. Another theme developed by Professor Johnson is the use of military intervention by civilian politicians and parties to enhance their own political objectives. Finally, a discernible trend is seen of the military preferring indirect influence over direct control, and the types of indirect influence are described through various country examples.

*The Changing Role of the Armed Forces: An Analysis**

EDWIN LIEUWEN

Militarism and Politics

Earlier chapters have shown how the last few decades of rapid change and social crisis in Latin America brought the armed forces back into a position of political prominence they had not held since the nineteenth century. At the time of World War I, the fraction of the total area and population that was dominated by the military was declining, and by 1928 only six Latin American countries, containing but 15 per cent of the total population, were ruled by military regimes. Then, abruptly, following the onset of the world depression in 1930, there occurred a striking relapse into militarism.

A rough measure of this phenomenon, though not always foolproof, was the number of presidents in uniform. Brazil, with its civilian traditions, managed to avoid it. But in Argentina, to take a different example, after nearly half a century of civilian rule, eight out of ten presidents between 1930 and 1957 were generals or colonels. To take a single year, in 1954

* Reprinted from Edwin Lieuwen, *Arms and Politics in Latin America* (New York: Frederick A. Praeger, 1960), Chapter 5 by permission of Council on Foreign Relations.

thirteen of the twenty republics were ruled by military presidents. In those countries which had never developed a civilian tradition in politics, like the republics of the Caribbean and Central America, the military tradition not only continued but was even reinforced.

This re-emergence of the armed forces upon the Latin American political scene was a by-product of the area's developing economic and social crisis, which the political institutions were not strong enough to contain. In the resulting political chaos the armed forces again and again were provoked or called upon to intervene. Their motives for so doing were not always the same. The devoted professionals might intervene in the name of their legitimate duty to preserve internal order, while the latent militarists might be motivated only by political ambition, and still a third group, the idealistic officers who believed it their duty to provide social justice, might compete with the other two.

The militarism of the postwar period, like that of the 1930's, has been principally a reflection of demands made upon the armed forces by antagonistic classes—by the traditional order attempting to maintain the *status quo* and by new social forces attempting to alter it. Examples already described will illustrate the point. In some cases, such as Argentina in 1930 and Peru in 1948, the armed forces intervened at the behest of the beleaguered civilian oligarchy. In others they acted on behalf of rising popular forces, as in Guatemala in 1944 and Venezuela in 1945. In Colombia, in 1953, the army took over when a stalemate appeared in the conflict of civilian groups. In El Salvador, where the strength of the civilian oligarchy declined after 1930 without a concomitant growth in responsible labor and middle-class groups, power went by default to the army, the only organized, disciplined force available for administering the affairs of the nation.

The environment in Latin America invited military rule. The decadence of the oligarchy, the political immaturity (not to mention the poverty and illiteracy) of the new groups aspiring to power, the lack of any strong, well-integrated group aside from the armed forces—all these combined to encourage militarism. In the words of one recent author:

> If there is no agreement on the right to command or the duty to obey, either because of ethnic heterogeneity or in consequence of an internal schism, naked force must remain the argument of last resort, and the distribution of military might must then be the principal determinant of the social structure.[1]

Had the armed forces remained neutral, or had they been unable to exercise effective control, unruly civilian elements would probably have made Latin America even more unstable than it actually became. The threatened use of force, for example, by rival, extremist civilian groups, such as the White Guard and the Red Militia in Chile, the pro-Prestes partisans and the Integralistas in Brazil, and the fascistic Gold Shirts and the labor militia in Mexico, made it most difficult for the regular army to remain aloof from politics.

Whenever the armed forces assumed political power, whatever their actual motivation, they maintained they were doing so only because the civilian government had failed. Ostensibly they were motivated by only the purest of patriotic intentions. In their own eyes, grave national circumstances made their intervention imperative.[2] Indeed, ever since independence, the military had developed the firm conviction that it was their duty to step forward in times of internal crisis to save the nation from itself. The changing social scene had not affected this basic concept, except in the few countries like Chile, Uruguay, and Colombia where professionalism had really taken root.

The armed forces were the arbiters of politics because it was they who controlled the means of violence, the *sine qua non* for political change in most countries. Advances in armament technology and improved military capabilities made them increasingly confident of their overwhelmingly superior power over unruly civilian elements; accordingly, they were less hesitant in putting that power to use. In addition, the newly modernized armies had no real military mission to perform. They were underemployed; the absence of interna-

[1] Stanislaw Andrzejewski, *Military Organization and Society* (London: Routledge and K. Paul, 1954), p. 128.

[2] For a typical military view, see Colonel Sosa de Quesada, *Militarismo* (Havana: Instituto Civico Militar, 1939), pp. 25–57.

tional wars, other than the Chaco struggle and Peru's border conflicts with Ecuador and Colombia, confined their military activities to routine peacetime maneuvers. Such meager military demands left surplus energies for extramilitary activities, and the social crises of the period since 1930 have offered unlimited political opportunities for the more clever, ambitious and energetic officers.

Finally, developments abroad—Nazism, fascism and Franco's victory in Spain—gave encouragement to militarism in Latin America.[3] Some officers, like Uriburu in Argentina, were attracted by pro-Fascist propaganda. Others, like Germán Busch and his colleagues in Bolivia, were indoctrinated in national socialism by German military advisers. The political appetites of still others, Perón, for example, were obviously whetted by travel and study in Europe. Quite naturally, considerations of national security during and after World War II encouraged the officer corps everywhere to assume a larger role in national affairs. Latin American officers could not help but be impressed by the prominence of military men in the governments of the great powers, and not least in the United States.

Militarism was contagious. The example set by Perón, and particularly his techniques, did not go unobserved by Major Arbenz in Guatemala, for instance, or by General Rojas Pinilla in Colombia. Similarly, General Odría's successful coup in Peru in October of 1948 probably served as an example for Colonel Pérez Jiménez, who emulated him the following month in Venezuela.

The Officer Corps

Essential to a deeper understanding of the social significance of the resurgence of militarism is a closer examination of the role of the military leaders. For, as might be expected, Latin America's twentieth-century economic, social, and political metamorphosis was clearly mirrored in the officer corps. The dramatic struggles that occurred between the old and the new, between farm and city, between vested interests and

[3] Eduardo Santos, "Latin American Realities," *Foreign Affairs*, January 1956, pp. 254–255.

newly organized labor, resulted in institutional upheavals in the armed forces as far-reaching and profound as those that occurred in civilian society.

After World War I, as we have seen, there began to appear in the lower echelons of the officer corps representatives of the rising urban middle groups. The sons of industrialists, bureaucrats, and urban professional men began to acquire the educational background and the modern, progressive outlook that made them superior cadets in the military academies. As in the past, men who chose a career in arms continued to come from the middle class, but the military representatives of these new urban groups, unlike the traditionally rural-oriented officers, had no ties with either the landed oligarchy or the church hierarchy. Consequently, they had, at least initially, little enthusiasm for perpetuating the role of the armed forces as a guarantor of the traditional social order.

The social identification of the new-type officer with the urban groups where he originated was probably the fundamental cause of the junior-officer uprisings that occurred in Latin America's armies in the second quarter of the twentieth century. In general, the ideological conflict was between the old and the new generation, between the generals, on the one hand, and the majors, captains, and lieutenants on the other, with the colonels often pulled in both directions. Such cleavages were nothing new in Latin America; what was new was their origins in social conflict.

Almost invariably, Latin America's popular revolutions of this century were led by the young officers. They became the sponsors of fundamental change and reform, the underminers of traditional institutions, the proponents of public-welfare measures. Democratic political institutions were of less concern to them. Indeed, they were often the leading advocates of militarized, authoritarian government and were apt to speak scornfully of "decadent" democracy. Their revolutionary zeal was by no means entirely altruistic, for changes in the make-up and role of the armed forces meant unparalleled opportunities for promotion. Militarization of government and extreme nationalistic policies meant new and important jobs for them, as well as expansion and enrichment of the state apparatus upon which the military was dependent for its income.

The new militarism, therefore, went much deeper than in the past. It was much more complex, as new social forces (labor and middle groups) and new military factors (politically influential navies and air forces) were added. Thus, those who stood for the old-type military dictatorship, backed only by the landed oligarchy and the upper clergy and often favored by foreign commercial or financial interests, had to face an entirely new, modern type of military competitor for political power.

Generally speaking, the new leader did not create the new sources of power. More often than not, the environment called forth the man, who rode to power at the head of a popular reform movement. A typical example was that of Arbenz in Guatemala. The new social philosophy was not primarily the brain child of the leader himself. His articulate expression of popular demands, demands in which he himself probably did not believe, was a weapon, a technique utilized for the enhancement of his personal power.

The new leader's relationship to the armed forces, the institution out of which he rose to power, was a curious one. He did not rise to be the head of a revolution by his own individual initiative, as had the *caudillos*. Rather, he represented a substantial cross section of the junior or middle-rank army leadership, concentrated in a conspiratorial clique, like the Group of United Officers in Argentina or the Patriotic Military Union in Venezuela. These young officers thought of themselves as enlightened members of a new, modern generation. Regarding the generals as unimaginative and behind the times, they sought to bring the armed forces into more sympathetic relations with the rest of the society. They were also interested in power, which could be had by gaining popular support, by playing the role of saviors of the downtrodden masses.

To win his battle against the oligarchy, the revolutionary leader had to pose as a representative of the lower- and middle-income groups. He had to make them believe that the enhancement of his power would lead to a parallel advancement of their interests. If the people responded to his vilification of the old regime and his Messianic promises, he was well on the way to the establishment of a kind of plebeian dictatorship, whether or not he had the majority of the people behind him. Opposition leaders could be effectively handled by simply condemning them as enemies of the people. Particularly troublesome elements, such as the conservative press, could be suppressed by organized violence, generally by police or security forces acting in "the people's" interest.

Every successful new leader announced a revolutionary reform program reflecting popular demands. The people supposedly would rule; they were the state; their new leader was its representative. He proposed to rebuild the national economy along modern lines, gave at least lip service to demands for agrarian reform, promised to curb the power of the landlords and the foreign capitalists, and pledged greater benefits to workers and peasants in the form of higher wages, better housing, and expanded social security.

In a typical case, the beneficiaries of these material gains were content with the vicarious enjoyment of political power through identification with the military dictator; but his colleagues were not. They had originally brought him to power; he was still dependent upon them. To decrease this dependence and thereby enhance his own power, he appealed even more to the people. Generally, to this end he built up organized labor as a counterpoise to potential rivals in the armed forces. The alliance with labor, the technique used by Perón, Arbenz, and others, was often as essential to the cause of fundamental reform as it was to the leader's drive for power. For in the frequent cases where his military colleagues began to lose their enthusiasm for drastic change soon after the revolution succeeded, labor was caught in a dilemma. Unless it shared in the aspiring dictator's drive for supreme power, achievement of its material and social demands was impossible. Generally, the lower classes chose to go along with him, as the only hope for more "economic democracy."

The first of these new-type military rulers, officers who rose to power as leaders of popular reform movements, was General Carranza in Mexico, who in 1915 appealed to the new social forces and gave lip service to—but did not fulfill—their demands. His successors, Generals Obregón and Calles, were more attentive to such demands. Prior to 1930, Major Ibáñez of Chile was the only other leader of the new type on the Latin American scene. Between 1930 and 1957, eleven of the fifty-six military men who held the presidential office in the twenty Latin American republics for as long as a year might be so described: Major Ibáñez (1930–1931), Colonel Perón (1945–1955), Colonel Rafael Franco (1936–1937) of Paraguay, Colonel Busch (1936–1938) and Major Villaroel (1943–1946) of Bolivia, General Rojas Pinilla of Colombia (1953–1957), Colonel Remón of Panama (1952–1955), Colonel Arbenz of Guatemala (1950–1954), General Cárdenas of Mexico (1934–1940), Sergeant Batista of Cuba (1933–1944), and Major Osorio of El Salvador (1948–1956). In three countries young officers who had conducted revolutions sustained reform-oriented, civilian-led regimes in power. This was the situation in Brazil under Vargas (1930–1945), Venezuela under Betancourt and Gallegos (1945–1948), and Ecuador under Velasco Ibarra (1944–1947).

Generally opposed to the military "reformers" were the senior officers. Their god was stability, and as its defenders they frowned upon social and political experimentation. They might be more partial to democratic institutions than their younger rivals, but this was likely to be the narrowly based "democracy" which had been allowed to function within the traditional order. Their political philosophy was understandable. Having arrived at the top of their profession, they were affected by the conservatism that came with rank, age, status, and the attainment of comfortable material circumstances. The exalted rank of general enabled them, unlike the junior officers, to enter politics without sacrificing their professional position.

In the events of the years 1947–1957 already described, every one of the reformist military regimes was overthrown, usually either by conservative army officers or by young officers, originally leaders of the revolution, whose zeal for reform had withered before the winds of labor-leftist extremism. Reactionary movements brought to the fore officers whose mission it was to halt the social revolution, although they were never completely successful, for the changes wrought by the reform regimes were generally too fundamental to be undone. In most cases labor-leftist political activity was sharply curtailed or prohibited, and although most of the social and material gains already attained were preserved, no new ones were forthcoming. In economic policy, however, the military leaders of the counterrevolution generally stole much of the industrializing, modernizing, and nationalistic programs of their predecessors.

It is difficult to make reliable generalizations about the socio-political attitudes of the officer corps in a single country, let alone in Latin America as a whole. Some military leaders did not conform to any type. The lines between groups were fluid, and there was seldom any permanent resolution of the struggle among those vying for power. Sometimes revolutionary young officers would win control, only to lose it to their more conservative seniors, as in Chile between 1925 and 1932. Sometimes senior officers would attempt a liberating revolution, as in Colombia in 1953. Sometimes junior officers originally liberal would turn conservative, as in Brazil between 1930 and 1945 and in Venezuela between 1945 and 1948. Sometimes the same officers that originally sponsored a military dictatorship would later bring it to an end, as happened when Perón and Rojas Pinilla were ousted.

Struggles within the officer class were complicated by ideological cross-currents and fierce personal and professional rivalries. Many officers in the lower ranks who talked of social reform really wanted increased pay and more rapid promotion. At times some of the senior officers, convinced of the inevitable political triumph of the new social forces compromised with them in order to preserve their own positions. This occurred, for example, in Guatemala in 1944. In the larger countries, generals interested in keeping pace with modern military technology in order to improve the capabilities of the armed forces, sometimes supported the new nationalism and industrialization.

Sometimes the three services were split along divergent political lines. The situation in Argentina under the Perón regime, for example, was most complex. There the army was the most powerful and the most politically inclined of the three branches of the armed forces. Within the army, whose officer corps had a middle-class background, there were two groups: one—the dominant—was nationalistic, socialistic, and politically minded; the less powerful group was more democratic in its outlook, inclined to accept the *status quo,* and relatively nonpolitical. A similar division characterized the navy, whose officers came from the upper middle class and the landed aristocracy. But in the navy, the democratic rather than the nationalist group held sway. Consequently, Perón never really had the navy on his side.[4] To compound the confusion, the air force was split about evenly. Only the police force, built up by Perón himself, revealed no broad internal divisions.

Throughout Latin America the armies were the strongest and the most politically active of the three services. They reflected social tensions most accurately, and therefore they were more seriously wracked by internal splits. Air forces had no significance in Latin America until World War II and have not yet achieved a major political role. Navies (important only in Brazil, Argentina, Chile and Peru), though less politically minded than armies, usually remained unified, fundamentally conservative institutions. A naval career, consequently, carried more social prestige.[5] The aristocratic tendencies of naval officers, however, often were moderated by the democratic views of the British and United States officers who were their professional advisers. Conversely, before World War II, authoritarian attitudes of some Latin American armies were reinforced by the influence of German, Spanish, and Italian military missions.

The Pattern of Revolution

In a number of Latin American countries, as we have seen, the pattern of revolution underwent radical change in the second quarter of the twentieth century. The former comic-opera, barracks-type revolts were superseded by revolutions of a genuinely social character, in which the military were

[4] Jorge Abelado Ramos, *América latina: un país* (Buenos Aires: Ediciones Octubre 1956), p. 193.
[5] This was not true in Colombia, however.

usually forced into taking a stand. The general picture was one in which the young officers, also frustrated in their ambitions, made common cause with the rising popular groups. Together they collaborated in bringing down, by force, the *ancien régime*. Revolutions of this type arose in some countries from direct military initiative, as in Bolivia in 1936; in others, *e.g.*, Guatemala in 1944, the young officers were inspired to revolt by civilian groups who were pressing for reform. In Argentina, in 1943, the colonels' clique took action in the belief that it had a continuing mission to manage the renovation of the nation. In Colombia in 1953, on the other hand, they intervened with reluctance and only after the traditional civilian leadership had amply demonstrated its incompetence.

However deep the causes, many of these twentieth-century revolutions appeared, on the surface, very much like the old palace revolts. Nearly always, preceding a revolutionary attempt, there was plotting by "disloyal" officers. As in the past, a secret clique did the organization and planning. In Bolivia in 1936 it was the Logia Santa Cruz, in Argentina in 1943 the Group of United Officers, and in Venezuela in 1945 the Patriotic Military Union. The leader of the conspirators circulated a reform program designed to attract his colleagues. Then, as the tensions inside the armed forces increased, officers who had no real desire to intervene in political processes had to weigh carefully the probable outcome of the impending crisis and make their gamble. Loyalty to the incumbent regime would be rewarded if the rebellion failed, punished if it succeeded. Neutral, innocent bystanders were apt to be suspected by both sides.

The revolt generally began with the carefully prearranged seizure of a key garrison, either in or near the capital. If a sufficient number of outlying garrisons joined the initial uprising, an assault was made upon communication centers, the presidential palace, and loyal military installations. If the revolt succeeded, the Junta Revolucionaria or a Junta Militar was set up as a transitional regime, allegedly administering the transfer of power to a "constitutional" government.

The *junta's* job was to remove from their official posts both the military and the civilian partisans of the defeated regime, in order to guard against counterrevolution. Usually the revolutionary *junta* reorganized all branches of the administration, decreed a certain amount of reform legislation, and, after an interim rule of one to three years, arranged for elections designed to restore a constitutional government satisfactory to the military leaders and more or less consonant with the wishes of supporting civilian groups. But the transitional period was generally far from smooth. Conspiring officers, no longer united against a common foe, found the aftermath of victory filled with conflicts, ideological and personal. In the jockeying for power, *junta* membership frequently shifted to reflect the changing balance of the forces, military and civilian, which had sponsored the revolution. There was always the temptation to stay in power and to postpone indefinitely any free election or return to civilian government.

Such were the surface manifestations common to nearly all twentieth-century Latin American revolutions. To determine whether they were of the "palace" variety or represented broadly based social movements, one must look at the forces supporting the rebels and their programs. Generally speaking, a *sine qua non* for fundamental revolution was a prior upheaval in the armed forces in which junior officers seized power from their superiors, as, for example, in Chile in 1925 and Brazil in 1930, in Argentina in 1943, and in Venezuela in 1945. When a revolt occurred without such an overturn in the armed forces, the revolution was generally superficial, a mere changing of the guard without social or economic reform. Such was the case in 1930 in Argentina, in 1943 in Bolivia, and in 1948 in Peru.

Despite the existence of popular pressures it was still no easy matter to conduct revolutions in the face of resistance by armed forces united in their loyalty to the government. On the contrary, the technological advance in weaponry—the machine gun, the tank, the airplane—and the development of modern systems of transport and communication notably increased the repressive power of the armed forces. Except in Cuba, Lenin's dictum that "no revolution of the masses can triumph without the help of a portion of the armed forces that sustained the old regime" applied to Latin America in the twentieth century. Each day, as armament grew more elaborate, as police organizations adopted modern equipment and new methods of surveillance, the possibility of successful civilian uprisings or local rebellions became more remote.

But the frequency of revolutions in Latin America underwent no notable alteration. For the new repressive powers of the armed forces were offset by defections of key officers or groups of officers. For example, as recently as January 1958, the heavily armed, dictatorial regime of General Pérez Jiménez in Venezuela was toppled with surprising ease when naval and air force officers made common cause with popular forces. What technology and modernization had done was to make it certain that the armed forces would always play a dominant role, on one side or another, in any revolutionary contest.

Contrary to what one might expect, the social revolutions, except for the unique upheavals in Mexico and Bolivia, were no bloodier than the palace revolutions. This was because the masses of the population, though they exerted pressure, did not generally participate in the actual fighting. Except in Colombia in the decade following World War II and in Mexico a generation earlier, social change fortunately took place in Latin America without civil war. For this result, the continued use in the twentieth century of nineteenth-century revolutionary techniques was largely responsible.

It was sometimes possible to launch insurrections and to keep them going although the armed forces remained loyal to the government. This could happen, however, only when the terrain suited the conduct of guerrilla-type warfare and when the rebels received clandestine support from sympathetic civilians.[6] These conditions enabled the famous Prestes column in Brazil in the mid-1920's to hold out successfully for more than three years against the government forces. Similarly favored Colombian guerrilla forces continued to operate for more than a decade after World War II. More recently, the rebel forces of Fidel Castro successfully defied the Batista regime. In these cases the strategy of the rebels was to wear down the morale of the government forces by long-term operations on an ever-increasing scale until defec-

[6] See Katharine C. Chorley, *Armies and the Art of Revolution* (London: Faber, 1943), pp. 49, 61.

tions or frustration made victory possible. Although this technique had heretofore not proved successful in defeating an incumbent regime, Castro's forces were able to carry through to victory in the first days of 1959.

Enlisted men played no leading or determining role in the social revolutions. Unlike the situation in Russia in 1917, extensive fraternization between regular troops and revolutionary elements of the civilian population did not occur in Latin America, for the commanders effectively isolated the men in the ranks by confining them in barracks, bases, and various military installations. Also, the illiteracy and general political apathy of the rank and file tended to make them docile instruments in the hands of the officer corps. As a result, many civilians tended to build up an emotional resentment to anyone in uniform and to condemn all soldiers as defenders of a hated regime.

Only in one brief period, the early 1930's, when economic depression brought discontent over loss of pay and deterioration in living conditions, did the men in the ranks become restless, and then in only a few countries. In 1931, the soldiers of the Fifth Regiment in Peru made an abortive attempt to seize the government; the sailors' mutiny in Ecuador in April of 1932 likewise failed. Success came in only one instance, in Cuba in 1933, when the enlisted men, led by Sergeant Batista, overwhelmed the officers, took over the government, and made themselves officers.

This Cuban experience was the single exception to the general rule that the Latin American officer corps kept the loyalty of the common soldiers and maintained discipline. Officers recognized that their own position depended on a contented rank and file, hence they usually ousted civilian governments which refused to provide for them adequately. Some reformist military presidents, in an effort to diminish their extreme dependence upon the officer corps and build up a defense against conspiracy, cultivated the men in the ranks with extraordinary emoluments and favors. Their aim was to secure from the enlisted men primary loyalty to the chief of state rather than to their immediate military superiors. But it did not work. Perón, Arbenz, Batista, and other military dictators who tried this technique ultimately failed.

Civilian revolutionaries, however, were sometimes able to gain support from special groups within the military. In several countries the military cadets, whose careers had not advanced sufficiently to give them a predominantly military outlook, and whose youthful idealism could be exploited by astute political crusaders, were attracted to revolutionary causes. In Colombia in 1948 and Bolivia in 1952, the police, who were in much closer, day-to-day contact with the civilian population than the armed forces, made common cause with the rebellious populace.

Revolutions were most sweeping when the regular army, the ultimate guardian of social order, was overwhelmed, as in Mexico in 1914, Bolivia in 1952, and Cuba in 1958–1959. These, however, were not primarily planned revolutions, but spontaneous outbursts of popular antagonism manifested in violent uprisings. Only in these three countries, moreover, was it possible in the aftermath of victory to deal with the basic problem of land reform, a matter which even the most radical military reformers elsewhere avoided. Genuine agrarian reform in Latin America was perhaps impossible without the destruction of the officer corps, recruited as it was from the middle and upper-middle social ranks which believed firmly in the sanctity of private property. A reform regime that attacked the latter soon forfeited the good will of the officers, as was demonstrated in Venezuela in 1948 and Guatemala in 1954.

Nature of the New Militarism

Militarism, an endemic political phenomenon in Latin America, has had two sides. It has been both progressive and predatory. The military have generally shown no great concern for such concepts as representative government or individual civil rights. That is not surprising. In a region of backward economies, extreme social stratification, and great political apathy among the masses, with little tradition of orderly, democratic, constitutional procedures, governments have necessarily rested upon force. Inevitably, therefore, the armed forces have played a determining political role, be it for good or for evil, for progress or for reaction.

Some military regimes, especially the reform-minded ones that came to power after World War II, have had a decisive influence in promoting economic development and social change, and indirectly even in furthering political democracy. The late Vernon Fluharty has described the significance of this type of militarism in Colombia, a not untypical example:

> Rojas Pinilla has turned the clock forward on social achievement for the masses. He gave them status and a sense of their importance, if only because his government has emphasized their welfare. That lesson they will never forget, and nothing less will be acceptable from other governments to come. . . .
>
> In this sense, paradoxically, the military dictator is making a substantial contribution toward democracy. Every social, educational, political, and economic gain in status is a step toward the creation of the substantive basis upon which true popular democracy may one day rise in Colombia. . . .
>
> Ultimate accomplishment of this process may require many Rojas Pinillas. . . . But the military dictatorships make their necessary contribution, a lasting one, with their emphasis upon substantive democracy. Nothing can be the same after they have come, spoken to and for the masses, and gone their way. It does not even matter, in the long run, whether they were sincere in their solicitude for the people, or merely self-seeking. The important thing is that the masses will not forget. They will slowly grow into the new concept that they, too, are men, and they will demand more from the parties in the future than ever they dared demand before.
>
> Sooner or later those demands will be met. . . . Even though it may appear negative and temporary, this contribution is a gain for the future of popular democracy in Latin America.[7]

Until the appearance of reform-minded young officers, governments in Latin America had paid little attention to the masses. Although the new-type military leaders were any-

[7] Vernon Lee Fluharty, *Dance of the Millions: Military Rule and the Social Revolution in Colombia, 1930–1956* (Pittsburgh: University of Pittsburgh Press, 1957), pp. 316–317.

thing but practitioners of genuine democracy, their new policies tended to bring about greater equality in income and social position, without which political equality could never have a solid, long-term basis. Many of the military regimes, moreover, regardless of whether they had popular backing or were reform-minded in a social sense, achieved a certain amount of material progress by fostering industrialization, the development of communications and public-works projects, and by enforcing political stability.

An officer's professional training often equipped him for the ministry of communications or of public works or other technical posts. In Brazil it was the army that explored the virgin interior, set up telegraph and wireless stations, developed agricultural colonies, and helped the Indians to advance in civilization. The army undertook similar tasks in Peru in the 1940's and in Bolivia in the 1950's. In Mexico and Argentina it played a key role in economic development by opening up new roads and constructing schools and hospitals. In Cuba, after 1936, it assumed a pedagogic and social function when it took charge of the new Escuelas Rurales Cívico-Militares designed to combat illiteracy and improve rural living conditions. In Chile, during World War II, the army helped alleviate the import crisis by manufacturing agricultural implements and bicycles.[8]

It can be also said in behalf of the armed forces that they often played an antidespotic political role, intervening to terminate the tyranny of one of their own errant colleagues or to supply a corrective to the excesses of civilian politicians. For example, they brought an end to the Vargas dictatorship in Brazil in 1945 and that of Perón in Argentina a decade later. To take an earlier example, they served the cause of genuine political democracy in Chile in 1924 when they stepped in, on behalf of the people, to break the deadlock between popular President Alessandri and the oligarchic Congress.

In many cases, genuine patriotism and a desire to prevent political excess have been the dominant motivations for mili-

[8] José Cavero Bendzú, *El ejército en las democracias hispanoamericanas* (Chorillos, Peru: Imprenta de la Escuela Militar, 1944), pp. 7–10.

tary intervention in politics. The stabilizing role of the army in Brazil has been aptly described by Alan Manchester:

> That the nation has been able to survive the incredibly rapid transition to industrialization without discarding its basic political structure is due in no small part to the army. Under the leadership of the General Staff the army has been the stabilizing factor which has stopped the political pendulum from swinging too far from the center. It terminated the dictatorship when the need for that regime was over and stood aside while the civil leaders laid the foundations for a real democracy. It stepped in again when the political leadership swung too far to the opposite extreme. It has played a conservative, stabilizing role since its rise to decisive influence in 1930.[9]

What might be called the predatory side of militarism, however, far overshadowed its beneficent and progressive aspects, even when military regimes rode to power on a program of social reform. One has only to compare their actual exercise of power with the legal provisions defining the position and function of the armed forces. The constitutions of the Latin American countries contain clauses along the following lines:

(1) The president of the republic is the commander in chief of the armed forces.
(2) The armed forces are a professional, nonpolitical body, which may not deliberate on matters relating to the service.
(3) The fundamental aim of the armed forces is to guarantee the defense of the nation, to maintain internal order, to guarantee constitutional rights, and to enforce the laws.

Yet in most Latin American countries the president was effectively commander in chief of the armed forces only when he was a military man who had come to power by revolution. Duly elected civilian presidents were generally powerless to call erring generals to order; the latter considered successful

[9] "Brazil in Transition," *South Atlantic Quarterly*, April 1955, p. 175.

politicians ephemeral rulers, whereas an officer's position gave him continuing and assured power until his retirement. With few exceptions, the armed forces were in fact not strictly professional, no matter what the law said, and they were anything but "nonpolitical." They "deliberated" on all matters, but particularly "on matters relating to the service," that is, on their needs for funds, manpower, and equipment. Finally, they frequently flouted the constitutional rights they were supposed to "guarantee" and ignored the laws they were pledged to enforce. Whatever role the armed forces played in a revolution itself, the new civilian government was never permitted to alter the armed forces' traditional role as the ultimate arbiter of political disputes, to trim their customary share of the budget, or to interfere with their pay, benefits, discipline and promotions. Reform regimes were obliged to confine their reform activities to nonmilitary matters. Presidents Bustamante of Peru and Gallegos of Venezuela learned this lesson the hard way in 1948. Similarly, Presidents Velasco of Ecuador and Vargas of Brazil in the 1940's and again in the early 1950's failed in repeated attempts to exert executive authority over their respective nation's armed forces.

In brief, the armed forces have generally held themselves above the law. True, there might be lengthy constitutional discussions between the lawyer-politicians and the officers, but the latter always won with the incontrovertible argument of force. The central issue was: Are the functions of the armed forces delegated to them by the state, or do they already possess, inherently and permanently, rights and functions independent of those specified in the ephemeral constitutions?[10] The armed forces in most Latin American countries insisted, as regards military matters, on being a state within a state, demanding complete autonomy for the armed forces. As to politics, with the exception of only a few countries, they were in fact above the state in claiming for themselves the inherent right to change governments at will.

Accordingly, the military arrogated to itself the power of deciding when constitutional rights had been violated and when the time had arrived to enforce the law. Though there

[10] Javier Bazán Pérez, *El ejército en la constitución y en la política* (Mexico City, 1952), pp. 16–17.

were obvious cases where military intervention was needed to curb the excesses of military or civilian *políticos,* in most instances its justification was highly questionable. On all too many occasions the armed forces acted arbitrarily and in utter defiance of the duly constituted authorities and the popular will. A particularly notorious case occurred in 1948 in Venezuela, when the armed forces took it upon themselves to substitute a military *junta* for a popularly elected government. Then, in 1952, when the military were overwhelmingly defeated in an election, they simply refused to honor the popular mandate. Similarly, in Peru in 1948 and in Cuba in 1952 military leaders overthrew democratic governments, then kept themselves in power by force in the face of popular opposition.

Predatory military governments could maintain their rule only by tyrannical methods; accordingly, they set up bodies of secret police, ostensibly "to enforce the law," but actually to throttle opposition. While such rulers were actually stifling freedom and democracy, political expediency often prompted them to conduct their despotisms behind a constitutional façade. Most Latin American constitutions sanction, in time of grave national emergency, the declaration of a state of siege, making legal the "temporary" suspension of constitutional rights. Under such conditions, after all the potential rival parties and candidates have been effectively suppressed, a military dictator can be elected "democratically," without opposition. This was the technique used effectively by Generals Odría, Rojas Pinilla, and Batista.

Military training obviously did little to equip an officer with the skills necessary for running a modern state. Because his professional career isolated him from the main currents of society, his understanding of national problems was apt to be defective. And as technical advances made military affairs more complicated and as new economic tasks and social responsibilities had a similar effect on the tasks of civil administration, it became each day more difficult for a soldier to become also a statesman. Eduardo Santos, a political leader concerned with democratic values and procedures, has written:

The military profession is poor schooling for learning the

> difficult art of government, for to govern well means to interpret, to reconcile, to respect the rights of all, to give freedom of expression to every opinion, to abide by the laws and never subordinate them to personal caprice, to have the courage to rectify mistakes, to ask for and listen to advice, to have patience, to realize that one owes one's power to the will of the people. . . . All this is difficult for the military to understand and accept, accustomed as they are to the blind obedience of their inferiors, the dry voices of command, and the narrow horizon of their profession, which rarely encompasses the element of humanism.[11]

As he wrote this in 1956, the ex-president of Colombia was witnessing, from exile, an example in his own country of how a fine professional soldier could prove utterly inept in the business of running a government. Rojas Pinilla, a devoted, conscientious, career man, had risen to the number-one post in the army by sheer dint of energy and professional excellence. As one of the more promising middle-grade officers, he had been selected for advanced training abroad. Having brilliantly led the Colombian Battalion in the Korean War, upon his return he became minister of defense. Unhappily, his country, ever since 1948, had been in the throes of a near civil war, with crime and violence widespread. Confronted by a deadlock between the Liberal and Conservative parties, public opinion demanded that something be done to stop the bloodletting.

The only individual in a position to act was Rojas Pinilla, who seized the reins of power with broad popular approval. But, since he had no experience in the complex business of governing, he was forced to seek advice from other generals; and he also compounded his difficulties by often stubbornly following mistaken civilian advice. He knew how to meet opposition only with force. His crude efforts to launch a popular political movement of his own ended in failure. Each day he marched more rapidly down the path of error. Frustrated by repeated failures (a severe blow to his pride), he became increasingly tyrannical, thus rekindling furious civil strife in

11 "Latin American Realities," cited, p. 256.

the countryside. In 1957 public opposition had reached the point where his military colleagues had to unseat him.

Below the presidential level, also, the competence of military men for high political posts was open to serious question. In the aftermath of the military revolts that occurred after 1930, and particularly after those of 1948, there was a tendency to assign to men in uniform cabinet posts heretofore held by civilians.[12] It was not surprising that the Fascist-inspired revolutions in Bolivia in 1937 and Argentina in 1943 should produce all-military cabinets, but the trend was noticeable elsewhere too. The war ministry had always been an army post, but under the Ibáñez government in Chile in the mid-1950's, for example, the ministries of labor and interior, also, were headed by army officers. In Venezuela, after the 1948 revolution, army officers headed the interior and communications ministries, and acted as governors of the Federal District. The extreme was reached in Peru with the all-military cabinet of General Odría, in which colonels headed the ministries of public health, education, labor, interior, treasury, and justice, and a rear admiral conducted foreign relations. Obviously, these officers' professional training did not include the schooling in medicine, economics, law, politics, diplomacy, and public administration that their official tasks demanded. Mexico under Cárdenas had an all-military cabinet, but the ministers had no real responsibilities. Cárdenas appointed old revolutionary generals merely as figureheads, so as to be better able to control them. Actually, competent civilian technicians ran his ministries.

Despite the fact that young officers led social revolutions in many republics at certain stages of their history, especially in the 1943–1953 decade, the conclusion is inescapable that, on balance, the armed forces have represented a static or reactionary social force in Latin American politics since 1930. Military regimes which really promoted reform were the exception; political intervention by the armed forces was more often than not a conservative holding action, even to the point of dissolving popular political parties by force.

[12] Jesús Silva Herzog, "Las juntas militares de govierno," *Cuadernos Americanos* (Mexico City), July–August 1949, pp. 9–10.

As suggested earlier in this chapter, moreover, even when idealistic young officers led a genuine social revolution, in the end they nearly always perverted and distorted its aims. Reform-minded military leaders generally came to power with a majority of the people behind them. During a brief honeymoon, drawing on their reservoir of popular support, they launched ambitious projects of economic development and enacted social-welfare measures. Yet, somehow, such regimes moved away from political freedom and eventually from social reform as well. It was as though the new military rulers were psychologically unprepared to accept authentically popular solutions to their nation's problems. Why?

Let us describe a generalized case which is hypothetical but quite typical. A young officer leads a military *coup d'état* and announces a program of reform. His head is then turned by his sudden attainment of tremendous personal powers; he is reluctant to let it go. Then, too, his revolutionary zeal is nearly always greater than that of his colleagues, whose ardor for reform cools fast in the aftermath of victory. Consequently, the social program begins to slow down. Also, the victors, in accordance with accepted traditions, demand spoils, and the illicit enrichment of the new military elite, including the reform-minded dictator, soon makes his government appear to the populace more and more like that of its exploiting predecessors. The dictator's mounting problems are complicated by his political incompetence and his often ill-conceived, ruinous economic policies. All of this gives new courage to the traditionalist opposition, increasingly joined by many who had originally supported the liberal revolution. Faced with mounting resistance, the dictator tightens his control and increases its brutality in a desperate attempt to hold power. Ultimately, the armed forces split, and when that happens the days of the dictator are numbered.

Such was the fate, in a general way, of Ibáñez (1930–1931), Franco (1936–1937), Busch (1937–1938), Villaroel (1943–1946), Perón (1945–1955), Arbenz (1950–1954), and Rojas Pinilla (1953–1957). Neither they nor their military colleagues gave proof of possessing the ability, or the determination, to solve their nation's problems in an orderly, progressive fashion.

Reform-minded military rulers showed little competence in dealing with economics. They were particularly inclined toward ruinous financial policies. Almost invariably they were poor planners. Their drive for economic independence often led to over-hasty industrialization programs. The case of Perón in Argentina is a good example. His short-sighted emphasis upon industry led him to foster it at the expense of agriculture, the principal source of funds for investment in industrialization. Lopsided economic policies brought the nation to the brink of disaster. In the comparable case of Colombia, Rojas Pinilla's ambitious programs of public works and economic development left the country near bankruptcy.

One of the chief impediments to real economic progress in nearly all Latin American countries, whether the regime was military or not, was the inflated demands the armed forces made upon government revenues. Traditionally, since the turn of the century, the armed forces' reported share of the national budget has averaged about 20–25 per cent annually in most Latin American countries.[13] Official figures of war and navy departments, however, do not tell the whole story. Sizable appropriations for the armed forces, amounting to perhaps 5 per cent of the total budget, were often concealed in appropriations for the ministries of interior, public works, and communications. In Paraguay, after the military coup of 1954, the share of the armed forces went up to 50 per cent, and in Colombia and Cuba, due to the civil wars, military budgets also rose sharply. In the total Latin American picture, however, these increases were at least partly counterbalanced by sharp declines in Mexico after 1938, in Bolivia following the 1952 revolution, and in Costa Rica following the abolition of the army in 1948.

Although budgetary percentages generally remained constant, the expenses for Latin America's armed forces in absolute figures grew tremendously. This was because total

[13] According to the *Inter-American Statistical Yearbook* (New York: Macmillan, 1940), pp. 512–541, the armed forces' percentages of the national budgets were as follows: Argentina–18, Bolivia –30, Brazil–24, Chile–26, Colombia–16, Costa Rica–9, Cuba–22, Dominican Republic–17, Ecuador–22, El Salvador–21, Guatemala –19, Haiti–24, Honduras–19, Mexico–21, Nicaragua–11, Panama –0, Paraguay–38, Peru–23, Uruguay–12, Venezuela–12.

national expenditures, with the rise of statism and big bureaucracies, had risen rapidly. For example, national budgets were several times larger in 1958 than in 1939. To some extent the armed forces' increase reflected the high cost of modern military equipment.

The resources that annually went into the armed forces' salaries and equipment obviously contributed little to the economic development of a country. Civilian reformers like Arévalo of Guatemala, Paz Estenssoro of Bolivia, and Betancourt of Venezuela found it hard to condone expenditures which seemed so wasteful—wasteful because in their view the armed forces had no commensurate military function to perform: there was no danger of invasion, and the maintenance of internal order was being capably handled by the nation's police forces. In addition, the continued high military budgets served to enhance the political power of the military. Yet these were fixed expenditure items which no government, either civilian or military, could alter. The minister of war or of defense, always a representative of the armed forces rather than of the government, made it unmistakably clear that the military would brook no curtailment in their traditional budgetary share. Whenever a military regime was established there usually occurred a further build-up of the armed forces, with stronger emphasis upon military items in the budget. Only in the four Latin American states where civilian governments had brought their armed forces under control (Mexico after 1938, Bolivia after 1952, Costa Rica after 1948, and Uruguay since before World War I) were substantial reductions made in the military's percentage of the budget.

Inflated expenditures for the armed forces absorbed funds needed for technical progress. Except in a few countries, military men tended to eschew engineering and public-works functions. And certainly the side effects of predatory militarism—tyranny, ruinous economic policies, and intensified social cleavages—hampered technical progress. In some cases peculation, graft, and corruption were still more injurious.

In the Latin American tradition, military dictators used their office for purposes of illicit enrichment. Almost inevitably military dictatorship led to corruption. Not that civilian governments were clean in this regard, but the record of some of the military regimes is rather more spectacular. Immediately after a successful revolution the most pressing demands on the national treasury came from the new leader's military supporters. This was usually the first stage of corruption. The second came when the problem arose of consolidating power through the attainment of popular backing for the regime. For this purpose funds were needed which would be free from legal control. Established political parties already had resources of this kind, but military regimes did not, and so they naturally dipped into the national treasury.

A new leader generally did not hesitate for long to join his associates in their peculations; in some cases he set the example. Nearly all military rulers prepared for the inevitable day when, their power having collapsed, they would have to live out their days in exile. The conduct of Venezuela's military dictators was brazen but none the less typical. The corrupt pattern was fixed by General Juan Vicente Gómez, who during his long rule appropriated for himself hundreds of millions of dollars from the public treasury and substantial amounts for his family and military associates. After his death in 1935, his successors, Generals Eleazar López Contreras (1935–1941) and Isaias Medina Angarita (1941–1945) carried on the dishonorable tradition. Each, during his term of office, made off with about $13 million, then, following the 1945 revolution, retired in New York.[14] Yet the young officer who helped lead that revolution (Pérez Jiménez), and emerged as dictator in 1948, far outdid his predecessors.

In the five-year period from 1954 to 1959 Latin America's fleeing military dictators carried out of their countries hundreds of millions of dollars. Indications are that Perón escaped with as much as $700 million, Pérez Jiménez with more than $250 million, Batista with $50 million in 1944 and $200 million in 1959, and Rojas Pinilla, Paul Magloire, and Arbenz with smaller, yet sizable fortunes. Meanwhile, those still in power were providing for their retirement. General Trujillo, in the neighboring Dominican Republic, had over the years

[14] Venezuela, Ministerio de Relaciones Interiores, *Sentencias del jurado de responsibilidad civil y administrativa* (Caracas: Imprenta Nacional, 1946), v. 1, pp. 303–334; v. 2, pp. 3–46.

perfected his systematic graft until his annual income was estimated in the neighborhood of 30 million. In similar fashion, corrupt use of political power has made the Somoza family of Nicaragua one of the richest in Central America. But thievery by the heads of state was only part of the story. Under the Perón regime, favored generals like Humberto Sosa Molina and Franklin Lucero became multimillionaires. Colonel Pulido Barreto, Pérez Jiménez' ordnance chief, amassed millions from parking-meter collections and transportation concessions.[15]

Not all politically powerful military men were dishonest, nor was corruption limited to military leaders.[16] Colonel Remón of Panama, though he had enriched himself considerably as police chief, was a model of integrity in the presidential office. Also General Ubico of Guatemala (1930–1944) and certain leaders of the armed forces in Brazil earned reputations for honesty. But these examples were exceptions to the general rule that peculation on a large scale was characteristic of militarism.

Corruption in high places, like the inflation of military budgets, hindered economic development. As Stanislaw Andrzejewski has observed, the armed forces' "parasitic appropriation of the surplus produced by the economically productive civilian sectors of the society was one of the most powerful factors inhibiting technical progress."[17] This "surplus," in countries with exceptionally predatory military re-

[15] The figures here are merely rough estimates gleaned from a variety of newspaper reports. Obviously, statistics on the volume of peculation are unreliable and cannot possibly be well documented. For figures, there is little to rely upon save the charges of the victorious opposition. However, the notorious affluence of the exiles and their accumulated properties, both at home and abroad, provide irrefutable evidence of illicit gain of great proportions.

[16] Batista justified his 1952 coup with the charge that his corrupt civilian predecessors, Grau San Martín (1944–1948) and Prío (1948–1952) had misappropriated over $200 million. Also, it was estimated that Mexican President Miguel Alemán and the high officials of his administration had deposited $500 to $800 million in foreign banks between 1946 and 1952. See *New York Times,* September 19, 1952; March 24, April 9, April 28, 1953; March 25, 1954.

[17] Cited, p. 162.

gimes, like those in the Dominican Republic, Nicaragua, and Paraguay, might be any amount in excess of the bare subsistence requirements of the mass of the population. Corruption was contagious; its spread caused would-be investors and entrepreneurs to lose confidence. The breakdown of many a nation's economy under corrupt military dictatorships was hastened by the flight of private capital.

Growth of Professionalism

There was, however, at work in Latin America a strong counterforce that reacted against militarism. This force was professionalism, which, despite the post-1930 upsurge of militarism, continued to build upon the initial advances that took place largely under the influence of European military missions around the turn of the century. Another and more basic factor in this trend was the antimilitaristic pressure exerted by the civilian population. In Mexico in 1914, in Costa Rica in 1948, and in Bolivia in 1952, the people destroyed militarism by violent revolution. And though in Mexico and Bolivia it reappeared in the post-revolutionary period, civilian authority eventually emerged supreme. In twentieth-century Uruguay, civilian leaders tethered the militarists, restricting them to proper military functions, notably the preservation of internal order.

In some other countries the armed forces retreated at least partially from the political arena and thus into a professional status as a result of pressure from hostile civilian groups. In Chile and Colombia the armed forces had developed a nonpolitical tradition. In each case the military intervened on one occasion (in Chile in 1924 and in Colombia in 1953) to arbitrate a current political crisis, and in neither case did intervention achieve its objective. Popular animosity, aroused by bungling and failures, ultimately forced the military to abandon politics (in Chile by 1932 and in Colombia by 1957). After 1955, similar antimilitaristic pressures exerted by the mass of the people were evident in Argentina, Brazil, Peru, Ecuador, Venezuela, and Cuba.

Since the military, however, still had a monopoly of physical power, the principal impetus toward professionalism had to come from within the armed forces. In almost every country the military organization was torn by two struggles: One reflected the country's social crisis; the other, but equally important, was the contest between the professionalists, the group of officers who held that the military should confine themselves to military duties, and the militarists who insisted on playing politics. In the first quarter of the century the former seemed to be in the ascendent, but in the period of continuing crisis that began in 1930 the militarists held sway. Only in the last few years, with the collapse of military dictatorships in Argentina, Peru, Colombia, Venezuela, Haiti, and Cuba, largely because many officers saw which way the wind was blowing and themselves aided in the overthrow of irresponsible military regimes, do the professionalists again appear to be gaining the upper hand.

Curiously enough, militaristic regimes gave stimulus to professionalism, not, to be sure, by the example they set, but because the dictators themselves feared the militarism that had given them power and might take it away again. For this reason rulers like Perón and Pérez Jiménez encouraged professionalism, advising young officers to stick to their military business and stay out of politics.

A growing element in the officer corps was becoming conscious of the proper role of the armed forces in the nation's affairs. The concept of the "good soldier" began to be more clearly understood, and was reinforced by travel and training in Western Europe and the United States and by the activities of foreign military missions in Latin America. Officers began to recognize that modern military technology required increased specialization, that genuine military *expertise* called for the digestion of a tremendous body of knowledge and years of training and experience, that gaining the technical proficiency necessary to qualify as a superior professional soldier was a full-time job that left no room for dabbling in politics.[18]

[18] The growing volume of professionalist literature emanating from the pens of Latin American officers well illustrates the steady growth of a professional *esprit*. See, for example Colonel Guillermo Prado Vasquez, *La carrera del oficial* (Santiago, 1952) and General Tomás Rueda Vargas, *El ejército nacional* (Bogotá: Comacho Roldán, 1944).

The rise of military professionalism was not an indigenous phenomenon. Rather, Latin America's armed forces were continuing their acceptance of ideas and programs already adopted in more advanced countries. During the 1930's German professionalist influence continued to prevail in southern South America; French missions were active in central South America (Brazil and Peru), and Italian missions, particularly in Ecuador and Bolivia. The United States, which did not establish military missions until the eve of World War II, achieved a monopoly of such activity in Latin America soon after hostilities began. The attitudes of United States officers toward their profession and their role in society, and indeed the very training in the arts of war which they imported, could not have failed to influence in some degree the outlook and the attitudes of their Latin American colleagues.

*The Soldier as Citizen and Bureaucrat**

JOHN J. JOHNSON

The role of the armed forces has not changed basically under the impact of the massive transformation that has taken place since World War I. It has been argued from time to time that they figure in the defense of the Hemisphere and serve as deterrents to aggression from the outside, but it seems apparent that their primary goal, as in the past, is to maintain internal order as a second-line police force. As in the past, they have engaged in politics as the surest way of fulfilling their "obligations to country and self." The depth of involvement varies from country to country (currently it is negligible in Uruguay, Costa Rica, Mexico, Bolivia, Chile, and Colombia), but the fact that they are so involved cannot seriously be disputed. But if the role of the armed forces has not changed, the attitude of the officers has, and how this new attitude came about and what it means in terms of military

* Reprinted from *The Military and Society in Latin America* by John J. Johnson, pp. 101–33, with the permission of the publishers, Stanford University Press. © 1964 by the Board of Trustees of the Leland Stanford Junior University.

behavior, especially in the extra-military areas, warrant elaboration.

The substitution of technically trained managers of violence for the heroic leaders of the past has had much to do with the growth of the new military. That substitution is now completed except in Honduras, where some officers entered the services without prior technical training (one high-ranking officer has had only three years of formal education) and the nation's military school did not graduate its first class until 1960. In Argentina, on the other hand, members of the permanent officer corps pass upon all admissions to the military colleges and no reserve or non-career officer can hope to rise to a top rank.

As might be expected, the level of achievement among graduates of the military academies in the several republics varies considerably. Graduates of the academies in Argentina and Chile, for example, have the equivalent of twelve to sixteen years of academic training; in Mexico, Venezuela, and Ecuador ten to twelve years; and in El Salvador and Honduras, six to ten years. All the states provide for postgraduate training in war colleges, command schools, and universities, and by foreign missions. The republics also make some kind of advanced training a requirement for promotion to the higher ranks. Venezuela, for example, sends a relatively large number of officers to colleges and universities in the United States, where they take as much as four years of undergraduate training in engineering, and Honduras proposes to permit approximately one-third of each class graduating from its Escuela Militar to continue on to the university. Several hundred Argentine officers are in constant attendance at civilian institutions of higher learning; in 1958 there were 514 members of the armed forces registered in the University of Buenos Aires alone.[1] But what is important is that whether the training has been good, bad, or indifferent, the tendency has been for control of the armed forces to pass to "laboratory

[1] Universidad de Buenos Aires, *Censo universitario, 1959*. This census is examined in some detail in K. H. Silvert's contribution in John J. Johnson, ed., *Continuity and Change in Latin America* (Stanford, 1964).

officers" who in most of the republics have raised the level of military expertise immeasurably.[2]

Better training has not been the only attraction held out to the new generation of officers or the only one shaping their thinking. Their salaries, which compare quite favorably with those of civilians of comparable age and training, are now paid with clock-like regularity. Promotions at the lower levels have been made automatic with the result that officers are free from political pressures for at least the first ten years and ordinarily the first fifteen years of their careers. Chile makes interest-free building loans available to commissioned officers and the government provides housing in many areas, including Santiago, where in 1960 the Commander-in-Chief of the Navy lived in a house that rented for $1,000 per month, paid by the government. In Venezuela, where interest commonly runs to 12 per cent and up, the government makes loans to both commissioned and non-commissioned officers at 4.5 per cent. This author knows of one Venezuelan officer who has received $50,000 under such terms, and it is general knowledge that majors in the Army and lieutenant commanders in the Navy have qualified for loans up to $40,000. President Betancourt said in 1960 that by the time he retired (1964) every commissioned and non-commissioned officer in the Venezuelan armed forces would have a home of his own if he wanted one.

Furthermore, attractive retirement plans for those who have served out their careers have become commonplace. Argentina retires its officers at full pay after thirty years of service. Chilean officers also retire at full pay after thirty years and in addition can borrow funds for business purposes from the government at favorable interest rates. Upon retirement, Ecuadorian officers receive full pay plus a lump sum (to which they contribute while in the service) of approximately $10,000, which they commonly use to go into business or loan out at rates of 10 to 15 per cent. A Venezuelan officer retires after thirty years at full pay one rank above his last

[2] See Victor Alba's articles on the Latin American Military in *Combate*, Nos. 1–6 (San José, Costa Rica, September 1958–June 1959) and in John J. Johnson, ed., *The Role of the Military in Underdeveloped Countries* (Princeton, 1962).

active one. In Colombia an officer can retire voluntarily after twenty years of service and can receive 80 per cent of his basic pay and allowances.

The system does not always work as it is supposed to. Officers are, in general, still a mediocre, if improving, group. They repeatedly violate the military codes. They feel that their services should be requited with more than pension plans. They tincture their greed with vanity and personal grievances. And civilian politicians constantly interfere with the system. At those ranks (general and colonel in the Army and Air Force and captain in the Navy) where congressional approval for promotions becomes necessary, politics rather than technical competence is often decisive. In Venezuela in 1963, for example, certain officers believed strongly that association with the Democratic Action Party was sufficient recommendation for promotion, and the same officers were convinced that President Betancourt was disregarding both seniority regulations and the best interests of the services in order to place officers oriented toward the Democratic Action Party in key positions. And there is no denying that in countries more highly developed than Venezuela promotion by seniority from time to time continues to be tempered by sycophancy and nepotism, with the result that young officers become easily disgruntled.

Despite the failings of the system, recent developments have been highly favorable to the average officer. As a member of a group, he now has a sense of security that he could not have reasonably expected a few years ago. And the armed forces have become institutionalized pressure groups with channels for maintaining close links with the civilian population.

C. Wright Mills once said that "social origins and early background are less important to the character of the professional military man than to any other high social type."[3] This may apply to countries with highly professionalized armed forces, but is not applicable to Spanish America. There, although the situation is changing, a uniform still does not always make an individual first of all a soldier, and at

[3] C. Wright Mills, *The Power Elite* (New York, 1959), p. 192.

least until that stage is reached the officer's social background will remain one of the keys to his behavior.

One component of this background is racial origin. It is known, for example, that in the armed forces, as in Latin American society as a whole, opportunities have favored men of European ethnic background over the "people of color." Everywhere except in Haiti, which may be considered solidly Negro and mulatto, the percentage of white officers is greater than the percentage of whites to the population as a whole. While observing a military parade in Tegucigalpa, Quito, or Lima, the whitening process beginning with the conscript and proceeding through the various levels to the top ranks can be seen taking place before one's eyes. This is not to suggest that there are not exceptions or that people of color are always kept from becoming officers. As early as 1960 the Peruvian army had at least one general who was a "full-blooded" Indian. In Mexico, El Salvador, and Paraguay, officers are overwhelmingly mestizos, and there is no discrimination against them at any rank. In Venezuela there are a few high-ranking officers who are part Negro. And everywhere except in Colombia, where an undetermined but obviously large percentage of officers still come from upper middle-class and elite families, there is evidence that the white predominance is breaking down within the armed forces, as it is in the political area; but for what it is worth, "whiteness" will continue, short of revolution, to be a factor for many years.

A major reason why the "whites" will not indefinitely continue to exercise their traditional influence is that everywhere the tendency is to dip deeper into the social strata for officers, and it is in the lower social strata that the mestizos, Indians, Negroes, and mulattoes are most often found. In Ecuador, where both civil and military personnel agree that 5 per cent of all officers are from the working classes (the same percentage as is estimated for the upper middle class and elite), the author was told of a cobbler's son who was making a distinguished record in the military school. Colonel Oscar Osorio, the dictator-president of El Salvador (1950–56), was "strictly peon," having come up from the enlisted ranks. The first class to graduate from the military school of Honduras had three Negro cadets "whose parents were obviously from the lowest middle sectors or working groups." A Venezuelan army officer spoke with considerable pride of the fact that his parents were from the working classes. Examples could be cited endlessly.

There would appear to be two principal reasons why more officers now come from the lower sectors than at any time since the mid-nineteenth century, when the armed forces were in near-total disgrace. First, economic and technological developments and the tremendous expansion of civilian bureaucracies have broadened the opportunities for the best-educated in the non-military areas. Second, public schools have given the lower classes the opportunity to receive the academic training needed to qualify for the military schools. Reasonably accurate figures show that in Ecuador 90 per cent of the cadets enter the military academies from the public schools, and this figure would seem to be reasonably correct for all of the republics. In Mexico, at least theoretically, the government will provide a child of sufficient aptitude with all of his academic and professional training without charge.

In the first half of this century the major source of officer material appears to have been the well-established small town families–professionals, shopkeepers, state and municipal bureaucrats. In El Salvador, for example, very few officers of the present generation came from the capital city; most came from "villages," which in many cases are little more than settlements linked to coffee plantations.[4] In Honduras in 1960, the small towns were especially well represented in the military school and in the officer corps. Because Venezuela throughout nearly all this century has been controlled by a military clique from the farming area of the Andes, bordering on Colombia, perhaps as much as 90 per cent of its officers have come from the non-industrialized states of the republic. The protocol list of officers for Caracas and vicinity published by the Minister of Defense in September of 1954 contained seventy names, for twenty-four of whom biographical information was available. Of that group twenty were from the agricultural and livestock-raising Andean states, including

[4] It has been said that the officers in El Salvador today owe their positions to plantation owners who knew them as cadets and recommended them to the military as trustworthy potential officers.

fifteen from the single state of Táchira, whose largest city, San Cristóbal, had a population of 56,000 in 1950. Only one officer was from the populous Federal District. Since 1950 the government has made a conscious and apparently successful effort to break the Andean monopoly over the armed services, and all sections of the country are now reasonably well represented in the military schools. On the basis of considerable reliable evidence, it is apparent that in Colombia the armed forces hold a very strong attraction for young men from the agricultural regions, which provide at least 70 per cent of the officers in the three branches of the service.

Ecuador presents a somewhat different situation. There, one is not so much impressed with the fact that a large percentage of officers come from small towns, which they do, as by the fact that they come in overwhelming numbers from the economically backward highlands with Quito as the hub; the more advanced coastal area, which Guayaquil dominates, is weakly represented, even in the navy. This situation has helped to keep alive the rivalry of the two regions; *guayaquileños* insist that they produce the revenue used to support the national army which is in turn employed to suppress them politically.

In Chile, the small town thesis begins to break down, and in Argentina it simply does not apply. The officers in the Chilean armed forces come from the various states more or less in relation to their share in the total population, and approximately 70 per cent of the Argentine armed forces come from the highly developed Federal District and the province of Buenos Aires.[5] Robert Potash, who has worked extensively

[5] See the contribution by Lyle McAlister in John J. Johnson, ed., *Continuity and Change in Latin America*. McAlister, drawing upon Potash, also points out that as late as 1951 only 12 per cent of the generals were from Buenos Aires. Two facts go far toward explaining the Argentine situation: there has been a heavy concentration of immigrants in the Federal District and the province of Buenos Aires; and the nation's large army bases and schools are also located in and around the capital city. The military have been swelled by men from this region because immigrants have used the Argentine armed forces as a springboard to social prestige, and because the sons of officers display a strong tendency to follow in their fathers' footsteps and become officers.

upon the Argentine military, holds that in recent years Argentine generals have been big city products.

The potential officers from the small towns appear to be motivated primarily by three factors. First, the military academies offer far better opportunities for education than are ordinarily available locally. Second, a military career affords a chance to break out of the provincial settlements, where economic opportunities are few. Third, military careers provide a chance to improve one's social-economic status. Another consideration, but one not easy to measure, is the "glamor appeal" of the armed forces for young men in hundreds of drab interior towns, cut off from contact with the pageantry and diversions of the cities.

The young man from a provincial settlement takes into his military career attitudes that almost certainly affect his thinking as an officer. In many cases the detachment of six to a dozen officers in his home town provides him with his only direct contact or acquaintance with the national government. The troops and the national flag flying from the presidio thus come to symbolize the nation. The troops, too, command youthful respect in a society that places considerable emphasis upon force and violence. And the ready response of enlisted men to the orders of their commander presents an apparent aura of power and influence bound to fascinate an impressionable mind. That mind is also impressed by the fact that the *comandante* is accepted as an equal of the village priest, the *alcalde* (mayor), the president of the Rotary Club, and the large landowners and their daughters. The association of the armed forces with social prestige is consequently strong among village youth.

The boys or young men of the rural towns grow up in an environment far more strongly shaped by Roman Catholicism than is the environment in which their city cousins are reared. Historically, the strength of the Catholic Church has been in the countryside, while the cities have taken the lead in anticlerical movements. It has been the well-established provincial families who have provided the hard core of the narrow and at times almost medieval Catholicism found in the outlying regions. In this regard, it is worth noting that in the Venezuelan presidential election of 1958, the state of

Táchira, which in this century has provided an estimated 80 per cent of all army officers, gave over 55 per cent of its vote to the candidate of the Social Christian Party (the most conservative of the four major parties), who obtained only 14 per cent of the total presidential vote.

Finally, the provincial youth ordinarily comes from a non-propertied family or one that associates property with land, if only because its fortunes are closely related to the welfare of the agricultural community. The importance of this economic background is that the provincial youth becomes an officer without a firm understanding of corporate industry and little appreciation of the problems, including labor relations, of technological development which his professional training as a soldier inclines him to support. The agricultural orientation that the cadets from the small towns take into their military careers may be strengthened, and cadets from other social backgrounds made aware of the "agricultural" problem, when as officers they marry into the provincial "aristocracy." This apparently occurs with some frequency, because new officers are often assigned to the least attractive garrisons of the interior and the frontiers soon after they have finished their academy training. In the provinces, their prestige as officers brings them into contact with the socially prominent and marriageable young ladies whose fathers control the countryside, and who, incidentally, are on the lookout for opportunities to escape the boredom of the interior.[6]

A second major source of officers, and one which is becoming increasingly important, is the sons and brothers of officers. Everywhere the academies have a strong contingent of army and navy juniors. A highly placed naval officer in Chile, for example, insisted that 60 per cent of the sons of officers go to the Naval Academy and that 20 to 25 per cent of all officers in the Chilean navy were navy juniors. Available evidence indicates that a figure of 20 to 25 per cent

[6] A careful estimate of the frequency with which such marriages take place has not been made, but civilian responses to direct and related questions suggest that the public, at least in the lesser developed republics, is convinced that the rate of such marriages is abnormally high. This point, which must be considered tentative for the moment, deserves more thorough research.

would hold throughout those republics where the armies and navies are now well established. Thus, there is some truth in the statement that children of officers are born to privilege in Spanish America. The air forces in most of the republics are of such recent origin that it is impossible to determine with any degree of certainty whether or not they will follow the pattern of the armies and navies, but on the other hand, there is no reason to believe that they will not. Military families, meanwhile, are becoming commonplace. In Ecuador, Venezuela, and Mexico research turned up several cases of four or more brothers in the armed forces, and two brothers in a single branch of the service is quite common. When one adds to the sons and brothers the cousins and second-cousins and ties resulting from marriages, the influence of a few families can become decisive, particularly in the smaller forces.

The opportunities for one or a few families to control a service is illustrated by the situation in the Venezuelan Navy and Marine Corps, and by the Cuban Army under Fulgencio Batista. The Venezuelan Navy in 1962 had six admirals; two of them were the Larrazábal brothers, Carlos and Wolfgang; a third, Sosa Ríos, was married to a sister of the Larrazábal brothers and a second Larrazábal sister was married to a commander in the marines, Oscar Nahmens. Also, the Carúpano and Puerto Cabello revolts of mid-1962, led by the marines, tended to be family affairs. The Carúpano uprising was headed by J. T. Molina, who "jumped the gun" on what was supposed to be a general revolt, when his brother, J. J. Molina, a high-ranking marine officer, was arrested for plotting. The same J. J. Molina is married to one of three Bermúdez sisters, the other two of whom are also married to marine corps officers. Furthermore Lieutenant Commander Morales, who deserted when the revolt broke out in Carúpano but who returned to the barracks the night of the Puerto Cabello outbreak, is a brother-in-law of Lieutenant Commander Francisco Avilan, one of the navy officers who backed the marine uprising at Puerto Cabello.

In Cuba, dictator Fulgencio Batista was well aware that the Cuban armed forces were essential to his continuance in power, and he accordingly made great efforts to insure the loyalty of the forces. The Tabernilla family played a dominant role in his plans. The leader of this family was Major General Francisco J. Tabernilla y Dolz (with five stars, the only Cuban officer of the rank). A career army man, he was a second lieutenant when Batista staged the "Sergeants' Revolt" in 1933. Tabernilla threw his lot in with Batista and subsequently became one of his closest friends. Promoted to lieutenant colonel in 1934, he made brigadier general in 1942. When Batista forces lost the election in 1944, Tabernilla was promptly "retired." Batista staged his last coup on March 10, 1952, with the active participation of Tabernilla, who was promoted to Major General and made Chief of Staff of the army. In January 1958 he was made Chief of the Joint General Staff and given the rank of General-in-Chief. He fled Cuba with Batista on January 1, 1959.

General Tabernilla had three sons, Francisco, Carlos, and Marcelo. During 1957 and 1958 they held the following positions: Brigadier General Francisco H. Tabernilla y Palermo (two stars) was commanding officer of the Mixed Tank Regiment, which included all the tanks in the Cuban armed forces. Brigadier General Carlos M. Tabernilla y Palermo (one star) was commanding officer of the Cuban Army Air Force which, with the exception of a few antiquated navy planes, contained all the military aircraft Cuba had. Lieutenant Colonel Marcelo Tabernilla y Palermo, "the baby of the family," was commanding officer of the Cuban Army Air Force Bomber Squadron, which included all of the bombers Cuba possessed. In addition, the older Tabernilla's sister was married to Brigadier General Alberto Del Río Chaviano (two stars), who spent most of the crucial years 1957 and 1958 as commanding officer of the Southern Military Zone of Oriente Province, which included the city of Santiago (Cuba's second largest) and the Sierra Maestra mountains, the center and heartland of Fidel Castro's operations.

Like the young men from the small towns, those sons of officers who follow in their fathers' footsteps doubtless take into their careers certain attitudes and biases that influence their behavior when they step out of their purely professional role. For one thing, their early training has conditioned them to think in essentially bureaucratic terms. Like the youth from the provinces, the son of an officer may have little understanding of the workings of industrial capitalism simply because his parents, if they were typical, would have had very little or no personal experience in that economic area. And the officer's son may well have grown up a superpatriot if only because it was dinned in his ear that the armed forces are the guarantors of the nation's sovereignty and defenders of its dignity, not only against the foreign enemy but also against those who would destroy the nation from within.

The relatively recent arrivals from Europe and their heirs constitute the third and last important source of officers that requires special mention here. The influence of this group has been most pronounced in Chile and Argentina. In Chile, the Germans, who began to come into the republic in the mid-19th century, had begun to infiltrate the armed services by the outbreak of World War I; by World War II their importance in the Chilean army (which had been under German influence for half a century) was of major concern to the Allies. Since World War II a sprinkling of Syrian and Jewish and a rather larger number of Yugoslav names have appeared on the registers of the military academies. But the influence of the newcomers in the Chilean armed forces has been insignificant compared to their influence in Argentina. There, both armed forces personnel and civilians claimed in 1960 that not less than 40 per cent of all officers were first and second generation Argentines, overwhelmingly of Italian and Spanish origin.[7]

The newcomers have looked to careers in the military for several reasons. The services are technical, and submerged social groups see technical training as an avenue to social mobility. The armed forces, because of their strong nationalistic leanings, provide a sanctuary for newcomers who fear being looked upon as anything less than 100 per cent patriotic. And these Argentines only one or two generations removed from Italy and Spain are quite comfortable in an army

[7] Robert Potash, in a personal communication, reports that in 1961 only 20 per cent of Argentine generals were second-generation Argentines. However, his information indicates that as late as 1951 approximately one half of the generals were sons of immigrants. See Lyle McAlister's contribution in John J. Johnson, ed., *Continuity and Change in Latin America* (Stanford, 1964).

that apparently enforces an unwritten requirement that all officers be at least nominal Catholics.[8]

We may now ask how institutionalization and increased professionalization on the one hand and the changing social character of officers on the other have been manifested in military-civilian relations since World War II. In terms of the relationships between the armed forces and civilians, the junta of government has been the most important by-product of institutionalization. In its civilian context the junta goes back to the colonial period, but it has been a regularly employed military device in Spanish America only since the 1920's. In their simplest forms the military juntas are boards or committees that assume power and rule by decree following the removal of a regime by force. They represent joint efforts on the part of dominant groups in the various branches of the military establishment to present a unified front against dissident elements within the services. This is what occurred in Peru in July 1962 when the Manuel Prado government was driven from power: a junta representing a substantial cross-section of the officer corps in each of the branches of the armed services took over the leadership of the republic. The juntas are by definition transitory and several have terminated their rule in favor of civilians but rarely without first laying down the terms under which the successor government is permitted to be selected.

As far as the evolution of the armed forces is concerned, the military junta is a manifestation of the decline of individualism and the growth of an *esprit de corps* or group identification that has accompanied the greater institutionalization of the services. The Venezuelan situation perhaps best illustrates this point. Under the old tyrant Juan Vicente Gómez, the armed forces were used against civilians repeatedly, but at the command and pleasure of the dictator. Their long-range interests were incidental to the immediate interests of Gómez. But under the tyrant the armed forces did take on a national character and did evolve institutional objectives, and

[8] K. H. Silvert, "Political Universes in Latin America," *American Universities Field Staff Reports*, VIII, No. 6 (Dec. 1961), p. 10.

when Gómez died in 1935 these developments manifested themselves. Following a number of internal crises that resulted in the younger professionals supplanting the older nonprofessionals in key positions, the armed forces began to act in the name of the various branches and to claim the role of custodians of the national interests. The juntas of 1945, 1948, and 1958 were the results. Although the junta may now be considered a well-established political device of the armed services throughout Spanish America, it does not follow that strongmen will not appear from time to time, as in Argentina where Perón emerged supreme two years after the military took over the government in June 1943.

Professionalization has produced officers, who, when they act politically, do so for reasons and in a manner that clearly distinguishes them from their pre-World War I counterparts. First of all professionalization has almost completely destroyed the fluidity that existed when officers moved in and out of the military life at will. Then, too, as Lucian Pye has so ably established in reference to areas other than Latin America, professionalization has created an intellectual atmosphere within the armed forces that makes the leadership acutely sensitive to the advantages of modernization and technical advancement.[9] The new officer's belief in the need to modernize involves him so deeply with the welfare of the nation that he feels obliged to take a position on all major issues. This view can place him in an unusual position at several levels. Although nationalistic, he is, for example, required to obtain his weapons abroad. Also, he can be forced to look outside his own society for models upon which to fashion his own career, which can make him painfully aware of the extent to which his own country is economically and technologically retarded. Or his impatience to see the complete modernization of the armed forces and of the nation may tear him emotionally between those values held over from his

[9] See his excellent contributions in Gabriel A. Almond and James S. Coleman, eds., *The Politics of the Developing Areas* (Princeton, 1960), and John J. Johnson, ed., *The Role of the Military in Underdeveloped Countries* (Princeton, 1962). Pye's thinking is apparent throughout Max F. Millikan and Donald L. M. Blackmer, editors, *The Emerging Nations; Their Growth and United States Policy* (Boston, 1961).

youth and those that tend to align him with intellectuals and students and others most anxious to bring about change rapidly. For better or worse, the emotional conflict has held up the playing out of the contest between the military bureaucracies, which have traditionally represented the countryside, and the civilian bureaucracies, historically centered in the cities and inclined to look outward for guidance. This is why when the cities appear to triumph politically, as they have on many occasions since World War I, there has remained a strong residue of rural-mindedness, which erupts from time to time either at the instigation of or with the collusion of the armed forces, who have held the balance of power more or less continuously in all republics except Uruguay, Costa Rica, Chile, Colombia, Mexico, and Bolivia.

The commitment of the new generation of officers to modernization has also meant that the traditional social-economic gap between the leader and the led has been reinforced by differences in acculturation to modern life. This, plus the fact that in contemporary military establishments there is little or no comradeship between officers and men, has created a void that tends to prevent commissioned officers from being fully aware of the concerns of the non-commissioned officers and troops. Accordingly, non-commissioned officers and troops have been encouraged to look to civilians to fill the vacuum of representation between them, their superiors, and the public. This gap also tends to keep the officers divorced from that part of the populace in which democratic aspirations are nourished. Modernization and its implications, it would seem, weigh so heavily in Spanish America's future that the "pay, promotion, pension" argument–so often used at one and the same time to discredit the armed forces and to account for their participation in politics–loses much of its significance. In the final analysis, the republics will not be made or unmade on the basis of their military expenditures, although their future may well be determined by how important the armed forces consider modernization to be.

In some respects professionalization has made the modern armed forces officer less qualified than his World War I predecessor to run the governments of the republics. The officer of an earlier generation was first of all a civilian who thought as a civilian; he could, if he chose, keep his finger on the pulse of the narrowly based civilian ruling element through direct contact—although in actual practice the military tyrants in the latter stages of their dictatorships often lost all touch with the civilian elite and depended entirely on crudely repressive tactics. And the state, which was charged with little more than defending the national sovereignty and protecting private property, could be managed with only a primitive knowledge of administration. The modern officer-statesman, on the other hand, is never free for more than a brief moment to rule exclusively in the interests of a single sector of society, and government has become extravagantly complex as the state has committed itself to action in many social and economic areas.

The contemporary officer, furthermore, must spend at least twenty years in the service before he can expect to be called by his peers to lead them when they challenge politicians on their own ground. During those twenty years he lives in near-isolation from civilian concerns. Consequently, when he plunges into politics without ethical, moral, or legal support, he must not only speak for the armed services and try to keep them happy; he must also, because of the isolation that the military life imposes, depend for advice on his military friends, who live by the same kind of conventional wisdom that he does. These advisors, like the junta member himself, are usually win-the-war-and-to-hell-with-the-cost men, and as administrators they have been inefficient planners and inclined toward ruinous financial policies, as witness Perón in Argentina and Rojas Pinilla in Colombia. Carlos Ibáñez of Chile is an excellent example of a military man elected to the presidency of a politically sophisticated republic in a free election who by the time he left office had surrounded himself with a disproportionate share of military men because he felt he understood them and they understood him.

During his first twenty years as a soldier, the military ethic teaches the modern officer that man is weak and irrational and must be subordinated to the group, a position which at times has induced officers to disdain the civilians whom they propose to rule. Furthermore, the officer is, for nearly all of his professional career, himself a subordinate, taking orders rather than giving them, carrying out someone else's ideas rather than his own, and fitting himself into the well-defined hierarchical organization of the military. Subordination, and the narrow range of alternatives that subordination in the military permits, make the officer decisive and build up in him a faith in his ability to demand decisive action from others. The professional soldier's ordered and disciplined life has unquestionably made it difficult for him to tolerate the unsettling effects of social change, the "wasted effort" and divisiveness that accompany the workings of the democratic process. Perón, for example, in addressing a class of Argentine cadets before the war's end, accounted for France's military collapse on the grounds of internal disorder resulting from its political system. Above all, it has been the officer-politician's propensity to reject democratic institutions, polemics, and personal rivalry, and to apply military regimentation and modes of thought to all types of civilian situations that has ordinarily kept him in conflict with important elements within the civilian population. In this climate of opposition, he has not been able for extended periods of time to make effective use of his best qualities—self-confidence, experience in taking orders before giving them, the ability to accept rapid modernization, and the disposition to think in national terms.

Finally, the modern officer-politician runs into difficulties never experienced by his predecessor when he insists, as he ordinarily does, on imposing not only his person but a whole system upon the nation. Officers of an earlier generation, assuming control when strains developed, simply "declared for the general will" and were content to exercise personal political power. Despite their apparent ruthlessness, they were haphazard in enforcing their will upon the public, and they invariably proclaimed representative democracy to be their ultimate objective. But the modern officer often enters politics because of ideological differences with the civilian elements in power. When he achieves power as a representative of his branch of the service he feels compelled not only to rule but to define the content of the general will, as did Perón under what he called *justicialismo*. The modern officer may attempt to brainwash his subjects through mass media of communications. He may use the schools and government-controlled labor organizations for the propagation of the ideological position he seeks to impose. He may employ economic sanctions, one of the more easily applied political weapons in a "planned" society. He may lump representative democracy with imperialistic capitalism and reject both as undesirable.

The officer-statesman's confidence in his ability to formulate and implant ideological doctrines arises from two basic causes: contact with officers from other countries, and a conscious effort on the part of the armed forces in the most advanced countries to make officers aware of contemporary developments. Thus, the rise of a totalitarian attitude in the Argentine Army in the 1930's and 1940's can be accounted for in large part by its close connections with the armies of Nazi Germany and Fascist Italy, which at that time must have seemed almost invincible. Today, middle- and senior-grade officers in all the leading countries of Latin America are expected to have instruction in both national and world affairs; as a result, they become convinced that they are qualified to play a leading role in the economics, international relations, and government of their countries. It is still too early to determine how successful these training programs will be. As yet there has not appeared an officer who has publicly displayed a greater grasp of national and world problems than have civilians. But to the consternation of the anti-military elements of the area, the armed forces have won some highly placed individuals over to the military point of view by using them as instructors and extending to them some of the privileges (free air travel, for example) that the armed forces enjoy.

The officers who rush into politics to protect their professional or ideological interests may be no more responsible for prolonging the military interference in politics than are those officers who permit themselves to be used by civilian politicians. Regardless of which side is more effective, civil-militarism in politics is a reality throughout most of Spanish America. In June of 1959, Rafael Caldera, the presidential candidate of the Social Christian Party in the 1958 elections, formulated the problem well when he said, "Venezuelans are so accustomed to see the army as a factor in their daily lives, so accustomed to make the army the arbiter of their political contests, that at each moment the most varied groups for the most dissimilar ends attempt to involve the army in new adventures to change our political reality."

There is a vast body of evidence to support Caldera's statement. The new political parties that arose in Venezuela after the death of the tyrant Gómez sought support in the armed forces for their demands, and Rómulo Betancourt and his Democratic Action Party first achieved power in 1945 by a military coup. When the armed forces removed his successor, Rómulo Gallegos, who belonged to Democratic Action, and set up a junta, the opposition parties approved—if they did not actually welcome—the role of the junta because of their intense dislike of the party. Then, in one of his campaign speeches during the presidential campaign of 1958, victorious candidate Betancourt listed the names of "soldiers who died in the name of Democratic Action." Betancourt was also charged, probably with considerable justification, with using his office to place officers sympathetic to Democratic Action in key positions in the various branches of the armed forces.

Civil-militarism is unusually pronounced in Venezuela, but it exists everywhere except in Costa Rica and Uruguay. In Honduras, "the army officers belong to the Nationalist Party," according to a prominent figure in that organization, "and we would all be dead if the army did not protect us from the Civil Guard." According to another member of that party, "Everybody praised the military junta for its role in removing Julio Lozana Díaz from office after two years of inept rule and then conducting a free election." Victor Paz Estenssoro, twice president of Bolivia, prior to achieving that high office for the first time in 1952, encouraged young nationalist officers in the army and air force to promote the interests of the Movimiento Nacionalista Revolucionario (MNR) by surreptitiously opposing the "irresponsible older officers." When the MNR achieved power, all officers in what remained of the armed services were MNR Party members. Between 1946 and 1957 the Conservative Party was predominant in Colombia, and it insisted that the majority of students entering the military academy, from which all officers come, be from Conservative Party families. In Mexico the Partido Revolucionario Institucional (PRI) uses armed forces officers as referees at the local level, and the free-wheeling *comandante* is courted if not respected in such modern provincial cities as Guadalajara.

José María Velasco Ibarra, four-time president of Ecuador, who was removed from office by the army in 1962, used to speak of "mi ejército" (my army). He bought the air force a number of jets during his 1952–56 term and, in an excellent display of non-coordination, sent officers to study abroad in at least twelve different countries. In Peru, Fernando Belaúnde Terry, presidential candidate in 1962 (and victor in June 1963) let it be known after the 1962 elections that he would as soon see the armed forces take control of the country as to have the presidency go to either of the leading opposition candidates, and a few days later his alternative to his own election came to pass. At the same time the politically powerful Miro Quesada family, which controls the newspaper *El comercio* in Lima, also urged intervention by the military.

One may dip into the history of Argentina anywhere and expect to find examples of civil-militarism. Hipólito Irigoyen, the first "people's president" of Argentina, during his initial term in office, paid off one debt after another to officers who in the 1890–1916 period had helped to counteract the ruling oligarchy's use of the army as a praetorian guard to manipulate elections. Before 1930 nationalist groups in Argentina found in General José F. Uriburu a possible vehicle for their rise to power, while conservatives, Anti-Personalist Radicals and Independent Socialists gravitated to General Agustín P. Justo.

Marvin Goldwert, in an unpublished manuscript, writes of a secret Argentine decree dated November 25, 1930, "which seems to have been an out-and-out attempt to bribe the official body of the army."[10] According to Goldwert, the decree called upon all officers to draw up a list of their outstanding debts to be submitted to the government, with the understanding that all approved ones would be paid by the administration headed by General Uriburu. The decree contained provisions for repayment over a ten-year period, but "this never seems

[10] "The Argentine Revolution of 1930: The Rise of Modern Militarism and Ultra-Nationalism in Argentina" (Ph.D. dissertation, University of Texas, 1962).

to have been done." This decree, it was later recorded, had cost the Argentine people 7 million pesos, and led one historian to call it "perhaps the cleverest wholesale bribery scheme ever witnessed in South America."

On the eve of the 1943 coup in Argentina, Radical Party politicians were in contact with General Pedro Ramírez and other key officers who took part in the ouster of President Castillo. Civil-militarism in Argentina since the overthrow of Perón has been so notorious that only three points of some interest need be recorded here. Admiral Isaac Rojas, who had steadfastly opposed Perón, according to the son of the president of a very staid and conservative club in Buenos Aires, was made an honorary member of the club "in appreciation." Arturo Frondizi wanted the presidency badly enough in 1958 to accept the terms laid down by the armed forces, including the outlawing of the *peronistas,* who apparently constitute at least 30 per cent of the electorate. And although the Popular Radical Party, whose presidential candidate in the 1958 elections ran second to Frondizi, feigned dismay when the armed forces ousted Frondizi in early 1962, high officials of that party in 1960 were said by well-informed sources to have urged a military takeover of the government. To these examples of civil-militarism must be added the actions of all those civilian authorities who rely upon the armed forces to maintain themselves in power and in so doing invite military interference in civilian affairs.

Caldera's statement for Venezuela, then, has rather general applicability. From it follows logically the proposition that until the armed forces develop as strong a moral fiber as have the civilians with whom they must deal, civil-militarism will be part of the political reality in large areas of Spanish America. Civilians will probably continue to appeal to the military for at least three reasons. The first, and obviously most justified one, is that in certain instances the military becomes an important means of removing a group in power. In this sense, the military coup is part of the democratic process, and has been freely acknowledged as such in Latin America.

The second reason that civil-militarism will continue is that violence, although diminishing, remains a definite feature of the political process in most of the republics. In such an environment, the politicians, the parties, and ultimately the people must from time to time choose from among five alternative sources of force: the armed services, the police, the civil guards, armies constituted and supplied by political parties, and forces raised by retired officers. The regular services, under such circumstances, will retain an extremely strong appeal.

The third reason is that the armed forces will continue to be divided by inter-service and intra-service rivalries which can be exploited by civilians in much the same way as they have been historically. Although inter-service differences certainly cannot be discounted, it should be realized that they have not been as important as they might have in view of the fluid situation that has persisted in the republics. This has been true primarily for two reasons. First, in most cases the armies have been so strong vis-à-vis the other military services that they have had the final say. Only on one occasion—the Chilean revolution of 1891—has a Spanish-American navy emerged clearly on top in a showdown with the army. And as yet no air force in Spanish America has attained either the strength or standing that would permit it to meet the corresponding army head-on, unless the Ecuadorian air force action against the army in 1961 may be considered an exception. Second, the political impact of inter-service rivalry has been still further reduced because, unlike in the United States, the armed forces of Spanish America are not pioneering advanced weapons, and their professional futures, therefore, are not constantly at stake.

Intra-service rivalries have had political repercussions more often than have inter-service differences. Such rivalries most often break out into the open in the army, because there the stakes in terms of power are higher than in the other branches of the armed forces, and also because in the navies officers are constantly being broken up into small groups aboard ships, which discourages the formation of cliques.

Differences of a politically important nature often arise between the young officers and their seniors. The reasons for the differences vary widely. Sometimes the younger men feel that as members of the technically trained and "virtuous" generation, they are better qualified than their seniors to represent the services. On some occasions they feel that ranking generals have lost touch with the troops and the field-grade officers are the real representatives of the military consensus. Sometimes they want to involve the armed services more deeply in politics; this is the case particularly with those who have authoritarian leanings. And sometimes they are simply discontented because for one reason or another promotions and privileges have not come to them as expected.

In order to strengthen their position in respect to the senior officers, the younger men are forever forming cliques or secret organizations. Thus a group of junior officers, for example, was responsible for the Venezuelan coup of 1945, and junior army officers, in cooperation with the Venezuelan navy and air force, likewise played an important role in the overthrow of Pérez Jiménez. They were clearly exasperated with Pérez Jiménez because he had consistently followed a policy of showering upon senior officers privileges, political appointments, and opportunities to grow rich by corruption while neglecting junior men.

Secret organizations have been common in the military history of Spanish America. The first known *Logia* (Lodge), which had Masonic connections, was founded as early as 1808 to promote the independence of Spanish America. Since then Masons have with varying success infiltrated the armed services in all of the republics; the Argentine navy had the reputation of being a stronghold of Masonry during the Perón dictatorship. In Argentina the military Logia San Martín dictated key assignments during President Alvear's administration (1922–28) and also won acceptance for an armaments expansion policy during Alvear's tenure.

More recently the secret organizations have taken on a professional or nationalistic coloration. The highly nationalistic, fascist-oriented Grupo de Oficiales Unidos (GOU) in Argentina, of which Perón was a member, is the best known of the secret military organizations that attracted younger officers, but there have been many others that have had some influence since the GOU came into prominence. In Bolivia the Radepa (Razón de Patria) reached its peak of influence during the war years, when it participated in the overthrow of President Enrique Peñaranda in 1943. It was made up of young officers who blamed Bolivia's defeat in the Chaco war on corrupt and greedy politicians, and its leaders reportedly accepted fascist authoritarianism as well as financial assistance from the Perón government of Argentina. In Chile the Pumas (Por un Mañana Auspicioso) and the Linéa Recta, two military parties that came out in the open in 1955, were made up of young officers who were impressed with the growing influence of the Argentine army after 1943 and sought to secure the same influence for themselves. They chose to improve their position first by dedicating themselves to the election of Carlos Ibáñez to the presidency in 1952 and, after that was achieved, to giving him dictatorial power to solve the country's problems. In Ecuador, young officers who claimed to be interested only in professional improvement, but who had ties with civilian politicians, created a secret organization known as Forme (Formación de Oficiales Revolucionarios Ecuadorianos), which in 1959 engaged in terrorist activities, but to no avail.[11]

The antagonism and bitterness that have led to inter- and intra-service rivalries and have served to involve the armed forces in politics have at the same time weakened them as cohesive political organizations. When acrimony leads to military executions, as it did in Argentina during the interregnum following Perón's overthrow, it seems unlikely that the armed forces can be expected to act with unity in any given situation; and if this is true, it follows that division in the armed forces will be exploited by civilians for their own purposes.

The police, except perhaps in Argentina and Chile, are not an acceptable alternative to the armed forces when political decisions start to be resolved by force. The police are in general a sorry lot. They often receive only a bare minimum of

[11] Robert Potash, who has made the most thorough study yet of the Argentine army, has come across a number of secret organizations in it: Los Dragones Verdes, Los Gorilas, El Pistón (military engineers), and Los Cuarenta (the forty colonels), to name a few. His tentative conclusion, however, is that in the Argentine case information about the cliques is unreliable, and that more often than not the cliques are short-lived associations set up to advance the personal ambitions of certain officers. Potash also holds that the cliques involve civilians as well as officers.

technical training. Not unusually illiterate and shabbily dressed, they can hardly command civilian respect, except the respect born of fear. They are so poorly paid that they live by various forms of blackmail, and intellectually they are completely unqualified to deal with the abstractions that arise in political life, and thus are subject to innumerable pressures from politicians and political appointees.

The national guards and the armies of political parties are ordinarily the products of revolution or highly unstable conditions. The national guards of Bolivia and Cuba became "permanent" organizations upon the destruction of the national armed forces under revolutionary circumstances, and if they become institutionalized they may be expected to assume nearly all the functions ordinarily reserved to the armed forces. And like the armed forces they will be able to influence social and political policies. The civil guard in Honduras arose from a less revolutionary atmosphere than those in Bolivia and Cuba, but for much the same reason: to defend the Liberal Party from possible attack by the predominantly conservative army. The Liberal Party, in effect, caught the Honduran armed forces in a fit of indecision and was able to create what they hoped would be a counterpoise to the army, a situation which the Guatemalan and Argentine armed forces did not permit to arise when Jacobo Arbenz and Juan Perón, in 1954 and 1955, respectively, attempted to arm the proletariat which could then have been converted into a national guard. Only the civil guard of Costa Rica, by and large remaining out of politics and accepting the decisions of four successive presidential administrations on matters directly affecting it, has set an example that one might wish other military establishments to copy.

The armies of the political parties usually have their origins in guerrilla bands, but they may be converted into national guards if their party attains power, as occurred in Cuba and Bolivia. The civil war that raged in Colombia for a decade after 1947, for example, was in part sustained by bands who fought in the name of the Liberal Party, although that party organization did not recognize them publicly (the Conservative Party, of course, had the armed services at its orders). More recently, other bands in Venezuela and Ecuador have been associated with Communist and *fidelista* groups. It was in an effort to provide the armed forces of the republics with better training in anti-guerrilla tactics that President Kennedy in 1961 proposed greater military assistance to Latin America. Thereafter the number of commissioned and noncommissioned officers receiving instruction in anti-guerrilla warfare at U.S. bases in Panama was stepped up significantly.

The quip that when officers retire they conspire seems to have had almost universal validity for over a century in Spanish America. It still does in those countries (e.g., El Salvador, Guatemala, Argentina, Ecuador, and Venezuela) where officers are continually being retired for political reasons. In order to emphasize the point that officers "driven" into retirement, unless imprisoned and under guard, are a constant threat to political order, one need only recall those Argentine officers who from exile fought Perón throughout his long term in office; or those Guatemalan officers who from a half-dozen countries plotted the overthrow of Arbenz in 1954; or the Venezuelan officers who from the Dominican Republic, Colombia, and perhaps the Dutch West Indies harassed the Betancourt regime during its first months in office.

But officers who retire in the system today seldom remain politically important, and they almost never successfully conspire. A few do run for office; some win elections, particularly if they have "connections" in the rural areas, or in Mexico with the PRI. The institutionalized armed forces have their own interests to serve, and those interests can be represented as well or better by officers on active duty and in a position to keep in touch with the rapidly shifting currents of change. Furthermore, retired officers today receive pensions that enable them to live at approximately the level to which they became accustomed in the service; thus one of the age-old worries of the professional soldier has been removed, and with it one more reason why most retired officers can be expected to avoid conspiracy.

In terms of the evolution of the armed forces a developing tendency for them to withdraw from direct control of the government in favor of exercising indirect influence could become of as great significance as has been the substitution of the junta for the man on horseback. Despite the many cases which seem to prove the contrary, such a trend is discernible. Officers are definitely becoming unwilling to assume direct responsibility for administration at the national level, particularly in the more politically sophisticated republics. There are basically two reasons why the military men are taking this position: the rise of the popular masses, and the many opportunities that modern governments provide for decision-making away from public scrutiny. The emergence of new, politically articulate elements has produced several conditions which have caused the armed forces to re-evaluate the merits of gaining their objectives through direct action. No longer, for example, can they struggle with civilian politicians for power over the neutral masses simply because the masses are no longer neutral. Nor will the newly articulate voters any longer permit power alone to be decisive. This has meant that when soldiers seize power they must test their political conclusions, and this, as we have suggested, they prefer not to do. Also, the armed forces realize that the struggle of the masses against the more privileged sectors will intensify before it subsides. Under such circumstances the suppression of the popular will become increasingly difficult. All this means closer and closer relations between the rulers and the ruled. It follows that if the armed forces maintain prolonged and close relations with the people, the working classes will lose the awe and respect which up to now has ordinarily permitted the armed forces to move in and stabilize situations that have gotten out of the hands of the police, whom the public had learned to scorn through day-to-day contact. To the armed forces this is a situation that must be avoided at almost any price.

Meanwhile, attractive alternatives to direct control of government are playing an increasingly greater role in discouraging the armed forces from seizing power. One of the most important alternatives is the ability of the armed forces to act as pressure groups. As in the United States, they can affect budget-making by playing up the danger, real or imaginary, of attack from the outside. A good example of this technique was the development of an Argentine army ski patrol, which supposedly would be advantageous to have in case of war with Chile or against an enemy stationed in Antarctica. Also, many officers–active, inactive, or retired–often hold governorships and seats in the national legislature, where they can be effective on behalf of the military. The *Directorio del Gobierno Federal* of the Mexican Government for the year 1956 showed 16 per cent of all state governorships, 20 per cent of the Senate seats, and 6 per cent of the Chamber of Deputy seats held by men with military titles. Since the PRI controls all elections in Mexico, the selection of officers is not accidental and the opportunity for them to affect decision-making on the national level is considerable. In 1959, during the civilian government of Manuel Prado, there were three officers in the Peruvian Senate, seven in the Chamber of Deputies, as well as an army officer as head of the Atomic Energy Commission. Officer intervention during both military and civil regimes in Argentina is so notorious that it need not be reviewed here.

As the republics have moved prominently into economic and social welfare programs, the opportunities for officers to affect decision-making indirectly have multiplied at a fantastic rate. Officers have moved freely into top-level positions in state-controlled enterprises and autonomous and semi-autonomous agencies that have been created to promote national growth and provide public services. In Argentina in 1958, for example, the General Director of Military Factories ran ten operations, some of which competed directly with private enterprise, and in addition the Argentine navy was engaged in commercial shipbuilding and produced gunpowder in competition with private industry. As of 1963 the army controlled the new iron and steel plant at San Nicolás, which is expected to develop into the largest of its kind in all of Latin America; it has been said that a civilian government "would not dare to oust the military from steel."

The story is much the same in many of the republics. As of October 1962, active and retired officers were known to be serving President Betancourt's civilian administration in Venezuela in the following capacities: Minister of Communications; Director, Merchant Marine; Chief, Technical Division, Merchant Marine; Director, Civil Aviation; Director, Cajigal Observatory; President, Venezuelan Corporation of Guayana;

Director, National Institute of Water Resources; Chief of Production, Venezuelan Navigation Company; Director, National Institute of Railroads; and Director, National Institute of Canals. The post of Director of the Venezuelan Airmail Line was vacant "but normally filled by an Air Force Officer." In addition "about fifteen" officers were serving as ambassadors and consuls. In Chile the army manufactures small arms, agricultural machinery, and hardware. In 1960 an army officer headed the state-controlled railroad of Ecuador. Needless to say, when the armed forces take over direct control of a government, the use of officers in non-military areas is much more widespread than when civilians are in control. In Venezuela under Pérez Jiménez, for example, it was said that "Officers controlled nearly all of the top positions in government at all levels and in all enterprises in which the government had an interest."

The question naturally arises as to why officers hold the key positions they do in non-military areas during periods of civilian rule. There are many reasons, some general and some specific. Three of a more general nature are ordinarily set forth as follows: (1) the influence of the armed forces is so great that they "cannot be overlooked"; (2) civilian politicians use such appointments as a means of paying off past debts; (3) the armed forces' responsibility for the national defense makes them acutely concerned with the development of major areas of the economy, including the heavy industries, all forms of transportation, and power. The particularized reasons, if no more complex, are at least more novel. In the case of the Argentine armed forces, control of the iron and steel industry goes back to 1941, when General Manuel N. Savio determined that the national defense called for an iron and steel plant and since there was no Minister of Commerce and Industry, and since domestic private capital was unavailable and it did not seem advisable to permit foreign capital to come in, the armed forces were put in charge of planning. They have been in control ever since, and if the operation remains unprofitable, as it is expected to, private capital will not be interested in taking over. There was, in 1960, no public disposition to see the industry surrendered to any other agency of the government. "Within the government the military is the best qualified to run it," was the way a professor of economics felt.

In Mexico, military participation in the non-military areas of government is closely associated with the pay officers receive, which is the lowest in Latin America, except possibly in some of the Central American armies. Because of this, it is common in Mexico for officers to hold more than one job. There is a provision for them to be "a disposición" (something between active and inactive status), in which case they can continue to receive full army pay and accrue time credit toward promotion and retirement while holding another appointment with the government or in private industry.

Officers are often called upon by governments because a job is "too hot" for the politicians. The officer, being "above the local battle" and not seeking public office, is a likely candidate to head an almost defunct government-owned railroad or steamship line or to direct an unprofitable enterprise that is about to arouse public indignation. Or, as a Chilean army officer insisted in the course of berating the Ministry of Public Works, "The army is requested to take over government construction that cannot be done with modern machinery." An added consideration is that the armed forces officer may do his job for a small part of what a competent civilian would demand as salary.

By any concept of effective government, ability alone should determine an officer's competence to direct non-military activities, and on that score the soldier-manager in Latin America does not fare well. In every republic there can be found quite responsible citizens who insist that the officers do have qualifications that are not available or are in short supply in the civilian sectors. However, the weight of evidence is overwhelmingly on the side of those who insist that today civilians have equal or greater competence than the officers. Furthermore, there is nowhere in Spanish America a situation comparable to what is found in some of the new nations of Africa, the Middle East, and Southeast Asia, where officers can claim the right to direct government activities on the basis of both acquired skills and moral leadership.

A representative sampling of remarks from notes taken during a tour of the area in mid-1960 indicates the extent to which public opinion downgrades the capabilities of the officers of the armed forces. An Argentine newspaperman observed, "I know many officers, but I would not want a single one of them to head an industry of mine." He added that "officers are excessively free with public funds and the army will produce low-grade steel at the highest prices in the world." An Argentine businessman said angrily, "they will take any damn job, they think they know everything." A Venezuelan newspaperman, asked whether officers in the armed forces were capable administrators, simply replied, "Pooh." A Honduran lawyer was sure that "There is nothing that an army officer can do that a civilian cannot do better." An Ecuadorian banker contended that "They have no systematized training to prepare them for important non-military assignments." And the banker was in effect substantiated by an Ecuadorian officer who said, "Honestly, we have very few skills of use in industry and commerce." A Chilean secretary at the United States Embassy in Santiago disqualified officers for civilian posts on the grounds that "the army and navy are still very old-fashioned." An ex-president of one republic who volunteered to query an acting president of another republic on this subject reported that his friend had said, "I have no faith in men of the armed forces in any post of responsibility." Positions held by retired officers in the business community would seem to bear out the prevailing civilian opinion of them. Except for the unusually capable one, or one with good family connections, those who enter business after they retire do not hold positions of major responsibility.

THE MIDDLE SECTORS

Until the writings of John J. Johnson, Professor of History at Stanford University, the significance of the middle sectors in Latin America had been minimized and their beliefs poorly described. The selection that follows incorporates the first and last chapters from Professor Johnson's important book on this subject. The first chapter discusses the strength, composition, and amount of cohesiveness of the middle sectors and then describes their support of and role in advancing urbanization, public education, industrialization, nationalism, state intervention in the economy, and political parties. The last chapter traces the changing relationship of the middle sectors to other important groups in society and analyzes their potential for future political influence.

*The Emergence of the Middle Sectors**

JOHN J. JOHNSON

In the late nineteenth century a number of the republics of Latin America began to undergo technological transformations. By 1920 the impact of those transformations was widely felt. One of the most profound developments to come from them was the emergence of the urban middle sectors of society as an aggressive political force. Today these groups hold a prominent position in the social-political amalgams that con-

* Reprinted from John J. Johnson, *Political Change in Latin America: The Emergence of the Middle Sectors,* Chapters 1 and 9 with the permission of the publishers, Stanford University Press.

trol Argentina, Brazil, Chile, Mexico, and Uruguay. These five countries contain two-thirds of the land area and two-thirds of the population, and produce more than two-thirds of the gross product, of the twenty Latin American republics.

The behavior of the urban middle sectors as political entities has been determined by the changes they have undergone as a result of the technological transformations and by their bid for popular support outside their own groups—a support that has ordinarily come from the industrial proletariat. The constant search for a balance between values they hold to be basic and those dictated by political expediency has been a primary characteristic of their political conduct in this century.[1]

Before the five republics began the transition from neo-feudal agriculture to semi-industrial capitalism, the composition of the middle sectors was essentially static: they were members of the liberal professions, such as law and medicine; they were writers, publishers, and artists, they were professors in secondary schools and institutions of higher learning; they were bureaucrats; they were members of the secular clergy of the Catholic Church, and of the lower and middle echelons of the officer corps. This composition began to change as soon as the technological transformations gained momentum, and it continues to change as the component groups remain fluid and as movement in and around them accelerates. Before 1900, representatives of commerce and industry were notably absent from the composition of these middle sectors; the same technological developments that gave the other components an opportunity to improve their political status also created the conditions for the emergence of the commercial and industrial elements—owners as well as managers, applied scientists, and highly trained technicians.

Numerically, the middle sectors formed, until well into this century, a small minority. Until 1900 they might be described as a thin intermediate layer separating the elite from the inarticulate masses; their growth after 1900 was stimulated by the requirements of technology and by the expansion of edu-

[1] The reasons for using the terms middle sectors, middle elements, and so on, rather than middle classes or middle strata are discussed in the Preface [not included].

cation and of the functions of the State. Even so they remained, for the first two decades of this century, a small percentage of the total population in each of the five republics. The sharp upswing in their growth curve coincided with World War I. Since 1919 their numerical expansion has been large both in absolute figures and relative to the other elements of society, except the industrial proletariat. Today the middle sectors probably constitute at least 35 per cent of the population in Argentina, 30 per cent in Chile and Uruguay, and 15 per cent in Brazil and Mexico.

In the course of the middle sectors' rapid expansion since World War I their ranks have been infiltrated by appreciable numbers from other levels of society. As long as the demand for their skills rose gradually, as was the case throughout the colonial period and the nineteenth century, the increments to middle sector positions came almost wholly from the middle elements themselves, although occasionally individuals from the elites would drift down and become permanent members, and isolated individuals belonging to the working groups could and did lift themselves up—usually via the Catholic Church or the military. Generally, though, the sons of middle sector families followed in the footsteps of their fathers or moved horizontally within the middle groups. There was nothing approaching the vertical social mobility, limited as it remains, found in the republics today.

When the members of the middle sectors could no longer satisfy the increased demands for skills associated with their status, individuals from other groups began to bid successfully for recognition. In Argentina, Brazil, Chile, and Uruguay many naturalized citizens or sons of immigrants entered the ranks of the middle sectors as the owners of commercial and industrial establishments. Others came from the old rural families who for various reasons—as, for example, scarcity of land in Chile—had invested in urban industry and commerce. The salaried elements—teachers, bureaucrats, technicians, managers—drew an important share of their accretions from the working groups.

Clearly, the middle sectors are anything but a compact social layer. They do not fulfill the central condition of a class: their members have no common background of experience.

On the contrary, among them are representatives of nearly the entire cultural and economic range. Members of old Spanish and Portuguese families co-exist with mestizos, mulattoes, Negroes, and newcomers from Europe. Some are members of the middle sectors because of their intellectual attainments; some, because they have combined education and manual labor in proportions that meet the standards of those middle sector elements that still look askance at men who depend upon their hands for a livelihood; others, more because of their wealth than because of their learning. Property owners are associated with persons who have never possessed property and have little prospect of ever operating their own businesses. Some members are strongly committed to the defense of personal initiative and private property; others may be little concerned with property rights or infringements upon what are often considered the domains of private enterprise. Some take their status for granted: their lives are organized, they know where they are headed and what they want when they get there. Others are undergoing the frustrating and unsettling experiences and tensions inherent in passing from one socio-economic group to another. Some have only a paternalistic interest in, and a theoretical understanding of, the working elements. Others know the lower levels of society because they have risen from them, and their feeling for those groups is likely to be highly personal.[2] They are all the more aware

[2] In Latin America the privileged groups are strongly inclined to look for cultural symbols rather than biologically inherited characteristics. Race, consequently, tends to be subordinated to human and social values. For this reason racial differentiations are dealt with only obliquely in this study. In any event, only in Brazil was the racial composition of the middle sectors notably changed when workers began to find their way into them. There, although most of those entering the middle sectors from the working elements have been European in racial origin, for the first time the mestizos, mulattoes, and Negroes in substantial numbers have been provided opportunities to improve their social status. In Argentina, Uruguay, and Chile the new members of the middle sectors have been almost wholly European or mestizos with a decided preponderance of European blood. In Mexico, the new elements entering the middle sectors from the laboring groups have been basically mestizo, but the mestizo has been entrenched in the middle sectors there at least since the mid-nineteenth century. (The term "mestizo" in Spanish America is used to refer to persons of mixed European-Indian

of the existing social and economic inequities because as new members of the middle sectors they are more often confronted by them than they were as members of the lower levels. Some have inherited an almost congenital abhorrence for the labor movement, while others come from families that have depended upon the labor leader as their sole representative before their employers and public officials.

The differentiations in their social backgrounds and economic interests have prevented the middle sectors from becoming politically monolithic. Individual members have reserved the right to act independently. At times large components find the prevailing middle sector attitudes unacceptable and either refuse to exercise the suffrage or make *ad hoc* arrangements with the elites or the workers, or both, in order to oppose the dominant elements. But the differences have not prevented large and ordinarily major segments of the middle sectors from finding common ground for joint political action.

To the extent that the middle sectors have had political cohesiveness and a continuity of common interests, this cohesiveness and continuity seem to have been due to six characteristics they hold in common. They are overwhelmingly urban. They not only have well above average educations themselves but they also believe in universal public education. They are convinced that the future of their countries is inextricably tied to industrialization. They are nationalistic. They believe that the State should actively intrude in the social and economic areas while it carries on the normal functions of government. They recognize that the family has weakened as a political unit in the urban centers, and they have consequently lent their support to the development of organized political parties.

1. *Urbanization.* Whether they are salaried persons, self-employed professionals, or property owners and *rentiers;* whether they belong to the middle sectors because of their learning or their wealth, the members of the intermediate groups are almost solidly urban. It has been thus historically. The great and rapidly expanding centers—Mexico City, Rio

---

blood. In Brazil those of mixed European-Indian descent are normally referred to as *caboclos.*)

de Janeiro, Buenos Aires, Montevideo, Santiago—where the middle sectors are presently found in large numbers were, from their beginning, the centers of concentration for professionals, educators, bureaucrats, and other components of the early middle sectors. The metropolises were first of all administrative centers with revenues that provided the means for their becoming oases in what was otherwise largely a cultural and intellectual void. As industry developed it too has, in general, concentrated in cities, and thus the new components of the middle sectors have been added to the old. Since the middle sectors are predominantly urban, they favor, as they traditionally have, national policies that promote urban growth and economic development and assign a disproportionately large per capita share of public revenues to the urban centers.

2. *Public education.* Before 1900 all other determinants of middleness paled before the educational requirement. It was assumed that the student who entered school would eventually go on for a higher degree. Consequently primary and secondary schools were viewed not as ends in themselves but as steppingstones on the way to a university. In the universities logic and dialectics were emphasized. Empiricism and pragmatics were slighted in favor of deductive reasoning. A humanistic education was the trade-mark of nearly every member of the middle sectors. The rigid quantitative and qualitative requirements of education gave ground to the conditions created by the economic transformation and the entrance into the middle sectors of the commercial and industrial elements. Members could no longer be expected to hold a degree from an institution of higher learning. The needs of industry and commerce provided the impetus that made scientific training an acceptable substitute for the traditional humanistic training. Trade schools and high schools began to turn out semiprofessionalized graduates able to use their limited educations along with their other qualifications to achieve middle sector status.

Although middle sector families have themselves shown a strong preference for private schools, their leaders have for a century used the political forum to champion mass public education. In the nineteenth century they associated education with representative government and national progress. As industrial and commercial proprietors began to wield their influence upon political thinking, they added a demand that public schools provide the trained personnel needed to operate their plants more efficiently. Political leaders of the middle sectors have continued their demands for public elementary and secondary schools to ensure a literate electorate and a supply of semiskilled and skilled industrial artisans.

3. *Industrialization.* Industrialization has become an obsession within the middle sectors. The urgent need to industrialize further is accepted as a self-evident truth by all components, although in periods of stress differences may arise as to the degree of urgency. The cries for industrialization have mounted to a crescendo since World War II. Today it would be political suicide for a member of the middle sectors publicly to recommend a national policy founded on the economic doctrine that holds that each geographic area should produce only what it can turn out most efficiently. In each of the republics such a position would be interpreted by the political opposition as advocating that the nation remain a producer of unfinished goods and hence an economic colony of the industrial powers.

The middle sectors reached their present views on industrialization in four stages. In the late nineteenth century those concerned with industrial development were by and large content to promote the extractive and processing industries and to support technological development as requisite to continued industrial expansion. Ordinarily, the major enterprises were foreign financed and managed. In the second stage came the clamor for more processing industries. The breakdown of normal trade channels during World War I showed the inconveniences that nonindustrial countries could expect in periods of international catastrophe. The politicians made capital of proposals to avert any recurrence of widespread shortages resulting from dependence upon outside sources of supply. Meanwhile the economics of industrialization remained largely unaltered, although the nature of the new enterprises, many of which required only limited amounts of capital, opened the way for considerably greater domestic financial and managerial participation.

Industrialization and politics became increasingly entwined in the third stage, which corresponded to the world depression of the 1930's. Domestic ownership of natural resources and industry was the cliché of politicians in Uruguay and Mexico and to a lesser extent in the other republics. Substantial expansion in the production of semidurables requiring raw materials as well as capital goods from abroad increasingly involved the politicians in the economic sphere, particularly when foreign-exchange shortages developed. But the important increment to the industrial environment in this phase was the politicians' discovery of the power and appeal of their solicitude for the protection and welfare of the industrial workers. The new concern for the workingman had many facets. He had won a new status throughout the Western World. An aggressive labor movement in Europe had spread to other nations and had helped to strengthen the bargaining power of working groups in Latin America. The laborer had become more politically articulate. His vote was in large part responsible for the success of the political amalgams that the middle sector leadership headed.

Since World War II, in the fourth stage, two aspects of the political-industrial scene have become particularly pronounced. The demands that industry be expanded to include heavy industry have become incessant. The iron and steel plant has become the symbol of progress. On the other hand, serious doubts have been raised whether the republics can achieve the industrial development they seek without a greater price to labor than it has been asked to pay since the 1930's. Differences of opinion on this question have provided the fuel for political fireworks, particularly in Argentina, Brazil, and Chile.

4. *Nationalism.* Nationalism of an assertive xenophobic nature is for all intents and purposes a twentieth-century phenomenon in Latin America. In the course of their drives to power, the middle groups in the five republics have raised nationalism to the level of a major political ideology. Its effectiveness in arousing the emotions of a broad segment of the electorate gives every indication that it will remain a weapon or a potential weapon in the arsenal of the middle sector politician.

During the relatively brief period that it has enjoyed currency, the concept of nationalism has had several dimensions as it has responded to stimuli originating at home and abroad. It was initially nourished by individuals acting in a private capacity. In that stage its juridic and cultural features were presented in abstract terms by intellectuals. The two aspects were often viewed as independent.[3] Not unusually, the advocates of cultural and juridic nationalism condoned the alienation of natural resources and the granting of long-term concessions of a monopolistic nature to foreigners as the price of technological development. As long as private individuals supplied the driving force and the concept remained abstract, nationalism was largely devoid of political appeal because of the narrow audience reached.

In Uruguay and Mexico between 1910 and 1920 and in Argentina, Brazil, and Chile in the 1930's the State replaced the intellectual as the chief propagandist for nationalism. Under the sponsorship of the State two outstanding current characteristics of nationalism soon manifested themselves. Its economic aspect was given greater stress than its cultural and juridic aspects. No longer confined to the abstractions of a few intellectuals it was brought down to the masses in its dynamic and politically charged form.

5. *State intervention.* Statism and middle sector political leadership have become closely linked. The middle sectors early in their bid for political recognition rejected the laissez-faire doctrines of the nineteenth century. As a substitute they offered planned societies. When their recommendations were popularized, the middle sectors rode to new political heights.

Social welfare and industrialization have been the first concerns of the state interventionists. Under the sponsorship of the middle groups the states by 1940 had taken over many of the responsibilities for the welfare of the distressed elements formerly delegated to private and semipublic institutions. The duties of the State in providing educational facilities, medical care, food, and housing for the working groups were written in minute detail into the laws of several of the republics. Also, "in fulfillment of the State's social func-

[3] Economic nationalism commanded only sporadic attention at that stage.

tions" the governments of Argentina, Brazil, and Mexico took over the direction of the labor movement. As a result the laborer was encouraged to view any benefits he received as coming from the State and to conclude that his well-being and that of his fellow workers lay in political action rather than in direct negotiations with management. With their welfare written into law, laborers ordinarily have preferred to ally themselves with the groups in power, reasoning that only through support of those who administer the laws could they hope to attain what by law is theirs.

State intervention in the economic sphere has been justified on the basis of three socioeconomic tenets upheld by the middle sectors: (1) Industry cannot survive without protection from outside competition, and only the State can provide this protection. (2) Since the accrual of domestic private capital is slow, the State, with its ability to accumulate capital relatively rapidly through taxation and foreign loans, must intercede in the industrial sphere in order to maintain the highest possible rate of development, at the same time that it reduces the share of private foreign capital in the economy. (3) Solicitude for the working groups requires that the State exercise some control over prices of necessaries.

6. *Political parties.* After World War I, important elements within the urban middle sectors began to substitute the organized political party for the family as the focus of political thinking. When this transformation is completed, a whole era —politic, social, and economic—will have passed.

For over three centuries after the initial phase of the conquest ended and the stabilization of the social order began (about 1580), the family—or, more properly speaking, the extended family, kin group, or clan—was traditionally a social, economic, and political institution. The status of each member within the family and his relationship to every other member were rigidly defined. After winning independence (1810–1825), the patriarchal heads of families often became political bosses wielding control over sprawling domains. Political leadership ordinarily passed from father to eldest son.

But the family as a political entity probably never operated as effectively in the cities as it did in the country. In this century it has been progressively less successful as new social and economic forces have undermined the interdependence of the members. The mobility offered by modern means of transportation has encouraged the younger generation to make associations outside the family. Cinemas, clubs, public parks and beaches, and social activities sponsored by the schools increasingly compete with the family for the leisure time of its members. Women have won new freedoms and have taken on new obligations. In ever growing numbers they leave the home to engage in education, business, and the professions, and return with the information that permits them to reach political decisions independently of the male members of the household.

The appearance of large and impersonal businesses has tended to reduce the role of the head of the family in finding employment for the various members of his immediate and extended family. The large corporate enterprises, which are becoming ever more common and which often offer the greatest opportunities for advancement, are inclined to consider individual qualifications more than family credentials. A similar condition is developing in government, which also has become more impersonal as it has become more complex. In the process, nepotism has gradually given ground to civil service systems and professional bureaucracies. The independence which has come with obtaining and holding positions on the basis of merit has helped to sunder allegiances to the family as a political unit. There has been a strong tendency to transfer allegiances to political parties, which provide a common ground for those who have similar objectives based on educational and occupational interests and on social relationships outside the home.

During the decades that the middle sectors have shared power or controlled political decisions in the five republics, the influence of their several components has fluctuated significantly. The pattern of these shifts of relative influence emerges most clearly when the political trends of the five republics are viewed in the long range. Viewed episodically, the trends dissolve into mere political maneuverings in search of short-range solutions, and the main currents of middle sector thinking lose their distinct outlines.

Until World War I, the members of the liberal professions constituted a numerically large segment of the middle sectors in each of the republics. As a group they were learned, and learning conferred considerable prestige. They held a near-monopoly on the formulation of political theory, and, to the extent that the middle sectors participated in practical politics, they were the most active component as well. In recent decades, the influence of the professions on middle sector thought has declined, partly as a result of their loss of relative numerical importance, partly because of their very success: indeed, as the middle sectors as a whole gained in political stature, the rewards of practical politics increased and groups other than the liberal professions began to compete for them.

The role of the Catholic clergy in politics has also been in a general decline in recent decades. This would seem to be true despite the evident part that the Catholic Church played in the overthrow of Juan Domingo Perón in Argentina in 1955, of Gustavo Rojas Pinilla in Colombia in 1957 and of Marcos Pérez Jiménez in Venezuela in 1958. The decline has been more the result of the changing functions of the clergy than of its composition.

The middle sectors continue as always to provide an important part of the Catholic clergy. But the place of the Church in society has been modified and in the process its activities have been circumscribed. This development has been particularly apparent in the urban centers. The urban elements are less inclined than formerly to look to the Church for leadership in those "extra-spiritual" areas on which it traditionally depended for much of its prestige and influence. The State has taken over many of the welfare functions previously performed by the Church. Public elementary, secondary schools, and institutions of higher learning have reduced its share in the field of education. It has lost its semimonopoly on learning in the smaller cities and towns as persons educated and professionally trained at secular institutions have filtered outside the centers of heaviest population. Mass communications have also lessened the dependence upon the clergy outside the large cities. To a considerable degree the popular groups have substituted the motion picture, radio and television, public recreation, and the diversions offered by the labor unions for the holy days and feast days that for four centuries were the accepted source of release from the humdrum activities of everyday life.

As the Church's temporal responsibilities have been circumscribed, the ministering to the spiritual needs of the people has taken up a larger share of its activity, and the opportunities have been reduced for the clergyman to be an individual personality dispensing personal ideas and expressing personal convictions on nonspiritual issues. Consequently clergymen normally are not today politically influential in any of the five republics except inasmuch as they reflect the thoughts of the Church hierarchy, whose thinking may or may not conform to that of the politically dominant segments within the middle sectors. When the political policies of the hierarchy are acceptable to the middle sectors, as they appear to be more and more often, they are disseminated more by Catholic lay organizations than by the clergy.

While the influence of the professional groups and the clergy declined, teachers acquired added political prestige with the public recognition of the importance of universal education. Where schools have been used for the propagation of political ideologies among the masses, the teachers have become essential parts of the political machinery. In recent years, as elementary school teachers have become better trained, they have been accorded middle sector standing in growing numbers. Teaching staffs in high schools and institutions of higher learning—groups traditionally included in the middle sectors—have expanded.

The bureaucrats too have proliferated and their influence has grown accordingly. As the responsibilities of government expanded, the bureaucrats carried out new functions and assumed many of those previously performed by private citizens.

Given the great number of imponderables involved, it would perhaps be impossible to establish whether the political influence of the officer corps has increased or decreased since World War I. There is some indication that the proportion of officers engaging in politics has declined in recent decades. In the author's opinion, however, there is no doubt that at least since 1930 the social and economic orientation of the politically active officers has been away from that of the old ruling groups and toward that of the civilian middle sectors. The new position of the officers stems primarily from three circumstances: (1) The various branches of the military have become more professionalized and, consequently, less attractive to the old elite groups. But since they continue to offer security at reasonably high salaries, they open up opportunities to men from the middle sectors. (2) As the civilian middle sectors have improved their political status vis-à-vis the elites, military officers have inclined to retain their social contacts with the middle sectors rather than to associate with the elites, as they did in the past. (3) The economic policies of the middle sectors, emphasizing industrialization, conform to those held by the armed forces. Under the widening impact of nationalism, both the civilian and the military elements have tended increasingly to equate industrial growth with national progress. Officers, thanks to their training in organization, have found employment as directors of State-controlled economic enterprises, and the armed forces look forward to domestic production of war matériel. Thus, despite differences in their approach to politics, the military and the civilian components of the middle sectors tend to agree on their broad social and economic objectives.

The swift rise of the commercial and industrial segments has profoundly affected the composition of the middle groups since the end of World War I. The acceptance of industrialization as national policy in each of the republics made the owners of industrial and commercial enterprises a highly effective force both as a constructive and as a veto group. Commercial and industrial leaders today exercise the most powerful influence on middle sector politics. The scientists, technicians, and managers, benefiting as they do from industrial development, have in general identified themselves politically with their employers. The growing role of the industrial and commercial leaders as decision-makers on the national level is a major theme of this study.

So seemingly spontaneous was the political emergence of the middle sectors after 1920 that one is inclined, however momentarily, to disregard the nineteenth-century antecedents of the development. To do so would leave untold vital chapters in the political metamorphosis of these groups, for the foundations from which they sprang into the spotlight after World War I were firmly embedded in the past century. The following two chapters establish those nineteenth-century experiences of the middle sectors which help most to explain their political, social, and economic conduct in this century.

Retrospect and Prospect

The middle sectors of Argentina, Brazil, Chile, Mexico, and Uruguay contributed brilliantly to the fight for freedom and to the cause of liberalism during the independence movement (1810–25). Once independence was achieved, however, they were unable to prevent the locus of power from shifting to the reactionary elements whose leaders were drawn from the elites of the land, the Church, and the military. The reactionary elements remained in unchallenged control until mid-century. To the extent that the middle sectors participated in politics and government they were limited essentially to justifying, refining, and administering the policies formulated by caudillos, whose power was based upon force and who spoke for those committed to retain the status quo.

After 1850 the middle sectors began to benefit politically from the economic transformations that were stimulated by ideas, investment capital, and technological know-how flowing from abroad and from immigrant labor. In particular, the transformations underwrote a considerable expansion of the middle sectors, primarily from among the commercial and industrial elements. The entrepreneurs, managers, technicians, and scientists associated with commerce and industry represented a new and dynamic type of wealth and influence. They were the intellectual-professional middle sectors' strong allies in the sharpening contest for power with the traditional ruling elites. But even with the additions to the commercial and industrial elements the middle groups remained numerically small, and in order successfully to challenge the elites they had to seek popular support outside their own ranks. They found it ordinarily in urban labor.[4] Thus were formed the political compounds that in this century have been so instrumental in breaking the monopoly of the traditional ruling elites.

The survival of amalgams composed of such disparate groups as owners of industry on the one hand and factory workers on the other was contingent upon their ability to produce results. Their social, economic, and political achievements—at least over the short range—were substantial in certain cases. The purpose of these final pages is not to summarize or conclude, but to analyze the major developments of the past several decades in terms of the middle sectors' political role in the foreseeable future. In this instance the foreseeable future is taken to mean the next decade or so.

Since the middle sector-led amalgams have asserted themselves, government by law and by the people—the nineteenth-century political trade-mark of the middle groups—has enjoyed wider acceptance than ever before in the five republics. Also, appreciable progress has been made toward institutionalizing the electoral process. The electorate has been expanded manyfold as the masses have been recalled from the political wilderness and brought inside the orbit of national affairs.[5] The national political parties founded upon ideological principles have made headway against the regional groupings and the personalist cliques.

On the other hand, demagoguery and the centralization of power, both of which the middle sectors have held to be antithetical to their political welfare, not only have survived but may have become more firmly entrenched. In the century following independence, demagoguery was widely employed but it was directed to a politically sophisticated element that was reasonably capable of separating the fact from fancy. Furthermore, it was of such a nature as to leave the socioeconomic structure essentially unaffected. The new demagoguery

[4] It will be recalled that to date the middle sector–urban labor alliance has been less pronounced in Brazil than in the other four republics.

[5] It is perhaps worth pointing out again that in Mexico "agrarian revolutionaries" provided the first impetus in expanding the electoral rolls and that in Argentina it was the dictator Perón who took the lead in broadening the electoral base.

in which the middle sector leadership finds itself involved is directed to persons whose minds are ruled more by their immediate material needs than by reason. It emphasizes social rather than legal justice—in which the middle sectors have greatest faith. It stresses social rather than political equality—which the middle sectors traditionally have insisted is the prime requirement for social progress. It insists upon a more equitable distribution of income and, in certain extreme cases, of wealth.

Also, in order to live politically with their working sector allies the middle groups have surrendered, at least for the present and immediate future, their objective of an "equitable division" of public power and responsibility. Historically they have held that the balanced distribution of power at the various levels of government and among the three branches of government can provide the only practical guarantee against the usurpation of authority by a single individual or region. But the urgency involved in meeting the immediate minimum demands of their worker allies has resulted in the middle sector leadership's accepting the concentration of power in the central authority and in the executive branch as the most direct means of putting the meager resources of the nations to work. Under governments responsible to the amalgams, the concentration of power in the central authority and in the executive branch may have reached the point where a reversal of the trend has become little more than a remote hope. Except in Brazil, the states and towns have been deprived of nearly all financial independence. When the gains in the political area are weighed against the permanent threat to those gains both from demagogic appeals to the politically immature and economically underprivileged masses and from the concentration of power, the gains become more apparent than real.

In general, the middle sectors have been effective in popularizing public responsibility for training heads as well as for counting them. Appropriations for public education have grown. Enrollment has increased. The time spent in schools has lengthened. The percentage of illiterates has dropped, that of the functionally literate has risen. In the process the arts and attitudes of civilization to some extent have triumphed over ignorance and violence. Secondary schools and institutions of higher learning have shown a growing awareness of their responsibilities in training persons capable of contributing more fully to societies that are in the throes of a social and economic upheaval.

But the middle sectors have paid a price for the achievement in public education, and the future may well extract an even higher toll. In order to attain a share of their educational goals the middle sector leadership has sanctioned the transfer of responsibility for education from the local to the central authorities. The school curricula prepared in cosmopolitan capitals carry the threat of being woefully out of touch with the environment of the student. The opportunity for the use of the classroom for nation-wide dissemination of currently popular ideologies and the promotion of the interest of dominant political parties and groups has been enhanced. In many instances the education of the youth and at the same time the neglect of adult education have proved socially disruptive. Roles have been reversed in the home. Children have become the teachers of their parents, thereby creating some social confusion and resentments.

Despite the middle sectors' championship of public education, they have not created public elementary or secondary school systems to which they as groups by preference send their own offspring. Thus far their preference for the private training of their own children has not had significant political implications. In the not too distant future the implications may be appreciable. By keeping their children in private schools, the middle sectors are tending to perpetuate the social distinctions that, for purposes of politics, they have insisted for some time must be obliterated. Meanwhile in the public schools there is growing up a generation of citizens who are socially and economically tied to the working masses. This new generation in general is being exposed to more radical interpretations of social and economic ideologies than the offspring of the middle sectors ordinarily receive in private institutions. The "more earthy products" of the public schools who become politicians may well pose the first serious threat to middle sector control of the popular masses.

A sense of social obligation and the need to pay off political debts have combined to induce the middle sectors to support advanced labor and welfare legislation in favor of the industrial working groups. While it is true that much of the legislation still represents little more than statements of aspirations, it is also true that considerable advance has been won in terms of workers' rights and the uplifting of the dignity of the popular masses. Among the solid achievements have been the outlawing of the company store and payment in scrip, the recognition of the right to organize, the right to a contract, and, under specified conditions, the right to strike.

What of the middle sectors' well-being? How long can or will they continue to support the demands of the industrial workers? Originally the workers were unable to finance a labor movement and the movement as it developed in its modern form was brought into being by politicians in the control of the several governments. In turn, the State in a supervisory capacity regulated the activities of the organizations to such an extent that ordinarily the central authorities in an independent capacity determined which labor laws would be honored. The price to labor for the benevolent interest displayed by the public officials was political backing of the group in power. Labor organizations consequently were encouraged–as they still are in most instances–to place far greater emphasis upon political activities than on straight union effort as it is generally understood in the United States. But the laborers have been growing muscles and are becoming more capable of paying the costs of their trade-union movement. As their improved economic position permits them to become more concerned with wages and working conditions and less concerned with the political framework within which their economic problems are resolved, the price of their continued support may well reach the point where the dominant elements within the middle sectors will find it unbearable.

The popularizing of the suffrage in the near future may also be expected to place strains upon middle sector–labor alliances. When the middle sector leadership first turned to the workers, the factory employees were capable of exercising political influence far out of proportion to their numbers. They were vocal. They paraded. In a society in which the practice was to restrict rigidly the number of qualified voters on the basis of literacy, a relatively large percentage of the urban workers met the legal requirements for the franchise. By the 1940's, however, the process of broadening the base of the political pyramid had reached out to make voters of many individuals before they had won for themselves a secure place within the organized industrial working movement. These additions to the electorate have reduced the relative influence of the industrial worker's vote. The expansion of the electorate to include a much larger percentage of the nonindustrial labor force has required the politicians to measure the industrial worker's share of the national income less in political terms and more in terms of his productive capacity. And the industrial worker's productive capacity, in relation to other workers, has not been increased outstandingly during the recent past.

The political relationship of the middle sectors and industrial labor is also being affected by the changes that have taken place in the ownership of industrial and commercial enterprises. When political cooperation between them began, a considerable share of machine industry was in foreign hands. Foreigners also had important holdings in commerce and particularly in transportation and foreign trade. Consequently, the foreigner and the foreign-domiciled company were made to bear directly a large portion of the original financial burdens of increased wages and other benefits that were awarded the working elements. Under such circumstances the middle sector politician could offer himself as a friend of the workers and as a watchdog against possible abuses from foreigners.

For at least two decades the trend has been for commerce and industry in the five republics to become domestically controlled. Domestic capitalists, as a result, have been called upon to carry an augmented share of the costs of wage gains and other benefits to labor. As the pressure upon them grows, they increasingly insist that the public good requires that the concern should be on expanded production rather than on equalitarian distribution. They use their legal rights and economic power to dissuade the politicians who would curry the favor of the workers by disregarding the economic realities. They have contended that it is the State's duty to alert the workingman to the fact that he cannot expect the same friendly consideration when he fights local interests as when he served as the protagonist against "foreign rapacity." The growing political influence of the industrial and commercial elements of the middle sectors has already forced the politicians to take cognizance of the argument to the current disadvantage of the laboring components.

Industrial development, which in actual practice has often meant simply the development of factory industries, has been since about 1930 the political mainspring of the middle sectors. Their leaders have ridden to giddy political heights as the champions of industrial expansion. Urban labor has given its enthusiastic support to economic emancipation. Under friendly governments the contribution of manufacturing and processing to the gross product of the republics has been expanded appreciably. Factories have been made symbols of progress.

Despite the large reservoir of favorable public opinion it enjoys, however, industry has in some cases reached the point where it has become a political bugaboo. In other cases it is rapidly approaching that point. In large part the dilemma lies in the fact that industry has not measured up to the predictions that politicians made for it.

In sponsoring industrial development, the middle sector leadership insisted that it would raise the workers' level of living. Until the late 1940's the steadily increasing output of consumer goods contributed appreciably to that end. By that time it had become apparent, however, that the expanded capacity to produce consumer goods was not built upon firm economic foundations. Rather, the increased production had resulted largely from the siphoning of available resources into the manufacturing industries to the neglect of adequate maintenance of capital investment in such vital segments of the economies as transportation and agriculture, and in Argentina, Brazil, and Uruguay agriculture has historically provided the only notable source of foreign exchange. Once the governments acknowledged that further economic progress must be predicated on heavy investment in basic industries and agriculture the rate of flow of capital into factories declined, the production of consumer goods leveled off, and the earning power of the working elements began to erode as they bid for goods in short supply. During the past half-decade the trend has been for the worker's earning power to decline.

The politicians had predicted that new industry would resolve the problem of providing employment for those entering the labor pool. In this regard industry has proved a disappointment, for although it has absorbed substantial numbers of employees, it has been the services, including the government services, and the construction industries rather than the manufacturing industries that have provided the safety valve for those entering the labor market. In the case of Mexico the demand for cheap farm labor in the United States has served a similar purpose.

The leaders also assured their electoral supporters that equalitarian distribution of income and rapid acceleration of production could be achieved simultaneously if the central government entered directly into the development of industry and the regulation of public welfare. The State has played a major role in industrial growth but it has not justified the original assumption upon which public participation in industry was predicated. Although the popular masses have undoubtedly profited from industrial development and State interference in the social field, the gap separating the rich from the poor has widened. Millionaires are being created at an ever increasing speed while millions remain economic zeros.

The politicians likewise assured the public that State participation in industry would strengthen public confidence in that segment of the economy. That assurance has been only partially fulfilled. The public has lost confidence in the utilities field as an area of private investment. The ownership of public utilities consequently has tended to pass from private to public hands. Industrial investment continues to be unattractive to the small investor who, in general, shuns the stock markets, while he displays a strong propensity for urban mortgages and speculation in real estate. Meanwhile, and to a considerable extent as a result of public intervention in the social and economic fields, the cost of government has risen faster than national income. This has served to alter the composition of the gross product. In relative terms the volume of services has increased and that of consumer and capital goods has declined. It has also led to deficit budgeting and currency depreciation.

The leaders further justified industrialization on the grounds that it would emancipate the republics from the more materially advanced countries of the world. But the fact is that industrialization, reliant as it has been to date upon equipment and raw materials from abroad, has increased their dependence on the outside. This has created complex industrial problems. The increased dependence comes at a time when the past neglect of agriculture in each of the republics except Mexico has reduced their capacity to earn foreign exchange at the rate required to maintain even a significantly reduced tempo of industrial growth. Meanwhile nationalism, which has accompanied the expansion of domestic industry, has reduced the republics' ability to attract badly needed foreign capital.

Because industrial development has in fact failed to satisfy either of the two groups most directly concerned, the republics during the foreseeable future may be expected to live under the dual threat of: (1) labor erupting against the immediate price it must pay for greater industrialization and (2) owners of industry seeking more forceful solutions to their foreign-exchange problems. The resort to direct action by either labor or capital could destroy the political amalgams that since World War I have played such an important part in the social and economic reorientation of the five republics.

Modern-integrated nationalism represents the collective demand of frustrated people for direct action by the State. In each of the five republics the middle sectors have played a leading role in lifting nationalism in its modern form to the level of a major political ideology. The nationalism of the new leadership has been of an essentially economic nature—the nationalism of people impatient for more rapid material progress. This type of nationalism gave the new leadership, in its bid for office, the opportunity to associate the old ruling elite with foreign exploitation and raw-material economies while they presented themselves as the promoters of indigenous values and modern-diversified economies. As policy-makers the new leaders placed themselves in the forefront of those who demanded legislation that would protect the national workers, capitalists, and resources from foreign exploitation during the transitional periods that would lead to the republics' emancipation from foreign domination. The leaders asked that during the transitions the workers, in return for the material and political sacrifices nationalism entailed, accept the spiritual and emotional rewards the ideology offered. But the question arises: Has nationalism reached the point where the presently dominant middle sector elements can no longer benefit from it to the extent that they could when the ideology was going through its formative stages? There are reasons to believe that such may be the case.

The middle sectors have done such an excellent job of selling nationalism that they can no longer claim an option on it. The ideology is today embraced by all the articulate elements, some of whom hold to it more ardently than do the dominant element within the middle sectors. In fact it may be that the middle sectors in certain instances have assumed—and in other instances in the near future will assume—a moderator's role on the nationalist issue. Already in Chile the Communists have seized the nationalist label and are running with it. Meanwhile, the Chilean middle sector leadership has urged moderation and has cleared the way for greater foreign private participation in economic development. In Brazil, João Goulart, the Vice-President of the republic and head of the Labor Party (P.T.B.), at a convention of the Party in late 1957 declared that "we [the workers] have *de facto* authority and the legitimate right to exercise the function of the vanguard in the nationalistic struggle in which the Brazilian people are involved."[6] What Goulart was saying was that labor must assume the responsibility for seeing that the middle sector leadership does not weaken on nationalistic issues. In Mexico the xenophobic nationalism of the agrarian radicals under Lázaro Cárdenas has been modified under the middle sector leadership of the past decade to the point where Mexico is currently hailed as one of the more favorable areas for foreign capital investment and foreign business. In Argentina an exaggerated nationalism has left very little room for rational thinking. That small space, however, appears to be occupied almost exclusively by middle sector components.

Both internal and external developments seem to favor the middle sectors' holding for the most part to a moderately na-

[6] *Correio da Manhã,* October 4, 1957, and *Estado de São Paulo,* October 4, 1957.

tionalistic position in the foreseeable future. The record repeatedly reveals that they are less radical in office than in seeking office. Many within the increasingly influential commercial and industrial components have come to appreciate that nationalism, when carried to extremes, can be economically disruptive. The leadership in general has recognized that assertive nationalism is often incompatible with the desire for international prestige and the expectation of assistance from major powers of the West.

Several developments and changes in attitudes abroad may encourage the middle sectors' pursuit of moderate nationalistic courses. In international relations narrowly defined, the growing interdependence of the nations of the Western world has made the less-developed nations feel that their cooperation is urgently desired. From that point they have argued with considerable success that cooperation is possible only among equals. Having attained equality, at least theoretically, they have been able to contend that their backwardness is not exclusively their own problem but also a problem of those with whom they cooperate. The acceptance, especially by the United States, of the republics as equals and the recognition that under-development is an international problem may serve to make easier the justification of international cooperation.

Developments in economic relations also favor the lessening of the antipathies and tensions that first bred nationalism and then were nurtured by it. Governmental and particularly international lending agencies are replacing private foreign lenders in many areas of economic activity. These new agencies attach fewer safeguards in their financial transactions than do private investors and, especially in the case of the UN agencies, are scarcely susceptible to the charge of imperialism. To the extent that public agencies replace the private lender, one of the favorite whipping boys of the Latin American nationalists will be removed from the scene. Directly related to this consideration is the evident decline of foreign private-capital investment in public utilities. In terms of the lessening of tensions this change may be particularly significant. Nearly every citizen living in urban areas must make use of utilities that, because of their public nature, are subject to regulation by the politicians. The charges and countercharges resulting from regulation of the utilities have served as a constant irritant. The sooner that all Argentines, Chileans, and Mexicans can pay an electric-light bill without believing or being reminded that they are paying "a hidden foreign tax" the sooner the nationalist politicians will have to discard one of their popular weapons. Finally, the fact that science and technology have reached a point where the borrowing of an idea is often more important than the borrowing of personnel or capital holds promise of healing some of the national wounds caused by what often in the past have been considered abrasive economic practices.

Meanwhile, as the ties that have bound the middle sectors and the workers together politically are being tested, changes have taken place which seem to insure the middle sectors a continuing prominent role with or without the support of the industrial laboring elements. The steady extension of the political base would appear to promise the middle sectors an increasing maneuverability in any situation dominated by civilian groups. Most significantly an enlarged electorate offers the middle sectors the possibility of finding popular support among voters whose price, at least in the beginning, would be lower than that of the industrial laboring elements, whose members are often looked upon and resented as the "aristocrats of labor" by other workers.

On the other hand, as public responsibility moderates the middle sectors' views, the middle groups have become more acceptable to the old elites. The middle sectors in general have systematically protected domestic property and have reserved an important segment of commerce and industry for individual initiative. This fact has tended to obscure their social and economic radicalism in the eyes of the conservative monied elements. The amelioration of the clerical issue since 1930 has reduced tensions to the point where the enlightened representatives of the Catholic Church can successfully cooperate with the progressive middle sector leadership. Such cooperation is currently effective in Chile and appears to be gaining strength in Argentina and Mexico. The Church and Catholic lay organizations in league with the middle sector political leadership might inject into politics a moral force for the most part lacking at present. They also might be highly effective in discouraging workers from deserting to the extreme Left Wing organizations, especially to the Communists, for many workers have a deep and abiding loyalty to the Roman Catholic Church.

The middle sectors may in the foreseeable future expect to exercise considerable influence in policy-making during those "unfortunate interludes" when the republics suffer from the incubus of military domination. The officer corps of the armed forces come almost entirely from middle sector homes. The military in each of the republics appears to be as committed to industrial progress as in the middle sector leadership. In the past the military associated itself with the old elite elements because of their influence and prestige. The armed forces may be expected to remain associated with the middle sectors as those groups continue to gain in prestige and influence vis-à-vis the old elites. Furthermore, the day has passed when the military in any one of the five republics can usurp power and rule in disregard of civilian wishes. Military rulers will have civilian advisers who have their fingers on the public pulse. At the moment individuals from the middle sectors would seem most often to satisfy this requirement.

The middle sectors' political position is also strengthened by the fact that interested foreign powers, in general, have come to accept them as providing the most responsible leadership that can be expected from the republics at this time. The direct and indirect support offered the Western bloc in the UN by the middle sector leadership of the five republics has been basically, if not uniformly, satisfactory. On all major issues the republics have voted with the Western bloc or have abstained. Perhaps more important, the remaining fifteen Latin American republics have shown a strong tendency to follow the leadership of the five republics, especially that of Mexico and Brazil.

Past and present developments directly affecting the middle sectors themselves offer abundant evidence that the future holds considerable political promise for them. They are in their present state the legitimate product of an evolutionary process which they played a major role in initiating and subsequently in guiding. They are experiencing rapid numerical growth in each of the republics. It is almost literally true that each new set of statistics makes them a larger segment of the total population. Publications of international agencies commonly fix the middle sectors in Argentina and Uruguay as constituting approximately 50 per cent of the total population of those republics, and in Chile 40 per cent. More important than any statistical designation is the recognition that they are finally receiving from the experts.

Their economic significance also promises them an important political role in the future. The age of the farmer is giving way to the age of the merchant and manufacturer. As the shift of wealth toward the urban economies develops the voice of the commercial and industrial elements in decision-making will become firmer. To their voice will be added that of high-level bureaucrats who direct the towering structure of government-controlled institutes charged with the protection and promotion of industry. Government participation in the economic field has given thousands upon thousands of bureaucrats the prestige of being associated with the planning and management of industrial and commercial undertakings–a prestige that their own financial resources deny them. They have become, consequently, firm converts to progress through technological advance. Their underlings look to governments for security in their jobs.

The solid body of political experience the middle sectors have acquired in this century also strongly suggests that their political influence will grow rather than decline in the next decade. In a society where economic concerns have become the primary political concern the middle sectors have had an opportunity to learn practical lessons in political economy. Their experience has taught them that it is easy to stimulate demands but that it is difficult to satisfy them. They have also learned some of the problems involved in attempting to telescope the economic process. These lessons will neither prevent them from making honest mistakes in the future nor prevent them from exploiting economic misfortunes for political ends. Undoubtedly they will often be guilty of placing their collective head in the lion's mouth in order to operate on a sore tooth. Progress does not move in a straight line but deviously, and the middle sectors will from time to time probably compete with both the Left and the Right in exploiting the nadirs. But more than any other groups, they possess the equipment for dealing with realities; consequently, they may not be confused by the economic fictions they formulate for political purposes.

Included in the body of political experience the middle sectors have accumulated in this century are valuable lessons in the art of compromise. In an area where, prior to the middle group's appearance in a major role, political compromise was unknown or distasteful, the middle sectors have elevated to a new level the art of achieving some equilibrium by balancing a mass of political antagonisms. They have consequently become stabilizers and harmonizers and in the process have learned the dangers of dealing in absolute postulates. Their political experience has also given them a positive psychology as opposed to the negative one so often held by opposition groups.

The middle sectors' cultural experience may be their greatest political asset. It gives them access to the great avenues leading to the past. But it also gives them, more than any other group, faith that the golden age lies not behind but ahead. Their faith in the future may keep them from becoming the slaves of antecedent circumstances. If it does, they may in the years ahead be up to the herculean task of providing the type of leadership requisite to advance before the fires they themselves lighted overtake them.

THE CATHOLIC CHURCH

The Catholic Church in Latin America has become increasingly involved in political and social activities. The Church itself, however, is badly split in its viewpoints, and this complexity is often overlooked when commentators are describing actions of the Church. In the selection that follows, Thomas G. Sanders, Professor of Religious Studies at Brown University and associate of the American Universities Field Staff, is able to get at this complexity through a fourfold typology of religious elites that include Reactionaries, Conservatives, Progressives, and Radicals. Professor Sanders focuses on these types in Brazil and Chile and describes their composition, strength, and differences. The differences between the four are developed with perception and objectivity. Professor Sanders also explains why such great diversity can exist within the Catholic Church in Latin America, and concludes by commenting on how the Catholic elites can exert influence upon politics.

Types of Catholic Elites in Latin America

THOMAS G. SANDERS*

Analysts of Latin America agree that the Catholic Church has a significant political influence, but its precise role is often obscured by images that do not consider the diversity and

* This is a revised version of Thomas G. Sanders, "A Typology of Catholic Elites," Institute of Current World Affairs Report (February 21, 1968), the revision written for this book of readings. Permission from author and Institute of Current World Affairs.

complexity of what has occurred in Latin American Catholicism, especially since World War II.

These images in turn are based on faulty historical generalizations. The Church has never been as simple as many of the interpretations of it. If representatives of the Church acquiesced in the cruelties of the *conquistadores,* others like Father las Casas humanely defended the rights of the Indians. Many Church leaders condemned the movements of Independence, but certain priests became outstanding leaders in them.

The modernization of Latin American Catholicism is not a totally recent phenomenon. As early as the 1930s many Catholics began to rethink their social and political views under the impact of fresh ideas mediated by Fascism and neo-Thomism. As a result the leading Latin American Catholic thinker and writer between 1930 and 1960 was not a clerical reactionary, but a layman, the Brazilian Alceu Amoroso Lima, who considered himself an authentic follower of Maritain's neo-Thomism. Neo-Thomism, the progressive Catholic thought of that era, had a profound influence on clergy and laymen in such countries as Brazil, through the Centro Dom Vital, and in Chile, where it shaped the outlook of a group of young men who were to become the founders of Christian Democracy. In the past two decades and especially since the Vatican Council, Catholics in Latin America have appropriated radically different political concepts and explored new approaches to social change which have divided the Church and whose ultimate consequences we cannot foresee.

Such variety in the Church may seem a puzzle to those who look on Catholics as unquestioning conformists. Though the Church insists on a certain unity in theological belief and basic ethical principles, Catholics in practice exercise a high degree of freedom in their social judgments, where many complex factors are involved that can be solved only by the individual conscience. To be sure, the Church inculcates an interpretation of the nature of society and government, based on the social encyclicals of the papacy, but the perspective is vague and claims only to present generalized principles which faithful Catholics then must apply to their own situations.

Two emphases of the Vatican Council, moreover, have stimulated diversity among Catholics. One is the impulse given to initiative and responsibility by laymen. More and more, thoughtful Catholics are following their own judgments in social decisions. The second is the opening to the "modern world," which has broadened the theories and movements in which Catholics feel in good conscience they can participate. The Latin American Church has not lagged in the universal problem which Catholics face today as they seek to come to terms with the modern world; in fact, it has acted in the vanguard, especially in problems of development, social change, violence, and political participation.

What do we mean by the "Catholic Church" when we discuss its relation to politics? The 90 percent of the Latin American population that has been baptized? The bishops? Educated laymen? Catholic institutions? For purposes of this discussion it is useful to introduce the sociological concept of *elites,* as distinguished from the masses. In a Catholic framework, an individual who participates in an elite has internalized Catholic beliefs and values to a sufficient degree that he justifies his social and political outlook and actions chiefly by his Catholicism rather than by other norms, institutions, or pressures. The most cursory observation of Latin American culture reveals that the overwhelming majority of those who call themselves Catholic, though often deeply religious, adhere to forms of culture religion that reflect only a slight, confused understanding of normative Catholic belief and no understanding of the social teachings of the Church which supposedly provide the framework for political action. We cannot then ascribe the political functioning of the masses to Catholic conviction, though in some instances they may be mobilized for actions, usually defensive, that certain Catholics rationalize as expressions of Church interests.

It is among the elites, then, those who have been trained in and thought about their beliefs and who are trying to apply them to decisions, that a genuine relationship between Catholicism and politics appears. Elites are usually educated and have participated in Catholic institutions where they absorbed a perspective that modified the unreflective culture religion common to Latin America. Bishops, priests, or laymen can compose elites. In general, though, bishops are more limited in their capacity to assume unusual political and social positions than priests and laymen, because they symbolize the unity of the Church in their dioceses and have pastoral responsibility for all the Catholics there.

A typology will help clarify the various Catholic political outlooks common today in Latin America. While typologies are useful in ordering modes of human thought and action, they should not be absolutized. They are heuristic, inviting criticism, and subject to change as human beings change. Moreover, some individuals do not easily fit a given type, or they may include in their outlook characteristics of two types. Nevertheless, four types illustrate political tendencies in contemporary Latin American Catholicism. From Right to Left they are Reactionaries, Conservatives, Progressives, and Radicals. In my discussion of these types I will refer to the Churches of Brazil and Chile, where recent developments in regional Catholicism have achieved a special clarity.

I. The Reactionaries. Both Brazil and Chile have small, militant, anti-modern Catholic organizations called the Society for the Defense of Tradition, Family, and Property. Their major vehicles of expression, *Fiducia* in Chile and *Catolicismo* in Brazil, are newspaper-like journals of limited circulation with an obviously planned similarity of appearance.

The Reactionary position has much greater strength in Brazil than in Chile—for two reasons. (1) In Brazil it has the active support of two bishops, Msgr. Antônio de Castro Mayer of Campos and Msgr. Geraldo de Proença Sigaud of Diamantina. The Chilean Reactionaries have had no hierarchical spokesman since the retirement of Msgr. Alfredo Cifuentes, former archbishop of La Serena, several years ago. (2) The leading lay advocate of the Reactionary position in Latin America is a Brazilian, Dr. Plínio Corrêa de Oliveira, a former professor in the Catholic University of São Paulo and the author of numerous books on a variety of theological and social topics. The Chileans, in fact, depend strongly on Brazilian inspiration, many of the articles in *Fiducia* being reprints from *Catolicisma*.

The Reactionaries burst into public attention in recent years through two widely discussed books. One was *Reforma Agrária: Questão de Consciência,* published in Brazil in 1960, whose four authors included the two bishops and Dr. Corrêa de Oliveira. This book charged that proposed plans for an agrarian reform were "socialist" and "anti-Christian" and called on its readers to oppose the reform as a "question of conscience." A more recent work, whose sale was prohibited in Chile because of its attacks on the president of the country, was called *Frei, El Kerensky Chileno*. Its author, Favio Vidigal Xavier da Silveira, denounced the Christian Democratic administration of Eduardo Frei and suggested that it represented a prelude to a completely Communist regime.

Although most of the Reactionaries come from the upper class, many of their most militant participants are youth, who appear on the streets—well-dressed and articulate—to gather signatures for petitions against such things as agrarian reform or "Communist" tendencies in the Church.

The most notable quality of the Reactionaries is a *militancy* in the defense of certain religious and social principles that they find rooted in the Church tradition. They opposed the changes discussed by the Vatican Council, and since the promulgation of the conciliar decrees they have done their best to ignore or rationalize them away. All of the phenomena that the reformers found obnoxious—authoritarianism, clericalism, scholasticism, curial control, Latin liturgy, defensive preoccupation with heresy—are precisely what the Reactionaries glorify. More than anything else they exult in authoritarianism, symbolized by the structure of the Church, its descending hierarchical sequence from pope and bishops down to laymen. Yet ironically the Reactionaries' estrangement from contemporary trends is forcing them into an ever more sectarian posture at variance with the authorities of the Church. The *Fiducia* group, for example, has been repudiated by Cardinal Silva, the primate of Chile.

The Reactionaries have a strong theological emphasis, but their interpretations depend heavily on the Council of Trent and the formulations in traditional scholastic manuals. With little sense of change or historical context, or better, an unwarranted commitment to certain selected periods, they will quote the nineteenth century Pope Pius IX with more enthusiasm than Popes John XXIII and Paul VI.

The public image of the Reactionaries does not derive as

much from their religious as from their social position. Yet the two dimensions are linked, since the idea of a "Christian" society dominates their socio-political views. With frank admiration for the confessional state and the traditional Latin American Conservative Parties, the Reactionaries deplore the loss of Christian values in modern culture and regard the chief culprits as the more liberal Catholics. As a statement by the Chilean group puts it, "Not in apostasy, nor destruction of the family, nor in violence and confiscation, but solely in the sacred ways of Christian civilization, can Chile attain its longed-for development." Among their chief emphases is a traditional concept of the integrity of the family based on the social prohibition of divorce and birth control. The appearance of legislation to allow divorce (which is forbidden in both Brazil and Chile) finds them campaigning and petitioning against it. It is not surprising that they often get a support disproportionate to their real membership by appealing to the assumption of conventional Catholics that "Christian civilization" will preserve morality and stability.

The arch-enemies of the Reactionaries are "Communism" (which they find active in the Church as well as in society) and "socialism" (they often cite older papal statements referring to the incompatibility of Christianity and socialism). Any initiatives toward reform in Church or society they place in these categories. The absolute which they defend is private property, divinely sanctioned by natural law. Their vehement opposition to agrarian reform stems from its effect on the property structure. A 1965 letter to President Frei of Chile illustrates their point-of-view: "Private property, one of the foundations of Christian civilization and one of the conditions of the liberty of the Church, is exposed to mutilation and death in the Chilean Constitution." The letter goes on to argue that private property is inalienable, an essential corollary of the dignity of man, and "one of the rights emanating from the natural order instituted by God which no human authority can violate."

The Reactionaries combine their defense of private property with a vision of society as authoritarian, organic, and unequal in classes. They charge that socialism seeks to level the divinely ordained distinctions of function and class. The harshness of this system they assuage through the charity of the superior classes toward those who are inferior.

It is not surprising that this position has a strong attraction among the landowning upper class. In Brazil, some bishops, clergy, and laymen actively support it, but in Chile it is a lay movement. Even though certain priests in Chile are reputed to sympathize with it, none of stature serves as its spokesman. The real influence of the Reactionary position is hard to judge, since its organizational strength is slight. Its greatest impact comes on isolated issues such as opposition to divorce and agrarian reform, where it can appeal to innate sympathies in a large segment of the populace.

II. Conservatives. Although Conservatives hold many of the same positions as the Reactionaries, they differ from them chiefly in their lack of militancy. The Conservatives do not campaign for a return to a traditional Catholic society, but they believe in it. They represent the relatively unreflective participants in an unrenovated Catholicism, the conventional, those who lack the imagination or energy to move into one of the other groups. They do not consciously oppose changes in the official teaching of the Church; they simply find it easier to continue as they always have functioned.

In both Brazil and Chile Conservatives may be the largest group among clergy and laity. Of them we genuinely can speak of the Church as a cultural force that supports past structures and does not contribute to modernization and development.

One rarely finds Conservatives among the publicly prominent bishops, because Progressives hold the initiative in interpreting the role of the Church today. Many bishops in Latin America are unknown except in their dioceses, because they are not outstanding. They accept without tension the older theology and practice and do not question the Church's linkage with the powerful, its estrangement from the majority of the population. They yield to the innovations of the Vatican Council out of respect for the voice of the Church, but they make little effort to apply them. They usually sign progressive statements of regional and national bishops' conferences, which are dominated by more liberal prelates because they do not sense the contradictions between them and their own ideas. These bishops, however, will frequently insist that reformist statements be balanced by warnings against extremism, Marxism, or immorality. Thus, the famous 1962 Pastoral of the Chilean bishops, which threw the weight of the episcopate on the side of basic reforms, gained acceptance by including an equally lengthy denunciation of Communism.

The parishes of Brazil and Chile are full of Conservative priests. They often wear a cassock, not because they oppose more modern dress, but because they have always worn one. Many are over forty-five years old. They have a paternalistically aloof, often kindly relationship to their parishioners, but they do not innovate. They teach traditional concepts and follow timeworn pastoral practices, because they lack the initiative and imagination to criticize and replace them. They worry about a lot of things: Communism, secularism, Protestant competition, loss of authority, the restlessness of youth, new things. They often become facile instruments of conservative political and social groups, repeating their slogans, because they honestly fear the consequences of change.

Private schools are also centers of Conservative members of religious orders. The clergy who teach there believe that they are rendering a great service by giving a Christian, moral, and humanistic training to the children of the privileged classes who can attend these schools.

The middle class is the base of one of the most conscious Conservative lay groups. A symbol of their political action occurred in Brazil in March, 1964, when hundreds of thousands of more-or-less Catholic, basically middle class women participated in "Marches of the Family with God for Liberty," protesting against the "Communism" and "corruption" of the Goulart government and indirectly assuring the Army that a coup would receive their backing. In both Brazil and Chile they fear extremism, immorality, and vote on issues of corruption and inflation, using their Catholicism to justify their position. In Chile they are those anxious mothers who attend forums to applaud right-wing politicians and who urge former President Jorge Alessandri to re-enter politics "because we want union, tranquility, and faith to return to the Chilean family, because we want less change and more work . . .

fewer projects and more realizations, more sincerity and less demagoguery."

III and IV. Progressives and Radicals. These final two types deserve careful parallel examination because they represent the elites through which the Catholic Church can participate in development and change in Latin America. Often lumped together, they actually differ in temperament and on many concrete issues.

The Progressive has absorbed the changes in the official thinking of the Church since 1960, believes that the Church is making significant adjustments and suggestions to the modern world, and wants to follow the Church's guidance. While he assumes that further innovations will come in the future, he thinks that the Vatican II documents and subsequent encyclicals, as well as major hierarchical statements, outline a sound position for the present. He tries to work carefully within the framework of the Church. His intellectual inspiration on social matters tends to be the reasonable, balanced neo-Thomism of Jacques Maritain, which also happens to be reflected in the episcopal documents.

The Radical considers himself as good a Catholic as the Progressive and quotes encyclicals where he can, but he stretches the obvious meaning of the Church's position. He considers the changes only a partial adjustment to what is necessary. In terms of certain vital social interests—relevance to development, political effectiveness, modernity—he regards the consensus as lagging. He sees himself active on the frontier of new problems and knows that the Church must learn from the ideas and experiences of innovating Catholics like himself.

Many Radicals are now moving toward a position that considers the Church's social teaching an anachronism which in time will disappear. They do not envision social and political action in terms of applying moral norms and generalized directions, but as the conscientious participation of faithful Christians in given movements. They do not believe that bishops and theologians, because of their class background, can understand, for example, the problems and aspirations of the poor. For them the voice of the Church on social matters does not lie in the hierarchy, but in another aspect of the

Church, the People of God, that is, the Latin American masses who are in process of a critical awakening and will in time participate in the building of a new Latin America. Social truth often is not found in the consensus of various interests that episcopal documents represent, but in the extremism undertaken by sensitive and oppressed groups.

The Radicals relate their Catholic faith to motifs drawn from existentialism, Marxism, sociologists like Mannheim and Mills, or psychoanalytic theory. This is the "modern world" opened up by the Vatican Council, and the Radical faces it unafraid. Some are strongly influenced by Protestantism and radical New Testament primitivism, with its emphasis on poverty and simplicity. Maritain they consider an important transitional figure, but now irrelevant and out-of-date.

The Latin American Bishops' Council (CELAM) and the national episcopal conferences embody the Progressive position. Two meetings, those of Mar del Plata in 1967 and Medellín in 1968, set forth the Church's solid support for development, economic integration, and basic reforms. Among individual bishops, however, there are representatives of all the types. For many years the Chilean Church, more than any other, symbolized a unified Progressivism linking bishops, clergy, and laity. The Brazilian Church, on the other hand, was known to be divided, harboring what was long considered an aberrant Radicalism. Since 1966, Chile too has developed a strong Radical wing, and the division between a more moderate and a more Leftist modernizing position now seems to be the general Latin American pattern.

Outstanding Progressive Brazilian spokesmen are Agnelo Cardinal Rossi of São Paulo and Eugênio Cardinal Sales of Salvador. The symbolic leader of the Radicals is Msgr. Helder Camara, archbishop of Olinda and Recife, though more consistent representatives are Msgr. Jorge Marcos de Oliveira of Santo André and certain young bishops of the Northeast like Msgr. Antônio Batista Fragoso of Crateús. Raúl Cardinal Silva Henríquez of Santiago typifies Chilean Progressives, while a younger group of bishops, though not as extreme as the Brazilians, on some points lean toward Radicalism. An example is Msgr. Carlos González of Talca.

In Brazil the journal most typical of the Progressive position is *Síntese,* published at the Catholic University in Rio de Janeiro. Associated with *Síntese* is a highly respected Jesuit, Father Fernando Bastos de Avila, who typifies the intellectual side of Progressivism, while Father Paulo Crespo, the labor union organizer in Pernambuco, represents its activist side. The clerical symbols of Radicalism, in both theology and politics, are the Dominicans, along with a number of secular priests and a few Jesuits, notably Father Henrique C. de Lima Vaz. Their most sophisticated publication, until its abolishment by the government, was *Paz e Terra,* which in a typical gesture was a joint publishing effort with political Leftists, Protestants, and other sympathizers. The principal lay Radicals have come from Catholic Action since 1959, and many participated in an organization called Ação Popular (Popular Action).

Until recently the leading symbols of Chilean Progressive clergy were the Jesuits of the Centro Bellarmino, especially Father Roger Vekemans, while the Christian Democratic Party contained the chief laymen. *Mensaje,* published by the Centro Bellarmino and the only quality religious journal in the country, effectively diffused the Progressive outlook. The recently emerged Radical wing developed especially among priests working in slums, students, and the Rebel or Left segment of the Christian Democratic Party. Two recent actions mark the organizational maturity of Radicalism. One was the seizure of the Santiago cathedral in August, 1968, by a group of priests, nuns, and laymen who called themselves the "Young Church." The other was the withdrawal in May, 1969, of many of the leading figures in the Christian Democratic Party to form MAPU (Movimiento de Acción Popular Unitario).

While many theological differences divide Progressives and Radicals, one is of especial importance, their view of the nature of the Church in Latin America. The term, Church, to be sure, is ambiguous, referring to a structure, the People of God, and the minority of dynamic Catholics. Radicals emphasize that the Church, in the sense of convinced Christians, is a permanent minority rather than a majority in Latin America. This conviction draws not only from observation, but from the theological belief that the conscious Church has always been an elite. This does not make them, however, less appreciative of the People of God. Rather they feel that focus on the Church as structure and hierarchy has led to an acceptance of conventionality for conviction, as well as lack of respect for the simple faithful and for those alienated from the structure.

The Progressives agree that convinced Christians represent a minority and that the Church as institution lacks influence on the majority of the population, but they consider this a temporary condition. They want to modify pastoral methods, recapture the masses, and give the Church a new voice in society.

If the Church is a minority, what will be its shape in the future? Both Progressives and Radicals have come to emphasize the promotion of small groups of conscious, dynamic Catholics, often apart from the parish structure. We can sense the significance of this change, only if we recognize that Catholic groups were traditionally linked to the parish and often composed of pious women who came to mass frequently, gave time to charity, and helped keep the edifice clean and orderly. If I may generalize perhaps too broadly, the Progressive is inclined to think of the new groups as vehicles for reconversion of society. The Radical, on the other hand, thinks of the groups as a Christian presence, no more, because society will not be reconverted. For the Progressive the Christian life cultivated in small groups will lead eventually to greater participation in the Church's cultus and sacramental life; for the Radical this external manifestation of Christian life is less important than the values of responsibility, love, solidarity, and social concern that Christians (and non-Christians) manifest in their lives. While the cultic life has its permanent significance, one does not judge the depth of religious spirit by participation in it.

Assuming that the real Christian community is a minority, the Radical differs from the Progressive in his institutional approach to problems. The Progressives have especially worked through "organizations of Christian inspiration," of which labor unions and the Christian Democratic Parties are leading examples. Such institutions are based on natural law principles and in practice are composed of a majority of Catholics. Their theoretical justification reflects a strong sense of the inappropriateness of secular institutions to fulfill the distinctive aims of Catholics in society. While some organizations of Christian inspiration became directly related to public policy, others served as institutions for "training leaders with an orientation according to Christian principles" so that they could in turn shape secular groups in which they participated.

Radicals reject these Catholic organizations in favor of participating with non-Catholics in organizations of clearly secular orientation. Thus hierarchical control over Catholic Action in Brazil led the Radicals to form Ação Popular, a nonconfessional political organization dedicated to the transformation of Brazilian society. Likewise, in Chile tensions within the Christian Democratic Party led to the formation of the Movimiento de Acción Popular Unitario, although long before, many Catholics had refused to participate in the Party because they objected to its theoretical foundations.

On social matters Radicals often define their function as *conscientizacão*. This concept, which developed in Brazil and has now spread to many other parts of Latin America, refers to an "awakening of consciousness" among the masses, on the assumption that the lower classes, as the majority, and not the existent power groups, must shape the future of Latin America. Catholics and others should engage in non-paternalistic activities which will lead to a critical reflection among the people and a quest for vehicles of participation and revolution. This is *conscientizacão*.

Questioning the concept of organizations of Christian inspiration leads to an additional set of presuppositions separating the Radical from the Progressive.

(1) Whereas the Progressives who promote organizations of Christian inspiration believe that they are developing a distinct Catholic approach to Latin American problems, usually in opposition to Marxism, the Radicals seek cooperation with "popular movements" that may among others include Marxists. That is, the Progressive tends to see Marxism as the opposition, while the Radicals regard it as a potential partner in effecting the transformation of society. The Radical readily

adopts, as well, many concepts often employed by Marxists, such as class conflict, imperialism, and revolution.

(2) The Progressive takes an evolutionary and cooperative approach to development, whereas the Radical takes a revolutionary and critical one. The Progressive, for example, supports enthusiastically educational, housing, and economic programs carried out by existing governments in conjunction with North American aid, because he regards gradual improvement as a normal road to effective change. The Radical, contrariwise, assumes that only an abrupt revision of political and social power can achieve development, and he believes that the developed world, especially the United States, is fundamentally concerned with dominating rather than helping Latin America. He looks with sympathy on various revolutionary models. For example, Msgr. Antônio Batista Fragoso, bishop of Crateús, once argued at a meeting of Northeast Brazilian bishops that "the courage of little Cuba in face of international imperialism, can serve as an example to Latin America, since almost all the countries are afraid of opposing international imperialism, especially North American imperialism." The Radicals vary in their strategic proposals, but they consider the Colombian priest, Camilo Torres, who became a guerrilla fighter, a symbol of legitimate Christian response.

(3) The Progressive inherits the longtime Catholic reservations about capitalism and proposes an alternative system that will avoid the problems of both capitalism and socialism. In Chile, Christian Democrats call this "communitarianism." The Radical, on the other hand, rejects capitalism and does not hesitate to adopt a socialist position which may reflect the influence of many models, from Scandinavia to China. The "Manifesto of the Bishops of the Third World," an interesting episcopal document of 1968, signed among others by eight Brazilian bishops, reflects the hostility to local and international capitalism among the Radicals: "The Third World is still seeking to escape the dominion of the powerful to develop itself freely . . . The Church greets with pride and joy a new humanity in which honor does not belong to money accumu-

lated in the hands of a few, but to workers, urban and peasant . . . If the workers do not become in some way owners of their work, all reforms of structure will be ineffective. . . . The government must agree to end that struggle of classes, which, contrary to what is ordinarily contended, the rich have frequently unleashed and continue against the workers, exploiting them with insufficient salaries and inhuman conditions of work."

Those unfamiliar with contemporary trends in Latin American Catholicism are usually surprised to find there a political outlook with revolutionary, socialist and anti-North American themes. It seems the very antithesis of the common image of the Church. For a long time its restriction to Brazil made it a curiosity, but it is now clear that two types of modernizing Catholic thought and action have emerged, that they have representatives in most Latin American countries, and that the Radicals currently seem to be gaining strength at the expense of the Progressives. Their growth reflects the intense quest of Catholics and other Latin Americans to work out an autonomous strategy for dynamizing the frustrating pace of development and replacing the deep rooted misery of the people.

The outlooks represented by Reactionary, Conservative, Progressive, and Radical elites are common to large institutions that include people from diverse social economic, and educational backgrounds, especially when the demand for change presents itself. They represent those who fight against change, those who ignore it, those who proceed prudently with it, and those who criticize radically and take advanced positions. The Latin American Church includes patterns of analysis that can be found in non-Catholic institutions as well as in Latin America. It is interesting that the much smaller Protestant Church has similar tensions and types.

Latin American Catholics, whether they be bishops, priests, or laymen, are affected by many factors that determine how they will interpret the Christian tradition and the problems of society. The Catholic teaching and experience are diverse, and people with different interests can often find in them what they want. Contemporary teaching conveys an obvious "line," essentially that of the Progressives; but the fact that this teaching represents an adjustment of contradictory principles and pressure groups in Rome, Rio, or Santiago does not render it the clear guide that many Catholics claim it to be. All of the positions we have outlined find some justification in the tradition and teaching, although the Radicals discern the inadequacies and lament the contradiction between the pious claims and the compromises of the Church.

At the same time, participation in the Catholic community does not protect an individual from the tugs of other factors shaping his perspective: social class, peer groups, educational influences. It is not surprising that the Reactionaries attract youth from upper class private schools, while priests working in slums, or students subject to Marxist ideas in the universities, incline toward Radicalism.

What, then, is the distinctive contribution of Catholicism? Fundamentally, Catholics derive from their life in the Church *energy* or *motivation* to take positions and act. They may also absorb such values as social concern, the dignity of human life, the significance of community, or the defense of special Church interests; but these are very general. In practice, Catholics draw from the Church a *sanction* for ideas and actions which are shaped in large part by other social and psychological factors. Those who fear change can easily discover statements and actions by the highest Church authorities to cite. Those who for various reasons believe in reasonable and cooperative evolutionary reform gain security from the recent positions of the Church. The impatient youth, those who feel deeply the offense of misery and underdevelopment in Latin America, and doubt the capacity of existent institutions to overcome them, become Radicals and manage to find justification in the comprehensive umbrella that is the Church.

While this sociological rather than theological analysis of the Catholic role may seem minimal, we should recognize that the motivation generated within the Church has such strength that Catholics constitute some of the decisive elites in Latin America. Especially those who have participated in organizations like specialized Catholic Action have a discipline, social concern, and capacity to work together that multiplies their influence beyond their numbers. The few hundred Catholic Action products who from 1930 to 1950 built Chilean

Christian Democracy, or the Catholic University Youth and a few sympathizers who shook the Brazilian Church by creating a Leftist movement, are examples.

If the Progressives and Radicals are the Catholic modernizing elites in Latin America, which are more important? In a dialectical way both contribute to the Church's policies and influence, because in the final analysis the fact that the Church presents to the world is composed of Catholic faces. The Progressives are in closer touch with present centers of decision and possibilities, and they usually get credit for the changes. The Radicals, on the other hand, are basically the Innovators, those who live in the future, sometimes wrong but often right, those who discerned the problems first and proposed fresh answers. The long range role of the Church cannot be judged by what seems acceptable now.

The significance of Progressives and Radicals is also bound up with what happens in Latin America. Catholics are not simply Catholics with a separate position, but also Latin Americans–and Brazilians, Chileans, Colombians, or Mexicans. We cannot anticipate the roads that various countries will choose for development. Some may resolve their problems through joint government and private enterprise, gradual reform, and cooperation with the United States. We may expect strong Catholic institutional and elite support for this avenue. On the other hand, some countries may follow more abrupt routes, eliminating the traditional ruling groups, adopting socialism, and taking an anti-North American stance. The evolution of recent Latin American Catholicism suggests that in this eventuality as well, Catholics will participate in good conscience.

In the modern world Catholicism will not determine the fate of Latin America, nor will it give the region's development a distinctive stamp. Its contribution will come from the support and participation of its spokesmen and faithful in the movements offered by the context.

THE LABOR UNIONS

Labor unions in Latin America are recognized as being capable of influencing politics. Specialists of the area disagree, however, on whether the unions have had any real political significance in the past. There is also controversy about whether the unions are conservative or revolutionary, with increasing research indicating that their concern rarely goes beyond narrow bread and butter economic issues that affect only their status.

Victor Alba, a specialist on labor and many other aspects of Latin America, points out the weakness of unions and their narrow concerns in the following selection. He blames the weakness of the unions on their types of members, their fractionalization, their tendencies toward bureaucratism, and their unquestioned willingness to accept middle class leadership. He illustrates their narrowness by showing that they are isolated from peasants and Indians and have little concern for land reform issues. It could also be added that the close affiliations of the unions with political parties have not been completely advantageous. There has been a tendency for opportunistic politicians to misuse the unions, and too many of the affiliated parties never do attain influence or lose it rather suddenly, leaving the unions bereft of any power. Finally, the military strongly dislikes unions in Latin America, and even the union relationship with students is usually rather short-lived, strained, and one of expediency on immediate goals.

Labor in Latin America

VICTOR ALBA*

There is much talk these days about the Latin American middle class, about students, intellectuals and oligarchs. But, except when there are strikes, little talk about the industrial working class.

There are some 15 to 20 million industrial workers in Latin America and labor unions exist in every country, even under the dictatorships. Latin American labor legislation is, generally, advanced (and as often as not, not carried out).

The industrial workers must cope as best they can with a multitude of complex problems stemming from industrialization, rapid urbanization and the prospect of automation. Their interests as workers force them to consider such problems as agrarian reform, inflation and the planning of economic development.

Nevertheless, it is the middle-class parties that spell out the orientation, study the problems, and propose the solutions. The labor movement as such rarely voices an opinion on these general questions. It is satisfied to fight for wages and working conditions. Only recently have any attempts been made to give the labor movement a voice of its own.

This has not always been the situation and it probably will not remain so in the future. But at present it may be said that the destiny of Latin America is taking shape without the decisive intervention of the industrial working class. To understand this we must briefly examine the character of the Latin American working class and the history of its labor movement.

I

a) *A considerable percentage of illiterate workers and, perhaps still worse, a great number of people whose formal edu-*

* Reprinted from Victor Alba, "Labor in Latin America," *Dissent* (Autumn, 1962), pp. 387–392 by permission of publisher and author.

cation does not go beyond knowledge of the ABC's, who have no interest whatever in any cultural activity, and who are impervious to and suspicious of complicated explanations. Such is the reality, and any program of workers' education must take this into account. This low educational level helps stir up differences within the working class. It creates castes of better educated workers, it establishes a hierarchy of wages and weakens trade-union solidarity.

b) *The peasant origin of the huge majority of industrial workers.* In a period of economic crisis or unemployment, they return to their villages where they are at least assured of food and shelter. In many areas workers abandon their work during protracted village festivals and at harvest time; hence there is a constant fluctuation of manpower, as well as of union strength. Educating these workers becomes a problem as does training them to fill skilled and specialized jobs.

c) *Persistence of an isolated, peasant mentality in the city worker.* He is often mistrustful, uninterested in social problems, and indifferent toward culture. A special study alone would be required to explain the influence this has on the psychology of the Mexican worker in his work and in his union, as well as his attitude toward his children, home, and pleasures. We would find no doubt that alcoholism, use of harmful herbs, emotional and family instability stem largely from the peasant's failure to adapt to urban life.

d) *The Latin American worker is in a transitional stage between artisanship (work performed in small workshops) and rationalized assembly-line work.* This creates problems of psychological adaptation which are reflected in his attitude toward his union.

e) *Women scarcely take part in industry.* One out of 233 among Mexican women as compared with one out of 153 in the professions and with one out of 213 among university students. This disproportion also leads to friction in work and home and frequently provokes union injustices.

f) *The great number of children who work before reaching the legal age at which they are permitted to.*

g) *General lack of interest in social problems and the absence of documentation (magazines, libraries, books, lectures, workers' study circles, etc.), in virtually all of Latin America.*

II

Basic needs in Latin America are so pressing that there is neither time nor possibility for disguising them in idealism. The workers are satisfied to fight for immediate aims. Exploitation is so blatant that any theoretical explanation is useless. While the European labor movement, particularly at the beginning, was preoccupied with the future, the labor movement in the New World concentrated exclusively on the improvement of existing conditions without bothering about tomorrow. Hence, its weakness in theory.

Toward the middle of the 19th century a few dreamers imported European socialist utopias. In Argentina, Esteban Echeverría, founded the Association of May in 1838 and wrote the *Socialist Dogma.* In Chile, in 1850, Francisco Bilbao created the "Society of Equals." Two poets in Mexico, Pantaleón Tovar and Juan Díaz Covarrubias, propagated utopianism, while in Brazil a Frenchman, Taudonnet, began to publish the *Socialist Review* in 1845. In Colombia the first socialist clubs were organized.

The old guild corporations of the colonial period disappeared or adopted a trade-union form. This development took place more rapidly when it received the help of European immigrants already familiar with trade unionism. That is why Argentina, with its mass immigration, experienced working-class struggles first.

The first union in Latin America was created in Buenos Aires in 1853. The *Unión Gráfica* (Printers' Union) won a ten-hour work day for newspaper shops in 1878, the first limitation of the working day accomplished by strike action. Nine years later the railwaymen went on strike to protest a foreman's mistreatment of one of their men.

It was the socialist *emigrés* who after the Paris Commune, led the way to coordination of the until then scattered unions. Several sections–French, German, Spanish and Italian–of the First International were established at Buenos Aires. Their members exercised influence in various trades so as to found the General Workers' Union of Argentina on May first, 1890.

This organization disappeared in 1896, weakened by a conflict between authoritarian and anti-authoritarian elements. In 1901 the Argentine Regional Workers' Federation (FORA) was organized. Exclusively trade-union elements left this in 1902 to found the General Workers' Union (UGT). In spite of a law permitting the expulsion of *emigré* agitators, the unions were very active. In 1902, 1904 and 1905 there were three general strikes, and in 1910 the Argentine Regional Workers' Confederation (CORA) was established. CORA and FORA merged in 1914, but split a year later. By the First World War the normal work day was ten hours (16 hours, however, for commercial employees), and wages kept up with price increases.

By 1918 FORA had 70,000 members and UGT had 80,000. Then, in 1929, after vain efforts to unify the unions, the General Confederation of Labor (CGT) was started. FORA remained independent. Trade-union cooperatives, certain of which lend economic support to strikes, have developed on a wide scale. In Uruguay and Paraguay similar movements developed.

As for Chile, thanks to foreign loans it was one of the first Latin American countries to become industrialized. British capital, followed by North American investments, built the railroads and worked the nitrate and copper mines in the inhospitable Northern regions. The working class developed rapidly, migration from the country into the cities was constant, contributing to the creation of a more democratic regime. The landed oligarchy was forced to permit universal suffrage in 1874, without any condition but literacy.

The nitrate region of Antofogasta, first exploited by combined Anglo-Chilean investments in 1866, saw thousands of peasants become miners. The solidarity which grew up among them was such as one rarely sees on the continent. The first strikes in the country were by the *salitreros* of Tarpacá in 1890 who wanted to be paid in cash, not in company-store vouchers. José Manuel Balmaceda, president of the Republic, refused to act against the strikers and went so far as to suggest nationalizing the mines as well as the railroads. But in 1891 an oligarchical rebellion ended Balmaceda's regime and he committed suicide.

Chile today is still the country with the most highly developed cooperative movement. As early as 1900 there were 240 cooperatives. Starting in 1905, the anarchist movement organized the first groups and so energetic was their action that by 1907 a law establishing Sunday rest was promulgated. In 1910, out of 3,200,000 inhabitants listed by census, 55,000 were affiliated to 433 groups. A year later a large number of them had formed the Greater Workers' Federation of Chile (FOCH). The mass of workers affiliated in the north rapidly gained control and weakened the influence of the anarchist unions affiliated with the IWW. In 1921 the Federation constituted itself along industrial council lines, abandoning organization according to profession. Thanks to mutual-help organizations which it had created at the start, FOCH was able to sustain prolonged strikes such as the 1921 coal strike which lasted two months and which won an 8-hour day in the coal pits. After 1923 political events forced the FOCH into a crisis. The railroad workers' union split away from it and a number of other unions followed. Until 1936, when the Chilean Workers' Confederation (CTCH) was established, FOCH led a rather monotonous existence; independent unions conducted the principal struggles.

In 1924 a military government was established which decreed, for demagogic reasons, a Labor Code giving legal recognition to the unions and to joint industrial committees. It also abolished night work for women and children, made health insurance obligatory and set minimum wages. In 1925, Arturo Alessandri issued a constitution recognizing the right of union organization and setting a 48-hour week.

Bolivia's first trade union made its appearance in 1906 and was called the Workers' Social Center. In 1912 the FOI (International Workers' Federation), changed to the FOT (Workers' Labor Federation) after 1918, was set up. This organization and the FOL (Local Workers' Federation–an anarcho-syndicalist movement) often form united fronts. In Peru also, anarchists were the initiators of the labor movement, taking leadership of the Confederation of Artisans

("Universal Union") which existed since 1884. The union instituted several agrarian communities for artisans. The CGT came much later and was dissolved, together with the "Universal Union," by the 1930 military dictatorship, at the moment when the APRA movement, founded in 1924 by Victor Raúl Haya de la Torre, began to develop. In 1922 Ecuador had its first union. As in the other countries, the central trade unions changed according to changes in the working-class ideologies and as the Communists formed their party–hereby splitting with the socialists; or, as in Brazil, from anarchist groups.

In Central America the labor movement came late and has little influence. Costa Rican unions were unified only in 1943; in Guatemala two movements merged to form the Workers' Federation for Labor Protection; the Guatemalan Confederation of Workers was created in 1944.

By contrast, labor struggles in Cuba early acquired importance. In 1812, the Negro Juan Aponte led a slave uprising of 20,000 with the aim of establishing a Black Republic; in 1813 the *vegueros* refused to plant tobacco unless their wages were increased. In 1831, the copper mine workers rebelled and, in 1868, during the first war of independence, a group of Spanish anarchists founded the Society of Tobacco Workers. The work day then lasted 16 hours. In 1892 a Regional Workers Congress met to demand the 8-hour day. After independence from Spain, unions were rapidly formed and in 1925 joined together in a national Confederation which was successively dominated by the Communists and by democrats, then subjected to Batista from 1952 to 1959. Under Castro it is used to raise productivity and control the workers.

III

There are three different stages in the development of the Latin American labor movement:

a) *The period of origins:* Anarchists or socialists create unions, they have a life of their own, import European ideas and, without becoming political, take part in national problems.

b) *The period between the two world wars.* A withdrawal from active politics, but the unions become a battleground for Communists, socialists and anarchists. They rarely take part in the anti-imperialists' struggles except when these are conflicts with foreign enterprises (the most important being those in the Colombian banana plantations in Santa Marta in 1929, the Chilean mine strikes and, in 1938, Mexican oil).

c) *The post-war period:* The unions become completely unpolitical in their activities, while splitting into anti- and pro-Communist groupings.

Several major conclusions may be drawn from this sketch of the Latin American labor movement.

First, the Latin American proletariat is numerically weak. In recent years, as a result of industrialization, it has increased in size, but its consciousness remains undeveloped and non-political. Except for Chile, the once powerful socialist and anarchist influence has vanished. Communist influence has always been slight, although during certain periods such as the Popular Front days and after the Second World War, Communists directed the central unions of a majority of Latin American countries. At present, Communism influences primarily intellectuals, students and the middle class. The Communists often succeed in making use of the working class, but have failed to obtain appreciable results in recruiting.

A majority of the labor movement is led at present by elements of the popular and revolutionary democratic parties (Peru, Venezuela, Bolivia, Costa Rica), by a Socialist-Communist alliance (Chile and a section in Ecuador), by a Peronist-Communist alliance (Argentina), and by leaders who are to all intents state functionaries (Brazil). Within all these movements a very active struggle between democratic and Communist tendencies goes on. The outcome of these struggles depends more upon the leaders' personal popularity than upon their ideological views. In Chile, Venezuela, Colombia and Ecuador, the Christian-Democrats have begun to gain a measure of influence.

In the second place, the labor movement has lived in a state of isolation from other social forces. It has almost never collaborated with peasant organizations in the few countries where they exist. There is even the example of the "Red Battalions" formed by Mexican workers during the 1910–1917 Revolution which helped the city forces crush the insurrectionary peasantry. Although on several occasions the unions have attempted to organize peasants, they have rarely succeeded. The same indifference is found with respect to the problem of the Indians. The unions have neither a program nor a viewpoint to help in the solution of this problem despite its considerable importance for the labor movement, one reason being that Indians are easily mobilized as strikebreakers. It is only recently that in a few countries—Peru, Venezuela—the unions have shown an active interest in the agrarian question.

This isolation sometimes takes on a politically reactionary character. Since industrialization takes place almost everywhere without any prior or parallel agrarian reform, it is the peasants who must pay for it. Thus, to a degree, the working class becomes a parasitic class living off the peasantry. Even without a conscious realization of this, the unions have often sided with the feudal oligarchy against the peasantry or have become the latter's accomplice through indifference toward the peasants. Suffice it to recall that the Cuban unions did not participate in the anti-Batista struggle. It is only lately that the unions, almost without exception, have taken a stand in favor of land reform. But even then it is only a platonic position which leaves to the popular and middle-class movements the brunt of the struggle against the *latifundists*.

Finally, such isolation creates very marked tendencies in the labor movement toward bureaucratization, the perpetuation of "leaders" in their posts, a fiction of democracy at meetings.

The result of this isolation and bureaucratism is the indifference of the unions toward important national questions. Not only a lack of interest in the agrarian and Indian problems, but no participation in planning where it exists, no struggle against dictatorships with the exception of some groups in Venezuela and Peru, no support to cultural activities, no help in the forming of workers or popular universities despite the fact that forty years ago such schools were common in Latin

America and, particularly those under anarcho-syndicalist leadership tied to the labor movement.

IV

Despite these shortcomings, the labor movement has a part to play in Latin American life. Growth of Latin America's economy and politics requires that the unions participate.

It seems clear that the Latin American "revolution" about which everyone talks is nothing but a typical bourgeois revolution. It seems also clear that the weak and politically inexperienced Latin American proletariat, lacking any doctrine, can play only a subordinate and secondary role in this revolution. But if it cannot lead the revolution, it does have sufficient weight to limit to some extent the freedom of movement of the bourgeoisie which itself is still in process of formation. Limits to exploitation can be established to prevent the repetition in Latin America of the worst characteristics of industrialization in Europe and the United States. Particularly, the labor movement ought by its action to prevent the bourgeoisie and the forces that support it (the technicians and the younger army people who possess a rather developed sense of efficiency) from attempting to force the nation's development by non-democratic means; that is, to prevent over-exploitation of labor according to the Soviet model. This model, moreover, has a greater attraction for the bourgeoisie and the young military men and technicians than for the working class which mistrusts the Communists.

Very likely the major task of the unions at present is to win the right to actively participate in the economic planning about which everyone now talks and which the United States has finally come to accept. The cultural and technical level of the Latin American trade-union leadership is generally rather low. To prepare leaders, to renew the union teams by infusions of young blood, to attract intellectuals, students, technicians and especially young workers into the unions, to support the organizing of peasants and to help Indian groups become modern without losing their identity are among the many phases of union activity which still remain unexplored. Latin American labor needs to reform itself, needs to fall into step with the evolution of Latin America and make a reality out of the workers' movement's old slogan: to make itself the representative of all of society's interests precisely because it represents the interests of the workers.

(*Translated by* STANLEY PLASTRIK)

POLITICAL PARTIES

Latin America's great variety of political parties and party systems has led many scholars to formulate typologies on this subject. The typologies are supposed to systematically distinguish between types of parties for the purpose of deriving meaningful generalizations. However, most of the typologies have differed and many have been so poorly constructed that they may be more misleading than suggestive. One of the difficulties of past typologies have been the factors chosen by each author to construct his typology. Factors stressed in the past have covered ideology, personalism, the left-right continuum, whether a party is traditional, European-copied, or indigenous, and a variety of others based on the predilections of each author as to what is important in Latin America.

The typology of parties by Peter Ranis, Professor of Political Science at York College of the City University of New York, is an improvement over the others in many ways. He discards most of the factors previously utilized and argues that a party should be judged on how it actually acts in concrete situations, regardless of its ideology, or supposed leftism or rightism, etc. The way it actually acts can be determined first by its mobility–the willingness to ally with other parties and ability to compromise, and secondly by its perception of societal problems and what it would actually do to resolve them. Professor Ranis then sets up triangles for each country, enabling him to show how the parties of each country fit into the mobility/perception categories, and how parties may be changing from one category to another. The triangles thus allow the author to make observations about the party systems of various countries, especially in respect to changes which cannot be done in many of the other static typologies. Finally, an over-all generalization is made that most important Latin American parties are of an aggregator-innovator type, contrary to generalizations of other specialists who have arrived at different conclusions by emphasizing other factors in their typologies.

*A Two-Dimensional Typology of Latin American Political Parties**

PETER RANIS

Throughout recent decades important changes have taken place in Latin America that appear to have altered aspects of political party competition. The growth of the middle class, urbanization, industrialization, greater literacy, better means of communication, and a higher standard of living all have had deep and vital impacts upon Latin American society in general and upon political parties in particular.

It may be too early to speak of a newly-acquired accommodating attitude in politics, but obviously there has been a shift in public attitudes, political activity, and governmental concerns. The important issues of the day vary from those of pre-World War II years, as does the general mood of the political participants. It is difficult to pinpoint the change,[1] but it becomes noticeable when we approach political party activities in the past decade.

The more dynamic, larger, more industrialized, wealthier Latin American nations are maturing both politically and eco-

* I am very grateful to Professors Tom P. Wolf, John F. McCamant, Michael J. Francis and Kalman H. Silvert for their helpful suggestions on earlier drafts of this article. Reprinted from *The Journal of Politics* (August, 1968), pp. 798–832, by permission of publisher and author.

[1] Survey research conducted with mass publics, responding to questions about their views on political issues, is largely untapped in Latin America. One exception to this is Gabriel Almond and Sidney Verba's *The Civic Culture* (Boston: Little, Brown, 1965), a cross-national study, which includes a survey of Mexican attitudes regarding their level of political cognition, their sense of competence, and the impact of government on their lives.

nomically. They have generally overcome severe internal crises and have lived through deep disturbances to their social fabric. Latin American development, partially evident from social, economic and political modernization indices,[2] has engendered a spirit of political incrementalism, that is, of not going too fast and too far afield from tried formulas nor violating abruptly that which has been achieved.

Vast sectors of Latin America's politically socialized[3] groups appear to have reached a level of cooperative and mutual political bargaining regarding some of the hitherto most deeply-divisive social issues. Institutionally, few groups in Latin America would opt for implanting a dictatorially-conceived totalitarian political structure. Bonapartist Fascism of the Perón variety has been largely discredited, as have the harshness and dislocations of the Castro-led experiment. The nineteenth-century version of unencumbered capitalism is as out-of-style with Latin America's political culture as is an all-controlling state supervision over every aspect of the domestic market. Complete disengagement from U. S. investments and U. S. political interests is considered unrealistic today, but so also is the acceptance of an unchecked flow of U. S. investment and U. S. assistance. The Church-State issue has been reasonably interred. Although the Church is recognized symbolically as part of the nation's official personality and accepted as an influential partner in political socialization within

[2] Seymour M. Lipset, "Some Social Requisites of Democracy: Economic Development and Political Legitimacy," *American Political Science Review,* Vol. 53, No. 1 (March 1959); Karl W. Deutsch, "Social Mobilization and Political Development," *American Political Science Review,* Vol. 55, No. 3 (September, 1961); and Bruce M. Russett *et al., World Handbook of Political Social Indicators* (New Haven: Yale University Press, 1964).

[3] It is difficult to say just who makes up these groups but there are some helpful statistics: voter turnout figures are given in the *Statistical Abstract of Latin America* (Los Angeles) and there are various county electoral analyses by the *Institute for the Comparative Study of Political Systems* (Washington, D.C.); urbanization indices are provided by *United Nations Demographic Yearbook;* figures for total work force in the industrial sector are included in *United Nations Statistical Yearbook.* There are many economic indices surveys published by the *Economic Commission for Latin America* (New York).

essentially private sectors of political life, its public force has been relegated to a perceptibly smaller role. This is exemplified by the positions taken by Christian Democratic parties, both in and out of power.

Centralism versus decentralism, the federal-unitary struggle that for so long immersed many Latin American nations in tragic internal conflicts, has also been resolved. The acknowledged winner in every case has been the central government which has acted moderately and reasonably enough to avoid secessionist movements or extreme domestic discontent. Certainly in the federal systems of Mexico, Brazil, Venezuela, and Argentina, a bargain among unequal powers has been forged which has not deterred the increasing control and competence exercised by national governments. Advocates of complete parcelization of land are as infrequent as those who would leave the nation's natural resources in the control of unproductive hands. The military's institutional role in society has been generally accepted as a possible force for good, despite its inveterate backsliding into learned reflexes of intervention. "Welfare socialism," or a "regulated capitalism," is the popular image of the future economy. Democratic procedures liberally sprinkled with guided governmental authority is the expected political system.

This portrayal of growing political conciliation by no means is meant to discount certain quiet, but nevertheless, alienated sectors in almost every Latin American society. However, the integration of these neglected groups is a challenge that the majority of Latin American political leaders have agreed to meet.

Contemporary Party Typologies

Within the context of party politics, there has been an evident development both in the types of parties evolving and their concomitant political behavior. This investigation is concerned with recent party evolution in seven important Latin American nations, i. e., Mexico, Venezuela, Colombia, Peru, Brazil, Chile, and Argentina; the purpose is to arrive at a tentative redefinition of party types.

The social systems of these Latin American countries all

sustain and support competitive political parties. There are no very powerful social institutions or political mechanisms for inhibiting a fairly free and open exchange of political ideologies and programs. Despite current military predominance in some of the countries, few barriers exist to the free interaction among political parties. Even where parties cannot formally participate in the political process, repressive measures have been taken not against the presence of parties in the political system, but rather temporarily against some of the programs of those parties. Parties in these countries, whether or not they are in positions actually to wield power, or whether or not they represent significant portions of the population, are visible and functioning political units. They offer the public a variety of meaningful political alternatives to governmental policy.

A current view that the "essential regional pattern is one of multi-partism, while minor qualifications are precisely that—reservations, not contradictions"[4]—is a broad scheme that efficiently and accurately represents the political party panorama of Latin America. Since much of the past instability of the Latin American political systems has occurred because of the activities of institutional interest groups (e.g., the military), it does not seem overly optimistic to label the majority of Latin American party systems as essentially "working" multi-party systems.[5] Based on the gradual supercession of old

[4] John D. Martz, "Dilemmas in the Study of Latin American Political Parties," *The Journal of Politics*, Vol. 26, No. 1 (August, 1964), p. 517.

[5] This phrase, used by Dankwart A. Rustow, "Scandinavia: Working Multiparty Systems" in Sigmund Neumann (ed.) *Modern Political Parties* (Chicago: University of Chicago Press, 1956), has come to mean that certain political systems with a minimal amount of societal consenses and no major political cleavages can make multiparty systems function effectively. The chapters by Hans Daalder, "Parties, Elites, and Political Developments in Western Europe," and Giovanni Sartori, "European Political Parties: The Case of Polarized Pluralism," in Joseph LaPalombara and Myron Weiner (eds.), *Political Parties and Political Development* (Princeton: Princeton University Press, 1966), both caution against the tendency of Anglo-American scholars to write off working multiparty systems as some sort of aberration of more authentic two-party systems.

issues, on contemporary socio-economic development, and on the growing homogeneity of Latin American political culture, the party systems may be profitably examined in light of their increasing success at making multi-party systems work.[6]

Left-right classifications are no longer particularly useful. For instance, some parties which are benign in their relationship with the church are vigorous prosecutors of profound land reforms; some who are friendly to U. S. private investments demand nationalization of basic industries; some who favor the legalization of the Communist Party oppose the basic tenets of the progressive tax reforms proposed by the Alliance for Progress; and so on, indefinitely. Who is to say then which is left and which is right? It is also not very meaningful to cite a party's social identification (e.g., workers–socialists, landowners–conservatives, church–Christian Democrats, trade unionists–Peronistas, and so on) or to refer to "economic" groupings, such as "statists" *vs.* "free enterprisers," or ideological groupings, such as Marxists *vs.* Democrats. Such party pigeonholing may obscure the cooperation which appears to have been reached as to the apolitical role of the church, the avoidance of totalitarian forms of institutional controls, and the requirements of a mixed economic partnership. More recent typologies have neglected factors which must be considered pertinent in the assessment of Latin American political parties. The typologies are usually rather static, though often sophisticated, analyses of party systems and party functions. Part of the problem may arise from the notable classifications which found their birth in Maurice Duverger's *Political Parties* (1954) and its most famous successor work, Sigmund Neumann's *Modern Political Parties* (1956). These works have tended to place the burden on Latin American scholars either to demonstrate exceptions to the rule or to place Latin American parties into the dictatorial one-party or unstable multi-party systems. The latter approach has found much favor in Latin American political party analyses.

[6] See Gabriel A. Almond, "Introduction," p. 42 in Gabriel A. Almond and James S. Coleman, *The Politics of Developing Areas* (Princeton: Princeton University Press, 1960), for Scandinavian version of the multi-party system.

A further explanation may lie in Duverger's description of the inherent instability of the center position in party politics. He said:

> A duality of parties does not always exist, but almost always there is a duality of tendencies. Every policy implies a choice between two kinds of solution, the so-called compromise solutions lean one way or the other. This is equivalent to saying that the center does not exist in politics. *There may well be a center party but there is no center tendency, no center doctrine.*[7] [Italics mine.]

This may have implied that in a multi-party system parties must always take a relatively extreme political position as either a conservative "particularist" party or a radical "ideological" party. Duverger, however, was not that categorical. He allowed for a center party to exist for an indefinite time until the political dialogue had reasserted itself.

Duverger, however, did not make clear why a center party should exist in the first place. Its very presence makes it as "natural" to the party system as parties which function on one or another end of the political spectrum. Moreover, a "duality of tendencies" is too rigid a concept. Though there are bound to be party differences, they are almost invariably accompanied by certain party agreements. These overlapping variables occur on almost every major or minor inter-party issue. Interaction among parties must necessarily occur somewhere close to the center of the system. This continual interaction in or near the center may itself provide the center-orientation with a political life of its own.

Neumann's dual classification of parties of "individual representation" and parties of "total integration" has also weighted the scales in the interpretation of Latin American parties. So much of the writing on Latin American political parties (including many textbooks) speaks of the limited amount of party activity between elections, the absence of party organization, and the inability to aggregate large sectors

[7] Maurice Duverger, *Political Parties* (New York: John Wiley, 1963), p. 215.

of the civic community, all attributes of parties of "individual representation."[8]

A typical recent classification, for example, divides ". . . Latin American political parties into those which are traditional, that is, which came down from the earlier years of these countries' independence; those which are of European inspiration; the national revolutionary parties; and those which can be classified as totalitarian."[9] This is an adequate classification but it risks losing sight of the alterations and metamorphosis under which these parties align and the frequent divergences within each party, not to speak of shifts within the total political system. It is not fruitful to speak of parties in isolation from each other (especially in multi-party systems). Rather we need to study party interaction *within each political system.*

John Martz, for example, divides typologies into party system approaches (measuring the relative competitiveness of the political system), legal-institutional approaches (measuring electoral and constitutional mechanisms), and intra-party structure and programmatic schemes (interpreting internal party qualities such as leadership, interest articulation, recruitment, organization, political education, etc.).[10] He suggests that it is this third approach which may be the best avenue for further research.

Gabriel Almond and James Coleman, some time ago, and more recently, Joseph LaPalombara and Myron Weiner, have dealt essentially with the relative competitiveness of political systems. They have brought forth interesting typologies which provide a convenient jumping-off point in further assessments of parties. Almond, for example, speaks of three types of parties, "pragmatic," "ideological," and "particularistic."[11]

[8] Sigmund Neumann, (ed.), *Modern Political Parties* (Chicago: University of Chicago Press, 1956), pp. 403–405.

[9] Robert J. Alexander, *Latin American Politics and Government* (New York: Harper and Row, 1965), p. 49.

[10] Martz, *op. cit.,* pp. 509–530. This study gives an excellent review of the literature on political parties in Latin America and, therefore, I have decided against a redundant compilation of existing typologies.

[11] Gabriel A. Almond and James S. Coleman, *The Politics of Developing Areas,* Introduction.

This is a helpful categorization because it employs the value structures of different parties. Belief commitments are then related to their political activity (political aggregation and articulation of interests). Though Almond's taxonomic device went no further it has generated more dynamic methods of comparing political processes in general.

A more complex method of comparing political parties cross-nationally is provided in the typology formulated by LaPalombara and Weiner.[12] It pertains not only to the relative competitiveness or openness of the political system (hegemonic as against turnover regimes) but to a second characteristic classifying competitive systems along an ideological-pragmatic continuum. This opens up greater possibilities for developing typologies that deal with more dimensions.

A Mobility/Perception Scheme

In this typology of political parties, the concepts of *party mobility* and *party perception* are used. Political parties are here defined as identifiable, autonomous organizations with known values and programs which they propose to promulgate upon achieving political office. Though the selection is for the most part composed of better known national parties that consistently compete in elections, it also includes parties whose activities from time to time have been politically restricted though their political organization remains intact. Party mobility refers to the likelihood with which a party tends to ally with another party or parties. It describes the means and methods considered legitimate in a party's attempts to attain power and influence. It refers to self-imposed rules governing party activity vis-à-vis other organized seekers of authority. Party perception refers to the manner in which a party views societal problems and their resolution. It implies something about the values adhered to by a party and the general nature of its commitment to social change and the degree of certainty with which it creates definite and prescribed goals for the whole society.

In the *party mobility* category, three groupings encompass

[12] Joseph LaPalombara and Myron Weiner (eds.), *Political Parties and Political Development*, p. 35–6.

all parties acting within the confines of any particular political system:

1. Aggregator Party
2. Resistor Party
3. Isolator Party

Under *party perception*, we similarly list three groupings:

A. Preservator Party
B. Innovator Party
C. Rejector Party

1. An *Aggregator Party* is extremely flexible and adaptive. It finds itself comfortable in wide-ranging and loosely-conceived party alliances. In its relationship to other parties, it is both purposeful and ambiguous. It is anxious to maximize the possibilities of "other-party" cooperation. It recognizes the importance of combining political groups until a sufficient plurality of political support has been amassed. It is preoccupied with constructing enough cooperation among other parties to allow it to possess a minimum amount of political power.

2. *A Resistor Party* is highly competitive and derives the resources for its policies and actions mainly from carefully prescribed internal formulations. It acquires strength from acting in an autonomous manner and usually refuses commitments that it fears are inherent in a multi-party arrangement. It looks upon inter-party arrangements as weakening its capacity to achieve power alone. It finds it difficult to adapt its means of competing for power to those of other political parties. It opposes the "conventions" of inter-party agreements.

3. An *Isolator Party* represents a relative "outsider" in the political arena, both from necessity and choice. Its assessment of political conciliation makes it incompatible with its political competitors. It eschews the mediation required for party agreements and dislikes the features of political compromise and political bargaining. Preferring to act in opposition, it is most amenable to refutation and confrontation.

In the category of *perception*:

A. The *Preservator Party* resists any deep-seated alterations of society and identifies its political life with the existing socio-economic relationships. It distrusts any basic readjustment of societal patterns of development. Committed to the continuation of present patterns of social stratification, it is likely to support the trend of contemporary allocations of goods and services.

B. The *Innovator Party* demonstrates an essentially empirical approach to socio-economic problems. It is willing to experiment with varying political formulae and does not overly commit itself to an absolute view of society. It will bend to the political exigencies of the moment in order to resolve political impasses or economic obstacles. It seeks to accommodate the largest possible sources of interest.

C. The *Rejector Party* does not accept the basic suppositions of other parties and considers contemporary societal adjustments and adaptations as poor substitutes for a profound restructuring of society's institutions. Suspicious of incremental, reformist approaches to economic and social problems, it prefers seeking solutions through measures not easily accepted by most societal interests.

The perception categories should not be confused with traditional typologies of left-right-center. They do not describe the relative extremism or moderation in party pronouncements or party dogma but rather the capacity and/or willingness of parties to react flexibly and non-doctrinally to changing socio-economic conditions affecting the political system. Any given party that has been classified within the traditional left-right-center can be placed into any one of the three perception categories. For example, a left-wing party may be an innovator or a preservator. A right-wing party may be a rejector. This will become apparent from the discussion below.

It is also important to distinguish our definition of aggregator from Almond's concept of the aggregative input function. Our wording is strictly confined to the aggregation, in some kind of bargain, alliance or coalition, with other parties and not necessarily to the act of incorporating social strata and interest sectors into political participation via political parties. It is an inter-party definition, not a socio-political concept.

In a multi-party system, it is easier to win an election in aggregation with other parties. Since it is probable that *all* parties want to aggregate (in the Almond sense here) more and more of the public as adherents of its party's formulas, to aggregate with other parties presents a short-cut to aggregating social sectors because it can be assumed that the party with which one aggregates also has its constituents. If a party is really trying to aggregate social sectors, then it might be expedient to make agreements with parties that represent those sectors of society. This is particularly true in a multi-party political system. If one party does not make such a move to initiate party aggregation, then other parties will, striving as they are (most of the time) to preserve or gain influence over governmental decision-making–a *sine qua non* of party politics.

No distinction has been made here between enduring alliances and temporary electoral "fronts." Electoral alliances are the specific factors that are considered, though coalition governments can also be treated since they are significant indicators of a similar aggregative predisposition. Parliamentary alliances and joint voting behaviors can *not* be considered because of the repetition of such agreements by all parties in a multi-party system. Voting in common in the legislature is not indicative of party mobility or perception. Party members often vote with members of other parties simply because, limited by a positive, abstention, or negative vote and with more than two parties participating, there are few voting alternatives for the legislator.

Figure I demonstrates the relationship between the mobility/perception categories, using the vertical columns for perception and the horizontal rows for mobility. A triangular diagram has been utilized as the most appropriate visual aid when dealing with party mobility/perception moves. The triangle gives a graphic representation of an ever widening base for party interaction. Furthermore, it may indicate where the power center of a stable political system lies. Approaching the apex of the triangle, there is less maneuverability while the inverse is true as one moves toward the base of the triangle. Within the context of the ebb and flow of parties in the triangle, it may be possible to relate a party's political power potential to its mobility/perception function.

With greater agreement present in Latin America over issues and ideology, there is a discernible movement to comply with a developing electorate's predisposition for the pragmati-

FIGURE I

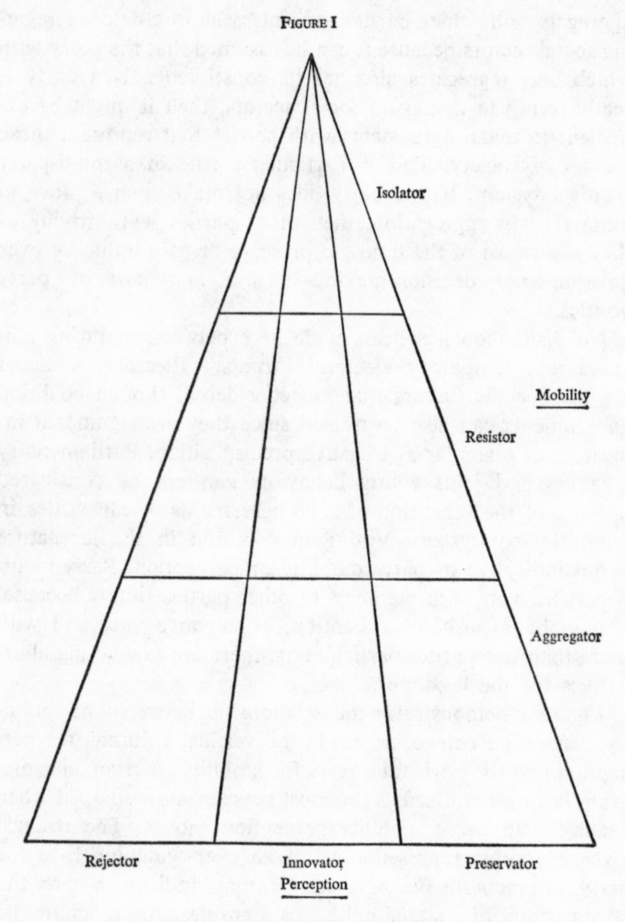

cally resolvable issue rather than the ideologically bifurcating issue. The major parties are competing for what they feel is the center of the political spectrum—the aggregator-innovator box—where, it is likely now and increasingly so in the future, the bulk of the votes are. The tendency to merge toward the "power centers" appears to be just as strong in a multi-party system as in a two-party system. As the landed classes are slowly weakened and as the organized urban and rural workers move up the economic scale (albeit slowly) it is from the growing middle sector of the population that support must be increasingly gained.

It may therefore be relevant to note how Latin American parties have changed in their mobility/perception orientation, how they are changing and probably will change in the future. Two avenues to political power appear to be related to the potential mobility and perception of parties. Figure I shows one route along the vertical innovator perception column and the other along the horizontal aggregator mobility continuum. There are three boxes from which political parties may directly move toward political power: the aggregator-rejector, the aggregator-preservator, and the resistor-innovator. Parties moving toward the aggregator-innovator position face the three possibilities of either assuming power, being eventually absorbed by larger and more effective aggregator-innovators within the same position, or establishing themselves as viable oppositions.

There seems to be a relationship between the capacity to achieve and hold power and the success at reaching the aggregator-innovator box. Successful attempts at governmental control have also been constructed in the three adjoining (gateways to power) boxes, but they have not been maintained. Those positions appear unstable and a party in one of these "slippery" categories must either make a move toward power or get off the vertical (innovator) axis or horizontal (aggregator) axis. It is as if there were a gravitational pull upon any party which reaches the aggregator or innovator continuum regardless of whether it is at the top-center or bottom corners of the triangular diagram. Thus only a society with a party in power that has entered the aggregator-innovator box can be expected to achieve long-range stability.

Once an opposition party decides to make a bid for power, it may move along the aggregator (mobility) continuum; or it may lose equilibrium and become, for example, a resistor-preservator, or a resistor-rejector. Or it makes its bid for power on the innovator (perception) column and moves quickly down to the aggregator box or again loses equilibrium and also becomes, for example, a resistor-preservator or a resistor-rejector or categories even more removed from power further up toward the apex of the triangle (isolator boxes on the preservator or rejector vertical columns).

Parties can probably survive indefinitely in the preservator or rejector vertical columns (outside the aggregator corner boxes), but once they make a bid for power, it seems they must move toward the aggregator box and once in that horizontal continuum, their shift toward the center (the innovator box) is almost automatic.

Parties that remain in the upper preservator and rejector boxes seem unable to adapt their perceptions toward an innovative view of society. This keeps them concomitantly in the resistor and isolator categories. If their mobility factor would allow them to move down to the bottom where they would be willing to aggregate, they would probably soon find it necessary to make a perception move toward innovation or re-ascend to a stable but powerless upper-strata box.

For a party to move down the sides of the triangular model implies a willingness to aggregate or work with other parties. Though this change in mobility need not give rise to an immediate perception shift toward the innovator continuum, once a party has decided politically to cooperate with other parties within the system it is only a matter of time until this influences its perceptions toward a more innovative view of society.

Similarly, a party that alters its perception first to one of innovation will then be normally available to extra-party alliances which forecasts a mobility shift on the part of that party. In both of the above cases, a party once having decided on a mobility move to aggregation or a perception move to innovation must make the compromises involved (though the political pay-off is usually worth it.)

As parties aggregate and innovate they tend to reinforce habits of compromise and accommodation. This increases the amount of inter-party consensus and lessens the need for confrontation. Distinct from that of the aggregator-preservator and of the aggregator-rejector, the alliance of aggregator-innovators is grounded on a continual expansion of the points of ideological contact. This alliance breeds majoritarian aspirations. The other two are content with holding some power through a significant minority. The continuing search for consensus subjects aggregator-innovator parties to inner stresses and strains. This internal dimension is one of adaptation to the political ecology as varyingly interpreted by its leaders. Given such a party's unwillingness to abort experimentation, these conflicts and internal dissensions will continue. Should aggregative-innovative coalitions break up, it is predictable that the parties concerned will have gained valuable experience from the partnership in terms of having a new taste for power, acquiring more tolerance for political compromise and developing sensible programs grounded in reality.

Minor parties within the isolator-rejector and isolator-preservator categories continue to persist not only because of their consistent interpretation of society but also because they provide status, jobs, and psychological gratification for their permanent membership. This sustains their dedication to a uniformity of perception.

In the following sections, the mobility/perception scheme will be related to observable political party activity in Mexico, Venezuela, Colombia, Peru, Brazil, Chile, and Argentina. This is not meant as an all-inclusive, definitive interpretation of party behavior in specific Latin American countries but rather a demonstration of the usefulness of analyzing parties by a two-dimensional typology.

Mexico

Mexico has a one-party dominated political system, though, as in other Latin American examples, the roots are present for an extension of that system to include other parties. The existence of Mexico's single-member electoral system leaves room for the development of a second major political party in opposition. As Kenneth Johnson states the case:

> Principal foci of the PAN [the major opposition party] attack are the anti-clerical provisions of the Constitution and the extension of state capitalism into the traditionally private sectors. Today's *panistas* include the *abolengo*, old established families whose wealth and position have been reduced or threatened, certain of the *nouveaux riches* who aspire to greater places, many of the upwardly mobile mid-

dle class who "never quite made it," and an uncertain base of peasants and artisans whose susceptibility to clerical propaganda has placed them within the PAN ranks.[13]

Mexico, though it has not yet established viable alternative governing parties, has a stable political system, and *Partido Revolucionario Institucional* (PRI) can be classified as an aggregator-innovator. (See Figure II) *Partido de Acción Nacional* (PAN) has not, until very recently, demonstrated any willingness either to aggregate or innovate and has, for the most part, remained in the resistor-preservator category. However, PRI, growing sensitive to the accusations of "one-party dictatorship," now appears to be making overtures to the PAN party as evidenced by the awarding of governmental jobs. Also a new electoral provision gives PAN representation of up to twenty seats in the Chamber of Deputies for votes over 2.5% of the total cast (which usually cannot alone assure them victory in *any* single-member district). In return PRI hopes that PAN will respond by recognizing basic democratic features of Mexican institutions. PAN may face the dilemma of absorption, an apparent risk of aggregation-innovation. Presently in the resistor-preservator category, PAN is being increasingly invited to aggregate (in terms of receiving governmental posts). This will mean a move down to the aggregator-preservator category from where, if PAN adjusts itself to the goals of the "Mexican Revolution", it stands to be absorbed by the PRI party. PAN has indicated resistance to this move and has thus remained a resistor-preservator–safe but powerless. On the other hand, PAN may choose to innovate its policy views. Once having shown the predisposition to innovate, it will then be in a position to come to terms more easily with PRI. At this point the party may be able to challenge PRI effectively *or* it may be absorbed as a distinct political party.

PRI's dilemma is that while searching for a "loyal opposition" party, it threatens either to absorb PAN or to maintain it as a resistor-preservator which means it will have no real

[13] Kenneth F. Johnson, "Ideological Correlates of Right Wing Political Alienation in Mexico," *American Political Science Review,* Vol. LIX, No. 3 (September, 1965), p. 659.

FIGURE II

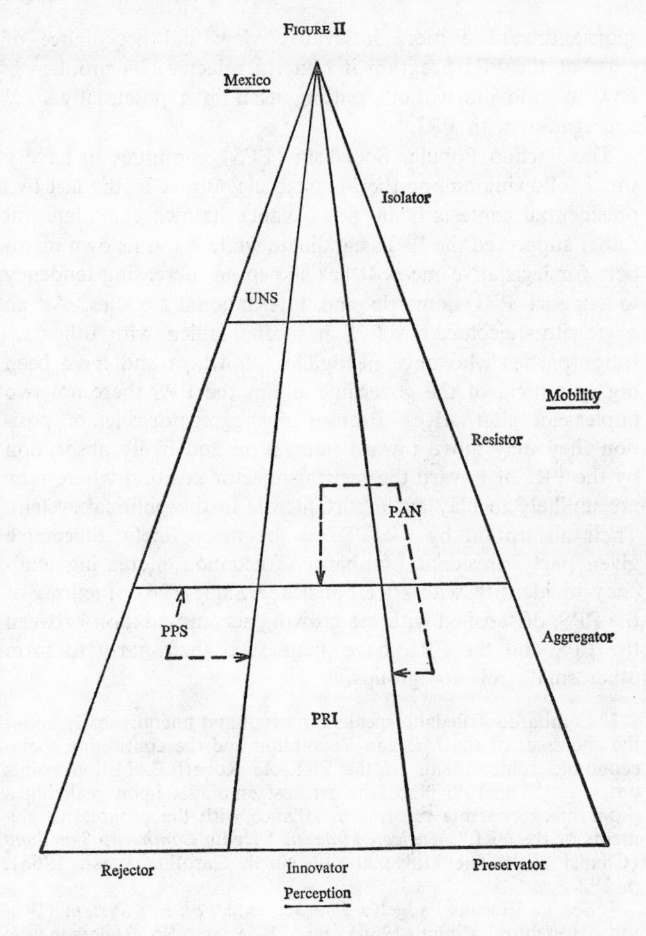

opposition and again will be susceptible to cries of "dictatorship."

Johnson affirms that PAN has already been partially co-opted into the Mexican single-party system and that the Unión Nacional Sinarquista (UNS) now serves as the principal catalyst for the articulation of alienated restorationist sentiment in Mexico.[14] PAN has shown of late a perception re-

[14] *Ibid.*, p. 661.

sponse toward a more innovative view and acceptance of parts of the PRI program it hitherto rejected. Its problem is how to innovate without putting itself in a potentially fatal aggregation with PRI.

The Partido Popular Socialista (PPS) continues to have a small following among the Mexican electorate. In the last two presidential contests it did not advance its own candidate but rather supported the PRI's candidate while it ran its own members for legislative races. It has shown an increasing tendency to support PRI domestic and international policies. As an aggregator-rejector, the PPS has often allied with other rejector parties who have negligible followings and have been highly critical of the government. For the PPS there are two unpleasant alternatives. From their aggregator-rejector position they may move toward innovation and likely absorption by the PRI or toward the resistor-rejector position where they are unlikely to play an important role in the political system. Their absorption by the PRI is the more likely alternative given party president Lombardo Toledano's increasing tendency to identify with PRI policies.[15] Since 1961, factions of the PPS, dissatisfied with the growing accommodation between the PPS and the PRI, have abandoned their party to form other small, rejector groups.[16]

[15] Lombardo Toledano speaks out often and unequivocally about the successes of the Mexican Revolution and the continuing socio-economic achievements of the PRI. As Robert P. Millon points out, . . . "The PPS places its greatest emphasis upon realizing a program of concrete reforms in alliance with the progressive elements of the PRI." *Mexican Marxist: Vicente Lombardo Toledano* (Chapel Hill: The University of North Carolina Press, 1966), p. 192.

[16] See L. Vincent Padgett's *The Mexican Political System* (Boston: Houghton Mifflin, 1966), pp. 75–78 and Bo Anderson and James D. Cockroft, "Control and Cooptation in Mexican Politics," *Journal of Comparative Sociology*, Vol. VII, No. 1–2 (March 1966), pp. 11–28. The latter study is particularly helpful for an analysis of the relationship of radical urban and rural groups (e.g., The MLN, The Movement of National Liberation, and the CCI, The Independent Peasants Association) to the PRI party. The leader of the MLN, Lázaro Cardenas, eventually supported Diaz Ordaz's candidacy in 1964. By making certain concessions to the CCI, the PRI leadership forced a split in the peasant movement. The core group returned to the PRI fold by mid-1965.

Venezuela

In Venezeuela the three major parties are aggregator-innovators. *Acción Democratica* (AD), *The Christian Democrats* (COPEI), and *Unión Republicana Democrática* (URD) all represent this mobility-perception orientation. All have been willing to aggregate in the recent past (1958). COPEI and AD continued in definite coalition until 1964. AD and URD renewed their erstwhile coalition (1958–1960) in 1964 which subsequently lasted until 1966. Both COPEI and URD have not only shown a predisposition to aggregate with AD but also to innovate their perceptions as well. This accord in political perceptions is attested by the fact that "all three of the principal parties expressed their interests in land reform, better housing, and more participation by Venezuela in the oil industry."[17] Furthermore, the major parties tend to act in coalition to defend the regime from extremist parties,[18] parties that we would classify as isolator-rejectors. Venezuela has effective government and loyal, effective opposition parties. Other parties (e.g., MIR, PCV) are isolator-rejectors within the political system and are far from power via what seems to be the normal mobility-perception route. The perception distinctions among the major three parties are so minimal that "a broad consensus in Venezuela has been formed on the major issues of the times, and the party system has provided both the leadership and personnel whereby problem areas have been confronted."[19]

In Venezuela democratic experience has been gained through coalition arrangements, both in the legislature and in the government. Coalition imposes upon the political parties greater awareness of the complexities of government and the responsibilities of opposition. COPEI and URD, both former

[17] Leo B. Lott, "Venezuela" in Martin Needler, *Political Systems of Latin America* (New Jersey: Van Nostrand, 1965), p. 251.

[18] Robert E. Scott, "Political Parties and Policy-Making in Latin America" in LaPalombara and Weiner, *Political Parties and Political Development,* p. 351.

[19] John D. Martz, "Political Parties in Colombia and Venezuela: Contrasts in Substance and Style," *The Western Political Quarterly,* Vol. 18, No. 2, Part I (June, 1965), p. 330.

FIGURE III

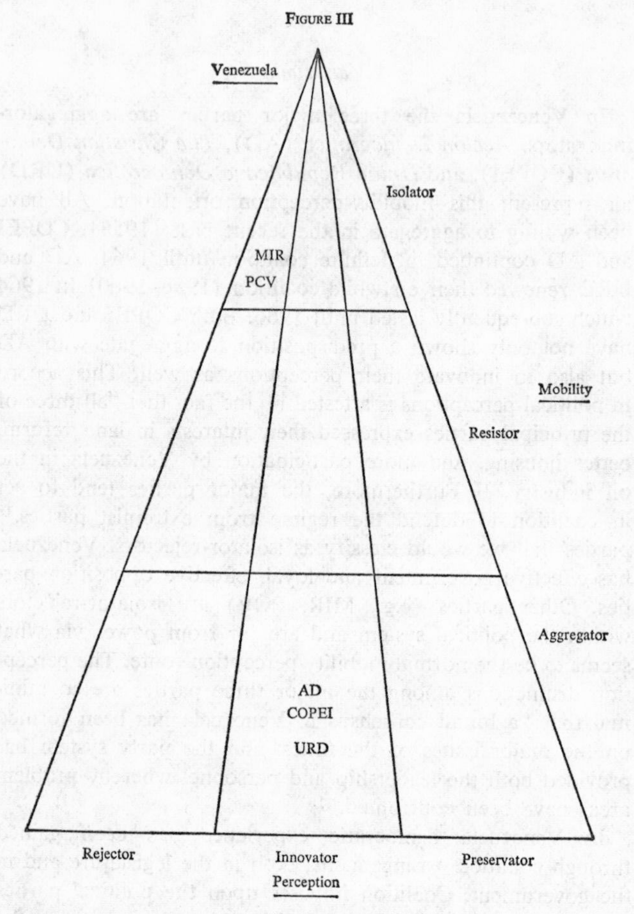

members of government coalitions, have benefited from their governmental apprenticeship and have gained a large measure of popular legitimacy.[20] The legitimization process aided in the development of responsible opposition positions. AD con-

[20] See John D. Martz, *Accion Democratica: Evolution of a Modern Political Party in Venezuela* (Princeton: Princeton University Press, 1966). See also Franklin Tugwell, "The Christian Democrats of Venezuela," *Journal of Inter-American Studies,* Vol. 7, No. 2 (April 1965), pp. 245–269.

sequently has had to make the kind of adjustments required of a dominant party which must face organized democratic opponents.[21]

Evidenced by the growth of political consensus and the mature aspects of its viable party system, Venezuela is developing a sound and stable political system. There is no indication that urban terrorism, or organized subversion and violence are causing either socio-economic disintegration or political decay.

Colombia

Colombia has imposed a two-party mechanism upon its political structure with its "paridad" formula by which the two principal parties share equal representation in the legislature while alternating in the presidential office. This has merely served to cover up the unrepresentative nature of the party system and the potential proliferation of political parties.

Both the parent Conservative and Liberal parties (disregarding the latter's MRL faction) are aggregator-preservator parties. There is much room for the development of an aggregator-innovator party or even a rejector party willing to aggregate. Because of the unresponsive nature of the preservator government, military forces or a "personalist" leader may find access to the control of government. Both the Conservatives and Liberals have, of course, shown a propensity to aggregate which has proven effective as a preservator combination, apparently because no real innovator party has appeared on the horizon. Here we have two preservators forming a coalition to ensure their joint power. However, this power is tenuous. These two parties off "in splendid isolation" may be carrying on an unreal dialogue between themselves. Both parties have a limited popular base, have homogeneous inbred support, and make no pretenses at forming really national or inter-party-based coalitions. Should they choose to form far-reaching, broadly-based political alliances, then they would of necessity begin to innovate, thus stabilizing the political system. The influence of the Movimiento Revolucion-

[21] Martz, *ibid.,* p. 379.

FIGURE IV

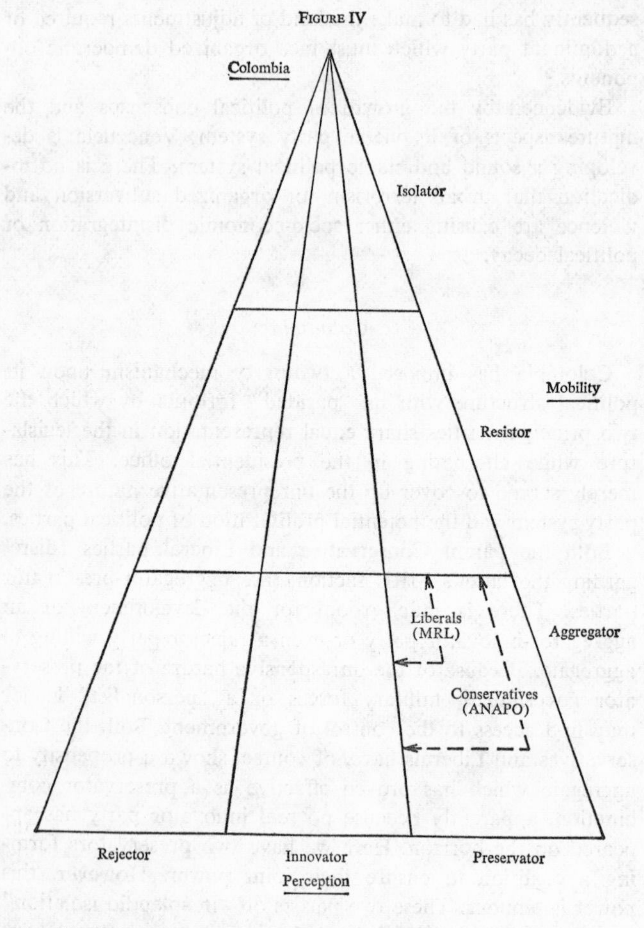

ario Liberal (MRL) faction of the Liberal party may act as a catalyst serving to move the Liberals toward an innovative position.

Within the Conservatives, a faction has been organized, the Alianza Nacional Popular (ANAPO), under the sponsorship of former dictator Rojas Pinilla. It is a loosely conceived grouping committed to the personal claims of Rojas. However, both the MRL and the ANAPO are further undermining the static basis of the Conservative-Liberal alliance. Regardless of any substantive contributions, these factions may thus help to shape Colombian party perceptions in the near future. As of the Congressional elections of 1966, the ANAPO has won one-third of all lower house seats allotted to the Conservatives (46%) and the MRL over one-fifth of the Liberal seats (54%).[22]

Apparently neither of the parent parties has mobilized broad sectors of the society and neither seems able or willing to give the populace a reasonable choice.[23] One can expect the coalition to break up given the need for one of the parties to take a more innovative position before popular discontent brings in the military or before a third party co-opts the aggregator-innovator role.[24]

Until such an "opening toward the center occurs," probably by the slightly more innovative-inclined Liberals, Colombia remains in the unique situation of having basic cooperation between two parent bodies while their own factions are pulling and tugging so that the parent parties can be pulled apart from a non-innovative aggregation. It is really a question of which party will make the innovative move toward ending a preservator political front.

Peru

Peru has recently seen the emergence of the Acción Popular (AP) as an aggregator-innovator party. Prior to the victory of AP candidate Belaúnde Terry in 1963, Peru had an unstable political system. The Prado government, represented by

[22] Ronald H. McDonald, "Electoral Systems, Party Representation, and Political Change in Latin America," *Western Political Quarterly*, Vol. 20, No. 3 (September 1967), p. 700.

[23] Ronald McDonald cites voter abstention figures for eligible voters of 59% for the most recent legislative election and 63% for the last presidential election. "Political Protest and Alienation in Voting: The Case of Colombia," *Inter-American Economic Affairs*, Vol. 21, No. 2 (Autumn 1967), p. 21.

[24] This view is supported by another recent study of the Colombian party system. Robert H. Dix, *Colombia: The Political Dimensions of Change* (New Haven: Yale University Press, 1967).

the Movimiento Democratico Peruano (MDP), was an aggregator-preservator. The Aprista Party (APRA), occasionally collaborating with the government, maintained an aggregator-rejector position. The aggregation between the MDP and the Apristas did not endure because neither party made lasting innovative concessions. This can probably be attributed to the fairly inflexible nature of President Prado and MDP's political perception, since it appeared that the Apristas, after years of unbending opposition, were ready to aggregate with a truly innovative political party.

The contemporary situation points to a rather stable political party system. The AP and the Christian Democrats have had a governing alliance with a growing predisposition to bring increasing numbers of Apristas into governmental posts. The Apristas, understandably cynical about the possibilities of gaining power on their own, have shown a predilection for collaborating with the governing AP.

The fourth important party, under the leadership of former dictator, Manuel Odría, the Unión Nacional Odriísta (UNO), is an aggregator-preservator. It has been allied with the Apristas since the election of Belaúnde Terry in 1963.[25] However, as the Apristas move toward closer ties with the AP and Christian Democrats, the Odriístas may be forced into a resistor-preservator position. Odriísta intransigence may be responsible for the fact that the post-1963 Aprista-Odriísta Alliance has not been based on a really conciliatory attitude. The Apristas are evolving toward an aggregator-innovator position.

> . . . Haya [de la Torre] (Aprista leader) in 1960 implied that new technological developments had given to the presently directing classes of Peru the necessary means to bring about the redemption of the country. He no longer saw the need for a social revolution, provided the influential classes would take advantage of what could be learned in other sections of the world. . . .

In regard to the means for bringing about social better-

[25] Belaúnde himself is a former member of the Aprista movement.

FIGURE V

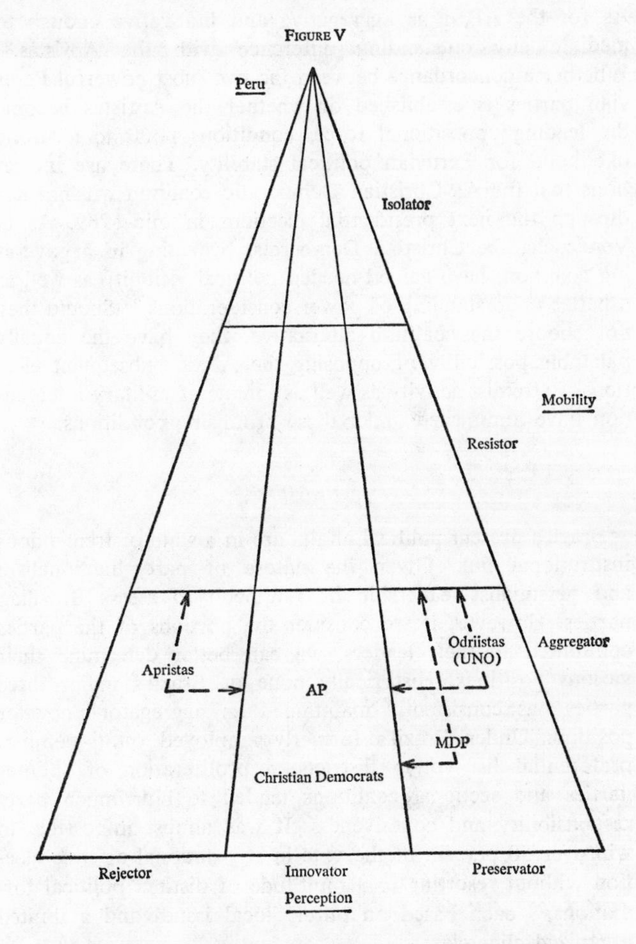

ment, the new APRA has rejected experimenting with innovations aimed at the immediate redistribution of wealth and instead seeks to strengthen the processes that have been tried and found effective in generating capital. . . .[26]

[26] Frederick B. Pike, "The Old and the New APRA in Peru: Myth and Reality," *Inter-American Economic Affairs,* Vol. 18, No. 2 (Autumn, 1964), pp. 30–45.

As for the AP, it is aggregative and innovative enough to mediate any outstanding difference with the Apristas.[27] Whether a concordance between the two most powerful Peruvian parties is established or whether the Apristas become the leading oppositional force, conditions point to a strong likelihood for Peruvian political stability. There are indications that the AP-Christian Democratic coalition will not last through the next presidential elections in mid-1969. As in Venezuela, the Christian Democrats, by acting in a governing coalition, have gained needed political visibility as well as a better understanding of power considerations.[28] Should they not choose the coalition alternative, they have the equally palatable possibility of opposing the AP in subsequent elections. Extremist activity as well as threats of military intervention have diminished under these promising conditions.

Brazil

Brazil's present political affairs are in a state of tremendous institutional flux. Given the nature of party factionalism and personalist leadership it is difficult to assess Brazilian parties. However, if we consider the portions of the parties committed to their leaders, we can better determine their various positions. Historically none of Brazil's major three parties has consistently maintained an aggregator-innovator position. Under Brazil's formerly employed multi-member, preferential list voting districts, a proliferation of splinter parties and sectional coalitions tended to blur much party responsibility and cohesiveness. It was almost impossible to win over 50 percent of the vote in any national or state election without resorting to a multitude of distinct political formations,[29] each based on purely local issues and a limited organized clientele.

[27] This was brought out by Belaúnde's top-level meeting with both Haya de la Torre and Manuel Odria to discuss Peru's inflationary spiral and lagging exports in the Fall of 1967.

[28] See the assessment of the Peruvian Christian Democrats in Edward J. Williams, *Latin American Christian Democratic Parties* (Knoxville: University of Tennessee Press, 1967), pp. 209–214.

[29] Phyllis Peterson, "Brazil: Institutionalized Confusion" in Martin Needler (ed.), *Political Systems of Latin America,* p. 483.

FIGURE VI

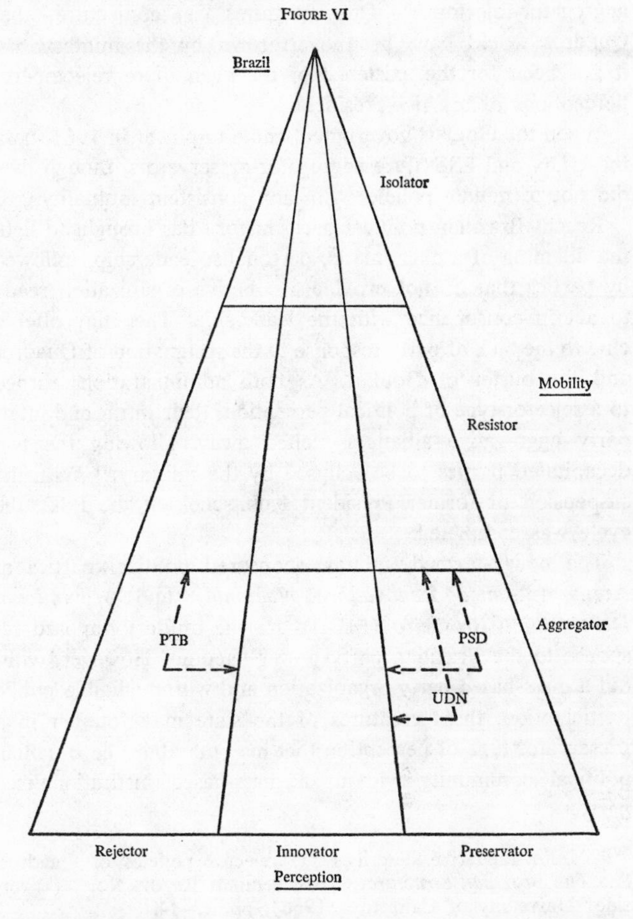

The Kubitschek *Partido Social Democratico* (PSD) government was essentially aggregative-innovative, allying both electorally and administratively with the *Partido Trabalhista Brasileiro* (PTB), from whose ranks Vice President João Goulart arose. However, both the *Uniāo Democratica Nacional* (UDN) personalist government of Jañio Quadros and Goulart's PTB administration after Quadros' resignation, though each began as an aggregator-innovator, became aggregator-rejectors.[30] One ventures a conjecture that Quadros would have been overthrown by the military had it not been for the existence of the even more rejector-like perceptions of his vice-president.

When the Goulart government came to power in 1961, both the UDN and PSD were aggregator-preservators, though they did not formulate policies with any consistent mutuality.

Recent Brazilian political party history has brought to light the dilemma of a charismatic, personalist leadership, followed by parties that do not provide a cohesive organization ready to act in consonance with the leadership. This may offer a clue to the lack of party response to the resignation of Quadros and the ouster of Goulart. As both administrations turned to a rejector-type of political perception, their intra- and inter-party aggregative alliances melted away, allowing the two decapitated parties to be eclipsed by the military.[31] With the suspension of former President Kubitschek of the PSD, the cycle was completed.

The newly-formed, military-sponsored political parties of Arena (*Aliança Renovadora Nacional*) and *Movimiento Democrático Brasileiro* (MDB) are the military-imposed response to the Brazilian party power vacuum. However, without a mass-based party organization and with negligible public participation, these creatures of the state may founder in a preservator-type of perception that may maintain the Brazilian political community without a mass-based institutionalized party.

[30] Hélio Jaguaribe describes the rejector policies of Quadros. See *The Brazilian Structural Crisis,* Seminar Report No. 1 (Riverside: University of California, 1966), pp. 12–14.

[31] "The ideological confrontation of Left-wing and Right-wing blocks, expressing the radical polarization of the big cities, powerfully contributed to the sliding of the Goulart government from its initial (and viable) Center-left position to its later (and non-viable) Radical-left posture. This confrontation also exerted a similar effect on the army, as the most representative and effective political agent of the middle class." Helio Jaguaribe, *Political Strategies of National Development in Brazil,* Studies in Comparative International Development, Vol. III, No. 2, 1967–8 (St. Louis: Washington University Social Science Institute), p. 40.

Chile

The Christian Democrats of Chile are an aggregator-innovator party, with a solidly-based mass support and a politically dominant position at the center of Chile's party politics. They have moved toward the center of the political spectrum for a decade and now appear to be firmly en-

FIGURE VII

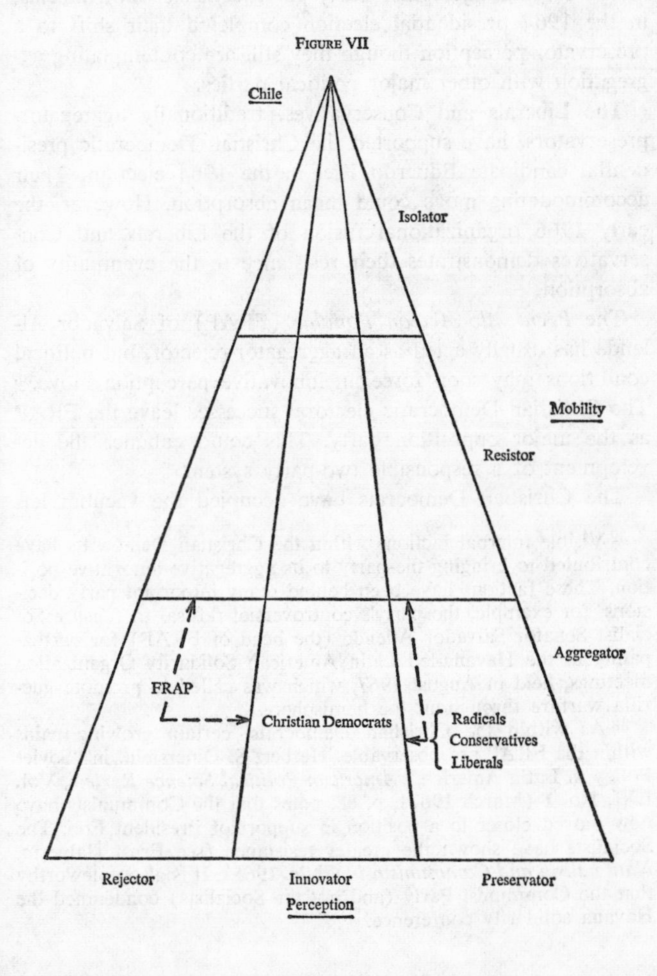

trenched, at least as much so as the aggregator-innovator Acción Democratica of Venezuela and the Acción Popular of Peru. The Christian Democrats moved from resistor-preservator in the mid-1950's to a resistor-innovator position under the Alessandri administration. By 1964 they had evolved toward an aggregator-innovator position from whence they made their successful bid for power.[32]

The original aggregator party *par excellence*, the Radicals, in the 1964 presidential election completed their shift to a preservator perception though they still are contemplating aggregation with other major political parties.

The Liberals and Conservatives, traditionally aggregator-preservators, have supported the Christian Democratic presidential candidate Eduardo Frei in the 1964 election. Their accommodating move could mean absorption. However, the early 1966 organizational fusion of the Liberals and Conservatives demonstrates their resistance to the eventuality of absorption.

The *Frente de Acción Popular* (FRAP) of Salvador Allende has usually acted as an aggregator-rejector, but political conditions may soon force an innovative perception move.[33] The Christian Democratic electoral successes leave the FRAP as the major opposition party. This could enhance the development of a responsible two-party system.

The Christian Democrats have occupied the vacuum left

[32] Visible internal factions within the Christian Democrats have contributed to bringing the party to its aggregative-innovative position. These factions have been behind many important party decisions, for example, the party's controversial refusal to censure Socialist Senator Salvador Allende (the head of FRAP) for participating in the Havana-led Latin American Solidarity Organization meetings, held in August 1967, which was called to promote guerilla warfare throughout the hemisphere.

[33] As within the Christian Democrats, certain growing pains within the FRAP are observable. Herbert S. Dinerstein, in "Soviet Policy in Latin America," *American Political Science Review*, Vol. LXI, No. 1 (March 1967), p. 88, notes that the Communists have now moved closer to a position in support of President Frei. The Socialists have shown the greater resistance (see Ernst Halperin, *Nationalism and Communism in Chile*, 1965). It is also noteworthy that the Communist Party (and not the Socialists) condemned the Havana solidarity conference.

by Radical and FRAP lack of innovation. As Federico Gil and Charles Parrish have said: "The roots of this decline of the Radical Party lie in the 14-year period between 1938–1952, when the party held the presidency. Lack of effectiveness in dealing with the accelerating inflation . . . greatly reduced the party's popularity. . . ."[34]

The Radicals have aggregated easily but have found it difficult to maintain their original policy of innovation initiated with Socialists and Communists in 1937. The three-way aggregator-preservator alliance among the Radicals, Liberals, and Conservatives (Frente Democrático) of 1961[35] again diverted Radicalism from any innovative perception it may have contemplated and left the Christian Democrats a free field as an innovative party mobilizing toward aggregation.

A crucial demonstration of the innovative perception by the Christian Democrats became evident after the Radicals had demonstrated their weakened electoral strength in important local elections in March, 1964, the year of the presidential elections:

> It is possible, however, to discern a shift in propaganda by the Christian Democrats after the Curico election, when they recognized the dilemma of the Right; they became more outspokenly anti-Communist. In a meeting of the major Christian Democratic leaders at Millahue in the middle of April; a general policy declaration was adopted which maintained the reformist attitude of the party but also averred that now only two roads presented themselves to Chile: that of Allende, which is to Communism, and that of Frei, which is to liberty. . . . Liberal and Conservative party reacted favorably to the statement. *Shortly*

[34] Federico G. Gil and Charles J. Parrish, *The Chilean Presidential Election of September 4, 1964: An Analysis* (Washington, D.C.: Institute for The Comparative Study of Political Systems, 1965), p. 19. Anibal Pinto states that the Radical Party refused to consider important fiscal and land reforms in the post-war period and became more and more the prisoner of its traditional wing and its commitment to the largest landowners. This eventually undermined the Popular Front. *Chile: Una Economia Difícil* (Mexico: Fondo de Cultura Económica, 1964), pp. 172–177.

[35] Gil and Parrish, p. 19.

thereafter the leaders of the three parties held a series of meetings, as a result of which both the Liberal and Conservative parties gave their official support to Frei.[36] [Emphasis mine.]

In the post-1966 period, all the major parties have been attempting to readjust policies and assuage internal dissatisfactions. The fluidity and flexibility of the Chilean party system has never been more apparent. Indeed a formidable alliance may be developing to challenge the aggregator-innovator position of the Christian Democrats. Despite occasional interparty difficulties, the Socialists and Communists will probably continue to aggregate. FRAP, under moderate Communist or Socialist leadership, is consciously attempting to innovate its perceptions. The Radical Party, despite its aggregative tradition,[37] still retains a preservator mentality that appears likely to restrict it in any long term innovative alliance whether with the government or rejector groups.

Argentina

The People's Radicals (UCRP) of Argentina were a minority governing party before the military intervened in June 1966. The main concern of the UCRP was to develop a working majority party. The UCRP faced the dilemma of either aggregating, something which has been traditionally distasteful to them, or facing political eclipse at the hands of the Peronistas who were split momentarily between factions favoring innovation and others supporting rejection. Events since the March 1965 election indicated that the Peronistas as a massive, consolidated bloc were more likely to innovate than the resistor-conscious UCRP were apt to aggregate.

The Peronista Intransigent Radicals (UCRI) and other smaller parties alliance in 1958 and the Christian Democratic

[36] *Ibid.*, p. 36.

[37] Michael Francis and Eldon Lanning see the Radical Party as having enough flexibility to coalesce with the FRAP in order to challenge the Christian Democrats in the 1970 presidential elections. "Chile's 1967 Municipal Elections," *Inter-American Economic Affairs,* Vol. 21, No. 2 (Autumn 1967), p. 36.

and other smaller parties alliance of 1963 have amply demonstrated the Peronista propensity toward aggregation. The Peronistas had moved toward aggregation and were innovating toward respectability and thereby the possible assumption of power. A certain amount of Peronista innovation was already apparent in Peronista moderation both before and after their March 1965 Congressional victory. Peronistas, as in the past, were receiving support and aggregative feelers from the UCRI,

FIGURE VIII

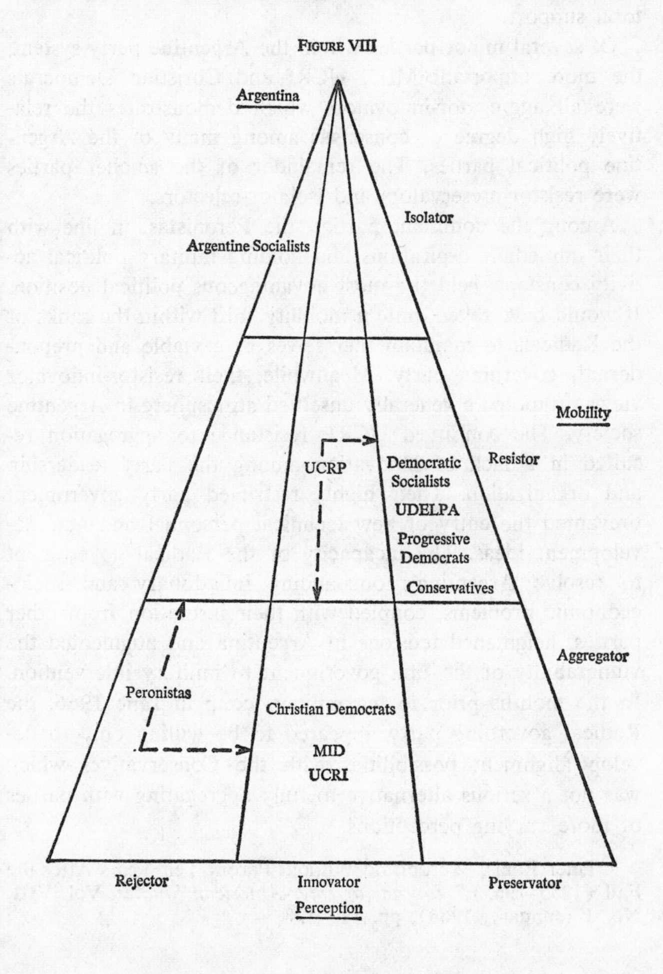

Movimiento de Integración y Desarrollo (MID) of Arturo Frondizi and the Christian Democrats.[38]

The governing Radicals hitherto had been unable to aggregate, though apparently a party struggle over this issue was about to commence before the 1966 military coup. The Radicals found themselves more and more isolated in their resistance and forced to aggregate with the Conservative Party, a resistor-preservator party, in order to broaden their electoral support.

Of several minor parties within the Argentine party system, the more important MID, UCRI and Christian Democrats were all aggregator-innovators which demonstrates the relatively high degree of consensus among many of the Argentine political parties. The remainder of the smaller parties were resistor-preservators and isolator-rejectors.

Among the dominant parties, the Peronistas, in line with their immediate aspirations and holding military political activity constant, held the most advantageous political position. It would have taken quite a mobility shift within the ranks of the Radicals to maintain themselves as a viable and preponderant, governing party. Meanwhile, their resistor-innovator views promoted a generally unsettled atmosphere in Argentine society. The continued UCRP resistance to aggregation resulted in a lack of innovation among the party leadership and organization. Their highly restricted party government prevented the entry of new technical personnel and new development ideas. The incapacity of the Radical government to resolve Argentina's outstanding inflationary and socio-economic problems, coupled with their insulation from other parties, heightened tensions in Argentina and augmented the vulnerability of the Illia government to military intervention. In the months prior to the military coup in June 1966, the Radical governing party appeared to be willing only to develop alignment possibilities with the Conservatives which was not a serious alternative to fully aggregating with parties of more varying perceptions.

[38] Peter Ranis, "Peronismo Without Perón: Ten Years After the Fall (1955–1965)," *Journal of Inter-American Studies*, Vol. VIII, No. 1 (January, 1966), pp. 112–128.

Summary

We have been attempting to describe political parties in Latin America by means of a two-dimensional typology based on party mobility and party perception. The typology has been applied to political systems in flux. The aggregator-innovator position seems to represent the large, basically unvarying field of power. It is as if there were a continual gravitational attraction emanating from this political power center which accounts for party coalitions as parties vie for power within a multi-partism situation.

Parties give indication of moving toward the center as they seek to approach political influence and enjoy greater expectation of being awarded power. The more influential parties tend not to be narrowly based, ideology appears to be playing an ever-declining role, and parties are sharply aware of the political facts of life.[39] Furthermore, an increasing number of sectors of the political community are becoming less and less tolerant of any sort of "ideological flamboyancy."[40]

Because of the flux of Latin American party systems, the direction in which parties move vis-à-vis other parties bears particular observation. Ideological classifications are not true indicators of the ability of a party to compromise. Some examples are in order: in Argentina the Peronistas were willing to compromise and the Socialists were not, yet within ideological typologies both might be lumped as leftists. In Chile the FRAP is defined as "left wing," yet it is moving toward innovation—an ingredient much less visible under an ideological categorization. In Peru, the Apristas are momentarily undergoing

[39] Our country examples may put in question Lipset's estimation about the importance of ideology in developing countries. See Seymour M. Lipset, *Political Man: The Social Basis of Politics* (New York: Doubleday, 1960), pp. 454–456. Nor is it certain that the LaPalombara-Weiner theory of narrowly-based, highly ideological parties, not easily inclined to the give and take of political interaction, holds true in many Latin American countries. See LaPalombara and Weiner, *op. cit.*

[40] Charles W. Anderson, "Central American Political Parties: A Functional Approach," *Western Political Quarterly*, Vol. 15, No. 1 (March, 1962), p. 136.

doctrinal change. Thus, an understanding of where the party has been and where it is going is needed. It is necessary to distinguish among parties hitherto often banded together because of a similar "ideology."

What has been discussed here is the degree to which certain parties are able to reject ideological rigidity, thereby gaining greater mobility and interaction with other parties. Said another way, the more strongly the "nondoctrinal element"[41] in the party emerges to the forefront, the greater is the possibility that the party will be able to aggregate and innovate. Views that the modern type of "integrating party" is rare within Latin American party systems seem overly pessimistic.[42]

All types of parties want to win votes and thus all act, to a degree, pragmatically in appealing to the voters. However, the acid test of true pragmatism is a willingness to aggregate with ideologically distinct parties, thereby giving up some of their own doctrinal concepts. Blanksten speaks of two types of pragmatic parties–narrowly-based and broadly-based.[43] With this two-dimensional typology the narrowness or broadness of a party is a function of whether they are truly aggregative and innovative. If a party is just personalistic or develops a following on just one issue, then that party undoubtedly will not withstand the test of time that a truly aggregative-innovative party will.

In the application of this typology of parties, we note the following political characteristics: first, there is nothing *de facto* in a multi-partism situation that will prevent party coalitions or even rule out the eventual formation of a bipartism party system.[44] Second, party perceptions are both a sub-

[41] Neil A. McDonald, *The Study of Political Parties* (New York: Random House, 1955), p. 32.

[42] Scott, for instance, lists two examples. PRI and Uruguay's Colorados and Blancos. See Scott, *op. cit.* p. 336. One could add to his list such parties as the various Christian Democratic parties of Chile, Venezuela and Peru, the Acción Democratica of Venezuela, the Acción Popular and Apristas of Peru, the Peronistas and MID of Argentina, and more.

[43] George Blanksten, "Politics of Latin America," in Almond and Coleman, *op. cit.*, pp. 482–483.

[44] One of Duverger's key exceptions to his general rule is that multi-party systems do not preclude the development of one or two-

stantial basis for party action and tools toward gaining governmental control. This is the case in Latin America as elsewhere in politicized national communities.[45] Third, in a multiparty system, there is usually a necessity to coalesce or ally with other parties either before or after elections. With electoral victory as a rational party goal, electoral coalitions present a flexible and normal mechanism for its achievement.[46] There a meaningful correlation between the propinquity to political power and the propensity to form alliances and coalitions. Fourth, the process of aggregating and innovating serves the double stabilizing function of either providing a second innovating party that will loyally oppose a similar party or of absorbing smaller aggregating parties which do not have a sufficiently identifiable policy or have too small a popular base of support.

From our triangular diagrams, we can conceivably calculate the relative strength and weaknesses of a given political system. It could be determined which parties are far from power and which potentially close. The diagram might indicate the degree of consensus present which, in turn, may offer a clue to potential political stability. All nine boxes could logically be filled with the type of party that would fit that mobility-perception category. Thus a corresponding number of boxes could be filled in for any political party eventuality. It might then be possible to predict party changes within a political system and perhaps anticipate any broad recasting of the political scene.

This two-dimensional typology has been devised in order to

---

party dominance and the possible stabilization implied in such a political system. Duverger, *op. cit.*, pp. 314–315.

[45] In *An Economic Theory of Democracy* (New York: Harper and Row, 1957), Anthony Downs hypothesizes that political parties are interested in gaining office per se, not in promoting a better or ideal society. These parties employ varying ideologies in order to maximize their vote potential. Dr. Downs, agreeing with Neil McDonald, explains that the attempt within parties to "modernize" will cause a conflict between those adherents to former ideological dictates and those members whose prime concern is to win elections. See pp. 96–113.

[46] William Riker spells this out in detail in his stimulating treatise on political coalitions, *The Theory of Political Coalitions* (New Haven: Yale University Press, 1962), pp. 21, 184–186.

complement other approaches to the study of parties in the political process. It has attempted to formulate a scheme readily applicable to cross-national research in the developing countries. This method of viewing political parties has not been directly concerned with a party's organization, its leadership, or the degree of its grass-roots support. Rather it has been assumed that the more institutionalized, the broader-based parties will gradually come from the aggregator-innovator categories. It is parties with these mobility-perception attitudes that are likely to attain longevity and gain or retain popular-mass support via organized interest groups and the general participating electorate.

REVOLUTIONS AND VIOLENCE

The topic of revolutions and violence in internal politics has been of interest to more and more scholars in recent years. The subject is no longer restricted merely to the politics of underdeveloped countries. Moreover, violence and revolutions are no longer looked upon as aberrations of many political systems but rather as a basic attribute of their functioning. This would be especially true of Latin American politics, where revolutions and violence seem to be endemic. In Latin America one is able to find both revolutionary and violent patterns common to almost all of the countries, and unique varieties pertaining to merely one country. The two selections that follow have been chosen to illustrate both facets—the regular patterns, and the unique variety that can be seen from the description of rural violence in Colombia.

In the first selection, the late William S. Stokes, previously Professor of Political Science at the Claremont Men's College, describes the way governments are overturned and violence carried out in Latin America through *machetismo, cuartelazos, golpes de estado,* and mass revolutions. His typology developed in 1952 still has use for classifying overthrows today and for understanding the strategy behind each technique. Professor Stokes also skillfully explains the peaceful methods of *imposición, candidato único,* and *continuismo* by which leaders are able to hold on to power.

In the second selection Richard S. Weinert, Professor of Public Law and Government at Columbia University, attempts to explain the causes that he believes have brought about extended rural violence in Colombia. The immensity and uniqueness of rural violence in Colombia has led many scholars to study the phenomenon, resulting in a bewildering number of conflicting interpretations. Thus Professor Weinert not only elaborates on causes he believes to be instrumental but also discards theories he finds inapplicable. He does recognize that the types and causes of violence changed according to different postwar political periods in the country.

*Violence as a Power Factor in Latin American Politics**

WILLIAM S. STOKES

Introduction

Violence seems to be institutionalized in the organization, maintenance, and changing of governments in Latin America. The methodology of force is found in advanced and in backward countries, in Indian, *mestizo,* and white republics, in the large states and in the small ones, in urban and in rural areas, in agricultural and in industrial organization, in the beginning of the twentieth century, in the present period, and in the early, middle, and late nineteenth century–in a word, wherever and whenever Hispanic culture is to be found in the Western Hemisphere.

Force is a unifying factor in Latin-American political culture, yet the fact of geographical and ethnic differences and of varying rates of social and economic development leads to the logical inference that the mobilization of violence for political purposes is not likely to revolve around one simple formula. This is, however, exactly what is done when the general term "revolution" is employed to describe all use of force in Latin-American politics. Violence is, instead, a highly developed technique for obtaining power. Direct action procedures include *machetismo, cuartelazo, golpe de estado,* and revolution. The monopolization of the power factors of the state by a single political leader, a group, or a class sometimes renders unnecessary the direct employment of violence,

* Reprinted from William S. Stokes, "Violence as a Power Factor in Latin American Politics," *Western Political Quarterly* (September, 1952), pp. 445–69. Reprinted by permission of the University of Utah, copyright owner.

and in such cases the methods of *imposición, candidato único, continuismo* and election (in the Anglo-American sense) may be selected. These are, of course, outwardly peaceful methods of obtaining and maintaining power, but they rest upon a foundation of force.

"*Machetismo*"

Machetismo is a crude, primitive method of mobilizing violence primarily in local, rural politics but occasionally in national, urban areas as well. The term emanates from the word "machete," the general utility knife employed widely throughout Latin America. In an extractive, agricultural economy guaranteeing little more than subsistence to the majority of the people, poverty is seldom or ever so great as to deny the rural resident his machete. It is a major implement in the construction of habitation, the production of foodstuffs, and in the establishment of political power. To survive, the rural inhabitant must develop proficiency in its use, and the process of becoming expert begins as a child. Whoever can command the authority represented by the machete in rural areas possesses political power of an important nature and automatically constitutes a factor to be reckoned with in the affairs of government.

If it could be demonstrated that no political leader has exercised sufficient discipline over the rural masses to employ their collective strength in direct action, then it might be possible to argue that *machetismo* no longer characterizes Latin-American rural politics. However, leadership of a highly personal nature can readily be observed in Latin America. The matters that vitally concern the rural resident include distribution of government patronage, rights to water holes and grazing areas, military service to the central government, road building in lieu of payment of taxes, and adjudication of social disputes. In many instances, the leader who exercises authority and issues judgments on such issues is the *alcalde, jefe de operaciones militares, comandante de armas,* or official in the church hierarchy. But on the other hand the political leader might very well possess no official position at all. That his power exists there is no denying; his authority is so well known that almost anyone in the area of his jurisdiction can identify him as *el que manda* (the one who commands). This kind of absolutist personal leadership is local, rural *caudillismo.*

Many writers, Latin Americans included, have associated *caudillismo* with the violent struggle for leadership among the generals in the early independence period, and hence terms such as the "Age of the *Caudillos,*" and "Men on Horseback" are common in historical literature. It is correct to define *caudillismo* as a principle of personal leadership in politics, but it cannot be restricted to any one age or period in Latin-American history. Indeed, its origins are to be traced in part at least to the feudal institutions of Spain and Portugal and to the nature of government in the colonial period. *Caudillismo* as personal authority, as a substitute for direction and control by institutional means, such as law, is to be found in all periods of Latin-American development, including the present. Nor is it accurate to think of the *caudillo* solely as a man on horseback, for he may be a civilian, such as Carlos Antonio López of Paraguay, García Moreno of Ecuador, Estrada Cabrera of Guatemala, and Fulgencio Batista of Cuba (who although a sergeant in the army did not even learn to ride a horse until after he had first achieved power!).

The determinants of leadership in Latin-American politics have never been investigated with sufficient objectivity and scholarship to permit definitive generalizations. How are personal qualities, education and professional training, religious and other social beliefs, location in a rural or urban area, and affiliation with organizations and institutions related to the development of leadership? We do not know. In my own field experience I have known *caudillos* who fitted various physical and psychological patterns. The *caudillo* exists, however, and exercises an almost omnipotent personal authority in his designated area, an authority his people will respect without question to the point of enforcement on the field of battle. He is in his own person law, constitution, party, flag, and political principle.

Although Latin-American rural communities are frequently isolated by poor communication facilities, the local *caudillos* are thrown into contact from time to time (to divide the spoils of government, for example), and occasionally, in activities such as drinking, card playing, carousing, and brawling a man so stands out that the others automatically accept his authority and extend to him their loyalty. When this occurs for an area as large as a province or a department, institutional means for resolving major issues of public controversy have been created which frequently may be entirely disassociated from the formal structure of government. The sectional *caudillos* are usually the group from which "available" presidential candidates are to be found. When a sectional leader commands the loyalty of all other major *caudillos* in the country, then a *jefe máximo* (or *caudillo supremo*) is recognized, and if he wants the presidency he will have it; he assuredly will determine who *will* have it. This procedure for the establishment of executive power is one that is essentially based upon violence, because any leader at any time may challenge the hierarchy of power, with immediate local, sectional, or national conflict resulting. Indeed, case studies of *machetismo* can be discovered somewhere in Latin America at all times, although most frequently in the local areas.

Widespread evidence of *machetismo* at the national level can still be observed among backward and advanced countries alike from time to time. Thus, for about half of the year 1947 Paraguay was in what news dispatches termed "civil war," and ever since April, 1948, Colombia has been in a state of violence that includes geographically almost the entire country. When no one *caudillo* can peacefully subjugate existing opposition, when one or more challenges claim to "supreme power," *machetismo* becomes a costly and time-consuming methodology for establishing authority. Among seventy nation-wide examples of *machetismo* in Colombia in the nineteenth century, one conflict alone took approximately 80,000 lives, and the struggle which covered the years 1899 to 1903 took about 100,000 lives.

Local and regional violence which produced national leadership in the persons of *caudillos* in the nineteenth century has been given ample account by historians,[1] but there have

[1] José E. Iturriaga, *El Tirano en la América Latina* (Mexico: Jornadas 15, Fondo de Cultura Económica, n.d.); Lucás Ayar-

been a large number of national *caudillos* in the twentieth century as well, although not all obtained power directly through *machetismo*. Some of these, with dates indicating periods of formal or informal dominance, usually as president, include: Getulio Vargas of Brazil; Juan Domingo Perón of Argentina; Arturo Alessandri of Chile, 1921–24, 1925, 1932–38; Carlos Ibáñez of Chile, 1925, 1927–31; Augusto Leguía of Peru, 1908–12, 1919–30; Oscar Benavides of Peru, 1933–39; Juan Vicente Gómez of Venezuela, 1908–35; Eloy Alfaro of Ecuador, 1895–1901, 1907–11; Germán Busch of Bolivia, 1938–39 (who committed suicide or was murdered in the latter year); Higinio Morínigo of Paraguay, 1940–48; Plutarco Elías Calles of Mexico, 1925–34; Manuel Estrada Cabrera of Guatemala, 1898–1920; Jorge Ubico of Guatemala, 1931–44; Maximiliano Martínez of El Salvador, 1931–44; Tiburcio Carías Andino of Honduras, 1933–49; Anastasio Somoza of Nicaragua; Gerardo Machado of Cuba, 1925–33; Fulgencio Batista of Cuba; Rafael Trujillo of the Dominican Republic. Federico Tinoco of Costa Rica (1917–19) and Gabriel Terra of Uruguay (1931–38) might well be included in the list. *Caudillos* from Colombia are not represented. Except for a brief period of coalition government, however, the Conservatives shifted power among themselves for fifty years (up to 1930), although not without a great deal of violence.[2]

The *caudillo supremo* produced by *machetismo* may govern by means of harsh measures including *estado de sitio* (state of siege), but on the other hand, his stature may be such that no challenges of importance may be directed against him, and he might well become *un presidente simpático*. In

---

ragaray, *La anarquía argentina y el caudillismo* (3d ed.; Buenos Aires: Talleres gráficos argentinos de L. J. Rosso, 1945); Alcides Arguedas, *Los caudillos bárbaros* (Barcelona: Viuda de L. Tasso, 1929); Carlos Octavio Bunge, *Nuestra América* (6th ed.; Buenos Aires: Vaccaro, 1918); *see also* the works of A. Curtis Wilgus, Charles E. Chapman, W. S. Robertson, J. Fred Rippy, H. G. James, P. A. Martin and others.

[2] Former President Alfonso López represents the attitude of the Liberal Party in respect to the methods employed by the Conservative Party in maintaining itself in power over this period. República de Colombia, *Documentos relacionados con la renuncia del señor Presidente de la República* (Bogotá: Imprenta Nacional, 1937), pp. 29–30.

any event, it is doubtful that a *caudillo* can long maintain himself in power, no matter how mechanized and up-to-date his military and police systems, unless he has a large body of popular support (*tiene gente*). Detailed analysis of the politics of the republic of Honduras convinced me that the major reason the Liberals of that country were not a force in government in the period 1933–49 was that they lacked the kind of leadership required to capture support. They simply did not have a national *caudillo*.[3] The defection of the Liberal party in Colombia in recent years with such tragic consequences lies primarily in divided leadership, with no one man sufficiently strong to command. For the *caudillo* is, above all else, a man who can command (he is *muy hombre,* or *un presidente macho,* literally, a stallion president). In his Labor Day speech of May 1, 1944, General Perón declared: "I believe that programs, as revolutions, should not be announced, but simply carried out."[4] What a magnificent exemplification of authoritarianism! The *caudillo* thinks and acts in terms of absolutes, and in active politics "for" or "against" are sole choices. In the language of speeches, and in day-to-day communication words like "inflexibly," "inexorably," "unchangeable," or "instantly" appear frequently. The president refers to his "supreme power"; he is not merely president but *el Presidente Constitucional;* all the symbols of power and status he puts forth openly; if he has a Ph.D. degree he is "doctor"; and if he is a general as well, he will be *El Presidente Constitucional de la Republica de . . . el doctor y general. . . .* The *caudillo* meets situations with lordly equanimity; he can't be an ordinary president; he heads a "Restoration Movement" (for example, General Odría of Peru, 1950); he is a regenerator, *benemérito,* restorer, defender of the constitution, pacificator. Government by *caudillo* tends to be authoritarian, intolerant (law of *desacato* of Argentina), personal ("my government," "my administration," "my people," nepotism, graft), antiscientific, and vio-

[3] William S. Stokes, *Honduras, An Area Study in Government* (Madison: University of Wisconsin Press, 1950), pp. 206–64.

[4] Republic of Argentina, *Argentina News,* April, May, 1944, Ministry for Foreign Affairs and Worship, Department of Information for Abroad, p. 8.

lent. But it should also be pointed out that in most instances it probably tends also to be representative of majority opinion.

"Cuartelazo"

Cuartelazo (sometimes called *sargentada* or *golpe de cuartel*), a more highly developed, complex method of organizing and changing governments than *machetismo,* has its focus in the barracks (cuartel). Its classic pattern is the treason of a single barracks, the *pronunciamiento, manifiesto* or *grito,* the march on centers of communication, sites of military supplies, the exchequer, government headquarters, and ultimately the capital itself, the announcement to the populace that the government has changed hands, and finally the appointment of a patriotic *junta* to guide the country in the interim period. Even the most cursory examination of illustrative *cuartelazos* reveals that it is a mistake to think of the technique as involving massive, overpowering military force repressing the legitimate desires of the people. To be successful the *cuartelazo* requires consummate skill in the selection of leadership, the drafting of a program, the equating of the power factors, the technical problems of logistics, and the drafting of at least a temporary series of policies to meet the most pressing problems of government when power is obtained. He who would play barracks politics must know his fellow officers and men well indeed to suggest that they follow his leadership in a calculated plan of treason. Betrayal by a single officer or soldier means at least ignominious failure in the venture and possibly death by firing squad.

The *cuartelazo's* success depends upon capturing the support of other centers of military power as well as that of public opinion. This is a problem which effectively deters all but the most well prepared politician. Many Latin-American armies, particularly those in the South American area, have been trained by German technicians, whereas the navies have been trained or inspired by the British. In the century of air power, the plane must be considered, and as a competing unit with the older vested interests in the area of defense, it can constitute a delicate source to be placated. Even assuming that a barracks has been captured and that it is able to obtain sufficient support from other segments of the armed forces to justify some optimism for success, what about the civilian *caudillos* in both the rural and urban areas? As has already been demonstrated, they also command power in politics, including from time to time the authority to plunge an entire country into civil war. Thus, it usually develops that the successful *cuartelazo* involves substantial support from the sectional leaders, the leading university and professional men, and the leaders of several of the principal political parties in the country.

When the politics of the *cuartelazo* have been organized with skill, the change in governments is likely to occur with a minimum loss of life or property. Excellent illustrations of well-planned and maturely executed *cuartelazos* include those of Argentina in 1930 and 1943. General José F. Uriburu combined a section of the army with strong civilian groups and announced to the acting president on the morning of September 6, 1930 that he was marching on the capital. When he reached the *Casa Rosada* that evening about six o'clock, the acting president resigned and fled. Then General Uriburu demanded the allegiance of the military commanders who had not participated in the *cuartelazo* (which he promptly received), issued a manifesto detailing his general policies, dissolved the legislature, and issued a decree making himself provisional president.[5]

Not all successful *cuartelazos* follow the advanced formula of these in Argentina. Tomás Guardia of Costa Rica (1870–82), for example, promoted his *cuartelazo* by secreting himself and a handful of followers in a fodder-filled oxcart which he employed to gain access to the *cuartel* where his eloquence won over the soldiery.

Cuartelazos may thus involve a single *cuartel*, as in Argentina in 1943, or a series, as in Venezuela in 1948. They also gravitate naturally to the capitals where military, political, and economic power are usually concentrated. Even in a large state like Venezuela control of the capital is likely to determine dominance of the rest of the country. The Gallegos government, for example, which owed its existence to the mul-

[5] *See* A. Hasbrouck, "The Argentine Revolution of 1930," *Hispanic American Historical Review* (August, 1938), pp. 285–321.

tiple *cuartelazo* of 1945, progressively lost the military support that made its existence meaningful. By November 22, 1948, rumors were circulating freely (even published in Carácas newspapers) to the effect that Gallegos was under arrest. At midnight on November 23 Lieutenant Colonel Mario Pérez Jiménez, chief of staff of the Army, Lieutenant Colonel Mario Vargas and others led the Army in a *cuartelazo* which ousted Gallegos without a shot being fired. Pérez Jiménez announced officially on November 24 that the Army was in control, and on November 25 the militarists revealed that Lieutenant Colonel Carlos Delgado Chalbaud was made president of the military junta.[6]

In a small country like Nicaragua the influence of the capital is even more noticeable because of shorter communication lines to the other centers of power. It is probably fair and accurate to say that the primary determinant in Nicaraguan politics is control of the National Guard, which Anastasio ("Tacho") Somoza employed in his successful *cuartelazo* of 1935. Even with the support of the National Guard General Somoza has had to maneuver adroitly in recent years to neutralize the blunt pressures against him. To this end he sponsored the *imposición* of Leonardo Argüello in February, 1947. Almost immediately upon being inaugurated on May 1, Argüello demonstrated unexpected and disconcerting independence, which precipitated the May 26 *cuartelazo*. General Somoza called a special session of Congress which declared Argüello "incapacitated" to hold office and named Benjamín Lacayo Sacasa provisional president with Somoza as minister of war, navy and aviation.[7]

[6] República de Venezuela, *Documentos oficiales relativos al movimiento militar del 24 de noviembre de 1948* (Carácas: Oficina Nacional de Información y Publicaciones, 1949), pp. 118 ff.; Chalbaud was the victim of political assassination (by Rafael Simón Urbina) in November, 1950. The politics of force in Venezuela are interestingly and frankly discussed by critics of the Gallegos, Betancourt, and *Acción Democrática* administration in Mister X, *Rómulo Betancourt, Estadista y Diplomático* (Carácas: n.p., 1948), p. 195, and Roldán Bermúdez, *Aquella Farsa* (Carácas: n.p., n.d.), pp. 74 ff.

[7] Ovidio Gondi, "All Nicaragua Is His Hacienda," *United Nations World* (March, 1948), pp. 30–33.

On the other hand, *cuartelazos* have been consummated successfully which bypassed the capital in the initial stages of the violence. General Manuel Odría of Peru, for example, by his "Proclamation of October 27" (1948) began the "Revolution of Restoration" from Arequipa, about 470 miles southeast of Lima, the capital.[8] General Odría's three-day almost bloodless march persuaded President José Luis Bustamante to flee first to Argentina and later to New York. The *cuartelazo* of May 30, 1944, in Ecuador is in point, but less dramatically so, for it had its inception in Guayaquil, which although about 150 miles from Quito, the capital, is nevertheless the country's largest and most important city. The supporters of José María Velasco Ibarra, who was conducting his campaign *in absentia* (being in exile in Colombia), gained control of an artillery regiment, won over draftees performing compulsory military service, captured the *cuartel* of the *carabineros* (a corps of rural police and customs guards), and by midnight of May 29 occupied the telegraph offices and blocked communications with the capital. Resistance was centered mainly in the Guayaquil police department, and estimates of casualties (almost always inaccurate) ran from fifty dead and two hundred wounded to eight hundred in all. The rebels controlled Tulcan, Riobamba and Cuenca by May 30. President Carlos Arroyo del Río resigned, took refuge in the Colombian embassy and prepared to depart by plane for Colombia. Velasco Ibarra returned to Quito in an armored car from Colombia at 4:20 P.M. May 31 and took over the presidency at 5:30, after the junta of the Democratic Alliance delivered the government to him in the name of the people. Velasco Ibarra was a weak *caudillo* and was forced to flee on August 23, 1947, by Colonel Carlos Mancheno, who in turn lost power through a *cuartelazo* which began on August 30 in Riobamba, about one hundred miles south of Quito. It spread to garrison towns in the interior and then to Guayaquil. At Ambato, about seventy-five miles from the capital, the rebels fought and defeated Colonel Mancheno's tank corps in a six-hour battle that reportedly resulted in thirteen killed and one hundred wounded. With this defeat President

[8] República de Peru, *Message to the Nation* (Lima: Talleres Gráficos de Editora Médica Peruana S.A., 1950), p. 3.

Mancheno resigned (September 2, 1947) and took refuge in the Venezuelan embassy in Quito. According to President Mariano Ospina Pérez of Colombia there were "constant uprisings"[9] against him during his term of office which if analyzed might cast additional light on the life-cycle of the *cuartelazo.*

"Golpe de Estado"

The *golpe de estado,* frequently called the coup d'état, and sometimes referred to as *golpe militar,*[10] with the noun *derrocamiento* being occasionally employed along with the descriptive phrase *desplazar del poder,* is the fastest, the most difficult to plan and implement successfully (short of genuine revolution), and potentially the most dangerous of the forceful methods of establishing and changing governments in Latin America. The *golpe* is a direct assault on power—almost always personal in Latin-American countries—which means the immobilization of the president either through assassination or detention. The possibilities of success are obviously enhanced if the president's cabinet, high-ranking members of the armed forces, and the head of the police system can be seized when the assault on the president is consummated. The *golpe de estado* is distinguished from the *cuartelazo* by the fact that professional military experience is less needed, and by the procedure of attack which bypasses the *cuartel* entirely. Whereas considerable military skill is required to capture the loyalty of troops and lead them successfully against a major *cuartel,* even a civilian with literary, professional or scholarly training can, assuming ingress to the *casa presidencial,* blow out the president's brains and proclaim a change in governments. The *golpe,* then, is a forceful method of organizing and changing governments which definitely permits, even encourages, civilian participation.

Inherent in the technique is ecstatic excitement for leaders

[9] República de Colombia, *The Political Situation in Colombia* (Bogotá: n.p., 1950), p. 26.

[10] República de Venezuela, *Documentos oficiales relativos al movimiento militar del 24 de noviembre de 1948* (Carácas: Oficina Nacional de Información y Publicaciones, 1949), p. 38.

and masses alike, for the *golpe* guarantees that a "bad" *caudillo* can be replaced by a "good" one, that "justice" can be substituted for "injustice," *immediately,* without the time-consuming and demoralizing limitation of such institutional restraints as law or constitutions. To the predilection toward extremism in politics in Latin America is added the factor of extreme speed and flexibility. The leader can ascertain easily and quickly the extent to which public opinion has been conditioned to the kind of change in administrations he is attempting. Politically, his status might well be nothing one moment, everything the next; his *golpe* might be rejected upon its announcement and he, himself, put to flight or captured and subject to penalties that might include death.

Yet the *golpe* is not spontaneous combustion in the field of organizing and changing governments. As with the *cuartelazo,* mastery of the elements of politics within the environmental framework of each Latin-American country is required by the successful politician (some of whom have participated in many *golpes* during a lifetime). The first step in the process is almost invariably the organization of the cadre of leaders and sub-leaders. To cement loyalty and guarantee incentive, the *jefe supremo* of the proposed *golpe* is likely to appoint his key personnel in advance. Sometimes there is no need to carry on any propaganda whatever prior to the assault; public opinion might be favorably disposed toward a change by the ineptitude of the incumbent. If this is not the case, however, then media of communication are required to attack the government, more frequently than not (unfortunately for the research scholar who faces the task of separating objective evidence from falsification), through lies, slander, and license. As insurance against failure, the *caudillo* should have an airplane, an automobile, or other means of locomotion ready for immediate departure. Recognition by the United States and other major powers is no longer a primary determinant, if it ever was, for the existence of a government, yet it is undeniably true that immediate recognition of a new regime might have a positive effect on public opinion in the Latin-American country concerned. The leaders, therefore, endeavor to plant competent diplomats in the several capitals to negotiate speedy recognition. Timing is of the utmost importance, and although circumstances vary from country to country, Sundays and holidays, when the official offices are closed and the president probably is separated from his major supporters, are to be preferred. Colonel Kurt Conrad Arnade, former military advisor to the Government of Bolivia, described a well-timed *golpe:*

> I once received an invitation to attend a party at the house of a high government official. On entering the house I discovered that the *Junta* had originated the invitation, and, after assembling the entire government in one reception room, locked the doors and assumed power.[11]

The recent political history of Bolivia provides excellent case studies of the *golpe de estado.* Eight different men occupied the presidency from 1930 to 1943. One resigned under pressure, one committed suicide or was murdered, two transmitted power peacefully, and the others were forcibly ejected. The most dramatic and the most completely analyzed *golpe* in recent years took place on July 21, 1946, in connection with the government of President Gualberto Villarroel who obtained power by *cuartelazo* on December 20, 1943, possibly with official aid from the Argentine government.[12] It was so well planned and executed that when the junta's assassins cornered President Villarroel in his own offices and shot him, then threw him, still alive, from the second-story window where a mob seized the body and hanged it from a lamp post, the belief was common in the United States, despite very convincing evidence to the contrary, that this was a popular movement.[13]

[11] Colonel Kurt Conrad Arnade, "The Technique of Coup d'État in Latin America," *United Nations World* (February, 1950), p. 25.

[12] Secretary of State Cordell Hull so contended. *See Chicago Sun,* January 8, 1944, p. 3. Under-Secretary of State Sumner Welles also argued that the Argentine government had aided in the plot. *Ibid.,* February 2, 1944, p. 10; May 15, 1944, p. 8; May 10, 1944, p. 10. *See also, Consultation Among the American Republics with Respect to the Argentine Situation* (Washington, D.C.: U. S. Government Printing Office, 1946), pp. 20–22.

[13] *See* Ernesto Galarza, "The Case of Bolivia," *Inter-American Reports* (No. 6, May, 1949), pp. 32 ff. This well-documented pro-

Other examples of successful *golpes* based upon personal assault include the well-organized effort of the Argentine minister of the interior and the commander of the *Campo de Mayo cuartel* who forced President Pedro P. Ramírez ("with a gun leveled at his head") to resign February 24, 1944, in favor of General Edelmiro Farrell, who had been vice-president under Ramírez. On August 23, 1947, Colonel Carlos Mancheno obtained entrance to the *casa presidencial* in Ecuador and forced President José María Velasco Ibarra to resign (at gun point) in his favor. At the time of the assault the Army and the police supported Mancheno, and public opinion appeared conditioned to the *golpe* by the unfavorable publicity given President Velasco Ibarra's alleged preparation for the *imposición* of Mariano Suárez Veintimilla. Felipe Molas López became president of Paraguay through a time-tested variation. He invited most of the government of General Raimundo Rolon to a dinner on February 26, 1949, surrounded the house with his own supporters, and is reported to have announced, "Gentlemen, the jig is up."[14] The leaders of the *Colorado* party (the dominant power group in Paraguay) supported Molas López in his presidential aspirations, but on September 10, 1949, they ordered him to resign, and then appointed Federico Chaves to the presidency.

Revolution

The history of Latin America from independence to the present time is a history of violent struggles of "ins" versus "outs," but it is not a history of revolutionary movements designed to remold the institutional bases of Latin-American life. By "revolution" I mean ". . . fundamental change in the nature of the state, the functions of government, the principles of economic production and distribution, the relationship of the social classes, particularly as regards the control of gov-

vocative study attempts to prove that the *golpe* was in reality supported by conservative, banking, and mining interests which stood to profit from destroying the Villarroel government which was a genuinely popular administration.

[14] *Havana Post,* September 11, 1949, p. 1.

ernment–in a word, a significant breaking with the past."[15] Revolution so defined is rare in Latin America, and even mass participation in violence is only occasionally found. It is an obvious and inescapable fact that revolution is too big and too difficult a power mechanism to employ in Latin America with any frequency. Problems of leadership, ideology, policy, planning, logistics, and timing are all maximized in genuine revolution.

Profound institutional transformations have taken place in Uruguay since the first decade of the twentieth century, but such changes have not occurred in an atmosphere of revolution, despite the ferocious violence of the nineteenth century. The Liberal revolution in Central America which began in the 1870's dramatically established in theory the doctrines of the liberal-democratic state and attempted some institutional changes, such as relations between Church and State. But the revolution lacked sustained vitality and continuity, and its effect was shadow rather than substance. Systematic research might well reveal that revolutions have been under way in various Latin-American countries in recent times, such as in Brazil from 1930 to 1945, in Argentina since 1943, and in the Dominican Republic from the 1930's to the present. The Cuban revolution assuredly deserves study.[16] But I would also argue that the only clear-cut illustration of revolution in Latin America since independence is the Mexican revolution, which began in 1910–11 and which continues to exist as the dominant characteristic of Mexican economic, political, and social life today. Despite the difficulties of mobilizing violence in revolution, of all the forceful methods of organizing power in Latin America, it is probably the most democratic. Revolution is the only method which invites mass participation and renders imperative the formation of decisions on basic issues of public policy by virtually all members of the state.

[15] William S. Stokes, "The 'Cuban Revolution' and the Presidential Elections of 1948," *The Hispanic American Historical Review* (February, 1951), p. 37.

[16] *Ibid.*, pp. 37–79; *see also* Raul Roa, *15 Años Después* (La Habana: Editorial Librería Selecta, 1950), pp. 645 ff.

"*Imposición*"

Imposición is a nominally peaceful method of organizing power in which the dominant political element in the state hand-picks a candidate and then rigs the election to guarantee victory. Its major principle is the presupposition of success for the privileged candidate. That being the case, the opposition must never become convinced that an *imposición* is operating because then there logically is no further premium in maintaining peace and force is likely to result. The conditions under which *imposición* enjoys maximum possibilities for development include: (1) the existence of a *caudillo* of such stature, power and personal popularity that no opposition dares stand against him; (2) a government firmly in power; (3) the principal parties or major elements of political strength in the country in agreement on the same candidate for supreme power. Even under the most favorable conditions, however, *imposición* is exceedingly difficult to exploit, and only the most mature, prepared, and experienced individuals or groups have been able to utilize it successfully.

A firmly established, confident government can, of course, openly announce support for a particular candidate and successfully carry through a campaign. On the other hand, such a course invites the opposition to unite and opens the way to charges of official unfairness which might result in undesirable violence. The typical *imposición* usually begins, therefore, with an official announcement from the highest sources in the state that the government is neutral and will guarantee free, fair elections. These protestations of impartiality and fairness are repeated continually throughout the campaign through all the media of communication. The president frequently will issue an impressive order to all government personnel calling attention to the principles of representative democracy and outlining specifically the provisions of the electoral law relating to proper conduct by government employees.

The government is likely to encourage a large number of candidates to offer their names in the election. The politically ambitious *caudillo* can reason thus: if the election is really fair, perhaps the vagaries of public opinion will favor his candidacy; if an *imposición* is under way perhaps he is the chosen candidate of those who are manipulating power. All during the campaign the perpetrators of the *imposición* carefully select and sharpen for effective use the methods required to insure success, whether they be control over the nominating machinery, registration fraud, appointment of key personnel at the polls, intervention in the *escrutinio* (official check of balloting), or cruder techniques involving purchase of votes or employment of violence through party workers, the police, or the armed forces.

If the election in an *imposición* is adroitly rigged, power will be maintained or changed peacefully, and the press and even scholars will hail the experience as a final demonstration of the democratic aspirations of the country. On the other hand, long experience has made most Latin-American politicians and the politically conscious citizenry exceptionally sensitive to fraud, and an *imposición* has to be very ably executed to forestall violence. In Mexico, for example, every change in power from the fall of Díaz to the *imposición* of General Manuel Avila Camacho in 1940 was followed by armed revolt. Another good illustration of improper handling of *imposición* is President Carlos Arroyo del Río's attempt in 1944 to transfer the presidency of Ecuador to Miguel Angel Albornoz. His ineptitude permitted the opposition to execute a successful *cuartelazo* and install José María Velasco Ibarra in power. Velasco Ibarra attempted the *imposición* of Mariano Suárez Veintimilla in 1947 and failed.

Imposición can be used by a president to perpetuate his own power, an excellent example being the re-election of Dr. Alfonso López of Colombia in 1942. Or the president may prefer to transfer power to one of his close friends (*compadrazgo*). I found many such examples in the political history of Honduras,[17] and this technique was plainly the determinant in the important presidential election of 1948 in Cuba.[18] However, even *compadrazgo* can frustrate the ob-

[17] Stokes, *Honduras, An Area Study in Government, op. cit.*, pp. 29–58, 228–64.

[18] Stokes, "The 'Cuban Revolution' and the Presidential Elections of 1948," *op. cit.*, pp. 48–58.

jectives of a *caudillo*. General Somoza of Nicaragua established Leonardo Argüello in the presidency through an *imposición* in February, 1947, but when Argüello betrayed Somoza's friendship by his independent policies the latter had to oust his own candidate by *cuartelazo* and begin again the task of selection.

When an *imposición* is unsuccessful, it is revealed for what it is and can be studied by the research scholar. To distinguish the successful *imposición* from an honest election, however, is frequently a difficult problem. The evidence would seem to indicate that *imposición* was present in the following changes of governments: Juan Arévalo, Guatemala, December, 1947;[19] Jacobo Arbenz, Guatemala, November, 1950; Rómulo Gallegos, Venezuela, December, 1947;[20] Salvador Casteñeda Castro, El Salvador, January, 1945; and the elections in El Salvador in March, 1950.[21]

"Candidato Único"

Candidato único, or an election in which there is but one candidate running, occurs occasionally when a *caudillo* develops who is so overwhelming in stature that no other political figure dares oppose him. An excellent illustration is General Manuel Odría of Peru who obtained power by *cuartelazo* in October, 1948, then developed his position so strongly that he was able to run for the presidency on July 2, 1950, without opposition. It is true that General Ernesto Montagne offered his name as an opposition candidate, but the National Electoral Board refused to accept it, and the general wisely did not persist in his presidential aspirations. President Felipe Molas López of Paraguay achieved power in a *candidato único* election of April 17, 1949. When so employed, however, it becomes an open, blunt repudiation of representative democracy and opens the administration to attack at home

[19] Departamento de Publicidad de la Presidencia de la Republica, *Trayectoria de la Revolución Guatemalteca* (n.d.), p. 3.

[20] República de Venezuela, *Documentos oficiales relativos al movimiento militar del 24 de noviembre de 1948* (Carácas: Oficina Nacional de Información y Publicaciones, 1949), pp. 37, 43.

[21] Rafael Antonio Tercero, *La verdad sobre las elecciones de marzo de 1950* (San Salvador: Imp. La República, 1950), pp. 72 ff.

and abroad. More frequently the astute *jefe supremo* of the country will select *imposición* as a more subtle, mature method of realizing his objectives. For an outstanding *caudillo* it is a relatively simple matter to persuade a respectable, distinguished man to run against him, with the understanding that the dummy candidate will receive enough votes to make the campaign appear authentic and to maintain his honor.

Candidato único is used much more frequently when one major party is unified, the other hopelessly fragmented. When victory for the latter seems utterly impossible it commonly will refuse to campaign, and will count its strength by the number of people who stay away from the polls. Utilizing Colombia as a case study, the following men won the presidency in *candidato único* elections in recent years: Dr. Miguel Abadía Méndez, a Conservative, in 1926; Dr. Alfonso López, a Liberal, in 1934; Dr. Eduardo Santos, a Liberal, in 1938; and Laureano Gómez, a Conservative, in 1949. In instances in which it appears that neither of two *caudillos* will give way *candidato único* may be resorted to in order to preserve the peace by awarding the presidency to a third man.

"Continuismo"

Continuismo is a peaceful, constitutional methodology for maintaining a chief executive in power beyond the legal term of his office. From time to time a *caudillo* will discover at the termination of his tenure that no one wishes to challenge him. He might even be approached by representatives of major power groupings in the country with the appeal that he continue in office. If the constitution prohibits re-election, then *continuismo* must be embraced. This usually involves amending the constitution, drafting a new document (in which the major change will be a section providing for temporary abrogation of the no-re-election article), enactment of legislative statute, plebiscite, or judicial interpretation. Russell H. Fitzgibbon's important study of *continuismo* in Central America and the Caribbean presents in detail some of these techniques.[22] But *continuismo,* like the other forceful and peace-

[22] Russell H. Fitzgibbon, "*Continuismo* in Central America and the Caribbean," *Inter-American Quarterly,* Vol. 11, No. 3 (July,

ful techniques for organizing political power, was in use before the period covered by the Fitzgibbon study, and it applies not only to the small countries in the Caribbean and Middle American area but to the larger countries of South America as well. The new Argentine constitution of 1949, for example, eliminated the no-re-election clause of the document of 1853 in order to permit General Juan Domingo Perón a second term of office.

Elections

Finally, the electoral method of organizing power has been employed at least once in all of the Latin-American countries. It is my hypothesis, however, that elections in the Anglo-American sense for the determination of executive leadership are resorted to mainly in Latin America when more satisfactory methods have for one reason or another proved inadequate. Election under such circumstances is not likely to produce a strong, popular leader, but the technique may provide time for reassembling and again bringing into play the more fundamental bases for determining political power.

If the assumption of force in Latin-American politics possesses validity, the question quite fairly can be raised: Why have elections at all? The reasons include the following: (1) The need for the friendship and financial assistance of the United States dictates at least superficial respect for the idiosyncrasies of that country in the field of organizing and changing governments. (2) Elections have a public-opinion role to perform for the government. Through the media of communication the government can help to strengthen the conviction that it has chosen the right candidate. (3) Elections are also useful to the opposition which can employ the campaigns to build up moral justification for revolt. (4) There is the belief that the electoral technique of the liberal-democratic state should be developed as the most satisfactory procedure for organizing and changing governments.[23]

1940), pp. 55–74. *See also* Stokes, *Honduras, An Area Study in Government, op. cit.*, pp. 256–62.

[23] Support for representative democracy is found in the literature of all the Latin-American countries.

Concluding Implications

The thesis of violence in the organization, maintenance, and changing of governments in Latin America is susceptible of considerable demonstration through ample objective evidence. As democracy is assumed to be imperative to American foreign policy in the Western Hemisphere, and as it is evident that violence tends to characterize politics in the Latin-American countries, it is only logical that a strong effort should be made by the Department of State of the United States to eliminate violence. Two main approaches stand out for consideration. One is associated with the name of the late Laurence Duggan, who argued that we could never further the development of democracy in Latin America by supporting the landed oligarchs or the reactionary army and church groups. Instead, he insisted, we should extend our aid and assistance to the labor unions, which, if they achieved a position of power in Latin-American politics, would strive for democracy.[24] What Mr. Duggan did not make clear was that the major unions, during the time he was advocating his policy, were dominated by militant communists. If they were to achieve power it seems reasonably clear that they would offer modest support indeed for such principles of the liberal-democratic state as individualism, the basic freedoms, and parliamentary organization. It is fair, however, to agree with Duggan that failure to support the labor unions in all probability would mean retention in some countries and development in others of clerico-military authoritarianism, almost as much opposed to democracy as is communism.

The other approach, one that seems to be widely accepted, is that political instability in Latin America finds its origins in economic distress among the masses. The concomitant argument is that if the Latin-American countries are assisted in raising their living standards, democratic procedures will in some way result. The fact that violence has a long history even in the most advanced Latin-American countries, such as Argentina, negates for me so simple an explanation. Further-

[24] *See* Laurence Duggan, *The Americas—The Search for Hemisphere Security* (New York: Henry Holt & Co., 1949), pp. 242 ff.

more, it is instructive for us to observe that right-wing authoritarianism as exemplified by Perón's *justicialismo,* and left-wing authoritarianism, as exemplified by the Mexican Revolution or *Aprismo,* also call for higher material standards of living for the masses.

My own research has led me to the conviction that the problem of violence is much more basic and a good deal more complicated than either of these approaches would suggest. There is much evidence which leads one to believe that there is no one simple cause for violence, which, if removed or corrected, would produce stable, democratic politics in the Anglo-American conception. It seems more defensible to me to argue, first, that Hispanic culture tends everywhere in Latin America to dominate in the power sense; second, that the institutions of Hispanic culture such as the family, church, army, educational institutions, and economic systems, are essentially authoritarian in nature, hence, conditioning the individual to more frequent acceptance of processes of dictatorship, including violence, than processes of political democracy.[25]

The Hispanic family, characterized by stratified inequality of rights, duties, and responsibilities based upon differentiations of age, sex, and other factors; the Church, hierarchical, authoritarian, and absolutist in both organization and dogma; the educational system, with its theories of exclusion which reduce the extent of educational services to a few, its segregation of the sexes, particularly in the primary and secondary fields, its discouragement of women in higher education, and its widespread retention of scholasticism in method; the exaggerated importance and influence of the Army in social and political life; and an economic organization which discourages individual initiative, imagination, and enterprise, and which seeks solutions through collectivism—all these are data in support of the generalization that the individual is constantly conditioned to authoritarianism. If the hypothesis here presented

[25] *See* Fernando de Azevedo, *Brazilian Culture* (New York: The Macmillan Co., 1950), pp. 24, 109, 117, 119, 334, 382, 385, 432, 491; Gilberto Freyre, *The Masters and the Slaves* (New York: Alfred A. Knopf, 1946), pp. 26–27; Francisco García Calderón, *Latin America, Its Rise and Progress* (New York: Charles Scribner's Sons, 1913), p. 365; Frank Tannenbaum, *Mexico; The Struggle for Peace and Bread* (New York: Alfred A. Knopf, 1950), p. 19.

is valid, then it is possible to say that Point Four and the program of the United Nations in respect to Latin America, both of which assume that modification of one aspect of Latin-American culture—the economic—will produce attitudes conducive to the development of democracy, are doomed to confusion and disillusionment.

Indeed, the eradication of force and violence takes on monumental proportions, for it implies fundamental reorganization of large parts of an entire way of life. Effective exploitation of those few aspects of Hispanic culture which tend toward the development of political democracy, and modification or elimination of the many that do not, presuppose almost unlimited time, power, and material resources, which are denied to any one state, such as the United States, or collection of states, such as the United Nations or the Organization of American States.

In this connection the question might well be raised as to whether the employment of violence in organizing political power in Latin America necessarily negates the principles of representative democracy. Or, to put the issue in another way, to what extent have governments established by force lacked majority support? Is it possible that Latin-American political culture has developed procedures for measuring and representing opinion different from but as valid as the techniques of election, initiative, referendum and plebiscite of the Anglo-American and Western European states? This is a subject on which firm judgments already exist, but I submit that it is an area of research which might profit through comprehensive elaboration. Systematic analysis of the pathology of violence in Latin-American countries is a necessary introduction to mature and meaningful speculation on the meaning of the phenomenon in terms of both comparative government and international relations. The definition of terms and the survey of selected case studies found in this paper point to the obvious conclusion that other facets of the broad, fundamental problem of the nature of power in Latin-American politics require research. The most important of such areas include: (1) the development of techniques for determining accurately where power is to be found in such areas as the appointment of personnel, the formulation of policy, the administration of the functions of the state, and the adjudication of competing interests; (2) an analysis of the nature of power and its classification and application to given circumstances, including the extent to which it is personal; the extent to which it is institutional, associated with the family, church, army or economic organization; and the extent to which it is structural and found in federal, unitary, executive, legislative, or judicial forms; and (3) an evaluation of the pattern of power from the standpoint of its relationship to forms and philosophies of government.

*Violence in Pre-Modern Societies: Rural Colombia**

RICHARD S. WEINERT

Violence is a common phenomenon in developing polities which has received little attention.[1] Clearly a Peronist riot in Buenos Aires, a land invasion in Lima, and a massacre in rural Colombia are all different. Yet we have no typology which relates types of violence to stages or patterns of economic or social development. We know little of the causes, incidence or functions of different forms of violence. This article is an effort to understand one type of violence which can occur in societies in transition.

Violence in Colombia has traditionally accompanied transfers of power at the national level. This can account for its outbreak in 1946, when the Conservative Party replaced the Liberals. It cannot account for the intensity or duration of rural violence for two decades. This article focuses primarily on the violence from 1946 to 1953, and explains its intensification and duration as the defense of a traditional sacred or-

* Reprinted from *The American Political Science Review* (June, 1966), pp. 340–347, by permission of the publisher and the author. I am indebted to Oscar Delgado, Fernando Guillén Martinez, Nelson Kasfir, Juan Linz, Peter Landstreet, John Plank and Thomas O'Leary for their suggestions on earlier versions of this article.

[1] An excellent discussion of the present state of our ignorance and the most urgent needs for concepts and research is Harry Eckstein's introduction to Harry Eckstein, (ed.), *Internal War* (New York: The Free Press of Glencoe, 1964).

der against secular modernizing tendencies undermining that order. We shall discuss violence since 1953 in the concluding section.

I. Violence in the Period 1946–1953

From 1946 to 1953, rural violence ranging from physical assault to brutal inhumanity engulfed most of Colombia, and touched every social institution from the family to the Church. It was so widespread and pervasive that the most appropriate name Colombians found for it was generic: the Violence. Though it varied in intensity among regions, violence was present in all of interior Colombia; only regions near Colombia's borders with the Atlantic, the Pacific, Venezuela, Ecuador, and Peru were exempt. The destruction and disruption of life caused by the violence is difficult to overstate. Careful estimates indicate 135,000 deaths from the violence between 1949 and 1958.[2] In a town in Tolima to which many fled to escape the violence, investigators found that 503 of 509 families had suffered the loss of some close relative, that one-third of immigrant families had been landowners, and that violence in the town itself around 1950 had destroyed its four coffee mills and five iron foundries.[3] Doubtless similar conditions prevailed in scores of other towns.

The violence existed for the entire 1946–53 period. It began on a small scale in 1946–7 shortly after a Conservative assumed the presidency after thirty years of Liberal rule. In April, 1947, Liberal leader Gaitán presented a memorandum protesting acts of violence in 56 towns in eleven of fifteen states.[4] In February, 1948 he made an "Oration for Peace"

[2] Mons. German Guzmán Campos, Orlando Fals Borda, and Eduardo Umaña Luna, *La Violencia en Colombia,* Ediciones Tercer Mundo, Bogotá, 1963, Vol. I, pp. 287–293.

[3] In the late 1950's when the questionnaires were distributed, 36% of the sample had resided there less than seven years. See Roberto Pineda Giraldo *El Impacto de la Violencia en el Tolima: El Caso de El Líbano,* Monografía Sociológica No. 6, Departamento de Sociología, Universidad Nacional, Bogotá, 1960, pp. 14, 16–17, 18, 25.

[4] See Guzmán, *op. cit.,* Vol. I, p. 29.

at a large Bogotá rally asking for public order.[5] Violence increased following the Bogotazo in April, 1948, and reached a peak 1949–53 during the presidential period of Laureano Gómez. Violence since 1954 has differed from earlier violence and will receive attention later.

Two outstanding characteristics of the violence are that it was rural and that loyalties to multi-class parties defined the lines of conflict. That the violence was rural is undisputable. No major city was affected. Of the 56 towns mentioned above, 30 had fewer than ten thousand residents; eight had between ten and fifteen thousand, nine between fifteen and twenty, and nine over twenty thousand. These figures themselves understate the point, since they are based on census definitions of towns, many of which contain a municipal seat and several hamlets, which together might total twenty-five thousand people, but contain no large concentration of population.[6]

The violence pitted Liberal peasant against Conservative peasant, and does not seem to have had a class basis. Rather than poor looting rich or rich oppressing poor, Conservatives attacked Liberals in similar social situations. Guzmán, for instance, reports no relation between incidence of violence and either patterns of land tenure or levels of education.[7] In lacking a social class basis, the violence was similar to Bendix's characterization of political and social protest in premodern Europe.[8]

Considerable documentary evidence supports the suggestion that traditional party loyalties and not class hostilities underlay the violence.[9] A chief of one band of antagonists in

[5] The speech is contained in *Las Mejores Oraciones de Jorge Eliécer Gaitán,* Editorial Jorvi, Bogotá, 1958, pp. 434–436.

[6] Sahagún in 1951, for example, contained 37,000 people. It is composed of 12 hamlets in addition to the town.

[7] Guzmán, *op. cit.,* Vol. I, p. 139.

[8] See Reinhard Bendix, *Nation-Building and Citizenship* (New York: John Wiley and Sons, 1964), pp. 40–48. This characteristic will receive further attention below.

[9] It may be noted that there were some cases of class-motivated violence. The Communist Party organized a campaign of "mass self-defence" through which several autonomous "republics" were established. See Partido Comunista de Colombia, *Treinta Años de Lucha del Partido Comunista de Colombia,* Ediciones Paz y Socialismo, Bogotá, 1960, pp. 93 ff. These were very isolated and limited

Antioquia wrote in July, 1953, of having seen a man's tongue removed by police who explained to their victim, "We're cutting it out so you won't ever again shout vivas to the Liberal Party, you dirty politician s.o.b." He continues, "They amputated genital organs of others so they wouldn't create any more Liberals."[10] A local organization of Liberals was formed in a town in Boyacá "to begin immediately the tasks and functions which the struggle against the falangist dictatorship implies."[11] Guzmán writes of the violence in one region of Tolima, "The Violence there was initiated by official elements. Its promoters were mayors, councilmen and police inspectors."[12]

It is striking, moreover, that no author has suggested that the basis for the violence was class hostility; even Marxist authors concede the primacy of political hostilities as motivations. Colombia's most imaginative socialist, Antonio García, wrote in 1953 of the violence,

> We are harvesting the only crop which our "historic parties" have sown: in this spilling of blood, in these odious crimes, in this unpunished cruelty, is summed up the sense of our party-laden history. Those truly responsible for this blood-letting are not the vulgar delinquents, . . . [but] the political system which takes them as its instruments. . . .[13]

An official history of the Communist Party referred to "the reactionary violence on the one hand and the illusions of Liberals in the effectiveness of assaults on the other. . . ."[14]

Because of its precarious political position, the Conserva-

---

in scale, however, and do not alter the analysis of the modal pattern of violence presented in the text.

[10] Quoted in Guzmán, *op. cit.,* Vol. I, p. 94.

[11] Quoted in *Ibid.,* p. 84.

[12] *Ibid.,* p. 62.

[13] Prologue to Daniel Caicedo, *Viento Seco,* Editorial Nuestra América, Buenos Aires, 1954, p. 17. See also his *Gaitán y El Problema de la Revolucion Colombiana,* Bogotá, 1955, pp. 294, ff.

[14] Partido Comunista de Colombia, *op. cit.,* p. 93. For a similar view from another leftist author, see Camilo Torres Restrepo, "La Violencia y Los Cambios Socio-Culturales en Las Areas Rurales Colombianas" in *Memoria del Primer Congreso Nacional de Sociologia,* Asociación Colombiana de Sociologia, Bogotá, 1963, pp. 147–148.

TABLE I. CONSERVATIVE AND LIBERAL URBAN VOTE, 1946-1949

City	Index of 1949 Vote with 1946 = 100			Liberal % of 1949 Vote
	Lib.	Con.	Total	
Armenia	118	99.5	93	66.8
Barranquilla	96.5	92	93.5	82.5
Bogotá	132	116	127.5	75.6
Bucaramanga	150.5	115	138	73.3
Cali	145.5	118.5	137.5	67.5
Cartagena	122	114	120	77.7
Ibagué	121.5	110.5	120	69.6
Manizales	128	110.5	119.5	54.4
Medellín	138	127	135	56.2
Pereira	136	94	118.5	74.5

tive Party initiated violence against Liberals. Conservative Ospina Perez won the presidency in 1946 when two Liberal candidates split the Liberal vote, but the Liberals retained their electoral majority in congressional and local elections following 1946 and posed a serious threat to regain the presidency in 1950. Moreover, Liberals were increasing their urban vote more rapidly than were Conservatives. Table I shows the comparative growth of the two parties in ten leading cities and the percentage of the vote captured by Liberals in 1949. In every case, the Liberal vote grew significantly more than did the Conservative vote 1946–1949, and the Liberals won majorities in the 1949 elections.

In part to counter increasing Liberal urban majorities, Conservatives resorted to rural political repression. They were assisted in their efforts by political resentments with roots in previous conflicts, which had been reinforced 1930–32. Traditionally in Colombia, the transfer of national power from one political party to the other has been shortly followed by local fights over bureaucratic power, inevitably won by the ruling party. Such conflict had broken out when the Liberals assumed power in 1930 after forty-five years of Conservative hegemony. In Boyacá and Santander, two interior states which were scenes of later violence, this led to sporadic fighting between Liberals and Conservatives in small towns. Whether this violence was due to Liberals taking revenge on Conservatives or Conservatives resisting newly-appointed Liberals is unknown; probably both factors were present.

In any case, this violence strengthened political resentments on local levels. In some areas, Conservative peasants were even forced to move to other towns, though the extent of this migration is unknown. In 1946 when Conservatives regained the presidency, hostilities similar to those of 1930 appeared. Boyacá and Santander were among the earliest scenes of violence.[15]

The violence of the 1930's was short-lived, however. One reason was a brief war with Peru in 1932 which elevated nationalist over partisan passions and drew attention from local violence.[16] But a more basic reason was the difference between the Conservative opposition in the 1930's and the Liberal opposition in the 1940's.

Conservative Party leadership prior to the Liberal victory was old. Moreover, the young Conservative leadership under Laureano Gómez supported Liberal President Alfonso López until a break between them in 1935, by which time the Liberals were firmly entrenched in power. Consequently, Liberals faced no vigorous opposition on a national level and had no reason to stimulate or encourage local violence. Liberal opposition following 1946, however, was quite vigorous. Led by Gaitán, it presented powerful opposition on a national level and threatened to regain power in the next Presidential elections.

To retain political power, Conservatives were therefore obliged to counter Liberal urban mobilization with rural mobilization. Stimulation of rural violence, assisted by the legacy of the 1930's, accomplished this goal in two ways. First, it aroused Conservatives and intimidated Liberals: in elections in rural areas, more Conservatives and fewer Liberals would

[15] The best account of this is contained in Jorge Enrique Gutiérrez Anzola, *Violencia y Justicia*, Ediciones Tercer Mundo, Bogotá, 1962, pp. 21–25.

[16] See J. A. Osorio Lizarazo, *Gaitán*, Ediciones Lopez Negri, Buenos Aires, 1952, p. 149.

vote. Further, growing violence in the countryside would justify stronger national measures which would permit repression of Liberals in cities. Though Ospina resisted this move, a state of seige was declared in November, 1949.

Repression, however, is not a startling political weapon. What sets the Colombian violence apart is the resonance which very traditional appeals found in stimulating so much violence for so long. Typical of such appeals is this excerpt from a speech in 1950 by Conservative Laureano Gómez:

> When they erased the name of God from the preamble to the Constitution, when they adulterated the wise principles which reigned over the concordance of the spiritual and civil power, when the youth in the University and secondary schools was submitted to unmasked instruction in naturalism and atheism, there emerged a process of disfiguration of our national soul and destruction of our noble Christian and free country, giving us instead a structure which forced the people to pass over red paths of revolution.[17]

The heavy reliance on traditional symbols of religion and mystic nationalism, and the powerful resonance it found are puzzling in a modernizing nation, in which manufacturing—apart from artisan industry—accounted for more than 17% of the national product in 1953,[18] and which had seven cities with more than 100,000 population according to the 1951 census.

II. Explanations of the Violence

The search for a coherent and convincing explanation of the violence has been nearly as frustrating intellectually as was the violence destructive physically. A detailed two-volume study ends by listing four "remote causes," five "proximate causes," four "immediate causes," and seven "auxiliary causes"; some of the "causes" listed are as general as "precip-

[17] From speech published in *El Siglo* (Bogotá), August 8, 1950.

[18] ECLA, *Analyses and Projections of Economic Growth,* Vol. III, *The Economic Development of Colombia,* United Nations, New York, 1957, p. 17.

itant factors" or "social deficiencies."[19] The list of factors frequently cited is formidable: regionalism, lack of national unity, traditionalism, fanaticism, institutional rigidity, poverty, psychopathic tendencies, political and military involvement, erosion of family, inadequate socialization, etc.

To this diverse collection, an American sociologist, Robert C. Williamson, has brought coherence in a suggestive article.[20] He relies primarily on two interrelated hypotheses, deprivation and atomization: "[I]nternecine warfare has been the end-result of social, political and economic frustration as well as of personal *anomie*."[21] These two factors, he argues, created a potential for aggression, and other features of the Colombian system translated potential aggression to internecine warfare. He suggests specific links between potential aggression and political and military involvement, breakdown of traditional institutions, inadequate socialization, and ready availability of coffee crops for looting during harvesting.

While this is an admirable effort at a synthesis of diverse factors and integration with social theory, two major characteristics of the violence are unexplained by the theory and even tend to controvert it. First, the violence was rural. Second, the lines of division of conflict were determined by party loyalty and pitted peasant against peasant.

Williamson notes "the relative immunity of the city to this kind of warfare,"[22] but makes no attempt to relate this to his theory. This is most surprising because both the hypotheses he offers, deprivation and atomization, imply greater urban than rural violence. While objective deprivation is perhaps greater in rural than urban areas, only *perceived* deprivation produces frustration which drives men to violence, and this is probably heightened in cities. Migrants to cities characteristically have higher aspirations than the folk they left be-

[19] See Guzmán, *op. cit.*, Vol. II, pp. 381–417, especially 410–417.

[20] "Toward a Theory of Political Violence: The Case of Rural Colombia," *Western Political Quarterly* (March 1965), 35–44. A related view is suggested by Orlando Fals Borda in an unpublished paper presented to the Fifth World Congress of Sociology, 1962, "The Role of Violence in the Break with Traditionalism: The Colombian Case."

[21] *Op. cit.*, p. 36.

[22] *Ibid.*, p. 41.

hind, and become more acutely aware than they had been of what they lack. Perceived deprivation is thus probably higher in cities and can more readily lead to the social, economic and political frustration of which Williamson speaks.

This is especially true since relative deprivation may not have been acute in coffee-growing areas where violence was particularly heavy. Coffee prices were frozen during the War, but rose sharply afterwards. From an annual average of 15.9 cents per pound in 1945, they rose to 30.1 in 1947, 37.4 in 1949, and reached 58.7 in 1951.[23] While coffee growers did not receive all of this increase, living conditions for thousands of small growers were surely not worsening during years of increasing violence.

Likewise, atomization is usually intensified by rapid modernization, in which traditional structures are eroded or left behind and not immediately replaced. Urbanization and industrialization are two of the most powerful motors of such modernization. William Kornhauser has noted that

> the very rapid expansion of cities and industries has constituted perhaps the most general source of social atomization in the modern world, insofar as they have inhibited the growth of new forms of group life to replace the vil-

TABLE II. GROWTH OF FIVE LARGEST CITIES, 1938-1951

City	Population 1938 (hundreds)	Population 1951 (hundreds)	Index 1938 = 100	Index of Rest of Corresponding State 1938 = 100
Bogotá	330.3	648.3	196	115
Medellín	168.3	358.2	213	119
Cali	101.9	284.2	279	161
Barranquilla	152.3	279.6	184	128
Bucaramanga	51.3	112.3	219	113

[23] FAO, *The World Coffee Economy,* Commodity Bulletin Series No. 33, United Nations, Rome, 1961, p. 73.

TABLE III. ECONOMIC GROWTH 1945-1953[24]

Sector	Rate of Growth 1945-53	Composition of Product 1945	1953
Agriculture	2.7%	47.0%	36.9%
Mining	5.7	3.7	3.7
Manufacturing	9.2	13.4	17.2
Artisan Industry	8.4	3.1	3.8
Construction	2.7	6.1	4.8
Transportation	13.7	4.2	7.4
Energy, Utilities, etc.	12.7	.7	1.2
Government	8.9	5.5	6.9
Trade	9.0	10.2	12.9
Rents	3.8	6.1	5.2
Total	5.9%	100.0%	100.0%

lage community, extended family and guild which they destroyed.[25]

As Tables II and III demonstrate, both rapid urbanization and rapid industrialization were taking place at this time; the five largest cities increased rapidly, far outstripping their surrounding areas, and predominantly urban activities like manufacturing and trade increased their share of the total output from 23.6% in 1945 to 30.1% in 1953 while the whole economy was expanding at an annual rate of 5.9%. Thus Kornhauser's remark is acutely pertinent.

Thus Williamson's hypotheses point to urban violence, while Colombia's violence was rural. Further, Williamson's hypotheses suggest a class basis for the violence. If men are driven to violence by frustration and deprivation, then they are motivated in part by social resentments and can be expected to assault the "establishment." Yet, as we have seen, political rivalry and not class hatred was a major root of the con-

[24] Taken from ECLA, *op. cit.,* p. 16.

[25] *The Politics of Mass Society* (New York: The Free Press of Glencoe, 1959), p. 157. For a full discussion of the effects of urbanization and industrialization, see *ibid.,* pp. 142–158.

flict.[26] Williamson's hypotheses, however, suggest social resentment as a root, and thus once again fail to explain a major characteristic of the violence.[27] The search for an alternative explanation should begin with consideration of the party system and political loyalties which produced the violence.

Prior to the rise of the urban sector, the party system was based on traditional legitimacy. Liberal and Conservative strength varied between states and within states, but the identification of a town with one or the other party was probably accidental. It perhaps began with the association of a patron in the 19th century with one party, which implied the association of his peons with that same party. Colombia's 19th century feudalism thus produced political groupings similar to those produced by European feudalism as described by Bendix:

> In this [medieval] setting the lower strata of the population are fragmented. Each community of peasants belongs to the jurisdiction of its lord, each group of craftsmen to the jurisdiction of its guild and town. Thus, peasants participate in medieval politics only indirectly, . . . ; as subjects they are bound up for better or worse with the jurisdictional rights of their lord to whom they are bound in loyalty and service.[28]

By the early 20th century, the original reasons for the association had died, but the association persisted, stimulated oc-

[26] For a similar stress, see Fernando Guillén Martínez, *Raíz y Futuro de la Revolución,* Ediciones Tercer Mundo, Bogotá, 1963, pp. 188 and *passim:* Vernon L. Fluharty, *Dance of the Millions* (Pittsburgh: University of Pittsburgh Press, 1957), pp. 110–211; and John D. Martz, *Colombia* (Chapel Hill: University of North Carolina Press, 1962), pp. 117–118.

[27] Williamson's theory may, however, go quite far in explaining the urban explosion in 1948 known as the Bogotazo. High inflation in the first part of 1948 heightened deprivation, and the violence did have a class basis; objects of attack were typically symbols of social power: public buildings, churches, hotels, businesses, newspapers, etc. See Alfonso López Michelsen, *Cuestiones Colombianas,* Impresiones Modernas, México, 1955, pp. 73–74.

[28] Reinhard Bendix, *op. cit.,* pp. 42–43.

casionally by strife along party lines and by partial mobilization for elections.

Party legitimacy then was traditional, and loyalty took on quasi-religious overtones. One of Colombia's most perceptive social observers suggests this view in a novel set in the mid-1940's: "in this country there didn't exist political parties properly speaking, but religious sects, closed churches into which one was born and died without real convictions, in the same way as one inherits a religious creed which . . . must be defended ardently unto death."[29] If this characterization is correct, one would expect minimal party organization in rural areas, since organization is unnecessary to retain traditional loyalty. Occasional stimulation through party violence—as in 1900–03 and 1930–32 in the twentieth century—and elections would be sufficient to maintain it. Several observers have noted such scant organization of parties.[30]

Traditional legitimation is characteristically upset when people move to a modern urban context.[31] Choosing to leave the region and economic activity of one's father often leads one to question traditional identifications. Moreover, demands of new occupational and social relationships of an urban area typically imply new legitimation, often linked to satisfaction of demands based on social position. For this reason, urbanization and industrialization tend to produce pressures for achievement-oriented political appeals and more penetrating political organization.

[29] Alfonso López Michelsen, *Los Elegidos,* Editorial Guarania, México, 1953, p. 313. This explication is also based on conversations with the Colombian historian Fernando Guillén Martínez, but it is only a hypothesis. It would require for its verification detailed anthropological work in several communities and an attempt to see whether strong correlations are indeed absent between party identification and sociological variables in rural areas. A cursory glance at regional party strength did not suggest any correlations to the author, but this is clearly a fruitful area for research. The view suggested here is also contained in Eduardo Santa, *Sociología Política de Colombia,* Ediciones Tercer Mundo, Bogotá, pp. 74–76 and *passim.*

[30] See Santa, *op. cit.,* pp. 81–82; and Martz, *op. cit.,* p. 12.

[31] This has been treated widely in the literature on African states. See for example Immanuel Wallerstein, *The Politics of Independence* (New York: Vintage Books, 1961), pp. 29–43.

A reform movement in the 1930's produced the first of these. The Liberal Party sought support of new urban groups by granting economic and social privileges, not by arousing traditional symbols, which say, in effect, "We are both Liberals; therefore follow me."

At the same time, it is obvious that this change was only a partial one, that there were (and are) many areas in which a traditional, not modern, appeal was most effective. This suggests a characteristic of societies in transition noted by other authors: the coexistence of a modern and traditional sector.[32] This coexistence of the modern with the traditional applies not only to legitimation of party authority, but also to many features of the economic and social systems.

By the close of World War II, then, Colombia was in the midst of transition. A generally rural traditional sector coexisted with a predominantly urban modern sector. The modern sector, strengthened by industrialization and urbanization, was gradually replacing the traditional sector; political power had swung to an urban-oriented Liberal Party as a result of the reforms of the 1930's.

Hobsbawm, in his study of primitive social movements, suggests what he terms "populist legitimism" as a characteristic reaction of a traditional sector to such a threat. He describes its logic as follows:

> First, the ruler (or an institution like the Church) in some sense symbolizes and represents the people and its ways of life, as uninstructed public opinion sees it. . . . But if this stable order, poor though it should be, should be threatened from outside or inside, then, unless the ruler has produced or tolerated more than the expected measure of poverty, injustice and death (to use the Chinese phrase, 'the mandate of heaven has run out'), the people will rally round him, since he is in a symbolic sense, 'themselves,' or at least the personification of the social order.[33]

[32] It has perhaps been developed most fully by Gino Germani in *Política y Sociedad en Una Epoca de Transición,* Editorial Paidos, Buenos Aires, 1962, pp. 69–126.

[33] E. J. Hobsbawm, *Primitive Rebels.* (New York: Frederick A. Praeger, 1959), pp. 118–119. See also Bendix, *op. cit.,* pp. 45–47 for a discussion of populist legitimism and its relation to political life in pre-modern Europe.

Post-war Colombia satisfied some conditions for populist legitimism, since a traditional order was being undermined by urbanization and industrialization–in short by modernization. But modernization does not always beget violence on a grand scale. Colombia's political parties, however, differed in two respects from those of most other Latin countries. They dated from the mid-nineteenth century and virtually all peasants identified with them; and they diverged sharply in their commitments to modernization.

The Liberal Party represented an attack on the traditional sacred order. Liberal identification with secular forces of urbanization and industrialization in the 1930's placed the party squarely on the side of modernization. Its latent anti-clericalism reinforced this identification, especially when attacks on churches took place in several sections of the country following Gaitán's assassination in 1948.

The Conservative Party stood for the traditional sacred order in the sense of Hobsbawm's ruler. Since the late 1930's, Conservatives had been stressing the moral superiority of the traditional peasant over urban masses.[34] Laureano Gómez in the late 1940's and early 1950's intensified the appeal to such symbols as the Church, family and Hispanic heritage. These became the bases of his proposed constitutional reforms in 1953, and he devoted about half a radio speech discussing those reforms to a historical sketch in which the erosion of values was traced to 1930, the year of the Liberal accession and the beginning of modernization.[35]

Rhetoric of this sort stimulated traditional identifications and intensified resentments toward the modern sector. Violence motivated by political hostilities on a local level was thus transformed into wider violence directed against perpetrators of moral and spiritual decay. Thus violence became a

[34] See, for example, Silvio Villegas, *No Hay Enemigos a la Derecha,* Manizales, 1937; and Gilberto Alzate Avendaño, *Sus Mejores Páginas,* Editorial Renacimiento, Manizales, 1961. The latter is a collection of newspaper articles and speeches from the late 1930's.

[35] Gómez later passed to world history, seeing the crisis of Western civilization as emanating from the French Revolution. The speech was printed in *El Siglo* (Bogotá), May 21, 1953.

kind of holy war, defending a traditional order against those who were undermining it.

The key to this process was to identify Liberal peasants with modernization, which was difficult since they were no more modernized than Conservative peasants and probably shared the latters' resentments. Traditional loyalties to the Liberal Party, however, associated some peasants with Liberal efforts toward modernization. Traditional political hostilities were thus reinforced in rural areas by the conflict over modernization. This explains the unusually strong partisan rhetoric of the period, in which traditional values of Church and family were juxtaposed with Liberal efforts at modernization. Liberal peasants fought back, partly to defend themselves, partly in response to traditional appeals from Liberal leaders.[36] In a context of insecurity which stemmed from intense hostility between the parties, rural violence rose to unprecedented and unintended heights.

The existence of national political parties which differed in their commitments to modernization and with which nearly all peasants identified were thus crucial ingredients in the violence. The absence of such institutions in other countries explains why the Colombian violence has few parallels among modernizing nations.[37]

[36] One Liberal Senator is reported to have exhorted Liberals to "break even social and family relations with Conservatives." See *El Siglo* (Bogotá), July 30, 1952.

[37] An article by Orlando Fals Borda which came to the author's attention after the completion of the manuscript hints at a view similar to that presented. Fals refers to "the hypothesis that the appearance of violence in the countryside in Colombia since the late 1940's has been an irrational but effective political response to efforts to preserve essential aspects of the same old 'sacred' order. . . ."He does not, however, follow out this suggestion to account for the duration or intensity of the violence; he refers only to the fact that "the use of violence could not be held within reasonable bounds and it got out of the control of the political leaders who had sought to use it and became a monster of malfunctioning based on unanticipated structural faults and cleavages," and leaves that phenomenon unanalyzed. He also asserts that the peasants "were unable to take the next step toward the social revolution that they unconsciously desired," indicating his implicit agreement with the Williamson thesis which he had articulated in "The Role of Violence . . ." *op. cit.* See Orlando Fals Borda, "Violence and the

III. *Conclusion*

We may summarize the argument. Colombian violence was rural and pitted peasant against peasant, and thus cannot be understood as generated by social deprivation or anomie. Rather, it was a feudal or premodern conflict, generated by modernization. Modernization begun in the 1930's presented a threat to a sacred traditional order, and created a potential for populist legitimism, or violent defense of that order. This potential was realized because of four additional factors: traditional and universal loyalty of peasants to the Liberal or Conservative party; the identification of the Liberal party with modernization; a legacy of political violence accompanying transfers of power at the national level; and the Conservative party's political interest in exploiting violence. Violence against Liberals widened and intensified into a holy war against modernization, with which Liberal peasants were associated through traditional party loyalty.

This view explains why the violence was so intense for so long, and can account for several features of the violence which the Williamson view leaves unexplained. First, it explains why the violence was rural: only that sector could be mobilized against modernization. Second, it explains why there was no class basis to the violence: feudal political affiliations with no class basis associated some peasants with modernization and defined the lines of conflict. Third, it explains the political overtones of the violence: peasants rose to the defense of a traditional order personified by the Conservative party, against Liberal peasants whose party affiliation identified them with modernization. Fourth, it explains the potency of messianic, quasi-religious political rhetoric: only this could mobilize tradition-bound peasants against an enemy whose most visible difference was party loyalty. Fifth, it explains why national leaders incited the violence: political imperatives of the Conservative party complemented loyalties of peasant adherents to traditional values. Sixth, it explains why

---

Break-Up of Tradition in Colombia" in Claudio Veliz, ed., *Obstacles to Change in Latin America.* (London: Oxford University Press, 1965). Quotes are from pp. 189, 197 and 198 respectively.

a figure like Gómez, in essence struggling vainly against the French Revolution, could attain political eminence in an industrializing and urbanizing nation: his attacks on modernization resounded powerfully in the sector being threatened by such changes.

There is a seventh feature of the violence also better explained by our view than by Williamson's. It is generally acknowledged that an evolution in the violence occurred from the late 1940's to the late 1950's. Prominent among the motives of later violence was family vengeance.[38] Another was that orphans of the violence raised among antagonists knew no other life and continued killing. Economic motives have also been present, from robbing coffee crops to kidnappings.[39] No dates may be given for the replacement of "traditional" violence by this latter pattern, but the best empirical study of the violence suggests that such factors were relatively minor in the late 1940's but important in the late 1950's.[40] Williamson recognizes these factors as part of the violence, but makes no attempt to account for an evolution.

Our view implies that the violence could not maintain its original character for long. Not only was it fighting a losing battle against modernization, but was also destroying its roots, the traditional society. Three features may be noted. First, thousands of peasants fled the violence, some to urban areas, others to new rural areas. Second, new local institutions arose as peasants banded together for protection from aggression. Third, upward mobility became possible for many peasants who came upon abandoned land.[41] Each of these effects of

[38] Biographies of four leading outlaws of the late 1950's and 1960's suggest the killing or violation of a close relative as the catalyst which induced them to begin looting and killing. See Brian Moynaham, "La Violencia," *Cromos* (Bogotá), October 18, 1965.

[39] One common practice in some areas for instance was to hire bandits to terrorize a finca, whose owners would then be forced to sell at a low price. Theft of coffee crops was also common. See Guzmán, *op. cit.*, Vol. I, p. 130, and Vol. II, p. 276.

[40] *Ibid.*, Vol. II, pp. 267–279. Colombians generally speak of the evolution as having occurred.

[41] These and related points are brought together by Camilo Torres Restrepo, *op. cit.* Also see Fals Borda, "Violence and the Break-Up of Tradition . . ." *op. cit.*, pp. 199–201, Pineda, *op. cit.*,

the violence tended to erode the traditional society out of which it was born and consequently to weaken its roots.

There is some reason to believe that rural violence is now entering a third stage, that of fidelista-inspired guerrilla activity.[42] The first incident which was clearly fidelista-inspired occurred in January, 1965; such activities may increase in the future. This suggests a dialectic of Colombia's violence, in which feudal conflict undermined the social structure which produced it, leading to a decade of unstructured and diverse violence, which in turn may be followed by modern conflict which could not have prospered in the traditional society.

---

passim, Gutierrez, *op. cit.,* pp. 15–50 and Guzmán, *op. cit.,* Vol. I, pp. 154–156 and 412.

[42] See James Nelson Goodsell, "Colombia's 'la violencia'," *The Christian Science Monitor,* January 14, 1966, in which the rise of fidelista activity is discussed. A statement to the same effect by Colombia's Minister of War, General Reibeiz Pizarro, may be found in *El Tiempo* (Bogotá), November 6, 1965.

Part II

The Politics of Separate Countries

MEXICO

Mexico's political system in recent decades has been characterized as highly stable. This stability was questioned to a certain extent with the student demonstrations of 1968, but the political system showed no major disruptions in its basic functioning and the discontent did not lead to any sizeable worker or peasant activism. The student demonstrations were certainly minor compared to the chaotic Mexican politics of the 1800s and the revolutionary turmoil from 1911 to 1921, and raises the question of what accounts for the stability and makes the regime so assured of itself and somewhat insensitive to any popular discontent.

One of the reasons for the stability and self-assuredness is that the military is not a threat to the regime and thus does not function as a channel to articulate discontent upwards or press changes upon the decision makers. Military non-involvement at present is a distinct change from most of Mexico's history, and in the first selection Edwin Lieuwen, Professor of History at the University of New Mexico, describes how the military was taken out of active decision making. Professor Lieuwen clearly shows that the task was a difficult one, taking a whole generation and the combined efforts of a number of presidents, and the use of every conceivable Machiavellian technique. By 1940, however, the military was effectively curbed.

Mexico in the last four decades has been governed by a highly centralized political machine centering on the President and an inner circle of leaders of the Revolutionary Family. This is described in the second selection by Frank Brandenburg, an expert on Mexico who published the first original dissertation on the PRI party and who has had many contacts with Mexican officials. Professor Brandenburg's conceptualization of the political system is that of one huge patronage machine that provides rewards for all of its members as long as instructions are followed from the person immediately above. Since mobility upwards towards the most coveted offices is possible, a strong incentive is provided all of the members, leading to a certain amount of competence in the machine, and a type of built in stability. Professor Brandenburg is by no means aghast at this system, feeling that it is an improvement over what Mexico had before, and can never really completely ignore the accomplishments of the Revolution.

Nevertheless the selection is realistically frank in its description of who governs in Mexico. Professor Brandenburg argues that the PRI party is negligible in important decision making, thus differing from other specialists. In following through on the choice of presidents and governors, he emphasizes how little a role the public plays. His description of the twelve rungs in the hierarchy of political power and prestige illustrates the positions worth aspiring to, of which the Mexican politicans seem to understand all too well.

THE CURBING OF THE MILITARY

*Curbing Militarism in Mexico: A Case Study**

EDWIN LIEUWEN

Probably no country in Latin America has suffered longer and more deeply than Mexico from the curse of predatory militarism. More than a thousand armed uprisings plagued this unfortunate republic in its first century of nationhood. Here were compounded nearly all the evils associated with undisciplined, irresponsible armed bodies of men on the loose. The word "army" in the popular mind more often than not

* Reprinted from Edwin Lieuwen, *Arms and Politics in Latin America* (New York: Frederick A. Praeger, 1960), Chapter 4 by permission of Council on Foreign Relations, Inc.

was associated with crime, violence, ignorance and corruption.

The sword and the rifle were the weapons of politics as opportunistic officers disregarded the constitution, broke laws with impunity, and provoked civil wars. Political turmoil engendered economic chaos, rampant peculation of public funds, deficits in the national budget, and loss of public credit abroad. The vigor of the private sector of the economy, small business especially, was sapped by monetary mismanagement, burdensome taxes, and confiscations. Thus the parasitic military caste added appreciably to the already deep-seated miseries of the Mexican people.

Yet Mexico has been able to rid itself of the plague of militarism. A quarter-century ago no Latin American army was more political than the Mexican; today the armed forces are virtually out of politics. Mexico has moved from one extreme to the other.

Although Mexican militarism actually was not born until after the country achieved independence, by the end of the colonial era conception had taken place and gestation was well advanced. Spanish monarchs had long fostered the growth of a military caste by restricting commissions as a rule to men of social position and by endowing the officer corps with special legal privileges. Clever and ambitious young men of limited means found in the career of arms opportunity for self-enrichment.[1] Officership was not a profession, it was a privilege. A late eighteenth-century observer noted:

> . . . The king had more officers than privates . . . [and] most of the former purchased their place to mock justice, to escape paying debts, to indulge in gaming and live a life of libertinage under the protection of the epaulettes. . . .[2]

In such armies standards of military honor could mean little, hence it was easy for leaders of independence movements

[1] Lucas Alamán, *Historia de Méjico* (Mexico City: J. M. Lara, 5 v., 1849–1852), v. 4, pp. 445–448.

[2] Hipólito Villarroel, *Méjico por dentro y fuero bajo el gobierno de los virreyes, o sea enfermedades políticas* (Mexico City: A. Valdés, 1831), p. 170.

to persuade a large fraction of the officer corps to betray their sworn allegiance to the king in exchange for quick promotions and new opportunities for graft. During the revolution of 1821, many young captains in the Spanish army were advanced to generals in the Mexican army as a reward for inducing large numbers of privates to desert with them.[3]

The dissolution of royal authority accelerated the breakdown of discipline in the armed forces. Three months after independence was declared, an audacious young officer, Augustín Iturbide, led a march on the constituent Congress and set himself up as Emperor Augustín I. Thus began the tragic spectacle of ambitious, undisciplined, irresponsible army officers competing with each other for short cuts to wealth, power, and influence.

For nearly sixty years political processes in Mexico were dominated by military violence. Hundreds of barracks uprisings and rebellions were led by army officers and backed by the political out-groups. Incumbent regimes were toppled at an average of better than one a year.[4] In 1821 there were nearly five thousand officers for the eight thousand enlisted men stationed in the capital. In 1823, when total government revenues were five million dollars, the budget of the armed forces was nine million. During Mexico's first quarter-century of independence, the military budget exceeded government revenues two out of every three years.[5]

The armed forces were completely beyond civilian control. The legal privileges and exemptions granted them in the colonial era continued in force. By threats of rebellion they got the lion's share of the national budget. The philosophy that predominated among the ambitious is described by Ernest Gruening as follows:

> . . . Good faith, merit, constancy and hard work were not only unappreciated but detrimental to an ambitious young man. Chicanery brought richer rewards. A lieuten-

[3] Ernest Gruening, *Mexico and Its Heritage* (New York: Century, 1928), pp. 289–291.

[4] Frank Tannenbaum, *Peace by Revolution* (New York: Columbia University Press, 1933), pp. 75–76, 92–93.

[5] Alamán, cited, v. 5, p. 499; Francisco Bulnes, *Las grandes mentiras de nuestra historia* (Paris: C. Bouret, 1904), pp. 210–211.

ant who participated in a half dozen *cuartelazos* [barrack uprisings] almost certainly emerged a general. A successful *levantamiento* [uprising] erased a previous defalcation. The risks were not great—except for a few hours—and far preferable to years of patient drudgery. Thus was the atmosphere of public life vitiated. Honorable men had no chance in it, for the successful tricksters wanted men of like stamp to further their common base ends. Even civilians were given high army commissions. So the officer caste grew, exempt from and above the civil law, an arrogant coterie of debauchees, reveling by night and conspiring by day.[6]

The most notorious of the predatory military adventurers was General Antonio López de Santa Anna. For over a quarter of a century he capriciously made and unmade governments. In fact, the domestic political history of Mexico up to 1855 is practically a narrative of General Santa Anna's revolutions.

In the 1850's and 1860's, a group of civilians led by Benito Juárez made some progress subordinating the military to civil authority. After a generation of conflict over this issue, a military man, General Porfirio Díaz, finally established control over the army and achieved political stability. Frank Tannenbaum explains that he did this "by replacing instability and disorganized violence with tyranny and organized violence."[7]

Pacifying and disciplining the hitherto untractable officer corps took patience, astuteness, and a wide variety of Machiavellian techniques. Díaz quieted rivals too dangerous to crush by providing them with unlimited opportunities for graft and plunder. Those that he was prepared to tackle he deliberately offended, then discharged and exiled. Gradually he ousted a quarter of the army's one hundred generals and dismissed some four hundred officers of lower rank. He attempted to purchase the loyalty of the remainder with generous salaries, expense accounts, and opportunities for self-enrichment. Further to insure their fidelity, he established a system of shifting commands in the nation's eleven newly

[6] Cited, p. 26.

[7] Frank Tannenbaum, *Mexico: The Struggle for Peace and Bread* (New York: Knopf, 1950), pp. 81–82.

organized military zones. To prevent any officer from gaining the allegiance of a large body of enlisted men, he extended the periodic change of officer duty as far down as the regimental level. Potential rivals he either "promoted" to governorships, or cashiered on charges of corruption. By 1892, after a dozen years of effort, the army was finally under Díaz' firm control.[8]

Díaz accomplished the miracle of disciplining the Mexican army not only by his remarkable courage, his astuteness and his administrative talents; in addition he owed much to the great influx of foreign capital in the late nineteenth century, which came in partly as a result of his pacification of the country. The new investments enabled the dictator to provide would-be rivals with the material benefits so essential to subduing their latent aspirations to power. Moreover, the rapid development of modern communications had made it far easier to stamp out incipient rebellions.

Díaz may have disciplined the military, but he failed to create an efficient and loyal fighting force. The armed forces were adequate, along with the *rurales* (mounted constabulary), for performing police functions and quelling isolated disturbances, but when in 1910 a popular revolution broke out the vaunted capabilities of the Díaz army and the asserted loyalty of his officer corps proved to be fictitious. The army in reality proved to be but a fragile shell.

On the eve of the revolution, when the total population was about fourteen million, the Mexican army consisted of some four thousand officers, twenty thousand enlisted men, and four thousand rural mounted police. Organized on a caste system, it was led by middle and upper-middle class white officers, most of whom were graduates of the Chapultepec military school. Although French influence was noticeable in the army and some of the equipment was German, Mexico did not entertain any foreign military missions and rarely sent officers abroad to study. Consequently, it lacked modern military techniques and equipment. The ranks were filled with primitive Indian conscripts, among them a good number of

[8] Carleton Beals, *Porfirio Díaz* (Philadelphia: Lippincott, 1932), pp. 223–255, 287, 289; Hubert Herring, *A History of Latin America* (New York: Knopf, 1955), p. 342.

vagabonds, beggars, and criminals. The small navy was weak and insignificant.[9] Ostensibly, the mission of the armed forces was to repel foreign invaders; their actual mission was to crush all internal opposition to Díaz and perpetuate the dictator in power. They lacked the capabilities for doing either.

The storm that broke in 1910 was not just another local rebellion or barracks revolt, but a fundamental social revolution with broad popular participation. Ultimately it was to bring about sweeping changes in Mexico's economy, its social organization and its political structure. Nevertheless, the country was doomed first to return to chaotic pre-Díaz conditions. Again irresponsible militarism was to hold sway over politics and to prey upon the nation's economy and civilian society.

The electoral dispute of 1910 was the spark that set aflame the latent popular antagonism to the Díaz regime. Under the leadership of middle-group citizens spontaneous uprisings began in scattered areas. When the weakness of the regular army became apparent, the movement began to snowball. An increasing number of officers deserted the regime and joined the revolutionary forces, impressed by their power and by their popular support. Their object obviously was to emerge on the winning side.[10] Thus, with the help of the regulars, the Díaz regime was overthrown and Francisco Madero assumed the presidency. Almost immediately, however, he was plagued by the problem of the army. Only those regulars who were loyal to Díaz had been crushed. Most of the army regulars, who had joined the rebels in ousting Díaz, now claimed their rewards. They were challenged, however, by revolutionary citizen-generals demanding to be made generals in the regular army.[11] Madero made the mistake of siding with

[9] Charles M. Jerram, *Armies of the World* (London: Lawrence and Bullen, 1899), pp. 206–207, 299; Thomas A. Janvier, "The Mexican Army," in *The Armies of Today* (New York: Harper, 1893), pp. 366–396; Percy F. Martin, *Mexico in the Twentieth Century* (London: E. Arnold, 1907), v. 2, pp. 42–43.

[10] Gruening, cited, p. 302; Tannenbaum, *Mexico: The Struggle for Peace and Bread,* cited, p. 50; Jesús Silva Herzog, *Un ensayo sobre la revolución mejicana* (Mexico City: Ediciones Cuadernos Americanos, 1946), pp. 28–29.

[11] Charles L. Cumberland, *Mexican Revolution: Genesis under Madero* (Austin: University of Texas Press, 1952), pp. 159–160; Silva Herzog, cited, pp. 28–29.

the regulars and disbanding the revolutionary army. His reward was assassination at the hands of former Díaz henchmen; thereupon General Victoriano Huerta attempted to reimpose a Díaz-type regime.

This action not only stirred to action the outraged former revolutionary generals, but stimulated the rise of new leaders as well. Thus the Constitutionalist army was formed in March of 1913. In this force were almost no regulars, but many civilian leaders like Alvaro Obregón who had displayed a natural talent for soldiering, and skilled military adventurers like Pancho Villa. A former state governor, Venustiano Carranza, assumed command of the movement. The revolutionary force drove down from the north, virtually annihilated the regulars, and took command of the capital.

But the citizen-generals were no more immune to political rivalry and ambition than their more class-conscious predecessors. Almost immediately the victors were squabbling over the spoils. Militarism returned to Mexico with vengeance as Pancho Villa, whose private army was even larger than the entire regular army had been under Díaz, challenged Carranza's authority. But by making use of nonpolitical, professional officers, and by enlisting the support of urban labor and the peasants to whom he promised reforms, Carranza was able to crush Villa in March of 1915.

Though Carranza was now dominant, he by no means had absolute control. The nation was armed to the teeth and equipped with a superabundance of improvised generals. The regular army had disappeared, but there was no real national army to take its place. Instead, there were a whole series of separate revolutionary armies, each claiming and exercising a large degree of autonomy.

Carranza, after desperately trying to establish firm centralized control of the army, was finally forced to sanction a certain measure of regional autonomy. Then, too, he was overly tolerant of the excesses committed by a large, irresponsible group of "loyal" young officers in the capital. This, along with Carranza's attempt to dictate his successor, turned Generals Obregón, Calles, and the bulk of the army against him. Driven from office, he was murdered by one of his closest military colleagues.[12]

1920, a crucial year in the evolution of Mexico's armed forces, marked their last successful coup. The militarism of the revolutionary period had reached its high point. Thereafter the tide ran out. The Mexican army, which had been one of the most political and unprofessional in all Latin America, had become by 1940 one of the most nonpolitical and professional. Credit for this reform must go mainly to four strong revolutionary generals (Obregón, Calles, Amaro, and Cárdenas), who together spent an entire generation in accomplishing this extremely difficult task.

What was the army like in 1920? After ten years of revolutionary turbulence the curse laid by militarism on the Mexican political scene was at its worst. Carranza had been unable to bridle the generals. Around 80,000 men were under arms, more than double the number in 1910. The army, which still consisted of poorly organized, badly disciplined, semi-autonomous revolutionary bands, was notoriously overstaffed. Its volunteer ranks were filled with a motley assortment of adventurers, vagabonds, bandits, and loyal followers of various revolutionary leaders. It lacked regulation uniforms, arms, training, and tactics. Its numbers rose and fell with fluctuations in the ambitions and power of its leaders.

The officer corps, a most unprofessional body, was headed by the scandalously young, bellicose generals of the revolution. Though Díaz-trained professionals were scattered through the various units, they wielded relatively little influence in comparison to the victorious political officers of the revolution. The latter, of course, were completely without professional training and were ignorant of modern military science.[13]

The main tasks facing the central government were somehow to curb the regional *caudillos,* to cut down the heavy military expenditures, to reorganize the army and to build it

[12] Gruening, cited, pp. 311–315; Tannenbaum, *Mexico: The Struggle for Peace and Bread,* cited, pp. 62–63.

[13] Vicente Blasco Ibáñez, *El militarismo mejicano* (Valencia: Prometeo, 1920), pp. 177–192; Virginia Prewitt, "The Mexican Army," *Foreign Affairs,* April 1941, pp. 609–612.

into a truly national institution. To inaugurate this difficult program there was probably no better man than General Obregón, one of the best of the revolutionary generals, who had succeeded Carranza as president. His heroic role in the revolution had gained him widespread popular support and great prestige in the army. He alone commanded sufficient respect, combined with the necessary force of character, to have a chance of tethering the young mustang generals of the revolution. Somehow he had to convince them that the army was no longer a revolutionary instrument, that henceforth their careers depended upon their loyalty and service to the incumbent government.[14]

Obregón moved cautiously, but deliberately, to establish control at the center. He first incorporated all revolutionary generals into the regular army, putting them on the federal payroll. These attempts to extend his authority, however, provoked resistance among a number of generals who believed their real interest lay in a continuance of a semi-autonomy and unbridled militarism. In 1923, the Obregón government was very nearly toppled by a generals' conspiracy led by Adolfo de la Huerta.[15] Obregón promptly followed up his narrow victory by a thorough purge of all suspects. After many officers had been shot and others sent into exile, a number of the vacancies thus created were filled by young professionals from the newly organized officers' training-school. For Obregón, in addition to curbing militarism, had energetically promoted professionalism. Already, in 1917, under Carranza, he had set up a general-staff school, in which officers of the revolution received technical training from officers who had served in Díaz' army. And when he became president in 1920, he reopened the old Colegio Militar at Chapultepec for newly enlisted officers, with a three-year curriculum offering specialized training for the infantry, the cavalry, and the artillery.[16] In addition, he dispatched prom-

[14] Tannenbaum, *Mexico: The Struggle for Peace and Bread,* cited, p. 63; Gruening, cited, pp. 319–322; Prewitt, cited, p. 612.

[15] Gruening, cited, pp. 319–322; Tannenbaum, *Mexico: The Struggle for Peace and Bread,* cited, p. 63.

[16] Prewitt, cited, p. 613; Fritz T. Epstein, *European Military Influences in Latin America* (manuscript in possession of author in Library of Congress, 1941), p. 206.

ising young officers to Spain, France, Germany, and the United States to study modern military methods and techniques. He also succeeded in easing the military burden on the federal budget from 142 million pesos in 1921 to 117 million in 1924, by reducing the size of the army, and by curbing graft and corruption. Despite this progress, militarism was to remain a major problem for his successors. For in the course of crushing the Huerta revolt, Obregón found it expedient to promote twenty-three generals and create fifty-four new ones, in order to ensure their loyalty.[17]

General Calles' views on militarism, though similar to Obregón's, were somewhat more advanced. Obregón had relied for his success on personal prestige, but Calles, far less a hero among the revolutionary officers, initially sought to deemphasize *personalismo* and instill in the army a sense of loyalty to their profession and to their country. This, he correctly believed, was the only real cure for the disease of militarism. The secretary of war selected to transform Mexico's semi-feudal army into a truly national body was Joaquín Amaro, a young Indian general of the revolution whose professional and antimiltaristic zeal was unmatched.

In the six years during which Amaro had a free hand to straighten out the army he did a truly remarkable job.[18] Wisely avoiding a direct challenge to the old revolutionary generals whom he was determined ultimately to break, he began his reforms in the ranks, by improving recruiting standards, living conditions, and military equipment. To cut down costs, he disbanded the most unreliable armed groups and discharged the least desirable individuals in other groups. By 1930 he had reduced the army from about 75,000 to 50,000 men and had slashed military expenditures from 107 million pesos to 70 million. He put the troops to work, employing them on road-building and other public-works projects.[19] He also launched an educational and recreational program,

[17] Gruening, cited, pp. 322–323.

[18] Carleton Beals, "The Indian Who Sways Mexico's Destiny," *New York Times*, December 7, 1930, sec. 5, p. 8.

[19] Same; Prewitt, cited, p. 613; Gruening, cited, p. 322; Mexico, Ministerio de Guerra y Marina, *Memoria* (Mexico City), 1930/31, p. 10, 1931/32, p. 10.

hoping it would pay off in patriotism and loyalty to the central government rather than to the regional *caudillos*.

To discipline and organize armed peasants so that they would be a dependable military force in times of internal crises, the cooperation of the officer corps was necessary. Again General Amaro avoided a direct onslaught on the revolutionary generals; instead he bored in from the bottom. He stepped up the training of young officers abroad and sent missions to France, Spain, Italy, and the United States to study foreign military organization and methods. Upon returning to Mexico, they became Amaro's advisers, assisting him to build up a more efficient general staff. The first step toward this goal was the creation in 1926 of a Commission of Military Studies; the last was the organization in 1932 of a War College, under French professional influence, to train superior senior officers for general-staff duty.[20] Meanwhile, the newly organized Colegio Militar was rapidly improving as the officer trainees returned from abroad to provide modern technical instruction to the cadets. The latter, upon receiving their commissions, were deliberately assigned to regiments of doubtful loyalty, the object being to interpose a shield of loyal officers between the revolutionary general and his private army.[21]

As soon as Amaro's reforms were well advanced, General Calles was ready to challenge the generals. He deliberately provoked them by launching a policy of shifting commands. This decisive move in breaking the force of *personalismo* and militarism met with resistance as Calles and Amaro had expected, but they were ready for it. When the first uprising came, in 1927, they promptly crushed it and dismissed all the conspiring generals. In 1929 another revolt took place, the General Gonzalo Escobar rebellion, with the same results.

[20] Epstein ms., cited, p. 206; *Memoria,* 1930/31, cited, pp. 9–10; Mexico, Ministerio de Guerra y Marina, Dirección General de Educación Militar, *Los estudios de la escuela superior de guerra* (Mexico City: Imprenta Nacional, 1934), pp. 24–25, 65, 73–175.

[21] Tannenbaum, *Mexico: The Struggle for Peace and Bread,* cited, p. 91; Beals, "The Indian Who Sways Mexico's Destiny," cited, p. 8; Virginia Prewitt, *Reportage on Mexico* (New York: Dutton, 1941), p. 76.

This time thousands of loyal peasant troops came quickly to the government's assistance.[22]

The success of the Obregón-Calles reforms is revealed by the progressive decline in the number of disloyal officers. In the outbreak of 1923 nearly half of the officers went over to the rebels, in 1927 less than a quarter; a decade later, the final major uprising attracted practically no support from regular officers. In breaking the power of the regional *caudillos* Calles had surmounted the most dangerous obstacle to genuine military reform. To his successor, General Lázaro Cárdenas, he left the task of completing the job. There was still much to be done, but the day of the military chieftain, the regional *caudillo,* had passed.

After crushing the Escobar rebellion Calles rapidly consolidated his dictatorship. He arranged for a "figurehead" to succeed him, remaining until 1934 the real power behind the scenes. Most people expected the Callista dictatorship to continue, but Cárdenas, the new president and also a general of the revolution, soon asserted, and won, his independence. Cárdenas insisted on deepening the revolution by sweeping social and economic reforms, whereas Calles would have limited the government's task to pacifying the country and consolidating the completed revolution. The break came in June 1935, when Cárdenas openly refused to accept Calles' suggestions on economic and political policies. The outcome depended primarily on the army. Calles still had the support of most of the active revolutionary generals, but Cárdenas had the backing of a few of the more influential ones, plus the young elements in the army—both officers and men. In addition he had much broader popular support. The tension continued to mount in the latter half of 1935 until December 15, when Cárdenas suddenly began dismissing pro-Calles senators and top generals, including General Joaquín Amaro. The victory was completed in April of 1936 when Calles and a number of supporting generals were forced into exile.[23]

[22] Prewitt, "The Mexican Army," cited, p. 613; Beals, "The Indian Who Sways Mexico's Destiny," cited, p. 8.

[23] *New York Times,* June 23, sec. 4, p. 11; December 16; December 22, sec. 4, p. 6, 1935; April 11, 1936; Tannenbaum, *Mexico: The Struggle for Peace and Bread,* cited, pp. 74–76, 82–84.

Cárdenas knew he had little chance of getting the army's cooperation in his plans for land and labor reform. For one thing, many revolutionary generals had utilized the opportunities of the continuing turmoil to become large property owners and big businessmen themselves. Naturally they would oppose reforms that might affect their vested interests. Then there was the growing conservatism of men like Amaro, devoted to the profession of arms, who felt that Cárdenas' radical policies would give rise to domestic disturbances and thus undo the great progress already made toward pacification of the country and consolidation of the revolution.[24] Thus Cárdenas, anticipating army resistance to his policies, began to build up powerful labor and agrarian organizations to serve as counterpoises. He played down the role of the military as guardians of internal order, emphasizing instead their functions in education and public works. Refusing to increase the size of the regular army, he proposed instead to organize all peons in federal army reserves and advocated the formation of an independent labor militia. He revealed his fear of ambitious generals by shifting commands frequently, by building up support in the ranks through new material and educational benefits, and by providing promising young soldiers the opportunity to become officers.[25]

Cárdenas also did his utmost to spur professionalism and to remove the army from politics. In 1934 he inaugurated a six-year program for "the moral and professional advance of the army." The following year all infantry officers below the rank of colonel were given examinations in military science; those who failed were sent back to school. In 1936 he made competitive technical examinations requisite for officer promotion; the same year he issued a *reglamento* which proscribed all forms of political activity for officers. The following year he made it mandatory that officers on active duty give up all civilian employment.[26]

[24] *New York Times,* December 22, 1935, sec. 4, p. 6; Frank Kluckholn, "The Army Keeps Hold in Mexico," in same, May 29, 1948, sec. 4, p. 6.

[25] Kluckholn, cited, p. 5; *New York Times,* July 18 and August 17, 1935; Prewitt, "The Mexican Army," cited, p. 614.

[26] Mexico, Ministerio de Guerra y Marina, *Memoria,* 1933/34, pp. 10, 13, 1934/35, p. 14, 1935/36, p. 16; Mexico, Presidente,

His master stroke at the army's political power came in December 1937 when he organized a new federated revolutionary party composed of four equal sectors–labor, peasant, military and popular. When his critics accused him of bringing the army into politics he replied: "We did not put the army in politics. It was already there. In fact, it had been dominating the situation, and we did well to reduce its influence to one vote out of four."[27] Now the army could always be outvoted. Cárdenas and the party leaders could curb its accustomed political strength by balancing it against the other three forces.[28]

The president's military reforms and his radical land and labor policies provoked a certain amount of rightist reaction. General Nicolás Rodríquez, leader of the "Gold Shirts," an incipient Fascist movement in northern Mexico, tried to start an uprising but could get no army backing. The movement was easily crushed by the Cárdenas regime; its leader was arrested and cashiered. Similarly, General Laura Rocha's "anti-Soviet" campaign in the western states of Guadalajara and Jalisco against Cárdenas' "socialistic" agrarian and educational reforms was more annoying than dangerous to the stability of his regime.[29] A far more serious threat came from General Saturnino Cedillo, the last of the regional *caudillos.* Breaking with Cárdenas over both personal and policy differences, Cedillo in 1937 resigned from the cabinet and returned to his native state of San Luis Potosí where he began drilling a personal army, estimated at 8,000 to 15,000 armed peasants. But again the army remained loyal and Cárdenas, taking command in the field in the spring of 1938, had little trouble in crushing the uprising, thereby enhancing the prestige and authority of the central government.

Despite their unwillingness to join an armed revolt, some of the top revolutionary generals and a certain number of the new professional officers continued to balk at and protest

---

Reglamento general de deberes militares (Mexico City: Imprenta Nacional, 1936); Prewitt, "The Mexican Army," cited, p. 614.

[27] William C. Townshend, *Lázaro Cárdenas* (Ann Arbor, Mich.: George Wahr, 1952), p. 216.

[28] Prewitt, *Reportage on Mexico,* cited, pp. 167–169.

[29] *New York Times,* February 11, March 24, August 12, 1936.

against Cárdenas' radical land and labor policies. They were especially apprehensive about the new breed of extremist labor leaders, like Lombardo Toledano, and about the formation of a uniformed workers' militia which outnumbered the army by nearly two to one. A congressional bloc, led partly by revolutionary generals, bitterly fought the Cárdenas-sponsored legislation proposing to strengthen the agrarian organizations and the labor unions.[30] The army's fear of the rising power of labor was revealed in the following public statement released by a group of army colonels on June 29, 1938:

> Lombardo Toledano cannot hide now that he seeks the dissolution of the revolutionary army, and one proof of this is the formation of the so-called workers' militia in order to install a proletarian dictatorship in Mexico. The army is tired of the anti-army calumny by labor leaders like Lombardo who are seeking to fool the workers into starting a fight like that in Spain. The Mexican public may have the secure knowledge that the military officers will put and end to the calumny and violence of perverse leaders who are exploiters of the working class. In good time the army officers will answer their aggressors. We wish it to be known that if our brother officers, in defense of our armed institutions, punish Lombardo we are not guilty since we have been provoked.[31]

Army-labor tensions threatened a crisis in the summer of 1938. In a very real sense the issue was control of the party, the revolution, and the state. The battle was between the old revolutionary army generals in the north, who had been dominant since Carranza's victory in 1914, and the rising new political elements (the peasantry and the urban workers) in the central region. The latter, having grown to maturity during the mid-1930's, were now, with Cárdenas' backing, challenging the generals. Toledano's central Confederation of Labor (CTM) boldly attacked General Juan Yocupicio, the anti-labor governor of the state of Sonora, and demanded his dismissal. The Revolutionary party, no longer controlled by the

[30] Same, May 2, 1938; Kluckholn, cited, p. 5.
[31] Same, June 30, 1938.

generals since Cárdenas reorganized it in four sectors in late 1937, moved to expel "congressional" generals who seemed to be resisting labor-agrarian advances. The CTM's aggressiveness in Monterrey, Mexico's leading industrial center, prompted General Andreu Almazán, the regional military commander who was the highest-ranking officer in the army and one of the ablest of all the old revolutionary generals, to call on Cárdenas and urge him to curb the activities of pro-labor groups.[32]

When Cárdenas refused to intervene in behalf of his old colleagues, the lines were drawn for the political battle centering on the election of 1940. On one side, now outvoted and therefore outside the official party, were ranged the old leaders of the revolution and the conservative landed and business interests. Their candidate was General Almazán. Thirty-four high-ranking officers, mostly old generals of the revolution, took leave from active service to campaign for him. The government party also had a general as its candidate, Manuel Avila Camacho, Cárdenas' secretary of defense. But Avila Camacho was no revolutionary hero; instead he represented new labor and agrarian forces. Cárdenas appears to have chosen him to run because his influence with younger officers gave him the best chance of combating, in the army, the support still enjoyed by the clique of old revolutionary generals.

General Almazán and his supporters were well aware that they had no chance of winning elections managed by the incumbents. Consequently, they began making charges of electoral fraud early in the campaign. They accused the Cárdenas regime of "imposing" an unwanted official candidate on the people. They issued warnings and veiled threats of revolt, but the bulk of the army, in contrast to its past attitude, now seemed thoroughly bored by politics. The result was that the threats of Almazán and his supporters proved empty. General Avila Camacho and his labor-agrarian backed party were proclaimed easy victors over the revolutionary generals and their conservative supporters in the 1940 elections. After several minor post-election conspiracies had been easily

[32] *New York Times,* July 17, August 11 and October 16, 1938.

quelled,[33] the shift was complete. Control of Mexico's politics had been taken away from the generals of the revolution and placed in the hands of the labor-agrarian forces. Avila Camacho delivered the final blows to politically minded generals soon after his inauguration when he eliminated the military sector from the government party, broke up the military bloc in Congress, and placed a number of revolutionary generals on the retired list.[34]

With militarism finally throttled and internal order no longer a serious problem, the Mexican army could now devote its attention to its orthodox function—namely, to protect the nation against possible foreign enemies. And it was primarily for this purpose that the armed forces were built up, with United States assistance, during World War II. Under President Avila Camacho the armed forces were further reorganized, modernized, and professionalized. With political stability, accelerated economic development, and the increasing strength and influence of middle-class and professional groups, military officers played an ever-declining role in public affairs.

In 1946 and 1952 the party in power put up civilian candidates which easily defeated the still present and ever-threatening political generals of the opposition. The 1958 elections were again won handily by the civilian candidates without serious incident. By this time the die-hard generals of the revolution were no longer in evidence.

Compared with other Latin American armies, the Mexican today is a model institution. In accordance with the constitution, it devotes its energies principally to two fundamental functions: (1) the maintenance of internal peace, and (2) the provision for external defense. Incidentally, it performs an important function in collaborating in the country's public-works program. It builds barracks, schools, and hospitals, manages reforestation and irrigation projects, and helps keep the roads in good repair. It does not carry out its internal-security duties autonomously, as in so many Latin American

[33] Same, January 4, February 12, July 4, August 11, August 20, September 14, October 2, and October 3, 1940.

[34] Howard Cline, *The United States and Mexico* (Cambridge, Mass.: Harvard University Press, 1953), p. 276.

countries, but acts only under the orders of the president and the authority of Congress as provided in the constitution.

In accordance with the law, military personnel in active service surrender their political rights. They may neither participate in public political discussions or meetings, venture their opinions publicly on political matters, nor attempt to exercise political influence over their subordinates. For such illegal action the law provides penalties, including dismissal from the service.[35]

The armed forces are by no means completely removed from the business of government, however. All the commanders of the nation's thirty-three military zones are political in the sense that they are agents of the central government. They keep the state authorities in line and preserve order during elections. The growing strength of parties independent of the central government reveals, however, that the tyrannical rule of the zone commanders over the state governors and manipulation of elections by the army is rapidly becoming a thing of the past. Although some high officers are very influential in the Mexican government today, the military men are definitely in the minority. In 1958, only seven out of twenty-nine state governors and only two of eighteen cabinet ministers (defense and navy), were military men.[36] Inside the ruling party and inside the government itself civilian professionals predominate; they are the real policy-makers. The army is under their control. On issues that do not concern the military establishment they can act without consulting the armed forces, and they can, and do at times, oppose it on military issues. For example, despite the armed forces' desire for outside assistance and modernized equipment, the civilian authorities overruled the military and rejected the proposed Mutual Defense Assistance Pact with the United States.[37]

[35] Javier Bazán Pérez, *El ejército en la constitución y en la política* (Mexico City, 1952), pp. 11–54; William P. Tucker, *The Mexican Government Today* (Minneapolis: University of Minnesota Press, 1957), p. 194.

[36] Tucker, cited, p. 193; Walter H. Mallory, ed., *Political Handbook of the World, 1957* (New York: Harper, for the Council on Foreign Relations, 1957), pp. 134–135.

[37] *Hispanic American Report,* September 1950, p. 13; January 1952, p. 8; July 1953, p. 10.

In accordance with the limited functions and influence of the military, the civilian authorities have deliberately kept the military establishment small (around 50,000 over the past quarter-century) while the rest of the nation has grown rapidly. Consequently, the armed forces have received a declining percentage of the national budget (only about 12 per cent in 1957 as compared with 21 per cent in 1940). They absorb, also, a smaller percentage of the gross national product than do the armed forces of any other Latin American country except Costa Rica.[38]

Though the Mexican army ranks very low in Latin America with respect to its political influence, its professional rating, based on modern methods of organization, instruction and discipline, is high. Since the beginning of World War II the United States armed forces have served as Mexico's model for the organization of the army, its arms, methods of instruction, and discipline.[39]

The officer corps, only 3,500 strong, comes mainly from conservative middle-class families. A competitive entry examination and a 500-peso admission fee screen out the uneducated and the poor. Officership is now an established and respected profession. The young men plan their careers carefully and obtain promotions through professional competence rather than through political influence as in the past. No longer are their aspirations blocked by "revolutionary generals" with no knowledge of modern military methods.

The capabilities of Mexico's armed forces, although limited by their size and by shortages in equipment, are adequate for their principal mission—preserving internal order. For defense against threats from a major foreign invader, Mexico knows it can count on the United States.

For an underdeveloped Latin American country that is trying to modernize, it is important that the armed forces neither act as a serious drag on the economy by inflated budget requests nor pervert and corrupt politics. The Mexican armed forces now do neither. Discipline and control are firmly in

[38] *Inter-American Statistical Yearbook* (New York: Macmillan, 1940), pp. 512–541.

[39] Prewitt, "The Mexican Army," cited, p. 612; Tucker, cited, pp. 193–194.

the hands of a government and a political party, both of which are dominated by civilians. Inasmuch as the political influence of the officer corps has continued to decline over the past quarter-century while professionalism has risen, it is difficult to see how in the foreseeable future militarism can again plague Mexico. The counteracting trends are firm and steady and unlikely to be reversed. Mexico is over the hump. Fortunately, it has solved the problem of militarism. That is a major reason why it has become one of Latin America's most progressive nations.

In dealing with militarism, Mexico has set an example which other Latin American nations might be well advised to follow. Its experience has shown that, once a major social revolution has taken place, determined executives can launch a comprehensive program to mould the armed forces into a disciplined, professional army that would shun political activities. The task involved a liberal use of Machiavellian techniques to break the power of the citizen-officers of the revolution and a well-planned educational program designed to instill in the new young officers the concept of the "good soldier." An integral part of the project to achieve civilian supremacy in politics was the development among the urban workers and the peasants of counterpoises to the armed might of the military. The task took a generation to accomplish, but the results have proved more than worth the effort. For the past generation the entire nation, including the armed forces, has been reaping the rewards of this basic political reform and will almost certainly continue to do so.

THE MEXICAN POLITICAL MACHINE

*The Liberal Machiavellian**

FRANK BRANDENBURG

Good, bad, or indifferent, the means and ends of public policy under Revolutionary Family leadership depend squarely on the executive branch of government. When the President of Mexico simultaneously controls the Family, "the power of a President of Mexico has no limit but that of time, his six years in office."[1] All political publics uphold executive dominance. The publics not on the extremes–Revolutionary (Left, Center, and Right), Independent Left, and Traditional Conservatives–adhere to the principle of no re-election for the presidency and governorships, which in accord with Mexican constitutionalism means a change in executive leadership every six years. On the other hand, the political theories of the Radical Left and the Reactionary Conservatives suggest that if these groups were to capture the government, the principle of no re-election would be abandoned in favor of unlimited tenure. There are virtually no restraints by legislative and judicial agents. Checks and balances, separation of powers, pressure groups, effective federalism–all the elements of the United States system–have little more than paper counterparts in Mexico. Dictatorship of the Díaz variety has slowly given way to six-year authoritarianism of the Revolutionary

* Reprinted from *The Making of Modern Mexico,* by Frank Brandenburg, copyright © 1964 by Prentice-Hall, Inc., by permission of the publisher.

[1] Statement made in 1953 by Enrique Parra Hernández, an inner-circle politician in the Alemán epoch. Quoted in *The New York Times,* July 23, 1953.

variety, directed by executives of relatively liberal mold dedicated to the broad lines of the Revolutionary Creed. Within the Mexican milieu, the political sun rises and sets every six years on the presidency, and in identical cycles on gubernatorial offices. Mexicans avoid personal dictatorship by retiring their dictators every six years.

Such executive supremacy may cause Americans to think that the political system of Mexico, like its economy, is underdeveloped and backward. But trying to judge Mexico by American standards–presuming that interest groups support political parties which in turn compete for public power–engages an observer in a fascinating game of mental gymnastics that invariably terminates in a victory for irrationality, partial truths, and falsehoods. U.S.-style democracy is not willed into existence anywhere in the world unless some sturdy requisites are present, and many of them were absent in the Mexico of 1910, 1935, and 1964. Mexican political realities are radically different from those north of the Rio Grande. The Mexican system is equally underdeveloped as regards the Revolutionary Creed objective on political liberalism. We know it; the Mexicans know it. But we and the Mexicans look on democracy in different ways. The perfect system for Americans would have marginal utility for Mexicans, and vice versa. Because of the insuperable differences, it is well to reject comparability scales and concentrate on precisely how and why the Mexican system operates the way it does. Behind the whole complex subject looms the impact of preceding centuries which, coupled with the nature of Mexican temperament, presents an inheritance that in all probability neither the Revolutionary Family nor another elite will ever overcome.

Mexico's Official Party: Theory and Reality

The President of Mexico and state governors must walk with their feet on the ground, with a firm sense of the direction they are taking in time and space. Doomed is the leader who loses sight of the urgency to rule and reign in the context of yesterday's and today's as well as tomorrow's stage of development. Both Cárdenas and Calles possessed transcendent power, but the latter fell from the Revolutionary throne because his sense of the direction of the nation's development proved completely outdated. Both men were strong presidents, powerful heads of the Revolutionary Family. Both believed in executive dominance. Both arbitrarily unseated governors and hand-picked officeholders. In the interests of legitimizing government, Calles propounded a theory of "institutionalizing" Mexican politics which, stripped of its pragmatic aura, meant that Calles would pass his orders on public policy through the President of Mexico and his selection of presidents, governors, senators, and deputies through an official party. The political ambitions of poor and rich, of lawyers and intellectuals, of militarists, regional chiefs, and politicians were to be channeled through central party headquarters, where the aspirants were to flex their political muscles before a trusted Calles lieutenant presiding over the PNR. The high point of official-party domination was reached in 1933 under Gen. Carlos Riva Palacio; not before or since has the official party wielded such supreme authority over the nomination process.

Cárdenas, on the other hand, conceived of public policy and selection of officeholders as centering in an official party based on a four-part elite of trade unionists, communal agriculturists, military men, and "politicians". In Cárdenas' plan, these four sectors would "democratically" select candidates whose nomination assured election. Both theories, those of Calles and Cárdenas, subsumed governance by partial and fragmented incorporation of important social groups into the active decision-making process. Cárdenas, however, came closest to constructing a broadly based political mechanism—one that might have succeeded if Moscow had not raised havoc with trade unionism, if Mexico had been prepared for a popular-front democracy, if the general populace had subordinated other interests to supremacy of the proletariat, if literacy had been higher, if . . .

Despite Cárdenas' own rejection of the principal features of his model, as we have observed in Chapter 4, the paper outlines of his design persist today. The theory of the official party in the 1960's varies slightly from the Cárdenas conception, even though several structural changes in the 1940's altered sector alignment. Today there is an official party composed of three sectors—organized labor, communal agriculture, and "popular" elements—which theoretically nominate candidates to public offices through a functional, proportional-representation, intraparty process structured from local to national levels. Unions, federations, and associations formally affiliated with the official party purportedly take over the sectors and appoint party officialdom. A number of local "ward" committees are subject to district committees, which in turn fall under the jurisdiction of state executive committees that answer to national organs of the official party. At all levels, party-affiliated interest groups are to assume control of the party's three sectors. Theoretically, the sectors then decide among themselves which elective offices are to be apportioned to each sector, each sector selects the candidates for its designated offices, and all three sectors collectively support the nominations in the name of the official party. National organs presumably take direct charge of nominating a candidate for the office of President of Mexico, while state-level party organs select governors and senators, district organs select federal and state deputies, and local organs select municipal presidents and councilmen. In the Cárdenas plan, this kind of institutionalization was to assure "majority rule," since sector leaders during his administration represented an absolute majority of the Mexican electorate.

Cárdenas wanted interests outside official-party ranks to channel political demands through organized chambers, associations, leagues, political parties, and similar groups. As we have seen in Chapter 4, he created a series of semiofficial groupings corresponding to specific socio-economic interests, and he permitted the establishment of the National Action Party (the PAN), spokesman for the Traditional Conservatives. Yet in Cárdenas' view, all the interest groups and political parties outside the official organization would play a minor role in Mexican politics, because the government itself would be run by the majority inside the official party. What opposition, thought Cárdenas, what combination of interests outside the official party could possibly render the official party ineffective once it had entrenched itself in public power? An official party oriented toward and directed by the proletariat would guarantee perpetual control by selecting officeholders and by formulating public policy.

That the official party never fulfilled the role originally or subsequently assigned it frequently misleads observers of Mexican electoral patterns. Accepting party propaganda at near face value, one study of Mexican politics contended: "As long as the present official party continues to work out a formula for satisfying a majority of the strongest influence associations, dissatisfying as few as possible, not only the aggregating function but the decision-making process itself will reside in it and not in the formal government."[2] Contrary to this line of thought, however, the official party cannot "continue" interest satisfaction, since this role in the Mexican political system has always been performed elsewhere, whether under Cárdenas, Ávila Camacho, Miguel Alemán, or under the two Adolfos. And as for "the decision-making process," if this had actually resided in the official party instead of in the Revolutionary Family inner council and in the formal government, Mexico probably would have become a workers' state long ago. Such contentions regarding an omnipotent official party prompted the author of this book to make the following comment in *The Annals of the American Academy of Political and Social Science:*[3]

> Organized industrial and communal agricultural labor wish . . . [the claim of official-party omnipotence] were true. Party leadership dreams of it, indeed, even speaks of it once a week on its regular television program. But, once again, this time at the party's third national assembly, held the last week of March, 1960, party membership was restricted by and large to the laboring classes and popular masses. Industry and commerce, banking and insurance, top-level bureaucrats, university and normal school administrators, and military men—in short, the interests which really prospered since 1939—are still excluded from official-party ranks. Are we to believe . . . that a proletarian oriented and staffed party would sponsor two decades of government favoring its adversaries . . . ?

[2] Robert E. Scott, *Mexican Government in Transition* (Urbana, Illinois: University of Illinois Press, 1960), p. 29.
[3] July 1960, pp. 188–89.

Belief in official-party control of Mexico is clearly fallacious. It is an idea that observant Mexicans shrug off philosophically. Not until the official party works out a formula for satisfying a majority of the strongest influence associations—and perhaps not even then—is there the slightest possibility that the political decision-making process will reside in the party instead of in the Revolutionary inner circle and the formal governmental apparatus. This does not imply that Mexico's political system as a whole does not or cannot approach majority rule or "functional democracy" through other channels. Nor does it necessarily mean that Mexican leadership has been unresponsive to basic popular needs and demands. It merely indicates that misleading, partial explanations of Mexican politics and government—including measurements of majority rule, elections, rule-making, and the responsibility of governors to the governed—will emerge from studies that credit too much of what happens in the Mexican political system to its official party.

One of the biggest discrepancies between what the official party claims and what happens in reality involves transfer of presidential power. Therefore, let us examine this subject in some detail.

Presidential Succession

The Revolutionary Family has advanced certain tenets of political liberalism by lodging the real political power, the effective decision-making power, in a small elite directed by the President of Mexico or, in his stead, by the head of the Revolutionary Family. Improvement of the political climate flows directly from limiting a given "administrative team" to six years of total power. Political recruitment and political advancement operate on the principle of opening up many thousands of bureaucratic positions every six years. And everything else is subordinated to the president-designate, for it is he, in concert with the Family's inner council, who decides on the next administrative team. Superseding other presidential responsibilities is that of designating a successor according to a power formula of liberal authoritarianism in six-year doses.

The transfer of power from one president to the next–that is, the entire process of the presidential succession–involves nine steps. The first three are known in Mexican parlance as (1) *el tapado,* (2) *el verdadero tapado,* and (3) *irse a la cargada.* These initial steps collectively represent the designation and band-wagon stages. The show begins unfolding when the president (or Family head) inquires of the Revolutionary Family's inner circle, of vested interests outside the official party, and sometimes of sector leaders inside the official party what their dispositions are toward Señor X, General Y, or Lawyer Z. Aspirants are circumscribed by several constitutional provisions of which the most compelling are age (at least 35 years of age at the time of election), birth ("a Mexican by birth of Mexicans by birth"), residence (one year in the country before becoming president), and an absolute prohibition on re-election to the presidency. (The proviso that both parents must have been born in Mexico eliminates such competent men as Jaime Torres Bodet and Manuel Gómez Morin.) In reality, the narrowing-down process rarely concerns more than a half-dozen cabinet officers, with the final nod in earlier decades favoring the incumbent defense minister (Calles, Cárdenas, and Ávila Camacho) and of late the *gobernación* minister (Alemán, Ruiz Cortines, and Díaz Ordaz). The ring today seems to be widening, so that virtually any cabinet post or directorship of a major autonomous agency or government-owned industry can qualify a man for stepping upward.

Insofar as the theory of the official party is concerned, it seems pertinent to note that not a single president ever headed a labor union or the *ejidatario* confederation, the two kingpins of official-party organization. Although Alemán and López Mateos served as campaign managers for their predecessors, Cárdenas, Ávila Camacho, and Ruiz Cortines did not. Only in the 1946 election did an official-party president, Pascacio Gamboa, simultaneously serve a president-designate as campaign manager; in 1940, Gen. Heriberto Jara made room for Miguel Alemán; in 1952, Gen. Rodolfo Sánchez Taboada stepped aside for Adolfo López Mateos; and in 1958, Gen. Agustín Olachea gave way to Alfredo del Mazo. It is interesting to note that from 1940 forward, both the party president and the campaign manager became cabinet members in the new administration. And although Cárdenas, Alemán, and Ruiz Cortines once served as state governors, Ávila Camacho and López Mateos never held a governorship, although the latter did serve one term in the senate. Only two of the five last presidents distinguished themselves in formal party officialdom–Cárdenas as PNR president and López Mateos as PRI secretary-general, both for a short period of time.

In terms of place of birth, presidents since the Sonoran Dynasty have been selected from the populous entities of central Mexico: Cárdenas from Michoacán, Ávila Camacho from Puebla, Alemán and Ruiz Cortines from Veracruz, and López Mateos from the state of México. In the 1960 census, these four entities, plus the Federal District and Jalisco, comprised the most populous in the republic. There is good reason to suspect that regional pressures for seating a native son of Jalisco, third in population, or of Guanajuato or Oaxaca, seventh and eighth entities, respectively, in the presidency may prove convincing in future elections. About the only rule of thumb that seems pertinent is that those born in a heavily populated entity of central Mexico enjoy a decided edge over those born elsewhere.

The Revolutionary Family has placed less emphasis on the religion of presidential candidates than the casual observer may suspect. At one time or another in his life, every president seems to have dabbled in Catholicism, although Ávila Camacho is considered to be the only Revolutionary who became a "Catholic" president. Some Presidents of Mexico never became Freemasons, but others achieved high prominence in Masonic councils. Five attained the highest, or thirty-third, degree in Scottish Rite: Francisco Madero, Emilio Portes Gil, Pascual Ortiz Rubio, Abelardo Rodríguez, and Miguel Alemán. Two others were associated with the Mexican or Cárdenas Rite (Lázaro Cárdenas, one of the lodge's founders and grand masters, and Manuel Ávila Camacho), and two other chief executives entered orthodox Freemasonry but took little interest in the rite (Victoriano Huerta and Plutarco Elías Calles). There is no evidence suggesting that Venustiano Carranza, Alvaro Obregón, Adolfo Ruiz Cortines, or Adolfo López Mateos entered Freemasonry. To compound the religious question, mysticism constituted a strong element in the religious thinking of Madero and Calles. Divorce did not prevent Cárdenas and Ruiz Cortines from winning the nomination, nor did the notorious attentions of Calles, López Mateos and Alemán, to the fairer sex affect their presidential ambitions adversely. The record of fifty years of Revolution suggests that religious moderation and opposition to fanaticism probably comprise the two "religious" qualities sought after in presidential candidates.

For every politician and high-ranking career bureaucrat, the months leading up to the designation are full of anxiety. All are trying to outguess the next man on who will be named, on the identity of *el tapado* (the hidden one). Guessing his identity early or wrongly identifying him can mean the difference between remaining or arriving at the top and falling into political oblivion. Uncovering *el tapado* too soon encourages the taking of advanced positions and may produce mass exodus away from the incumbent president. When the Family head finally arrives at the "correct" consensus, when the propitious moment arrives for revealing *el tapado,* the candidate becomes *el verdadero tapado* (the one and only true candidate). The first officials apprised of the identity of *el verdadero tapado* after the inner circle of the Family has concurred on the designation are the government minister and official-party president. Revelation to the general public comes shortly thereafter in the form of an announcement of support by the largest trade union, the CTM, or by the communal agricultural union, the CNC or by the FSTSE civil servants federation. Having one of these large organizations declare itself in favor of *el verdadero tapado* provides an aura of popularism not otherwise available. Whether the CTM, CNC or FSTSE will enjoy the privilege of being the first to announce the candidacy is determined by *el verdadero tapado* himself. The public announcement simultaneously sets in motion the *irse a la cargada,* or band-wagon stage. Unions, federations, associations, agencies, regional strongmen, artificial groupings—everyone everywhere proclaims that the only man who can continue the Revolution is the proposed candidate. All manner of virtues are ascribed to him, and complete silence shrouds his defects. There is no mention of his mistresses, of his divorces, of his mistakes, or of his shortcomings. Everyone expatiates, everyone promises submission.

The stage is now set for making the candidacy legal and for the president-designate to "campaign." A giant outdoor rally in Mexico City takes care of the formalities of making Señor X the candidate of the official party. With this out of the way, the official-party president sits back to await orders from his new chieftain, provided that the head of the Revolutionary Family (generally the incumbent President of Mexico) sanctions the passage of total political power to the president-designate. In actual practice, then, not only does the official party fail to select the candidate on a sector basis, according to the theoretical plan, but it is relegated to the position of simply rubber-stamping the choice handed it from above. One president-designate may incorporate the official party into his program just as he finds it; another may relegate it to the role of a minor formalism, borrowing the name of the party for his own personally directed propaganda apparatus.

The presidential "campaign" in Mexico differs substantially from its counterpart in the United States. Although the foreign observer is led to believe that the candidate is seeking votes to overwhelm the opposition, this aspect never enters into the candidate's "campaign," for by this point all Mexico knows that, barring an armed revolt, the president-designate will in fact become president. In this context, the heir apparent is not a candidate in the American sense; he is the favorite son of the Revolutionary Family. The president-designate utilizes the campaign to permit people to see him in person, to size up regional strongmen on their own terrain, to examine the credentials of aspirants to the posts of senator, federal deputy, and governor, to bargain with opposition elements, and to satisfy the hundreds of friends and relatives who pop up everywhere. At this stage in the presidential succession, it counts for one to be a friend of a friend of the president-designate. The "campaign" also affords those state and local elements that wish to retain, enhance, or acquire power their big opportunity to impress the president-designate by organizing meetings, by spending money, by oratory, by unfolding economic-development schemes, and by any other means they believe will pay off. Aided by the incumbent president and government minister, "opposition parties" horse-trade for concessions in return for supporting the official candidacy or, as the case may be, for not supporting it. For his usual opposition, Vicente Lombardo Toledano traditionally receives the right to name several deputies, ambassadors, or second-level bureaucrats; Lombardo himself is permitted to retain a diplomatic passport. For his opposition in the 1950's, Gen. Jacinto Treviño of the PARM party was given the powerful directorship of the governmental agency controlling free ports and, additionally, was permitted to seat some of his people in legislative bodies. The president-designate must become president: the whole Revolutionary apparatus depends on it. Bankers, industrialists, merchants, union leaders, intellectuals, foreigners, large farmers—everyone who wishes something in the coming administration has the "campaign" period to prove himself. Spokesmen for the several Mexican publics establish their worthiness by direct consultation with the president-designate.

Although the president-designate never need worry about his own election, he does face one pressing duty at this time. Deciding on 60 senatorships, almost three times as many federal deputyships, and, if gubernatorial terms are expiring, on several governorships is a mighty task involving the ingratiation of friends, relatives, official-party affiliates, regional strongmen, and opposition elements. Hasty decisions in the case of federal deputyships can be corrected after election day by giving these seats to "opposition" candidates. But Family prestige and the unquestioned leadership of the President of Mexico demand that all senators and governors come from the official slate. However, since nominations for senators, deputies, and governors are made months before election day, the immediate months before election day are free of appeals from office-seekers for these posts.

These last few months find the president-designate working in unison with the defense minister, the government minister, and his campaign manager (who may simultaneously be official-party president) to assure that the masses and classes will stay in line before, after, and especially on election day. The major task of this concerted effort is the judicious stationing of trusted election officials, government-ministry agents, secret police, and army troops.

The sixth and seventh steps in the presidential succession are the general election and legalization of the vote tally. These steps produce invariable results: The official candidate and his senatorial team receive overwhelming majorities, opposition elements cry fraud and point out electoral illegalities, and the chamber of deputies verifies the vote tally sent it by the Federal Election Commission through the government minister. Accusations of fraud are intended to suggest the authenticity of an organized opposition, of free and effective suffrage, and of a give-and-take electoral contest in which the official slate truly won by an overwhelming majority, even though a few minor electoral manipulations occurred.

Ever since *el verdadero tapado* was revealed, an eighth step has been unfolding—that of choosing the new administrative team. Unlike a senatorship or deputyship, the offices of cabinet minister, military chief of staff, military zone commander, or director of an autonomous agency or state-owned enterprise carry access to public monies, to patronage, and to real economic and political power. For politicians and interest groups alike, these are the designations that really count. Now that the "elective" posts are filled, the various elites engage in a new guessing game: speculating on who will become treasury minister, director of Pemex, director of the Nacional Financiera, and so on. When private secretaries, undersecretaries, bureau chiefs, ambassadors, diplomatic ministers, consuls general, assistant directors and agency heads, military zone commanders and chiefs of staff, official-party officers down to the local level, special assignments, and several assistants per position are added to ministry-level appointments, then more than fifteen thousand political plums are at stake. The process of *el tapado* and *el verdadero tapado* begins anew. Revealing a minister-designate too far in advance introduces numerous dangers, such as the probability of undermining the authority of the incumbent minister or the possibility of giving an enterprising fellow a chance to set up a construction company to do business with his uncle who is slated to become public works minister. The residual patronage accruing to cabinet ministers and directors of autonomous agencies and state industries is so great that merely being a friend of their relatives and close friends means enjoying an inside track. For these and other reasons, the president-designate normally awaits inauguration day, the final step in the presidential succession, to reveal the identity of the top-level bureaucrats who will rule under him.

Gubernatorial Succession

Power transfer from a state governor to his successor follows the presidential pattern. The final word belongs to the head of the Revolutionary Family, although in several instances he merely rubber-stamps the selection by a regional strongman. Under optimum "effective suffrage" procedures, the President of Mexico consults with the Family's inner circle, "opposition" factions, military zone commanders, incumbent governors, regional strongmen, and vested interests outside and inside the official party to reach the "consensus" of the important people in a given state. A senatorship, federal deputyship, military zone command, or cabinet post in the national government normally qualifies a man for consideration. *El tapado* becomes *el verdadero tapado* when the President of Mexico informs the government minister, official-party president, incumbent governor, and military zone commander of his choice, and when one of the vested interests affiliated with the official party formally announces that General X and only General X can carry on the Revolution in X's state. All important interests in the state then *irse a la cargada,* the official party legalizes the nomination, the governor-designate "campaigns," selects state legislators, and reaches a modus vivendi to govern his relationship with local *caciques* and municipal authorities. He subjects himself to the formalities of a general election whose results are verified by the state legislature, appoints his administrative team, and finally, has himself duly inaugurated.

From prenomination to inauguration, the gubernatorial succession is controlled from Mexico City. The President of Mexico selects, the government minister oversees, and the defense minister enforces. The theory of official-party sector nomination simply never enters the picture. The party's president and secretary-general may assist the President of Mexico in reaching his "consensus," but this depends on the president, not on convention. The pattern varies slightly in states where a regional strongman is permitted to call the plays; there, the president sanctions the puppet-designate of the strongman and makes the latter personally answer for government in that entity. Since López Mateos removed the holds of Gonzalo Santos over San Luis Potosí and Margarito Ramírez over Quintana Roo Territory (an appointed post), four states continue subject to strongmen: Michoacán (Lázaro Cárdenas), Puebla (the Ávila Camacho family), Nayarit (Gilberto Flores Muñoz), and Baja California (Abelardo Rodríguez). In seven additional entities, a commanding role is played by Javier Rojo Gómez (Hidalgo), Adolfo López Mateos (state of México), Gen. Gabriel Leyva Velázquez (Sinaloa), Marte R. Gómez and Emilio Portes Gil (Tamaulipas), Gen. Alfonso Corona del Rosal (Tlaxcala), Adolfo Ruiz Cortines (Veracruz), and Leobardo Reynoso (Zacatecas). Yet by 1964, of all regional chieftains only Lázaro Cárdenas in Michoacán and incumbent president Adolfo López Mateos enjoyed extraordinary power, with the latter choosing to share it in his home state with Dr. Gustavo Baz. (The regional *cacique* persists because keeping him constitutes less of a problem than removing him. At times, not removing a regional chief, such as Gonzalo Santos in San Luis Potosí, can also produce serious political tensions.) In completely ignoring Javier Rojo Gómez and Marte R. Gómez, Miguel Alemán caused serious political tensions in Hidalgo and Tamaulipas, which the two Adolfos resolved by bringing Rojo and R. Gómez back into prominence.

Miguel Alemán also illustrated another characteristic of executive succession in the states: A very strong personality in the presidency may not consult anyone on gubernatorial nominations—and, further, he may impose his personal choice over multiple objections. Alemán's treatment of labor unions was extremely harsh. Placing Sánchez Colín in the state of México governorship, for example, constituted an outright refutation of CTM leadership. Alemán ran counter to intense local antipathy toward Dr. Ignacio Morones Prieto by making this non-resident of Nuevo León governor of that important northern entity; Ruiz Cortines reduced tension there by bringing Morones Prieto into his own national cabinet. Alemán also reversed two decades of civilianism in Tamaulipas, overriding the personal objections of Marte R. Gómez and Emilio Portes Gil, by making Gen. Raúl Gárate governor. Alemán further selected unpopular governors for Guerrero, Oaxaca, and Yucatán, all of whom Ruiz Cortines subsequently removed. And Alemán highlighted the fact that the army had not been removed from politics by running the nation at one time or another during his six-year regime with fifteen military men in gubernatorial posts, including those of Baja California Sur and Quintana Roo. In short, the "consensus" may and frequently does reflect the disposition of important vested interests in a given federative entity, but it always reflects the prevailing attitude of the Revolutionary Family head (normally the President of Mexico)—and for Michoacán, Puebla, and Nayarit, the desire of regional strongmen.

Local government is based on the *municipio,* roughly analogous to a county, governed by a *presidente municipal* and *regidores,* or councilmen. In electing municipal presidents, the "consensus" is normally determined by the respective state governors or, as the case may be, governors-designate. Nonetheless, the national government minister, acting under instructions of the President of Mexico or president-designate, can intervene, overrule a governor, and impose an alternate for the official-party nomination. A state governor can never forget that regular army, navy, and air force contingents in his state are commanded from Mexico City. The national government often intervenes when a governor becomes *persona non grata* with the President of Mexico—not an unusual situation under the system of staggered gubernatorial elections. Although the Constitution provides six-year terms for both the presidency and governorships, election dates do not coincide. Thus the new president inherits state governors from his predecessor, and he rarely sees eye-to-eye on policy with all governors during the initial years of his administration—unless, of course, he legally removes uncongenial governors before their constitutional terms end. This drastic alternative may complicate yet improve state politics; it may upset political equilibrium in the inner circle of the Revolutionary Family or re-establish it. Nonetheless, except for those few states in which regional strongmen prevail, it is not difficult for the President of Mexico to unseat a governor; in the last instance, the military zone commander can insure the acquiescence of the governor. Lázaro Cárdenas removed a majority of the state governors by forced resignations, which he ordered through the national legislature, state legislatures, or achieved by direct pressure on governors to renounce their offices. Ruiz Cortines removed four governors, replacing them with politicians less enthusiastic about Miguel Alemán. A state governor in the Mexican political system either stands in the shadow of Mexico City or loses his position. *Gobernación* agents, military zone commanders, Masonic lodges, business chambers, labor, cooperativist, and agrarian unionists, Catholic prelates, and official-party representatives are continually reporting on a governor's conduct to their corresponding higher councils in Mexico City. Senators and federal deputies, themselves frequently competing for prestige with the governor of their home state, also exert an influence that keeps a governor loyal to the president. These multiple checks on a governor, plus his own normal ambitions to proceed up the bureaucratic ladder, mean that nominations for *presidente municipal* and *regidores* preferred by the national government minister in Mexico City will prevail. In general, however, the President of Mexico usually permits a governor in good standing to designate municipal presidents, who in turn select their own *regidores*. Local official-party organs finally proclaim these choices to be the party's very own candidates.

The Legislators

By now, the reader should anticipate the "consensus" patterns marking the election of legislators. Aside from *regidores*, who theoretically fulfill the legislative function at the local level, there are three sets of legislators in Mexico: state deputies, federal deputies, and (federal) senators. Deputies to unicameral state legislatures represent electoral districts mapped out on the basis of population. Who will sit in a state legislature depends on the whims of the governor, governor-designate, or regional strongman, who determines the "consensus" of a given electoral district. He passes the nomination of a deputy-designate along to the state minister of government and to the official-party state president, who in turn picks an interest group affiliated with the official party to make the candidacy known publicly. Finally, the official party legalizes the candidacy. Though official-party nomination resolves the succession question then and there, the fiction of effective suffrage is upheld by a general election, accusations of fraud, and the seating of official candidates, who invariably win thumping majorities. Some governors arbitrarily select all state legislators; others turn over the entire nomination apparatus to regional strongmen, and still others permit union bosses, *ejidatario* leaders, local *caciques,* and politicians in the official party to designate candidates. The last procedure results in local labor and *ejido* bosses grabbing as many seats as they can for themselves. Whether official-party sectors cut up the electoral pie or someone outside the party does it for them, no effective power is at stake anyway: a state legislature obsequiously follows the state leader, be he governor, regional strongman, or governor-designate.

Under these circumstances, why does anyone seek a state deputyship in the first place? For additional salary, for the privileges and immunities that the office bestows, and in the peculiar Mexican sense, to rise above the masses–to no longer be like the average man-in-the-street or peasant-in-the-field. A union boss or a peasant leader hardly looks upon his "election" to a deputyship as a mandate for representing the electorate or his own rank and file–he and everybody else knows that the legislature is an impotent branch of government. The material benefits that accrue to the interest groups whose leaders sit in legislative bodies come from the executive branch, completely independent of these deputies. Groups never bring their claims before a legislature unless they are putting on a show for the executive or for visiting foreign dignitaries. It is the executive who answers to Mexico City for the conduct of his legislature. Inside or outside the official party, groups seek and obtain governmental benevolence from the executive branch directly, not through the powerless legislature or official party. When union leaders become state deputies, they add a few thousand pesos to their regular monthly incomes and acquire fringe benefits in the form of immunity from the application of certain laws and the privilege of importing certain items tariff-free; union rank and file receive nothing. The leaders use the new prestige and extra money to live better and to facilitate their upward mobility in the Mexican political system and captive union network. For two decades, the union boss has kept the rank and file in line, loyal to Revolutionary regimes. His reward, besides the permanence of his tenure, sometimes comes in the form of a legislative office.

The practice of rewarding labor bosses in this fashion is nowhere more pronounced than in the designation and composition of the national senate and chamber of deputies. For more than two decades, the big bosses of the biggest labor union, the CTM, have regularly sat in both chambers, yet the proletariat which they avowedly represented gained few notable advances in real income. Since 1940, the CTM bosses have conveniently alternated from senate to chamber of deputies. (Immediate re-election to either house is prohibited constitutionally). This kind of deal originated in 1940, when Cárdenas decided that Lombardo Toledano would relinquish his leadership of the CTM on terminating his secretary-generalship in 1941. To replace him came four of the "five little wolves" who had deserted Luis Morones and the CROM in the early 1930's to back Cárdenas and ultimately form a part of the CTM core: Fidel Velázquez, Fernando Amilpa, Alfonso Sánchez Madariaga, and Jesús Yurén. Division of the spoils resulted in Amilpa and Sánchez Madariaga becoming senators in 1940, Velázquez becoming CTM secretary-general in 1941, and Yurén becoming secretary-general of the biggest "state" federation, that of the Federal District. Six years later, Velázquez and Amilpa switched places—the former became a senator, the latter CTM secretary-general for three years. In 1949, Velázquez reassumed the CTM secretary-generalship, a post that he had not relinquished by 1964. In 1952, Yurén took a senate seat, and in 1958, Fidel Velázquez was back once again in the senate. Meanwhile, Amilpa died and Sánchez Madariaga became secretary-general of the hemisphere-wide Inter-American Labor Organization (the ORIT), of which the AFL-CIO is a member. Throughout this score of years, the CTM chieftains also took federal deputyships; in addition to his senatorship during 1940–46, Sánchez Madariaga became a deputy in 1937–40, 1946–49, and 1955–58. In the states and, to a lesser degree, in the Federal District, other CTM and railroad, petroleum, and mining union bosses have followed an identical pattern. Whenever the labor sector is awarded the right to designate official-party candidates for legislative offices, the labor bosses nominate themselves. And why not? There is no real power involved in the federal legislature, and the President of Mexico keeps his captive labor leaders placated by permitting them to acquire the extra money, privileges, immunities, and prestige of an office that other labor leaders are denied.

Division of the spoils of the federal legislature is a principal responsibility of the president-designate during his presidential campaign; three years later, as President of Mexico, he again decides on the membership composition of the chamber of deputies. In all, 60 senators (two from each state and from the Federal District) enter the upper house for a six-year term, and 178 deputies (based on total population proportioned among the states) enter the lower house for a three-year term.[4]

The "consensus" for a senator depends on the president-designate who, after insisting on his personal choices, usually permits sector leaders to name the rest. Since 1940, labor bosses, CNC spokesmen, and other known regulars of the official party account for approximately two-thirds of total senatorial seats awarded. Translated into other terms this means that interest-group leaders in the official party were permitted to name about two-thirds of the senators, while the president-designate, with or without the advice and consent of

[4] The new election law of December, 1962, provides that any political party winning 2.5 per cent of the national vote, whether five of its candidates actually win or not, will automatically obtain at least five deputy seats. Any party will acquire another seat for each additional one-half of 1 per cent of the total national vote. The new formula, to be applied for the first time in the 1964 federal elections, will prevail up to a maximum of twenty deputy seats. No similar provision was written into the new law on senatorial elections.

governors, regional strongmen, factional leaders of the Revolutionary Family, or the incumbent President of Mexico, personally named the rest. But no single *tapado* from the official party becomes *el verdadero tapado,* whether he is a party regular or not, unless the president-designate gives his final approval. Once candidates are approved by the president-designate, the official party holds intraparty primaries to nominate these same candidates by "democratic process," after which the party's president makes the candidacies public. Thus formally and legally proclaimed the senatorial candidates of the official party, all senators-designate share the comfort of knowing that 32 years of precedent will not be reversed to seat any opposing candidates. Furthermore, the government minister, election commission, President of Mexico, president-designate, and Mexican army are at hand to guarantee their election. Regardless of what happens on election day, official-party nomination guarantees a seat in the senate.

With federal deputies as well, the "will of the people" is what the president-designate and President of Mexico say it is. Since 1940, the Revolutionary Family head, President of Mexico, and president-designate have hand-picked about 20 per cent of the deputies; governors and regional *caciques* have selected approximately 15 per cent; opposition parties have been given almost 5 per cent; and the remaining 60 per cent has emerged from sectors in the official party. Invariably, candidates picked outside the official-party sector arrangement have been conveniently made the choices of the popular sector. This means that every three years about 35 labor leaders and 40-odd *ejidatario* spokesmen become federal deputies, while the remaining seats in the lower house ostensibly go to the "popular sector." The nominations from the three sectors and those of governors and regional *caciques* reach the president-designate or President of Mexico or both, where they are approved or disapproved, other choices are added, and the final definitive slate is given to the official-party president. Intraparty primaries then "democratize" all nominations, and the candidates are legally registered with the government minister. A meaningless campaign culminates on election day with victory for 95 per cent of the official slate. The official party runs candidates for every federal deputy district in the republic, and a few official candidates lose to "opposition" standard-bearers. Not one instance of complaint from a "defeated" official-party candidate is on record. Opposition parties, on the other hand, variously accuse the official party, governors, electoral officials, and military men of manifold sins of omission and commission. These post-election-day antics are supposed to suggest that although the election was not entirely free, "effective suffrage" did materialize because opposition parties "participated vigorously" in the election. The token seats awarded to opposition parties are usually from election districts in which the official-party organization for historical causes is in fact weak—districts in Durango, the Federal District, Guerrero, Jalisco, Nuevo León, Oaxaca, and Puebla. But sometimes the president or president-designate hands over a deputyship to the opposition in order to discipline an official candidate who has fallen from official grace between the time of his nomination and election day.

A chief executive who wishes to strengthen the legislative branch into a real power factor faces insuperable problems. Mexican tradition expects, virtually demands, an omnipotent president. Official-party composition and electoral procedures further combine to seat legislators who are unrepresentative of Mexican interests as a whole. Few interest-group leaders who reach the legislature are truly dedicated to their respective interest groups; they merely authoritatively manage the interest group in their charge. In this context, magnanimous presidents who sincerely attempt to build up the legislature invariably run into trouble.

Political Prestige and Political Mobility

If new jobs made available through electoral procedures comprised the entirety of bureaucratic patronage, there is little doubt that a sad fate would befall Revolutionary Mexico. Recruitment of new elements in sufficient numbers to give the political system continuous vitality would become impossible, and ambitious, politically conscious young men, denied hope of ingratiating themselves before the ruling elite, would be forced to look outside the Revolutionary mechanism for opportunities to enter public offices. Periodic access to all top jobs constitutes the Revolutionary formula for avoiding political stagnation. The price of permanent revolution is bureaucratic job turnover and the creation of new jobs. Top wages for loyal public service come in the form of six years of golden opportunity at the head of a cabinet ministry, autonomous agency, government-owned enterprise, or state government. Even when the change amounts to little more than switching jobs among a certain set of individuals (as occurred during the switchover from Ruiz Cortines to López Mateos), whereby managers of state enterprises move to other state enterprises, directors of autonomous agencies become cabinet ministers, and some cabinet ministers remain but bring new undersecretaries and bureau chiefs into their ministries—even then, the principle of change for the sake of patronage and vitality is upheld. Old elements entering different offices are permitted a relatively free hand in selecting a new team to serve under them.

Providing an ever-increasing number of public jobs, if not in government service proper, then in government-owned enterprises, thus comprises a major ingredient of the permanent revolution. Some idea of pressures for jobs in the public sector is gleaned from the growing number of sons, grandsons, brothers, nephews, and cousins of big and near-big Revolutionaries who have appeared on the scene since 1910. Of course, many of these descendants forgo a political career for private business and the professions, but thousands of new Revolutionary offspring come of age every six years. More imposing is the increasing number of university graduates who prefer the security and promise of public service to private pursuits. Satisfying all Mexicans, or even a majority of Mexicans, is not the *sine qua non* of permanent revolution. Finding jobs for enough Revolutionary descendants and college graduates is an important matter, however—one in which the Revolutionary Family has been successful so far, either by providing posts in the public quarter or through public policies that have stimulated new and bigger opportunities in private industry, commerce, and the professions. Gearing continuance of the Revolution to job satisfaction for Mexicans in the twenty-to-thirty-year age bracket may never have comprised a conscious Revolutionary Family policy, but it is precisely one achievement of the past two decades that checked praetorianism and permitted a generation of Mexicans to enjoy greater political liberalism and a life free from ruthless suppression.

From the presidential office down to municipal governmental organs, from giant state industries to small regulatory agencies, from the official party to captive opposition parties, every six-year administration witnesses a turnover of approximately 18,000 elective offices and 25,000 appointive posts. Discounting most of the 12,000-odd local councilmen and the 8,000 appointive jobs in the official party because of the relatively low pay involved leaves some 6,000 elective and 17,000 appointive positions for which the politicians compete in full knowledge that success will bring higher income. The politically ambitious enter anyplace along the line—as private secretaries of ministers, as technicians in a state industry, as normal school teachers, or in one of hundreds of ways. The general tendency is for the educated, technically prepared young men, including the usual host of young lawyers, to enter the political system through the civil service, and for the less-educated to initiate a political career through the lower elective offices. Of course, there is a fair amount of crossover, with onetime career bureaucrats becoming senators, federal deputies, or governors. The president of the official party (since 1946, an army general) moves on to the national defense ministership. Local *caciques,* whose power position lies outside the normal pattern, usually grab off state legislative posts. Since Alemán, the bureaucratic machine has favored placing technically qualified individuals in high appointive positions as well as in the thousands of middle-rank positions in cabinet ministries, autonomous agencies, boards, and commissions, and in state industries, banks, and related business enterprises. Captive leaders of communal agriculture, civil service, trade, and other unions enter politics through the official party; their future rarely holds the promise of anything beyond a senatorship.

From this complex patronage structure, a hierarchy of political prestige has slowly emerged. Does a state cabinet office carry more prestige than a federal deputyship? A supreme court justice more than a state governor? A manager of a big state industry less than a senator? Does the Mexican ambassador to Washington deserve higher prestige than the private secretary to the President of Mexico? What is the relationship of members of the Family's inner circle to cabinet members? That of a big trade-union boss to an official-party president? The answers to these questions can be found in the scale of political prestige that applies to the Mexican political system as a whole. Excluding business elements, which exert political influence but rarely wish for "political" prestige, and understanding that some persons through special talents or influences are able to enjoy prestige and power beyond that expected from their specific posts, the ladder of political prestige has twelve rungs:

12. Local party officials and municipal councilmen.
11. Municipal presidents, local military commanders, and state and federal officials at the local level.
10. State deputies, state judges, district official-party officials, federal officials in the states, and local *caciques*.
9. Federal deputies; federal judges; the president and members of regional executive councils of the official party; leaders of minor opposition parties; labor, agrarian, and federal credit bank bosses at the state level; and state cabinet officers.
8. Municipal presidents in large cities.
7. Directors and managers of medium-size state industries; directors of secondary federal boards, commissions, and agencies; governors of medium and small states; ambassadors, ministers, and consuls general.
6. Supreme court justices; senators; undersecretaries of cabinet ministries and assistant directors of large state industries, commissions, boards, and dependencies; the secretary-general and sector heads of the official party, leaders of major opposition parties; and the secretaries-general of the CTM, CNC, and FSTSE.
5. Governors of the big states and the federal territories, ambassadors in prestige posts, regional strongmen not in the inner circle, the two presidential legislative spokesmen in the respective houses of congress, military zone commanders, and the official-party president.
4. Cabinet members, including the governor of the Federal District; the military chief of staff; the private secretary of the president; managers of major state

industries; and directors of large semiautonomous agencies, commissions, banks, and boards.

3. Members of the inner circle and factional leaders of the Revolutionary Family.
2. The President of Mexico.
1. The head of the Revolutionary Family.

Permanent revolution thus depends on a political system that opens top bureaucratic positions every three years at the local level and every six years at the state and national levels. Bright, competent individuals who miss the patronage boat with one administration know that the next regime will offer them another opportunity to hop aboard. For example, a Marxist economist in an advisory capacity to the president may not remain or obtain a better position when an avid pro-private-enterprise Revolutionary becomes president. What does he do? He returns to his classes at the National University, writes a few treatises on aspects of political economy, and participates in special research projects while awaiting the next administration.

Two notable exceptions to general mobility, both of them potential monkey wrenches in the Revolutionary mechanism, have occurred in trade unions and the Mexican army. Bosses of the largest labor central, the CTM, have not relinquished their control of the labor movement for more than two decades, not the least because no president since Cárdenas has emphatically supported syndicalism, hence no president has dared risk upsetting economic development by removing these captive leaders. But big troubles lie ahead for CTM leadership; the rank and file despise their opportunistic conduct and, permitted a free, honest vote, would unload the whole leadership forthwith. The blockade to mobility in the military is raised by the old Revolutionary generals who have run the army since 1940. Though near or over seventy years of age, they refuse to step down. Becoming a general has been denied virtually all officers who are not veterans of civil war days. With an estimated 11,000 "auxiliary" officers—officers who draw full pay but engage in private pursuits—the military today, as in the past, is top-heavy with officers. What will happen when the younger officer crew, professional soldiers by vocation, finally move into zone commanderships, cabinet posts, and governorships is anybody's guess. Defense ministers obviously will have to come from among those officers without active service in the 1920's. The army as an institution, instead of simply a means by which several thousand old military men drain from the public treasury enough to keep themselves personally content, has prospects of regaining a bigger voice in Mexican political life. The stockpile of several thousand younger officers probably constitutes the most concentrated force of highly educated and surely best-disciplined men in the entire nation. For many years they have observed as their senior officers shared in the allocations of contracts let in their respective military zones, or obtained low-interest loans from government banks. And they have noted that accountants, engineers, small businessmen, and even full-time university professors receive higher salaries than theirs. Without this officer core behind it, the Revolutionary elite cannot continue to direct the destiny of Mexico—and of late, much of the younger officer corps seems noticeably impatient for more authority and higher income.

It is doubtful whether the Revolution could continue if the individual bureaucrat, in addition to being socially responsible, were not also self-seeking and opportunistic. A bureaucrat helps himself from the public till—sometimes more, like the *alemanistas,* sometimes less, like the *ruizcortinistas.* But graft there is, and undoubtedly, graft there always will be. Reduction of grafting? Possible. Elimination of graft? A contradiction of human nature. Many Mexican career civil servants live almost solely on their biweekly paychecks from the government. Aside from picking up a few pesos here and there by expediting papers, temporarily borrowing minor papers in their charge, and accepting gifts at Christmas and before Easter week from middlemen regularly engaged in government work—all in all, totaling less than four hundred U.S. dollars annually—perhaps 90 per cent of the bureaucrats are "honest," and thus persons of modest incomes. Even if tempted by grafting on a grandiose scale, civil servants below the upper 10 per cent bracket rarely hold positions important enough to realize their dream. In case the American tourist suffers from the illusion that customs officials at the border pocket the ten or twenty pesos that they politely fleece from the American, let us make clear that the lion's share goes to higher officialdom. It is these higher positions to which ambitious bureaucrats aspire. The prospect of $120 monthly and, after forty years, retirement with a modest pension is not their goal. Some of the presumed career bureaucrats who possess high political acumen (and usually technical competence as well) rise to the top, take what they can, retire from public service forever, and engage in more pleasant, less painstaking pursuits. What truly keeps a large stockpile of bureaucrats loyal to the Revolution is the prospect of someday satisfying their personal appetites—the hope that through dedicated service they too can rise to the top, make a fortune, and retire, not at 62, but at 42.

The bureaucracy as an interest group seeking benefits for itself in return for loyal, continuous services by and large encompasses only those civil servants up to the top 10 per cent—the "policy-making" level. Government financing of low-cost housing projects for civil servants, government dispensing of foodstuffs, clothing, and medicines at reduced prices to civil servants, government-financed vacation hotels for civil servants, vacations with pay, pay bonuses, shorter work hours, all manner of fringe benefits—every advancement of this nature holds little attraction for the top 10 per cent of the bureaucracy. For this bureaucratic elite, a fashionable home in the Lomas or San Angel districts of Mexico City, a weekend cottage in Cuernavaca, Cuautla, or Acapulco, and vacations in the United States or Europe for their families—all achievements beyond the reach of the career civil service—are the awards worth striving for. Social prestige, and particularly the snobbishness of the high bureaucrat's wife, precludes his living in a mass-style housing development or vacationing in the same hotel with the bureaucratic rank and file. While the 90 per cent are thinking of working a lifetime for the government, the 10 per cent are usually thinking of ways to boost their incomes high enough to permit them to get out of government work—or out of work in general.

It is the spokesmen of the FSTSE (the civil servants' union) who proclaim the rights of civil servants before the President of Mexico and the upper 10 per cent of the bureaucracy. In the final instance, it is the president who rules on FSTSE requests for higher benefits and on the union leaders' ambitions for extra income. Seating a few civil-service union leaders in legislative chambers, which adds to their regular pay, takes care of the leadership; the vast majority of Mexican civil servants, perhaps like career civil servants elsewhere, are not very ambitious. Thus it is that the FSTSE, which avowedly speaks for the 90 per cent, manages to gain a few deputy and senator seats for men who are usually technically unprepared for ever reaching the higher positions in public administration.

The ambitious Mexican who rises to the top of the politico-bureaucratic heap, whether through the career civil service, the military, state industries, or state governments, by faithful political militancy in political parties, or merely by virtue of being a descendant of a great Revolutionary, rarely needs more than six years to accumulate sufficient capital to retire for life. Of course, many officials continue to serve in successive administrations. But unlike the first eight rungs of the political prestige ladder, the top four rungs provide the bureaucratic wherewithal to earn a comfortable retirement. A cabinet minister, for example, begins with his base pay and his privilege of importing certain commodities tariff-free; his salary is then greatly augmented by service on the boards of directors of government banks, agencies, dependencies, and state industries. For the finance minister, these extra "duties" on boards of directors pay handsomely: as much as $60,000 annually for six years. Even a minor cabinet minister will sit on ten or twelve boards and earn $15,000 yearly. Besides these sources of income, a cabinet minister can usually invest in companies doing business with his ministry and in other ways "honestly" increment his income by taking advantage of public works, changes in tariff schedules, new laws, etc. When all "honest" paths come to an end and a cabinet minister still lacks desired capital, he will find suppliers to his ministry anxious to kick back 10 per cent on large sales, more on small sales. The precise amount a cabinet minister or state-industry manager finally accumulates by the end of six years largely depends on himself, although when grafting becomes excessive and injurious to his rule, the President of Mexico may step in and close some sources of a subordinate's income. The average minister or director finishes his term with two or three houses, a good library, two or three automobiles, a ranch, and $100,000 cash; about 25 directors and ministers hold posts from which they can leave office with fifty times that amount in cash. In this perspective, it is clear why six years in a top office is long enough, why the politically conscious Mexican is willing to serve faithful apprenticeships, or why the indefinite terms of office characterizing pre-Revolutionary days have been replaced by firm adherence to the principle of no re-election.

Political Security

Why have Mexicans condoned the manner in which their Revolution has developed over the past two decades? The privileged, forming the top 20 per cent, naturally accept the present direction. Most of the rest probably do not accept it, but they are led by men from the privileged class. University graduates and politically ambitious youths find opportunities inside and outside the bureaucracy and soon join the top 20 per cent. Periodic opening of the bureaucratic machine absorbs substantial new elements every six years at the national and state levels, every three years at the local level. There is some doubt whether private enterprise is doing the same—that is, providing attractive jobs in sufficient number to satisfy the job appetites of college and technical school graduates. Meanwhile, what can the masses do about their plight? They may be conscious of long-range benefits brought by the Revolution—political stability; relative freedom of speech, press, religion, and assembly; education; roads; the promise of electrification; irrigation; sanitation—all of which tends to soothe day-by-day poverty. They may even think that they are contributing to the building of a greater Mexico, to national integration, and to other planks in the Revolutionary Creed. Put if they chose to force the issue of real-wage increases now, of easier access to credit, and of a bigger share in national income, how would they proceed? Would the central government order the army, navy, and air force to repress an armed rebellion of the peasantry and proletariat?

Would they choose to shoot down the very elements that the Revolution purportedly represents? So far the government has snuffed out armed factions founded on basic discontent before they could grow into serious threats. A look at the permanent channels of political security offers insight into the small chances of success internal rebellion holds so long as control points remain loyal to the President of Mexico.

In addition to the regular cabinet ministries, federal agencies and banks, government-owned industries, and the federal court system, the President of Mexico relies on dozens of other permanent channels of political communication and sanction application. Captive labor-union and agricultural-federation leaders report on their rank-and-file membership and on outside powers making attempts to divert the labor movement from Mexicanism. Senators, federal deputies, and state governors keep the chief executive advised on affairs in their respective constituencies. The official party and "opposition" political groupings loyally communicate information to party headquarters and the *gobernación* ministry. Masonic lodges serve as watchdogs over religious tolerance; the Catholic Church reports on Communist abuses. Foreign embassies and legations stalemate one another. Vested private interests, including the press, radio, and television industries, offer information voluntarily. To bring the security picture into sharper focus, the President of Mexico relies on seventeen principal agents: (1) the minister of the presidency and special presidential aides; (2) the military chief of staff, the presidential guards, the ministers of defense and navy, and the army and navy zone commanders; (3) *governación* agents; (4) agents of the Federal Security Commission (*Comisión Federal de Seguridad*); (5) treasury agents; (6) the attorneys general; (7) judicial police; (8) federal judges; (9) labor conciliators; (10) federal credit bank officials; (11) the minister of foreign affairs and the diplomatic and consular corps; (12) state governors; (13) official-party officials; (14) regional and local strongmen; (15) teachers, agricultural agents, and public-health officials; (16) telegraph and railroad agents; and (17) private bankers. The three essential, continuous key agents of the security apparatus are the armed forces, *gobernación* and secret police agents, and state governors. The armed forces, in turn, are watched by state governors and *gobernación* agents, who themselves are reported upon by military zone commanders. In comparison with the federal security system, the security apparatus of governors is relatively restricted. The whole mechanism draws heavily on the principle of divide and rule.

To say the least, the Revolutionary Family is in a strong position to meet opposition. The loyalty of the armed forces is buttressed by a variety of factors: professional status, the prohibition on military zone commanders taking their troops with them when transferred to another zone, faith in the continuance of the Revolution, the privilege of generals to graft on government contracts. The danger of any cabinet minister or other favorite building up sufficient personal power to challenge Family leadership is reduced by the changeover of the administrative team every six years. All in all, the success of liberal authoritarianism in six-year doses owes much to the security apparatus of the Revolutionary elite heading Mexico.

Politics and the People

Little by little, the gap between the President of Mexico and the people of Mexico is closing. Presidents have become less fearful of the people and the people less afraid of their presidents. This encouraging state of affairs improves tolerance and extends freedom. Violence is rarely employed by a president to sustain himself in power—although, on the other hand, opposition elements have never been permitted to acquire enough power to be in a position to challenge the Revolutionary elite. Personalism persists, however, and the President of Mexico still *gives* public works to the nation—"el señor presidente da a los mexicanos." The president, as final arbiter, must appear to be just and impartial and always "take from the rich (the bad) and give to the poor (the good)." When questioned on abuses of the ruling elite, the Mexican usually replies with a stock answer: Politics is that way; anyway, we have more freedom today, and we do not like the thought of returning to the cruelty and destruction of the first decade of the Revolution. Besides, Mexicans today have the good fortune of a turnover in dictators every six years.

The actual Mexican political system is far removed from theory and legality. The presidential, gubernatorial, and legislative nominating process varies greatly from the theory of official-party operation, effective political opposition, and legal norms. Significant interest groups affiliated with the official party are captives of the ruling elite, and the several interests that have really prospered since 1939 are outside the official party. Tradition, the expectation (and perhaps dire necessity) of a strong executive, civic apathy, illiteracy, an entrenched bureaucracy, and a host of other factors accentuate gaps between constitutionalism and practice. Fifty years of Revolution suggest that the appearance of effective interest groups and political parties unimpeded by constant governmental intervention is wishful thinking. In working toward the fulfillment of ideals in the Revolutionary Creed, the Revolutionary Family has brought a fair measure of political liberalism into Mexican life. It has also shown itself sensitive and responsive to many popular needs. But the future, like the past five decades, holds little promise of improving democratic goals beyond the expectation of placing in the presidential office a tolerant, powerful chief executive—of retaining the "liberal Machiavellian."

BOLIVIA

Bolivia, like Mexico before and Cuba afterwards, has had profound revolutionary changes since 1952. In this selection, Richard W. Patch, an anthropologist and member of the American Universities Field Staff, evaluates many of the facets of this revolution. He analyzes the important role of the National Revolutionary Movement (MNR) party, especially through a discussion of its leaders and strong groups within the party. The origins and results of land reform are given a thorough analysis, and the effects of nationalization of the tin mines, the austerity program, and United States aid are pointed out. In 1964 President Paz Estenssoro was deposed by the military, but this did not lead to the undoing of the basic changes brought about by the revolution.

THE BOLIVIAN REVOLUTION

*United States Assistance in a Revolutionary Setting**

RICHARD W. PATCH

Latin America has seen many kinds of political change that go by the name of "revolution," from trading offices between "outs" and "ins" to profound upheavals which remake

* Reprinted from Richard W. Patch, "Bolivia: U.S. Assistance in a Revolutionary Setting," in Richard Adams, etc., *Social Change in Latin America Today* (New York: Harper & Row, 1960), pp. 108–37, 157–68 by permission of Council on Foreign Relations, Inc.

permanently the political, economic, and social structure. Most "revolutions" are usurpations of power, conducted according to a well-understood and carefully observed set of rules. Often they have little popular support or opposition, are precipitated by a shift in the allegiance of key groups in the armed forces, and have little effect on the structure of the government or the condition of the governed.

Occasionally a revolution, in the sense of a sudden and radical change, does take place. For many years Mexico was unique in Latin America; it alone had undergone a revolution which struck at the roots of the previous order. The change that occurred after 1911 was in many ways more fundamental than that brought about by the wars for Mexico's independence from Spain. Then in 1952 Mexico was joined by Bolivia—the first South American republic with a large Indian population to undergo the upheaval of a revolution from which there was no return. The revolt was directed not only against a previous government but against the institutions that had made that government possible and even inevitable.

The revolution was a political success. The tin mines were nationalized, and the large estates were divided among the peasants who cultivated them. The Indians threw off their depressed status, and the entire class of wealthy landowners disappeared as a social power. The suddenness of the reforms, coupled with a sharp drop in tin prices and a devastating drought, brought economic disaster.

The United States recognized the new government and expanded substantially a modest program of assistances designed to help Bolivia achieve a measure of stability. But neither government nor economy achieved that goal, and U.S. assistance to Bolivia grew until it has now become the largest program of its kind in Latin America.

What is the present situation of Bolivia and how has it come about? And what are the purposes and the effects of the U.S. assistance programs? Only a careful, if brief, review of what the Bolivian government and the U.S. aid programs have done, have not done, and could not have done, can provide the basis for a realistic appraisal of U.S. policy in a revolutionary setting.

Divergent Approaches to the Bolivian Revolution

Until recently Bolivia was an almost unknown country, isolated in the center of a continent which has commanded less attention in the United States than its relative proximity and economic importance would lead us to expect. Yet from 1953 through 1959 economic aid and technical assistance to Bolivia by the United States amounted to $124 million. This total is exclusive of Export-Import Bank loans of $11 million disbursed during this period, authorized credits of $4 million from the Development Loan Fund, and a $15 million stabilization loan from the International Monetary Fund and the U.S. Treasury. It also does not include assistance from the United Nations, which has one of its largest missions in Bolivia.

The increase in U.S. aid to Bolivia–from $1.5 million in 1953 to $22.7 million in 1959, exclusive of loans–provides a rough yardstick for measuring the growing interest of the United States in Bolivia's future. This interest also is apparent in a growing volume of comment, some hostile to the new leadership, but most of it sympathetic.

The difficulty is that North Americans have known little of the deep-seated problems and wrenching social changes that are at the root of Bolivia's grave economic distress. Without a knowledge of the country's basic conditions it is impossible to estimate the wisdom of the aid program. U.S. policy must be appraised in the light of a new Bolivian nationalism, the Indians' struggle for emancipation, and other forces which very largely make the government a creature of the governed.

One major strand of these new processes can be examined only in the countryside, where the peasants have become a power to reckon with, and where agrarian reform has become the symbol and tool of social reform. The agencies to which we would normally turn for information do not have the experience or personnel necessary for gathering firsthand material on the village population, which is both different from and antagonistic to the city dwellers who alone meet and inform most foreign visitors.

A comprehensive United Nations report on Bolivia foreshadowed the revolutionary changes that have occurred since 1952.[1] Among analyses made by trained observers since the revolution of 1952, the most interesting is a brief study by Carter Goodrich, professor of economics at Columbia University, who headed the United Nations mission before and after the overturn.[2] Going beyond its title, his booklet throws much light on the social as well as economic transformation of the country. Because of the nature of Dr. Goodrich's work in Bolivia, his study is chiefly concerned with the population of the western plateau (the *altiplano*) and with the mines and tin miners.

Alberto Ostria Gutiérrez, a former foreign minister of Bolivia now in exile in Chile, has written a dramatic and reasonably sober indictment of the present government of Bolivia and its policies.[3] Written with an emphasis upon the injustices suffered by the Spanish-speaking middle and upper classes, it leaves out of consideration, as do many books by Bolivians, the positive benefits which the government's reforms have brought the Indians.

Lilo Linke, a German journalist, has written an informal history of the revolutionary changes which have taken place since the Movimiento Nacionalista Revolucionario (MNR) came to power.[4] It gives a number of interesting sketches of the personalities of the government. But if Ostria can see no good in the MNR party and government, Linke can see no evil. Her book is often an uncritical eulogy of Víctor Paz Estenssoro, re-elected president in June 1960 for a new four-year term.

My own approach to the study of Bolivia has been through

[1] UN Technical Assistance Administration, *Report of the United Nations Missions of Technical Assistance to Bolivia,* ST/TAA/K/Bolivia/1 (New York: Author, 1951), the report of the "Keenleyside Mission." Also, UN Economic Commission for Latin America, *Development of Agriculture in Bolivia,* E/CN.12/218/Add. 2 (New York: Author, 1951).

[2] Carter Goodrich, *The Economic Transformation of Bolivia,* Bulletin 34 (Ithaca: New York State School of Industrial and Labor Relations, 1955).

[3] *Un pueblo en la cruz* (Santiago de Chile: Editorial del Pacífico, 1956).

[4] *Viaje por una revolución* (Quito: Editorial Casa de la Cultura Ecuatoriana, 1956).

the methods of anthropology. When an anthropologist undertakes to interpret a total national culture, he encounters certain limitations, chiefly imposed by his usual preoccupation with preliterate or "primitive" groups who remain largely below the horizon of the national state. When he studies Bolivia, however, this avenue of approach offers certain advantages because the preliterate population, comprising some 60 per cent of the nation, is the principal object of the government's reforms and, in addition, it now wields much of the power which has been taken from the army and police.

The Indian populations of Bolivia have been studied by several anthropologists, notably Allan R. Holmberg, Weston La Barre, and the late Harry Tschopik. In addition to benefiting from these studies which were carried out before the revolution of 1952, I have been able to study the Spanish-speaking and Indian peoples of Bolivia in three periods–in 1954–1955, in 1956, when the full impact of the changed status of the Indian was making itself felt, and again in 1958–1959. My studies were concentrated in the major area of the Indian upheaval, the Cochabamba valleys, but I have also made less intensive studies of the Aymaras of the *altiplano,* the transitional population of the eastern boundary of the Andes around Comarapa and Valle Grande, and the people of the eastern lowlands of Santa Cruz and the Beni.[5]

Land and People

Compared with other Latin American republics, Bolivia is a large country, with a total area of 412,800 square miles, roughly equal to that of Spain and France combined. Its situation as the only American republic without access to the sea has contributed greatly to a sense of isolation from the outside world. The Dirección General de Estadística estimates that Bolivia had a population of 3,161,503 in 1954. According to the criteria employed by the census bureau, in 1950 it had 1,703,371 "Indians." With Indians making up some 54 per cent of the total, Bolivia has by far the largest

[5] My studies were made possible by grants from the Institute of Current World Affairs and the Grace and Henry L. Doherty Foundation.

proportion of Indian population of any country in Latin America.

The distinction between "Indian" and "white" (or *blanco*) is crucial to an understanding of Andean social life. Both the Spanish-speaking *blancos* and many of the Quechua- and Aymara-speaking Indians believe that the terms denote a real difference in race as well as an important difference in the cultures of the two groups. In fact, however, in the four hundred years since the Spanish conquest the two originally distinct races have so far intermingled that the racial difference has largely disappeared except in the most isolated Indian villages and in the largest cities, where many of the *blancos* are recent immigrants. Nevertheless, the fiction of the racial apartness and inferiority of the Indians has strengthened and preserved their very real distinctiveness of culture. Most writers, recognizing the inappropriateness of the word "whites," have adopted the substitute term *"mestizos,"* which, in fact, is sparingly used by "whites" and "Indians" of the Andes.

Thirty-eight per cent of "Indians" speak only Aymara. They are concentrated on the large *altiplano,* the level plateau of western Bolivia, which extends for hundreds of miles at an elevation of slightly over 12,000 feet. The Aymaras, living mainly in the heavily overpopulated areas near Lake Titicaca and also in the valleys of the Yungas, are surrounded by Quechua-speaking peoples, both to the west, where the Peruvian Indians also speak Quechua, and to the east, where the invading Quechua-speaking Incas settled in the richer agricultural valleys beyond the *altiplano*. Fifty-four per cent of the Indians speak only Quechua. Both Quechua and to a lesser extent the Aymara language are divided among numerous dialects, which limit the Indians' ability to communicate effectively with other Indians outside their immediate localities. And while Quechua and Aymara have many points of similarity in vocabulary and syntax, they are separate languages, mutually unintelligible. A few other independent languages, such as Uru are spoken by a very few individuals, most of whom also speak Quechua or Aymara. The diversity of languages and dialects creates a serious problem of communication within the population of Bolivia, for few of the

Indians speak Spanish as a second language. The 6 per cent of "Indians" who also speak some Spanish are found in predominantly *mestizo* areas near the cities of La Paz, Cochabamba, Potosí, and Sucre.

The majority of the total population, and practically all the Indians, live in the highlands. East of the plateau and the mountains and valleys lies the subtropical lowland, which makes up fully three-fifths of the national territory. The eastern lowlands shade gradually from the arid pampa of the southeast through the subtropical savanna and forest of Santa Cruz to the jungle and flood plains of the Beni and Pando in the northeast. Much of this lowland has a rich potential for agriculture and grazing, but is little exploited by the few Spanish-speaking inhabitants and the sparse and nomadic forest tribes, estimated at only 2 per cent of the total Indian population.

The region of the Yungas, which encompasses the precipitous valleys of northwestern Bolivia, is also sparsely populated. As the valleys of the Yungas fall off abruptly to the lower altitudes of the eastern slopes of the Cordillera Real, moisture-laden clouds moving west from the Amazon basin deposit a heavy rainfall in the subtropical gorges. In addition to coffee and bananas, the main product of the Yungas is the coca leaf, from which cocaine is derived; the coca leaf has been chewed by the Indians of the Andes since before the time of the Incas.

From the Chaco War to Social Revolution

During the colonial period and under the republic, Bolivia's economy has had a dual character. One part, oriented to the world market, has been concerned with exploiting resources which were not only exported but largely processed beyond its borders. The rest of the economy, mainly agricultural and centered around local markets, was traditionally organized in small subsistence farms or large estates—latifundia—whose produce flowed to local markets little affected by world prices. Land-tenure patterns, modeled after Spanish manorial customs, served to immobilize the agricultural workers in an unchanging way of life. The religious structure likewise placed a high value on acceptance of the traditional patterns and emphasized the rewards of a future rather than a present life. The social stratification of the society into caste-like categories fixed the tenure patterns and the economic and social behavior of different classes in a rigid system, in a traditional equilibrium which remained basically undisturbed down to the impact of the Chaco war which was waged against Paraguay from 1932 to 1935.

From this war the Bolivian government hoped to win a quick victory and to re-establish its prestige shaken by its previous losses of territory to Chile and Brazil. Bolivia's defeat was due largely to a weak government and an incompetent military leader, whose strategy proved disastrous in the unfamiliar terrain of the Chaco. Paraguay had the advantages of an able government, a shrewd military leader, and short supply lines into an area with which the Paraguayan soldiers were thoroughly familiar. Bolivia continued the fight with increasing desperation until, with both countries exhausted, the war was ended by a truce in 1935. Some 60,000 Bolivian and some 40,000 Paraguayan soldiers had lost their lives in the struggle.

During the war all classes of Bolivians volunteered or were conscripted into the army. For many of the Bolivians who called themselves "whites" or *gente decente,* it was an unparalleled experience to serve in an army with "Indians." The white and *mestizo* officers suddenly found themselves dependent upon the infantry of the once despised *indios.* For the Indians it was an equally strange experience to see unfamiliar areas of their country, to conceive of Bolivia as a nation, and to become the object of propaganda designed to persuade them that they were citizens of a single nation, no longer Indians, a people apart, but *gente,* or "persons," in the same sense as the "whites."

Bolivia was defeated, but it was neither the loss of lives nor the war itself which finally upset the country's social and economic equilibrium. It was rather the rise of a liberal image of the prospective role of the Indian within the nation, and a new sense of participation, real or frustrated, by the Indian population in the national life. In Bolivia, as elsewhere in Latin America, the universities often provide the wellsprings of new political movements, and in the early 1930's a new political ferment was introduced by the rise in the Bolivian universities of a group imbued with Socialist and Marxist ideologies. At that time, a related movement, called "liberal" in Bolivia, was becoming fiercely nationalistic and anti-imperialist.

The long-maintained equilibrium, which had depended on preserving the role of the Indians as serfs in a feudalistic society, had been disturbed. To pacify the new unrest, liberal governments enacted new laws from time to time, thereby encouraging the Indian to seek a new status for himself, only to be forgotten by later, tradition-dominated governments as they attempted to restore the old regime. With each swing of the political pendulum the disequilibrium became steadily more pronounced, until the revolution of 1952 crushed the mainstays of the traditional society.

A new political party, the Movimiento Nacionalista Revolucionario had been formed in 1940 by a group of intellectuals headed by Víctor Paz Estenssoro, at one time a professor of economics in the University of San Andrés at La Paz. The MNR favored the nationalization of the tin mines and called itself "anti-imperialist." At first it represented an uneasy alliance between upper-class "liberal intellectuals," products of the universities, and the right-wing Vanguardia, composed of young army officers dissatisfied with their seniors' conduct of the Chaco war.[6] As the new party gained influence, it absorbed the political activities of the tin miners and the remnants of a much divided Marxist party, the "Party of the Revolutionary Left."

After having declared war on the Axis powers in December 1943, the government of Enrique Peñaranda was overthrown almost immediately in a coup organized by a secret lodge of army officers who then installed Major Gualberto Villarroel as president. Villarroel took several leaders of the MNR into his cabinet and repressed both the traditional and the Marxist parties; Paz Estenssoro became Villarroel's minister of finance. When the U.S. government denounced the coup as having been instigated and financed by Nazis and

[6] The Vanguardia should not be confused with the Vanguardia Obrera Movimientista, a group of the left.

by Argentine nationals, its example in refusing to recognize Villarroel's government was followed by all Latin American republics except Argentina. Unable to withstand the pressure of continued isolation, the Villarroel government dropped the MNR members from the cabinet, and six months later it was recognized by the United States and other American republics. In July 1946, after the defeat of the Axis, discontent with the government exploded in La Paz. After several days of armed conflict in the capital, the presidential palace was stormed and Villarroel was hanged from a lamp post. Paz Estenssoro went into exile in Argentina, where he remained until he returned as president in April 1952. Throughout his exile Paz Estenssoro remained the symbol of the aspirations of the MNR and "The Revolution." In the meantime Bolivia was governed by a succession of weak cabinets of the right.

In the elections which were scheduled by the cabinet of Mamerto Urriolagoitia for May 1951, the government was expected to control the outcome by legal means, since the franchise was restricted to literate males, largely urban dwellers, who, it was thought, would split their votes among several competing candidates. Under the constitution, if no candidate received an absolute majority, the Congress could choose the president from among the three candidates receiving the most votes. Since the Congress was dominated by the government party, it would, it was assumed, proceed to choose the government's candidate, Gabriel Gosálvez.

The government party was more surprised than anyone when the voters gave Víctor Paz Estenssoro 45 per cent of the 120,000 ballots cast, and the MNR also elected six out of nine senators and ten out of fifty-five deputies. However, in spite of the MNR's impressive showing in a restricted electorate which was not generally regarded as favorable to it, Paz Estenssoro had not received an absolute majority. Although he had a five-to-three plurality over Gosálvez, there was no assurance that the Congress would not choose the government's own candidate as president.

Then, suddenly, on May 16 Urriolagoitia resigned, handed over the reins of government to a military junta, and fled to Chile. The reason given by the junta for the coup was the necessity of keeping the MNR from power. The MNR, they proclaimed, was "an unholy alliance" of Nazi, Fascist and Communist elements which would establish a dictatorial type of government, nationalize the mines and industry, and institute a campaign of terror such as had prevailed in 1943–1946.[7] The junta lacked both positive leadership and popular support. It accomplished little, and its unity steadily deteriorated until in April 1952 a member of the junta, General Seleme, defected to the MNR.

From April 8 to April 11 a struggle was joined in La Paz to determine what forces would control the government and the country. In it, according to some estimates, as many as 3,000 persons were killed. Irregular forces led by Vice-President-elect Hernán Siles and labor leader Juan Lechín, both partisans of the MNR, finally overcame the opposition. The provisional government which Siles set up was turned over to Paz Estenssoro as soon as he returned to La Paz from Argentina.

Juan Lechín, recognized leader of the tin miners and guiding spirit of the Trotskyite Revolutionary Workers party (POR), became a nominal member of the MNR and was made minister of mines and petroleum. One of the government's first acts was to nationalize the tin mines, taking over the three large corporations belonging to the Patiño, Hochschild, and Aramayo interests.

Despite the present pride of the government in its agrarian reform decree of August 2, 1953, there was at first little talk and less action about agrarian reform in the period following the success of the revolution of 1952. President Paz Estenssoro and Vice-President Siles were essentially moderates. If agrarian reform was a part of their political ideology, they apparently conceived of it as a gradual turning over of inefficiently cultivated latifundia to landless Indians. However, the Indians or *campesinos* (farmers), as they now came to be called, finding themselves for the first time in a position of power, embarked on a program of total land redistribution from below. It was their demands and their power which soon forced the government to recognize the serious nature of the problem and to appoint an Agrarian Reform Council. One

[7] *The New York Times*, May 17, 1951.

reason why the MNR avoided making any pronouncement on agrarian reform as long as it could was that its rightist Vanguardia wing, which formed the main strength of the party until it broke away in 1956, was opposed to land reform.

In the later months of 1952 the situation in rural areas had become unmanageable. The specter of a civil war of extermination between *campesinos* and "whites" rose to haunt the new government. A sweeping program of agrarian reform was now indispensable, both to put some order into the land redistribution which the *campesinos* were carrying out by direct action, and to prove by a convincing gesture that the MNR was indeed the friend of the *campesinos,* as it had so often proclaimed.

The Indians and Agrarian Revolt

The most striking and unexpected consequence of the revolution of 1952 was the rapid and organized emergence of the "Indian" *campesinos* as a decisive force on the national scene. The policy-makers, city-dwellers to a man, still thought of the *campesinos* as unorganized, leaderless, and susceptible to coercion. But this was no longer everywhere the case.

In the large interior valley of Cochabamba, located in west central Bolivia, with the highest ratio of Indian population to arable land, the *campesinos* had long been in close contact with the town-dwelling *mestizos.* They had become familiar with the norms of *mestizo* culture. As early as 1936, almost immediately after the close of the Chaco war, *campesinos* of one province, Cliza, in the department of Cochabamba, had established an agrarian "syndicate" (*sindicato*) with the aim of freeing themselves from the feudal obligations of service to the latifundium owners and advancing their status toward that of the *mestizo.* The first step was to arrange to lease their holdings from the landlords, thus escaping from the traditional obligations of rendering unpaid services to the *patrón.*

Very soon the *campesino* syndicate suffered a setback which, however, in the long run only served to weld its members more closely into a purposeful and determined group.

A number of large landowners of the area banded together to destroy the nascent syndicate and remove this direct threat to the customary pattern of landlord rule. As a first step, in 1939 five landlords purchased those latifundia which the syndicate members had succeeded in renting from the previous owners, took back the lands from the *campesinos,* and cleared large areas by destroying the houses of the *campesinos.* They then proceeded to "rationalize" the cultivation of the latifundia, retaining the services of those *campesinos* who were willing to become *pegujaleros* (a type of sharecropper serf whose obligations differed in minor ways from the older type of *colonos*). Those *campesinos* who refused to submit were driven from the lands which they and their families had occupied in usufruct all their lives, and often from father to son. This attack upon the syndicate members did more than any other one act to unify the Indian population and awaken it to political life. Treatment which had hitherto been endured as acts against individual peasants was now recognized for what it was, a concentrated attack by landowners upon the whole group of *campesinos.*

After this first defeat, the syndicate, now centered in the *campesino* community of Ucureña in the province of Cliza, turned from the direct attempt to secure the land for the peasants to a program of school-building and other improvements designed to organize and prepare the *campesinos* for what they now saw as an inevitable struggle with the landowners. Suppressed for several years, the syndicate reemerged in 1947 when a PIR (Party of the Revolutionary Left) member was elected deputy for the province of Cliza, and a young man, José Rojas, took over the leadership of the syndicate. A native of Ucureña, who had been driven from the latifundium on which his father had been a *colono,* Rojas escaped to Argentina, only to return secretly to Ucureña later in the 1940's. There he worked as a laborer while he assisted in organizing the *campesinos.* Rojas affected to speak no Spanish but was an eloquent orator in Quechua. Deeply impressed by the platform of the Marxist PIR, he soon became a forceful and determined leader of the *campesinos.*

In 1949 members of the MNR began a new campaign in the rural areas, attempting to identify themselves with the *campesinos* and to enlist their support against the vested-power groups. They assumed correctly that, if they could win broad support among the *campesinos,* no government could resist their right to rule. During those years José Rojas held the syndicate of Ucureña at arm's length from the MNR, possibly because of the gap between his own PIR leanings and the MNR's more moderate objectives. The syndicate, as it happened, took no part in the revolution of April 9, 1952.

After the MNR had assumed power in La Paz, the syndicate of Ucureña emerged, after a short interval, as the organized spokesman of the *campesinos.* At first its influence was challenged by the new regime. The regional command of the MNR in Cochabamba attempted to place another *campesino* leader, Simón Aguilar, at the head of a "Syndicate of the Valley." Aguilar belonged to another *campesino* community, closer than Ucureña to the city of Cochabamba, and was more sympathetic than Rojas to the MNR. The issue came to a head at the first meeting of the new syndicate, which was to unite all the *campesinos* of the Cochabamba valley. At the meeting, held in the provincial capital, Cliza, the delegates had to decide where the headquarters of the syndicate should be located. By a narrow margin they voted to remove it to Ucureña, and José Rojas thereby became the undisputed leader of the valley's hundreds of thousands of *campesinos.* In turn Rojas became resigned, at least outwardly, to cooperating with the MNR.

The early meetings of the Sindicato Campesino de Ucureña del Valle organized task forces of *campesinos* and young MNR students from Cochabamba, dispatching them to the farthest reaches of Bolivia. Often these teams of organizers were the first to bring news of the revolution to Indian villages of remote valleys and lofty plateaus. The syndicate groups showed the *campesinos* how to organize new syndicates of their own. Most of these later syndicates remain personally loyal today to Rojas, for they believe that he and no one else was responsible for their being established in the first place. As the wild fire of revolt and hope raced through the villages, the entire *campesino* movement was completely outside the control of the national government or the MNR party leaders. The only center it recognized was Ucureña.

In the early months after the revolution the national government in La Paz paid little attention to the rising tide of peasant unrest. It announced that the innocuous reforms decreed ten years before by the Villarroel government, which had placed certain restrictions on the exploitation of *pegujaleros* by latifundium owners, were again to be put into effect. The landowners were not much concerned over this mild gesture, and for a time the traditional landlord-peasant pattern seemed likely to remain unchanged by this as by so many previous revolts.

Then, on November 9, 1952, the syndicate of Ucureña demanded the return of eleven parcels of land to *pegujaleros* who had been driven from one of the latifundia a few years before. The landowner refused. Thereupon the syndicate called for a general uprising of the *campesinos* in the provinces of Cliza, Punata, and Tarata. It threatened to pillage the town of Cliza and burn the houses of the nearby landowners. This threat of direct action, reported to Cochabamba, the departmental capital, found the governor and his officials, with their limited forces, understandably reluctant to interfere. Only prompt action by the sub-prefect of Cliza finally succeeded in pacifying the *campesinos* and in preventing a general assault upon the latifundia and the smaller towns. The *campesinos* had now come to realize their strength, and acts of violence became more and more frequent.

The uprising of the *campesinos* could not but arouse the national government to the necessity for drastic action. If far-reaching concessions could no longer control but only channel the emergence of the *campesinos,* they would at least demonstrate that the sympathies of the government were on the side of the now irresistible movement. Fortunately, the *campesinos* also had a direct channel to the national leaders of the MNR in La Paz. The minister of *campesino* affairs, Ñuflo Chávez, was acutely aware of the government's dependence on the good will of the village population, and was in close contact with José Rojas and other *campesino* leaders. Ñuflo Chávez became an early and insistent advocate of an extreme type of agrarian reform. His concept, if carried out, would have divided all the land in areas of predominantly Indian population into *minifundios* (small parcels). A reform of this type would have converted the country's entire system of agriculture to subsistence farming, leaving little or no marketable surplus to feed the cities. Had the *campesinos* been left to their own devices this would assuredly have been the final upshot.

As it was, the syndicates rapidly took over the most accessible latifundia or *haciendas,* divided up the land among their members, and expropriated the vehicles, machinery, and houses of the former *patrones.* For example, at Ucureña the *casa hacienda,* or manor house, of one *patrón* was seized by the syndicate, which renamed it the "General Barracks" or village headquarters of Ucureña. Other houses were converted to serve as hospitals, schools or syndicate headquarters. By this time those landowners who had so far remained in the rural areas finally realized the full sweep of the revolution and fled for safety to the cities, especially to Cochabamba and La Paz. Since then most of them have not been able so much as to go near their former *haciendas.* Large areas of Bolivia have remained inaccessible for this class of *blancos,* often called *"la rosca,"* a bitter term applied to persons popularly believed to have used their wealth and power to exploit the Indians.

The Government and Agrarian Reform

The *campesino* uprising with its demand for agrarian reform posed several difficult questions to the MNR. As a political party, the MNR had risen to power as a congeries of groups each of which had its own purposes, and their amalgamation was not accompanied by a genuine unity of views or goals. The original inspirers of the MNR, leaders such as Víctor Paz Estenssoro and Wálter Guevara Arze, minister of foreign affairs until February 1956, were supporters of moderate, evolutionary "socialism." As such, they attempted to keep the use of force to a minimum. Hernán Siles, then vice-president and president of the republic from 1956 to 1960, also belonged to the moderates.

In the 1940's the moderate intellectuals had been joined by a group which called itself the Vanguardia of the MNR. The Vanguardia in turn was, in its origins, close to the

RADEPA, an organization of younger army officers, veterans of the Chaco war, who had turned against the higher officers, holding them responsible for Bolivia's defeat.[8] However vague the political platform of the Vanguardia, its leaders were more conservative in social outlook than the Paz Estenssoro group, and also more willing to resort to force.

The universities had been another source of recruits and ideas for the MNR. While some professors and students were close to the moderate views of the MNR, many other students, no longer attracted to the older MNR intellectuals, had formed their own groups. The Avanzadas Universitarias (Avant-Garde University Students), as they were called, were young enough to be strongly influenced by the Marxist thinking that had flourished at the universities in the 1930's and 1940's. These groups were far to the left of the rightist Vanguardia wing of the MNR, whose adherents were barely lukewarm toward agrarian reform. Other influential leaders within the MNR took strong positions for or against the peasants' demands. Among them, the very influential Juan Lechín was an advocate of extreme land reform.

As the pressure of the *campesinos* and their syndicates was rising explosively, President Paz Estenssoro decided to put the government and the MNR at the head of the movement. On January 20, 1953, he proclaimed Supreme Decree No. 3301, creating an agrarian reform commission to study the "agrarian-*campesino* problem" and suggest the best ways in which the reform could be carried out. The commission, headed by Vice-President Siles, was given 120 days in which to prepare a report and draft a decree dealing with all interrelated aspects of the reform. These included property and tenure patterns of agricultural and grazing lands; "an adequate redistribution of this land, in order to raise the standard of living of the *campesinos,* intensify agricultural and livestock production, and develop the national economy"; procedures for liquidating the latifundia and suppressing "semifeudal" exploitive practices in rural areas; the effect of these reforms on agricultural production, work patterns, and the payment and protection of the *campesinos; campesino* housing; technical assistance and credit for agricultural producers;

[8] RADEPA stands for Razón de Patria.

conservation of natural resources. While Paz Estenssoro assigned responsibility for carrying out the decree jointly to the ministers of *campesino* affairs, agriculture, and finance, the primary responsibility, significantly enough, was assigned to the minister of *campesino* affairs, Ñuflo Chávez, an intimate of the Indian leader, José Rojas, rather than to the minister of agriculture, Germán Vera Tapia, one of the stronger leaders of the MNR's Vanguardia wing.

Within the stipulated period of four months the commission completed a series of reports and prepared a draft decree which Paz Estenssoro enacted into law by Supreme Decree No. 3464. On August 2, 1953, the decree was signed with much pomp and ceremony by the president and the entire cabinet before a huge convocation of *campesinos* held in the village of Ucureña. Eduardo Arze Loureiro, who had aided in establishing the syndicate of Ucureña in the difficult years of the 1930's and 1940's, was named president of the Agrarian Reform Council.

The decree represented a compromise between two conflicting forces: the partisans of preserving productive and efficient agricultural units, whatever their size, and the advocates of distributing the maximum amount of land to the largest possible number of *campesinos,* regardless of the effect on production. On balance, the compromise favored the former. In addition, the decree recognized the overwhelming desire of the *campesinos* for individual private ownership, and had little to say of communal production cooperatives patterned after the Mexican *ejidos.* The decree, covering some thirty pages, may be summarized briefly:

> The Nation maintains the original right of the Nation over the soil, the subsoil and the waters of the territory of the Republic. The State recognizes and guarantees agrarian private property when it fulfills a useful function for society. The State recognizes only the following forms of agrarian private property: the peasant homesite, the small holding operated by the farmer and his family for subsistence purposes, the medium-sized holding operated with the help of hired labor or with agricultural machinery for the purpose of marketing most of the pro-

duce, the Indian communities, the agrarian co-operative holding, and finally, the agricultural enterprise.

Specifically the State does not recognize the legality of the latifundium—the rural property of large size which may vary according to its geographical location, that remains idle or is exploited inefficiently by the extensive system (low capital inputs relative to other factors), with obsolete tools and with practices which serve to perpetuate the serfdom and submission of the peasant. The semifeudal estates are subject to expropriation in their entirety.[9]

The newly outlawed latifundium is distinguished in the decree from the approved agricultural enterprise. The latter is defined as an intensive farm, operated with large capital investments per unit of land, producing for the market, with labor paid in cash wages and enjoying the right to organize and participate in collective bargaining, regardless of the amount of land held by the enterprise.

The decree fixes the maximum sizes of holdings, which vary according to whether the holdings are on the *altiplano,* on the *puna* (high areas mainly used for grazing), in the interior valleys, or in the eastern subtropical region; in fixing them, only the cultivable area is taken into account. The size of maximum holdings for different regions, based on studies and reports by agronomists and land-use specialists, was defined as the area necessary to satisfy the needs of a rural family. The decree established the rights of the Indian communities to recover lands which had been usurped from them. From the date of the decree, communities which claimed restitution rights could occupy the land on which they had claims. This article, in practice, recognized the *de facto* occupations of land which had already been carried out by the *campesinos.*

All Bolivian citizens, 18 years of age or over, of both sexes, who intend to work on the land will receive grants wherever there may be available lands, on condition that they cultivate it within a period of two years. Peasants who

[9] "Texto del Decreto Ley No. 3464 que dispone la reforma agraria en Bolivia," *Revista Jurídica* (Universidad de Cochabamba), nos. 63–66, 1953, pp. 460–462.

have been subject to a feudal regime of work and exploitation are declared the owners of the land they now occupy or work until the National Agrarian Reform Service has granted them the lands to which they have rights in accordance with the definition of a small holding. The preferential right of one individual to receive a land grant in a given area rests upon his permanent residence in the area and upon his being a farmer.

In those areas where there is enough land the grants per family will be made by allocating one unit [the "small holding" as defined for the particular region] to each family. If the lands [available] do not suffice to grant a unit to each family, the size of the grant will be reduced in the proportion necessary to accommodate all those who legally have preferential rights to the land. The peasants insufficiently provided for reserve their rights to receive new grants in other regions where there are available lands.[10]

It was these provisions of the decree that opened the way for multiplying the small subsistence plots or *minifundios*. As the framers of the decree foresaw clearly, in those densely populated areas which stood in greatest need of land redistribution, there was simply not enough land to give each family an allotment even approaching the prescribed "small holding." By reducing the defined minimum holding in order to satisfy all *campesinos* legally entitled to receive land, the decree made a gesture toward appeasing the greatest possible number of *campesinos*. But it thereby made the subsubsistence *minifundio* the dominant pattern in the more densely populated regions. Agricultural production and marketing have not recovered from this drastic change. That is the root of many of Bolivia's economic straits today.

Bolivia's Seven Plagues

The continuing march of the Bolivian *campesinos* to power was symbolized by the election, in July 1956, of the syndicate leader, José Rojas, to the Senate. Since then, for the first time in Bolivia's history, the business of the Senate has been conducted in a native language when the speaker is unable

[10] *Revista Jurídica*, cited, pp. 473–475.

to express himself in Spanish. In the same election the political figure most closely identified with the *campesinos,* Ñuflo Chávez, was elected vice-president.

After coming to power in 1952, the government had discovered, somewhat to its surprise, that it had no choice but to enact a drastic program of land reform. The same political realities compelled it to nationalize the tin mines in accordance with the MNR's electoral promises. The large vote cast for the MNR in 1951 showed how strongly the Bolivian people favored the nationalization, and the new government could not have survived if it had reneged on its promise. Meanwhile, tin mining, almost wholly dependent on world-wide economic factors outside Bolivia's control, was already encountering stormy weather.

For one thing, the Korean conflict had inflated the price of tin, and the price and cost of Bolivian tin were swept to abnormal heights. Suddenly, the turn came. On March 6, 1951, the U.S. General Services Administration announced that it would not pay the price Bolivia demanded for its tin, and suspended its purchases for stockpiling. On May 31, 1951, the U.S. Reconstruction Finance Corporation contract for the purchase of Bolivian tin also expired and was not renewed. Meanwhile, the quality of the Bolivian tin concentrate had been declining as the higher-grade deposits were exhausted. At the same time, the numbers of the tin miners, who enjoyed a privileged position during the Korean war boom and under the protection of Juan Lechín, had expanded out of all reason. The situation became so unfavorable that, before his retirement from the presidency in 1956, Paz Estenssoro reported that the production costs per pound of Bolivian tin averaged $1.25. In early 1959, in contrast, the world price was about $0.90 per pound. The full impact of this gap becomes apparent when it is noted that over 95 per cent by value of all exports from Bolivia is accounted for by metals, of which tin is by far the largest part.[11]

Apart from tin, the other main pillar of the Bolivian economy is agriculture. Yet Bolivia has been transformed into a

[11] Bolivia, Ministry of Foreign Affairs, *Economic Development of the Republic of Bolivia,* Memorandum II (La Paz: Author, December 1954; mimeographed).

country mainly of subsistence farmers who are unable to feed the cities. The resulting serious food shortage has been relieved only through U.S. aid which has been granted for both political and humanitarian motives. In 1955 the U.S. hopes were expressed in a Senate document:

> The Department of State, which constantly appraises political, social, and economic developments, has concluded that the Bolivian Government is now Marxist rather than Communist and has advocated United States support of this regime on the same premise that it advocated support of the preceding military junta–to prevent displacement by more radical elements.
>
> The administration has accepted the appraisal and the recommended policy of the State Department and is extending technical, financial, and material aid to support the Bolivian Government, at least until 1956. By then it is hoped by the State Department that political entrenchment and social and economic progress will have reached a point at which such support can be sharply tapered off and ultimately no longer required.[12]

The continuing instability of the moderate wing of the MNR was amply illustrated in 1956, when Hernán Siles publicly declared his reluctance, and at one point his refusal, to be put forward as a candidate to succeed Paz Estenssoro as president.[13] In turn, Foreign Minister Guevara Arze was forced by Juan Lechín to resign from the government. Finally, a series of riots in La Paz led President Siles to put an end to his policy of "pacification" and declare a state of siege.

Bolivia's failure to come anywhere near the economic goals which were envisaged in the U.S. aid program has been examined in detail in a report by the economic adviser to the American Embassy in La Paz and a member of the U.S. Economic Operations Mission. They placed the blame for

[12] *Critical Materials,* Report of the Senate Economic Subcommittee on Minerals, Materials, and Fuels of the Committee on Interior and Insular Affairs, Doc. no. 83, 84th Cong., 1st sess. (Washington: GPO, 1956), pp. 116–117.

[13] Paz Estenssoro was barred by the constitution from standing for a second term.

the failure, not so much on the dubious wisdom of the economic policies, but rather on the circumstance that the policies had been framed in terms of a society and an economy which had existed prior to 1952, and which have since then been changed even more drastically than most people realize.[14]

The crux of the matter is that Bolivia's political and economic difficulties have been intensified, not reduced, by the basic social changes of 1952. By 1956, the life of a majority of Bolivians had been transformed in a mere two or three years to an extent which is paralleled in Latin America only by the transformation of the life of the Mexican peasants. But the transformation has taken place in Mexico over a period of thirty to forty years.

The election of 1956 installed Hernán Siles as president. In April 1952 he, with Juan Lechín, had led the fighting in La Paz that brought the MNR to power. But it was Paz Estenssoro, who had waited hopefully at the Argentine border until the fighting was over, who became the first MNR president, while Siles, as vice-president, remained out of the public eye. As a result, little was known of Siles' administrative abilities or personal convictions when he became president in 1956. However, he soon demonstrated a rare courage and unswerving belief in orderly processes. The best example is his defense of the currency and exchange stabilization plan drawn up by U.S. experts, which was put into effect on January 1, 1957. A major difficulty in securing the adoption of the new plan was that many government officials were directly interested in continuing the old system, under which favored individuals could buy dollars at low "official" rates for importing scarce goods. Stabilization also brought a wage freeze, while prices continued to rise. Since this bore with special hardship on the tin miners, Siles soon earned the bitter opposition of both Lechín, with his fanatic following among the mine workers, and Vice-President Ñuflo Chávez, with his backers in the *campesino* organizations. Facing an uphill fight, Siles took up the struggle against inflation, large-

[14] Cornelius H. Zondag, *Problems in the Economic Development of Bolivia* (La Paz: U.S. Operations Mission to Bolivia, 1956; mimeographed).

scale graft, and the near-nihilism of the left wing of the MNR with remarkable determination.

Among the first to oppose Siles' campaign for economic reconstruction was Vice-President Chávez. When Chávez miscalculated his strength and backed an ultimatum to Congress with a threat to resign, Congress rejected the ultimatum and accepted his resignation. In December 1956 Lechín, a constant opponent of Siles, organized a miners' walkout at Llallagua as a demonstration against the proposed stabilization plan. By declaring a hunger strike, Siles rallied support and broke the demonstration. Again, in March 1958, Siles' harassment by Lechín, apparently seconded by Paz Estenssoro, who was threatening to return to Bolivia from his ambassadorship in London, was temporarily halted when Siles submitted his resignation and left the government palace. After six labor unions had struck in his support and a huge popular demonstration in the Plaza Murillo had urged him to withdraw his resignation, Siles consented to return. Speaking from the back of a small truck, he called for austerity and order, and warned his countrymen of the chaos that would follow any attempt to carry out Lechín's promises. Siles was carried back to the Palacio Quemado on the shoulders of the crowd. Shortly thereafter, a series of strikes which Lechín and his lieutenant, Mario Torres, attempted in the tin mines, ended in failure.

In 1956, a U.S. Senate committee described Juan Lechín as "Marxist-minded," and said of his former party:

> The POR (Partido Obrero Revolucionario) became the Bolivian Trotskyist Party, closely linked with the Peruvian and Argentine POR and with the Bolivian Central Obrero Boliviano, the principal labor union headed by Juan Lechín, who, in May 1951, denounced as unconstitutional the law outlawing the Communist Party in Bolivia. . . .[15]

In 1955, when the U.S. Congress was considering continuing aid to Bolivia, Lechín resigned as minister of mines. The sentiment has been expressed frequently in Bolivia that this

[15] *Critical Materials,* cited p. 115.

step was a condition for the extension of further aid by the United States.

Meanwhile the stabilization program had begun to have a dampening effect on the inflation. The boliviano, which had fallen to about 12,000 to the dollar under Paz Estenssoro, recovered to around 8,500. By the end of 1957 the cost of living had begun to decline slightly, thus interrupting a steep rise which had gone on since 1952. In January 1958, in the face of ineffective opposition, Siles again froze salaries and wages for another year. But by December 1958 the cost of living had resumed its upward climb, and at the end of the year the exchange rate was again 12,000 bolivianos to the dollar.

Meanwhile, Siles' political problems were growing worse. Before the congressional elections of July 1958, Paz Estenssoro returned briefly from London to participate in the campaign. In this instance, his role was not decisive, and Siles rode through the election without substantial gains or losses. In Bolivian politics it is now difficult, however, to distinguish who supports whom or who is elected to Congress because he may be less dangerous inside than out.

In August 1958, Siles issued a new ultimatum—his eighth—to Congress to maintain his "hold-the-line" policy, and for the eighth time he accompanied it by his resignation from the presidency in case the ultimatum was not accepted. For the eighth time Congress voted to support Siles, and for the eighth time he withdrew his resignation.

The opposition's reply to Siles' precarious success was strikes and more strikes. A transportation strike called by Lechín closed down the railroads for several weeks. By early 1959 it had become increasingly clear that Siles could not convince miners, workers, and farmers of the need of indefinitely prolonged sacrifices for the sake of stabilization. The white-collar workers, formerly a strong support for the moderate wing of the MNR, were losing faith as they attempted to live on $20 to $60 a month.

The right also opposed Siles' stabilization program. In mid-September 1958, Siles' half brother, Luis Adolfo Siles, representing the rightist PSD (Social Democratic party), signed a pact with Oscar Unzaga de la Vega, the leader of the

Falange, the bulwark of the opposition, for closer cooperation between their parties, emphasizing their opposition to the stabilization and *status quo* policies of the Siles faction within the MNR. In it they declared: "The nation finds itself under a government which survives by inertia, without faith in its men or methods and without hope in its ideas."

In late September 1958, the economy and the MNR received a harsh blow from a new quarter. During the previous year, Russia had been selling substantial quantities of tin in free world markets, at prevailing prices. Most of it was purchased by the International Tin Council, which was attempting to maintain a price of 91 cents a pound. When the Council's funds were exhausted, the price of this plunged for a time below 80 cents, while Bolivia protested in the United Nations against Russia's economic aggression. The imposition by the United States of lead and zinc import quotas also weakened Bolivia's economic position. The combination of unfavorable factors caused the boliviano to slip from about 9,000 to the dollar, at which level it had been held for nearly two years, to about 11,200 in September 1958.

In the presidential election scheduled for May, and then postponed until June 1960, Hernán Siles was debarred from succeeding himself. A comparatively young man, he will continue to be a force on the political scene. In 1959 Víctor Paz Estenssoro returned to Bolivia to campaign for the presidency. In 1960 Paz again demonstrated his control of the MNR, was elected to a new four-year term in an election marred by scattered violence and by many charges of stuffing and stealing ballots. The popularity of the Paz candidacy was undoubtedly bolstered by Juan Lechín standing with him for the vice-presidency. The main opponent to Paz was Wálter Guevara Arze, who had done yeoman service in the MNR since its founding, serving almost continuously in high office. Guevara had apparently concluded that 1960 was his year for the presidency, and several MNR moderates supported him, even tentatively organizing a new splinter party, the Authentic MNR, to oppose Paz Estenssoro's candidacy. For a time Guevara attempted to dissociate himself from this faction and from open opposition to Paz, but strong support from "political control posts" (a kind of urban militia) and urban residents of Cochabamba forced his hat into the ring.

Retiring President Siles was as usual in a difficult position. When Paz apparently forced Guevara's resignation as minister of interior in October 1959, Siles appointed him minister of foreign affairs, a position he had previously held under Paz. The moderates' support of Guevara, and Siles' initial refusal to remove him from the cabinet, inevitably drove Paz closer to the left, headed by Lechín, although Lechín has never enjoyed Paz's full confidence. Immediately after the election of June 1960 it was far from clear how great Lechín's influence would be in the new Paz administration. Ñuflo Chávez's fall in 1956 demonstrated that MNR vice-presidents are expendable, and Paz had once before struck down Lechín from cabinet rank. Paz's actions quite obviously will be subject to the pressures brought to bear upon him, and now it matters little that many of those pressures were of his own making.

In 1959 *campesino* leader José Rojas was named minister of *campesino* affairs, technically a step up, but in reality removing him from direct leadership. He remained in the cabinet only a few months before his resignation in November, thereupon returning to the Ucureña area to participate in virtually open warfare over the future leadership of the *campesino* movement. New patterns of peasant leadership had not emerged clearly by early 1960. Federico Alvarez Plata, one-time vice-president and president of the Senate, and Lechín's opponent in 1960 for the vice-presidency, has made little headway in his attempt to organize the Aymara-speaking *campesinos* of the *altiplano* to counterbalance the Rojas organization, which is strongest among Quechua speakers.

The Falange, the strongest adversary of the MNR, had meanwhile suffered a severe setback in April 1959, when, taking advantage of the economic discontent, it staged another of its abortive revolts against the MNR. In La Paz some two hundred persons were killed in street fighting, many of them the younger and more fanatic Falangists. This Sunday morning coup, in which much of the fighting centered around the Cathedral and the Church of San Francisco, further discredited the Falange. Party leader Oscar Unzaga de la Vega was killed, or accomplished the difficult feat of suicide by two mortal gun shots to the head. In the 1960 elections the Falange, as usual, gathered substantial support only in the cities.

In the early months of 1960 newspapers reported the Bolivian government as contemplating the establishment of diplomatic relations with the Soviet Union and the United Arab Republic. Simultaneously the Soviet government was reported to be offering a loan of $70 million to finance Soviet or Soviet-bloc exports, to help the state-owned Yacimientos Petrolíferos Fiscales Bolivianos build up the extraction and refining of Bolivia's promising but underdeveloped oil reserves. There were also reports of plans to withdraw Bolivia's diplomatic representatives from Panama and Costa Rica and to handle affairs with these countries through its ambassador to Cuba. Responsible newspapers in La Paz were critical of the rumored moves. But it was significant that the government found it necessary to plant the ominous rumors, if indeed the moves were not seriously contemplated, in order to dissociate itself from the accusation of slavish adherence to U.S. policy as epitomized in the stabilization plan. Unable for several years to secure U.S. government funds to develop its potential oil resources, in June 1960 Bolivia received its first U.S. government loan, in the amount of $2.7 million, supplementing private loans by U.S. business, to develop oil production.

Personal loyalties and ideological abstractions play major roles in Bolivian politics, but a central factor in the political struggle today is the persistent economic dilemma of the country. For the miners and white-collar workers a new round of inflation threatens their already meager livelihood, and political forces on the left and the right are awaiting the moment when economic despair may further erode the power of the moderate wing of the MNR. How have the *campesinos* fared in these turbulent years? Always insulated to a high degree against the fluctuations of the market economy, yet able to expand their subsistence farms after the land reforms, will their support offset the discontent of many urban groups, hard hit as they have been by the continuing crisis and perilously close to the seat of power? While much has changed since 1952 in the political power of the *campesinos*, they are, after all, only at the beginning of a complex process of social and cultural change.

* * *

Bolivia's Economic Prospects

Bolivia is confronted with problems common to many underdeveloped countries: dependence on a few basic exports, low productivity, lack of capital, and an absence of the spirit of enterprise. In addition Bolivia has had a history of political instability, violent social upheavals, and demoralizing inflationary cycles that have delayed the establishment of institutions essential for economic development. At the beginning of the 1960's the prospects for both political and financial stability seem far more promising than they were before. The moderate wing of the MNR has maintained itself in power for eight years, the country's currency has been stable for a year and a half, and internal prices have been kept under control.

With these essential conditions for economic health achieved, Bolivia still faces the hard job of increasing output and productivity in all sectors of the economy if the country is to live within its income and provide a better standard of living for its increasing population. Agricultural output must rise so that meager foreign exchange reserves need not be spent on food and fiber imports. About two-thirds of the population live by agriculture, but these people are concentrated in the Andean highlands and valleys, where land suitable for cultivation is badly eroded and low in fertility, and where many plots are so small and distribution channels so underdeveloped that little is produced for market. Some increase in productivity in the areas now under cultivation can be expected with the introduction of more advanced techniques, but the prospects for large-scale increases lie in the plans for opening up the vast and largely uninhabited areas of the fertile eastern lowlands. The Bolivian National Institute of Colonization is engaged in a program of resettlement in the Santa Cruz area, and the UN Special Fund is contributing $283,500 for surveys of the region. (Another contribution of $336,500 will go for training at two agricultural schools.) The Bolivian government has a broad program covering crop diversification, road-building, electrical power installations, and plants to process the products of the region. Exports of tropical products—oranges, bananas, and coffee—are already providing some foreign exchange, and Bolivia's rice and sugar requirements are being increasingly met from domestic supplies.

The future of tin is uncertain; its use has not kept pace with the growth of the world economy. As a high-cost producer Bolivia is at a competitive disadvantage in comparison with other major tin-exporting areas, and the declining grade of its ores and the prospective changes in world demand make reliance on this metal hazardous. In other metals Bolivia is generally a low-cost producer, and the prospects for some of them—particularly gold, antimony, and tungsten—are more favorable. The hopes of extractive industry lie chiefly in petroleum. Drilling concessions were granted to private foreign companies in 1956, and a pipeline across the Andes to Chile has been built. Exports of crude petroleum and gasoline have been rising steadily and an increasing share of the domestic market is being supplied from domestic production.

Manufacturing has made a very small contribution to national income, not only in absolute terms but also in comparison with other Latin American countries. A limited internal market, shortage of capital and skilled labor, dependence on imports for raw material supplies, and high transport costs have all contributed to a low level of industrial activity. The expansion and diversification of Bolivia's manufacturing and service industries are essential since the capacity of the agricultural and mining sectors to absorb additions to the labor force is limited, the first by the difficulties of reclaiming land in the *Oriente* and establishing the settlers there, the second by the surplus labor already underemployed in the mines. Until foreign reserves are larger and foreign funds more readily obtainable, Bolivia will have to develop those branches of industry that require small capital investments—processing of food and fibers, refining of ores, production of materials, such as cement and bricks, that are needed for development work, the manufacture of textiles and household goods. With an advance in agriculture from subsistence farming to the production of cash crops, new domestic consumers will be found for Bolivia's industrial goods.

The expansion of production in manufacturing and agriculture must be accompanied by even larger advances in two basic activities: energy production and transport. Bolivia has abundant hydroelectric and petroleum resources; it lacks the financial resources needed for their exploitation. And few countries have faced the transport problems that altitude and difficult terrain present in Bolivia, or a greater need for improvement in road and rail facilities. Here are two areas essential to economic development, in which foreign funds have traditionally been invested and where, for Bolivia, they are an indispensable supplement to its own efforts.

CUBA

Much of the writing on Castroism in Cuba has stressed its totalitarian nature, amalgamation with Communism, and dependence upon the Soviet Union. In this selection, George I. Blanksten, Professor of Political Science at Northwestern University, emphasizes instead the indigenous conditions within Cuba that helped facilitate the Castro movement. The conditions that are elaborated upon cover Cuba's long history of political instability, the antagonism between metropolitan Havana and the rest of the island, the persistent domestic problems such as a poor public morality and depressed agrarian living standards, and the country's long dependent and antagonistic relationship with the United States. Professor Blanksten points out that many of these same conditions are found elsewhere in Latin America and that this is precisely what explains the appeal of *fidelismo.*

FIDELISMO AND ITS ORIGINS

*Fidel Castro and Latin America**

GEORGE I. BLANKSTEN

An old Latin American political axiom has it that "every 'ism' is a somebody-ism." Putting the matter that way of

* Reprinted from George I. Blanksten, "Fidel Castro and Latin America," from *The Revolution in World Politics,* Morton Kaplan (ed.) (New York: John Wiley & Sons, 1962), pp. 113–36 by permission of publisher.

course exaggerates the situation. Nevertheless, "somebodyist" movements abound in Latin America. Paraguay has its *franquismo,* supported by the admirers of General Rafael Franco;[1] Brazil had its *querimismo;*[2] Ecuador its *velasquismo,* based on the followers of President José María Velasco Ibarra; Uruguay its *batllismo,* founded by President José Batlle y Ordóñez; and Argentina its *peronismo.* Cuba today has its *fidelismo,* with which this paper is concerned.

The *curriculum vitae* of *fidelismo* is readily provided. It began in 1947, when Fidel Castro Ruz, then a twenty-one-year-old Cuban law student, took part in an invasion of the Dominican Republic in an unsuccessful attempt to overthrow the government of Generalissimo Rafael Leónidas Trujillo Molina. The following year found Fidel Castro in Colombia, where he took part in the *bogotazo,* the tumultous rioting which began at Bogotá during the Ninth International Conference of American States. In 1952, Dr. Castro, during the course of his legal practice in Cuba, filed a brief with the Court of Constitutional Guarantees asking that body to declare unconstitutional the government of General Fulgencio Batista y Zaldivar, who had resumed power by a *coup d'état* in March of that year. When the court rejected Castro's legal plea, he turned to revolutionary activity against the Batista regime. On July 26, 1953–*fidelismo* is known officially as the 26th of July Movement–Castro led an unsuccessful attack on a military post at Santiago, in eastern Cuba. Imprisoned for this act, he was freed through an amnesty in 1955. He then left Cuba to spend almost two years in exile, principally in Mexico, preparing for his major contest with Batista. In December 1956, Castro and a small band of guerilla invaders landed in eastern Cuba. During the following two years the island was gripped by civil war, with Fidel Castro acquiring legendary stature as the guerilla leader of the rebels. Batista at length fell from power on January 1, 1959. *Fidelismo* then took up the reins of government. The last lines of this *curriculum vitae* remained to be written at the time this paper was prepared.

[1] Not connected with Spain's Generalissimo Francisco Franco.

[2] Literally, "we-wantism," a popular abbreviation of the "We want Vargas" movement launched in 1945.

No doubt, much of *fidelismo* is peculiar to Castro, and much is indigenous to Cuba. Yet, a substantial sector of the movement remains generalizable as a part of the revolution of our time. For the purpose of analysis of *fidelismo* in that context, it is helpful to examine the four major components of the movement. These components—let us call them the keys to *fidelismo*—are the historic political instability of Cuba, the political contrast between metropolitan Havana and the remainder of the island, the domestic, social, and economic changes in Cuba, and problems in the country's relations with the United States.

These keys are discussed below. They are also important to the politics of other Latin American nations and help to place the Castro revolution in context as a hemispheric phenomenon. None of this is intended to deny the totalitarian elements in the particular Cuban revolution—or the close relationship between Castro, Communism, and the Soviet Union. The totalitarian element, in particular, may provide Castroism with organizational means to discourage counterrevolutionary movements or *coups d'état*. Yet, these aspects of the Cuban problem have been much discussed to the neglect of the indigenous factors that helped to create the Castro movement and that help to give *fidelismo* hemispheric-wide appeal. To equate the appeal of Castroism with Communism, or even with totalitarianism, is to make as great a mistake as to ignore the Communist or totalitarian aspects of the present Cuban regime. To understand the indigenous factors, an analysis of their components is necessary. It is to their systematic examination that we now turn. Attention is also extended, where relevant, to these components as they function in the general Latin American context.

I

Cuba's historic political instability stands first among the four major keys to *fidelismo*. Political instability may be regarded as a condition characterized by frequent so-called "revolution" and recurrent dictatorship, much of it short-lived. Far from being peculiar to Cuba, political instability, thus defined, is a general Latin American characteristic. Each of its elements–frequent so-called "revolution" and chronic dictatorship–is worth consideration, from the twin standpoints of Latin America as a whole and Cuba in particular.

The American nations are famous for their "revolutions." Indeed, the Brazilian Emperor Dom Pedro II is said to have remarked, when he visited the Philadelphia Exposition in 1876, that many of the Latin American countries had more revolutions per minute than the machines he saw on display at the exposition. However, few words are more loosely and promiscuously used in the Americas than "revolution." An amazing array of dissimilar and unrelated occurrences go by this name in the Western Hemisphere. The Wars of Independence have been so dubbed, as well as minor changes in government, the promulgation of new constitutions, and political violence of almost any variety. Actually, true revolution –that is, a basic change in the political system or a recasting of the social order–is surprisingly infrequent in Hispanic America. But "typical revolutions"–changes in government brought about by other than constitutional means, usually not accompanied by fundamental changes in the social or political order–are constantly recurring. Violence, or the threat of it, is often present in such movements. Their frequency is a major Latin American political problem. "Since the turn of the present century," a student of this phenomenon has observed, "the governments of the nations to the south have been overthrown . . . seventy-six times. . . . Revolutions are still the order of the day. . . . Bolivia, for example, has had violent changes of government in 1920, 1930, 1934, 1936, 1937, 1943, 1946, and 1952."[3] Thus far during the twentieth century, on the bare mathematics of the matter, the average Latin American state has experienced four so-called "revolutions."

In this regard, Cuba is fairly typical of Hispanic America. Among the most recent of the states in the area to achieve

[3] Austin F. Macdonald, *Latin-American Politics and Government*, 2nd ed. (New York: Thomas Y. Crowell Co., 1954), pp. 11–12. See also Russell H. Fitzgibbon, "Revolutions: Western Hemisphere," *The South Atlantic Quarterly*, Vol. 55, No. 3 (July 1956), pp. 263–79; and George I. Blanksten, "Revolutions," in Harold E. Davis (ed.), *Government and Politics in Latin America* (New York: The Ronald Press, 1958), pp. 119–46.

national independence, Cuba has undergone somewhat more than the average number of "revolutions" since the island's national political career was launched in 1901. A violent uprising against the government of President Tómas Estrada Palma in 1906 brought military intervention by the United States, then acting under the Platt Amendment.[4] After the departure of the "North American" armed forces in 1909, the constitutional order was not again interrupted until General Gerardo Machado assumed the presidency in 1925. In a *coup d'état* three years later, Machado prolonged his period in power and intensified his dictatorship. Two "revolutions" occurred in 1933. The first overthrew Machado and installed Dr. Carlos Manuel de Cespedes as provisional president. The second, led by Batista, then an army sergeant, unseated Cespedes. Batista remained in power until the election of 1944, following which he went into voluntary exile in the United States. In a *coup d'état* in 1952, Batista overthrew the government of President Carlos Prío Socarrás to return to power. And it was this second Batista regime that Castro's "revolution" ousted in 1959. Measured against the general Latin American average, this Cuban record is a little–but not much–more than par for the course.

Involved in the problem of political instability, in addition to the frequency of so-called "revolution," is the phenomenon of recurrent dictatorship. While the situation is continually changing, it is generally true that at any given moment at least a half-dozen Latin American countries are governed by dictatorship, normally military in orientation. The reasons for this are many and deep-seated. Among them is the authoritarian political tradition the Spanish Empire imposed upon its American colonies. Itself historically governed by divine-right monarchy, Spain left a tradition of strong government in the Western Hemisphere. Indeed, this tradition was so marked that many of the nineteenth-century leaders of the movements for Latin American independence believed that monarchy should be retained as the newly independent states' form of government. In conformity with this reasoning, monarchies were in fact attempted in the nineteenth century

[4] The controversial Platt Amendment is discussed on pp. 399–406, to follow.

in Mexico, Brazil, and Haiti. Even those who advocated the establishment of republican systems in Latin America were convinced that they should be strongly authoritarian. In preparing the draft of Bolivia's first constitution, "The Liberator" Simón Bolívar produced an instrument providing for a president with not only lifelong tenure, but also the authority to choose his own successor.

> The President of the Republic becomes in our Constitution the sun, which, firm in the center, gives life to the universe [Bolívar wrote]. I have never been an enemy of monarchy, as far as general principles are concerned; on the contrary, I consider monarchies essential for the respectability and well-being of new nations. . . . The new states of America . . . need kings with the name of presidents.[5]

In seeking the keys to *fidelismo,* it is worth emphasizing that Cuba received much more than the average Hispanic-American dose of this Spanish tradition of political authoritarianism. Not only was Cuba one of the first places in the Western Hemisphere where Spanish colonial power was established, but it is also worth remembering that this island was the last place in the Americas to be freed from that power. Christopher Columbus, the celebrated Admiral of the Ocean Sea himself, visited Cuba during his second voyage in 1493. Spanish colonial government was established there shortly after, and remained in the island for four centuries. Cuba's history as a Spanish colony stands in marked contrast to that of, say, Argentina, where the Spanish Viceroyalty of the United Provinces of the La Plata River was not established until 1776, lasting only until the independence movement which began in 1810.[6] Not only did Cuba endure a longer

[5] Quoted in Blanksten, "Caudillismo in Northwestern South America," *The South Atlantic Quarterly,* Vol. 51, No. 4 (October 1952), pp. 498–99.

[6] Also worth contrasting with Cuba were the following colonial vice-royalties, with the dates of both their founding and the beginnings of the successful independence movements: New Spain (Mexico), 1535, 1821; New Castille (Peru), 1542, 1821; and New Granada (Colombia, Ecuador, Venezuela, and Panama), 1717, 1809.

history of Spanish colonial rule than any other American colony, but also the military and authoritarian orientation of that rule was heavier in the island than elsewhere in Hispanic America. During the colonial period, Cuba served as a military and supply base, first for the Spanish conquest and later for the government of the New World. Spain conquered Mexico from Cuba, and moved from the island to other parts of the Americas as well. No other part of Latin America has endured a longer or more heavily military tradition of political authoritarianism than has Cuba.

Since the achievement of Cuban independence, this tradition has been reflected in the recurrence of military dictatorship in the island's government. Among the most celebrated of the conntry's dictatorships was that presided over from 1925 until 1933 by General Gerardo Machado. His regime has been regarded as "one of the cruelest that Latin America has ever seen. Machado . . . ruthlessly oppressed his opponents, frequently by means of torture and murder. The . . . life of the republic was paralyzed."[7] Shortly after the fall of Machado, Sergeant Fulgencio Batista rose to national power, promoting himself to colonel during the process. Although Batista's first period in power, which lasted until 1944, bore many of the characteristics of dictatorship, the regime was mild as compared with Machado's, and a number of constitutional reforms were put into effect. These made possible the election of 1944, which ushered in an eight-year period of civilian constitutional government. During this time the presidency was occupied by Dr. Ramón Grau San Martín (1944–48) and Dr. Carlos Prío Socarrás (1948–52). Batista's second regime (1952–58), unlike his first, was a rigid dictatorship sufficiently ruthless to lead many Cubans to compare it with the Machado period. Castro overthrew this dictatorship. In establishing another, he presided over a continuation of, rather than a departure from, a four-century-old tradition of military authoritarianism. It was this consideration that gave point in 1959 to the widely-told joke to the effect that when the bearded Castro was secretly shaved he turned out to be Batista.

[7] Miguel Jorrín, *Governments of Latin America* (New York: D. Van Nostrand Co., 1953), p. 276.

Cuba's historic political instability thus stands as a first key to *fidelismo.* A number of the movement's basic characteristics derive from this tradition. The most obvious of these is that *fidelismo,* like a number of previous Cuban regimes, has embraced the continuation of government through dictatorship. Few lists of *fidelista* objectives have assigned significant priority to the restoration of constitutional government in the country. The holding of elections, while mentioned as a possibility early in the Castro regime, eventually lost its place among *fidelista* intentions. The Cuban press, censored by Batista and a number of his predecessors, continued in censorship during the Castro regime. Radio, television, the theater, and other mass-communication media were likewise controlled. While civil and political liberties were not much less curtailed by Castro than by many of the previous governments, neither were the liberties permitted by him in any way significant in contrast to the policies of Machado or of Batista's second regime.

As a military dictatorship, the Castro regime illustrated a curious phase in the evolution of Cuban militarism. Beyond providing a defense system for the community, the Cuban army has long performed domestic political functions. The frequency with which military officers have assumed the presidency of the republic has already been noted. High-ranking army officers have historically been important politicians, and the military influence has provided a species of backdrop for politics. In view of the fact that the significance of militarism in Latin-American politics has long been recognized, it is a curious circumstance that social scientists have only recently begun to turn their attention to this problem. Early studies indicate that the process of political clique-formation among army officers, correlations between military rank and the class systems, and relationships between military rank and political orientation offer potential insight into many aspects of Latin-American politics. In a number of the countries, for example, general officers tend to lead conservative political movements, while a significant radicalism recruits its political leadership from the group of military ranks bounded at the top by colonel and at the bottom by captain. Additional studies of these matters are sorely needed to test such hypotheses which are occupying interesting places in the as yet small and pioneering literature on the armed forces of Latin America.[8]

In any case, the story of Machado, Batista, and Castro suggests a curious direction in the evolution of Cuban militarism. Machado's military regime was dominated by general officers who exercised a conservative influence on national politics. Batista was a sergeant at the time of his first uprising in 1933. Securing the aid of junior army officers, his movement effectively liquidated the officer class which had ruled Cuba before and during the Machado regime. Batista's military government differed from his predecessors' in that it was based upon a lower-ranking officer group. The latent political coalition between the large landowners and the military command was markedly weakened in Cuba after 1933. While the first Batista government was of course a military regime, it was a lower-ranking group that exercised political power then than had been the case in earlier governments. After the election of 1944, Batista maintained his contact with the junior army officers. When he made his *coup d'état* in 1952, he confided that "I did it with captains and lieutenants."[9]

As Batista's revolution of 1933 was a military purge, so, too, in a sense, was Castro's revolution. Shortly after Castro came to power in 1959, his firing squads embarked upon a sensationally wholesale program of executing military men who had served Batista's government. Much has been written about these executions. Castro called them, and the trials that preceded most of them, "revolutionary justice." His enemies pointed to the executions as additional evidence of the ruthless dictatorship of *fidelismo*. It may not be amiss to suggest that they constituted a new military purge in a country historically governed by its armed forces. It has been estimated

[8] See Edwin Lieuwen, *Arms and Politics in Latin America* (New York: Published for the Council on Foreign Relations by Frederick A. Praeger, 1960), *passim;* and Robert J. Alexander, "The Army in Politics," in Davis, *op. cit.*, pp. 147–65.

[9] Stanley R. Ross, "Some Observations on Military Coups in the Caribbean," in A. Curtis Wilgus (ed.), *The Caribbean: Its Political Problems* (Gainesville: University of Florida Press, 1956), pp. 112–13.

that 557 men were executed by Castro's firing squads during the first few months of 1959. With very few exceptions, these had been soldiers and policemen of the Batista government. Again the question of military rank becomes significant. The overwhelming majority of the executed were junior officers and men holding non-commissioned ranks. Also prominent among the victims were army conscripts who had been assigned to firing squads. Of the 557 executions, the most widely publicized was that of Captain Jesús Sosa Blanco. Among his distinctions was the fact that he was the highest-ranking of the military people put to death at that time. Batista's "captains and lieutenants" were liquidated.

Fidel Castro's popular militia thereupon filled the military vacuum. The basic significance of this pattern of the evolution of Cuban militarism remained unclear at the time this paper was written. There appears to be a perhaps ironic democratization of the military, in the sense that its politically influential center of gravity has moved to progressively lower military ranks. Cuba remained under military rule, to be sure; but the progression from Machado's generals through Batista's junior officers to Castro's popular militia appears to reflect a broadening of the base of the country's militarism.

Cuba's historic political instability has also been reflected by remarkable difficulty in achieving political institutionalization, and this too throws light on the nature of *fidelismo*. Cuban opposition parties have been in the habit of accusing the groups in power of violating the country's written constitutions. These have indeed been violated, but traditional instability lies at the heart of the problem at least as much as does any personal skulduggery of men in public office. Since independence, Cuba has had two major written constitutions. Neither ever achieved genuine institutionalization. The first, promulgated in 1901, was violated in 1906, 1928, 1933 (twice), 1934, and in 1937. The second, a Batista instrument proclaimed in 1940, not only has been violated at least as often as the first, but also will probably never actually function in Cuba. Theoretically, the Constitution of 1940 provides for a variation of parliamentary government, with the president of the republic functioning as a species of figurehead, while major authority is to be exercised by a prime minister and his cabinet.

Batista found the parliamentary system, foreign to Cuban traditions and practices, to be the answer to a dictator's prayer. Serving as the "figurehead" president under the Constitution of 1940, he pursued the practice of obtaining the prime minister's and cabinet ministers' signed but undated resignations at the time he appointed them to office. When it suited his purposes, President Batista dated the resignations and delivered them to the press. Even during the eight-year constitutional period, from 1944 to 1952, the parliamentary system did not take genuine institutional hold. Because he declared that he expected the prime minister to exercise more power than he would himself, President Ramón Grau San Martín was berated by the Cuban press as a weakling unfit to hold national public office. Throughout the constitutional period, prime ministers generally entertained the political ambition of becoming president, a pattern contrary to the spirit of the parliamentary system. Batista again lived comfortably with his constitution when he returned to power in 1952. Castro's use of the parliamentary idea has been but a minor variation of Batista's. Theoretically, Castro has been prime minister, to be sure, and his presidents, powerless figureheads; but neither prime minister nor president—not to mention a parliament!—has been elected. The record is clear that constitutional government has yet to take root in Cuba, and that the Constitutions of 1901 and 1940 have both failed to establish a viable institutional framework.[10]

Civilian political parties have not had much more success in achieving stable institutionalization on the island. During the first generation of national independence, the Liberal Party enjoyed something of stability, but this was damaged by its support of Machado. The Cuban Revolutionary (*Auténtico*) Party emerged from the revolution of 1933 and endured to support the administrations of Presidents Grau and

[10] See Fitzgibbon, "Constitutional Development in Latin America: A Synthesis," *American Political Science Review*, Vol. 34 (June 1945), pp. 500–22; and William S. Stokes, "The Cuban Parliamentary System in Action, 1940–1947," *Journal of Politics* (April 1949), pp. 335–64.

Prío. Leftist participation has been provided by the Party of the Cuban People and the Communist Party. But civilian political parties, whether of the Right or of the Left, have exhibited a remarkable instability and a chronic incapacity to work with, and otherwise relate to, each other. *Fidelismo* clearly demonstrates this condition of the parties. Numerous attempts have been made to relate civilian political parties to the Castro government but all have failed. This has also been true of the opposition—it is more accurate to say "oppositions"—to Castro. Here too it has been virtually impossible for the parties to join together in a stable fashion in pursuit of a common cause.

Furthermore, the country's political instability has tended to intensify *personalismo* in Cuba and, with it, a popular tendency to respond to charismatic leadership. *Personalismo* may be regarded as the custom of following or opposing a political leader on the basis of his personality rather than on ideological grounds. Many students of Latin American politics have found this to be a widespread tendency in the area. Pierson and Gil, for example, point to "the high value placed on the individual and personal leadership," promoting "a disposition to vote for the man rather than the party or the platform."[11] Another student has said: "From earliest days the Latin Americans . . . have always been more interested in their public men than in their public policies. They have tended to follow colorful leaders, to the subordination of issues. . . . A picturesque demagogue is virtually assured a large following."[12] Expanded *personalismo* has increased the tendency of charismatic leaders to rise to national power in Cuba. Convinced that he is the only figure on the scene who can "save the country," the charismatic leader feels an "inner call." He is recognized by his followers as a "natural" leader of men. They "do not obey him by virtue of tradition or statute, but because they believe in him," Max Weber has pointed out. He governs through a species of divine right, but "his divine mission must 'prove' itself in that those who faithfully sur-

[11] William W. Pierson and Federico G. Gil, *Governments of Latin America* (New York: McGraw-Hill Book Co., 1957), p. 31.
[12] Macdonald, *op. cit.*, p. 2.

render to him must fare well. If they do not fare well, he is obviously not the master sent by the gods."[13]

Personalismo is clearly central in *fidelismo,* and Fidel Castro is one of Latin America's leading case studies in charismatic leadership. Two implications of this are significant. First, his role is defined by his charismatic hold on his followers, rather than by an institutional or constitutional position he might hold. Secondly, the magic of charisma is not easily transferable–Fidel Castro, and Fidel alone, heads *fidelismo.* From time to time during the course of his regime, rumors arose to the effect that he was about to be displaced by one or more of his associates as leader of his movement. Prominently mentioned as candidates for this leadership were his younger brother, Raul Castro, *fidelismo's* military commander; Major Ernesto ("Che") Guevara, chief of the National Bank of Cuba ("Che's" National Bank); and Antonio Núñez Jiménez, head of the National Institute of Agrarian Reform (INRA). It seemed likely, however, that none of these figures would be able to inherit Fidel's charismatic hold on his movement. It has been said that

> Fidel is the most charismatic figure produced by Latin America, at least in this century. . . . Castro's domination of Cuban events is virtually unique. . . . The history of Cuba in the last two or three years is the biography of Fidel.[14]

The island's historic political instability, then, stands as a first of the major keys to the nature of *fidelismo.* As such, this consideration points to the Castro revolution as one more upheaval in a country with more than the average Latin American predilection for "revolutions," and to the *fidelista* dictatorship as one more strong government in a culture historically given to political authoritarianism. As a military dictatorship, the Castro regime appears to have encouraged further de-

[13] Max Weber (H. H. Gerth and C. Wright Mills, tr.), *From Max Weber: Essays in Sociology* (New York: Oxford University Press, 1946), pp. 79, 249.

[14] Fitzgibbon, "The Revolution Next Door: Cuba," *Annals of the American Academy of Political and Social Science,* Vol. 334 (March 1961), pp. 113–22, especially pp. 114, 116–17.

mocratization of the political role of the armed forces, as evidenced by the emergence of a popular militia on the ruins of Machado- and Batista-style armies. The place of political instability in *fidelismo* is further attested to in the lack of institutionalization which has characterized the movement. This has been reflected in the absence of constitutionalism, in the inability of civilian political parties to relate to Castro, and in the heavily charismatic, rather than institutional, leadership which has given *fidelismo* much of its course and character.

II

A second significant key to the nature of the movement is to be found in the striking political contrast between metropolitan Havana and the rest of Cuba. Again, it may be helpful to compare the island with the remainder of Latin America. Throughout the area—indeed, in most underdeveloped areas[15]—sharp contrasts and conflicts characterize the relationships between urban centers and rural communities. These relationships appear to be a function of the process of economic development in two significant ways. First, urban centers in the developing areas serve as nuclei of commercialization and the beginnings of industrialization, as centers of "modernization" or "Westernization," and as focal points of secularization. In contrast, the rural areas live in a landed or agricultural, rather than commercial or industrializing, economy and tend to be more "backward," traditional, religious, and superstitious. In the underdeveloped areas, illiteracy rates are sharply higher in rural than in urban communities, and standards of living differ dramatically, being much higher in the cities than in their hinterlands.

Second, underdeveloped areas are theaters of rapid social and economic change. A major facet of this change is urbanization, the movement of people from the rural areas to the cities. This trend, intensified by the tendency of European immigrants to locate in the major cities of Latin America, has

[15] See Gabriel A. Almond and James S. Coleman (eds.), *The Politics of the Developing Areas* (Princeton; Princeton University Press, 1960), especially pp. 455–531.

been one of the area's major social phenomena of the twentieth century. There is no Hispanic-American country in which there has been a trend away from urbanization; everywhere the impressive fact has been the movement toward the city, the swelling of urban populations. This trend has given rise to what is sometimes referred to as the problem of *la cabeza de Goliat* (Goliath's head), characterizing a country in which a giant urban head rests upon a dwarf-like rural body. In Latin America this situation is by no means peculiar to Cuba. It is acute in a number of other countries, such as Uruguay, where more than half of the national population lives in the metropolitan area of Montevideo; Argentina, where a little more than one-fourth of the people are located in Greater Buenos Aires; and Venezuela, where approximately 20 per cent of the population lives in Caracas.

If the Cuban case is viewed in this perspective, a number of significant propositions emerge. In the first place, the island is no mere case study in *la cabeza de Goliat.* Rather, Cuba exhibits an exaggerated caricature of the problem. Fifty-three per cent–more than one-half–of the total national population is urban residing principally *in one city*–the metropolitan area of Havana! Far from being representative of the cultural life of the rest of the island, Havana–secularized, commercialized, "Westernized," sophisticated, and "modern"–stands not only as the metropolis of the Caribbean, but also, ranking with New York, Chicago, Buenos Aires, and Mexico City, as one of the major metropolitan centers of the Western Hemisphere.

Moreover, Havana has stood historically in a position of political opposition to the rest of the island. In the Americas, it has been pointed out, "Hispanic culture has always been strongly urbanized."[16] Throughout the imperial period, Spain treated its American colonies as a collection of cities, setting the pattern for the deep division separating urban from rural life. The seat of governmental power in colonial times, Havana provided "the chief centers of political activity of the upper classes and, indeed, the only community levels upon which they–rather than the home government in Europe–

[16] William S. Stokes, *Latin-American Politics* (New York: Thomas Y. Crowell Co., 1959), p. 502.

could exercise power."[17] Traditionally the headquarters of elite groups, in contemporary times Havana has come to be the home of those political groups which gained in strength as the island's economic development proceeded. Especially important among these groups were organized labor, the urbanized "middle sectors"–identified as "politically ambitious middle groups" active in commerce and developing industry[18]–and other newly emerging industrializing and entrepreneurial groups. Caught in the economic development of Cuba, these Havana-based interests frequently pursued courses opposed to the desires of rural sectors, feeding the historic fires of rural-urban conflict.

Against this background, *fidelismo* took shape as a rural movement at war against Havana interests. During his years as the leader of the rebels against Batista, Fidel Castro led rural Cuba in its historic, and now open, war against Havana. Castro's image as the champion of the back country grew after December 1956, when he set up rebel headquarters in the rural Sierra Maestra. The back country's enemies of Havana flocked to him in an intensely indigenous nationalism. Suffering real and imagined hardships at the cruel hands of the metropolis, the rural fraternity of the disadvantaged provided *fidelismo* with an agrarian popular base.

Thus, a second key to *fidelismo*. In a very real sense, Castro's rise to power was the triumph of rural Cuba over Havana. The imprisoned metropolis saw its interests crushed by Fidel. The industrializing "middle sectors" fell prey to the back country, and Cuba's economic development, insofar as it had depended upon urban leadership, was significantly retarded.[19] Seen as a rural victory over the metropolis, *fidelismo* was curiously reminiscent of the regime of General Juan Manuel Rosas which had ruled Argentina more than a

[17] Blanksten, "Problems of Local Government in the Caribbean," in Wilgus, *op. cit.*, p. 226.

[18] John J. Johnson, *Political Change in Latin America: The Emergence of the Middle Sectors* (Stanford: Stanford University Press, 1958), p. vii and *passim*.

[19] John J. Johnson, "The Political Role of the Latin-American Middle Sectors," *Annals of the American Academy of Political and Social Science*, Vol. 334 (March 1961), pp. 20–29.

century before. It, too, was a triumph of the "interior" over the urban capital, of the intensely indigenous over the secular.

III

Domestic Cuban social and economic conditions cannot be ignored as a major key to *fidelismo*. The island, like most underdeveloped areas, is a theater of remarkably rapid change. In combination with the country's historic political instability, this pattern of social and economic transformation has influenced the nature of *fidelismo* in two ways. The first is a matter of public morality. The second gives Castro's movement something of the flavor of the agrarian-populistic or *Aprista* parties common in a number of Hispanic-American countries.

The problem of public morality is widespread in the Latin American political culture in a form often difficult for "North Americans" to understand. In many of the countries, including Cuba, politicians and government officials are generally distrusted and popularly assumed to be guilty of a wide variety of forms of graft and corruption. Most Latin Americans are cynical about equating ordinary morality with politics, and *la mordida* (the "bite") is generally expected in the discharge of governmental functions. "They tell you that I am stealing your money," a Latin American officeholder is said to have told a public rally. "Who would you rather have steal your money than me?"

It is important to distinguish the charge or expectation of corruption from the question of the extent to which it takes place in fact. Much more is known about the former than the latter. Mass media in most of the Latin American countries indulge in the belief that their governments, or many of their officials, are corrupt. The public acceptance of this belief is widespread. On the other hand, it is as difficult to substantiate as it is to disprove such accusations, and little is objectively known of the extent to which they are justified. This writer's guess—and it is only that—is that graft and corruption in fact do occur in Latin America, but probably not on as large a scale as is popularly believed.

In any case, pre-Castro Cuba was characterized by the typical Latin-American situation in this regard. Government officials were generally believed to be corrupt and were often pictured in the press as enriching themselves at public expense. A few illustrations of this Cuban pattern might be mentioned here. During the administration of President Ramón Grau San Martín (1944–48), one of the more celebrated Havana sights visited by guided tours was a huge diamond set in the floor of the *Capitolio,* the building in which the Cuban Congress met. In 1947, the diamond was stolen, and the Havana press rose to the mystery-solving challenge with considerable zest. Many of the papers declared that it was inevitable that the diamond would be stolen, simply because it had been placed in the building where the national legislature, composed of Cuba's leading thieves, met. Some argued that President Grau himself was the culprit; many who disagreed pointed out that he could steal more without leaving the presidential office. Three years after the expiration of his term, Grau was formally charged with having misappropriated one hundred and seventy-four million dollars; the ultimate indictment was for forty million, "mainly because valuable evidence was apparently stolen by gunmen from a public office."[20] Many exiled Cuban ex-presidents have been reported as living handsomely because of self-enrichment at public expense while in office. Among the leading recent instances of this is Dr. Carlos Prío Socarrás, Grau's successor (1948–52) in the presidency. Both of Batista's regimes were similarly characterized by charges and expectations of corruption. With the expansion of the "North American" tourist trade during his time, luxurious gambling casinos and other entertainment centers, publicly supposed to be centers of dishonesty and immorality, flourished in Havana.

One significant side of *fidelismo* is its role as a crusade for public morality. Castro's movement has been a species of political puritanism, curiously Spartan-like in character. An amazing variety of charges and accusations has been hurled against the Castro regime, to be sure; but graft and corruption are significantly absent among them. Virtually no looting was engaged in during the tumultuous first days after the fall

[20] R. A. Gómez, *Government and Politics in Latin America* (New York: Random House, 1960), p. 67.

of Batista; money taken from the raided gambling casinos lay virtually untouched in the streets. *Fidelismo* has moved, often in naive ways, against gambling and other activities assumed to be corrupt, and the administrative morality of the Castro government seems strangely out of place in a Cuba grown cynical in such matters.

The following news story offers some insight into the stern and humorless extremes achieved in *fidelismo's* war against *la mordida:*

> Premier Fidel Castro has decided to revise the rules of baseball, it was disclosed today.
>
> Last Sunday, after cutting cane at a nearby sugar mill, Dr. Castro pitched in a sandlot game. But when a runner stole second base on him, the Premier ordered him back to first.
>
> 'In the revolution,' Dr. Castro said, 'no one can steal—even in baseball.'[21]

The face of *fidelismo's* Spartan-like public morality should be neither ignored nor underestimated.

The rural character of *fideslismo,* springing from Cuba's historic rural-urban conflict, has already been noted. From this standpoint, the Castro movement has acquired a substantial agrarian-populistic base and may be regarded as containing some of the elements of an *Aprista* party. Common in Latin America, *Aprista* parties have two distinguishing characteristics. First, they seek far-reaching social and economic changes in rural areas, usually including land reform. Second, they demanded the integration of the rural lower classes into the political process; indeed, *Aprismo* boasts a greater percentage of lower-class adherents than can any other Latin-American political movement. The chief prototype of this class of political party is, of course, the celebrated *Aprista* Party or APRA[22] of Peru. Other *Aprista* parties include the *Acción Democrática* of Venezuela and the National Libera-

[21] Quoted in *The New Yorker,* March 25, 1961, p. 29.

[22] After the initial letters of *Alianza Popular Revolucionaria Americana* (American Popular Revolutionary Alliance).

tion Party of Costa Rica.[23] In a sense, Mexico's governing PRI[24] is also a party of this type.

Rural conditions in pre-Castro Cuba were by no means the most severe in Latin America. Nevertheless, sufficiently inequitable circumstances to feed an agrarian-populistic revolt certainly existed. Forty-seven per cent of the national population was classified as rural, and 40 per cent of the island's work force was engaged in agriculture. In 1946, 8 per cent of the farmers owned 71.1 per cent of the land while 39 per cent owned only 3.3 per cent of the land. Many of the rural workers were the employees of the more than one hundred fifty sugar mills located throughout the country. Owing to the seasonal production of sugar, there was an average annual unemployment rate of 25 per cent.

> The typical Cuban agriculturalist [it has been pointed out] is not a peasant in the usual European sense of the term but rather a landless proletarian who customarily works for wages in groups or gangs under the direction and supervision of others. . . . He has traditionally been the forgotten man of Cuban society. For the most part employed only a few months during the sugar, tobacco, or coffee harvests, he has barely managed to exist the remainder of the year.[25]

Especially during the years when *fidelismo* was a rebel movement in the back country fighting against Batista's Havana, Castro acquired a strong agrarian following increasingly dedicated to rural reforms. The construction of schools and other educational programs, of benefit especially to rural Cuba, acquired significant status among the goals of his movement. Housing and medical programs also found their way into *fidelismo*. So, too, did land reform, and the pattern of land tenure faced significant changes during the Castro

[23] See Harry Kantor, *The Ideology and Program of the Peruvian Aprista Movement* (Berkeley: University of California Press, 1953), *passim;* and Robert J. Alexander, "The Latin-American *Aprista* Parties," *Political Quarterly*, Vol. 20 (1949), pp. 236–47.

[24] After the initial letters of *Partido Revolucionario Institucional* (Institutional Revolutionary Party).

[25] See Leo Huberman and Paul Sweezy, *Cuba: Anatomy of a Revolution* (New York: Monthly Review Press, 1960), *passim,* especially p. 80.

regime. Following the promulgation in May 1959 of the agrarian reform law, a government agency, The National Institute of Agrarian Reform (INRA[26]) was established under the leadership of Antonio Núñez Jiménez, to administer Castro's land program. It was estimated that, by mid-1960, INRA, then a gigantic administrative entity, held title to more than one-half the land surface of Cuba.[27] It thus seemed clear that substantial *Aprista*-like rural changes were contemplated by *fidelismo.*

Yet, the relationship of these changes to the economic development of Cuba is at best questionable. This development, properly considered, is not a vague or general umbrella covering all varieties of change. Rather, economic development is the more sharply defined phenomenon of technological innovation, resulting in greater efficiency on the part of the productive arts. A more effective technology draws a higher level of production—that is, a greater gross national product per capita—from a known initial input into an economy.[28]

On the eve of the fall of Batista, Cuba's standard of living, expressed in terms of gross national product per capita, was the third highest in Latin America.[29] To be sure, a degree of perhaps inevitable bias is built into the gross national-product figures. For one thing, international economic comparisons are never easy to make, as a number of significant factors are often difficult to reduce to quantitatively comparable terms. Moreover, translation of gross national-product figures into United States dollars catches aspects of trade relations and foreign exchange rates not entirely relevant to economic development and standards of living. Finally, Cuban national figures are distorted by the problem of *la cabeza de Goliat* —more than half the island's population lives in the metropolitan area of Havana, and other urban centers, where the standard of living is substantially higher than in the rest of the country. For example, 87 per cent of the dwelling units

[26] After the initial letters of *Instituto Nacional de Reforma Agraria.*

[27] Fitzgibbon, *op. cit.,* p. 115.

[28] See Blanksten, "The Aspiration for Economic Development," *Annals of the American Academy of Political and Social Science,* Vol. 334 (March 1961), pp. 10–19.

[29] See Table 1, p. 397, below.

in Havana have electricity, whereas only 9 per cent of the island's rural units are so equipped.[30]

Even after due regard is paid to these statistical pitfalls, pre-Castro Cuba's standard of living remained among the highest in Latin America. It did not seem likely, at the time this paper was written, that national living standards might be expected to rise under *fidelismo*. Indeed, such statistical changes as were in the making in 1961 seemed headed in the other direction. A number of propositions flow from this situation. In the first place, while revolutions and other political phenomena appear to flow from economic growth in the underdeveloped areas,[31] it does not seem possible to make a reasonable case for regarding *fidelismo* as deriving from, or contributing to, Cuba's economic development. The ties, if they exist at all, are not easy to find between Castro's movement and theories of revolutions of rising expectations or of "take-off" in economic growth.[32] The mainsprings of *fidelismo* must be sought elsewhere in the island's national life.

Moreover, economic development must depend heavily upon emerging industrializing and entrepreneurial groups. These groups—the so-called "middle sectors"—have developed in urban centers in Latin America, especially in Havana. Insofar as it has been an agrarian-populistic movement directed against Havana interests, *fidelismo* has warred against the urban "middle sectors," seriously paralyzing their ability to continue functioning. In this view, the Castro regime can be seen as opposing the country's economic development insofar as technological innovation is central to the growth process.[33]

[30] Huberman and Sweezy, *op. cit.*, p. 4.

[31] See Almond and Coleman, *op. cit., passim.*

[32] The reader may wish to consult the following works by W. W. Rostow: *The Process of Economic Growth* (London: Oxford University Press, 1953); "Trends in the Allocation of Resources in Secular Growth," in Leon H. Dupriez (ed.), *Economic Progress* (Louvain: Institut de Recherches Economiques et Sociales, 1955); "The Take-off into Self-Sustained Growth," *The Economic Journal* (March 1956), pp. 25–48; "The Stages of Economic Growth," *The Economic History Review*, second series, Vol. 12, No. 1 (August 1959), pp. 1–16; and *The Stages of Economic Growth* (New York: Cambridge University Press, 1960).

[33] See Johnson, *Political Change in Latin America: The Emergence of the Middle Sectors, passim;* and Johnson, "The Political

Domestic Cuban economic and social conditions, then, provide a third key to the Castro movement. As reflected in *fidelismo,* these have taken the forms of a puritanic crusade for the advancement of public morality and agrarian-populis-

TABLE I. ECONOMIC DEVELOPMENT IN LATIN AMERICA*
(Rank Order of Countries Based on Gross National Product per Capita)

Rank	*Country*	*Gross national product per capita (in U.S. dollars)*
1	Argentina	$ 688
2	Venezuela	457
3	*CUBA*	*454*
4	Uruguay	382
5	Panama	382
6	Chile	335
7	Brazil	278
8	Colombia	231
9	Costa Rica	203
10	Mexico	199
11	Dominican Republic	189
12	Guatemala	182
13	Nicaragua	168
14	El Salvador	167
15	Paraguay	166
16	Honduras	134
17	Peru	118
18	Bolivia	109
19	Ecuador	93
20	Haiti	62
For Comparison United States		2220

* Source: Blanksten, *op. cit.,* pp. 10-19, especially p. 11. See also Davis, *op. cit.,* pp. 50-93, especially pp. 60-71; and Almond and Coleman, *op. cit.,* pp. 455-531.

tic attempts to improve literacy, housing, medical, and land-tenure conditions in the rural areas. In view of the nature of Havana's economy and Cuba's overall level of economic de-

Role of the Latin-American Middle Sectors," pp. 20–29, especially pp. 28–29.

velopment, however, it does not seem likely that this aspect of the movement will make a positive contribution to the island's standard of living.

IV

Finally, Cuba's relations with the United States provide a fourth major key to the nature of *fidelismo*. Again, comparisons with the experience of other Latin-American countries might be useful. It is worth noting that, of the twenty states of the area, some are far removed from the "Colossus of the North." Simply in terms of air miles, no European capital, not even Moscow, is farther from the geographic center of the United States than is Buenos Aires, Argentina; and only one European capital, Athens, Greece, is farther from that center than is Brasilia, the new seat of the Brazilian government. On the other hand, the Middle American countries–Mexico, Central America, and the Caribbean islands–are closer to the "Yanquis" and much more subject to their influence. While there have been unhappy periods in the histories of the relations of the United States with most of the Latin-American countries[34]–it is instructive that Brazil is the only one in which a statue of James Monroe has been erected–the Middle American states have felt the influence of the United States much more than have the countries on the continent of South America. Many years ago, for example, a Mexican newspaper observed editorially that the United States "like everything big frightens us, like everything strong seduces us, like everything rich arouses our envy and makes us forget the clay feet of the Anglo-American colossus to focus our attention upon its head of gold."[35] General Porfirio Díaz is said to have complained thus: "Poor Mexico! So far from God; so close to the United States!"

Compared with the rest of Middle America, Cuba is once

[34] See, for example, Graham H. Stuart, *Latin America and the United States*, 5th ed. (New York: Appleton-Century-Crofts, 1955), *passim*.

[35] Quoted in Donald Marquand Dozer, *Are We Good Neighbors?* (Gainesville: University of Florida Press, 1959), p. 2.

more a caricature rather than a case study. Indeed, if General Díaz had had a second tear, he might well have shed it for Cuba. Lying less than one hundred miles off the Florida coast, the island has been showered with virtually everything "Yanqui" ranging from the fragments of the battleship *Maine* to the debris of a shattered dream launched from Cape Canaveral. The island was first occupied by the armed forces of the United States and then overrun by hordes of vacationing tourists sprawling on Havana's beaches by day and filling its night clubs and gambling casinos by night. "Yanqui" business firms have invested heavily in the Cuban economy and controlled much of it, and the "Colossus of the North" has provided the chief markets for the island's exports.

It was ever thus, throughout Cuba's national history. The United States, of course, played a major military role in the achievement of the island's independence from Spain. Although the first Cuban president Tomás Estrada Palma (1902–09) expressed "the immense gratitude which the people feel towards the American nation,"[36] it is worth remembering that Jose Martí, the major national hero of the island's independence, saw the United States as beginning "to bring into the open its latent spirit of aggression."[37] Martí's view of the "Yanquis'" part in the struggle for insular independence is much more widely held among Cubans than Estrada's attitude.

Indeed, the fateful Platt Amendment was to become the major symbol of their image of the United States. Adopted in 1901 by the Congress of the United States as an amendment to an Army appropriation bill, the Platt instrument was later written into Cuba's first constitution and also into a treaty between the Washington and Havana governments in 1904. The "Amendment" provided, among other things, for limitations on Cuba's authority to conduct its own foreign relations and to contract public debts. At the same time, the United States was guaranteed the right to intervene militarily in the island to maintain order there and to hold naval bases

[36] Stuart, *op. cit.*, p. 212.
[37] Dozer, *op. cit.*, p. 2.

in Cuba.[38] The first "Yanqui" military occupation was terminated in 1902. Under the Platt Amendment, however, "North American" armed forces returned four years later to occupy the country until 1909. During the administration of Presi-

[38] The Platt Amendment has become so controversial in the relations between the United States and Cuba that the relevant clauses of that instrument deserve quotation in full:

(1) That the Government of Cuba shall never enter into any treaty or other compact with any foreign Power or Powers which will impair or tend to impair the independence of Cuba, nor in any manner authorize or permit any foreign Power or Powers to obtain by colonization or for military or naval purposes, or otherwise, lodgment in or control over any portion of said Island.

(2) That said Government shall not assume or contract any public debt to pay the interest upon which, and to make reasonable sinking-fund provision for discharge of which, the ordinary revenues of the Island, after defraying the current expenses of the Government, shall be inadequate.

(3) That the Government of Cuba consents that the United States may exercise the right to intervene for the preservation of Cuban independence, the maintenance of a government adequate for the protection of life, property, and individual liberty, and for discharging the obligations with respect to Cuba imposed by the Treaty of Paris on the United States, now to be assumed and undertaken by the Government of Cuba.

(4) That all acts of the United States in Cuba during its military occupation thereof are ratified and validated, and all lawful right acquired thereunder shall be maintained and protected.

(5) That the Government of Cuba will execute, and as far as necessary extend, the plans already devised or other plans to be mutually agreed upon, for the sanitation of the cities of the Island to the end that a recurrence of epidemic and infectious diseases may be prevented, thereby assuring protection to the people and commerce of Cuba, as well as to the commerce of the Southern ports of the United States and the people residing therein.

(6) That the Isle of Pines shall be omitted from the proposed constitutional boundaries of Cuba, the title thereto left to future adjustments by treaty.

(7) That to enable the United States to maintain the independence of Cuba, and to protect the people thereof, as well as for its own defense, the Government of Cuba will sell or lease to the United States lands necessary for coaling or naval stations at certain specified points, to be agreed upon with the President of the United States.

(8) That by way of further assurance the Government of Cuba will embody the foregoing provisions in a permanent treaty with the United States.

dent Alfredo Zayas (1921–25), the "Amendment" was invoked repeatedly. At length, "North American" President Franklin D. Roosevelt abrogated the Platt Amendment in 1934 as an early step in his administration's Good Neighbor Policy toward Latin America. Provision was made at that time for the retention of the United States naval base at Guantánamo Bay, originally acquired under the "Amendment."

Following the abrogation of the Platt Amendment, United States influence continued in Cuba. As its forms changed, its volume increased. "Yanqui" investments in the island, already valued at $80,000,000 as early as 1901, rose steadily in the following half-century. Most of these investments were connected with the sugar industry, with "North American" firms owning or controlling 54 per cent of the island's sugar mills during the Batista period. United States interests invested heavily in other sectors of Cuba's economy as well, particularly in tobacco, fruit, transportation, docks, electric light and power, telecommunications, banks, luxury hotels, and steamship and air lines. Late in the Batista regime, the island's imports achieved an annual average value of $640,000,000, and exports were valued at $766,000,000. Approximately two-thirds of each of these figures represented trade with the United States.

Under Batista, Cuba—principally Havana—became increasingly attractive as a vacation resort for "Yanqui" tourists. Many, originally oriented toward the pleasures of Miami Beach, seemed suddenly to discover an even more beckoning playground less than an hour away by commercial airline. Crowding into the luxury hotels, night clubs, and gambling casinos of Havana, these fun-seeking vacationers fed a Cuban image of the "Yanqui" as a shallow and insensitive materialist with unlimited amounts of money to devote to amusing himself. This writer once visited a Havana night club whose management had secured the services of Jorge Negrete, then one

---

See *United States Statutes at Large,* Vol. 31, p. 897, or *House Document No. 2,* 57th Congress, 1st Session, p. 47. The reader may also wish to consult Raymond L. Buell, "Cuba and the Platt Amendment," *Foreign Policy Reports,* Vol. 5, No. 3 (April 17, 1929) and Stuart, *op. cit.,* pp. 186–230, especially pp. 213–14.

of Mexico's most well-known popular singers. The Cuban master of ceremonies was obviously moved in announcing his pleasure in being able to introduce the distinguished Mexican artist, about to interpret the music of Mexico he loved most. "No, no!" shouted the "Yanqui"-dominated audience. "No Mexicans! If we wanted Mexican music we would have flown to Mexico! Give us Cubans! *Viva Cuba!*" The celebrated Mexican's chagrin could not have approximated that of his Cuban hosts.

Such continuing "North American" economic, cultural, and social influence in Cuba has given rise on the island to a phenomenon that has been called "Plattism."[39] This might be defined as the circumstance that, despite the abrogation of the Platt Amendment more than a generation before the rise of Fidel Castro, Cuba has "continued to experience a significant degree probably of economic and certainly of psychological subordination to the United States."[40] No doubt, "Plattism" is essentially psychological in nature. It is widely believed in Cuba that the Platt Amendment is still in force. While quantitative data on this are not available, it is probably true that the overwhelming majority of the Cubans who have heard of the document have *not* heard that it was abrogated. The heavy economic and other influences of the "Yanquis," and the retention of the United States naval base at Guantánamo Bay are, for most Cubans, more than ample evidence that the Platt Amendment still lives. Legally and technically, it was put to rest in 1934; psychologically, it continues to dominate Cubans. This discrepancy is the soul of "Plattism."

And "Plattism" is a major element of *fidelismo,* governing many of its attitudes and policies toward the United States. What to many "North Americans" might appear to be quaintly unrealistic windmill-tilting against a long-dead dragon is to the Cuba of Fidel Castro an urgent, necessary, and just war against a living Platt Amendment. In this context it has been necessary to eliminate "Yanqui" economic influ-

[39] This writer is indebted to Dr. Russell H. Fitzgibbon for the term "Plattism," which was apparently first used in his article, "The Revolution Next Door: Cuba," p. 114.

[40] *Ibid.,* p. 114.

ence in the island. "Plattism," no doubt, has motivated much of the nationalization and expropriation of United States business interests in Cuba in 1960. The same psychological phenomenon strains to do battle at Guantánamo Bay. Such *fidelista* policies would certainly have brought renewed United States military intervention in Cuba if the Platt Amendment had still been in force. Such intervention, for the "Plattism" of *fidelismo,* is largely indistinguishable from the anti-Castro Cuban exiles' abortive "Yanqui"-aided invasion of the island in April 1961.

Furthermore, much of the interplay between *fidelismo* and Communism has derived its curious course and character from "Plattism." For one thing, it should be noted that the Cuban Communist Party had long been one of the four or five most important Communist organizations in Latin America, lagging behind only those of Brazil, Chile, and perhaps Argentina and Mexico.[41] It has been estimated that the Cuban Communists have from 20,000 to 30,000 members. If that figure seems small to "North Americans" accustomed to thinking in larger numbers, it would be, on a comparable basis, roughly equivalent to a Communist Party with more than 670,000 members in the United States.

Pre-Castro Cuban Communism, however, despite its influence among some of the rural sugar workers, was essentially an urban movement with its strength concentrated in, and almost restricted to, Havana. In the period before the fall of Batista—that is, when *fidelismo* was essentially a rural movement at war against the urban capital—there was little evidence of Communist association with the 26th of July movement. It is perhaps significant that those of Castro's lieutenants who were then reputed to be Communists, such as Raul Castro, Major Ernesto ("Che") Guevara, and Major Camilo Cienfuegos, acquired this reputation more from their foreign and international associations than from connections with the Havana-based Cuban Communist Party. It was not until *fidelismo* took Havana in 1959 that the island's Communist organization clearly threw its support to the already victorious Castro regime. "The Communists," it has been ob-

[41] See Robert J. Alexander, *Communism in Latin America* (New Brunswick: Rutgers University Press, 1957), *passim.*

served, "mounted the Castro bandwagon so late in its parade to success that their motives should have been suspect for that reason if for no other."[42] Fidel Castro reacted sympathetically to the Communists. Perhaps he would have been something less than human not to have appreciated their vocal, imaginative, and dedicated support and assistance. Furthermore, in the Cuban context, "Plattism" operated to present the *fidelistas* and the Communists with a common enemy, the United States.

The role of "Plattism" has been somewhat less spectacular in Castro's relationships with Cuban Communists than in the case of international Communism. Under *fidelista* leadership, Cuba's relations with the Soviet Union, Communist China, North Korea, and other states with crucial roles in the Soviet bloc have been redefined, sometimes under sensational circumstances. Formal diplomatic relations with these countries have become remarkably cordial. Trade and other economic agreements have been entered into with Soviet-bloc governments in an endeavor to fill the vacuum in the Cuban economy left by the departing "Yanquis." Castro personally attended the session of the United Nations General Assembly at New York in September 1960 as did the Soviets' Nikita Khrushchev, and made a major public spectacle of his endorsement of the Russian leader's opposition to the positions taken by the United States on a number of questions. Planes and tanks manufactured in the Soviet Union, machine guns and other small arms made in Czechoslovakia, and military aid from other Communist countries have flowed to Cuba. The value of these armaments in strengthening Castro's militia was demonstrated with devastating effectiveness by the defeat dealt the anti-*fidelista* invaders in April 1961.

The decisive climax of the Communist question came in December 1961, when Fidel Castro declared in a major address that he was a "Marxist-Leninist." He asserted that he had been so oriented since his student days, but that he had withheld public statements to this effect for fear of alienating anti-Communist Cubans from the *fidelista* revolution. By the end of 1961, Castro asserted, he no longer feared the consequences of such alienation. The complete significance of this

[42] Fitzgibbon, *op. cit.*, p. 117.

declaration remained unclear at the time this chapter was written. Some observers believed that Castro's statement was essentially an attempt to place the Soviet Union under obligation to offer greater aid to the Cuban regime in coping with its mounting domestic problems and the continuing deterioration of its foreign relations, not only with the United States, but also with most of the other American republics. Others saw the move as an attempt to offset the rising strength of "Che" Guevara by creating a "Marxist-Leninist" or Soviet counterweight against Guevara's apparent leaning toward Chinese Communism. In any case, and whatever the explanation, Castro's statement in December 1961 constituted a major step toward the identification of *fidelismo* with Communism.

The place of Communism in *fidelismo* is both crucial and subtle. It seems likely that this role is far more negative than positive, that is, that it is motivated more by rejection of the United States than it is by acceptance of the Soviet system. Insofar as this is true, Castro's posture toward Communism appears to be the consummate expression of "Plattism." It has been noted that the imbalance or discrepancy between the legal extinctness, on the one hand, and, on the other, the psychological persistence of Cuba's subordination to the United States is the essence of "Plattism." There is some possibility that the process of *fidelismo* itself might work out this imbalance. Such a solution cannot be depended on, however, because the road leading in that direction is replete with dangerous pitfalls.

V

In one sense the contribution of *fidelismo* to the revolution of our time is, in the Latin American context, but the donation of one more bottle for the same old wine. Little–indeed, surprisingly little–is new, creative, or original in the Castro movement. At bottom it is essentially the latest synthesis of elements which have been afoot in the Western Hemisphere since the opening years of the twentieth century. Yet this is precisely the appeal of *fidelismo* throughout Latin America. Fidel Castro strikes responsive chords in all countries of the

Americas because his movement is composed of old and familiar elements, most of which have long been at large throughout the American republics. *Fidelismo* is more than exportable from Cuba to other Latin American countries. Most of its components were already abroad in the Americas long before Castro seized upon them in Cuba.

Consider, for example, the various keys to *fidelismo*. The first of them, political instability, characterized by frequent so-called "revolution" and dictatorship, is as generally Latin American as it is Cuban. Political authoritarianism, although more deeply rooted historically in the Caribbean islands than elsewhere in the Americas, is by no means peculiar to Cuba. Neither does the island boast a monopoly on military dictatorship in the Western Hemisphere. A study published in 1960 indicated that no fewer than fourteen of the twenty Latin American countries were living with at least as much political militarism as was Cuba.[43] Indeed, approved textbooks used in the military schools of Ecuador did not hesitate to teach that "the last step in a military career is the presidency of the republic."[44] Difficulty in achieving political institutionalization is likewise as generally Hispanic-American as Cuban. Constitutions come and go in the area, where the basic law that lives for more than a quarter of a century is rare indeed. No fewer than eight of the countries have each had ten or more written constitutions, and two of the states, the Dominican Republic and Venezuela, have each had more than twenty.[45] The chronic instability of civilian political parties likewise belongs not merely to Cuba, but also to the entire Latin American world.

> In these times [a Bolivian has written of his own country's parties] nothing is simpler than to found a political party. To form a political party only three people and one object are necessary: a president, a vice president, a secretary, and a rubber stamp. The party can get along even without the vice president and the secretary. . . . There have been

[43] Lieuwen, *op. cit.,* pp. 154–168.

[44] Quoted in Blanksten, *Ecuador: Constitutions and Caudillos* (Berkeley: University of California Press, 1951), p. 36.

[45] See Davis, *op. cit.,* pp. 225–51.

cases in which the existence of only the rubber stamp has been sufficient.[46]

And Fidel Castro is probably not the last—he is certainly not the first—charismatic spellbinder to thrive on the *personalismo* of a Latin America that has known a Juan Domingo Perón, a Getulio Vargas, a Jorge Eliecer Gaitan, a Rafael Leónidas Trujillo Molina, and a Víctor Raúl Haya de la Torre. "Never before had I heard such a speech," an Ecuadoran legislator once said of one more "man with a mission." "When it was finished, the president and congress were unashamedly in tears, and we stood up and voted unanimously for his bill. . . . I [was] such a fool, such a fool, to vote for his insane measure! . . . I have been mesmerized by experts. . . ."[47] In short, to export the first *fidelista* key to other Latin American countries would be but to dump it on already badly glutted markets.

The second key, *la cabeza de Goliat,* the rural-urban conflict, will spread in Latin America with or without Fidel Castro's assistance. Goliath has already reared his ugly head in Argentina, Paraguay, Uruguay, and Venezuela. Urbanization is apparently the inevitable handmaiden of economic development in the underdeveloped areas. As the growth process proceeds, the ever-widening schism separating the secularized, commercialized, and industrialized urban centers from the traditional and agrarian rural areas will doubtlessly aggravate the conflict, often giving rise to intensely indigenous anti-urban nationalisms. Hear the roar of the rural cannon trained on Goliath in Peru:

> [the rural-urban] division is not merely physical. It pervades our entire social and economic life. . . . If it is true that no capital is really representative of the country that it governs, this is more than ever true in the case of Lima. . . . Lima is the center, but it is not central. It was the seat of Spanish colonial power; now it is the seat of the Government. . . . They founded it next to the sea, that it might look out toward Spain; ever since it has looked toward the

[46] Luis Teran Gomez, *Los Partidos Politicos y su Accion Democratica* (La Paz: Editorial La Paz, 1942), pp. 60–61.
[47] Quoted in Blanksten, *op. cit.,* p. 50.

> outside world, courting foreigners; it is the sweetheart of the sailors of the seven seas; but it is not ours.[48]

Essentially, the expansion of this conflict is a function of the increasing political modernization of Latin America. To lay this, too, at the door of Fidel Castro would be to give him even more credit than he has claimed for himself.

Fidelismo's third key, internal social and economic conditions, tends to straddle the exportability question. On the one hand, this key contains an element–public morality–which is probably more difficult to export to other Latin-American countries than any other aspect of the Castro movement. Expectations of graft, corruption, and other forms of dishonesty in public office are widespread throughout the area. The diminution of this public immorality in Cuba is likely to be one of the long-range consequences of *fidelismo* in that country. But it is extremely difficult to imagine any circumstance under which the Castro regime could export its Spartan-like puritanism to any other American nation. Even assuming the future rise of *fidelista* power and influence to ridiculously unrealistic proportions, the prospects of the indefinite tenure of *la mordida* seem safe, secure, and generally unthreatened in the other American republics.

On the other hand, the agrarian-populistic nature of the 26th of July movement is substantially exportable to many of the Hispanic-American states which have long been sensitized to problems of land tenure, illiteracy, poor housing, problems of health and sanitation, and generally low standards of living. Throughout Latin America, *Aprista* parties—APRA in Peru, *Acción Democrática* in Venezuela, the National Liberation Party in Costa Rica, and the PRI in Mexico—have preached that reforms in these areas are both necessary and long overdue. It has been noted that this aspect of *fidelismo* is not likely to contribute to the economic development of Cuba. But it is ironic that insofar as this element of the Castro movement makes itself felt in other American

[48] José Carlos Mariátegui, *Siete Ensayos de Interpretación de la Realidad Peruana* (Lima: Biblioteca "Amanta," 1943), p. 153; and Moises Sáenz, *The Peruvian Indian* (Washington: Strategic Index of the Americas, 1944), p. 8.

countries, reforms promoting their economic development might well be hastened in the states with more receptive standards of living. Throughout the Western Hemisphere, Fidel Castro has come to symbolize "the aspirations of the Latin American commoner for a better life," it has been pointed out.

> That economic and perhaps even social improvement, though certainly not political democratization, can conceivably be achieved . . . has been brought home to the Latin-American man in the street by the vastly improved communications of mid-twentieth century. He is not as devoted to the traditional democracy of the West as are most people in the United States because he has known less of it.[49]

There is, therefore, some likelihood that *fidelismo* might intensify demands, in many of the countries with lower standards of living, for greater speed in social and economic changes expected to promote the growth of the economies involved.

The final key to *fidelismo,* anti-United States sentiment, has, of course, long existed throughout Latin America. Indeed, a close student of such attitudes has reported in a recent study that "the normal state of Latin America is to be hostile to the United States."[50] Historically, this Yankeephobia has had its ups and downs. At the time of the First World War, a Latin American intellectual told the "North Americans" that

> What you people must get out of your minds . . . is the idea that we . . . want to be like you. We do not—in any respect. . . . We don't want your type of education, your kind of religion, your commercialized ideas of living. . . . Our civilization is older than yours by centuries. It suits us. Your paternalism, your continual oversight of Latin-American affairs is irritating to us. You assume too much, and the benevolent role fools none of us. . . . Why talk about a unity that does not live? Why keep up all this

[49] Fitzgibbon, *op. cit.,* p. 121.
[50] Dozer, *op. cit.,* p. 403.

> Pan-American propaganda unless—what we all believe—for your own purposes of exploitation and political dominance?[51]

During the "Good Neighbor Policy" of the administration of the "North American" President Franklin D. Roosevelt, particularly during the years of the Second World War, Latin American attitudes toward the United States were probably abnormally friendly. In the era of the Cold War, however, suspicion and distrust of the "Colossus of the North" have regained much lost ground in the Western Hemisphere.[52]

As a manifestation of renascent Yankeephobia, the "Plattism" of *fidelismo* has had a profound effect in a generally receptive Hispanic America. Although the formal declarations of some governments occasionally express a contrary view, it has been pointed out with considerable insight that "Castro is, to an uncomfortable degree, correct when he implies or states forthrightly that the governments in more than one Latin American state do not really speak for large numbers of those they govern."[53] Throughout the Western Hemisphere, admiration is quick and widespread for regimes that dare to express defiance of the "Yanquis." *Fidelismo* "is definitely a danger to our continued peaceful relations with Latin America," Robert C. Hill, a United States Ambassador to Mexico during the administrations of President Dwight D. Eisenhower, declared in a recent press interview. "They have traditional reasons for hating and fearing us and when one of their own can thumb his nose at us and get away with it, he has their sympathy."[54] This observation has been substantiated by demonstrations throughout the Americas in support of *fidelismo* against the "Yanquis."

The Castro movement thus looms as a formidable component of the revolution of our time. Most, although not all, of its major elements are readily exportable to other Latin

[51] Mexican diplomat Luis Cabrera, quoted in Frederick L. Schuman, *International Politics,* 2nd ed. (New York: McGraw-Hill Book Co., 1937), p. 347.

[52] This cooling of Latin-American attitudes is painstakingly documented in Dozer, *op. cit., passim,* especially pp. 188–354.

[53] Fitzgibbon, *op. cit.,* p. 121.

[54] Quoted in Chicago *Sun-Times,* April 30, 1961, Section 2, p. 2.

American countries, where *fidelismo* has acquired increasing numbers of sympathizers in the Americas. Yet, Cuba's involvement in the Cold War should not feed distorted views of the situation. Support for *fidelismo* should not be equated with Communism. Yankeephobia has achieved dizzying heights in the past in Latin America and, conceivably, might regain them in the future. But the gross error involved in the oversimplification that interprets anti-United States sentiment as Communism should be avoided. It is unlikely that the influence of *fidelismo,* however great, in Latin America could operate to win substantial support there for the Soviet cause should the chips of the Cold War be down.

CHILE

Christian Democracy in Chile and elsewhere has created a great deal of interest both among Latin Americans and specialists of the area. Many have looked upon it as a constructive alternative to Castroism, as a type of movement that adapts well with Latin American culture along with invigorating it, and as a force that can solve the area's deep seated economic and social problems in a peaceful democratic way. Much of the great enthusiasm that surrounded the party's election victory in Chile in 1964, however, has since dissipated. Some specialists are now wondering whether the enthusiasm was deserved in the first place, while others are reminding themselves that most reform movements in Latin America tend to bog down no matter what their coloration. Those who defend the regime, however, do so equally vigorously and tend to blame any shortcomings on an intransigent opposition.

What is needed is a balanced assessment of the administration, and this is provided in the following selection by Thomas G. Sanders, Professor of Religious Studies at Brown University and associate of the American Universities Field Staff. He begins by describing Christian Democratic ideology and explains how the party leaders have been able to add to it the technology of economic development and programs of social change without distorting the ideological premises. Next follows an analysis of how the party's policies of Latin American integration, Chileanization of copper, agrarian reform, Popular Promotion, housing, education, and birth control fit in consistently with the overall objectives of what it is trying to attain. Then Professor Sanders explains why the party has lost a certain amount of its popularity, mentioning higher taxes, the failure to solve inflation, little ideological enthusiasm, an overambitious program that was oversold, factionalization within the party, and the vigor of the other parties as reasons. The author is fair in apportioning blame on the party itself, the impatient Chilean public, and the opposition parties. Economic scarcity and drought could be added as another reason. At the end of the selection Professor Sanders touches on the question of whether the Christian Democrats have permanently altered Chilean politics and society, and reflectively takes a middle position.

THE CHRISTIAN DEMOCRATIC EXPERIMENT

*The Christian Democratic Regime in Chile**

THOMAS G. SANDERS

Christian Democracy surged into prominence in Latin America after 1960, at a time when many observers had lost faith in the older political movements and Cuban Marxism was frightening Washington and the Latin American Establishments. The rhetoric of the Christian Democrats, with their slogan of a "Revolution in Liberty" and vision of a new order in Latin America, nurtured extraordinary expectations, some of which now seem unrealistic. Thus when Eduardo Frei became the first Christian Democratic chief executive, all eyes turned to Chile. His regime became the object of an international scrutiny which placed an excessive burden on an inexperienced team wrestling with Chile's stubborn economic and social problems and with its exasperating political context.

Four years of Christian Democracy have achieved no miracles in Chile. The charisma of the movement has declined and talk of "Revolution in Liberty" now seems something of an embarrassment, as Mr. Frei has lost support among Chile's fickle electorate and even within his own Party. These years have underscored once again the internal and external limitations of Latin American reformist move-

* This is an original article, written especially for this volume.

ments. The problems and obstacles shatter enthusiastic aspirations.

Nevertheless, if we divest ourselves of utopianism, the contributions of the Frei administration stand out, even though its shortcomings are equally clear. The only other significant Chilean regimes of this century exhibit a similar ambivalence. President Arturo Alessandri, in his first administration from 1920 to 1925, brought the middle class into the power structure and instituted laws for labor security. The Popular Front governments from 1938 to 1952 stimulated the country's industrial infrastructure and development through state intervention. But neither transformed Chile into a modern, developed nation. The Frei administration, however cloudy its Party future in 1970, becomes the third of these innovating regimes because it has unquestionably initiated important new stages in Chile's economy, social structure, and political participation.

The Chilean Party is one of Latin America's oldest Christian Democratic movements. It traces its origins to the nineteen thirties, when a socially placid traditional Catholicism found itself challenged by new options such as Fascism and Maritainism which emphasized and claimed to interpret authentically the social teachings of the papacy. In Chile the key elite for the future, an exceptional younger generation of pious Catholics, embraced fervently Maritain's neo-Thomism with its emphasis on natural rights, religious pluralism, democratic participation, and limited government. At the same time their distaste for the capitalism and social irresponsibility of the traditional Catholics provoked a break with the Conservative Party and the formation in 1938 of the Falange Nacional, which was to become the Christian Democratic Party in 1957.

In its self-image Christian Democracy always begins with "ideology." Based on natural law principles mediated by the social teaching of the Church, the ideology has in practice served more effectively as a barrier against repression than as a guide for public policy. It places central emphasis on "Christian humanism," based on the concept of the *person*, who has intrinsic rights and responsibilities and is truly free when fulfilling certain divinely sanctioned natural functions:

self-development, participation in family and society, worship of his Creator. While this neo-Thomism stresses individual rights, it distinguishes itself from individualism by its focus on the social nature of human existence. Men function in *solidarity:* in friendship and love, reason and cooperation, they meet their mutual needs through formal and informal group activity. The intermediate groups created by men have priority in the functions for which they exist. The state (or government), which should be subordinate to society and seek the common good, protects the intermediate groups while undertaking for itself responsibilities consistent with its more global composition and power.

Throughout the forties and fifties Chile's Christian Democrats gradually refined these essentially restrictive norms into more dynamic policy principles. They retained an emphasis on the family, labor organization, and community initiative, but affirmed that government had to become the dominant agent of planning and justice. As economic developmental theory came to influence Chilean intellectuals after World War II, the Party absorbed without tension the central role of the government in the economy, even justifying the nationalization, if necessary, of basic resources, utilities, and industries. Likewise, when social obstacles to development and effective redistribution of resources led many critical Latin Americans to advocate a radical change of social structures, the Christian Democrats concluded that a "revolution" was necessary, though one in "liberty," respecting the rights of the individual and intermediate institutions.

The most difficult problem lay in defining a new economic and social structure that would sidestep the "individualism" and "materialism" of capitalism, while avoiding the pitfall of restrictions on personal and group rights ascribed to Marxian socialism. In the late thirties the founders of the Party flirted with corporativism, but by the fifties they espoused a "communitarian" society as their objective. The exact lines of "communitarianism" remain to be etched, though the numerous writings on the subject by Christian Democratic "ideologists" suggest a revision of present economic structures to allow for participation of all segments of the enterprise in ownership, management, and profit. The key disputes at present concern the relationship between existent capitalist and governmental structures, on the one hand, and communitarian enterprises, on the other—more specifically, the manner and pace at which communitarianism can become a reality.

Christian Democratic ideology, finally, is universalistic rather than nationalistic. Throughout their history the Chilean and other Latin American Parties have unashamedly drawn from European inspiration. Acknowledging that the nation constitutes an essential center of decision, they affirm that men have more universal links. Thus the Christian Democrats have supported with ideological fervor as well as on practical grounds the economic and political unity of Latin America and international organizations like the United Nations.

The facility with which Chile's Christian Democrats absorbed the technical suggestions on economic development and social change associated with the Economic Commission for Latin America and the Alliance for Progress has led some observers to emphasize the pragmatic or technocratic nature of its program and to wonder whether the ideology plays any role at all. The relationship is very simple. Because the ideology is not based on revelation but on natural human inclinations and rationality, it stands open to common wisdom on effective government. Technical policies are extensions of reasonable moral norms. For example, the Chilean Christian Democratic economic program drew much of its inspiration from *En Vez de la Miseria* (*Instead of Misery*), a book by the ECLA economist, Jorge Ahumada. The Party leaders easily discerned that the moral problem—the misery of much of the Chilean population—could not be resolved by platitudes and charity, but by programs like those proposed by Ahumada: industrialization, export diversification, economic stabilization, and agrarian reform, all leading to increased production and national income.

Even though many of the Christian Democratic policies seem well justified on sheer economic grounds, the ideology gives them a special "style." The leadership, for example, consistently seeks to avoid extremes and to work out a consensual, harmonious solution. Promotion of the family and other intermediate groups enters as a major objective in many programs. In areas like housing and agriculture, the government gives priority to group self-help, popular initiative, and cooperatives. "Social development" has a theoretical emphasis on a par with economic development.

The Frei government has centered its policies on releasing the economic—especially industrial—potential of the country. Like thoughtful Chileans since the forties, Christian Democratic planners believe that higher living standards and national significance can only be achieved through a relatively autonomous economic system that will free Chile from dependence on imports. This means that the country must gradually replace its traditional reliance on export of mineral and agricultural products by a more comprehensive industry. Even though two of the Christian Democratic policies, Chileanization of copper and agrarian reform, have received principal publicity abroad, they represent only aspects of an attempt to enter a new stage of productivity whose primary focus is industrial.

Chile suffers, however, from structural obstacles to economic autonomy. It has limited physical resources and, more significantly, its population of nine million does not provide a large enough market to attract and stimulate efficient and profitable large-scale industries. By 1964 Chileans had reached virtual self-sufficiency in internal production of light consumer goods and had established industries providing such intermediate commodities as cement, steel, chemicals, petroleum, and paper. The culminating stage, production of durable consumer goods like automobiles, complex industries like petrochemicals, and capital goods like machinery, seemed unattainable. Chile was doomed to remain a producer of frequently high-cost basic products for its own population, while it would have to import other items from the sale chiefly of copper. Alarmingly, planners noted that export earnings would not cover the demands of the country's consumer-oriented population and the requirements for maintaining the existent industrial plants.

The Frei administration has tackled this problem with great imagination by encouraging economic integration with other countries and by stimulating the manufacture of products in which Chile can specialize for sale largely to the Latin American market.

President Frei early recognized the structural deficiencies of the Latin American Free Trade Association and became a leading promoter of a common market composed of Venezuela, Colombia, Ecuador, Peru, Bolivia, and Chile. The "Andean Group" aims principally at industrial growth through common planning coordinated with an automatic reduction of tariff barriers. The first joint industrial step, which hopefully will eventually come to include automobiles, machinery, and electronics, was taken in petrochemicals, by distributing segments of this complicated industry among the member nations. In Chile, the government entered as a shareholder in its part of the petrochemical system. The Andean region in the early nineteen seventies will thus develop all the essential elements of a petrochemical complex by allowing free flow of products within the zone and erecting a common external tariff against outside competition. In this way the countries together will establish a major modern industry and achieve a freedom from outside sources that no single one of them could acquire by itself.

The full implications of petrochemicals and other integration industries will only materialize after 1970. The planning, energy, and investment dedicated by the Frei administration in this area may turn out in the long run to be its most important accomplishment; but the Chilean voters do not generally recognize its significance, nor has it been reflected in the figures on industrial growth, which sagged sharply in 1967 and 1968 after increases in 1965 and 1966.

The Christian Democrats have also encouraged specialized industries aimed at utilizing Chile's extensive copper and wood resources. The government has extended credit and other forms of assistance to private Chilean corporations producing wires, cables, automobile radiators, and other copper items. With similar encouragement paper and cellulose for the export market have been among the country's most vigorously expanding industries.

We must place the Chileanization of copper within this context of industrial aspirations. Chileanization involves a program of investment designed to increase production and sales so that the earnings can pay for an industrial structure that will replace copper as the mainstay of the economy. Chileanization represents an alternative response to strong pressure for nationalization, and even Christian Democrats seem to consider it a transitional stage. It opts for increased production as the primary need of the country and rejects nationalization because of risks like possible decline of production and loss of markets.

Even though the government's purchase of shares in the large mining companies has received the most publicity, other aspects of Chileanization—which in its full sense means control by representative institutions of the Chilean people over the nation's copper resources—have equal importance. These include the revitalization and expansion of small and medium mining enterprises, total smelting and refining of ore within the country, intensification of purchases by the companies within Chile, control of commercialization, and coordination of policies with other copper-exporting countries. Like the industrial program the Chileanization of copper will mature only in the seventies. In 1967 and 1968 copper production actually declined because of strikes and electricity shortages, but the investments carried out by the government and the giant foreign corporations, Kennecott and Anaconda, are on schedule and will in time transform Chile from third to first place among copper-producing countries. The movement toward public power of decision in this industry illustrates the willingness of Christian Democracy to respond to pressure for vigorous state action in a key sector of the economy, while bringing its own concern for a reasonable evaluation of priorities into play.

The Agrarian Reform, though always justified by the Frei government primarily on social grounds, intends likewise to increase production. In the mid-forties Chile changed from a net exporter to a net importer of food, and as productivity consistently lagged behind increases in population and demand, Mr. Frei inherited a situation in which the nation did not feed itself and food imports were consuming a fourth of the nation's foreign exchange.

The Chilean Agrarian Reform has three features that deserve emphasis: (1) Although operating under democratic

procedures the government has extremely rigorous policies of expropriation and compensation. The Corporation of Agrarian Reform can expropriate on grounds of abandonment, under-utilization, and size. The latter criterion indicates the intention of ultimately eliminating giant landholdings in Chile. Owners receive one to ten percent of the value of their land, which is determined by previous tax declarations, and the balance in bonds maturing in twenty-five or thirty years, with the bonds adjusted to only 70 percent of the increase in cost of living.
(2) The most distinctive characteristic of the Reform is the *asentamiento,* a transitional phase normally lasting three years during which participating peasants learn to function cooperatively under government supervision. True to the Christian Democratic ideology, the community of families, organized in a general assembly, makes the decisions in the *asentamiento* and chooses its officers and committees. At the conclusion of the *asentamiento* phase the peasants choose the future structure of the landholding, either dividing it into individual plots or continuing a communal scheme.
(3) The Reform emphasizes organization of the rural population not incorporated into *asentamientos,* such as peasants on unexpropriated estates, salaried workers, renters, and small landholders. The Frei administration has achieved impressive gains in unionizing the previously unorganized rural workers and in forming cooperatives among renters and smallholders.

The Agrarian Reform has fallen far short of the goal of placing 100,000 families on *asentamientos* within six years. At the end of 1968, in fact, there were only 15,000 *asentados,* and the Reform itself was buffeted by the criticism of conservative interests and the impatience of those who wanted it to move more rapidly. Delay in passing the law and the extreme costliness of this kind of Reform, involving as it does infrastructural investment, credit, and close supervision, have hobbled it. Unquestionably the Reform initiated an alteration of Chile's landholding system, raised the living standard of the rural population, and began the slow process of their organization and integration, but its long term fulfillment and directions remain uncertain. They depend on the continuity of the program, availability of financing, and the unpredictability of national politics. Nevertheless, if we remember that the agricultural sector in developing countries is especially intractable, the Frei government has constructed a sophisticated model combining economic, social, and political objectives and has attempted to avoid such pitfalls of other agrarian reforms as a drop in production and the indifference of the peasants.

The clearest economic failure of the Frei administration has been in its stabilization program. Mr. Frei inherited an inflation that reached 45.4 percent in 1963 and 38.4 percent in 1964, which he reduced in the first two years to 25.9 percent and 17.0 percent; but in 1967 it ascended again to 21.9 percent and in 1968 to 27.9 percent. Rejecting an all out austerity program, Frei's planners hoped that economic growth and social investment would unlock forces that would gradually reduce the inflationary rate. Even though the government curbed demand through a stricter system of tax collection and the stimulation of deposits in Savings and Loan Associations, its stabilization program foundered through failure to hold expenditures at anticipated levels, the refusal of many organized workers to adhere to guidelines for wage adjustments, and the unwillingness of Congress and even many Christian Democrats to support a proposed forced savings plan.

Unlike the mere structural aspects of the Frei economic program, inflation and its concomitant in capital accumulation, increased tax collections (up 90 percent between 1964 and 1968), shocked the consciousness of the electorate. The voters do not understand the significance of long range planning directed toward increase of national product, so they tend to judge the government on pocketbook issues like inflation and taxes. Nothing has contributed more to the decline of Christian Democratic popularity. Unfortunately the government has not succeeded in interpreting to the public the linkage between these phenomena and development. We thus encounter the first political dilemma of the Frei regime: certain concomitants of planned development clash with the immediate interests of the electorate and can undermine popular consensus.

Consistent with its ideology of social justice, but also with the suggestions of ECLA and the Alliance for Progress, the

Frei administration has undertaken a diversified program of social development in such areas as housing, education, and health. The government does not view these policies in isolation but as expressions of a "humanist philosophy"; that is, "man, as individual is the object of all the policies which are proposed and at the same time the subject of all the policies which are executed." The social programs anticipate that "the extensive sectors of the country's population which are submitted to diverse levels of *marginality* will attain a full *integration* in the national life, that is, an adequate access to enjoyment of goods and services and an authentic participation in decisions."

At the theoretical apex of social development, the Council of Popular Promotion tries to awaken and organize the lower classes. In practice the Council has focused on urban groups, giving them vocational and civic training, promoting organizations, and encouraging them to take responsibility for community betterment. In the summer of 1968 Congress passed a law of prime importance giving legal standing to neighborhood clubs and other popular organizations on a local, community, provincial, and national level, thus providing the foundation for a lower class interest and pressure mechanism.

Popular Promotion represents the Christian Democratic counterstrategy to the Marxist exploitation of class tension as the basis of social change. It assumes that the poor, once conscious of their rights and responsibilities, will peacefully assume their legitimate role in society. The government through its social programs provides access to adequate housing, health, and education, but the people should participate and contribute. By their own activity the people will cease to look to government, as they often have in Latin America, as an impersonal *patron*.

This ostensibly innocuous theory has evoked sharp controversy in Chile. Marxists object because they believe that it assuages the class conflict stemming from the genuine exploitation of the poor. Anti-clericals dislike its origin in Catholic social theory and more specifically its literal adaptation from the views of the controversial Jesuit, Father Roger Vekemans. Political parties claim that the civic training inculcated by Popular Promotion is constructing organizations for the

Christian Democratic intention of enlarging its base in the lower class. Some Catholic critics accuse the approach of being basically paternalistic, a middle class *noblesse oblige* which preconditions the manner and structures of popular participation in social change.

Popular Promotion, though it has fomented hundreds of new institutions and given instruction to thousands of Chileans, is difficult as yet to evaluate. It deals with a complex phenomenon: the psychological change experienced by a traditionally passive and exploited class. The congressional elections of 1969, which might have reflected some shift of the lower class electorate to Christian Democracy as a consequence of the program, did not do so. Within the government itself, Popular Promotion suffers from a lack of understanding on the part of those who consider it in political terms, from a budget whose size belies its theoretical significance, and from undistinguished personnel. Nevertheless, the Christian Democrats deserve credit for giving serious attention for the first time in Chilean history to the social and political participation of the unorganized lower classes. The program could have profound implications for the future by changing the balance of political power and by intensifying social mobility, or it could turn out to be a fantasy.

The Frei administration has chalked up impressive social accomplishments in other areas. Its housing program is perhaps the best in Latin America, its most distinctive feature being *Operación sitio* (site operation), which provides those who cannot afford the regular housing programs a plot of land on which they can place an inexpensive prefabricated house or build their own. In education, it has constructed unprecedented numbers of rural schools, trained teachers for them, and reformed the curricula on the primary and secondary levels nationally. Its adult literacy training received an award from UNESCO as one of the five leading programs of this type in the world.

Chile's hidden policy is family planning. Without fanfare a government whose principal leaders are practicing Catholics is carrying out what is probably the most effective public birth control project in Latin America. Set up originally as an alternative to alarming abortion rates, it has steadily grown and gained general public acceptance. Chileans are now training personnel for similar programs in other Latin American countries.

Family planning symbolizes the intertwining of economics and ideology in Christian Democracy. Obviously it regulates the population growth which undermines economic gains, but the Chilean policy tries at the same time through strict objectivity in presentation of methods to foster in the participants a consciousness of responsible parenthood and free choice consistent with human dignity.

This cursory survey of major programs underscores the scope and ambition of the Frei administration. For the first time in Chilean history a government has embarked on a program of economic development and social change reaching into every part of national life. Ironically, however, this did not produce mass support at the polls, but rather a significant drop in popularity. President Frei was elected into office in 1964 with an impressive 55.5 percent of the ballots, and in the 1965 congressional elections the Christian Democrats received an unprecedented 42.3 percent; but in municipal elections of 1967, the Party dropped to 35.6 percent and in the congressional elections of 1969, to 29.7 percent.

There are several reasons why the electorate did not respond to a government of clearly superior accomplishments. Some are intrinsic to its programs; others can be attributed to confusion within the Christian Democratic Party and still others to the nature of Chilean politics.

It was suggested that the Christian Democrats confront a dilemma involving the politics of development. Economic and social growth demands sacrifice—the postponement of immediate consumption to channel resources through policies like taxes and inflated government expenditures into productive investment. The dilemma arises—for democratic regimes in general—because a government may have to choose between intensifying developmental programs and currying political support. In theory the government could persuade the public and opposition politicians to accept these sacrifices through an appealing ideology, but the Christian Democratic experience in Chile thus far indicates that its ideology generates little enthusiasm. The intellectual framework drains it of the mythological charisma that successful ideologies like nationalism, Marxism, and personalistic populism often exhibit. To many of the Chilean public the Christian Democratic ideology does not seem rooted in human nature or even national reality, but represents the special position of one particular political group among others. In practice President Frei has often gained popular support most successfully when he appealed to the latent desire for national significance among Chileans.

The ambitiousness of the administration's policies has also added to its difficulties. Many of them, especially in the social field, are lagging behind announced goals or suffer from administrative defects and lack of financing. Perhaps the Christian Democrats tried to do too much. In failing to follow through in areas of interest to voters they created frustration and opened themselves to criticism and cynicism. Other countries also share this dilemma. The problems of an underdeveloped nation are so numerous and deep rooted that they demand greater skills and resources than are available. Should a government try to achieve a thorough transformation in a few areas or work toward small gains in many? The Frei administration contributed to its own difficulties by its messianism. It stimulated Chileans to hope for a new social order, but its unfulfilled promises and limitations have reduced it to the level of more conventional political parties.

Conflicts within the Christian Democratic Party have also wracked the Frei administration. Analysts tended to overlook the profundity of these divisions, even though some can be traced back to the nineteen forties. Like Christian Democratic parties in other countries, the Chileans shelter under the umbrella of their vague ideology sharply differing interpretations of policy. Some of the principal ones are the following: (1) The ideology of the Party is based on an interpretation of Catholic thought that was abandoned by many thinkers after the Vatican Council and evidently has little attraction to the younger generation. Neo-Thomism, the "progressive" Catholicism of the thirties and forties now seems antiquated alongside the more dynamic perspectives drawing from biblical, existentialist, and even Marxist themes. Although the Party in Chile is not "Catholic," its major leaders come from backgrounds in Church organizations like Catholic Action. The youth of the Party, as well as some older sympathizers, question such axioms of Christian Democracy as the concept of parties of Christian inspiration, the relevance of the Church's social teaching to Latin American problems, and the genuineness of a pluralism based on natural law principles interpreted by the Church. Rather than an ethic based on principles, they advocate participation in existent historical movements. They do not believe in "Christian" parties. They feel that the social outlook of Christian Democracy, with its emphasis on harmony and rationality, overlooks the significance of tension and conflict in social change. Many contend that the opinions of the lower class have not contributed to the formulation of theory and policy, that the presumed universal truths disguise the interests of the privileged groups.

(2) Since 1938 the Christian Democrats have differed on policy toward other parties. From 1938 to 1952 this referred to the question of cooperating with the Popular Front governments, led by the anti-clerical Radicals; but since 1957, with a new political alignment, many have urged a front with the Chilean Marxist parties. Against this the majority, as interpreted by President Frei and the leading Party ideologist, Jaime Castillo Velasco, has promoted a purist approach which defines Christian Democracy as a third way having little in common with either the Right or the Left. They claim that the Chilean electorate revealed its moderate reformism by choosing their Party in 1964 as an alternative to Marxism. After 1964, dispute over an opening to the Left intensified, culminating in May, 1969, with the withdrawal of many leading Party members, including two senators, to form the Movimiento de Acción Popular (MAPU). These in MAPU, as well as the many remaining in the Party who advocate collaboration with the Marxists, believe that only the united popular forces can stymie the resurgence of the Right and bring to fruition a genuine economic and social revolution in Chile.

(3) The Party was compelled to face more concretely its attitude toward capitalism, once it came to power. In 1966 a commission of the Party produced a controversial *Informe Político-Técnico,* which urged a "non-capitalist way" in future development and brought into center stage the simmering

problem of "communitarianism." In effect, the *Informe* advocated governmental initiative, including extensive nationalization. Leftist Christian Democrats want to eliminate capitalism in Chile, whereas President Frei and his wing insist that the private sector has an indispensable role in future development. The issue of capitalism had decisive importance in the MAPU schism and the misgivings of Radomiro Tomic, long the number two man of the Party, about running for the presidency in 1970.

(4) The Left wing of the Party, reflecting the critical nationalism common to Latin America, accuses the Frei administration of "dependence" on the United States and a generally accommodating attitude toward the developed world. They argue instead for a community of interests between Chile and the rest of the underdeveloped countries against those that are developed and in a position to exploit. Their criticisms center especially on two concrete issues: the refusal of the administration to restore relations with Cuba, and its unwillingness to nationalize the large North American copper companies.

The formation of MAPU chiefly by the group of Christian Democrats usually called "Rebels," has rendered outmoded the commonly accepted description of the Party wings as Oficialistas (exemplified by President Frei), Rebels, and Terceristas (a middle position concerned with maintaining Party unity). Many Terceristas frankly agree with the Rebels, but chose to remain in the Party as Leftists, alongside the more moderate group (Oficialistas). It is now clear, and the Christian Democratic Party reflects this, that progressive Latin American elites of Catholic inspiration are basically divided into two groups over the issues sketched out in the previous paragraphs. We may assume that Christian Democratic parties in other Latin American countries will also experience the consequences of this divergence of opinion.

The significance of the internal troubles of the Christian Democratic Party lies in the growing uncertainty about what it represents. The Chilean voters had a reasonably clear idea in 1964, as a result of the debate between Mr. Frei and the candidate of the Marxist Popular Front, but since then they have witnessed the deterioration of the Party's unity. Conservative citizens, shocked by the positions of the Left wing, claim to discern no significant difference between the Christian Democrats and the Marxists, while those who anticipated a new social order object to the moderation of the Frei administration. The certitude of offering an exciting new option, which provided the Christian Democrats much of their drive after 1957, has now deteriorated in Chile, and the Party image is significantly altered for the future.

The Christian Democratic hope of maintaining and extending its electoral base has also foundered on the continued vigor of the other Chilean political parties. The high degree of freedom which provides a forum for constant criticism of the government, the continued loyalty of many voters to the older parties, and the failure of the Frei administration in its public relations to explain away its mistakes and the Christian Democratic divisions, combine to handicap the development of a national consensus.

Chile has a long tradition of coalition government, but following on their impressive vote in 1964 and 1965 the Christian Democrats concluded that they had a mandate to govern alone and they spoke optimistically of "thirty years of Christian Democracy." This self-righteousness aroused resentment and reluctance to cooperate among the other parties. Nevertheless, without the aid of the opposition the Christian Democrats could not have succeeded as well as they have; for example, Chileanization of copper relied on the support of the Right, while the votes of the Left guaranteed the passage of the Agrarian Reform.

When the Christian Democrats were elected in 1964, many observers concluded that the Right was dying and that the Left was thrown on the defensive. It was generally believed that the reformist Christian Democrats and the Marxist Left would contest for power and that the Christian Democrats in a two-way competition could easily gain a working majority in Congress. Future alignments now seem much more fluid.

The dominant political fact in Chile since 1966 is the resurrection of the Right. Reduced to a mere 13.1 percent in 1965, the Liberals and Conservatives joined into the National Party in 1966 and augmented their share of the vote to 20 percent in 1969. The Right exploited public dissatisfaction with the programs and internal problems of the Christian Democrats and benefited from the impressive campaign to return Jorge Alessandri, president from 1958 to 1964, to national leadership. Many who voted for Frei and the Christian Democrats in 1964 and 1965 to avoid Marxism returned to their more natural home, the National Party.

The National Party is not reactionary. Although it includes the fearful opponents of change, its leadership comes chiefly from relatively progressive businessmen. The government of Alessandri was in fact, the first to undertake a large-scale public housing program. The National Party platform emphasizes reduction of inflation and the primacy of private enterprise in development. The Right, then, not only has the strength to influence policies, but may even elect a president, especially given the personalistic tradition in Chilean presidential elections.

On the Left, the longtime collaboration of the Communist and Socialist Parties in the Popular Action Front (FRAP) underwent severe strains after the defeat of the FRAP candidate in 1964. The Communists, conforming to the position enunciated in Moscow, abjured violence and advocated a gradual, reformist road to socialism through a united front, including some segments of the Radical and Christian Democratic Parties. The Socialists, on the other hand, under the inspiration of the Cuban Revolution, adopted an official line casting doubt on the possibility of victory through electoral processes and urging popular organization in anticipation of a violent introduction of socialism.

The proposals of the Left, which include nationalization of additional sectors of the economy, centralization of development in the government, destruction of the power of the traditional ruling classes, and an anti-imperialist foreign policy, have sympathizers among the Christian Democrats and the Radical Party. The Communists and Socialists continue to be the dominant components in Chile's highly politicized labor movement, and both have great strength among intellectuals and students. Thus, despite their conflicts, the organizations of the Left more than held their own in the congressional elections of 1969, and the Communist Party in particular continued its steady growth, receiving 15.9 percent of the vote.

The Radicals, Chile's fifth major political party, may hold the balance of power in the nation's struggle for the consensus necessary for effective government. A swing group that claims to be Left-of-Center, the Radicals at various times in recent history have participated in governments of both the Left and Right. Although they have declined in strength since 1960, they maintain an influential base centered in white-collar workers, government employees, and professionals. The diversity of opinion among its members could push it into joining a front with the Marxists, cooperating with the Christian Democrats, or supporting a personalistic president of the Right.

The ongoing vitality of these political groups suggests that, barring a genuine revolution or military intervention, the Chilean scene will be shaped by agreements, especially in Congress, between two or more parties and the interest groups they represent. On the surface, three options–the Right, Center-Left, and Left–seem to be struggling for supremacy, but none has a majority support in Congress or in the electorate. The fact that all the parties (except the Communists) manage to preserve a semblance of unity despite internal divisions provides experiences in the compromises necessary to agree on and implement policies. Chile has such a remarkable tradition of adaptability among its parties that surprising combinations may emerge, especially on specific legislation and presidential administrations.

The entrance of Christian Democracy into the political arena reflected popular pressure for experiments with new economic and social policies. The Frei administration has not revolutionized Chilean society or altered radically the interplay of competing forces, though it has probably reduced the power of large landholders and increased that of peasants. Christian Democracy will undoubtedly continue to be one of Chile's major parties, but the context in which it operates will be determined by characteristics that have marked the nation's political life for decades: coalition and compromise; personalism especially on the presidential level; arbitration by such pressure groups as industry, commerce, and the middle class; inconsistent and immature voting patterns by an electorate that seeks progress without restriction of its own immediate interests; flexibility, opportunism, and division within the parties. Yet this system does not stand still, and the Frei administration has given it a significant propulsion forward.

ARGENTINA

Primitiveness and turbulence have been long observed traits of the Argentine political system. In the three selections that follow, the first describes its actual working, the second evaluates the military power group that has greatly affected it, and the third analyzes the Onganía experiment to resolve the basic problems.

In the first selection, K. H. Silvert, Professor of Political Science at New York University and long associate of the American Universities Field Staff, does an extremely perceptive job in conceptualizing the system. The system is simplistic, consisting of an inordinate number of narrow orientated power groups pressing their demands directly on a president who usually fails in office due to a misuse of charisma, sheer incompetence, and/or an impossible task of trying to balance off and satisfy the conflicting power group demands. A sense of public welfare seems to be completely lacking, with power groups even going so far to approve or abet coups against presidents in order to further their own immediate goals. Professor Silvert in dissecting the Peronista regime convincingly argues that it was not totalitarian but rather much like other Argentine governments in its juggling of power groups, opportunism, and lack of accomplishing any major societal shifts with the exception of furthering labor.

In the second selection, James W. Rowe, an associate of the Brookings Institution and former member of the American Universities Field Staff, evaluates the military, the most important of the power groups in Argentina. He describes its size, composition, public image, officer background, and interservice and intraservice rivalries. The attitudes of the military toward their role in the political system are broken down into four different viewpoints. The complexity of the military is well brought out in this selection. The military has intervened in Argentine politics numerous times since 1930, and with its last two coups against Presidents Frondizi and Illia in 1962 and 1966 respectively, it has shown that it is not willing to stand aside when it feels the country needs its direction.

In the third selection, Mr. Rowe analyzes the reasons for the military overthrow of President Illia in 1966. The overthrow seemed to epitomise Argentina's major political problems, many of which were evaluated in the other selections. After the overthrow, however, the military brought General Juan Carlos Onganía from retirement, made him President, and decided to step back from politics for the next few years. Thus since 1966 Argentina has been run by General Onganía, and Mr. Rowe describes the man and his policies of the first year. Since 1966 General Onganía has continued his economic programs and has had a fair degree of success in economic stabilization. Also, his continued suppression of Congress and the political parties did not seem to overly disturb the Argentines. In May 1969, however, tightening student and labor union restrictions led to serious demonstrations in many cities, and the military complained that in being given the unpleasant job of putting these down it was assuming responsibility without being given any role in formulating policy by General Onganía. The discontent of students, union officials, and parts of the military is bolstered by that of a portion of the Catholic Church and party leaders, and possibly could lead to the end of General Onganía or at least to a change of his unique style of governing. Thus, the ten year experiment in solving Argentina's underlying problems may prove to be abortive. From all past experiences, however, a new government will probably prove to be no more successful.

THE ARGENTINE POLITICAL SYSTEM

*The Costs of Anti-Nationalism: Argentina**

K. H. SILVERT

The Articulation of the Political Mechanism

Simplicity is the most striking characteristic of Argentine politics. The lack of complication and the failure to achieve a high degree of articulation of the nation's power groupings are also in consonance with the set of traditional values still widely held. While the *structure* of the economic institution has managed a fairly high degree of modernization despite the continued rooting of certain *functions* in an older order, the political institution has remained much more intimately related to prenational structures as well as functions. Charisma, the charm factor of personalism, remains vital to the mobilization of widespread public support, and the essential fragility of the entire mechanism is demonstrated by the ease with which the military have been manipulating the state. Their freedom of action is not so much a demonstration of military might as it is of civilian weakness. Personalism and naked force have been the two essential ingredients of the mobilization of political power in the last three decades; the so-called "popular will," although often invoked and even occasionally called upon to act, has in truth been but the creation of the manipulations of essentially anti-democratic demagogues. Recent history unequivocally supports these statements concerning the essentially superficial nature of allegedly "national" Argentine politics.

Argentina's last truly free election of a civilian president occurred in 1927. This mandate, extended to Hipólito Yrigoyen, was revoked by the military in 1930; although the coup was

* Reprinted from K. H. Silvert (ed.), *Expectant Peoples: Nationalism and Development* (N.Y.: Random House, 1963), pp. 353–372 by permission of publisher and author.

based on a fair degree of popular support to begin with, the dictatorship of José E. Uriburu ended in 1931 as a mere military adventure with overtones of Italian corporativism. Succeeding Conservative governments depended on simple electoral fraud to give their governance a semblance of democratic legitimacy, but their authority rested directly on a combination of oligarchical economic and military power.[1] The baldness of the hypocrisy is revealed in the name commonly given to this epoch—the "Period of the Patriotic Fraud." The reason is that the Conservatives argued that they were forced, as a matter of patriotism, to falsify the vote, for otherwise the ignorant populace would vote against its true interests, knowledge of which was a merit only of the Conservatives. By the middle of World War II, the Conservative governments had entirely lost their ability to confront the changing local and national scenes. The military returned themselves to direct authority in 1943, a move made possible, and to military eyes "necessary," by the utter simplicity of the patterns of power distribution and the shrunken universe of political discourse recognized as pertinent. The emergence of Perón in 1944 and 1945 and his attractiveness to certain parts of the public —a political magnetism not seen in the country since the early days of Radical Yrigoyen during World War I—added other dimensions of power. Still, the fall of Peronism was essentially a response to changes in the views of certain leaders and not to the complex, sweeping movements which one attributes to truly national and popular politics. The succeeding provisional government of President Aramburu (1955 to 1958) made no pretense of being other than a military interregnum, even though it earned widespread praise and support among middle and upper-class groups. The election of the civilian Arturo Frondizi in 1958, a polling which did not permit the candidacy of avowed Peronists, appeared at first to

[1] It is not necessary to list the standard works on recent Argentine political developments. Specialists already know them, and any non-specialist can find them easily enough. I might mention only a fairly recent work of merit, Alfredo Galletti, *La realidad argentina en el siglo XX: La política y partidos,* Mexico: 1961. Otherwise, see Fillo, *op. cit.,* and the appropriate works of A. P. Whitaker, G. I. Blanksten, J. J. Johnson, J. J. Kennedy, R. Alexander, *et al.*

offer some promise of the complicating mechanisms of true party politics. But that administration chose not to attempt to develop and then rely upon the mechanics of a pluralistic society, but instead played about among the all too evident power centers to maintain a most precarious existence until its fall in early 1962. A highly confused and divided military leadership has once again arrogated to itself the responsibility for "maintaining the constitution" in the face of almost absolute public helplessness. The hard surface of military rule or the mottled aspect of Machiavellian balancing and intriguing have been the two masks of Argentine politics since 1930. The masks, most unhappily, do not disguise reality—they *are* the reality of Argentina's situation of weak government.

The political absoluteness which is a natural corollary of political simplicity is nowhere made so evident as in the manner in which political parties define their own functions. Instead of viewing themselves as the guardians of a part of the truth and as holding only a limited responsibility for the nation's destinies, party leaders see themselves as the vessels of universal truth and their parties as simple mechanisms with which to gain power. Even the quasi-official historian of the Radical Party, the most professional of all Argentine parties, permits himself these words:

> We are not just a political party . . . we are a force of national and continental history which consists in imparting constitutionality to Independence . . . in giving to the Nation through its people firm bases for its authentic development, which conceives of the Republic as a moral idea. . . .[2]

This Messianic view of politics leaves no room for a legitimate opposition; the erection of an ideological structure on moral grounds held to be universal condemns dissenting voices not as mere human error but as heresy. The dismaying inclusiveness of this view of Radicalism is really no less than the bald statement made by General Rawson the day

[2] Gabriel del Mazo, *El radicalismo: Ensayo sobre su historia y doctrina,* 2nd ed., Buenos Aires: 1951, as quoted in Galletti, *op. cit.,* p. 40.

after he led the military back to overt power in 1943: "Now there are no political parties, but only Argentines." In his turn Perón employed his newly erected party structure as a direct arm of government, as in totalitarianisms. Although the succeeding military government actually encouraged a limited play of party politics except for Peronists, official proclamations deplored such activities, clearly implying a belief in the innately evil nature of parties.

> And finally, we appeal to all the inhabitants of the Republic to postpone all tendentious and partisan interest to the higher interests of the collectivity. Let republican austerity be the guide of our conduct and let solidarity in the common effort permit the prompt gaining of those ends for which our people long.[3]

Even the professional politician Arturo Frondizi, when his turn came, demonstrated the same implied disdain for party politics by his constantly reiterated statement that he was the "president of twenty million Argentines," and not the exponent of a self-consistent and necessarily only partially valid set of views supported by a continuing, responsible, and extended party organization. President Frondizi demonstrated in much more basic manner the inefficacy of his country's political structure by the profound about-face he made after assuming office. During his campaign he projected the image of the classical Latin American left-leaning intellectual—anticlerical, anti-imperialist generally, anti-American specifically, economically autarchical, in favor of industrialization, opposed to foreign business, and so forth. After election, he allied himself openly with the Church, took Argentina into a close alliance with the United States, welcomed foreign investments, and turned his back on nationalistic recipes for economic development to embrace an austerity program, monetary stability, and other measures normally deemed sound in the United States and Western Europe, but viewed as anathema by Latin American proponents of economic nationalism. These new

[3] Message prepared by General Pedro Eugenio Aramburu on assuming the provisional presidency of the nation after the deposition of General Eduardo Lonardi in 1955, as quoted in Galletti, *op. cit.*, p. 209.

policies could be adopted only because his followers, though they were deeply opposed to them, were powerless to stop the executive. In turn, the taking of this line was a measure not of Frondizi's strength, but of his weakness. If the Radical Intransigent Party had not the power to prevent the change, then it follows that it did not have the strength to support its own president and that Frondizi had little national bargaining power with which to confront his ideological opponents—a fact borne out by the ease of his deposition, accomplished without a break in the normal rhythm of Argentine life.

Clear consistency also was shown by the successor government to the Frondizi administration, one of the earliest acts of which was to disband all political parties.

Evident within the structure of the government itself are the lack of pluralism and the directness of the manner in which public power is applied. The strong executive pattern is a constant; the judiciary is weak and without prestige; and the legislature has never at any time been able to exercise the deciding voice in the setting of public policy. Indeed, one of the earliest acts of the Frondizi administration was the destruction of the integrity of the Supreme Court and the criminal courts of the Federal District, and one of the first acts of the government which followed was to disband Congress. The expression of fundamental decisions comes from within the executive establishment itself, even though those decisions may have been made elsewhere. Although there are rudimentary interest groups established outside the formal organization of government, the institutionalized power centers extend their heads directly into the executive. The country's basic decisions are made *in camera,* the result of deliberation among the heads of the organized power groups. The armed forces, the single most obvious source and avenue of extra-state pressure, of course represent other groups and ideologies as well as their own professional interests. As a consequence, all aspiring interests attempt to exercise influence over the military establishment; even far leftists sometimes speak wistfully of the possibility of talking some disgruntled level of the army over to their point of view. The Church, agrarian interests, industrial groups, and the labor unions all bring their plaints and their points of view to bear directly on the executive and often upon the leaders of the other power establishments, at best using the legislature as a sounding board and the courts, when possible, as some kind of interim source of juridical legitimacy.

The workings of the mechanism are transparent, the channels of access clear, and the results apparent to all through the media of mass communications and the pronouncements of the interested parties themselves. Executive decisions, however they may have been reached and with what concessions and through what bargaining, may be in themselves the decisive political acts of the state, but they are limited in their scope and effectiveness by the very simplicity of the structure. In short, the Argentine government is intrinsically weak, a debility stemming from several fundamental causes:

First, the simplicity of the political institution of which we have been speaking not only makes for decisions which are a response to the crudest of pressures, but also inhibits the subtlety and refinement of measures which, by promoting general development, might work to strengthen government itself.

Second, the state is not firmly established as the ultimate secular arbiter of Argentine public life. The other institutions competing for men's loyalties permit a high degree of protection from the dictates of the state. Although the Church immediately springs to mind, the matter is much more complicated. A failure to recognize the supremacy of the state in the arbitration of secular dispute leaves many areas of life, such as the family, outside the reach of governmental determination. Class status also plays a fundamental part in the unequal and uneven application of the law, as does simple economic position. The impunity enjoyed by the far right scions of upper class families over the last twenty-five years for their racist demonstrations, shootings, bombings, and burnings are undeniable evidence of the truth of this statement.

And third, the combination of a simplified structure and a lack of acceptance of a broad social area as legitimate to political action reduces the amount of obedience or attachment to the rule of law which any Argentine government can expect, thus increasing the need for direct police and military enforcement of the law, or else permitting a wide latitude in such daily events of life as parking a car or painting political slogans on walls. This executive dependency on the police and the weakness of the legislature were well illustrated in mid-1961 when members of the national gendarmerie peppered the Congress building with small-arms fire in a protest concerning equipment and pay, incidentally at the time Congress was considering charges of police torture. Their punishment was a salary increase.

Simplicity, party weakness, the immediacy of action of pressure groups, and an exaggerated dependence on direct sanction within a severely limited sphere all describe not only Argentine politics, but also generic Mediterranean political thought and practice. An innate distrust of the state coupled with the direct representation of economic and occupational interest in the government are destructive of party strength, erode pluralism, and deny the sweeping grandeur possible to enlightened political action in its broadest senses. Such results stem directly from the conscious desire of leadership groups and the value structures of the societies involved—they are the politics of anti-nationalism indigenous to Spain and Portugal, but also clearly visible in Argentina and such other Latin American countries as Colombia. Syndicalism and falangism are two of the ideologies evolved in the Mediterranean world in the attempt to permit some economic development without the usual cost in terms of class structure and national organization.

The theory of Mediterranean syndicalism is essentially a complication of the idea of hierarchical order of medieval society. The Doctrine of the Two Swords is amended to become the Doctrine of the Six or Seven or Eight Swords, depending upon the number of institutional pillars created to become the fasces, so to speak, of quasi-modern traditionalism. The purpose of this institutional ordering is to subsume class to hierarchy, preserving a kind of Latin *Führerprinzip* and leaving inviolate the privileges and powers of the traditional, thus escaping the effects of "massification." While Marx was writing his attacks upon the evils of industrialism from the vantage point of the northern European, southern Europeans too began to attempt to protect themselves against the fully revolutionary implications of the changes of the last century. Mosca, Croce, and others were the intellectual scions of the period, reflected in Hispanic America by the work of Ortega y Gasset, whose *Revolt of the Masses* was not a kind of early *The Lonely Crowd* in Spanish, but rather an appeal against mass man from the stance of the traditional universalist whose humanism stems from a medieval base.

The good society pictured by the syndicalist would have the individual firmly rooted in his institutional place. His representation in government would not be a result of his individuality or of his mere citizenship, but rather a function of his place in the institutional order of events. Public decisions would then result from the interplay of the institutional oligarchs, and not from the deliberations of groups and men elected at large from a citizenry escaping its occupational bonds in an act of political selection and decision formally and somewhat substantially indicative of equality. The secular state could not become supreme in its area; mass man would be tamed by being herded into institutional kennels, safely under the tutelage of the leader.

Although it does not exemplify a pure form of falangist or syndicalist practice, the recent Argentine experience does exemplify it in modified form. The weakness of the state, the strength of competing institutions, and the accent upon class-bound politics wedded to hierarchy and obedience within the occupational function all define Argentine practice; and all are incompatible with the fluidity and self-adjustment required for the voluntaristic human mobilization of democratic development. Because the modern nation-state carves out an area of secular and impersonal politics, the traditional man with his notions of religious order, ecumenical and thus exclusivist and anti-democratic politics, and occupational hierarchy must dedicate himself to anti-national endeavors. The failure of Argentina to emerge into a relatively stable existence despite its high level of economic development can certainly be attributed in major part to the unwillingness or inability of decisive power groups to accept the necessary impersonal secularism of the modern, interdependent society.

It should be remembered that falangism and syndicalism are not fascism. The essential difference is that the fascist government does indeed attempt to establish the supremacy of the state, while the syndicalist subscribes to an extended oligarchical form legitimated by religious sanction. The Perón period in Argentina well exemplifies this difference, despite the many times that regime has been carelessly labeled as "fascist" in other countries. The following discussion of Peronism also illustrates the limitations of the leader-follower relationship of which we have been speaking, as well as the prenational politics of Argentina even in the throes of a harsher than usual dictatorship.

Peronism and Leadership

The Argentine leader cannot create a modern set of national values by signing a decree or speaking from a balcony. He can extend the effectiveness of his government by chipping at the power of rival institutions only through the exercise of great skill and effort. Unless he whips together a mass movement striving for frank and complete revolutionary change, the leader is restricted to the employment of two types of authority: he can be content with the immediately available power derived from the existing play of intra- and inter-institutional forces, or he can attempt to modify this situation by gaining a measure of external power through the mobilization of new domestic groups or the enlistment of foreign support. In matters of program, as distinct from the question of the composition of his sources of power, he is restricted either to the path of administering the tides of the *status quo* or to a mild reformism. In explaining his actions to himself and others, however, he can indulge in the strongest ideological statements from center-left to right in tone, or else be a simple eclectic. But no matter what the basis of his power, the profundity or superficiality of his program, or the style of his explanations, the non-revolutionary leader cannot escape the limitations inherent in the prenational orientation of the elite, nor the confining contradiction of leading a people of traditional values who are flexing the muscles of a substantially developed economy.[4]

[4] Little attention is given in this statement to the political left. The reasons are that we are not considering the possibility of social revolution and that, of course, all Argentine governments since 1930 have leaned more or less sharply to the right. The Argentine

These limitations apply to Perón as well as to his successors. The matter of categorization here becomes crucial to further analysis, for if the foregoing synthesis is correct, then the Peronist government was not effectively totalitarian, whatever other unhappy things it may have been. A totalitarian state employs the political institution to work its will directly upon the citizen without the interference of intervening buffer institutions or the restraints of a rule of law or a less than universal ideological justification. These conditions simply did not prevail in a total pattern in Argentina between 1946 and 1955, although the lack of juridical and ideological constraint did and still does exist.

If we use secondary criteria of totalitarianism derived specifically from the European fascist examples as our baseline, the Argentine experience diverges in significant points:

The middle-class base for German and Italian fascism must be contrasted in Argentina with the mass lower-class backing for Peronism. In Argentina, it is true that important middle-class groups were also involved, and even a significant number of persons of upper-class extraction made themselves available for leadership positions. The participation of the traditional rural elite was especially important in the culturally more colonialist provinces such as San Juan and Tucumán. In no class sense was Peronism revolutionary; the movement squeezed classes together, especially by raising the lowers, but

---

left has had scant chance to mount fullblown revolution in the last two generations, although the present chaotic situation and the availability of certain fringe Peronist groups are changing this perspective. But it should be remembered that leftist leaders are no less the captives of their culture than their political opponents. They have delivered themselves up to endless bickering, conspiratorial practices, unreal policies, and short-lived coalitions entered upon through wishful thinking more than a real concord of belief and interest. *Fidelismo* has also served to accentuate romantic dreams and to underscore the extranational nature of at least part of the left in a country crying for a healthful national integration. The fraying away of the left Socialists and Radicals, Communists, Trotskyists, and other left fringe groups was also hastened by the actions of ex-President Frondizi, who persuaded many of them during his campaign that he would be a left-leaning president, only to present them after his election with a conservative caricature of their own economic determinism, as mentioned earlier in the text.

did not change class order or strive for a substantial loss of class status among any groups.

The relatively high degree of technology necessary for police state control, eminently true of Nazi Germany, could not be said to describe Argentina. Even Italian fascism lost some of its effectiveness through an institutional "leakiness" caused by technological deficiencies.

Charisma was of great importance in the three systems, but in Argentina the full measure of organizational consequences did not flow from the personalism of Juan and Eva Perón, especially in the internal administrative operation of the government. Most of the persons holding important leadership positions of a formal nature in the Peronist hierarchy followed career paths normal both to the pre- and post-Perón epochs. Max Weber's definition of the charismatic corporate group does not describe the Perón administration:

> The corporate group which is subject to charismatic authority is based on an emotional form of communal relationship. The administrative staff of a charismatic leader does not consist of "officials"; at least its members are not technically trained. It is not chosen on the basis of social privilege nor from the point of view of domestic or personal dependency. It is rather chosen in terms of the charismatic qualities of its members. The prophet has his disciples. . . . There is no such thing as "appointment" or "dismissal," no career, no promotion. There is only a "call" at the instance of the leader. . . . There is no hierarchy. . . . There is no such thing as a definite sphere of authority and of competence, and no appropriation of official powers on the basis of social privileges. . . .[5]

A mystical ideology of nationalism was true of the three governments, but Argentine *justicialismo* was almost an afterthought, an intellectual appendage to justify the "leadership principle" and dignify the regime. Argentine nationalistic ideology was restricted largely to attacks on foreign countries in speech and press and to mystical glorification of the nation,

[5] Max Weber, *The Theory of Social and Economic Organization,* tr. by A. M. Henderson and Talcott Parsons, Glencoe: 1947, p. 360.

but devoted itself little to the task of assuring the relative position of the state as the supreme social institution. Only very late in the Perón administration was ideology designed to begin to grapple with the country's institutional organization over the issue of church-state relations. The result was an open break with the leaders of the Catholic Church, the burning of Church properties, excommunications, and the passing of a divorce law and other punitive legislation. The process ended with the overthrow of the government, forced back into its accustomed compliance in such matters.

Militarism was an important component of Peronism as of German and Italian fascism, for Perón assumed power primarily as a consequence of his military position and the previous actions of the armed forces. But of course both Hitler and Mussolini assumed power in some measure despite the military, and employed their armed might for war, a purpose alien to the ideas of Perón, despite brave words about Argentine hegemony in the southern part of the continent. It would not be unfair to state that the military functioned in almost directly opposite manners in the Argentine and European experiences.

A controlled economy—the total identification between economic and political interests and the growing indistinguishability of controlling personnel that came about in Italy and Germany—was not matched in Argentina. Despite a degree of governmental intervention unsurpassed in previous history, the Argentines did not reach the degree of control exercised in Chile, Mexico, and Uruguay. Although Peronism did recruit some new millionaires from among its own ranks, it is difficult to say whether such acts were substantially different from the same kind of political insurance practiced in other Latin American countries. In any event, Peronism contributed to building a new class of industrialists, but stopped far short of dispossessing pre-existing wealthy groups or instituting total mobilization of the economy for national ends. The motivation for the economic measures of Peronism rested in autarchical nationalism, as in the Mexican case, in statism, as throughout Latin America, in anti-capitalism, an almost universal article of faith among both traditional conservatives and leftists in

Latin America, and probably only in a very minor degree on any self-conscious ideological principles concerning the role of economics in a fascist society.

Racism was entirely incidental to Peronism, even more marginal than it was to Italian fascism. Indeed, the Perón administration defended certain ethnic minorities against the extreme measures desired by certain parts of the urban upper class.

Perón's search for support outside the existing power structure led him to herd the lower-class groups into captive trade unions. This black populism appealed especially to the less skilled workers, such as packinghouse employees, and to new migrants to the city, coming out of the countryside in response to the growing industrialization of the metropolitan centers. Despite the substantive difference between this process and the recruitment of déclassé middle-class persons in Germany, some observers have attempted to save the totalitarian category for the Peronist regime by labeling it as "Fascism of the Left." S. M. Lipset, for example, writes:

> [Another] . . . type of social movement which has often been described as fascist is Peronism. . . . Unlike right-wing antidemocratic tendencies based on the more well-to-do and traditionalist strata and those tendencies I prefer to call "true" fascism–centrist authoritarianism, based on the liberal middle classes, primarily the self-employed–Peronism, much like Marxist parties, has been oriented toward the poorer classes, primarily urban workers but also the more impoverished rural population. . . .
>
> The phenomenon known as Peronism–anticapitalist populist nationalism which appeals to the lower strata in alignment with the army–is, of course, not unique to the Argentine. In Brazil, Getulio Vargas developed the same theme a decade earlier, was also identified with fascism, and continued to retain the support of the workers after he left power. . . . If Peronism is considered a variant of fascism, then it is a fascism of the left because it is based on the social strata who would otherwise turn to socialism or Communism as an outlet for their frustrations.[6]

[6] *Political Man: The Social Bases of Politics,* New York: 1960, pp. 170–173, *passim.*

Several very serious quarrels can be picked with this statement, the most important being the loose and interchangeable use of "fascist," "authoritarian," and "totalitarian." All fascism and totalitarianism is of course authoritarian, but not all authoritarianism is totalitarian and fascist. Peronism employed the ideology and public style of fascism, but performed no revolutionary functions in a class or structural sense, governed internally by juggling already existing power centers in a fashion typical of states in immediately prenational situations, and above all was unable to establish the unquestioned supremacy of the state. The regime even toppled in traditional semi-developed Latin American style, victim of a *coup d'état* led by a military vanguard and supported by an important and significant body of public sentiment.

Much doubt also can be cast on the seemingly logical view that the persons who became Peronists would otherwise have become socialists or communists. Certainly Peronists have not flocked to the Marxist banners upon the collapse of their own movement. What is most probable is that, at least in any short or intermediate run, persons susceptible to following the traditionalist politics of syndicalism are not apt recruits to the essentially developmental and nationalist appeals of any of the modernizing camps, whether Marxist left or Liberal moderate. The intellectual atmosphere on this point might well be cleared by understanding that in Italy Mussolini presided over a mixed regime—part Mediterranean traditional syndicalism, part modern totalitarianism. The rather purer forms of the one are found in Portugal, and of the other in Nazi Germany. Both Mussolini and Perón, after all, were leading Latin peoples with Latin cultures.

But Peronism did succeed in setting class against class more sharply than in any other period of Argentine history. The movement clearly and self-consciously counterposed liberty and authority and opted for the latter; in more hidden fashion it also opposed honesty to dishonesty, and also chose the latter in all senses. Reason, too, was made to cede to demagoguery. If Peronism did not change the relative position of Argentina's social classes, only pressing them together in their economic aspects, it did temporarily reduce social distance in a psychological as well as economic sense. There is no contradiction in the fact that the more equitable income distribution and greater feeling of participation on the part of lower elements was accomplished in part through the fomenting of overt class antagonisms.

The regime, nevertheless, did not change the land tenure system or the prevailing patterns of distribution of great wealth. Although the style and ideology of leadership were novel, the recruitment patterns changed only slightly, and the sources of succeeding opposition leaders were unaffected after all was said and done. Not even the pre-Perón distribution of opposition parties was effectively destroyed, for they all returned to their usual sickly bloom within a year after the fall of the dictator. These "accomplishments" of Peronism simply do not describe the workings of a totalitarian fascism.

Peronism responded to many basic needs in Argentine political life, and succeeded eventually in betraying all of them. Any reasonably modern society must somehow recognize and make provision for the desire of large groups of citizens to participate in the civic experience; Argentina also needs some kind of national, integrated identity, and a means for the routine settlement of secular dispute. Perón gained outside support by promising to meet these needs and by devising a poor man's neo-fascist ideology to explain his actions. But he employed worker support only to construct a General Confederation of Labor as an added institutional pillar in the emergent syndicalist structure, not as a free labor movement. He did not change the institutional order; he only amended it by extending its already existing configuration. Through corruption and inefficacy, a failure to understand why he really had gained mass support, and his ultimate commitment to traditional values and sources of power, Perón perverted what might have been the positive developmental aspects of his policies and left his country with the twisting legacy of a lower class infected with neo-fascist political beliefs and an opposition stained with his own style. And by denying even the traditionally thin Liberalism to which middle and upper groups had become accustomed, his kind of authoritarianism guaranteed the hatred even of wavering Argentine democrats.

The Argentine political tragedy resides in the fact that

> the political integration of the popular classes was initiated under the sign of a totalitarianism which succeeded in providing, in its fashion, a certain experience of political and social participation in the immediate and personal aspects of the life of the worker, nullifying at the same time the political organization and the basic rights which constitute the irreplaceable pillars of any genuine democracy. The immense task to be carried out consists in gaining this same experience, but relating it in an indissoluble manner to the theory and practice of democracy and freedom.[7]

The importance of Peronism should not be underestimated, however. The effects were profound precisely in those two areas least strongly inhibited by institutionalized power—ideology and style. Unable or unwilling as Perón was to change the basic contradictions in the structure of social values, economic practices, and mass versus traditional politics, his ideological prods and his simulacrum of populism have left the problems inflamed, a continuing source of infection and pain. Not only did the dispossessed become aware of their status and taste some of the fruits of an artificial participation, but now even the integrated middle and upper groups are willing to admit the possible alienation of some of their fellow citizens.

Dismantling the work of the Perón administration in an organizational and immediate policy sense was not an inordinately difficult task, and certainly nothing to compare with what would have been a transition from totalitarianism to limited democracy. Despite the damage he wreaked on the nation's economy, there is good reason to believe that many of the difficulties would have existed even without the badly directed interventionism of the Perón era. The constitution of 1949 was calmly repealed, elections organized, and by early 1958 the government was legally re-established in regular constitutional fashion. Ideological confusion has hindered all politics since the end of Peronism, but since both policy horizons and public power remain limited, the play of politics continues to deal with problems superficially and merely manipulatively. Peronism was not born in social revolution, nor was it im-

[7] Gino Germani, *Politica e Massa,* Minas Gerais: Estudos Sociais e Politicas da Faculdade de Direito, No. 13, 1960, p. 189.

molated in it. And the politics of post-Perón Argentina remain traditional prenational and essentially syndicalist in nature.

The Heritage of Anti-Nationalism

The military government of 1955–1958, presided over by an unstable group of predominantly Liberal army officers, attempted to restore the politics of formal democracy based on a coalition of upper and middle groups. The armed governors, somewhat abashed at their role, sought to establish a kind of democratic market place without the Peronists, but otherwise characterized by a large measure of civil liberties. They succeeded in this end well enough to supervise substantively good and honest national elections for all groups except Peronists. Otherwise few decisive public acts were taken, the government assuming that its basic function was to provide a healing cushion of time between the fall of Perón and a constitutional civilian successor regime.

In early 1958 Arturo Frondizi, the candidate of the center-left Radical Intransigent Party and supported by the Church, the Peronists, and the Communists, was elected president. The military divided on the advisability of permitting the new government to assume office, but finally moderate counsels won the day with the understanding that Frondizi would be inhibited by the military from following policies of either an allegedly Marxist or allegedly Peronist nature. Thus began the uneasy three years, marked by three dozen attempted military *coups* of many political hues, which finally culminated in the collapse of the Frondizi administration in early 1962 and the assumption of power by the extreme interventionists among the military.

Frondizi was seen overseas as a progressive politician who followed free enterprise policies dedicated to a rapid healing of the nation's economic problems antecedent to a political reconstruction. He was considered inside Argentina as an opportunist and a Machiavellian juggler always ready to retreat when necessary to maintain his precarious hold on power. Whatever may have been his motivations and those of his inner group, the Frondizi regime, measured by any yardstick, was a total failure. Frondizi's economic policies did not succeed in raising productivity, distributing income more equitably, or reducing balance-of-payments difficulties, although inflationary pressures were stopped short of becoming run-away. His social policies did not reduce interclass tensions; indeed, the immediate reflection of his economic measures was to intensify such conflict, as was stated in the introduction to this chapter. And his political "integrationist" policy of attempting to woo Peronists into the Radical Intransigent Party failed before the absolute strength of the Perón movement itself and was, of course, the immediate cause of the military strike which removed him from power.

The Frondizi government can be best understood as yet another Argentine attempt at syndicalist organization. The government made no attempt to follow Liberal political policies, but instead fomented the very politics of institutional hierarchy employed so strikingly during the first seven years of the Perón administration. It is clear that Mr. Frondizi presumed that he could gain the support of enough of the organized power groups to be able to contain the military until such time as he could muster sufficient strength to submit them entirely to civilian control. To that end, he wooed the clergy, insisted upon turning the General Confederation of Labor over to Peronist control, and hoped that his economic policies would weld industrial and agrarian groups to his movement. He also sought to go outside the standard fasces to find extra support, much as Perón had done when he established his captive trade union movement in the first instance. The Frondizi government sought the added margin of power in the international sphere, soliciting and receiving strong support from the United States. All this maneuvering was still not enough, for the policies followed remained antithetical to the very economic development for which all the material and ideological sacrifices were being made. Traditional values and organization remained inconsistent with economic development; Argentina was not and is not in a primary economic crisis which can be solved by economic means. It is in a political and social crisis which has affected the formerly healthy economic machine.

The economic policies of Mr. Frondizi and his foreign advisers only exacerbated Argentina's problems, leaving the country much worse off after his truncated rule than before.

The political party system is now in shards, democratic procedures are even more discredited, the military have become ever more deeply convinced interventionists, and a national weariness has replaced the enthusiasm of the immediate postwar years. As yet no political solutions are in sight, despite the promised return to a moderate and civilian administration implicit in the elections of July, 1963. The basic sin of the Frondizi government was that it betrayed the democratic process in the ideological conviction that a policy of neo-syndicalist "integrationism" and naked economic determinism was the only viable solution. The self-delusion of the military that they are the ultimate defenders of the constitution against the Peronists and Communists proves itself in the utterly regressive nature of their politics of consolidation by force in the midst of delay, confusion, and vacillation. The failure of Argentina's large middle classes is their continued identification only toward the top instead of toward the total nation. And the insufficiency of major parts of the literate lower group is their yearning for a Peronist politics of romanticism and authoritarian leadership.

As there are Romance languages, so are there Romance politics. For long it has been a common saying that Europe stops at the Pyrenees. The Iberian peninsula and its offshoots, Western though they may all be, are the only part of the European cultural community so consistently lagging in integrating any effective degree of modernism. Underdeveloped, undefined, and understudied, they have gone their way, the subject either of neglect or of a beneficent Pan-Americanism of a rather sticky hands-across-the-border variety. But there can be little doubt that eventually, in the long and dolorous run, the Iberian community will emerge into the modern world. In the meantime, Argentina will probably continue to serve as one of the more striking cases of resistance in the Romantic world to the value and institutional requirements of development. All Latin America offers case after case of differing accommodations of traditional values to a certain ingestion of the modern, especially in the areas of industrialization and mimetic ideology. But Argentina's experience is still the most notable because of the country's extraordinary degree of urbanization, industrialization, and cultural Europeanization.

There will be no effective solutions in Argentina until that country puts aside its paradoxes, its attempt to have the best of the traditional and the best of the modern. Argentina clearly demonstrates that machines and Europeans and big cities do not guarantee self-sustaining development and stability. Equality before the law, public secularism, and guarantees of participation in the total nation remain ineluctable parts of the total situation that is the modern state.

THE ARGENTINE MILITARY

*Argentina's Restless Military**

JAMES W. ROWE

The Armed Forces Today

Soldiering and statecraft have been mixed in Argentina since the Republic was founded, as is amply testified by the careers of five generals: the Liberator José de San Martín, the Dictator Juan Manuel de Rosas, and three early Presidents, Urquiza, Mitre, and Julio A. Roca. The modern phase of politico-military relations dates from September 1930, when the Argentine military emerged as a major political force with its overthrow of the Yrigoyen government.[1] At that time the total personnel of the Armed Forces numbered approximately 50,000; by 1943, on the eve of another military *coup*, the number of men in uniform had doubled.[2] In 1945 military expenditures accounted for 1.5 billion pesos, over 50% of the national budget, and during the Peronist decade (1946–1955) officers' pay was raised to the highest level in Latin America.[3] As that decade ended, the Armed Forces reached a strength of nearly 200,000–100,000 in the Army, 22,000 in the Navy,

* Reprinted from James W. Rowe, "Argentina's Restless Military," *American Universities Field Staff Report* (May, 1964) pp. 4–11, 17–21, by permission of American Universities Field Staff, Inc.

[1] Robert Potash, *op. cit.*, p. 571.

[2] Horacio Sueldo, "Fuerzas Armadas" *Argentina, 1930–1960* (Buenos Aires: Editorial Sur, 1961), p. 174.

[3] Edwin Lieuwen, *Arms and Politics in Latin America* (rev. ed.; New York: Frederick A. Praeger, 1961), pp. 68, 70.

about 15,000 in the Air Force, and a total of 50,000 in the Border Patrol and Federal Police.[4]

Over-all Armed Forces strength decreased somewhat after 1955. Since 1960, officers and men of the three services (excluding reserves) have numbered just over 140,000.[5] Modernization in the Army is supposed to cut this figure further, but reductions have been delayed by the institutional disorder of the last two years.

The Army in recent years has had about 85,000 men–some 65,000 one-year draftees, 15,000 career noncommissioned officers, and about 5,000 officers. With rare exceptions, neither draftees nor noncoms have figured in political action. Neither have officers in the professional services branches (Medical, Judge Advocate, etc.) played much part. It is the Command Corps of the three services that make political news: an elite of about 3,500 officers from the Army, 1,300 from the Navy, and 1,200 from the Air Force. Among the 6,000 (about .03% of Argentina's population) there are nowadays about 40 Army generals, between 30 and 35 Air Force brigadiers, and 10 to 15 admirals.[6]

The Army is organized into six divisions, four cavalry brigades and two mountain detachments. These consist of 31 regiments of infantry, 15 of cavalry, 10 of artillery, and several engineer battalions. The country is divided into five military districts, which take on some of the qualities of political units during a military insurrection. In addition to the forces mentioned, the Army counts reserves of about 250,000. Military service of one year's active duty (two years in the Navy) is compulsory for most male citizens at around age twenty. The Military College for cadets was founded in 1869 and presently graduates over a hundred officers annually.

The Navy's fighting ships include one aircraft carrier, two cruisers, eleven destroyers, nine frigates, and two submarines. Principal power and prestige lie with the fleet, but a small Naval Air Force and Marine Infantry compete for funds and

[4] Arthur Whitaker, *Argentine Upheaval* (New York: Frederick A. Praeger, 1956), pp. 65–66.

[5] Sueldo, *op. cit.*, note 5, p. 175; *Statesman's Yearbook (1961–62)*, p. 817.

[6] *La Nación* (Buenos Aires), January 6, 1964.

attention and complicate the Navy's relations with the other two services.[7] The Navy School Academy is at Rio Santiago and the Navy Mechanics' School is in Buenos Aires.

The Air Force was founded in 1912 and gained autonomy in 1945. With about 300 pilots and 150 operational aircraft (including Gloucester Meteors and F-86 Sabre jets) the Air Force has five operational air brigades. It is organized into an Air Defense Command of two fighter groups, an Air Transport Command, and a Tactical Air Command. The Military Aviation College is in Córdoba.

Each of the services boasts a Ministry in Buenos Aires, but there is no equivalent of the Pentagon despite nominal unification under the Minister. Large and relatively modern War and Navy Ministries are within "glaring distance" of each other and of the Casa Rosada (government house); the Air Ministry is scattered through several handsome if decaying town houses in the Barrio Norte. Together, the Armed Forces account for around 30% to 40% of the Argentine federal budget–compared to 15% spent by the Ministry of Education and Justice and 3.5% by the agencies charged with public health and social assistance.[8]

Officers of the Armed Forces are generally regarded by civilian outsiders as a privileged group. Especially during recent years, as the once-prosperous middle and upper classes have experienced hard times, the pay, perquisites, and tenure of the officer corps have appeared especially generous. After August 1961 the base pay of generals, admirals, and brigadiers came to 50,000 pesos (about $600) monthly and that of second lieutenants and their equivalents was 15,000 (almost $190).[9] Not only are such earnings high according to

[7] Marine Infantry has had a strength of 8,000 in recent years. The Marines played a leading part in the unsuccessful Colorado-Navy revolt of April 2 to 6, 1963. Among the terms of surrender was a provision calling for reduction of Marine strength–according to unconfirmed reports in the Buenos Aires press, to about 2,500.

[8] Data are from the (mimeographed) "Joint Program [*Programa Conjunta*] of the Federal Council on Investment and the Institute of Economic and Financial Research of the General Economic Confederation, Vol. I" (Buenos Aires, 1962), pp. 324 ff.

[9] Sueldo, *op. cit.*, note 5, p. 175; Rogelio García Lupo, *La Rebelión de los Generales* (Buenos Aires: Editorial Jamcana, 1963), p. 21.

standards prevailing among Argentine professional and white-collar groups, but in addition the officers enjoy family allowances and fringe benefits which many estimate to be worth 60% or more of base pay.[10] Finally, officers enjoy a generous system of retirement and pension. They can retire with 100% pay after 30 years service (when perhaps less than fifty years of age) or 75% after 25 years.[11] A liberal system of pension rights for widows, orphans, and other relatives sometimes leads to the wry comment by those outside the system that "the officer can still make a good living after he is dead." In the Andean resort of Bariloche, the visitor is told that the more attractive chalets all belong to retired colonels, commodores, and captains.

Envious respect for the officer corps' privileged economic position does not mean widespread admiration for the social role of the military. In a public opinion survey commissioned by the Presidency in December 1962, 52% of the respondents believed that the Armed Forces—rather than some other group or person such as the President or "foreign capital"—were really "running" the country.[12] But when asked to rate five institutions as to "social utility" on a ten-to-one scale, respondents gave the Armed Forces the lowest rating of all (2.4), below the Rural Society (5.8), the General Confederation of Labor (5), the Stock Exchange (4.8), and even the low-prestige National Congress (4.5). Thirty-two per cent answered "yes" when asked "Is there any group, organization, or institution in Argentina which inspires absolute confidence?" But when respondents were asked to list the group offering such inspiration, only 1% indicated the Armed Forces —less than the number listing mutual benefit associations, political parties, trade-unions, or the Catholic Church.[13]

[10] John J. Johnson, *The Military and Society in Latin America* (Stanford: Stanford University Press, 1964), p. 166.

[11] Cámara de Senadores de la Nación, *Diario de Sesiones* (September 23, 1958), p. 1737.

[12] This was during the "interregnum" of quasi-military rule during the Presidency of José María Guido, and shortly after the brief Azul-Colorado war of late September.

[13] Seventh National Public Opinion Survey, December 1962. The survey was designed and conducted by a private commercial

Less is known about the public image of the Armed Forces as a fighting body. The problem for most Argentines is that there is little to measure their Army, Navy, and Air Force against, for the forces have not participated in a foreign war since that of the Triple Alliance against Paraguay (1865–1870). Domestic revolts and rebellions pit Argentine against Argentine, and, even so, most of the "little revolutions" are affairs of bluff, maneuver, and nose-counting, with light casualties and of brief duration. Among foreign military attachés stationed in Buenos Aires, opinion regarding the quality of Argentina's military forces is mixed. The Armed Forces are considered among the largest and best equipped in Latin America, but the attachés raise serious questions regarding training, discipline, and morale.

Where do the officers come from? For some years it has been apparent to even the casual observer that the old simplistic identification of Latin American officer corps with wealthy landowning families would not stand up in the Argentine case. On the other hand, there has been a dearth of reliable factual information regarding the social origins of officers. While it is a commonplace saying in Argentina that the Army has long been typically middle class in origin, with the "pro-British" Navy somewhat more closely linked to the cereal, livestock, and trading interests of Buenos Aires, the propositions remain unproven. Such disparate observers of the military scene as E. F. Sánchez Zinny and Carlos A. Florit agree that the social extraction of Navy officers does not differ significantly from that of their counterparts in the other services or the liberal professions.[14] Part of the difficulty lies in the frequent confusion of acquired political tastes with expression of inherited class interest. The cosmopolitan atmosphere of a Naval career may be more decisive an influence

---

group and used a sample of 3,290 persons taken from the capital, Buenos Aires Province, and Tucumán.

[14] E. F. Sánchez Zinny, *El Culto de la Infamia* (2nd ed.; Buenos Aires, 1958), Vol. II, p. 460; Carlos A. Florit, *Las Fuerzas Armadas y La Guerra Psicológica* (Buenos Aires: Editorial Arayu, 1963), p. 36. A naval officer who is a part-time sociologist with some interest in officer recruitment suggested to me that the remaining links of the officer corps with the great landed families of the past would be found in the Army, not the Navy.

on an Admiral's foreign policy convictions than the opinions of his "liberal" (or nonliberal) family connections. Some younger Army officers of modest background seem to experience a "pull" toward "conservative" attitudes by virtue of being stationed in the vicinity of Buenos Aires, with its more rigid status requirements.

A beginning has been made at collecting empirical data on the background of officers.[15] The tables below, limited to general-grade officers and to the Army and Air Force, indicate at each of several five-year intervals the proportion of generals born in Buenos Aires (city or province) and those whose fathers were foreign-born. Both services show a rapid rise during the post-Perón years in senior commanders born in the capital or its environs rather than in the "interior." The

ARMY GENERAL OFFICERS (COMMAND CORPS ONLY)
PROPORTION BORN IN OR NEAR CAPITAL AND
OF FOREIGN-BORN FATHERS, SELECTED YEARS

Year	*Number of Generals on Active Duty*	*Born in Buenos Aires (City and Province)*	*Of Foreign-Born Father*
1936	19	58%	32%
1941	32	61%	34%
1946	41	46%	42%
1951	78	49%	46%
1956	52	44%	31%
1961	54	65%	19%

AIR FORCE BRIGADIERS
PROPORTION BORN IN OR NEAR CAPITAL AND
OF FOREIGN-BORN FATHERS, SELECTED YEARS

Year	*Number of Active and Retired Brigadiers*	*Born in Buenos Aires (City and Province)*	*Of Foreign-Born Father*
1946	5	60%	20%
1951	28	57%	22%
1956	32	66%	29%
1961*	18	67%	39%

* Active duty only.

15 Data on file at the Institute of Sociology, University of Buenos Aires, from the Ministries of War and Air. The Navy Ministry did not furnish data.

Army shows a sharp decline during the 1950's in its second-generation generals—from almost half in 1951 to about a fifth in 1961—but the figures for Air Force brigadiers suggest the reverse of this trend.

Armed Forces Rivalries, Factions, and Cliques

Internal quarrels and tensions in the Armed Forces can be divided into two principal categories: interservice and intraservice rivalries, and conflicts between factions not defined by military tables of organization. The latter usually have at least a nominal political coloration. Since the Liberating Revolution of 1955, the political divisions variously dubbed *legalista*-vs.-*golpista* and *Colorado*-vs.-*Azul* have at times obscured institutional rivalries lying underneath.

Until 1955 the Navy's role in politics was a minor one. That year, with the Army divided, the Navy's solidly anti-Peronist officer corps[16] brought in the fleet to turn the balance of power in September's successful revolt against Perón. The Navy gained enormous prestige and the Vice-Presidency, which went to Admiral Isaac F. Rojas. The custom began of appointing a Naval officer as Police Chief of Buenos Aires, and Navy men filled numerous federal jobs. But the Presidency and the preponderant role in the administration remained with the Army, a source of resentment in the Navy, with lingering consequences. Navy leadership was involved in the Colorado uprising of April 2 to 6, 1963. Only two "acceptable" admirals were left for active duty after the swift repression of the revolt, which represented the nadir of post-Perón Navy influence.

The latecomer Air Force has had less chance to build a tradition of political action. It gained prestige through the adhesion of important sectors to the successful Azul revolt of September 1962, but it lost some of this when its Commander in Chief, Brigadier Cayo Alsina undertook an ill-starred, one-man rebellion the following December. Thus far, the Air

[16] One of the semiofficial historians of the Perón ouster recalls that no more than 14 senior Navy officers could be called "loyal" or pro-Peronist during the final months of the regime. E. F. Sánchez Zinny, *op. cit.*, note 17, p. 460.

Force has not been the successful initiator of politico-military action; the evidence tentatively suggests that its officers have been somewhat more concerned with balance-of-power considerations vis-à-vis the other services than with "ideological" alignments.

It is the more numerous and historically more "interventionist" Army that has provided the bulk of the military forays into political action. And it is the Army that has produced the jungle of fissioning factions and cliques of recent years.

Intraservice rivalry between the several combat arms may have provided a partial basis for shifting alignments during the quarrels of the past decade, but it is difficult to find a consistent pattern or rationale behind them. "Pro-legality" or Azul leaders (Solanas Pacheco, Onganía, Pistarini, Lanusse, Alsogaray) seemed to attest a high incidence of cavalry officers of this persuasion. Three prominent *golpista* generals, however, were also cavalry (Franklin Rawson and the brothers Toranzo Montero). The rest of the more prominent *golpista*-Colorado generals came from the infantry (Fraga, Labayrú, Zenaruzza, Lorio), the artillery (Ossorio Arana, Yornet, Turulo, Elizando), and the engineers (Bonnecarrere, Poggi, Martijena).

In previous years the most notorious vehicles for the expression of factional interests in the Army were the *logias* (lodges). They have a long history, going back to the Wars of Independence, coincident with the arrival of Freemasonry in Spanish America. The first lodge recorded in Argentine history was the Logia Lautaro, founded by San Martín in 1812.[17] Its neophytes swore: "Never to recognize as legitimate any government of the Fatherland except one elected through free and spontaneous will of the people; and since the republican system is the most suitable for governing the Americas, to work in every way possible to see that the people decide in favor of it."

After a long lapse, *logias* reappeared toward the end of the 19th century. The Logia Militar, founded in April 1890, included 13 junior officers and a sergeant among its charter

[17] Jorge Abelardo Ramos, *Historia Política del Ejército Argentino* (Buenos Aires: Colección La Siringa, 1959), p. 37.

members. Far from reactionary or hostile to the growing Radical movement, the Logia Militar was itself influenced by the ideas of Radical leader Leandro N. Alem and "tried to direct the Armed Forces toward democratization of political life of the country."[18] In considerable contrast was the Logia San Martín, founded July 1921, which played an important part in events leading up to the *golpe de estado* of September 6, 1930. During the first Yrigoyen administration this lodge gained control of elections in the important officers club Círculo Militar and turned its prestige against Yrigoyenist officers; during the administration of Marcelo T. Alvear its pressure was strong enough to ensure the selection of a strong anti-Yrigoyenist, Colonel Agustín P. Justo (President, 1932–38) as Minister of War. Though the Logia San Martín disappeared in early 1926, a number of its former leaders were involved in the overthrow of Yrigoyen four years later. Ironically, a lodge whose initial objectives were nonmilitaristic and sought to reduce political interference with military discipline became associated with the ultimate in political intromission.[19]

The best-known Argentine lodge remains the famous GOU founded by Colonel Juan D. Perón and others in 1942.[20] The GOU was an important part of the breeding ground for the nationalist military revolution of June 4, 1943, which overthrew the government of President Ramón S. Castillo. Later the GOU provided the nucleus of rightist officers who overturned the government of General Pedro P. Ramírez in a palace *coup* on February 16, 1944, and served as Perón's springboard to power. The GOU had a skillfully designed and executed organizational plan down to the "cell" level

[18] García Lupo, *op. cit.*, note 12, p. 54.

[19] It should be noted, however, that neither General José F. Uriburu, who assumed the Presidency in September 1930, nor his elected successor, General Agustín P. Justo, was ever actually a member of the San Martín lodge. Cf. Juan V. Orona, *op. cit.*, note 1, pp. 73–94.

[20] The initials stood for Grupo de Oficiales Unidos (Group of United Officers), which was occasionally called Grupo Obra de Unificación (Unification Work Group), and also for its slogan, "Gobierno Orden, Unión" (Government, Order, Unity).

and employed clever psychological devices to ensure secrecy, efficiency, and loyalty. The GOU was nationalistic and fascist-oriented, but it appears to have been more obsessed with the geopolitics of Haushofer than with Axis ideology.[21] "Like John the Baptist," Horacio Sueldo puts it, "the GOU sprinkled the plotters with water from new fonts, preparing the way for one who would baptize the people in the fires of revolutionary emotion."[22]

During the Perón era, the GOU disappeared; but by the early 1950's, the same Army officer corps which produced the GOU and gave Perón his start had developed currents of strong anti-Peronism. One of these centered in the Sol de Mayo (May Sun) lodge. Composed mostly of retired officers, it was headed by Colonel José F. Suárez and included former GOU as well as pro-Radical officers. Like the GOU, the Sol de Mayo lodge counted some adherents in the Navy. A conspiracy in the hatching by this lodge was uncovered and smashed by Perón in February 1952.[23]

After Perón's fall in September 1955, the number of lodges inside the Army appears to have increased; even the Army Engineers have a secret society–known as "The Piston." With this proliferation came a tendency for the lodge factions to degenerate into cliques–officer groups clustered around an individual rather than common principles or purposes. One exception was the lodge known as Los Dragones Verdes (The Green Dragons) headed by Colonel Manuel Reimundes. It was formed principally of officers who had taken part in an abortive 1951 anti-Peronist uprising led by General Benjamín Menéndez.[24] It served briefly in the late 1950's as a focal point for "legalism": the peaceful transfer of power from the Provisional Government of General Aramburu to a freely

[21] García Lupo, *op. cit.,* note 12, p. 56.
[22] Sueldo, *op. cit.,* note 5, p. 163.
[23] Sánchez Zinny, *op. cit.,* note 17, p. 465.
[24] Menéndez appears recurrently through four decades of Army lodge-and-conspiracy history. The "perennial *golpista*" was born 80 years ago and graduated from the Military College in 1904. As a major he was a founder of the San Martín lodge in 1921. Forty-two years later he was the figurehead leader of the Colorado revolt of April 1963.

elected successor, and later support of Frondizi against military conspiracies.[25]

Contemporary Views of the Military Role

Despite the occasional rhetoric of romantics—in the Peronist trade-union sector at one extreme or the pockets of literary nationalism at the other—it is safe to say that very few Argentines can tolerate the notion of outright dictatorship headed by a military *caudillo*. Similarly, except for a few of the more romantic Radical orators, no one talks of the shriveling of the military role to a status similar to that which is found, say, in Costa Rica, or even Uruguay. Within these outer limits, however, at least four views regarding the role of the military in Argentine society have some currency.

The first view, which was actual practice during the Provisional Government and came near to being re-established in 1962, holds that a period of tutelage is necessary while the country is being cleansed of totalitarian threats and corruption in preparation for full democracy. The military govern as trustee, but permit widespread civilian participation in the decision-making machinery, encourage impersonalism, and observe institutional forms if possible. This was the view of the more extreme elements of the Colorado movement inside the military, and during the anarchic months of 1962 it was embraced by a variety of civilian leaders more influential than numerous. The prestige of this school has been considerably diminished by the successive Azul victories of 1962 and 1963.

A second view is the "Doctrine of Vigilance" practiced during the Frondizi administration. It was enunciated bluntly by its chief practitioner, General Carlos Severo Toranzo Montero in March 1960.[26]

[25] Before Reimundes became Frondizi's Undersecretary of War, he had been Military Attaché in London, whence he sent his close associates a Christmas greeting depicting St. George slaying a green dragon—and thus a lodge was named! García Lupo, *op. cit.*, note 12, p. 60.

[26] *La Nación* (Buenos Aires), June 29, 1960, as cited in German J. Bidart Campos, *Grupos de Presión y Factores de Poder* (Buenos Aires: Colección La Siringa, 1961), pp. 77–78.

. . . The national government, with its initial "integrationist" political line,[27] stimulated Peronist appetites. This line was abandoned because of pressure of the Armed Forces. . . . Pressure action by the Armed Forces, acting within the constitutional order, contributed to the change. . . . In case of national catastrophe, of a succession crisis, or of the drift of government toward tyranny, the Armed Forces, disciplined in republican principles, are the best guarantee. . . . The Armed Forces, politically impartial and directed by men true to their word, can and do act from time to time as a legitimate force of gravitation in the institutional order, and contribute to the hastening of national recovery.

"Vigilance," then, permits the normal play of civilian politics and administration within certain boundaries. As conceived by Toranzo Montero, it implies circumscription by means of suasion, and within an order of institutions and legality–not mere fiat. It is questionable whether such a theory corresponded to the reality of 1959–1962, since the "vigilantes" usually needed the support of allies more interested in terminating the administration than controlling it. "Vigilance" also implies a degree of institutional coherence and unity which simply did not exist either in the Army or the services as a body. As a policy, it had to be abandoned in favor of a *golpe* to contain Frondizi, and slipped toward "tutelage" before the Azules struck in 1962.

A third view sees the military's role as that of "the great mute"–a highly professional corps dedicated exclusively to its "specific task." Professionalization and modernization of the Army took place around the turn of the present century under the direction of General Pablo Richieri. Despite the tergiversations of the past three decades, a persistent strand of thinking in the Armed Forces has insisted on the incompatibility of military and political activity. In 1962 this view received new impetus when the Azul sector triumphed and General Juan Carlos Onganía became Army Commander in Chief. Both Onganía and the Azul documents stressed repeatedly that the Armed Forces, after setting Argentina back onto the

[27] In current Argentine usage, "integration" means reincorporation of Peronists into political life.

path of law and constitutionality, should return to their specific professional duties.

A fourth view holds that the energies of the Armed Forces must be harnessed to the task of economic development. Argentina has a strong tradition of military involvement in industrial and developmental enterprise, dating from the activities of General Mosconi with the state oil monopoly (Yacimientos Petrolíferos Fiscales) in the 1920's and those of General Manuel N. Savio with heavy industry in the 1940's. The latter was largely responsible for laws establishing an infant iron and steel industry at San Nicolás and a complex of military industries known as the Dirección General de Fabricaciones Militares. The Air Force and Navy also established industrial activities extending well beyond mere arsenals. During the Perón era, individual officers and the services themselves entered a wide variety of paramilitary activities, and despite retrenchment during both the Aramburu and Frondizi periods, the influence of the military in state industrial enterprises is still heavy. In social development activities which other countries now call military "civic action," antecedents can be traced to Roca's Army of the Desert in the 1870's. Even such a beleaguered target of military intromission as Arturo Frondizi has indicated disagreement with the notion of Armed Forces limitation to the "specific task," and urges that they be enlisted in the struggle for economic development.[28] Although the semiofficial creed of the present military hierarchy is "professionalization and abstention," a number of younger officers appear to favor more vigorous paramilitary activity. Sometimes loosely termed "Nasserists" by the Argentine and foreign press, they include such officers as General Carlos J. Rosas and Colonel Carlos María Zavalla. In March 1964 this viewpoint was espoused by General Juan E. Gugliamelli, Director of the Superior War School, who suggested that a "third way"—between political intromission and professional abstention—could be found in the notion of "the Army at the service of economic development."[29]

[28] Felix Luna, *Diálogos con Frondizi* (Buenos Aires, 1963), p. 92.

[29] *Comentarios* (Buenos Aires), March 25, 1964.

In Conclusion–Some Propositions:

(1) The Argentine officer corps, in recent years, has constituted an elite by virtue of the power it has wielded, not because of the social class from which it is drawn. What scanty statistical evidence is available relates officers to the urban, middle-class mainstream from which professionals, politicians, and entrepreneurs are recruited. German instructors and texts were an extremely important influence on Army training between the two World Wars (as in Chile and other countries), but the interlude of fascist impact in Argentina was of relatively brief duration and always watered down by liberal British influence. For 20 years the predominant professional influence in the services has been North American. The popular interpretation that officers reflect the same divisions, virtues, and faults as the middle and professional classes generally has yet to be disproved.

(2) One of the most remarkable phenomena of the long series of military crises is a trend permitting directives to flow from the bottom up in the officer hierarchy. As Tulio Halperín Donghi remarks, "While representative government was disappearing as a reality in our political life, its principles were triumphing in the Armed Forces." Such bizarre decision-making, lacking norms for either form or content and put into a national setting of generalized and extended social crisis, makes the absurdities of 1962 more explicable.

(3) During the Frondizi administration and the Guido "interregnum," much of the responsibility for military threats and plots must lie with the ambitions of civilian political leaders. Unwilling to use the manifest mechanisms of political adjustment, or convinced of their inadequacy, opposition figures of every hue and some from the administration itself chose to go knocking on the barracks' back door.

(4) Of the several alternative roles the military may attempt during the Illía administration, that of energetic participation in paramilitary developmental activities would appear to be the most promising. Although it is too soon to say whether either military or civilian *golpistas* were as stung as they should have been by the comic-opera spectacle Argen-

tina presented to the world in 1962, the successive Azul victories and Illía's initial handling of military relations give considerable cause for optimism regarding a decline in *golpismo*. On the other hand, the traditions of the Argentine military suggest that it will not be easy for the Armed Forces to bide their time between planning defenses for the Soviet invasion and their annual field maneuvers. Officers still like to eat their bread believing they have earned it.

THE 1966 COUP AND THE ONGANÍA REGIME

*Onganía's Argentina**

JAMES W. ROWE

Part I: The Golpe in Retrospect

Whatever the justification of the June *golpe,* it was no ephemeral matter, and was linked to a long-maturing crisis of values and authority which has been under way for many years. The "revolutionary" ferment prior to the *golpe* went far beyond mere concern over the alleged impotence of the Illia government (manifest justification for the *coup*) or even the specter of Peronist success in the elections scheduled for next March (an underlying motive) and was importantly related to the anxious–sometime desperate–concern of heterogeneous groups of younger officers, middle management, professionals, and others, to break the political and institutional impasse of the last decade. Partly because of this, and partly because of the singular prestige of General Onganía–aloof, decisive, totally uncompromised–the *golpe* was received with widespread consent and even enthusiasm by diverse sectors, including such "progressive" elements as organized labor, post-Conciliar Catholics, Frondizi "developmentalists," and much of the business community (which in today's Argentina cannot be considered uniformly traditional or even conservative). To be

* Reprinted from James W. Rowe, "Onganía's Argentina, Part I: The Golpe in Retrospect," pp. 4–9, and, "Onganía's Argentina, Part II: Men, Words, and Deeds," pp. 1–4, 7–15, *American Universities Field Staff Reports* (November, 1966) by permission of American Universities Field Staff, Inc.

sure, the *golpe* was also supported by various groups on the Right (including nationalist circles, conservative Catholics, the *colorado* military faction, and others)—while among those opposing the *coup*, the most prominent were the university community and, of course, the Radical Party in power. "Onganía very nearly had a blank check on assuming the presidency," remarks a generally astute political observer; "he could have done almost anything he wanted." What accounts for the rapid deterioration? Is the "Revolutionary movement" itself endangered, or the command of President Onganía? A brief review of the *coup*, and of the "Revolutionary" performance and status of several "power groups" in Argentina, may help to provide some clues.

The Coup of June 28

One is tempted to begin with the assertion that this was no "ordinary" Latin American military *coup*—but then most of them these days are not, and it is doubtful if such a thing exists, except in a factionalized past where dashing, bandoleered generals toppled popular constitutional governments for motives of pure plunder, or else to protect the threatened interests of rich landlords and reactionary priests. Whereas some outside governments and business interests have in the past tended to exalt and romanticize military governments in Latin America as the "only solution for anarchic societies" or as "the best defense against communism," liberal democrats in the developed countries have at times been equally quixotic in permanently assigning the villain's role to the military and the hero's to the embattled civilians in highly complex situations often marked by legislative immobilism, electoral fraud, endless party quarreling, and the efforts of the civilian politicians themselves to recruit support in the garrisons rather than from the hustings. The Brazilian *golpes* of 1930, 1945, and 1964, and the Argentine *coups* of 1930, 1943, 1955, and 1962 were all "special" situations, responding to the pressures for the incorporation of new groups into the national society, or else "protecting and restoring" the liberal constitutional order from real or alleged deformations resulting from those pressures. Gino Germani and K. H.

Silvert, in their study of military intervention in Latin America, conclude that "military intervention in the political power structure always indicates . . . at the minimum, a relative incapacity of other social institutions to wield power efficiently, and at the maximum, an advanced state of institutional decomposition."[1]

Noteworthy features of the *golpe* of June 28, 1966–Argentina's fifth[2] in thirty-five years–included the following:

(1) It was a "clean" *golpe* and swiftly executed–without shots, government resistance, or state of siege. Extraordinary troop movements were minimal; there were no exiles or political prisoners; and the military commanders did not even bother to arrest the President. People went to work and children attended school as usual.

(2) Compared with previous Argentine *golpes,* the formal attributes claimed by the June 28 movement are pretentious and the institutional changes are drastic. The new regime claims revolutionary constituent powers; its spokesmen reject the image of a *de facto* or "caretaker" government. Informally, they have indicated that the new order will be of "long duration," perhaps five to ten years. The first pronouncements of the "Revolution" (i.e., the statement of the military junta of June 28 and the Statute of the Revolution issued the following day) decreed the dissolution of the national Congress, provincial legislatures, and all political parties, the granting of

[1] Gino Germani and K. H. Silvert, *Estructura social e intervención militar en America Latina* (Buenos Aires: Editor al EUDEBA, 1965), p. 228. For two sociological approaches to the problem of military intervention in Argentina–each basically an introductory statement–see Virgilio Beltrán, *El Ejército y los cambios estructurales de la Argentina en el siglo XX: Primera aproximación* (an unpublished paper read at the 6th World Congress of Sociology, Evian, September, 1966), and Dario Cantón, "Notas sobre las fuerzas armadas argentinas," *Revista Latinoamericana de Sociologia,* Vol. I, No. 3 (Buenos Aires, November 1965).

[2] The term *golpe de estado* is used here to indicate a successful internal attempt to oust government either by force or by threat of force. Unsuccessful attempts are not included in this count, nor are shifts of leadership within a *de facto* regime–such as the replacement of General Ramírez by General Farrell in January 1944 or the substitution of General Aramburu for General Lonardi in November 1955.

legislative powers to the President, and the dismissal and replacement of all members of the Supreme Court. Edicts of the government are called "laws" rather than "decrees," and the newly appointed provincial administrators are called "governors," as if they had been elected, rather than "inventors" (the name commonly applied to federally appointed provincial authorities). The Statute of the Revolution is paramount to the Constitution, although the latter is not explicitly abandoned.

(3) A classic military junta–composed of the commanders of the three services–executed the *golpe*, decreed the Statute of the Revolution, and "elected" Lieutenant General Juan Carlos Onganía President. In contrast to previous *golpes*, however, this junta was to dissolve itself within twenty-four hours, in accordance with a "basic plan" for the "Revolution," and the well-known insistence of Onganía that the military not dissipate its unity and professionalization through prolonged political involvement.

(4) For the first time, an Argentine *golpe* was prepared with widespread collaboration of mass communications media. A part of the daily press–particularly two weekly newsmagazines–had long painted a more dismal picture of the Illia government and the depth of the "crisis" than would appear to have been objectively justified, and it lost few opportunities of suggesting the imminence of a *golpe* and putting forth favorable images of General Onganía and a "military solution." Perhaps no other *golpe* had been so publicly discussed in advance, or made to appear such a foregone conclusion. The newsmagazine *Confirmado,* in its issue of August 26, 1965, carried an interview by Juan José Güiraldes[3] predicting the

[3] Commodore Güiraldes, who retired from the Air Force during the Perón era and was later head of the state-owned Aerolineas Argentinas, is a political independent with unusually wide contacts among diverse circles. An outspoken Catholic and nationalist with an old family name and the outward attributes of the *estanciero* class, he moves as easily among the Frondizi "developmentalists" and the more independent Peronists as among military circles or the *distinguidos* of the Jockey Club. He was a contact man and "bridge" between various sectors interested in terminating the Illia regime, but he does not appear to have been a prime mover of the "Revolution."

"revolution" in terms remarkably descriptive of the actual occurrence ten months later; and in its Christmas 1965 issue the same journal published an imaginary account of the future *golpe,* complete with a date–July 1, 1966! On the eve of the military take-over, another weekly, *Primera Plana,* ran a kind of straw poll of who was for and who against the *golpe* among the nation's power elite. Even for Argentina, this degree of candor and a "promotional" approach to sedition and subversion seemed little short of bizarre.

(5) Motives behind the revolutionary movement were varied. The "incidents" triggering the *golpe* (a series of "showdown" confrontations between the Illia government and the top military commanders, beginning on May 29 and culminating with the President's effort on June 28 to dismiss Army Commander-in-Chief Pascual Pistarini–an attempt rejected by the latter as "totally lacking in value") had little importance except in affecting the timetable of the take-over. The significant causes should be viewed on at least three levels:

(a) The overt justification was the familiar charge, cited endlessly by the pro-*golpe* press and also in the junta statement of June 28, that the Illia government was "without authority"–fraught with internal contradictions and archaic ways, and marked by increasing paralysis and frustration, thus permitting the country to drift into social anarchy and economic stagnation.

(b) The more important officers and civilian politicians behind the *golpe* had been increasingly preoccupied with the specter of Peronist victories in the March 1967 elections and the diminishing chances of cutting this decade-old Gordian knot of Argentine politics. (Peronists had won 36 per cent of the vote in the partial Congressional elections of 1965 while the remainder was split among some ten parties. In traditionally conservative Mendoza province, an off-year governor's election in April 1966 produced a total Peronist vote of 41 per cent and, more importantly, demonstrated the continued strength of Juan Perón himself, for his "loyal" faction won easily over the rival independent movement ["Peronism without Perón"] led by Augusto Vandor. And in 1967 not only would half the Congress be up for election, but also crucial provincial governorships including that of Buenos Aires, whose industrial suburbs still form the strongest Peronist redoubt. Peronist control of Buenos Aires province, like the return to Argentina of Juan Perón, is unacceptable to powerful sectors otherwise committed to the reincorporation of Peronism into the national life.) According to their reasoning, a *golpe* in mid-1966 would be infinitely preferable to a "military reaction" after the March 1967 elections, since it would be less nakedly anti-Peronist and could be justified on other grounds.

(c) At another level, support for the *golpe* went beyond merely anti-Illia (anti-Radical) or anti-Peronist considerations, and may be considered revolutionary in concept. Many influential Argentines believed that the impasse of 1966 represented not only the ineptness of the Illia government but also the unworkability of the whole system of parties, political divisions, and leadership of the post-Perón era, and that the self-correction of the system was unlikely or impossible. But while deeply critical of what they term "representative semidemocracy" (Mariano Grondona), or "constitutional fiction" (Mariano Montemayor), they insist that such ideas differ markedly from the elitist and corporativist antiliberalism of the 1920's and 1930's: it is not that democracy *per se* is impossible in Argentina, but that the particular kind of limited democracy practiced in Argentina since 1955 is unworkable—it was neither truly "participatory" (because of the restrictions on Peronists), responsive, nor responsible. At this level, the problem of the Illia government was viewed not just in terms of its ineptness, but rather of its highly questionable legitimacy;[4] and also at this level, the reaction to a probable Peronist victory in March 1967 represented more than anti-Peronist intransigence. It included an appreciation of the long-

[4] The difficult, contentious, and unresolved question of political legitimacy remains a root problem in Latin America. As the distinguished Catholic review *Criterio* recently pointed out, legitimacy involves not only a legal and moral dimension, but also a sociological and political state of affairs enabling authority to be exercised (legitimately). No realistic assessment of the legitimacy issue at hand could fail to note the slim vote (24 per cent of the electorate) which brought Illia's party to power in 1963, nor his government's loss of its military guarantee with the resignation of General Onganía as Commander-in-Chief of the Army in late 1965.

range dilemma, which would remain even if a formula could be found to permit Peronist participation next March without creating a violent reaction: the fact that, while they constitute the *largest* political minority in the country, the Peronists are still a *minority* (roughly 30 to 40 per cent of the electorate). The remainder of the political forces are too deeply divided to form a coherent majority, but they can occasionally coalesce for negative ends. The full and free participation of the Peronists as a first minority within present circumstances would very likely result in a continuous political impasse similar to that of the Fourth French Republic; and for the more revolutionary of the June *golpistas,* it is precisely political immobilism—rather than the intrinsic defects of Illia Radicalism or Peronism—that is the greatest deterrent to the modernization of Argentina. Among the specific problems which the "modernizers" believe can no longer be postponed, the most frequently cited have been containment of inflation; reform of the inefficient and costly public service; reduction of the enormous deficits of the railroads and other state-owned enterprises; restructuring of the unproductive and socially explosive sugar economy of Tucumán province; and some kind of reorganization of the universities. As a means to these and other ends, however, the most revolutionary and perhaps the most unifying aim of the June movement was "to put an end to the old political cycle."

(6) Despite prolonged anticipation of the *coup* and the peripheral involvement of diverse groups in the enterprise, the actual plan of action and formulation of immediate aims were the work of a limited group. This was essentially an Army *coup*—managed by generals such as Pascual Pistarini, Julio Alsogaray, and Alcides López Aufranc, retired officers such as Francisco Imaz and Eduardo Señorans, working with the collaboration of a few civilians, such as Jorge Salimei and José María Saravia. Ranking Air Force officers were sympathetic, while those of the Navy were indifferent, but both of these services were involved only marginally. One result of this limited participation and of the limited gestation period for the plan of action was the failure to produce a substantial corps of dedicated "revolutionaries" united by the special bonds forged during a lengthy conspiracy.

(7) As noted earlier, most organized sectors of the population—excepting a part of the university community and most of Illia's Radical Party—received the *golpe* favorably if not with wild enthusiasm.

(8) At its inception, the movement of June 28, 1966, could be termed a *golpe* with revolutionary pretensions. Ideological vagueness and the lack of an organized cadre of supporters raised some doubt from the beginning as to its ability to evolve into a true revolution. Ideological vagueness plus the heterogeneous participation and support given the movement also made the use of conventional labels—"right-wing" or any other—dubious at best. How much of a revolution—and what kind—were questions the new regime would have to answer by its performance.

Part II: Men, Words, and Deeds

An interim assessment of the new leadership in Argentina must judge three elements—the qualities of President Onganía himself, the structure and men of his government, and early policy directions.

The President:

General Onganía first came into national prominence in September 1962, six months after the *golpe* which ousted Arturo Frondizi from the presidency, when he was commander of the Campo de Mayo garrison outside Buenos Aires, and the Army's prestige was perhaps at an all-time low due to promiscuous political involvement, internal divisions, and eroded discipline. As the main factions wrangled over whether to continue indirect military rule behind a civilian façade or to depose President José María Guido outright, Onganía submitted a formal protest against the deformation of the Army's mission and the breakdown of discipline. For this he was dismissed. His answer was to lead a victorious armed revolt of the "Blue" (*azul*) faction over the "Red" (*colorado*) faction calling for a return to legality, for the holding of elections as soon as possible, and for a restoration of discipline in the armed forces and their return to their professional mission.

In the brief days of combat, Onganía showed himself a brave and decisive soldier and a man of few words, completely nonpolitical and practically obsessed with the restoration of professional competence and vertical discipline in the Army. In the months afterward, as Commander-in-Chief, he was virtually the guarantor of the elections of July 1963 and thus, indirectly, of Arturo Illia's government, formed by a minority Radical force which won the election more or less by accident. Illia prudently retained Onganía as Commander-in-Chief—any other course would have been unthinkable—and despite thinly veiled differences over international questions (e.g., Onganía favored sending Argentine troops to the Dominican Republic), the General was faithful to his standard of nonpolitical professionalism and no internal meddling. When Onganía's displeasure over the President's manner of appointing a new Secretary of War led to his resignation in November 1965, some observers saw the beginning of the end for the Illia government. Not so the Radical Party stalwarts in several ministries, who raised champagne glasses to toast the "end of the Onganía myth."

There was an obvious irony in the award by the June *golpe* of the presidency to an officer whose fame and reputation were built on his dedication to legality and the depoliticization of the Armed Forces. Still, some of the most qualified observers had long maintained that during Onganía's hegemony there would be none of the halfway measures—the military "meddling" involving "tutelage" and "veto powers" characteristic of 1955–1963—but an all-or-nothing situation calling for hands-off or a full takeover. And so it was. But Onganía's continued insistence that the military institution not be too deeply involved with the regime of its own creation presents special problems. Of all the military men who have held the Argentine presidency in recent years, Onganía is perhaps the most exclusively military in background and formation. General Uriburu was linked to the *estancieros* and the oligarchy; Colonel Perón built the C.G.T.; General Aramburu had a wide circle of friends and supporters in the business and civilian world—but Onganía, who does not come from a prominent family, has few close associates outside the Army. He is a soldier's soldier, "uncontaminated" by the connections that most important men have with the country's political and other elites. This uncommitted quality and his aloofness have no doubt enhanced the legendary character of his authority, but the plain fact is that Onganía assumed the presidency with very little being known about his political ideas, or about his skill at convincing—as distinct from commanding. Within the military institution, his insistence on discipline and vertical hierarchy gained him great respect; in the broader context of the presidency it is causing alarm. For example: in early October he was visited by General Alejandro Lanusse, a close comrade-in-arms during the *azul* rebellion, an active supporter of the June movement, and now one of the senior commanders on active duty. Greeting Lanusse, the President inquired whether the visit had been cleared through the Commander-in-Chief and, on learning that it had not (it was a social call), terminated the meeting with a curt "Good afternoon, General." Officers who have served with Onganía—as well as pro-"Revolution" civilians—have repeatedly expressed concern to this writer that Onganía will adopt an excessively rigid and military approach to all kinds of problems.

Onganía is a practicing (as distinct from nominal) Catholic, and much has been made of his presence at several *Cursillos*[5] (a kind of spiritual retreat with an evangelical tone where laymen and clergy share a weekend of meditation, prayer, and discussion) and of the presence of several prominent Catholics in the new government. Part of the press was quick to suggest a parallel between the regime and Franco's Spain—a strong-man government based on Army and Church—but evidence for such a conclusion is scanty. In itself, Onganía's Catholicism says little about his political or economic bent, since the Catholic hierarchy and lay movements are notably divided on the social question—with the reformist, post-Conciliar wing easily more influential than the conservative and nationalist traditional sectors. The weekend retreats apparently did serve as something of a recruiting-ground for some of Onganía's assistants: he is said to have become acquainted with the Minister of Economy Jorge Sali-

[5] *Cursos de Cristiandad,* an institution imported into Argentina by Spanish priests a few years ago.

mei and Undersecretary of the Interior Saravia at them; but the best evidence suggests that the *Cursillos* were themselves devoid of political or ideological content. As for the participation of nationalistic or right-wing Catholics in the adminstration, a few appointees might qualify: retired General Eduardo Señorans, the head of the intelligence service; Mario Amadeo, Ambassador to Brazil; and possibly the Minister of the Interior Enrique Martínez Paz, a law professor from Córdoba, who despite his conservative reputation says he is a "liberal" or "Maritain" Catholic. Actually, the influence of the Catholic right is less today than it was after the *coups* of September 1930, June 1943, or September 1955. One remembers, too, that the elitists and Catholic nationalists had a brief moment in the sun after those earlier *golpes,* but that in every case they were among the first power groups to decline in influence. This year, the more extreme Catholic nationalist groups are already running newspaper advertisements and editorials expressing "concern" over the trends they fear Onganía may be following.[6] Eventually, the Onganía regime may clash with the progressive, post-Conciliar Catholics; it is already skirmishing with the reactionary fringe groups.

. . . .

The "Revolution": Deeds

A month after the *golpe,* the new government–not yet fully organized, and with its policy aims still vaguely defined and at times obscure–took its first major action. The abrupt "intervention" on July 29 of all eight national universities (which, at least temporarily, ended the autonomy of the universities, placed them under the authority of the Ministry of Education pending reorganization, and terminated the "tripartite system" whereby students, alumni, and faculty had shared in their governing) was accompanied by police occupation and violence in two Buenos Aires faculties on the same night. The Rector and a majority of the deans of the Univer-

[6] See, for example, the "Open Letter to the President of the Nation" from the editors of *Cruzada* in *La Nación* (September 27, 1966); and "Somos Opositores," *Ulises* (No. 20/21; August-September 1966).

sity of Buenos Aires resigned in protest, along with the Rectors of four of the seven other institutions; and during the next few days heavy professorial resignations began (all of them in Buenos Aires, and mainly in the two schools that had been physically "invaded"), which eventually totaled several hundred teachers, including half the staff of the Exact Sciences Faculty and a third of that of Architecture. Much of the academic community was further affronted by the appointment of Dr. Luís Botet (a former federal prosecutor and judge best known for his *colorado* inclinations and aggressive anti-Communist and anti-Peronist convictions) as Rector of the University of Buenos Aires and of Dr. Carlos Gelly y Obes (a museum director) as Secretary of Education.

The first serious student manifestations, which began in Córdoba on August 18, resulted in the wounding of a student by the police, a boycott which closed the university for forty days, a hunger strike involving sixty-eight students, and renewed street demonstrations during which a *cordobés* student was fatally wounded by police gunfire. In Buenos Aires, three faculties were inoperative for lack of professors and deans until early October. A complete shutdown of the universities was averted, however, and by October the authorities strove painfully to restore a semblance of normalcy to academic operations, despite the temporary–and possibly permanent–damage inflicted on one of Latin America's largest (70,000 students) and most promising universities.

Indignation flamed, not only in the academic community but also throughout many other sectors, including numerous elements in the Armed Forces. Even President Onganía was reported to be irritated with the handling of the intervention. At the same time, it should be noted that this reaction–except for those directly affected–was milder than might be imagined in the United States, where a network television program, press accounts of police brutality, and the *cause célèbre* of an American visiting professor being among those beaten up on July 29 combined to give a somewhat exaggerated impression of the extent of the violence. There were also important differences among those objecting.

Except for the "McCarthyite" element among those with *colorado* and pre-Conciliar Catholic inclinations, there was a generalized abhorrence of the police action (the beating of fifty students and professors and the arrest of 150).

Concerning the far more important question of *why* the government intervened in the universities, reasonable men inside and outside both the university and the government can and do differ. If the lifting of autonomy (a temporary measure, the government claimed) was merely a means to an end–i.e., that of reorganizing the cumbersome university bureaucracy and terminating the tripartite system, or *tercio*[7] then a considerable number of professors, including many of the "modernizers," agreed with that end, while insisting on the immediate restoration of autonomy. (An important sector of professors and students, to be sure, disagree with the end itself, and hold that tripartite government has been, on the whole, beneficial.)

There is little doubt, however, that another, and perhaps stronger, motivation for the attack on the universities is the conviction that they are hotbeds of subversion. (It is only realistic to point out that this conviction is held in Argentina not only by traditionalist conservatives, pre-Conciliar Catholics, *Colorados* in the military, and the like, but that it is also found within relatively "progressive" circles: both wings of the Radical Party, the "developmentalist" military and industrialists, and much of the Peronist movement. This conviction has been buttressed by increasing political activism by students, and by the prominence of a number of Trotskyites and independent Marxists in several faculties.) Many of the "modernizing" professors, whether or not "leftist" in their own political convictions, base their concern for the future not on the act of intervention as such, but on their fear that reorganization will be used as a cover for the arbitrary

[7] This system, in effect since 1958, provides that each Faculty is governed by a Directive Council consisting of the Dean and sixteen members, of whom eight are elected by professors, and four each by graduates and students. In practice, the graduate or alumni representatives have tended to vote with the students, thus assuring the control–or at least veto power–by the student-dominated coalition of a body which among other things, hires the professors and sets curriculum policy. At the all-university level, a Superior Council is composed of the Rector, the deans, and five representatives each of the professors, graduates, and students.

elimination of nonconformist, progressive, and radical faculty members—that is, if left in the hands of such figures as Interior Minister Martínez Paz, Rector Luís Botet of the University of Buenos Aires, Intelligence Director Señorans, and Rector Ernest Gavier of the University of Córdoba (whose remark, after the wounding of a student was: "We lament the present victim . . . and also those to come"). A spokesman for a group of professors of the natural sciences believes that the military, even its "developmentalists," mistrust the work being done in basic science in the universities (some of which has gained world renown), hold that basic research is a luxury that Argentina cannot afford, and want to see the country's efforts in science and technology monopolized by the Armed Forces institutes.

In summary: although the Argentine university intervention was by no means the simple, black-and-white affair generally portrayed in the United States, the combination of aggressive means and questionable ends was sufficient to displease nearly everyone and risked alienating intellectuals and the youth from the new regime. A complete catastrophe was avoided, but months later the future of the universities is still in doubt,[8] many able professors have been temporarily or permanently lost, and student resentment smolders. The progressive and "revolutionary" elements within the June movement were dismayed that a problem of low priority on the revolutionary agenda both received first attention and was badly bungled, distracting energies and talents from the more important tasks and creating the image of a regime given to harsh reaction rather than to modernization and development.

Just as the university crisis developed, revolutionary zealots in the federal police and municipal administration of Buenos Aires undertook activities which, although relatively

[8] An eleven-man University Advisory Council was appointed on September 7, 1966, to draft a new university statute and report back in November. The composition of the Council was for the most part elderly and conservative. It was expected that a new statute embodying the Council's recommendations would be decreed during the summer vacations (December-February).

trivial and short-lived, helped to compound the image of a Draconian, illiberal and puritanical regime. Retired Navy Captain Enrique Green, a brother-in-law of Onganía's and an official of the Buenos Aires municipal government, after lecturing the city over television on the perils of "atheist liberalism" and the connection between pornography and subversion, launched a "moralizing" campaign directed against such phenomena as miniskirts, the sale of *Playboy* and similar magazines, kissing in public parks, and dimly lit cabarets. Meanwhile, the Minister of the Interior had ordered the closure of *Tia Vicente,* a perennially hilarious satirical weekly, which had mercilessly spoofed each successive government for nine years, but which finally tripped up by depicting the heavily mustached Onganía as a walrus. The disappearance of *Tia Vicente* (there has been no further overt infringement of freedom of the press) did not inhibit the oral circulation of a myriad wry *porteño* jests: e.g., "This is the government that turned the lights up in the bars and off in the university," or "Why is Onganía like a tube?" Answer: "Hard on the outside, empty on the inside."

Green's moralizing was soon curbed by his superiors; the creator of *Tia Vicente* now puts out a milder version called *María Belém,* and the specter of an Argentina run by censors and commissars of morality has all but subsided. Despite their lack of fundamental importance, these episodes provided tempting materials for journalists—partly because there was so little to go on regarding the eventual thrust of government action.

Of the four concrete problems most often mentioned in the pre-*golpe* rumblings—the railroads, the sugar economy of Tucumán province, an understanding with labor, and the universities—only the last had been confronted by mid-October, assaulted like an enemy battery but with inauspicious results. As for the railroad problem, for which a plethora of analyses and proposed solutions have existed for years, there is no sign that the government has yet found some magic new solution, nor that it is yet prepared to carry out those already drafted (which in order to eliminate an annual deficit of $450,000,000 would probably have to close 20,000 kilometers of track, separate 40,000 to 50,000 employees, and, above all, change the work rules). In Tucumán, where the government's plan is to replace dependence on the uneconomic sugar monoculture, nothing is yet definite about a diversification program, whereas preliminary actions–cutting the sugar quota, the expropriation of a few inefficient mills, and resistance to cutters' demands for wage increases–have succeeded in displeasing all sectors. In the labor field, the initial attitude of "watchful waiting" by both unions and government appears ever more strained, though a major confrontation has thus far been avoided. In addition to the compulsory arbitration decree (which received a negative but guarded reaction), the imposition of new work rules to rationalize cargo-handling at the costly and inefficient port of Buenos Aires (leading to a strike by the 15,000-man Longshoreman's Union, which was only partially effective), and the drive to "normalize" the badly divided C.G.T. (which met with the overt approval of the warring factions, each of which hoped to profit by the proposed redistribution of power within that body), other government actions affecting the total labor movement in a more general way caused great uneasiness. These were the drive to hold down wage increases (in the face of continually rising prices), the threat of unemployment implicit in the railroad and Tucumán rationalization schemes, and, curiously, the signs pointing to a consolidation and modernization of the social security system. Probably the main reason for the absence of a stronger and more coherent labor reaction was the preoccupation of the unions with their own internal jockeying–i.e., the Peronist unions versus the "independents," and within the Peronist group, the "loyal" Alonso bloc versus the "rebel" Vandor faction. Another reason was the ill-defined attitude of Juan Perón to the new regime, as reflected in the typically ambiguous and contradictory directives sent from Madrid, some of which apparently approved the June movement, while others were totally disparaging.

As of late October, most of the concrete steps to implement economic policy and to provide some kind of substitute structure for providing political "input" for the new regime had not yet materialized, but broad trends were apparent. The presence in the government of Alvaro Alsogaray, a long-time champion of an almost laissez-faire free enterprise, as Ambassador to the United States was variously interpreted either as a strong neo-liberal influence or as a mere "token" in recognition of the important services rendered the June movement by his brother, General Julio Alsogaray, the Commander of the I Corps. Other signs, however, pointed to the implementation of an orthodox stabilization-type economic policy: these were the devaluation of the peso, a strong push to export, the freeing of the exchange market, and a relatively "monetarist" approach to inflationary pressures, such as an emphasis on reduction of the budget deficit and holding down currency emission. Despite the presence of nationalists in the government, it appeared that such concrete steps to encourage foreign investment as the reopening of negotiations with foreign oil companies were materializing. In a number of ways, the economic approach resembled the program of the Brazilian *dictablanda* authored by Roberto Campos.

In the political sphere, the scene was murkier, but it appeared that the regime was stoutly resisting internal and foreign pressures to define itself in terms of eventual elections and the restoration of liberal representative institutions. The Minister of the Interior and others, including his newly appointed Secretary and Undersecretary of Government, frequently reiterated the theme of "basic organizations of the community" as the foundation for the new politics. A confidential plan, known by the code name of "TRANSPASS" and said to involve the creation of a Council of the Community linking some 60,000 local groups–unions, professional associations, co-operatives, neighborhood groups, and the like–was being discussed within the administration. As the astute political commentator Mariano Grondona, a disciple of José Ortega y Gasset and a former Undersecretary of the Interior (1962–63), pointed out: any such communitarian scheme would ignore two of the three classic functions of the governed–to oppose and to control their governors–while admitting only the third function of "participation" in a limited sense. Details are lacking as to how these cell-like structures would function–whether they would vote, serve as units for a possible plebiscite, or be the basis for regional assemblies. If such a restructuring materializes, the possibility of an evolution in the direction of either a Spanish-type Falange or a Mexican-type one-party system is obvious. Just as obvious are the enormous contrasts between Argentina's level of social development and that of Spain in 1936, or Mexico in 1916, and the tremendous price paid for revolutionary *mystique* in the other two countries in terms of lives and destruction, a price unthinkable in Argentina. The reiterated emphasis on a communitarian approach to political reorganization is easily one of the most enigmatic features of the Onganía regime.

The Problem of Support

The Argentine presidents who followed Perón did not possess charisma: the one who came closest was Frondizi, whose brilliance and verve created more of an intellectual admiration among various elites than an emotional bond with a mass followership. Onganía perhaps possesses something akin to charisma insofar as his extraordinary qualities have aroused deference, awe, and even "myth" within a limited circle, but this has not been converted into a direct link with the masses. With the inevitable evaporation of the initial and generalized "consent" which greeted the June movement–and in the absence of political parties or of new links (of information, direction, and support) between the governors and the governed–the giving or denial of support to the regime depends to a great extent on the behavior of traditional power groups, known in Argentina as *los factores de poder*–i.e., the Armed Forces, organized labor, the Catholic "establishment," and the business-industrial elites.[9] Each of the most important groups is deeply divided in late 1966, and an analysis of each *factor* is beyond the scope of this Report. But as of the end of October, it was possible to detect the emergence of two main clusters of tendencies, ideas, and men, not yet fully articulated but obviously diverging on the nature of the "Revolu-

[9] For an impressive pioneer study of Argentina's various elites, see José Luis de Imaz, *Los Que Mandan* (Buenos Aires: Editorial Eudeba, 1964).

tion" (the familiar division following a *golpe* supported by heterogeneous elements united only on the proposition that the previous regime must go).

The first is a broad and uneasy coalition of the *frondizistas* (a scattered but influential collection of newer industrialists, young intellectuals and journalists), the "independent" Peronist labor sector headed by Augusto Vandor, a number of "developmentalist" and pro-Frondizi Army officers, and a part of the "modern right" or neo-liberal business community (such as those represented by Julio Cueta Rua and Alvaro Alsogaray). These groups supported the June movement, but they appear extremely unhappy over Onganía's leadership, the signs of corporativism, and the possibility of a lengthy "political intermission." Binding them together, however tenuously, seem to be twin desires to push the regime more toward "pure economic development," with less pretensions about revamping basic institutions, and to speed up the timetable for calling elections and returning to political normalcy, possibly in two years.

The other cluster is even less homogeneous and clearly defined, but brings together elements convinced that the *golpe* can and should become a true "Revolution," with radical institutional transformations over a period of long duration. Within it are found nationalistic officers such as General López Aufranc, representatives of both the traditionalist and post-Conciliar sectors of Catholic activists (obviously for different reasons), a group of technicians and intellectuals associated with "Plan PASS" (Argentine Program of Social Security, an impressive research project which has been under way for the past six years, assisted by I.B.M. computers and Ford Foundation financing), and, at least temporarily, the Alonso faction of the Peronists. Although spokesmen for these sectors indicate a great diversity in motivation and emphasis, they appear inclined to accept Onganía's leadership, though several of them insist on the necessity of giving real social content to the "Revolution" and of providing for political expression, possibly through plebiscites, as soon as possible.

As was noted earlier, a number of conservative Catholics are serving Onganía, but both their prestige and their enthusiasm appear to be diminishing. On the other hand, voices of progressive, post-Conciliar Catholicism (for example, those of Bishop Podestá of Avellaneda, Bishop Devoto of Goya, and the review *Criterio*) have warned against identification of the Church with the new regime—or any regime—insisting that what is important is not that a government be "Catholic," but that it be just. (Bishop Podestá even remarked to friends that as so many of the "righteous" had been appointed to government, it might not be a bad idea to appoint a few "sinners.") No member of the hierarchy defended the government's intervention of the universities, whereas a number of prominent clergy protested the action; nor did the Bishops support the "moralizing" campaign of Captain Green. Withal, the sympathy of reformist Catholics appears to lie more with the group pushing full-fledged revolution—skeptical as they may be with regard to present performance—than with the Frondizi-Vandor cluster (partly out of mistrust of Frondizi's rather naked economic determinism, and partly out of older misgivings over the record of liberalism in Argentina). But these Catholics, who justified their acceptance of illegal institutional changes on the grounds of a "higher good," might withdraw their sympathies should the new regime prove immobile or regressive in its broad social policies.

The alignment of Peronist groups in the present constellation is highly tentative, tactical, and probably transitory. The struggle for control of the C.G.T. and for the rights of political "succession" within the Peronist movement occupies the energies of the local leaders who, paradoxically, also breathed a figurative sigh of relief at not having to face an electoral encounter in March. A military regime in itself does not scandalize the Peronist movement, which was born under one. But given the signs that the regime's economic orientation is toward orthodox neo-liberal austerity and stabilization measures, it will be little short of a miracle if the bulk of Peronist forces are not in vigorous opposition within months.

Within the politically significant sectors of the Armed Forces—mainly Army officers of field grade and higher—the picture is just as cloudy. Onganía's popularity appears to have fallen rapidly. Some of the older internal cleavages seem to have healed during the period of Onganía's tenure as

Commander-in-Chief, but there are still important differences, especially between the more nationalistic officers and those favoring more "liberal" and internationalist economic positions. Despite disenchantment with Onganía, he seems virtually irreplaceable, for no other officer combines personal and institutional authority sufficient to challenge him—at least at present. This fact, plus a widespread conviction among middle- and senior-grade officers that the "Revolution" is irreversible and that the Army must remain united at all costs, would seem to extend Onganía's credit, despite his pale showing to date.

Furthermore, the end of the year is approaching. December, January, and February—hot and humid for most Argentines not lucky enough to join the hundreds of thousands at the seashore—are traditionally "dead" months politically. The Onganía experiment is virtually assured of survival until March, but what will happen afterwards? A gradual slippage back toward the previous state of affairs seems much less likely than in the Brazilian situation following April 1964. There are those who merely ask whether a Colonel Nasser or a Sergeant Batista will appear in the next act, and others who maintain that Onganía's measured pace and grim obstinacy presage a burst of innovation and creative solutions.

For the North American observer, often committed to what Louis Hartz has called the "fixed, dogmatic liberalism of a liberal way of life," the Argentine panorama is clouded, and it is difficult for him to escape the traditional liberal exasperation over the reverses of democracy abroad, or to admit that there may be various roads to political development. Among twenty-three million Argentines, there are still progressive, humane reformists who hold out hope for a positive result from the June movement—despite the dangers arising from political naïveté, obsessive military style, and the potential threat (as occurred in Brazil during 1965–66) that a failure to produce a national "grand design" could permit the rise of a pathological anticommunism as an outlet for "Revolutionary" energies. Certainly the political question mark is the largest in a decade.

BRAZIL

In 1964 the Brazilian political system seemed to reach a turning point with the overthrow of President João Goulart. The military, largely instrumental in the overthrow, announced that it had saved Brazil from leftism and sheer demagoguery, and that its intention hence was to stay in politics until it could reconstruct the Brazilian political and economic system. The 1964 overthrow brought to the surface a number of controversial questions. Was the Brazilian political scene before 1964 actually that defective or did it also contain constructive forces? Was President Goulart by 1964 leading Brazil into a Communist system? Was the military intervention of that year unusual or predictable from increasing military involvement? Was the military justified in calling its 1964 action a real revolution instead of a regular coup? And finally, have the strong political repressions since 1964 by the military and Presidents Branco and Costa e Silva been necessary to "cleanse" the system and to allow a free hand in new types of economic programs? The selections that follow will attempt to shed light on these questions.

In the first selection James W. Rowe argues that Brazil up to 1964 has been controlled by a "System." His "System" incorporates elite groups, relationships among various parties, and certain styles of governing. What is so interesting about this "System" is its pervasiveness through periods as different as those of the Vargas dictatorship and the post 1945 liberal democracy. Mr. Rowe perceptively describes how the "System" governed, and although he mentions some accomplishments, he tends to be critical of what it has done to Brazilian political life as a whole.

In the second selection John J. Johnson describes the

relationship of the military to politics from the Vargas period through the postwar governments. The selection was written before the 1964 military intervention, but it is worth noting that even with that not in mind, Professor Johnson saw an increasing trend for the military to intervene. The types of interventions and the diverse reasons for them are carefully explained. He then discusses the attitude of the military toward regionalism and also the changing military relationship to the large landholders, industrialists, and emerging urbanized workers. Finally, he explains why the military has become the repository of Brazilian nationalism.

In the third selection James W. Rowe evaluates the 1964 overthrow of President Goulart. He describes the overthrow and carries on an analytical discussion of whether it can be called a true revolution. Mr. Rowe then attempts to describe the true nature of the controversial Goulart government that led to its downfall. The writing is objective since the author brings up all of the controversial viewpoints about the 1964 overthrow and the nature of the Goulart government and then justifies his own explanation.

THE BRAZILIAN POLITICAL SYSTEM

*The "Revolution" and the "System"**

JAMES W. ROWE

Part I: The Seeds of the "System"

The term *"o sistema"* has been popularized by the scholarly journalist Oliveiros Ferreira of *O Estado de São Paulo,* but the general notion is used in one form or another by various intellectuals and politicians. It is not to be confused with the concepts of general systems analysis as used in the

* Reprinted from James W. Rowe, "The 'Revolution' and the 'System', Part I: Seeds of the 'System'," pp. 7–14, and, "The 'Revolution' and the 'System', Part II: The 'System'—Full Flower and Crisis," *American Universities Field Staff Reports* (July, 1966) by permission of American Universities Field Staff, Inc.

behavioral sciences, but simply denotes the several elites which have dominated Brazilian political machinery during several successive governments and their pattern of joint action to maintain control and preserve "social peace" through heavy reliance on conciliation and paternalism. More specifically, the "System" refers to the institutionalization of a delicate balance of power between these elites during the Getúlio Vargas regime of the 1930's, which remained more or less intact until the 1960's. In the narrowest sense, the "System" refers simply to the political alliance between the Social Democratic Party (P.S.D.) and the Brazilian Labor Party (P.T.B.) which controlled the national government most of the time from 1950 to 1964. (If not for the curse of increasing jargon, it might be useful to refer to the "Greater System" and the "Lesser System." The former would include a wide range of attitudes, devices, stratagems, concessions, and alliances extending well back into the last century which have permitted Brazil to plant substantial features of a modern Western nation–liberal constitutions, great cities, and an impressive industrial plant–onto a society that is still markedly non-competitive, paternalistic, and semi-authoritarian. The latter would be limited to the ingenious coalition devised by Vargas to maintain a balance among labor bureaucracy, agrarian, commercial, and industrial interests through the ubiquitous arbitration of a "Provident State.")

The introduction of the "System" concept may be compared with the young Woodrow Wilson's insistence on a distinction between the "literary theory" of the Constitution and the informal pattern of "Congressional government" prevailing in the United States of the 1880's. In short, the term "System" helps to describe the informal power structure of Brazilian politics–confederal and elitist, as distinct from the liberal, republican, and federal formalism of the Constitution –through which professional politicians, bureaucrats, and their respective clienteles pursue their own ends more or less independent of presidential programs and policies.

The present is always fathered by the past, but the remarkable absence of major social upheaval during 400 years makes the thread of Brazilian history somewhat more continuous than that of many countries. The "System" as developed over the past thirty years is related to several historic factors in Brazilian development which deserve mention.

(1) Brazil, lacking a revolutionary tradition, also lacks a tradition of genuine liberalism. (The word "liberalism" is used here in the classical Lockian sense and not that of contemporary American usage, i.e., full of reformist connotations.) The contract theory, essential to liberal thought, was alien to colonial Brazil, where the state actually existed before a well-articulated civil society. The frequent weakness of Brazilian government must be laid to causes other than the liberal suspicion of the state characteristic of Jeffersonian America. And even when governmental machinery was weak, the state continued a long "interventionist" tradition in economic matters, uninhibited by laissez-faire dogma. The characteristic tendency of private interests in Brazil has not been to resist the state but to seek its favors. Thus, though Brazil's has been primarily a private-enterprise economy, capitalism there has developed in a different mold from its North American counterpart. Long marked by lingering features of mercantilism, in recent times it has managed to accommodate a great deal of intervention and mixed enterprise without many ideological traumas. A substantial portion of twentieth-century industrial entrepreneurship was recruited from the agricultural sector, bringing with it, some claim, the "rural ethos" derived from large-scale monoculture enterprises—a peculiar kind of rural capitalism which had long coexisted with slavery, neofeudalism, and paternalism.

Of course, formal liberalism of a sort has a history in Brazil. Under the Empire (1822–1889) Brazil developed a constitutional monarchy which superficially resembled the British parliamentary system, with ministerial responsibility and two parties—labeled Conservatives and Liberals—contending and alternating in office. But the real power and decision-making lay elsewhere, in the hands of the rural *fazendeiros* and the Emperor Dom Pedro II. Later, formal liberalism was conspicuously present in the thought of some of the founding fathers of the Republic, and in the Constitution of 1891, which was modeled after that of the United States. It had an important and puzzling place in the events of 1945–46 which brought the downfall of Vargas' Estado Novo (New

State), the ostensible return to "democracy," and another United States-modeled Constitution. But even on the formal level, for many Brazilians the liberal order appeared as an imported article extremely difficult to reconcile with the conditions and the heritage of the country. An apocryphal account recalls the agony of a nineteenth-century liberal *bacharel* ("bachelor," a degree-holder, usually in law): "Trying to live out his thesis that Brazil was really an outpost of Western civilization, he not only suffered frock coat and beaver hat in Rio's 100-degree heat, but mouthed the doctrines of 'liberty, equality, fraternity' at the same time he was a slave-owner." Labels could hardly obscure the thinness of the differences separating Liberal and Conservative parliamentarians of that period, just as they have hardly obscured them in recent years. The historian José Honório Rodrigues, in a comment directed to that earlier time, could almost have been describing any period when he characterized most legislators as, "Hard-boiled conservatives and indignant liberals—all of them Ciceronian, rarely dictatorial, but never libertarian."[1]

(2) Without real revolutionary or liberal traditions, organized Brazilian society has long remained essentially conservative in temper. Its conservatism, however, has differed markedly from the self-conscious conservatism with roots in Burke or the French Reaction, since that of Brazil displays little substantive content or reactionary quality (there being so little to react against). The scarcity of ideology, the absence of commitment to principle, and the relatively unimportant role of ideas in Brazil's historical turning points have frequently been noted by Brazilian analysts, along with the premium placed on practicality, empiricism, and talent for improvisation. The distinguishing feature of Brazil's "natural conservatism" is the degree to which it enshrines the notion of *conciliation* as a substantive goal, "not merely a means, but an end in itself."[2] Well-known Brazilian and foreign writers have expounded on the Brazilian's penchant for accommodation, tolerance, compromise, and the maintenance of

[1] *Conciliação e Reforma no Brasil: Um Desafio Histórico-Político* (Rio: Ed. Civilizaçao Brasileira, 1965), p. 124.
[2] *Ibid.*, p. 238.

"social peace." A lesser current of bloody violence and cruel repression is also found in the country's history, but the prevalence of "conciliation" is indeed characteristic of the mainstream. Brazilians have praised conciliation, often lyrically, but in recent years critical voices have been raised. Is conciliation compatible with reform? Brazil's positivists of the late nineteenth century, supplementing "natural conservatism" with the ideas of Comte and Spencer, believed in a "conservative conscience" informed by "conciliation and evolution." The new critics are asking whether "conciliation" has not smothered "evolution":

> The politics of conciliation and transaction has as its principal objective the smoothing out of divergences between dominant groups rather than conceding benefits to the people. The oligarchic domination of small minorities and their protégées, along with favoritism, cronyism, and patronage has prevented social transformation or structural reform. To this must be added the personalization, omission, or disinterest of political representatives with regard to the solution of problems, their impermeability to ideas, their mechanical imitation, first of Europe, then of America, and the inauthenticity and untrustworthiness of representation.[3]

(3) Public conciliation in Brazil is often attributed to an extraordinary blandness of social relations, and in turn to the fusion of races and cultures worked out in a tropical plantation society. Gilberto Freyre depicted the *fazenda's* amalgam of love, sex, and mutual indulgence transcending barriers of class and race in his classic *The Masters and the Slaves*[4] in a favorable although not uncritical light. Frank Bonilla's comment is as relevant today as it was when made in 1961:

> Whether or not Freyre's thesis is a faithful depiction of Brazilian slave society, few persons who know Brazil today will deny that the forms of domination elaborated by the

[3] *Ibid.*, p. 103.

[4] *The Masters and the Slaves: A Study in the Development of Brazilian Civilization.* Translated by Samuel Putnam (2nd ed.; New York: Alfred A. Knopf, 1963).

> groups who have traditionally held power here and in large part continue to do so have been singularly effective in mitigating and controlling violent social conflict. . . . In no other country in Latin America do such staggering inequalities (material, social, political, racial, and regional) seem so little productive of individual tensions and resentments or of intransigent, regimented, collective strife. This cannot be explained simply as mass apathy or fatalism, or as the incapacity of the exploited to mobilize themselves for the defense of group interests. All these are factors in the avoidance up to the present of more violent internal conflict, but the nation is not inert politically. . . . There is nevertheless an almost exasperating blandness underlying the public façade of combativity affected by politicians and a bewildering lack of rational connections among apparent interests, organized political groups, and points of view espoused. The disposition to yield among groups at the top, though not extravagant, seems often more than apparent pressures from below would reasonably demand, just as the disposition to accept small concessions among lower groups seems often out of line with the urgency of their need or their apparent power at a given moment. In short, there is an element of civility, a capacity and a disposition to work out dispute peaceably in Brazilian political life that one would hardly expect to find in conjunction with such harsh inequities, the generally low cultural level, the sad record of corrupt and irresponsible government, and the vulnerability and rudimentary organization of political institutions.[5]

One is tempted to suggest, after the tempestuous episodes of 1961–64, that there may exist a widespread if tacit acknowledgement among Brazilians of an awesome conflict potential in this country, given its size, distances, the "staggering inequalities" mentioned above, and the less publicized episodes of enormous cruelty and bloodletting in the past. Seemingly shared by middle and lower groups as well as the more privileged, and recently reinforced by the specter (whether myth or reality) of communism, such an awareness may well

[5] See Frank Bonilla, *Rural Reform in Brazil* (FB-2-'61), American Universities Field Staff Reports, East Coast South America Series, Volume VIII, No. 4, October 1961.

strengthen the doctrine of conciliation, at least temporarily, in an age which otherwise might be expected to erode it.

(4) Slavery and monarchy disappeared in the 1880's; but the demise of each and the advent of the Republic were accomplished in typically conciliatory fashion, without real mobilization of social forces, and the essential features of an old-fashioned, agrarian, patriarchal, and conservative Brazil remained. The introduction of the federal principle enhanced the power of local rural oligarchies, fragmenting the modicum of central direction that had existed under the Empire among the twenty states of the Old Republic. With twenty state party machines dispersing political currents irremediably, the result was the "Governors' Politics" which—in the absence of any possibility of alternating power according to national divisions based on program or principle—substituted a simple rotation of the presidency and its patronage among the more important states.

Another important feature of Brazil's informal, unwritten political code has its origins in the Old Republic—i.e., the extralegal assumption by the armed forces of the "moderating power" formerly the constitutional perquisite of the Emperor. Mainly through his powers to dissolve parliament and replace ministers at his own discretion, the Emperor implemented the constitutional charge that he "incessantly watch over the maintenance of the independence, equilibrium, and harmony of the rest of the political powers."[6] Since the bloodless *coup* which toppled the monarchy in 1889, the military have arbitrated every major political crisis to date, intervening frequently since 1930. Withal, neither the spirit of the military, in which the army is dominant, nor the character of its interventions has been reactionary—or revolutionary. Middle class in outlook, with a keen eye to legalism and public opinion, imbued with the doctrine of prime loyalty to the Constitution and the nation rather than to the government of the moment, the military (until 1964) have withdrawn from actual political participation immediately after intervention. The net effect of military intromission has been enforcement of the rules of the game, restoration of equilibrium, and reinforcement of the politics of conciliation.

[6] Constitution of 1824, Article 98.

Two archetypes, the *coronel* and the *bacharel* (the rural boss and the city lawyer), did much to set the tone of the Old Republic (1891–1930) and to transmit the culture of "archaic" ninteenth-century Brazil with only minor mutations into an outwardly bourgeois, urbanizing nation on the eve of industrialization.

Coronelismo was a kind of latter-day adaptation of feudalism to the conditions of republican Brazil. The setting was the vast spatial extension of the rural *municípios,* where even the minimal or "police" functions of government were difficult to provide, and into which had been introduced male suffrage (theoretically for literates only) without a secret ballot. The basic features were a code of mutual rights and responsibilities and a three-way understanding between the state government, the local chief (usually a large planter whose designation as "colonel" was inherited from the days of the National Guard), and the ordinary people in his domain. This untitled baron offered minimal protection and favors to his extended family, their respective tenants and croppers, and a variety of others in exchange for their votes, delivered in turn to the state party machine. In return, he had a free hand in his district, with patronage rights over state functionaries posted there and the possibility of locking economic, police, and judicial power into a single structure.

The role of the *bacharel* was more diffuse, and *bachelerismo* is not so easily defined as *coronelismo.* Two legacies for present-day Brazil seem important. First, the lawyers provided the bulk of the middle and upper bureaucracy. They continued and expanded the tradition of inflated administration inherited from the Portuguese, skirting the problem of an unemployed intelligentsia through the multiplication of offices, procedures, documents, and the stamping and notarizing characteristic of what has been called the "Cartorial State." With its numbers and prestige far in excess of what was socially necessary or even useful, this important segment of the urban middle class developed an outlook which, while different from that of the rural society, had little in common with the classical bourgeois ethos with its esteem for work, prudence, and thrift, and its hostility toward ostentation and luxury. Secondly, to the lawyers, deputies, and other professionals in the cities fell the burden of reconciling Brazilian reality with the ideas and ideals of modern Western culture. No longer embarrassed by slaves and a monarch, the *bachar-eis*—eloquent, cosmopolitan, imbued with French humanism—nonetheless faced a formidable task. Although they left accomplishments in the legal and literary fields, *bacharelismo* contributed importantly to the exaggerated formalism of middle-class thought in Brazil, which in less elegant terms may be called a "myth-system" conducive to a good deal of self-deception about both society and policy in this land of paradox and contrasts.

Part II: The "System"—Full Flower and Crisis

The basic features of the "System" were largely consolidated during the fifteen-year personalist regime of Getúlio Vargas (1930–1945), especially its latter phase, known as the Estado Novo. These features were readjusted and refined, but to a surprising degree they were retained following the "Democratic Revolution" of 1945 and during the subsequent administrations of Marshal Gaspar Dutra, Vargas (returned to power constitutionally in 1950), Juscelino Kubitschek, Jânio Quadros, and João Goulart. Descriptive accounts of the Vargas and subsequent administrations may be found elsewhere. Our concern here is limited to those events and trends essential to a depiction of the "System."

Techniques

Two well-worn techniques, adroitly used by Getúlio Vargas and his successors, help to explain the avoidance of class conflict in Brazil; techniques permitting limited readjustment of power balances and enabling "conciliatory conservatism" to weather severe buffetings by the winds of doctrine for thirty years—by those of communism and fascism in the 1930's, by neo-liberalism in the 1940's, and by nationalism, "developmentalism," and several variants of Marxism in the 1950's. These may be termed "anticipation" and "co-optation." Employing the first of these, the holder of power anticipates the demands of the presumed adversary and reacts with concessions–generally limited and formalistic–before the issue is forced. A well-known slogan attributed to Deputy Antônio Carlos in 1930 was, "Let us make the revolution before the people make it." As several students have pointed out, various innovations in the Brazilian social order have become legal realities before any social struggle forced them, and also before conditions existed for their practical application: labor legislation in advance of much experience with industrial life; a substantial Communist Party prior to a proletariat; and trade unions (if they can be called that) created from the top by government decree before a large, self-conscious work force demanded them.

When "co-optation" is practiced, a present or potential adversary is invited to join or collaborate with the dominant element. The personal charm of the leader or the overriding argument of "social peace" may be utilized to bring in those whose economic, geographic, or doctrinal ties should seemingly identify them with the opposition. Under the Vargas system, co-optation was practiced on the institutional as well as the personal level, notably after the formation of political parties in 1945. Each of the three large parties–the Partido Social Democrático (P.S.D.), the União Democrática Nacional (U.D.N.), and the Partido Trabalhista Brasileiro (P.T.B.) –contained contradictory elements or, as someone has put it, "each is conservative, liberal, laborite, capitalist, socialist and traditionalist." And insofar as the parties did display modest differences of emphasis in clientele or ideas, the long-standing coalition of the P.S.D. and the P.T.B., which Lacerda once called the "alliance between the traders and the ragged," produced still another union of apparent adversaries.

The Revolution of 1930

The Vargas Revolution of 1930 was a watershed between "Old Brazil" and the contemporary nation. Almost everyone agrees that its underlying causes lay in the widespread discontent of younger, urban elements with the social and political stagnation associated with the agrarian-dominated "Governors' Politics" under the hegemony of Minas Gerais and the São Paulo coffee squirearchy; and that its proximate causes were the weakening of the Washington Luis regime by the world market crisis and fall in coffee prices, coupled with São Paulo's violation of the "rules of the game" in attempting to impose a second *paulista* President in a row. There seemed to be progressive overtones in the *coup* which installed Vargas; for although he was backed by a new regional coalition (Minas Gerais and his native Rio Grande do Sul) and the *coup* was staged by the senior military who feared civil war, there were also reformist elements in his entourage, including the movement of nonconformist junior officers (the *tenentes,* who had twice raised protest revolts against the "old order" during the 1920's) which were vaguely reformist-liberal in their orientation.

But the astute and enigmatic Vargas did not choose the path of reform liberalism, although during the interim years, before his own *coup* of 1937 established the Estado Novo, such liberal trappings as the secret ballot, suffrage for women, and proportional representation were introduced. Even the Estado Novo, by re-establishing the unitary state, ended the regressive federalism of the Republic (obviously by nonliberal means). Vargas, himself a uniquely Brazilian product, produced the uniquely Brazilian "System," which, even when stripped of the exotic and nakedly corporativist features of the "New State," was never liberal. Remarkably durable, it may have been the greatest single obstacle in this century to genuine social change and political development.

As an individual, Vargas belied the stereotype of the South American "dictator"—he was personally honest, neither loquacious nor ostentatious, no military man and no fascist, highly conventional and middle-class in his personal life; and shrewd, skeptical, and slippery in his dealings with others. If his motives were complex, it is nonetheless clear that his drive for power was based on neither an ideological mystique nor the vision of a great modernized nation, but rather on an inclination to run the country like a huge *fazenda,* improving and centralizing its management. The heterogeneous forces which had put him in power had no common program beyond the deposition of Washington Luis, and the reformist *tenentes* among them either soon deserted the movement or settled down comfortably to promote each other.

Vargas' master stroke during the 1930's was in accommodating nascent industrial interests without a major struggle with agriculture, and at the same time accommodating the new urban labor force without a confrontation with industry. Other urban elements who had rebelled against superficial aspects of the old rural-patriarchal dominance were pacified by an increase in the already swollen middle-class bureaucracy concomitant with new welfare and social-assistance programs. These accommodations, accomplished without political parties or the free social process involving autonomous interest groups, depended on the state's role, not as a mere arbiter, but as an active participant in the affairs of each class. Paternalism was ingeniously transplanted from the countryside to urban, middle-class, and industrial activities.

Various measures were used in forging these accommodations. A rupture with agriculture was avoided in part through Vargas' continuation—although in a more imaginative manner—of the old policy of "valorization" of coffee, i.e., government stockpiling in years of excess supply to maintain price level. After the 1929 depression, industrialization based on import substitution expanded considerably. Industry flourished under the umbrella of government protectionism through favorable tariff and exchange policies, and later through direct government investment. The swelling ranks of urban labor were presented with a ready-made union organization, copied from Italian legislation of 1926, which was created and controlled by the Ministry of Labor. Organizationally weak but financially powerful by virtue of a mandatory union tax levied on all workers, the unions did not serve as collective bargaining agents but as social welfare agencies, brokers in the patron-client relationship established between government and worker. Increasing state intervention in the economy produced autarchies in a wide variety of fields, each with new opportunities for patron-client brokerage.

Things did not always go smoothly in establishing this elaborate balance. Armed revolts were mounted against Vargas by São Paulo separatists in 1932, by the Communists in 1935, and by the neo-fascist Integralists in 1938. These served to justify Vargas' own bloodless *coup* instigating the Estado Novo, under a corporativist constitution providing for "functional representation" and theoretically bringing "class organizations" of employers, employees, and professionals into one great phalanx of parallel *sindicatos.* Although the Estado Novo was fascist-modeled and is still known as the "dictatorship," it is important to recall that its grand design was never very fully implemented and that, while personal and political freedoms suffered, the regime resembled a modern totalitarian dictatorship less than an older kind of "despotism tempered by sloppiness." In one of the most significant "transactions" of the period, the continuing support of agriculture (in the face of that sector's relative decline in income) was gained with the *quid pro quo* of the exemption of rural workers from the new labor legislation, and no attempt to organize them. Still, the symmetry of the "System" was considerable, and, as Oliveiros Ferreira maintains, Brazil entered the fifth decade of the twentieth century with all classes "the prisoners of the state–politically, economically, juridically and administratively."[7]

"Democratic" Revolution

The 1945 "Democratic Revolution" eased Vargas from the Presidency, erased the corporativist constitution, freed political prisoners, called free elections, fathered a new liberal-democratic constitution, revived a modified federalism, and brought forth a welter of political parties. Key features of the "System" remained intact, however. Among the most important was the Consolidation of Labor Laws of 1943 (C.L.T.). It provided not only a code of working conditions similar to that found in industrializing countries (eight-hour day, minimum wage, etc.) and social-security institutes for several categories of workers, but also such distinctive features as the union tax,[8] the concept of employee tenure,[9]

[7] *O Estado de São Paulo* (São Paulo), November 14, 1965.

[8] The *imposto sindical,* a tax equal to one day's wages, discounted at the source once annually and levied on all workers regardless of union affiliation. Twenty per cent is earmarked for the Ministry of Labor, the rest divided among the union hierarchy.

[9] *Estabilidade* as provided in Article 477 of the Consolidation of Labor Laws makes it very difficult–or too expensive–to dis-

a system of labor courts, and the previously mentioned parallel structure of employer and employee organizations—a pyramid rising from *sindicatos* at the local level and state federations to an apex of national confederations, all linked to the Ministry of Labor. (Successive governments based on the "System" have scrupulously avoided creation of a single central confederation.) Strong criticisms of the resultant labor practices have been leveled from disparate quarters—of corruption and abuse of the union tax fund controlled by the Ministry of Labor; of corruption and inefficiency in the social-security institutes; and of the right of the Ministry to approve—and even to make—appointments of union leaders, leading to an aristocracy of *pelagos* (union leaders more dependent on the government than on their own labor following). Even insofar as it brought positive short-run benefits, the system remained limited to a small minority of workers. By 1963, twenty years after the C.L.T., there were only about 1,500,000 organized workers in 1,800 unions, out of a work force of around 25 million. Above all, the exclusive, government-sponsored, brokerage unionism of the C.L.T. stifled opportunities for an independent labor movement to arise in Brazil.

Another novel feature of the "System" was actually institutionalized after the 1945 Revolution. A set of paternalistic social services outside both the government and the unions was established by employers' organizations through the Serviço Social da Industria (S.E.S.I., or Social Service of Industry) and the Serviço Social do Comercio (S.E.S.C., or Social Service of Commerce). Financed by a compulsory employers' contribution of 2 per cent of payroll, these institutions frankly avow the goal of "social peace," and attempt to head off worker discontent which might benefit either the Communist Party or a militant labor movement. Both are decentralized, federative organizations, and their approach to "preventive charity" and the use of funds varies from state to state, but typical activities include medical and dental clinics,

---

charge an employee with ten or more years' service. In practice, many firms automatically fire employees with eight or nine years' service in order to evade this provision.

legal assistance, canteens, discount shops, recreation, and "social orientation."

Perhaps the most paradoxical feature of the post-1945 period was the way in which revived and improved formal structures of representative democracy served not to dismantle the balance achieved by Vargas but, in a sense, to ratify it. One technique, already mentioned, was the creation of two of Brazil's three major parties out of the Vargas forces, with the third being a conglomeration of anti-Vargas elements. The Social Democrats (P.S.D.) coalesced traditional rural oligarchs, state-machine politicians and bureaucrats from the Estado Novo, and a smattering of industrial *nouveaux riches*. The Labor Party (P.T.B.) was based on Labor Ministry and welfare bureaucrats, middle-class trade union *pelagos*, large ranchers from the South, and sugar interests in the Northeast. The National Democratic Union, originally an anti-Vargas "united front" including labor, socialist, and even Communist elements, evolved into a more coherent and conservative body appealing to the urban middle class, professionals, banking interests, moralists, and intellectual liberals, as well as to a part of traditionalist agriculture in the Northeast. Vargas, who appeared to see the P.S.D. as a "high road" attracting conservative interests and the P.T.B. as a "low road" with supposed appeal to urban workers, was personally ambivalent regarding the two—for a time serving simultaneously as P.S.D. Senator from Rio Grande do Sul and Party President of the P.T.B. (1948–1950). In any case, during most of the time between 1945 and 1964 the national administration was headed by the P.S.D. or the P.T.B., and a formal coalition of the two parties existed during a good portion of this period.[10] Social Democrats were preponderant in the cabinet of Vargas' "P.T.B. administration" (1950–54); the Vice President under Social Democratic President Jus-

[10] It is an irresistible temptation to suggest the meager differentiation among the three parties by reference to "conciliatory conservatism," a notion best represented by the P.S.D. The P.S.D. has been the keystone of the "System," the embodiment of "Historic Opportunism" the most successful of the polls. The U.D.N. has been conservative but not always conciliatory enough; the P.T.B. conciliatory but not always sufficiently conservative.

celino Kubitschek (1956–1961) was João Goulart, head of the Labor Party; and in the halls of Congress, with over a dozen party blocs, the prevailing coalition for most of twenty years was that of P.S.D. and P.T.B. Deputies—even though lack of party discipline made voting patterns something else again. This prevalent pattern was broken intermittently by "national union" coalitions of the P.S.D. and U.D.N.–under Dutra in the late Forties, under Cafe Filho in 1954–55, and as a counterweight to Goulart in 1961–63—but the traditional eagerness of Social Democrats to be "with" the government of the moment in the end always outweighed considerations of program or class identification that would seem to make it a more natural ally of the U.D.N. Hence the unique role of the P.S.D., at once a party of the "right" and of the "center," in circumstances which have bestowed on it that unflattering sobriquet, "the Dirty Center."[11]

Finally, "redemocratization" after 1945 added features to the formal liberal-democratic structure which in practice almost guaranteed the viability of an informal substructure in the hands of dominant interest groups. As if the welter of contradictions in the party system were not enough, the electoral laws combined an unusual form of proportional representation with provision for unlimited electoral alliances between parties, features conducive to the extraordinary unaccountability of legislative politics in Brazil. Allowed to pick only one Federal Deputy and one state legislator from a ballot commonly containing several hundred names from the state at large, the voter was already virtually doomed to an irrational choice; the fact that the name appeared on a party list was of little help, since that list might be sponsored by an electoral alliance of up to half a dozen parties, with no indication of the party adherence of the individual candidate. In such a system, each candidate is in a sense campaigning not only against the candidates of other lists, but against those of his own list as well. Once elected, he could switch to still another party bloc in the Chamber. Deputies, operating in

[11] With characteristic wit, a P.S.D. Deputy once remarked on the matter of ideology: "As between *Das Kapital* and Rerum Novarum, we had rather read the *Diário Oficial*–at least it's a government organ."

this system of profound irresponsibility, have been likened by a Brazilian analyst to "four hundred Sputniks, each in individual orbit: neither parties nor voters can control them."

Until 1966, however, the President (and the Governors) were elected by direct majority vote, and the nation, although dominated by the "System" is witness to constantly increased articulation by elements outside the "System" which demand something more than "conciliation" in response to Brazil's enormous problems. Hence the rise of presidential politics quite different from legislative politics, containing a highly personal element and generally demanding of the successful candidate a "reformist" program–whether wise or unwise, sincere or insincere. And hence, too, the seemingly inevitable impasse between an activist President–regardless of party or program–and the "System," flowering in the legislature. As someone put it, the latter's methods are "smiling and patient non-cooperation, crippling amendments, bills without budgets, administrative slowdowns, exhaustion of funds in the distribution of patronage and pork, and the like." A basic problem of any Brazilian president is simply that of gaining effective control of the Federal machinery, even if he has a large electoral mandate and personal charisma. The "System" has built-in methods of keeping the President relatively impotent in spite of the impressive powers vested in him by the Constitution.

Kubitschek and "Developmentalism"

The period of President Juscelino Kubitschek (1956–1961), especially the later years, was characterized by a dynamism, industrial expansion, and economic growth that temporarily obscured reliance on the "System" with all of the latter's impediments to rational modernization or "total development." In a word, this was the "System" at its best. The population–thirty-three million in 1930–had more than doubled to over seventy million by 1960. From the end of World War II to the early 1960's, Brazil registered an impressive rate of economic growth, over 6 per cent annually, or more than 3 per cent per capita. The largest gains were in industry, which increased as much as 12 per cent in some years, and whose contribution to the national product rose from 21 per cent in 1947 to 34 per cent in 1961. Per capita income, estimated at US $260 for 1957, was twice that ($520) in the industrialized states of São Paulo and Guanabara, as contrasted with less than half (around $100) in the Northeastern states. Earlier, industrialization based on import substitution had originally been a response to external factors (depression, war, balance-of-payments problems) in which government stimulants had played a leading part, but under Vargas in the 1950's, and especially under Kubitschek, the process shifted to a self-conscious drive toward industrial self-sufficiency through changes in the economic structure. This, along with the move of the capital inland to Brasília, constituted the essence of Kubitschek's "developmentalism," which promised "Fifty Years of Progress in Five."

Kubitschek, whose political career was launched in the very "cradle" of the "System"–the P.S.D. of Minas Gerais–displayed an underlying approach to development much in vogue a decade ago–i.e., pure "economic development" stressing industry, power, highways–but the implements used, particularly those for financing "developmentalism," were far from orthodox. Government techniques included direct investment in the economic infrastructure, direct operation of petroleum and steel enterprises, and promotion of the private industries sector through "protectionist" devices–tariff and exchange controls and preferential import treatment for manufacturing equipment. Substantial new capital investment was required, both foreign and domestic. With the fall in commodity prices and export earnings following the Korean War, and the consequent balance-of-payments problem and inflationary pressures, large international development loans were presumably out of the question, since they would have entailed stabilization and austerity policies (similar to those accepted by Arturo Frondizi in Argentina) which probably would not have been tolerated by the "System," and in any case were not deemed appropriate by most Brazilian policymakers. Foreign private investment, however, was massively attracted (over $500 million in 1955–1960, of which 40 per cent came from the United States), largely by advantageous exchange treatment and the absence of restrictions on the remission of profits abroad. At home, inflation contributed to capital formation in both the public and private sectors. Deficit spending financed government investment, and since both prices and profits rose in quick response while most wages lagged behind, the particular pattern of inflation in the Kubitschek years led to forced savings, a kind of hidden tax on wage earners, especially on the least organized.

The concomitant of "Fifty Years of Progress in Five" was "Forty Years of Inflation in Four," but the outward results were impressive. By the end of Kubitschek's term industrial production had doubled over 1952; over 90 per cent of consumer goods were of local manufacture and industry had turned to capital goods; steel production was up 100 per cent over 1955; an automobile industry started from scratch was ready to turn out 200,000 units per year; and electric power capacity and highway mileage had doubled since 1950. São Paulo recorded a new housing venture every nine minutes. Brasília, erected at a monumental cost, was brilliantly inaugurated in the wilderness, and a thin ribbon of highway stretched through the backlands connecting it with the far North.

Although the pros and cons of Kubitschek's "developmentalism" are beyond the scope of our analysis, three questions must be touched upon in view of widely held notions that equate industrialism with "development," economic growth with "modernization," and the rise of a dynamic urban-industrial complex such as São Paulo with the decline of the archaic sectors, and, by extension, erosion of the "System." First, economists themselves now suggest that import substitution cannot carry the development of Latin American countries very much further.[12] Even Brazil, with favorable conditions in terms of size of the internal market and an industrial plant with considerable depth and diversification, faces this quandary; higher income, unless accompanied by income redistribution, cannot provide the mass purchasing power necessary to match the growth in productive capacity. The kind of economic growth experienced during the years before 1961 produced severe imbalances at the sectoral, re-

[12] "The Growth and Decline of Import Substitution in Brazil," *Economic Bulletin for Latin America* (Vol. IX, No. 1, March 1964).

gional, and social level. The agricultural sector—except for traditional exports such as coffee and cocoa—was ignored, undergoing no structural or technological change and lagging in productivity. There is evidence that impoverished rural regions such as the Northeast declined even more due to the flight of local capital to the industrializing centers and to government incentives amounting in practice to a transfer of income from the less developed to the more developed regions. According to a study of the United Nations' Economic Commission for Latin America (E.C.L.A.), "the social imbalances appear to have worsened during the recent process of development . . . including the increase in the marginal populations in the cities and the gap between the income of those employed in the most backward sector—the primary—and those employed in the most developed sector—the secondary. This increase in social disequilibrium derives largely from the inability of the dynamic sectors to create employment opportunities at a pace sufficient to absorb the growing masses of population in the economically active age groups." Referring to the period 1948–1961, the same E.C.L.A. study concludes:

> The effect of the recent development model has been to transform the Brazilian economy into one of the most perfect examples of dual economy to be found in all Latin America . . . involving the existence of a dynamic capitalist sector, that expands rapidly, absorbs relatively little manpower, and has a comparatively high level of productivity, side by side with an underdeveloped sector in which is found the bulk of the population and which is to all intents and purposes excluded from the development process. The seriousness of this problem lies in the fact that not only do absolute differences in productivity between the two sectors exist, but that these differences have tended to increase as development proceeds.[13]

Secondly, when a sociological dimension is added to the analysis, there is reason to question the "dynamism" commonly attributed to the industrial sector of the São Paulo-Rio-Minas Gerais "triangle." Recent European immigration

[13] *Ibid.*, p. 54.

has formed a part of entrepreneurship, but the greatest recruitment came from large planters diversifying their investments, bringing their old attitudes and life-style along with them. And even immigrants have often absorbed the "traditional" more than they have disseminated the "modern." In 1960 there were only 380 firms in Brazil employing more than 500 workers—one-half of 1 per cent of all enterprises; most enterprises are not only small or medium-sized, but they also continue under family control and recruit management according to varied criteria—occasionally including proven ability.[14] Above all, industrial expansion took place in a hothouse of government protection, subsidies, and inflation, creating an owner-manager outlook which—with some notable exceptions—fears competition, domestic or foreign; is satisfied with high-cost, low-quality products as long as profits are maintained; shows little interest in market expansion; is nonideological, opportunistic, and dependent with regard to government and politics; and displays an almost single-minded concentration on the maximization of profits.

Because of the accumulation of several spectacular fortunes amid generalized corruption, some observers have likened the more aggressive industrial magnates to the North American "Robber Barons"—who, withal, changed a continent—but the Brazilian dependence on government pampering would seem to undermine the case. Brazilian intellectuals of the 1950's dreamed of a kind of neo-Bismarckian alliance between the "national bourgeoisie" and organized labor, collaborating under the banner of nationalism (and protectionism) to transform the country. It proved an illusion. Later there was talk of a "Modern Right," in which increased political participation by management and entrepreneurs might bring some of the rationality and impersonality of industry into national affairs. Until now, however, dominant elements of the new industrial class have shown little interest in political ideas or national goals; and apart from a brief flurry of mobilization to "fight communism" before Goulart's fall, they appear less inclined to alter the "System" than to seek a senior partnership in it.

[14] See Emmanuel de Kadt, "The Brazilian Impasse," *Encounter,* September 1965.

Finally, on the political level, it is evident that Kubitschek left the "System" untouched. Plagued by incipient *coups* and containment measures by the military during the first half of his term, he undertook no basic rearrangements of political forces and avoided supplementing economic growth with such unsettling ventures into social reform as education or the agrarian question. To buy support for his Brasília project, he coddled industry in the South, and offered the Northeast a regional development agency, originally viewed by the politicians of that area as little more than a vast gravy train of public works. He remained outwardly neutral as between capital and labor, and maintained the old P.S.D.-P.T.B. alliance, with Vice-President Goulart and the P.T.B. controlling government jobs in the labor and social security bureaucracies. Some of these jobs and slots on P.T.B. ballots were given to members of the Communist Party (illegal since 1947) in return for their support. In implementing his development programs, Kubitschek preferred to work outside the regular bureaucracy and party channels, creating new autarchies and administrative devices to get things done, and thus avoiding the immobilism of the "System" without confronting it.

Quadros, Goulart, and the "System" in Crisis

A record vote swept the mercurial Jânio Quadros, an independent endorsed by the U.D.N., into the Presidency (January-August 1961) in what may be viewed as a brief, contradictory, and unsuccessful attack on the "System." Quadros' promises to rationalize the nation's finances and administration attracted elements from outside the "System" and, with the orgy of inflation mounting, even certain groups within it. His moralism appealed not only to middle-class liberals of the U.D.N., but also attracted a temporary following among young radicals who had finally discovered that among the nationalists of "developmentalism" and the "Dirty Center" there were those who were taking bribes from German investors, profiteering from inflation, investing in brothels and illegal gambling, and pushing large-scale payola. Some serious nationalists, both within and to the left of the "System," responded to Quadros' call for genuine social reforms and espe-

APPROXIMATE ALIGNMENT OF BRAZILIAN POLITICAL FORCES, EARLY 1960's

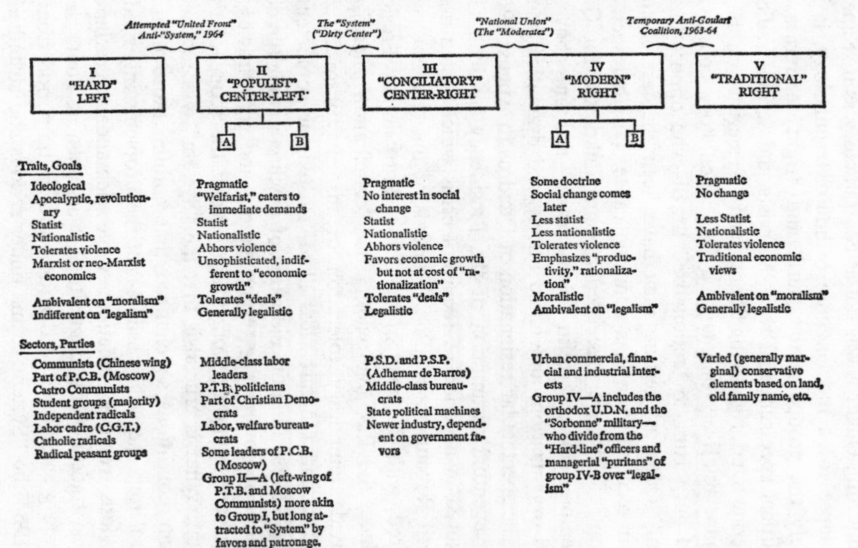

	I "HARD" LEFT	II "POPULIST" CENTER-LEFT	III "CONCILIATORY" CENTER-RIGHT	IV "MODERN" RIGHT	V "TRADITIONAL" RIGHT
Traits, Goals	Ideological Apocalyptic, revolutionary Statist Nationalistic Tolerates violence Marxist or neo-Marxist economics Ambivalent on "moralism" Indifferent on "legalism"	Pragmatic "Welfarist," caters to immediate demands Statist Nationalistic Abhors violence Unsophisticated, indifferent to "economic growth" Tolerates "deals" Generally legalistic	Pragmatic No interest in social change Statist Nationalistic Abhors violence Favors economic growth but not at cost of "rationalization" Tolerates "deals" Legalistic	Some doctrine Social change comes later Less statist Less nationalistic Tolerates violence Emphasizes "productivity," rationalization" Moralistic Ambivalent on "legalism"	Pragmatic No change Less Statist Nationalistic Tolerates violence Traditional economic views Ambivalent on "moralism" Generally legalistic
Sectors, Parties	Communists (Chinese wing) Part of P.C.B. (Moscow) Castro Communists Student groups (majority) Independent radicals Labor cadre (C.G.T.) Catholic radicals Radical peasant groups	Middle-class labor leaders P.T.B. politicians Part of Christian Democrats Labor, welfare bureaucrats Some leaders of P.C.B. (Moscow) Group II—A (left-wing of P.T.B. and Moscow Communists) more akin to Group I, but long attracted to "System" by favors and patronage.	P.S.D. and P.S.P. (Adhemar de Barros) Middle-class bureaucrats State political machines Newer industry, dependent on government favors	Urban commercial, financial and industrial interests Group IV—A includes the orthodox U.D.N. and the "Sorbonne" military—who divide from the "Hard-line" officers and managerial "puritans" of group IV-B over "legalism"	Varied (generally marginal) conservative elements based on land, old family name, etc.

Note: Any attempt to diagram forces so fluid, undefined, and in a state of perpetual motion must at best be rough.

cially to his "independent" foreign policy—despite the fact that the Communists officially supported the "System" candidate, a colorless and conservative Army marshal. Given the nature of the "System," the peculiar combination of forces supporting Quadros was not as contradictory as it seemed; for, to lapse for a moment into orthodox terminology, it is precisely the groups at the "left" and "right" extremes of the political spectrum in Brazil—Marxists and serious radicals on the one hand, right-wing liberals and "Nasserists" on the other; groups relatively unentangled in "conciliatory conservatism" and purporting to "rationalize" Brazil—who oppose the "System." Quadros' gesture may have been the last chance for their reconciliation in a common cause. Whether such an attempt could have succeeded remains unknown, for Quadros attempted to govern in "Bonapartist" fashion, above party and organization, and failed utterly and dramatically.

The spectacular resignation of Quadros in August 1961 and the eventual assumption of the Presidency by João Goulart ushered in a period of recurrent crisis which lasted until the April Revolution of 1964. The axis of the "System" was restored, with the head of the Labor Party in the Presidential Palace, the P.S.D. providing the "conciliation" necessary to provide temporary toleration of his investiture by hostile groups, and Goulart (less liked, trusted, or competent than Vargas) resuming the old game of juggling among the obvious centers of power. The tergiversations and conspiracies of his thirty-one months in office are beyond the scope of this account. What is crucial is that the "System" was restored, but under conditions so changed that nothing more than a political impasse was possible. Yet the problems inherited from previous regimes—inflation, wage demands, agrarian pressures, trade deficits, commitments assumed at Punta del Este—were greater than ever before, and in the period from 1961 to 1964 the "System" came under serious and sustained pressure, both from internal contradictions and external attack.

Over the years there had been alternating competition and collaboration between Brazil's "hard left"—Communists and independent radicals—and the left wing of the P.T.B., the latter solidly inside the "System." The forces of the left, although dispersed between the labor movement, several radical student movements, the two Communist parties (Soviet- and Chinese-oriented), peasant groups, Castro supporters, and independent revolutionary nationalists, grew rapidly after 1960. Although the events of 1964 showed them to be singularly disorganized and poorly led, the increasing militancy of these groups, particularly in labor, altered the nature of their relations with the Goulart group. Each tried to use the other for its own ends, but the bargaining power of the militants—whether working "inside" through their uneasy arrangement with the P.T.B. labor bureaucrats, or "outside" through strikes and disorders in defiance of "Jango"—became more that of an equal. At the same time, non-Communist labor groups, both radical and moderate, began to show independence of Goulart and the "System." "Sponsored" groups linked to the "System" were in a sense "escaping" into a certain autonomy.

At the other end of the spectrum, the traditional "outsiders" in the U.D.N. and an important sector of the military were reinforced by a wide variety of anti-Goulart elements. A group so diverse could be united only by a powerful myth, readily available in the "holy war against communism"—a myth given a semblance of credibility by the formation late in 1963 of a "united front" of radicals and Communists, and by Goulart's own swing to the left the following February. The "System" of conciliation, payoff, and pure maneuver—barren of ideas or convictions regarding national purpose—could no longer govern, even by doing nothing. It yielded to a blow from the "right," precipitated by Goulart's naïve condonement of mutinous acts in the Navy; but the blow could have come with almost equal logic from the "left," since the "System" had long constituted the greatest single obstacle to genuine reform in Brazil.

THE BRAZILIAN MILITARY

*The Military in Brazil**

JOHN J. JOHNSON

The revolution in 1930 propelled the armed forces into the center of Brazilian politics and the locus of power has resided in them ever since. Getulio Vargas, during his fifteen-year dictatorship, was never able to extricate himself from their influence. Since 1945, when the dictatorship was terminated, the president has had to have his *"dispositivo militar,"* a group of officers who "guarantee him." The record of the officers has been spotty. On several occasions they have seemed to play well the role they have assumed. On other occasions they have taxed the patience of those civilians who looked to the armed forces to guarantee the democratic process. More significantly, perhaps, within the last decade the representatives of the armed forces again have become increasingly prone to take public positions on policy conflicts rather than being content to arbitrate the differences that arise from civilian debate.

During the 1930's and early 1940's the armed forces drained the reservoir of good will they had filled by participating in the overthrow of the old regime. Vargas briefly catered to the *tenentes* who swarmed into administrative posts without reference to their capabilities or experience, but many of them had deserted him by 1932 and supported the São Paulo revolt. The dictator, meanwhile, appeased the regular officers by spending recklessly on guns, armored vehicles, airplanes, and naval vessels. When the São Paulo revolt broke out in 1932, the main body of the armed forces remained loyal to the government, but large numbers of officers individually deserted to the rebel forces. Shortly after the uprising was suppressed, a scattering of officers and non-coms became involved

* Reprinted from John J. Johnson, *The Military and Society in Latin America,* pp. 206–23, with the permission of the publishers, Stanford University Press.

in the abortive communist revolt of 1935, which was staged in an effort to seize control of the army preparatory to taking over the entire government. In that revolt the pro-communist forces relied almost entirely upon the regular forces for their fire power. The anniversary of the *putsch* is observed each year and serves to strengthen the military's aversion to communism; army officers who served in action against the communist attempt are entitled to a special one-rank promotion upon retirement. Two years after the revolt, and partly as a reaction against communism, both the regular forces and the *tenente* contingent, represented by Cordeiro de Farias, Juarez Távora, and Gomes, among others, did not raise their voices against Vargas when he decreed the "Estado Novo," which was in essence a neo-fascist corporate state with much of its fascist paraphernalia, including a "new nationalism" borrowed from the Old World. Then the armed forces sat back as the dictator redeemed his pledge of a "political renovation" by imposing severe curbs on civilian political activities.

By the outbreak of World War II some officers close to Vargas, such as Gões Monteiro, had become fascinated by nazism and fascism and they tried, without success, to dissuade the dictator, who had earlier been disposed rather favorably toward Germany and Italy, from aligning Brazil with the West. But once in the war, the prestige of the services soared as Brazilian troops became the first from Latin America to fight in Europe, and by the war's end not only had the Brazilian military come of age as a fighting force but its leadership was clearly pro-democratic. Meanwhile, the officers' nationalistic aspirations were satisfied somewhat by United States commitments to provide machinery, capital, and technicians for the construction of an integrated iron and steel plant at Volta Redonda following Brazil's leasing of land for airstrips along the "Hump." There were striking manifestations of the new military mind during the half-decade after the end of the war. In October 1945, officers, reflecting the general repugnance of the Western World to totalitarianism following the defeat of Germany and Italy, forced Vargas into retirement when it appeared that he might renege on his promise to hold general elections. Then they turned the government over to Chief Justice Linhares of the Supreme Court, who ordered that the election be held as scheduled.

The public, uncertain of what had occurred during the Vargas dictatorship, instinctively turned to the military. Both major parties named armed forces generals to head their presidential tickets and at the polls the public voted the colorless and unimaginative Eurico Dutra into office. The General's administration devoted itself to taking the nation's pulse as it returned to the democratic system. The armed forces tended to withdraw from public view, and their representatives remained undecided as to the meaning of the vastly broadened political base as indicated by the extended electorate and the strong showing of the communists, who captured approximately 10 per cent of the vote in the 1945 and 1947 elections.[1]

There was a recrudescence of military politics in 1950, and since then the armed forces have at ever-shortening intervals served notice that they consider themselves "the court of final political resort." Vargas had to have the tacit consent of the military in order to return to power through presidential elections in 1950. In 1953 some officers, in spite of strong opposition from their colleagues, intervened openly in political affairs for the first time since 1945 and in February 1954 forced the dismissal of Vargas's Minister of Labor João Goulart, who had been appealing demagogically to labor. And after an air force officer was accidentally shot in what appears to have been an attempt masterminded by members of Vargas's bodyguard on the life of Vargas-baiting Carlos Lacerda, editor of *Tribuna da imprensa,* and now conservative, publicity-seeking governor of Guanabara state, dominant groups in the three services demanded Vargas's immediate withdrawal from government. Rather than accede to their ultimatum, the President committed suicide on August 24.

Although civilians were permitted to head the government between Vargas's death and the election and inauguration of a new president, the armed forces were in complete control despite the fact that they failed in their demands for a single candidate. After the election in which Juscelino Kubitschek, the presidential candidate of the Social Democratic Party

[1] There was a 400 per cent increase in the number of qualified voters between 1930 and 1945.

(PSD), and João Goulart, the vice-presidential candidate of the Brazilian Workers' Party (PTB), were victorious, an army-led "preventive coup" or "anti-coup"—strongly opposed by a large majority of navy and air force officers and an important group of army officers—guaranteed that Kubitschek would be inaugurated. Five officers served in Kubitschek's cabinet and during his presidency Brazil spent more funds on the armed forces than on all public development programs, despite the fact that massive development programs were the hallmark of his administration.

Both the PSD and PTB nominated Marshal Henrique Texeira Lott as their presidential candidate in 1960. Goulart, who was named by the PTB to run for re-election as vice-president, in his acceptance speech said, "With Marshal Lott and [Minister of War] Marshal Denys, no one will fail to respect the will of the people," thereby inviting the armed forces to be the guarantors of the electoral process.

Marshal Lott was trounced in his bid for the presidency in 1960 by colorful, erratic Jânio Quadros,[2] just as General Juarez Távora had been beaten by Kubitschek in 1955 and General Eduardo Gomes by Vargas in 1950. But the public's rejection of Lott as presidential material no more deterred the military than had the setbacks suffered by Juarez Távora and Gomes.[3] Refusal of the armed forces to support his demands for broader powers was apparently one of the factors that led President Quadros to submit his resignation unexpectedly in August 1961, less than seven months after his inauguration. Thereupon the three top-ranking military men—one from each of the services—in Quadros's last cabinet moved quickly to prevent Vice-President Goulart, who was at the time on a state visit in the Far East, from returning to Brazil and fulfilling his constitutional duties. The ministers soon found themselves in a minority. The National Security Council, made up of high-ranking military and civilian officials, issued a statement disassociating itself from the anti-

[2] Quadros received 5,576,040 votes, which was a 48 per cent plurality in a three-way race. He defeated Lott by approximately 1.5 million votes.

[3] There was bitter opposition to Lott's candidacy in the air force and the navy, and the army was far from united in support of him.

Goulart manifesto of the service ministers, the general public voiced its disapproval, and the commander of the Third Army, in an act which served to emphasize the growing dissatisfaction within officer ranks, declared for Goulart. When the ministers found themselves without widespread support, they first wavered and they then drew back from plunging the country into civil war. In good Brazilian fashion a compromise followed which converted the country from a presidential to a parliamentary system with a severely circumscribed Goulart as president. But Goulart was not satisfied and began immediately to campaign for a return to the presidential system. The differing public statements of the officers during the debate on the issue not only called attention once again to the serious rivalry between the various branches of the armed services and within the army; it gave further grounds for believing that the Brazilian armed forces since 1954 have been moving in the direction that their Spanish American counterparts have historically pursued.[4] It is too early to guess whether this trend will be followed to its logical conclusion before an increasing lack of military agreement on vital issues destroys the military's capacity to continue its traditional role as the moderator of constitutional processes.

The armed forces' influence over policy formulation has been further enhanced through numerous individual officers holding elective and appointive positions at the national, state, and municipal levels. The extent to which these officers are distributed in government is suggested by a document prepared at the request of the author by an armed forces officer who must go unnamed, but who may be considered highly reliable. The document, dated May 20, 1959, begins as follows: "The number of Brazilian military now in the fields you mention must be in the hundreds.[5] There are no lists of such personnel available, but I will name as many of the more important ones as I can readily recall." According to the list

[4] It should be recalled that while the Brazilian armed forces have acted less responsibly in recent years, the military in many of the Spanish American countries have become somewhat more responsible, hence the gap between the Brazilian forces and their Spanish American counterparts has narrowed noticeably.

[5] I have another source for September 1961 that fixes at 1,100 the number of officers on detached duty and holding civilian positions.

that follows, officers were then holding the following key positions in national agencies related to industrial development: Minister of Transportation and Public Works; Director-General, National Mail and Telegraph Service; Executive Commission, National Post and Telegraph Planning; President, Radio Technical Commission; President, Merchant Marine Commission; Administrator, Leopoldina Railway Company (state-owned); President, National Petroleum Council; President, National Steel Company; President, National Alkali Company; President, National Petroleum Company; Superintendent, National Oil Tanker Fleet; Director General, Civil Aviation; Secretary General, National Coordinating Council of Food Supply; President, National Executive Commission for Coal Production Planning; Director, Food Supply Service; Chairman, National Price Control Board; President, National Commission on Nuclear Energy; President, National Transportation Council; "plus many more, particularly in Petrobras, the National Petroleum Company." In the National Legislature of the government there were two generals, one admiral, and one colonel, "plus at least twenty others who have not been active in the armed forces recently." At the state level a general was governor of Pará, a colonel was governor of Bahia, and two colonels held the highest political positions in the Territories of Rondônia and Fernando da Noronha, "plus an estimated fifty or more who are serving as state Directors of Public Safety and Public Works, etc." In the Federal District, a general and a colonel were respectively Chief and Assistant Chief of Police and a colonel was Fire Chief, "plus an estimated twenty-five more armed forces officers in police and fire units." The informant adds, "The police chiefs of all major cities are ex-colonels or generals." Although the source declined to estimate the number of ex-armed forces officers in private industry, he did observe, "I am sure that there are a great many, particularly in the engineering field."

In response to a question regarding why officers held positions in the civilian area, he wrote, "The main reason for so many military men accepting non-military positions is financial. . . . In most of the governmental positions listed above, an officer can draw one-half of his active-duty service pay in addition to the generally higher non-military governmental salary. Furthermore, he receives half credit applied to his army service for the time spent in jobs which have been decreed by the president to be 'of military interest.' The main reasons for the selection of officers for such positions, in my opinion, are their generally higher educational level, their administrative ability, and their honesty."

Other than the impact that nazism and fascism had on the armed forces and on Brazil in general, the military's changing conception of its responsibilities in non-military fields since 1930 can be explained in terms of the profound but uneven transformation that the republic has undergone. In turn, the developments most directly affecting the military mind lie within three major areas: (1) regionalism, (2) the rise of competing social-economic groups, and (3) the emergence of a perverted nationalism with a distinct economic bias.

Regionalism represents, as it has historically, a formidable obstacle to Brazil's development. When Vargas came to power in 1930 the republic gave the impression of seemingly infinite space fragmented into a number of distinct areas, each consciously seeking maximum self-sufficiency rather than coordinated growth through national unity. Since then, improved transportation, mass media of communication, and large-scale internal migration have contributed somewhat to the breakdown of sectional peculiarities. But at the same time uneven economic development of the regions has served to keep alive animosities that weaken the nation. Plagued by drought, critical shortages of transportation, power, and industry, its sugar, cocoa, and vegetable oil undersold on the world markets, the "Hump" has been too weak economically to respond to the relatively feeble assistance provided at first from Rio de Janeiro and now from Brasilia. The great Amazon drainage basin has not lived up to expectations. It may be a sleeping giant—a term often applied to the republic as a whole—which will have to await still further advances in technology and science before it will yield up its resources. It remains to be seen if the new national capital at Brasilia can serve as a hub from which will radiate the roads and economic stimuli required to develop the largely unexploited, temperate hinterland. Only the center-south has prospered; its three states, São Paulo, Guanabara, and Rio de Janeiro, produce over 50 per cent of the national income and pay over 60 per cent of the revenues collected by the national government. Paraná, Rio Grande do Sul, and Minas Gerais, also in the center-south, are expanding rapidly.

The armed forces become involved when provincialism is reflected politically, as when representatives of the economically advanced states oppose broad programs that their constituents would have to finance, and thereby make it difficult to get a clear-cut consensus on broad issues of public policy. In such circumstances the armed forces, national in scope as they are, and charged as they are with the nation's defense, do not feel obliged to stand aside indefinitely in favor of politicians whose thinking does not transcend issues of interest to their patrons. On such occasions the officers conceive of their role as "consolidators in a federation beset by regionalism." Furthermore, a disproportionate number of officers, as in the case of Spanish America, have come from the lesser-developed areas of the country, the areas that have felt most the need for federal assistance. Thus it was that officers during the 1930's favored Vargas in his successful effort to curb the autonomy of the states; today they support federal financing of development projects, such as for roads and power, that contribute to over-all national development. The national outlook of the armed forces ordinarily places them politically closer to the president of the country, who is elected by popular vote and who is more likely to hold a national point of view, than to legislators, who find it difficult to resist local pressures.

Still, it is apparent that the social, regional, and economic divergencies which characterize Brazilian society are reflected in the military establishment, and there is some evidence that military personnel tend to group themselves more or less unconsciously along regional lines and to maintain some of their natural ties with the regions from which they come. As long as regionalism continues to be a factor in Brazilian society, tendencies toward division along regional lines may be expected to continue in the armed forces, although almost certainly on a decreasing scale.

The ideological crosscurrents resulting from the emergence of industrialists and urban laborers as politically competing groups after 1930 were of interest to the Brazilian military from the first and had become an overriding concern by 1950. Prior to Vargas's seizure of the government, the latifundia oligarchy, occasionally assisted by the mercantile oligarchy with whom they often had family ties, held a firm monopoly on political power. Aspirants to power who reached their goal were automatically absorbed into the oligarchy-controlled Republican Party. The uprisings of 1922 and 1924, the Prestes Column, the Liberal Alliance, and the Revolution of 1930 were all forerunners of the struggle that had been waged by the new groups against the latifundia oligarchy, who, through their control of state and municipal government, continued to exercise power at the national level far out of proportion to their numbers or to their total contribution to the economy. The unpredictability of the armed forces in this heated struggle has served to make Brazil one of the most politically complex countries of the Western Hemisphere.

The armed forces were able to develop cordial relations with the rising industrial community while remaining on good terms with the landed elements. Reflecting their historical relationship with the agricultural sector, the armed forces were reluctant to support rapid industrial expansion during the early years of the Vargas dictatorship. However, by the outbreak of World War II, the officers had discarded, in principle, their historic willingness to rely upon foreign sources for war matériel in favor of a policy calling for an industrial buildup at home, in the hope that domestic industry might eventually satisfy all of the nation's military and civilian requirements. But the rate of expansion that the armed forces favored after World War II was such that it could not be met by private Brazilian capital, and as an alternative the armed forces urged direct state participation in basic industries such as railroads, electric power, petroleum, and steel, "the backbone of contemporary civilization."

The military's advocacy of state intervention in the economic sector might have led to a conflict of interest with the industrialists, but two considerations operated to prevent such an occurrence. In the first place, Brazilian private industrial capital always had been attracted to the production and distribution of consumer goods rather than to the basic industries which, as a consequence, had been neglected or had been left largely to foreign capital. Thus when the armed forces called upon the state to assume responsibility for developing the basic industries, the officers were nowhere treading upon the interests of local private capital. In the second place, the moneyed class simply did not have the investment capital needed to finance the rapid expansion of heavy industry, which was, of course, very much the situation that existed throughout Spanish America.

The armed forces welcomed industrial expansion, but they have been deeply distrustful, for the most part, of the rapidly growing and increasingly articulate urban labor forces that have been an inevitable by-product of industrial growth. When Vargas first came to power the labor force was numerically small, weakly organized, and politically ineffective. The dictator, conscious of the privileged group's attitude toward the workers, paid little attention to them during his early years in office, and they in turn were unresponsive to his occasional gestures of good will. But when the institution of the neo-fascist Estado Novo in 1938 cost him support among the middle and upper classes, he opportunistically set out to capture labor's backing with promises of better wages, shorter hours, more jobs, and by appealing to their latent nationalism. The *tenentes* applauded the dictator's decision, but officers of the regular armed forces looked askance at the maneuver. By the end of the war Vargas had made the proletariat an indispensable element of social cooperation, and labor was firmly tied to and dependent on the government. The dictator's ouster produced stirrings of labor discontent, but the workers did not dare challenge the armed forces' action.

By 1950 there were approximately five million urban workers of all kinds, most of whom were crowded in the half-dozen largest cities. They were generally underpaid and underfed, as were workers elsewhere in Latin America. They were politically unsophisticated because their leaders and irresponsible politicians had consciously kept them that way. But despite their political immaturity they had come to realize that politics was a means of getting what they wanted, and as they qualified for the vote the electorate swelled quickly to twelve million. The new voters were easily appealed to by demagogues, including students, who were in revolt against the established order. As voters they noisily but with little violence demanded more of the comforts and benefits that the privileged elements took for granted. They gave bread, shoes, and freedom precedence over God, country, and family.

It was the clamor of the urban masses and the proliferation of politicians demagogically soliciting their votes that brought the military back into politics in 1950. Their response to what they viewed as a threat to the status quo was to make Vargas's return to the presidency contingent upon guarantees by him that he would not attempt to overstep the constitution by going directly to the masses for support. That was what Vargas, who had won election as "the father of the poor," in effect did in 1953 when he assigned Goulart to bring about a rapid resurgence of popular support for the government, with reckless promises to the workers. Early in 1954 the armed forces determined that Vargas could not be trusted and as "defenders of the constitution" they drew up a memorandum of grievances against the administration. Thereafter the officers were relentless in their attacks upon the administration and finally drove the President to take his own life.

Vargas's death marked the beginning of a new era in relations between the armed forces and labor. Up to that moment, despite occasional indications of radicalism in the Clube Militar (Officers' Club), the military, for all intents and purposes, had presented a united front against the workers. Since then an ever-growing number of officers, most notably in the army, have aligned themselves with political elements who favor incorporating the workers more fully into the body politic.

At least until 1960 Marshal Henrique Lott was the principal spokesman for those officers who were prepared to grant the masses a greater political role. Lott came into public prominence when, as Minister of War, he gave unstinting support to Café Filho, Vargas's successor in office, for his policy of refusing to interfere in the electoral process or to prevent the election of a Vargas-type president. When officers representing the air force, navy, and more conservative elements of the army and civilian groups threatened to prevent the inauguration of Kubitschek, who had won election as the heir of Vargas, Lott engineered the "anti-coup" or "preventive coup" to assure that Kubitschek would be permitted to take office. The Minister's action had a two-fold impact. It produced wounds in the military that had not healed eight years later, and it initiated the courtship of labor by powerful and perhaps dominant elements in the army.

Lott, who had resigned as War Minister to run for the presidency in 1960, was replaced by Conservative Marshal Odilio Denys. After Jânio Quadros's landslide presidential victory over Lott, Denys was joined in the cabinet by equally conservative navy and air force ministers. When Quadros resigned the presidency in August 1961, it was this triumvirate of officers who, in violation of the constitution, sought to prevent labor-backed, leftist-leaning Vice-President Goulart from becoming President. The air force and navy stood firm behind the ministers, but the army split and those favoring constitutionality were sufficiently strong that the ministers backed down rather than risk the possible consequences of resorting to force in order to see that their directives were carried out. Thus in a clear test of strength–the second in six years–the Brazilian army by its actions refuted the oft-repeated allegation that the military in Latin America is committed to the defense of the conservative position. And afterward they were consistent when they upheld the results of the plebiscite held on January 6, 1963, that by a five-to-one margin favored a return to the presidential system.

As of early 1963 it appeared that the army's response to the growing power of the masses had resulted from a conviction that those groups must be given a greater voice in government. Lott and certain other officers may have acted opportunistically or demagogically in their desire to achieve political recognition, but such a charge could not be leveled at the armed forces as a whole. Officers had accepted with equanimity the people's mandate when they voted for Quadros rather than Lott. They had refrained from taking advantage of the extreme instability resulting from the severe deterioration of the nation's economy and the ineffectiveness of the parliamentary system to assume direct control of the government. Still, one could hardly think that the opposition elements in the armed forces would remain content with their respective roles. Civilian politics were becoming progressively complex as students injected themselves more forcefully into the political picture and poverty-stricken, politically immature rural workers clamored for recognition. Privileged groups were wondering if they had been pushed to the point where they must strike back or surrender. Officers were wearying of standing by as the nation marked time; some of them would favor using the armed forces to renovate the country, much as the *tenentes* had proposed to do four decades earlier. Within all of the more politically conscious groups there was an increasing feeling that Brazil had not lived up to expectations. Short-run disappointments were reinforcing more profound self-doubts and anxieties to produce an ever-sharpening sense of hostility toward politicians as a class. In many a Latin American republic, where weak governments mean a strong military, such a combination of circumstances, at least until recently, would have constituted an open invitation to intervention by the armed forces on their own account. In Brazil tradition argued against such a development, but it was apparent that if its officers were to continue on the course that they had pursued since Vargas's death—a course which involved them more and more in policy conflicts and less and less with legality—intervention on their own behalf sooner or later would become a necessity which no amount of civilian façade could conceal. There was no question but that the Brazilian armed forces had been moving in the direction of their Spanish American counterparts. The only question was whether or not over the short range the victorious element would have popular opinion on its side, as in 1889 and 1930, or whether conservative elements would triumph over the popular will, as happened in 1954.

The course that the army follows in all probability will be determined in the Clube Militar, a recreational and mutual benefit society comprised of a majority of Brazilian army officers. Established in 1887 in an atmosphere of crisis, as a direct result of the military's desire to express itself on the issues of slavery and republicanism, the Clube historically has provided a forum for debates on political issues between army factions. It was closed temporarily by President Pessôa (1919–22), when its president, Marshal Hermes da Fonseca, recommended that military units stationed in Pernambuco ignore presidential orders relating to an internal security matter in that state. Later the Clube was a hotbed of *tenentismo.* It was kept under a fairly tight rein during the Vargas dictatorship, but since the early 1950's it has reflected the crosscurrents of social and political thought found in the army. Debate in the Clube becomes particularly heated during the elections, which are held biennially (in even years) and are usually contested by two slates of candidates, one of which ordinarily represents the views of the War Minister, while the other is likely to speak for the opposition. On occasion a successful candidate may claim to be apolitical, but in most instances the election is fought out and the outcome determined by views of the candidates on matters of national policy rather than army welfare. The War Minister's candidate, ordinarily an officer with a general's rank, is usually but not invariably successful. The Clube thus has served at least two purposes. Watched closely by the Brazilian press and politicians, it is at all times a microcosm of the attitudes and antagonisms of the various factions within the officer corps, and it provides a sounding board for the opposition, usually made up of younger officers of field command rank. Serving these functions as it does, the Clube tends to discourage the formation in the Brazilian army of the "secret" organizations that have been so commonplace and disruptive in the armies of Spanish America.

Nationalism, the third of the developments affecting the military's conception of its non-military role, has been the most significant addition to the ideological field since 1930. Brazil's major political ideology for over a decade, nationalism has now become institutionalized. But in its current social appeals and economic-political emphasis, this nationalism is a far cry from the type inherited from "the old regime." Three decades ago nationalism was practically a monopoly of a few intellectuals, who were interested in it primarily as an abstraction. And by the outbreak of the war, Vargas, taking his cue from the nazis and fascists and with encouragement from the *tenentes,* had usurped the ideology from the intellectuals and assigned civilian bureaucrats to give it a concreteness which would be meaningful to the urban masses and as such could be translated into political capital.

Since the war nationalism has undergone three major modifications, more or less simultaneously. First, as a sense of personal identification with the country, it has become generalized to the point where it is felt by individuals belonging to all sectors of society. This in turn has given the Brazilian people a sense of destiny, and they have come to think of their country as a future world power. Second, nationalism has been given a sharpened economic focus, and as such has become the central rallying point for all those who feel that the nation has not lived up to its potential. Third, the hard core of nationalism's support has passed from the civilian bureaucrats to the armed forces, and they have been primarily responsible for its institutionalization.

The military became the depository of nationalism largely by default. The elite groups, constrained as they were by regional obligations and still unable to think about things not related to the coffee market, remained essentially internationalists. They looked for closer ties with the United States, at a time when the submerged peoples of Africa and Asia were insisting upon their political and economic emancipation. The communists, who would have been logical contenders for the role of nationalist leaders, were outlawed as the cold war became hotter. Labor, as noted above, remained under the domination of the state. Thus only the armed forces possessed the necessary qualifications. Their organization, as has been pointed out, was national in scope and they had primary responsibility for national defense. Officers had associated themselves with local industry during the war and claimed the iron and steel plant at Volta Redonda as their brainchild. They were trusted by the industrial community. They needed only an issue, and they were given one when the cries of the underdeveloped areas made protection of natural resources a national obligation of the first order. The officers took control of Petrobras, the national oil monopoly, and made it the symbol of the republic's determination to become economically independent.

Until 1955 Brazilian nationalism was of a mild variety. It

involved primarily identifying the individual with the nation and as such it might have been termed patriotism. It seldom manifested the xenophobic or anti-American characteristics associated with nationalism in certain other countries of the developing world. Public opinion and national legislation favorable to the more nationalistic elements in the industrial community and the armed forces were countered by quite close relations between the governments and the armed forces of Brazil and the United States. The nature of Brazilian nationalism during this phase of its development is explained by the fact that it was regulated by the armed forces.

Since 1955 a number of developments have lent themselves to a somewhat more xenophobic, anti-American type of nationalism. As was discussed above, there has grown up in the armed forces an element that is prepared to give the radical masses a greater share in government. The World War II generation of officers, who had a close attachment to the United States, is rapidly being supplanted by a new generation of officers who have not formed such an attachment and who are less inclined than their superiors to associate themselves with the United States. The rapid rise of the prestige of the U.S.S.R. following its launching of the first satellite in 1957, and the subsequent success of Fidel Castro, with Soviet support, in withstanding the pressures applied from the United States, have encouraged the growth of neutralism vis-à-vis the East-West conflict. Neutralism, a by-product of nationalism, may have become more important than the nationalist ideology itself. In early 1964 it was still too soon to determine for sure whether or not the armed forces would influence neutralism to the same extent that they had influenced nationalism, but the probability was that they would not, simply because the students and the rural masses, as well as traditional pressure groups, were insisting that they also share the demagogic political capital that neutralism promised.

THE 1964 OVERTHROW OF PRESIDENT GOULART

*Revolution or Counterrevolution in Brazil?**

JAMES W. ROWE

A basic problem of terminology arises in discussing the Movement of March 31–April 2. The new government and the preponderantly sympathetic press style it a "Revolution." Critics and skeptics—including some social scientists and the important Rio de Janeiro daily *Correio da Manhã*—insist that it was a *golpe*, a mere military *coup d'état*. This controversy in turn raises questions about the labels applied to the anterior situation—the social and political upheavals during the Kubitschek-Quadros-Goulart years. (Observers convinced that Brazil was on the brink of vast structural changes gave titles such as *Revolution in Brazil*[1] and *The Brazilian Pre-Revolution*[2] to their works; critics of the Goulart-leftist alliance warned of "revolution from above.") The lack of uniform criteria for distinguishing a "revolution" from a golpe is painfully apparent in most of the discussion, and some criteria cited are of limited relevance. Carlos Lacerda, for example, is probably right in insisting that swift and bloodless victory did *not* deprive the Movement of a revolutionary character, but this alone proves nothing.

The basic elements of the April Movement combined certain

* Reprinted from James W. Rowe, "Revolution or Counterrevolution in Brazil?, Part I: The Diverse Background," pp. 2–3, and Part II: From 'Black Friday' to the New Reforms," pp. 9–13, *American Universities Field Staff Reports* (June, 1964) by permission of American Universities Field Staff, Inc.

[1] Quoted in Irving Louis Horowitz, *Revolution in Brazil: Politics and Society in a Developing Nation* (New York: E. P. Dutton, 1964), p. 96.

[2] Celso Furtado, "Reflexões sôbre a pré-revolução brasileira," *Revista Brasileira de Ciências Sociais* (Minas Gerais: March 1962).

features of a golpe with others of a revolutionary character, and still others of a counterrevolutionary type. They included:

(1) Widespread belief among Brazilians of diverse political persuasion that the legal, constitutional government of President Goulart had demonstrated clearly its intent to radically alter the legal and power structure by means of agitation, strikes, military insubordination, and at least tactical collaboration with trained subversives of various Communist factions;
(2) Overthrow of that government by a military rebellion, to which leading elements of the armed forces and governors of the most important states quickly adhered;
(3) Indications of widespread (though not universal) popular support for the revolt in major cities, contrasted with the apathy, disorganization, and indifference displayed by the groups (students, the trade-union rank and file, enlisted men, peasants) which the Goulart regime had considered its bulwarks;
(4) A forthright statement of aims by the victors, including subordination of the Constitution of 1946 to the "constituent power inherent in victorious revolution," in its Institutional Act proclaimed April 9, 1964;
(5) Adherence by the new government—apart from the illegal act of revolt—to juridical norms already existing (most of the 1946 Constitution is retained intact) or to new ones provided by the Institutional Act, a temporary measure due to expire January 31, 1966;
(6) The stated intent of the Castelo Branco government, already partially confirmed, to undertake basic reforms of Brazilian society, including a number of those reforms vocally espoused by the Goulart government.

It now seems clear that the breadth of support given the revolt and the degree it shifted the power base make it difficult to dismiss the Movement as a mere golpe. In view of the admittedly negative origins of the uprising (based on fear of communism and the desire of at least some elements of the revolutionary regime to erase most of the thirty-five years' influence of Getúlio Vargas and his followers from Brazilian life), there was a real temptation to call it a counterrevolution. But the "reformist" and "modernist" strands of the Movement have thus far saved it from a reactionary or even traditionalist cast, and they may yet succeed in earning the "Revolutionary" sobriquet it claims.

A Rightist "Terror"?

The Question "Revolution or Golpe?" is dangerously simplistic because of the varying objectives pursued by three strands of the anti-Goulart movement–one dedicated to ridding Brazil of Goulart and the worst of his accomplices, but otherwise pretty much satisfied with traditional structures; another intent on a sweeping moralistic crusade to eradicate populism and paternalism along with "Jango"; and a third reluctant to move against Goulart until virtually forced to do so, but once having acted, determined to use the occasion for positive and progressive ends.

The immediate postvictory period provided similar complexity; the phrase "Rightist 'Terror'" suggests the principal ambiguity. A "Terror," of sorts, there was. But as Castelo Branco's government rounded its mid-June corner, most signs were that the "Terror" was over and that the government's direction was anything but traditional-rightist. If the extent and swiftness of arrests and purges (especially the banishment of Celso Furtado) was sufficient to dampen the euphoria of official Washington, the bills Castelo Branco was sending to Congress a few weeks later must have caused second thoughts by the three United States professors who had written on April 10 to The New York *Times:* ". . . What is so distressing is that our Government has once again allied itself with the social and political forces, represented by Governor Carlos Lacerda and the rebel generals, that have long opposed precisely those sweeping reforms advocated by João Goulart and which alone could bring Brazil fully into the modern era."[3]

The revolt which overthrew Goulart was almost without combat deaths; the three or four reported were either accidental or the result of personal vendettas. Goulart and Brizola

[3] Letter to the editor, signed by Herbert Marcuse, Barrington Moore, Jr., and Martin H. Peretz, April 10, 1964. The New York *Times* (April 19, 1964).

sought asylum in Uruguay; their principal extremist accomplices also fled the country, except for the military figures such as Admiral Aragão and General Assis Brasil who turned themselves in and are awaiting court-martial. The main elements of the "Terror" were: (1) The arrest of a large number of Brazilians—generally believed to be around 10,000—by military and security forces in the days of the revolt. "All but a few," say responsible sources have now been released. Many of the arrests were "preventive" or interrogatory; security forces admit that many mistakes were made. The prize captives still in prison are Miguel Arraes, Governor of Pernambuco before his arrest and impeachment in the first hours of the revolt, and Francisco Julião, the Bible-reading, Castroite messiah of the Peasant Leagues and Deputy for Pernambuco. (2) Considerable unstructured violence and abuses in the first few days, much of it in the northeastern states, including the destruction of UNE (National Students Union) headquarters in Rio. Deaths, if any, were few. Scattered charges of police torture are difficult to assess. (3) Removal from office and cancellation of political rights of a total of 337 persons, including over 10 per cent of the deputies in the Federal Chamber, six state governors, several of Goulart's cabinet ministers, and ex-President Quadros. The most obviously political purges were those of Kubitschek and Furtado. Purge decrees were based on summary proceedings of Marshal Taurino Rezende's Central Investigating Committee (a creature of the National Security Council), conducted without prior advice to the "accused" or right of defense. Dom Hélder Câmara, Archbishop of Olinda, led the Brazilian Council of Bishops in criticising the proceedings—which he conceded were necessary—for ignoring "the sacred right of defense."

The picture would not be balanced without some additional comment: (1) If viewed alongside upheavals of comparable proportions and complexity in other times and places, the April Movement appears to have kept its "Terror" phases within livable bounds. It is widely expected that a general amnesty in one or two years will remove many of the political proscriptions. (2) Quite clearly an internal struggle within the Castelo Branco government took place over the severity of the "Terror," especially over the purge of Kubitschek. Castelo Branco seems to have been under great pressure from the "hard line" (*linha dura*) officers such as Costa e Silva and Cordeiro de Farias to extend the deadline for the purges; he held out successfully but gave in on the Kubitschek and other cases as *quid pro quo*. (3) After the first few days, the "Terror" shifted its fire from elements accused of Communism, pro-Communism, and subversion to those accused of corruption or Brazil's recent mismanagement. This not only led to charges of deformation of ends (the revolt had been mounted on the theme "save Brazil from Communism") but left the new regime open to a damaging appearance of hypocrisy, given the prominent place in its midst of such old-time manipulators as Adhemar de Barros and Vice-President José María Alkmim. The problem for the Castelo Branco government was a simple one of power: De Barros and São Paulo had played a crucial part in the uprising and the Governor could not be cast aside easily. Nonetheless, there were sufficient omissions of the notoriously corrupt to cloud the moralistic purity of the housecleaning. (4) Attempts by the revolutionary regime to censor foreign news dispatches in the early days were short-lived, although many of its leaders pout over the critical press coverage in the United States, Britain, and France. The management of the pro-Communist Rio daily *Ultima Hora* was thrown out, but the paper continues to be published. Freedom of the press varies from state to state, but the acid and vigorous attacks of *Correio da Manhã* on the government attest its existence in Guanabara. In matters related to the "Terror," many officers are quick to admit a variety of mistakes and abuses, and to ridicule its excesses—as, for example, the case of the Rio bookseller arrested because he prominently displayed a Portuguese edition of Suzanne Labin's violently anti-Communist exposé of Red subversion in the Americas, *Encima da Hora*. Why? The cover displayed a hammer and sickle!

How Close Was Brazil to Communism?

The failure of General Assis Brasil's supposed "Red Machine" to provide resistance in the armed forces, the inability of the CGT to mount an effective general strike on

April 2, the non-appearance of Brizola's much-talked-about guerillas, and the shift of the revolutionary attack from Communism to corruption have caused some observers to wonder if the Communist subversion menace was not a myth. Indeed, the new leaders have a great responsibility to document the case on which they based the call to revolt in March. Such documentation is promised in a *Livro Branco* (White Paper) scheduled for release by the Foreign Office in July. Until its contents are known, the outside observer can form only fragmented and tentative conclusions.

A sifting of more responsible and dispassionate opinion in and outside the government reveals agreement that: (1) Neither Goulart nor his more reckless brother-in-law Brizola was a Communist ideologue or under Communist discipline, but they believed that they could use a wide variety of Marxist, leftist-nationalist, and *sui generis* extremists—including the official Communist apparatus of Carlos Luiz Prestes—to break existing structures and build a new power base. (2) The Communist Party of Brazil (PCB), outlawed in 1947, had only about 40,000 members at the time of the Moscow-Peking schism, and the Party itself did not furnish those major figures in Goulart's entourage who were known as his "links with Communism": Press Secretary Raúl Ryff, Cabinet Secretary Darcy Ribeiro, General Assis Brasil, Admiral Candido Aragão, labor leaders Oswaldo Pacheco, Dante Pelacani, and Clodsmith Riani. Goulart, however, proposed to legalize the Communist Party and had frequent contacts with Prestes, who urged the March 13 rally. (3) Since the split of the Moscow and Peking factions, Brazilian Communism has splintered into a bewildering variety of groups. Representatives of some of these held key positions in labor and student organizations, radio, and telecommunications. (4) A total of approximately 850 trained Communist subversives were at work in Brazil during recent months. According to the Army's secret service, 40 were graduates of the Lenin Institute, 350 had attended the Latin America Institute in Prague, and the rest had taken the "Short Course" in Havana. Guerilla training had begun in the states of Rio de Janeiro and Rio Grande do Sul by late last year. (5) A plan existed for concerted action on May 1 by Communist factions and Goulart's pressure groups; versions vary as to authorship and ultimate ends.

The Communist threat to Brazil had a definite basis in reality, but seems to have been more a product of local adventurers flirting with Chinese theories than of an international grand design. Its leadership was divided and largely disreputable, and presumably jumped the gun on the disciplined subversives. Though the needs of Brazil's rural masses and marginal groups are great and their miseries frightful, the "revolution from the top" failed to capture a mass base. On the other hand, the Communist threat was obviously exaggerated and exploited as a catalyst for the varied anti-Goulart forces—with a degree of cool cynicism rivaling that with which Goulart used "reformism" to pursue his own ends. Whatever the moral implications, the example of those carefully organized housewives marching with their rosaries is not likely to be soon forgotten.

PERU

In this selection, James L. Payne, Professor of Political Science at the School of Advanced International Studies of Johns Hopkins University, has a conceptualization of Peruvian politics that is especially interesting. He sees political power residing almost completely in the presidency, with a strong opposition ready to use any means to overturn this power center if necessary, and the military ready to step in if the President cannot keep order. The strategy of labor unions in this type of system will consist of using the threat of escalating strikes instead of collective bargaining, for labor demands will be met by the President if he feels that violence prone strikes bring the danger of military intervention. Thus the whole system operates within the context of, not random or isolated violence, but politically structured violence. Professor Payne does not necessarily deplore this, but rather is more interested in explaining why it has to be this way considering the underlying conditions.

Professor Payne developed this conceptualization of Peruvian politics from a book focusing on labor issues. A study of other issues conceivably might refine the conceptualization or perhaps even make major modifications of it.

THE PERUVIAN POLITICAL SYSTEM

*Peru: The Politics of Structured Violence**

JAMES PAYNE

At first glance, Peruvian politics presents a chaotic scene to the political analyst. Demonstrations, riots, rebellions, electoral irregularities, *coups* and dictatorships: the political panorama unfolds so rapidly that there seems to be nothing permanent on which to base an analysis.

The recent political history of Peru has been kaleidoscopic. From 1939 to 1945 the country experienced a repressive government under Manuel Prado. In 1945 elections were held and a period of free government under Jose Luis Bustamante y Rivero ensued. In 1948 Bustamante was removed through a military *coup* and General Manuel Odria headed a dictatorship which lasted until 1956. Elections were held and Manuel Prado took office as President of a free regime once again. In 1962 his term was ended a few days short of the constitutional six-year period by another military *coup* which grew out of the election crisis. A military government—which observed political freedoms—ruled for one year, elections were held again, and Fernando Belaunde Terry emerged as President of a free regime in 1963.

It might seem, after gazing at this record, that the pattern of Peruvian politics is simply incoherent, that there are no regularities. The problem lies, however, in defining the system

* Reprinted from James L. Payne, "Peru: The Politics of Structured Violence," *The Journal of Politics* (May, 1965), pp. 362–374 by permission of publisher and author.

This paper has been prepared from a full-length study of labor and politics in Peru. Research was conducted in Peru during the entire year of 1961. Most of the information on which this study is based has come from over one hundred interviews with labor leaders, party politicians and government officials, supplemented by personal observation of meetings, assemblies, demonstrations and strikes. The writer is grateful to Drs. Aaron Wildavsky and Robert Anderson of the University of California (Berkeley) for their assistance in the preparation of this article.

to be analyzed. An American, familiar with the regular constitutional procedures of the United States, tends to look at the same institutions in Peru. Finding these practices atrophied or abused, he would become discouraged, concluding lamely that the *system* is 'unstable' or 'perverted.' But his discouragement and his lame conclusions are simply the result of adopting an inadequate theoretical perspective.

Analytically it is impractical to view Peruvian politics in a constitutional framework, for constitutionalism is not the modal pattern of interaction. To treat violence and the military *coup* as aberrations places one in the awkward position of insisting that practically all significant political events of the past half-century are deviations. Demonstrations, clashes with the police, military take-overs: these are *normal* in a purely descriptive sense. They happen frequently and they are significant.

Consequently, we must identify as a system for analysis the pattern of interaction characterized by violence and other extra-constitutional practices. In the same way that elections are central components of a constitutional democracy the military *coup* is considered essential to the functioning of the system in Peru. Riots are fully a part of the Peruvian pattern, not merely distasteful, peripheral incidents—as they are considered in the United States. When we make violence the focal point of analysis the behavior of the participants becomes understandable and—over a certain range—predictable.

In treating Peruvian politics in a short essay we must narrow down our scope of concern. Two explicit restrictions are placed on our analysis. First we shall deal with patterns of decision-making in which violence plays an immediate, critical role. Such issues include: most labor disputes, both specific wage demands and many general laws on such subjects as discharge and length of the working day; some university student-administration (or faculty) conflicts; numerous specific agrarian conflicts (land occupation by peasants, strikes of plantation workers); occasional conflicts over the cost-of-living in general or over prices of specific commodities (cement, meat, gasoline); and certain positions involving foreign policy which organizations of journalists and lawyers as well as workers and students might seek to defend violently in a particular case.

Deciding such violence-connected issues is a substantial part of the activity of government, and as such these cases merit study. In addition, an understanding of these cases is extremely useful in analyzing most of the other decisions of government, since decisions on most non-violent issues are made with the possibility of future violence in mind. For example, the decision made in late 1961 to raise the export tax on fishmeal—opposed by both the producers and the longshoremen's union—was not accompanied by violence. But decision-makers were influenced by the knowledge that to disappoint the longshoremen would engender their animosity and make future violence more probable. By analyzing the decision-making process on issues of violence we thereby gain insights into many other decisions as well. However, we make no attempt to give a complete account of all patterns of conflict resolution.

We shall further limit our analysis to a discussion of interaction during a free regime. A "free regime" may be defined as characterized by the actual freedom of all major political parties and interest groups to exist and operate, and the actual observance of freedoms of speech, press and public protest. Naturally, as in the United States, these freedoms are not absolute; nevertheless there is a wide difference in the degree to which these freedoms are observed in a free regime and in what may be termed a "dictatorship." It should be pointed out that our conception of a "free regime" does not include the idea of permanence. It is simply one phase of a global pattern.

Under a free regime groups may organize and communicate. They may mobilize opinion and gain adherents. Under a free regime groups are able to develop and stage violent attacks upon the government.

The violence to which we refer is not random or isolated; it is politically-structured violence, violence which is meaningful in the political context. In the Peruvian context politically significant violence must have the following characteristics: 1) it must be directed against significant political leaders and/or parties. In nearly all cases the object of the attack will be the President; 2) it must involve a prominent political issue on which there is wide disagreement. A simple murder, for example, does not have these properties and consequently it is not politically relevant.

In its ultimate form structured violence involves a physical attack upon agents of the government over some issue of political concern. An illustration is provided by the assault of the Congressional building in October, 1961 which occurred during the strike of the public school teachers. A group of about 300 demonstrators rushed at the entrance, the guards fired, the demonstrators fled, but one lay behind, killed by a bullet. Were this event isolated it would have been generally condemned as either silly or repugnant. But because it was structured within the political context it had highly significant repercussions.

The teachers' strike—during which this episode occurred—had become a national issue. Opposition parties and newspapers, along with the left-extremists (Communists, Trotskyites, and others) had condemned the government for its stinginess. When the demonstrator was killed it was taken as proof of the cruelty of the government. In spite of the decree suspending Constitutional guarantees (which formally prohibited all public gatherings) a gigantic funeral demonstration was held. Striking teachers joined opposition forces and gathered in the Parque Universitario. The situation was explosive. The slightest incident would have led to a massacre of serious proportions. The army troops carefully kept their distance, waiting in side streets away from the crowd. On this occasion the demonstration ended peacefully. But it could easily have been otherwise.

Uncertainty, as the reader can see from this example, is a feature of this structured violence. No one knows exactly when violence will take place. But all the participants are acutely aware of the relative probabilities of violence occurring at any particular moment. In this sense the violence is structured. Each event bears a relationship to the next so that we must speak of a pattern and not of isolated events. The congressional attack had serious overtones because it led to an even more explosive situation. But the attack in turn had its antecedents in earlier demonstrations, in newspaper invective, in opposition party meetings, in extremist activity on the issue, in the hunger strikes of some teachers, and so on. Structured violence, then, is an entire pattern of interaction, the end product of which is significant physical violence directed against the government.

Why does this pattern exist? How does violence fit into the processes of decision-making and leadership change? These are the questions which we shall attempt to answer. Our discussion will center around five propositions about political interaction during a period of free government:

1. The conflict for control of the Presidency is intense.
2. Opposition forces are disposed to employ extreme methods to destroy an incumbent President—including the use of physical violence.
3. The armed forces will remove a President when widespread "dissatisfaction" exists and incidents of violence become frequent.
4. The President, when his tenure is threatened by the use of violence, will attempt to prevent violence by making concessions to those groups which threaten its use.
5. Therefore politically structured violence is a highly effective weapon for those groups which can employ it.

The underlying drive for the Peruvian system—the mainspring, as it were—is the intensity of the conflict between the opposition and the President. Opposition forces do not view politics as a gentleman's game played for moderate stakes in an atmosphere of restraint. They see it as a struggle of overwhelming significance. The intensity of conflict explains, in large part, the frequent use of violence. Opposition forces see the outcome of this struggle against the executive as *more significant* than constitutional norms, moral injunctions or physical safety. We have in American history occasional examples of conflict so intense that it transcended the usual moral and constitutional norms—the Civil War, for example. But in Peru such intense conflict is not occasional; it is the permanent condition of political society.

We may briefly suggest certain conditions which produce this high level of conflict intensity between opposition forces and the President.

1. The Peruvian government is, and has been since colonial

times, highly centralized. At the apex of the system is the President. State and municipal governments, Congress and the courts are, in practice, subordinate to him. The chief executive can and does issue authoritative decrees on almost every conceivable subject. As a consequence of this centralization the President is considered omni-competent and hence, omni-responsible. From the price of meat to the backwardness of agriculture; from holes in streets of a provincial town to the profit rate in the mining industry: when anything goes wrong the executive is considered to have committed a sin of commission or omission.

Needless to say things do go wrong, many things. And the affected groups hold the incumbent President responsible. In a free environment the dissatisfied sectors will organize and concentrate their opposition on a single point: the executive. Whereas in most of the established Western democracies opposition is directed at diverse points in the various decision-making matrices, in Peru the President and his immediate subordinates, being the only decision-makers of consequence, receive its full impact.[1]

In addition to broadening the responsibility for policies, a dispersal of the decision-making processes also serves in countries like the United States to mitigate the opposition to the existing regime. Because opposition forces have, in one way or another, a foothold in the existing system, because they are contained within the government, their hostility to it is never total. In the United States a Southerner may be disappointed with the incumbent President, but he knows that he

[1] It is interesting to note that Alexis de Tocqueville, in discussing the causes of the French Revolution, noted a similar centralization under the *ancien regime:* "In times of dearth—and these were frequent in the eighteenth century—everyone expected the Intendant to come to the rescue as a matter of course. For the government was held responsible for all the misfortunes befalling the community; even when these were 'acts of God' such as floods or droughts, the powers-that-be were blamed for them." *The Old Regime and the French Revolution* (Doubleday, 1955), p. 71. In discussing the stability of the American system, de Tocqueville praised the federal arrangement which insured that "political passion, instead of spreading over the land like a fire on the prairies, spends its strength against the interests and individual passions of every State." *Democracy in America* (Mentor, 1956), p. 85.

can make his views felt in the Senate as well as in local decision-making and administration. But in Peru a group excluded from the executive has no other arena in which to exercise influence. Consequently such a group finds its only practicable alternative is that of attempting to unseat the President.

Groups which formed a permanent opposition during the Prado government (1956–62) included the Popular Action Party of Belaunde, the Odria Party, the Christian Democratic Party, seven left-extremist groups–Communists, two Trotskyite factions, the APRA Rebelde, the Progressive Socialists, the Leninist Committee and the Socialists–as well as interest groups in which these parties had a controlling position: the Federation of Students of San Marcos University, the Federation of Bank Clerks, the Lima Union of Construction Workers and a number of others. Consistent with their position of isolation these groups maintained a posture of total opposition to the President.

2. The large amount of patronage which the President dispenses is another factor contributing to the isolation and intensity of the opposition. Whereas in a country like Sweden or Switzerland few posts go to political appointees, in Peru the civil service is based largely on the spoils system. Job hunters (and their friends and relatives) are numerous. In the above-named countries a change of government leaves public employees practically unaffected; in Peru it creates a horde of angered ex-office holders who see the new President as directly responsible for their loss of employment.

3. Another condition which contributes to the intense conflict found in Peruvian society is the existence of exclusive, partisan communication patterns. Holders of different political views tend to locate themselves in the communication channel which reinforces their position. This phenomenon is most clearly seen in the case of the Aprista party organization. The Apristas have their own cafeteria and barber shop, their own medical assistance staff, soccer teams, and party newspaper, *La Tribuna.* In addition there are numerous secondary groups within the party: university students, workers, high school students, artists, lawyers, and so on. Hence an Aprista may live within the party's world and never have his party loyalty

weakened by contradictory communications. The other parties, to varying degrees, tend to provide their adherents with similar unified opinion environments.[2]

Two of the three major Lima newspapers, *La Prensa* and *El Comercio,* are part of the partisan channels of communication. The former supported the government in the period 1959–1962, the latter attacked it with skill and venom. Those individuals who sided with the opposition found in *El Comercio* a copious supply of criticism and invective which served to reinforce their dissatisfaction with the Prado government.[3]

Political conflict in Peru, then, is intense and bi-polar: between the In's and the Out's. Those groups which are excluded from the executive become intensely opposed to the incumbent President and are willing to take extreme measures to depose him. Centralization places in the hands of the President practically all formal decision-making power; consequently he is a significant target. Excluded from this pin-point of power opposition forces have no alternative but to work for his downfall. Deprived of patronage and reinforced in their animosity by partisan channels of communication, opposition groups see the destruction of the President as a noble and necessary task.

The visitor to Peru does not pass many days in the country before grasping the polarized nature of political conflict and the intensity of the opposition to the executive. A chat with a

[2] The analysis here draws upon the general theory of cross-pressures and attitude formation. For specific reference to the problem of political conflict see: David B. Truman, *The Governmental Process* (New York, 1960), pp. 157 ff., 507 ff.; Sigmund Neumann, *Modern Political Parties* (Chicago, 1956), p. 404; Seymour Martin Lipset, *Political Man,* (Anchor, 1963), pp. 74–79.

[3] The third Lima daily, *La Cronica,* was more mass consumption-oriented and tended to avoid partisan political issues. The television stations were also relatively nonpolitical, again apparently because they were attempting to reach the largest possible audience and thus realize the greatest return on their investment. One might expect that *El Comercio* and *La Prensa* may also be forced by economic necessity to 'tone down' partisan politics. For a discussion of the relationship between political cleavage, economic variables and the mass media the reader should consult Otto Kirchheimer, "The Waning of Opposition in Parliamentary Regimes," *Social Research,* Vol. 24, No. 2 (1956), pp. 149–150.

taxi driver, a newspaper headline: the American soon realizes that politics is a serious, even deadly, business. The desire to destroy the incumbent President is of paramount significance. The intensity with which this objective is pursued results not only in the use of violence, as we have suggested, but also in the formation of seemingly incongruent alliances. The Christian Democratic Party (in the opposition in 1961) had a peasant affairs bureau which worked closely with members of the Trotskyite and Rebel APRA parties who were attempting to foment a revolution through rural violence. That the Pope's sworn enemies should walk hand-in-hand with his disciples testifies to the overwhelming importance of the struggle against the executive in the eyes of these participants.

The picture, as far as we have presented it, leaves out an important component: the armed forces. They maintain the chief executive in office; they protect him from the enraged opposition. The guards one finds outside the homes of most high officials are mute testimony to the military's role. And when demonstrations and riots reach excessive proportions, it is the Army which contains and disperses the mobs.

Although the armed forces tend to establish broad limits to the actions of the executive, they are characteristically uninterested in details of policy. What they are interested in is peace. It is incorrect to suppose that the military is the enemy of peaceful free government. Direct military intervention in politics has taken place only in times of acute crisis, in times when civilian political conflict threatened to lead to dangerous extremes. The military *coup* of July, 1962, is a case in point. None of the three major presidential candidates–Odria, Haya de la Torre, and Belaunde–obtained the requisite one-third of the ballots for election. Belaunde, seeing his position was weakest, agitated for annulment of the elections on the grounds of fraud. He was joined by the extremists and *El Comercio*. The other two candidates could not agree–until it was too late–on a coalition. After civilian politicians had struggled for nearly a month and produced only greater uncertainty, the armed forces stepped in and put an end to the chaotic scene.

The logic of the situation dictates that intervention should occur at such times of crisis. The armed forces, composed of different factions holding conflicting ideological and political sympathies, can act unanimously only if the civilian government has demonstrated its inability to keep order. When things are going along smoothly an attempted *coup* by one faction would be opposed by other factions of the armed forces which sympathized with the incumbent regime. A *coup* attempted in times of peace, when the armed forces are divided in their opinions, would be very dangerous. At best it could mean a court martial for the losers; at worst, internecine war.

Consequently, as long as the executive manages to keep unrest at a minimum the military tends to support the incumbent regime. But if the armed forces are repeatedly engaged in clashes with agitated mobs and armed demonstrators, they will come to believe that the wisest course is to depose the object of civilian dissatisfaction, the President. When civil war threatens, the armed forces become united in their disapproval of the existing government and a bloodless *coup* can be quickly executed.

The President of a free regime, then, while all-responsible, is by no means all-powerful. He is situated between a ravenous opposition on one side and an ambivalent military on the other. As the political temperature rises–strikes, solidarity strikes, demonstrations, clashes, deaths, protest demonstrations–the tenure of the chief executive becomes increasingly uncertain. Since the first object of the chief executive is to stay in office, the manner in which he must behave is quite clear: he must attempt to pacify, undermine or at least contain the groups employing violence against him. The most obvious manner in which he can forestall violence is to give those who threaten it a part of what they want.

This leads us to consideration of the dynamic impulse given to the system by interest groups. We have identified three actors with interrelated roles: the opposition, the President, and the military. But what sets these participants in motion? We have shown how violence cannot be random if it is to be politically effective. A group of political party members cannot simply rush out onto the street and attack a policeman. Successful violence must be structured; it must be meaningful. The opposition political parties require substantive issues of conflict on which to construct their attack upon the government.

Interest groups, particularly labor unions, provide these issues. These organizations, through their specific, substantive demands, provide opposition forces with a cause around which violence may be structured—as well as an additional supply of agitators. Once a conflict has been initiated by worker organizations—or less frequently by groups of students or peasants—the opposition forces may swing into action. It follows therefore that if these interest groups are relatively quiet or if the President meets their demands rapidly with adequate concessions, violence has little opportunity to build. The crucial, "violence-initiating" position of interest groups under a free regime explains why, first of all, they are successful if they are able to initiate violence and, secondly, why control of these organizations is so important to political parties.

Opposition forces wish to control these groups in order to initiate and extend violence. In the case of labor unions opposition party (or left-extremist) control results in exorbitant demands, prolonged strikes and the frequent use of the solidarity strike for a wide range of political issues. Government-supporting parties (e.g., the APRA party during the Prado regime) wish to control interest groups to prevent their use against the executive. Worker organizations influenced by these forces tend to make their demands moderate, to avoid or curtail strikes whenever possible and to refrain from solidarity strikes except when such strikes clearly involve limited worker objectives.

In practically all major political crises worker organizations play a key role. The June 1961 strike of the construction workers provides a typical example. Called by the Communist-controlled Federation of Construction Workers, the strike was immediately given full and sympathetic coverage by *El Comercio*. The issue began to build. One worker was killed when a group of strikers attacked two policemen guarding non-striking workers. In the Chamber of Deputies members of the Popular Action and Progressive Socialist parties presented a motion to censure the Minister of Interior. The opposition-extremist Federation of Bank clerks held a one-day sympathy strike. The extremist-led regional federations of workers in

Callao and Arequipa threatened to strike. University students, under the leadership of a member of the Christian Democratic Party, staged a 48-hour protest strike.

In view of the agitated political atmosphere the Ministry of Labor issued a decree granting a 12 to 15 percent (depending on the category) wage increase for construction workers. Interest waned. The construction workers had received substantial gains and were uninclined to remain on strike. Extremist leaders of other unions, although they might have wished to add to the tension, realized that rank and file workers would not obey a solidarity strike order in support of the already successful construction workers. So opposition forces withdrew to wait for the next opportunity which a worker organization conflict would provoke.

The support of political parties which have strength in the labor movement is an important asset for a President since these parties will attempt to moderate the violence which worker organizations will use. One of the major reasons for the 1948 *coup* against Jose Luis Bustamante y Rivero (President from 1945 to 1948) was the 1947 shift of the APRA party, and the many labor organizations it controlled, from support to opposition of Bustamante. The repeated use of violence-oriented strikes and demonstrations by these APRA-led unions greatly added to the political tension which finally resulted in a military *coup*. The support of the APRA party and its labor leaders provides one explanation for the relatively long term of Manuel Prado (1956–1962). This is not to say that APRA labor leaders did not threaten or use violence. But they were careful to circumscribe overt union activity so that their threatened crises seldom materialized.

Through his control over the timing and content of conflict-resolving decrees, the President has another important asset. As we pointed out above, the limits on presidential action are broad. He is not bound by constitutional constraints or similar legal trappings. He (or his ministers with his authority) may issue any decree, which has the force of law, on almost every conceivable subject. By carefully adjusting each decree to a series of variables–preference intensity of the interest groups involved, cohesiveness of these organizations, the possibility of solidarity strikes, the popularity of the cause, and the general political temperature–he can carefully circumscribe violence while not making extravagant, and eventually dangerous, concessions.

In dealing with labor conflicts, the executive has a highly institutionalized procedure to accomplish this dual objective of low violence and sound economics. When a local union voices a demand, it bargains first with management. When it fails to receive satisfactory concessions from the employer it appeals to the Ministry of Labor for a decree and, at about the same time, begins a strike. The Ministry allows time to elapse (3–10 days) in order to gauge the severity of the threat. If violence seems unlikely, the Ministry issues a modest sub-directoral resolution which awards the workers about as much as, perhaps slightly more than, the employer was willing to grant. If violence becomes imminent–solidarity strikes, newspaper agitation, opposition party rallies, university student parades–then a second (directoral) resolution is issued, usually on the eve of a solidarity strike or proposed mass demonstration.

This two-step process makes it possible to allow the assaulting union to expend most of its resources so that it might be disposed to accept a relatively low offer. At the same time the executive has a second, more generous resolution ready which may be used if the situation moves to the brink of full-scale agitation.

In order to absolve itself of the enormous responsibility inherent in 'dictating' employer-employee relations throughout the country, the Ministry attempts to maintain that it employs objective criteria for its decisions: cost of living index, comparable wages, "subsistence level." But of course this is mere verbiage. Wage increases are each carved out to fit particular conflict situations, generosity being proportional to the violence potential.

For example, a tiny group of workers for the small shop Ciurlizza Maurer struck in December 1961 for higher wages. The Ministry of Labor granted a 4.26 percent increase (the rise in the cost of living index for that year). The workers were not satisfied and continued striking. After nearly thirty days of strike the Ministry made a second offer of 6 percent which the workers eventually accepted. Although there were minor instances of local violence (fist fights, for example), there was no major incident. The group of workers was very small, they belonged to no higher organization which would carry out a solidarity strike and the issue was virtually unknown to the public.

In the case of the strike of the San Miguel factory textile workers the situation was quite different. This relatively large union belonged to the Federation of Textile Workers which can muster nearly 20,000 workers into the streets in a solidarity strike in support of a member union. And behind the Federation stood the Confederation of Peruvian Workers, the national labor center. The general secretary of the Confederation was a past officer of the Federation and ties between the two organizations were quite close. When the San Miguel workers went on strike in August 1961 the Ministry of Labor granted an 11 percent wage increase, which the workers would not accept. Then, two and one-half weeks after the strike began, during a meeting of the Federation of Textile Workers where a solidarity strike was being discussed, a messenger arrived from the Ministry with a decree granting a 14 percent increase. This the workers accepted. Only by taking into account the political environment can we explain the difference between the outcomes in the case of these two unions.

Violence which is structured into the political context, then, is an eminently successful political weapon in the Peruvian free regime. A President threatened by its use will make generous concessions to the assaulting groups. And it must be thus. Many Americans fail to understand the role of the executive. They complain about his supposedly "unconstitutional," "unnatural" intervention in such affairs as labor disputes. But he must intervene to survive. It is suicidal for a President (and his Labor Minister) to "stand aloof" from such conflicts for the ever-widening circles of violence would quickly engulf him. He could, of course, attempt repression, but the road to and through dictatorship also has its dangers, not the least of which is the problem of military disunity.

The President acts as he must, as do the workers in employing violence. For them violence is a highly successful weapon. The alternative of collective bargaining, a tactic of economic coercion, offers little promise. Successful use of collective bargaining requires that numerous economic variables be favorable, particularly that the supply of unemployed labor be small. In Peru where migration has created severe unemployment, economic strikes would, in most cases, be undermined by replacements. To ask Peruvian unionists to use collective bargaining and refrain from violence is tantamount to urging dissolution of the labor movement.

The leverage of these interest groups comes, in turn, from the intense, bi-polar conflict between the opposition and the President. The role which the military plays as arbitrator must also be interpreted in light of this conflict. Were Peruvian political society characterized by friendship and tranquility, the military would not find itself encouraged, even forced, to effect *coups*.

The intense conflict between the President and his opponents, then, we identify as the force which structures the entire pattern of interaction. We have briefly discussed some of the institutional and social variables which contribute to this conflict, but the problem is clearly one which invites further analysis.

URUGUAY

Uruguay's long-standing democracy has been debilitated in past years by a number of extremely serious financial and administrative problems. In this selection, Philip B. Taylor, Jr., Professor of Political Science at the University of Houston, argues that this situation has been caused mainly by certain characteristics of the political system. He is particularly concerned about the proliferation of pressure groups and factions of parties that have pressed their narrow self-interest demands directly into the legislature with little regard for aggregating their interests beforehand. Professor Taylor's comments leave one with the strong impression that Uruguay is no longer the innovator in Latin America.

URUGUAY'S DYSFUNCTIONAL POLITICAL SYSTEM

*Interests and Institutional Dysfunction in Uruguay**

PHILIP B. TAYLOR, JR.

Small in size but great in influence on Latin American intellectuals, Uruguay has been regarded as the most progressive of the twenty countries of its heterogeneous area. The "western" nature of its political system invites the application

* Reprinted from Philip B. Taylor, Jr., "Interests and Institutional Dysfunction in Uruguay," The American Political Science Review (March, 1963), pp. 62–74 by permission of author and publisher.

of recently devised analytical concepts, and preliminary analysis suggests that many of these concepts can be exemplified in its highly developed political institutions.

The titles of books devoted to Uruguay seem to suggest an approach to the millennium there: *Uruguay, South America's first Welfare State; Uruguay, Portrait of a Democracy;* and *Utopia in Uruguay,* among others.[1] They imply that despite the feudal obscurantism of the colonial era, and the incapacity and abuses of the nineteenth century, that country has achieved redemption of a sort. Yet the idealist who seeks his goal there may be disappointed. Despite all the hopeful arguments that a stable middle sector based on professionalism and technical proficiency may prove the strongest ally for democratic practice and progress (and hence for the Alliance for Progress), an examination of this particular specimen may suggest the opposite. Or worse, Uruguay may actually offer an example which is simply irrelevant.[2]

Current conditions in Uruguay suggest many problematical questions. All must be considered within the context of a democratic, social welfare-oriented system which has produced the highest average level of living in Latin America commensurate with national resources. Has emphasis on political and personal freedom created conditions in which political institutions perform functions quite different from those normally allotted them in traditional institutional analyses? If this is so, are these institutions actually dysfunctional, even within the unique Uruguayan context? To what extent have the demands of interest groups created this dysfunction, and to what extent have they defeated efforts to undertake institutional improvement or correction? Does Uruguayan political experience demonstrate any special and transferable genius which can be employed by the sister republics to their own advantage?

[1] Respectively, by George Pendle (London, Royal Institute of International Affairs, 1952); Russell H. Fitzgibbon (New Brunswick, N. J., Rutgers University Press, 1954); and Simon G. Hanson (New York, Oxford University Press, 1938).

[2] John J. Johnson, *Political Change in Latin America* (Stanford University Press, 1958), pp. 1–14, states the general thesis regarding the "middle sectors"; pp. 45–65 discuss Uruguay specifically.

I

To a greater extent than most Latin American countries, Uruguay is divided into three distinct and unequal parts. The urban metropolis today includes at least 50 per cent of the total population, and is known as the largest capital in the world relative to the total population of its country. In material terms all but its slums offer more attractive living conditions than most rural housing, and public health and educational facilities, together with the well paying jobs, are concentrated here. The livestock-based "interior"—the second part—encompasses the great *estancias* or estates which tend to operate as if this were a past century. The available data show clearly that progressively fewer owners possess progressively more acreage there. The mood of the leaders of this area has been unremittingly individualistic and conservative, although the flow of lower and middle-class immigrants to Montevideo, both from Europe and from the interior, had given the city political predominance even before 1900 and so forced semi-cooperation from the interior. In between, in the suburbs and along the coasts and rivers—the third part—are the farms and the slums which grow continuously through city-ward migration. Their inhabitants have sought political spokesmen in the past with some success, but their small average income and comparatively small population have made the affiliation tenuous. The government's resettlement, colonization and land reform program has had small resources, and has been unable to turn peasants into self-reliant farmers in sufficient numbers. The area therefore has prospered politically only in transitory alliance with the interior's greater wealth and influence.[3]

The city and the interior each possesses its own "pecking order" and goal, although the unremitting civil strife of the

[3] Support for these generalizations is presented in the author's *Government and Politics of Uruguay* (New Orleans, Tulane Studies in Political Science, Vol. VII, 1962).

The racial composition of the cast of characters in Uruguay is almost entirely white. The folk-myth of the plainsman or *gaucho*, the semicivilized mestizo, is retained today in diet and in the *semana criolla* (in other countries, Holy Week), but in little else.

nineteenth century was fought largely above the heads of the indifferent majorities and without much reference to any geographic strongholds. Almost unthinking demands on government were channeled through two pseudo-parties, the *Blancos* and the *Colorados,* which were the personal gangs of momentarily dominant *caudillos* rather than conscious articulators of genuine interests.

The peace treaty of 1851 was the first formal aggregation of interests in the country's history, a *modus vivendi* which also established geographic spheres of influence for the two. Succeeding outbreaks produced similar formal agreements, to which governmental institutions responded without the slightest display of independent action.[4]

Starting about 1880, immigration began in significant numbers. In the 1890s the Colorado party came under the influence of José Batlle y Ordóñez, whose rejection of the previous national social and political *status quo* was based on both humanitarian and tough-minded political analysis. His election to the Presidency in 1903 brought on the last great civil war; and definitive government victory, for the first time, led to the Pact of 1904. By its terms the Blanco-controlled interior recognized that resort to arms was no longer possible against the national government, and unification occurred.[5] Since that time the pacts have become somewhat more sophisticated in appearance, although the purposes have remained largely the same. The changing power balances among Colorados and Blancos, as well as among their respective warring factions, have been reflected by division and redivision of the spoils in never-ending institutional and constitutional change, although the breakdown of agreement actually produced mild *coups d'état* in 1933 and 1942.

Until 1959, the Colorado party largely controlled the fate of the country. Its majority faction was principally urban, liberal, and lower and middle class-based. A conservative wing found its strength in the interior and the coastal farm coun-

[4] Eduardo Acevedo, *Anales Históricos del Uruguay* (Montevideo, Barreiro y Ramos, 3d printing, 1933), Vol. 3, pp. 9–364, discusses the details.

[5] Juan E. Pivel Devoto and Alcira Ranieri de Pivel Devoto, *Historia de la República Oriental del Uruguay* (*1830–1930*) (Montevideo, Editorial Medina, 1945), pp. 540–542.

try, and was assured some elective offices by the introduction of proportional representation (PR) in the election of all public officers; but it never controlled the executive branch nor national social and economic policy.[6] The party's urban organizational machinery was tightly knit, and its strength preserved the party's advantage within the urban areas generally, and in Montevideo especially. The Blanco party always remained the largest minority. Although its great *caudillo*, Luis Alberto de Herrera, tried many times to achieve power by election, pact and *coup*, he succeeded only in winning terms in the nine-member national executive council, and in the legislature, because to most urban voters he symbolized the traditional past and the great *estancieros*. The Blanco party machinery could deliver majorities in most rural Departments, but never in Montevideo. The Colorado party's social and economic policies brought health and a solid share of the available wealth of the country to the urban majorities, and disparities between economic classes shrank in the cities. Little legislation penetrated deeply enough into the interior to disturb seriously the continued dominance of the conservative rural elites. As time passed the gap between the rural mass and elite widened further. Although the Blancos could not prevent the enactment of policies with which they were in disagreement, they could temper their administration by obtaining a proportionate share of bureaucratic positions. The *Pacto del Chinchulín* (literally, "pork-barrel") of 1931 essentially confirmed this allocation of power for the indefinite future.[7]

[6] Briefly, the election law of 1924 allows the "most-voted" sector of the "most-voted" party to control the accumulated votes of all sectors of that party. The same is true for the corresponding sector of the "second most-voted" party. This rule applies to election of the executive officers. PR is employed without gimmicks for election of legislative officers. 1924 *Registro Nacional de Leyes y Decretos del la República Oriental del Uruguay*, pp. 81–122; 1925 *Registro*, pp. 27–59. The operation of the law is discussed in detail in Taylor, *op. cit.*, pp. 43–49.

[7] The agreement, and several accompanying understandings, were enacted into law. The Pact is #8,765, October 15, 1931 (1931 *Registro*, pp. 577–580).

Blanco electoral control of interior Departments increased steadily after 1946. In the 1954 election, only Montevideo Department

The middle sector of society—of which some professionals and the enormously over-developed bureaucracy were the backbone—appered to see in the Colorado party's various factions satisfactory channels for presenting most of their rather simplistic demands on the government. The highly unionized lower class, which generally rejected the seductive call of the left, whether Socialist or Communist, shared this evaluation. José Batlle's reforms actually had created these groups as politically sentient elements, and the *batllista* wing of the party retained their loyalty long after his death. The moderate Independent Blanco party, which was composed largely of more conservative professionals and which bitterly opposed Herrera and his followers, often threw its support to liberal Colorado initiatives. The completely *laissez faire* political climate, which encouraged highly vocal discussion of government policies in the party-owned newspapers as well as in the legislative chambers and the Executive Council, produced sophisticated examination of most interest demands for government action, although the general public actually was rather ingenuous. This process also forced the major parties to make somewhat broader commitments to the voters than their leaders might have preferred, in attempts to prevent an unbearable proliferation of parties through the use of PR.[8]

Popular reliance on the political system thus created produced a national political psychology in sharp contrast to that of most of the country's neighbors. By 1920, Uruguayans (at least, urban Uruguayans) believed explicitly in the reality of all of the fundamentals of the democratic-republican process. Political utopia did, in fact, appear to have developed. Beneath this popularly satisfying façade, however, untested conservative and fundamentally anti-democratic strengths lay quiescently, awaiting the time when circumstances would permit reversals.

---

returned a Colorado majority. Uruguay, Corte Electoral, *Elecciones Uruguayas* (Montevideo, 5 vols., 1948–1959), by Julio T. Fabregat.

"Pacts" among political parties are rather common in the history of the republican period in Latin America. They are recognition of the real *loci* of power, and of the fact that constitutionalism is no deeper in penetration than the depth of agreement at the moment among the leaders of the more important political groups.

[8] Taylor, *op. cit.*, pp. 45–49.

II

The opportunity began to develop in the 1950s. Batlle had taken control of a modestly vigorous economy, operating within a primitively organized but slowly modernizing society, and had projected it toward limited but imagination-capturing goals. Although in the long run the devices adopted have had a limiting effect on subsequent economic development, Batlle's abiding sense of integrity and appropriateness always restrained the urge toward innovation of social provisions, or nationalization, for their own sakes. Yet there could be no mistaking his strong commitment to the urban and lower class groups of the country. His reforms rested implicitly on the development of respect for law and on the development of rational administrative processes; it may well be that neither would have been entirely possible had it not been for his dominant personality. The reforms moved successfully along the tightrope of feasibility until his passing in 1929. He created a new *modus vivendi* for the majority of the population, and out of it grew a middle sector—perhaps one of the largest, proportionately, in Latin America—based on limited socialism.[9]

Batlle's successors and opponents seemed not to share his intellectual and tactical capabilities. The social and economic role of the government was broadened rapidly and was debased simultaneously by mismanagement, peculation and bureaucratic inflation. The new leaders, many of them related to him by blood or marriage, seemed unable to respond to

[9] The most comprehensive and authoritative Uruguayan work on Batlle is Roberto M. Giudice and Efraín González Conzi, *Batlle y el batllismo* (Montevideo, Editorial Medina, 2d Edition, 1959). The disintegration of the system is described in many polemic works; perhaps the best of them is Gustavo Gallinal, *El Uruguay hacia la dictadura. Preparación del golpe de estado* (Montevideo, 1938). Milton I. Vanger, *José Batlle y Ordóñez of Uruguay, the Creator of His Times, 1902–1907* (Cambridge, Harvard University Press, 1963), covers the early years of his political control. See also Hanson, *op. cit.*, pp. 19–26; and Antonio M. Grompone, "Las clases medias en el Uruguay," *Materiales para el estudio de la clase media en la América Latina* (Washington, D. C., Pan American Union, 1950, vol. I, pp. 76–91).

increasing urban and labor demands except through blindly enacting more social legislation. They could find no techniques for paying the new bills except the enactment of greater tax demands on the interior (administered as export taxes, fundamentally) or bothersome excises on domestic commerce. The movement lagged during the depression of the 1930s, but this was momentary. Socialism became sterile and unimaginative conservatism; the political system became one in which no appeal was ever denied, no problem ever solved definitively, no issue ever faced candidly on its merits. The obvious fact that the country was living beyond its means as early as 1933 was never met by policy conducive to production and export. Thereafter, only during major foreign wars, when Uruguay's agricultural exports were in profitable demand, were international trade balances in surplus, let alone the total payments balances.

As the interior's spokesmen found decreasing satisfaction in the formal institutions of government as instruments for even the limited fulfillment of their interests, they engaged in mounting civil disobedience.[10] Thirty-five years of Herrera's semi-responsibility, and the political demagogy of his newspaper, *El Debate,* had contributed little to urban public confidence in him. Simultaneously, urban groups, which had been the mainstays of the Colorado party, now began to reconsider the utility of their old fealties. The sectors of the major parties began to regroup under new alignments, and the coalitions began to form in 1956.

Two elements became the nuclei of political change during the 1950s. One was the Independent Blanco party. Tired of wandering in a political no man's land, this small group combined with the Blanco political leader in Montevideo, Daniel Fernández Crespo, who in turn defected from his long-time support of Herrera. The newly formed *Unión Blanca Democrática* (UBD), as a sector of the Blanco party, could perhaps hope to capture control of the parent party in the 1958 election. Later, a substantial number of Colorado conservatives also defected; it was correctly anticipated that some of them would vote Blanco. An added factor, of completely unknown political valence, was the recently arrived slum-dwell-

[10] Taylor, *op. cit.,* p. 140.

ing migrant in the suburbs of Montevideo. The social benefits of the city had not yet reached him, and the rural patterns of behavior, which tended toward a Blanco vote, were probably overlaid only with bitterness about his underprivileged status.

Herrera was alarmed by the growing threat to his dominance. He turned to coalition with the second nucleus group, the Federal League for Rural Action, or *ruralistas,* which was led by Benito Nardone.[11] Herrera's bid came at a low spot in Nardone's fortunes, and he joined with alacrity; stoutly maintaining the nonpolitical nature of *ruralismo,* he nevertheless claimed to control the votes of thousands. But disturbed by his ingenuous and fickle new partner,[12] Herrera also patched up a short-lived split with an unprincipled and skilled infighter and former ally, Eduardo Víctor Haedo, in self-protection. The UBD indeed had joined a strange set of bedfellows.

While this regrouping occurred, the Colorado leadership failed to resolve the differences which had been developing from the late 1940s. José Batlle's nephew, Luis, demagogic and left of center, controlled the Executive Council of Government and the Cabinet. Batlle's sons, César and Lorenzo, who were more conservative in some ways and who tended to consider any variation from the preachments of their father as mild treason to the party, would not permit their followers to participate in Luis' government, and they held enough legislative votes to prevent the passage of bills. As the 1955–1959 term neared its end, Luis finally realized the need for remedial

[11] Nardone's first political activity was as a leftist. In the early 1940s he made an unsuccessful effort to join and control the Asociación Rural, an old and respected organization of *estancieros.* In 1951 he broke openly with this group and began to espouse the cause of the coastal and small farmers. In 1954 he joined with Luis Batlle, the Colorado leader, in an unsuccessful effort to attain power. Batlle accepted his aid but refused the favors demanded. By 1956 Nardone was ready to seek other allegiances. The record is reported in a useful article in *Visión,* February 27, 1959.

[12] Evidence of Nardone's naïveté rests in his failure to offer supporting candidacies for legislative or local governmental posts when he came to the coalition. As a result, Nardone stood alone except in the executive branch when the Blancos unexpectedly won.

tax and social legislation to deal with the domestic inflation resulting from previous efforts to counter the effects of recurrent adverse foreign payments balances. César's faction refused its cooperation. Public opinion became impatient at the sight of the self-frustrated and impotent Colorado party. Yet the party remained confident that it could indulge itself. A poll of Montevideo voters which suggested a Blanco victory might occur was attacked as biased, but the final electoral results vindicated the prediction.[13]

The Blanco tenure of power, 1959–1963, obviously was a period of partisan maneuvering, regrouping and reconsideration of policy. Herrera died within weeks after the inauguration of the government for which he had worked so long. Even before the inauguration, Nardone's unreliability and ambition were in evidence, when he tried to make a deal with Luis Batlle to wrest control of the Executive Council from Herrera. Later, as President of the Republic for one year, in the rotational pattern established by the constitution of 1952, Nardone gave abundant evidence that his concept of leadership was fundamentally caudillistic rather than responsible; his constant use of his radio station for daily programs of bitter political attack and innuendo supports the conjecture that he may represent a serious threat to due process and political balance. On the other hand, the UBD came within a very narrow margin of defeating the Nardone-Herrera-Haedo ticket, and must be considered as a political force of insight

[13] Instituto Uruguayo de la Opinión Pública (IUDOP), *Elecciones de 1958 en Montevideo; Un estudio sobre las posibilidades de predicción electoral a través de los métodos de muestra representativa* (Montevideo, 1958); and IUDOP, *Un estudio sobre las posibilidades de predicción electoral y de las caracteristicas socioeconómicas de los grupos partidarios. Efectuado en la ciudad de Montevideo por el método de muestras representativas* (Montevideo, 1959). The first study presents the pre-election survey and offers tentative analysis. The second reports on the reinterview of the first group of respondents, and suggests the major reasons for errors which occurred in the analysis. There is a full report of sample construction as well as the logical reasoning employed in the analyses.

The second analysis shows clearly that the suburban vote, which had not been represented adequately in the sample, threw the results more heavily to the Blancos than had been anticipated.

and salutary resourcefulness if it can retain its coherence. It received as many parliamentary seats as Herrera himself, and devoted the term of office to strenuous efforts to retain its popular vote and find additional acceptable partisan partners. Nardone sought the same goal, however, and with much less restraint; his speech and action as *ruralista* leader revealed his comparative willingness to employ violence as a means which is denied to his more professionally inclined opponents.

The inexperienced members of the new Blanco government could remark sincerely, as one did to this writer, "unfortunately, we won!"

If partisanship is the keynote of political campaigns, sober reflection is necessarily the keynote of legislation and administration. Serious attempts have been made at economic retrenchment, policy change and bureaucratic adjustment. Recommendations of the International Monetary Fund (IMF) have been followed in large part in this process, and austerity has been imposed, with its unwelcome but necessary restraints on popular appetites. Though some of the Fund's recommendations are too unpalatable politically to be adopted in full, the government has attempted to meet others. A first major evidence of good intent was the appointment of a Cabinet composed in part of professionals of both stature and vigor. A second was enactment of a reform law concerning foreign exchange and trade controls, which proved less than ideally effective partly because of its shock on the economy.[14]

On the whole, the government did about as well as could have been expected, although good intentions alone could not suffice. Economy in government operation has special difficulties when an estimated 28 per cent of all workers are employed by the government, and at least 30 per cent of the population depend almost exclusively for their livelihood on

[14] The appointee to the central position in the new Cabinet, Minister of Treasury, was Juan Azzini, Professor of Economics in the University of Montevideo. Azzini's performance has been courageous, at least, and has demonstrated considerable capacity for personal growth in a difficult position. Several other appointments have been of equal stature. The Monetary Reform Law of December 17, 1959 (1959 *Registro*, 1378–1385) is discussed in some detail in Taylor, *op. cit.*, pp. 141–146.

government pensions.[15] The failure of the University of Montevideo to train social scientists prepared to be administrators, planners and investigators has been a glaring disservice to the country, and very few members of that scholarly community appear to have understood it. The 1959–1963 political leadership seemed not to have been able to present to the general urban public, in entirely understandable terms, the need for total reconsideration of past economic and social policy. This is scarcely surprising, since certain aspects of current policy came close to liquidating the position of the lower middle class, and pushed many of the lower class to the wall. Further, many of the Blanco leaders appeared to be more intent on personal preeminence within the party than on solving the country's problems; Blanco leadership therefore inspired little confidence and this demonstrably appeared in response to the recurrent failure of political office-holders to support the more professional Ministers in the Cabinet.

The well-laid plans of the interior elites, to manipulate this trifurcated Blanco party so as to recoup their positions of the late nineteenth century, presently have been partially frustrated by the hard realities of the world in which they are no longer independent agents. These economically powerful interests have been able to achieve many legislative goals, and have been very influential in affecting bureaucratic action; but complete success would result either in the loss of their apparent gains through inflation or the deterioration of the competitive position of the country in international trade.[16]

[15] IUDOP, *Una incógnita nacional, El empleado público* (Montevideo, 1956), pp. 15–20, discusses employment figures. IUDOP, *La austeridad y los problemas económicos-familiares* (Montevideo, 1959), pp. 64–70, discusses pensions and social legislation.

[16] The Monetary Reform Law of 1959 freed all exports and imports from administratively controlled exchange rates, and left the peso free to seek its own level in international money markets. The peso value of lands and animals immediately rose spectacularly. At the same time, all agricultural exports were subjected to "retentions" (export taxes), which cut back on profits to the ranchers and slaughterers. Cattle raisers also sought free access for privately slaughtered beef to the Montevideo market; a decree of February 1, 1934 (1934 *Registro,* 215–216) had closed it to all but the government-owned Frigorífico Nacional. The ranchers scored a

Nevertheless, the combination of rural pressures and market considerations was influential in depriving well-meaning Ministers of requisite legislative support.

Currently, while some political groups bicker over writing a new constitution—as if a new document could solve their problems—others clamor for another *caudillo*. There also is pressure from the left, since the romantic absolutism of *fidelismo* appeals to young student malcontents whose argumentativeness often is matched only by their ignorance. Through all this, a few genuinely thoughtful men in all parties consider what must be done to face the demand for economic and social change while yet retaining the country's genuine and worthwhile characteristics of freedom, fairly adequate social adjustment, and political stability and regularity. The pain of the recent government's tenure of office was conducive to useful thought, but domestic and international currents run swiftly, and interest demands on the government proved difficult to reconcile with the national interest.

An analysis of the system today therefore takes place at a time of crisis and of some drama. An Uruguayan Professor of Constitutional Law remarked to this writer in 1960 that his position was akin to that of a diagnostician who remarks, after examining the patient, "What a divine cancer!" Perhaps no better time could be chosen for an attempt to apply recent analytical concepts.

III

All theories of national development recognize that political change goes hand in hand with social and economic evolution.[17] Marx asserted the primacy of economic factors. More

momentary victory when this market was opened on June 5, 1959 (1959 *Registro,* 520–528), but within 18 months all previous controls had been reimposed by indirect methods or by urban public pressures.

Ranchers have been able to curtail or even eliminate some retentions, but the country has been subjected to the penalties of mounting price inflation as a result. Bank of London and South America, *Fortnightly Review,* February 12, 1961; December 2, 1961.

[17] See particularly, Edward Shils, "Political Development in New States," *Comparative Studies in Society and History,* Vol.

recent students suggest that the interrelations of the three common classifications of forces are so close that differentiating theories, the Marxian included, tend to be ingenuous when carried beyond the most elementary level of discussion. "Western" societies, in contrast with "traditional" societies, it is argued, begin to appear when a population becomes pluralistic as the result of the operation of forces and interests materializing from a nearly infinite universe of possible decisions. Some "western" societies become "democratic" while others do not; yet whether they become "democratic" or "authoritarian," interests will out and change will occur even after the initial configuration has been achieved. The "democratic" society's change may be less orderly in the short run, but it will necessarily involve more freedom and dignity for its participants in the long run. The "authoritarian" society not only will afford fewer of these advantages, but its changes ultimately will come in styles which may well be destructive and jarringly unpredictable.

Recent writing on the analysis of political systems urges that comparisons of functions performed by social institutions are more useful than comparisons solely of the institutions themselves. The most recent and complex formulation of this type of thesis proposes several major categories. These comprise the formulation of claims upon the political system, their communication to it, and the means of satisfying them. If sufficient study ultimately will permit the development of specific quantitative, and not only qualitative, data regarding the elements involved in this interplay, then probabilities of behavior should be calculable.[18] Obviously, the testing of available information against such a proposal offers challenge.

2, nos. 2 and 3 (April and July, 1960), pp. 265–292, 379–411; and Max F. Millikan and Donald L. M. Blackmer, *The Emerging Nations, Their Growth and United States Policy* (Boston, 1961).

[18] Gabriel A. Almond and James S. Coleman, eds., *The Politics of the Developing Areas* (Princeton University Press, 1960), pp. 16–17, 58–64. A useful discussion of Latin America which examines the area from the general approach developed by the S.S.R.C. Committee on Comparative Politics is found in George Blanksten's "Political Groups in Latin America," in [*The American Political Science Review*], Vol. 53 (March, 1959), pp. 106–127.

It also suggests that the general satisfaction with Uruguay's political system usually expressed by area specialists may be reexamined in the light of a set of possibly more sophisticated criteria than those employed to date.[19]

There can be little doubt of the institutional complexity of the Uruguayan political system. In some important respects it can be said that the system achieved its most important goals three decades ago, and today functions only from the momentum of that achievement. The virtual absence of violence over most of a century, and the stability of established families and interests within a small territory, have resulted in a closely knit community which resembles not so much a "city-state" (the figure Uruguayans are fond of applying to themselves) as an overly prolific extended family. It is almost literally impossible, for example, to find a native Uruguayan of the third generation who cannot claim blood relationship with a large percentage of the population. While the country is not uncongenial to immigrants it does not hold out great hope for immediate upward mobility. Much of this is not unusual in a small Latin American country; it *is* unusual in a democratic and western country (although typical of Latin America) to find that such relationships are not only socially meaningful (in the ordinary sense of the word) but also intimate keys to power, to the degree found here.

The personal and organizational elements that participate in the political interplay are deserving of both introduction and examination. To paraphrase the satiric line, (nearly) every little Uruguayan is born a Blanco or a Colorado, however intermittent his political activity may be. Certain family lines have a tradition of great political activity. The mobility of the average citizen among the multitude of parties, fractions and subfractions which bid for his support, particularly in the cities, relates to the unique interests in which he be-

[19] An example of interesting, but only moderately useful studies is the series of articles prepared each five years by Russell H. Fitzgibbon on the basis of polling a selected group of specialists on Latin America. The most recent of these, growing out of the fourth round of questionnaires, is written with the collaboration of Kenneth F. Johnson: "Measurement of Latin American Political Change," [*The American Political Science Review*], Vol. 55 (September, 1961), pp. 515–526.

comes involved. Personal realignment seldom means ostracism by kin today.

Parties and their subgroups flourish in a beneficent legal climate; electoral honesty is of high order and the continued wide if not wanton use of PR has tended to blur the distinction between parties and pressure groups. No would-be politician is precluded from participation. Few active politicians are as compliant to the demands of ambition as are Nardone and Haedo; few are as stubborn as César Batlle. The political scene is populated with enough prominent and high-minded figures, past and present, to make corruption somewhat less common than in most Latin American countries.

It may be supposed that a political system becomes significantly democratic–*i.e.*, combines intermittent popular participation by ethical and legal right in the making of public policy decisions with the assured recognition of some basic freedoms–as it realizes both the ideal of election procedures whose reputation for integrity inspires some general confidence, and the ideal of free and active intercommunication among a literate mass and its leaders, whether in interest groups, parties, or elective office. Ease of communication is essential to the process. It is facilitated in Uruguay by a press which is completely uncensored and is moderately subsidized as well, although there are no nonpartisan newspapers anywhere in the country. Experience, rather than court actions, has taught the limits of expression, and the popular journals are less reluctant to take strong positions than in the United States. A degree of consensus does exist regarding taste, however, and even the most bitter satire in Uruguay seldom reaches the extremes found in Chile and Argentina. Obvious demagogy is somewhat dysfunctional in Uruguay; this lesson had to be learned repeatedly by the extreme *herrerista* wing, as possibly it is being learned today by other groups. On the whole, information and feed-back in the political process are facilitated by the press and also by the determined observance of other personal freedoms. The most extreme groups are able to communicate with each other, even amid quarrels. This marks a significant contrast with other Latin American countries.

As elsewhere, education and economic status are central

to the recruitment of potential political leaders. Universities are the traditional training grounds for most future Latin American activists; Uruguay does not differ in this respect. Matriculation is free, but there is little scholarship aid for other expenses. Residence in Montevideo is essential, for all colleges are located there. Roughly two per cent of the country's population now is able at some period to attend classes, and therefore to qualify potentially for the professional degree which is the hallmark of most national leaders outside the labor unions. The potential circle therefore is quite small, although graduates of secondary and preparatory schools may aspire to middle level positions. The circle must also supply business, education, the arts and the professions.[20] The University cannot be fully effective as a recruitment arena for other reasons than curriculum deficiency. A nucleus of "professional" students enrolls–a group only a few hundred in size but one that makes use of the cloak of "academic freedom" as a cover for participating in lawless manifestations designed to bring legitimate students and the University into disrepute. Their organizational locus is the Student Federation, to which all students belong automatically under the University's rules. They dominate the Federation by devices well known to any student of Communist techniques. In the past few years they have made use of the obvious sympathy of a Socialist Rector, as well as the *"cretines útiles"* who might be considered Uruguay's counterparts of the "angry young men" of other countries. While few students come to such gatherings, in proportion to the total student body, they often bring about action to close the University in a strike. It is common for serious-minded students to complain that they would like to go to classes but cannot because of extremist action.

A second factor contributing to the University's decreased usefulness as a recruitment arena is the longevity of the country's population. Opportunities for young professionals are limited; government incomes are not attractive, even at the professional levels, and private employment at rewarding salaries is not found easily. Wealthy families often send their young men to Europe or to the United States for University work. Many graduates of the University of Montevideo seek

[20] Taylor, *op. cit.*, pp. 126–129.

quicker monetary success than is possible in their own country, and emigrate to presumably greener pastures elsewhere. Figures are impossible to obtain and even specialists in demographic data differ. But there can be little doubt of the phenomenon. It contributes to the comparative social stasis which has been noted elsewhere.

An analysis of Latin American political systems must consider the Catholic Church and the armed forces. In many countries these two are still functioning elements of the government, even though the formal constitution may not so provide. In other countries, less parochial groups have supplanted them as societies have become more "western." No country has progressed so far as Uruguay in this respect. The displacement of the Church in Uruguay began in the 19th century, and was completed officially in the constitution of 1918. The Church was forced to take it calmly, and religion —in the cities, at least—tends today to be a private matter.[21] The army, on the other hand, was never much more than a small militia banded together behind warring *caudillos*. The last of these was exiled in 1887, and José Batlle systematically curtailed military power after the last civil war of 1903–1904.[22] Three generations of Uruguayans now have reached maturity free of the manic characteristics instilled by constant political meddling by these groups, and a certain objectivity exists.

In a country in which the political process is as open as in Uruguay, interest groups are bound to proliferate. If the existence of such groups be a criterion of "westernness" in a polity, Uruguay can be said to meet all tests. Their existence and range have filled in any gap which might have developed through the weakness of the Church or armed forces as power centers, and testify to the pluralistic nature of the society. However, the effort by interest groups to influence pol-

[21] The position of the Church is discussed in useful detail in J. Lloyd Mecham, *Church and State in Latin America* (Chapel Hill, N. C., The University of North Carolina Press, 1934), pp. 331–339; and in Fitzgibbon, *op. cit.*, pp. 230–244.

[22] Fitzgibbon, *op. cit.*, pp. 24–25, and Maj. Theodore Wyckoff, "The Role of the Military in Contemporary Latin American Politics," *Western Political Quarterly*, Vol. 13 (September, 1960), pp. 745–763, discuss the role of the Uruguayan military.

icy is regarded as so normal a phenomenon, and it is so easy to organize a political party to contest an election, that many ordinary citizens find it difficult to distinguish between the groups and parties. Nardone, for example, continued to maintain the "non-political" (*i.e.*, non-partisan) nature of *ruralismo* until some time after he had been elected to office through its voting strength. And the groups which support governmental commitments to intervention in the economy and broadening of social welfare measures jointly comprise by far the largest lobby in the country.[23]

Over the past decade one clear change has occurred. Here as elsewhere in the world the increasing incidence of street disturbances and other irregular interest manifestations appears to evidence a decreasing willingness to be content with the normal communications machinery for presenting interest group demands. On the right, *estanciero* disobedience has been noted; this is within narrow bonds, involves little overt violence and is intended as a means of obtaining desired types of administrative acts. Yet it indicates a lack of respect for the capacity of the government to enforce the law.

At the opposite end of the spectrum, noisy leftist and *fidelista* street demonstrations began sporadically in 1959. As the relation of the Cuban revolution with international Communism became more direct in 1960, these demonstrations ceased to be anomic and became, rather, a calculated series of incidents. Many participants are students; Latin American tradition has long accorded young people the privilege of abusing the tolerance of their elders. The systematic nature of Communist-*fidelista* actions however, suggests that the goal is not regularized change within usual bounds but revolution.

Another novel experience for Uruguayans in recent years has been the carefully planned activities of *ruralismo;* these evoke the aura of the plains and the farm, while steadfastly refusing to deal with most important issues on their merits. They also imply revolution, although this would be rightist reaction rather than leftist change. The implicit or explicit violence of all of these groups suggests the need for re-examining the institutional guarantees of free assembly and ac-

[23] Taylor, *op. cit.,* pp. 53–59.

tion and the permissive attitudes which have been regarded as sacrosanct in Uruguay. The very existence of the groups also suggests some rejection of the system of socio-political values which has developed in the country and stabilized it during the past half century.

Urban Uruguay therefore is significantly free, in a *political* sense, from many of the checks on socialization and recruitment, and on communication of demands and information, which are often found in other parts of Latin America. Rural Uruguay is retarded in serious degree in many areas, however, and this is basic to a consideration of values and of the functioning of institutions. Two of the three institutionally disturbing elements which have developed in the past decade have been based on rural interests. The rather deliberate pace of the development of social and political institutions in Montevideo has contributed both to stability and to popular confidence, however, and the adaptation of values has permitted comparatively comfortable accommodation. The net product is the existence of much social and impersonal loyalty to the prevailing system. In comparative terms, this is a notable achievement.

IV

Both governmental and nongovernmental institutions function in any national political system in styles and for purposes unique to that system. This is the more likely to be evident when economic matters are considered, and the real demands on government which appear in the articulative and aggregative processes are almost invariably couched in economic terms. This phase of the system must be examined if interests, appearances and actual functioning are fully to be understood. Three sets of factors therefore are proposed as of central importance.

First comes capital formation. It has already been observed that in Uruguay the State owns the public utilities and certain other crucial elements in the economy. Many other sectors are open to private enterprise, however, and few manufacturing or industrial plants are State-owned. Therefore, government ownership is not the sole source of the rigidity which limits growth and change in the economy, or which curtails opportunities for rapid advancement for University graduates.

A serious limit on the economy is the lack of a private capital market. Funds are always in short supply for either private or governmental borrowers. Ultra conservative laws limit the lending capacity of banks unnecessarily, and there must be excessive resort to rediscounts with the central bank. Interest rates are high. The modest expanse of the national territory, the small size of the potential domestic market for any industrial product and the even more modest mineral resources, are limiting economic features of the country in the present and future.[24] The country has lived beyond its overseas trade earnings for many years; deficit financing of government expenditures is so chronic that government securities sell regularly at a discount of nearly 30 per cent.[25] The depth and breadth of social welfare commitments have contributed to economic rigidity. These programs cause the average untrained person to find only limited incentive to seek personal improvement, since there is far less personal deprivation than prevails in most neighboring countries. Although international disaster has been skirted, domestic stability has been maintained. This is the reverse side of the coin of unlimited practice of utopia-oriented democracy.

Uruguay has "two tyrants," says one writer: "Their names are Cattle and Sheep."[26] Their power has been demonstrated;

[24] The country's area is 72,172 square miles. Its population was declared officially to be 2,538,734 in 1944, with a continued rise estimated annually by the census bureau. University of Montevideo sociologists estimate it, however, at not more than 2.4 million in 1960, while other, partial, censuses place it at about 2.25 million. A recent *Visión* estimate, reported without attributed source, shows Montevideo as having 1,363,000 population (February 9, 1962).

Comprehensive studies for the government petroleum company, ANCAP, have failed to discover exploitable oil, *Fortnightly Review*, October 24, 1959. Studies concerning iron and other ores have been similarly unencouraging, *El Debate*, February 22, 1960.

[25] In the period 1954–1960 the country suffered deficits on current foreign trade accounts in all seven years. The total deficit was $385,218,000 or approximately three times the value of exports in 1960. Banco Comercial, *Información económica del Uruguay* (Montevideo, April 1961), #18, p. 1.

[26] Fitzgibbon, *op. cit.*, p. 71.

yet at the same time they are (to change the metaphor) the country's Achilles' heel. The growth of capital-intensive agriculture has been unnecessary since the climate is mild enough to permit animals to pasture freely and without cover, and since most land is so marginal as to require irrigation and fertilization for effective cultivation. Absolute agricultural production figures, with few exceptions, grow progressively smaller. Rural depopulation has progressed because of urban advantages; radicals and *fidelistas* to the contrary, most Uruguayans would consider land reform as a goal irrelevant to the country's needs. It is evident that José Batlle's reforms, which skimmed the cream from agricultural exports, and directed it toward social equalization rather than toward industrialization, had a stunting effect on the future growth of the economy.[27]

Obviously the fault is shared with "politicians" by "bureaucrats." It is true that in any "western" society this latter group competes for available resources, but Uruguay's bureaucracy may be regarded as unique, at least in degree. By law and custom its members are virtually immune from removal. Party pacts assure its continued growth. It is more effective at creating problems than at solving them. Its inertia frustrates the few who seek its reform. Its incapacity to plan and execute government policy is evident, its inefficiency the butt of innumerable jokes. Yet it is the heart of the middle sector, and therefore highly functional both as a means of sharing the available national wealth and as a support for the present political system. Relocation of this enormous staff would be impossible; no private alternatives exist.[28]

The basis for resolving many of the limiting conditions which have been described would be a potentially vigorous private sector. After all, small population and territory, and

[27] W. W. Rostow suggests a general thesis concerning economic development in his *The Stages of Economic Growth* (London, Cambridge University Press, 1960). It may be suggested, somewhat facetiously, that in terms of Rostow's stages, Uruguay chose to pass from the second stage (transition, or precondition for takeoff) directly to the fifth, one of the alternative forms of which is the stage of high mass consumption.

[28] The problem is discussed in detail in Taylor, *op. cit.*, pp. 99–105.

even a pronounced lack of mineral resources, have not determined genteel poverty for some small European States. These either have benefited by being natural or artificial *entrepots* (which could be possible on a small scale for Uruguay), or by the possession of industries producing high-value articles for international trade. In either case, large capital investment would be needed. In Uruguay, all salary and wage earners find habits of individual savings and investment frustrated by the very heavy taxes which they pay to the retirement and welfare funds, and by the equally heavy indirect taxes which support the bureaucracy.[29] Moreover, virtually all lines of insurance which would enable the insurer to develop large cash reserves out of premium payments are monopolized by the State Insurance Bank. Capital formations therefore are controlled by the State's entities. The retirement funds must invest 80 per cent of their reserves in government securities, under the law; a part of the balance must be maintained in cash, and much of the remainder must be invested in social benefits, such as housing, for the beneficiaries of the fund. Therefore there is no real capital market. The great majority of transactions in the Montevideo securities market is in government securities bought by the retirement funds. The cash holdings of private banks are modest, and the laws concerning reserves and loans are very conservative. Many businesses normally avoid paying interest rates which are usurious under the law (usury is defined as starting at 12 per cent annual interest) only by engaging in an alternative illegality, withholding from the retirement funds the

[29] Social security and retirement contributions apply to all earned income. They are graded upward so that higher incomes pay at a higher rate. Rates also have increased as benefits have become more generous. A law of October 6, 1919 (1919 *Registro,* vol. II, pp. 293–302), established a four per cent deduction from all wages of certain employees. Law 11,496, September 27, 1950 (1950 *Registro,* p. 1000), raised this to 7% for salaries up to 300 pesos monthly and 9% for salaries over 900 pesos monthly. In law 12,380, February 12, 1957 (1957 *Registro,* pp. 253–262), the range became 8% on salaries to 150 pesos monthly, to 13% on salaries over 1,200 pesos monthly. In all cases employers at least match the employee contributions, and in the lower brackets must do better. Additionally, all contribute to funds for subsidies to lower-income employees.

sums which they have deducted from the wages of their employees as compulsory contributions, in order to use them as short-term capital funds.[30]

The IMF has urged that the economy could be revived by a combination of astringent measures: austerity regarding the bureaucracy, subsidies and social guarantees, so as to permit balancing the government budget; a thoroughgoing overhaul of the taxation system, to include taxes on earned personal income; elimination of currency and quota controls so that foreign trade could benefit by a single exchange rate set by the open market; encouragement of economic activities which would contribute to exportation and thus to the country's trade balances; and stabilization of the peso.[31] The Fund implied it would give assistance if these steps were taken. But in the long run, the real issue is not economic but political; can the interest groups be brought to heel?

A second important factor relates to the relative success of interest group activity and to the extreme difficulties encountered in the legislative process. If lawless and irregular phenomena have been rather rare in Uruguayan politics until recently, it has been principally because of this factor. Not all interest groups endure, of course; but enough represent enduring economic and social interests to have made deep impressions on formal governmental institutions. No systematic research has been undertaken yet on the degree to which they have colonized legislative committees, the Executive Council, or the parties, although interviews suggest their great effectiveness.[32] Study of successful legislative initiatives serves to relate many bills to declared interest group positions. Further, it is clear that interest groups have been very successful in influencing administrators in their execution of the laws, or in obtaining their non-execution, when vital interests were considered at stake.

[30] Not surprisingly, granted the climate of Uruguayan thought about rewards and punishments, this practice is condoned in periodic amnesties which absolve the employer if he pays within a specified period. Taylor, *op. cit.*, pp. 146–148. In the meantime, only 7% interest is charged.

[31] *Fortnightly Review*, March 14, 1959; September 26, 1959. *Hispanic American Report*, September, 1959.

[32] Taylor, *op. cit.*, pp. 57–58.

Although the Executive Council is empowered by the constitution to introduce bills in the legislature, it has no monopoly of this privilege, nor even preferential treatment in many instances. José Batlle's plan for an Executive Council was designed deliberately to curtail its efficiency; he saw the presidency in the light of its past contributions to dictatorship or *caudillismo*. If the results of his reforms prior to his 1913 proposal of a *colegiado* realized his expectations—and it seems that in large part they did—then the council plan was an anachronism at birth. Its revival in 1951 was in large part the result of a pact between elements of the Colorado and Blanco parties to sidetrack Luis Batlle and to bolster Luis Herrera; it foisted uncertainty and dispersion of power on a political system which could afford little more of either. A decade of experience does not suggest that the Executive Council, which was mildly disastrous when first employed in 1918–1933, is better in its reincarnation.

Demands from both anomic and organized groups are introduced in increasing measure directly into legislative hoppers, without first having passed through any preliminary aggregative processes. The normal procedure is to clarify and implement these bills in caucuses of the parliamentary party delegations before submitting them to legislative committees. Executive Council inability to perform its responsibilities regarding legislative initiatives is only part of the government's functional problem in this regard. The necessity for party involvement stems from several causes. The first is the use of PR, which has been carried virtually to the extreme. Necessity demands some amalgamation of groups pretending to some common party label, once the legislative sessions commence, but party effectiveness at aggregating interests is dependent on frequent intra-party negotiations. A second cause is administrative incompetence. Operating bureaus seldom are permitted, nor do they have the qualified personnel, to prepare either statements of genuine national needs, or legislative proposals which meet these needs. Even occasional well conceived plans seldom receive detailed implementation. Interest spokesmen therefore are permitted (if, indeed, not required) to do this job. A third cause is that legislators themselves have no staff, and little experience in drafting bills, and therefore originate little legislation.

A third set of factors relates to the popular tendency to regard the country as a proliferated family. Denial of demands is not necessarily regarded by the disappointed groups as a decision in the national interest, but rather as caprice or discrimination. As such it is not accepted as definitive, and no decision is ever viewed as final. If negotiation among the parties cannot change it immediately, then the next election may facilitate later accommodation. "Hard" decisions are notable for their absence from the record.

The result of economic factors, fused with political and social forces, therefore has been to render the normal "outputs" of government–rule-making, definition and adjudication–subject entirely to aggregative activities by the parties rather than by the government. This is not to say that party dominance does not appear in other countries, but rather that few countries have witnessed such an extension of this condition as has Uruguay. The country's system of "inputs" is such as to make party effectiveness mandatory. The fact of executive incapacity has exposed the legislature to unusual pressures, which it is not able to transcend.

V

Cynicism and leisure were the elements which conditioned the development of conservative politics during the colonial and early republican periods in Latin America. The elaborate structure for the defense of established interests held back forces for change, and provided much of the fuel for the fiery Zapatas and Fidel Castros. Against this tradition, José Batlle's mild but nevertheless fundamentally effective social revolution was one of the great developments of the area's history. A master among the politicians developed in this politics-ridden area, he employed the art of the transaction, already so well developed, for his own purposes. He has been criticized for leading toward a nationalist and socialist State, and ultimately perhaps toward a total readjustment of the country's economic and social system. It has been suggested here that these steps may have made the society now too rigid, with the middle sectors committed to the preservation of a largely government-controlled, rather than a privately controlled economy; and that the functioning of the system now is dominated by pressure groups. It may follow that these groups are not potential friends of the reformist Alliance for Progress, if that organization advocates development of the private sector beyond what Uruguay is prepared to accept—especially if this should imply the loss of government jobs.

Comparative study of national societies has shown that standards vary so widely as to make it possible to speak advisedly of "corruption" as a highly relative matter. It is the essential "grease" for the governmental machine in Mexico; it has been "democratized" there to the extent that it pieces out inadequate government salaries, enables bureaucrats to support the existing government, and makes possible the existence of the sophisticated power structure called the Partido Revolucionario Institucional—which really *is* the government in functional terms. Perón's Argentina and Cuba of the 1940s and 1950s, on the other hand, were characterized by massive payoffs to a political elite, so that both power and wealth grew more concentrated as the respective systems flourished. Whether or not these political systems have been "democratic," they have proved that what is corruption by conventional Anglo-American standards may serve necessary and useful purposes.

What has occurred in Uruguay has been quite a different type of generalized "corruption." The State undertakes to pay something to everybody, although it may be only a little. It maintains a bureaucracy intended to be inefficient, while producing a maximum number of sub-sinecure jobs. It refuses to enact a law which means what it says, since there is the attendant implicit promise to review and revise it if it ever becomes inconvenient. It establishes an electoral and vote-counting system which permits the widest possible suffrage but which rigs the results so that the majority often does not rule. The great advantage, from the viewpoint of democratic development, is the degree of popular commitment to the system as it has developed. The growth of impersonal loyalties, so important in democratic practice, and so lacking generally in Latin American societies, can be matched in few other countries. Corruption therefore may be an evil by some criteria, a benefit by others. It is doubtful if reforms, spurred by the Alliance for Progress, which might endanger these aspects of the Uruguayan system, could be there regarded as beneficial.

Economic problems and frustrations today are forcing changes. The government is abandoning some of its previously sacrosanct subsidies. General price inflation has pinched Uruguayans at all levels. Morale has begun to deteriorate, and the effect on elections remains to be determined.[33] Today, ordinary corruption is beginning to appear; innumerable instances can be cited.[34] Possibly the most serious effect of all has been the passage of power into the hands of people who indicate by their actions that they regard as inconsequential the essential freedoms which the country has symbolized throughout the world. For the present all the ordinary nongovernmental functions which contribute to democratic practice continue. But the degree to which the boundary lines between institutional and noninstitutional groups or organs have broken down, under the pressures of intense ambition and some austere living, is revealed by the functioning of the system.[35] The 1962 general elections in

[33] The elections of November, 1962, produced a paper-thin Blanco plurality for a joint UBD-*Herrerista* slate. In effect, the 1963–1967 government will merely continue the tight-rope-walking act of the past four years.

[34] A damning (but at least partially verifiable) indictment of the pensions system is contained in "El Problema de las Cajas de Jubilaciones," published in the official journal of the Communist party of Uruguay, *Estudios Políticos-Económicos-Filosoficos-Culturales* (August–November, 1956), pp. 70–73. The article is by the party's specialist on the Pensions Funds, Héctor Cerruti. A second article by him appears in the issue for September, 1959 at pp. 17–19, "La Defensa de las Cajas de Jubilaciones y de sus Afiliados."

In another instance a private businessman offered evidence of having been approached by a highly placed official for collusion in fraud in connection with the importation of machinery. The amount involved would have been about $140,000 to be split between the two.

[35] The concern for the implications of Benito Nardone's rise to prominence is stated by Carlos Rama in "La crisis política uruguaya," *Combate #5* (Marzo–Abril, 1959), pp. 3–6.

some respects indicate the impact of the events of the past few years is still ambiguous.

The urban-rural split in living levels and styles in the past facilitated the creation of a firm, comparatively stable, and objective urban middle sector, with a commitment to legal and political regularity and some indifference to land reform *per se*. The temptation to regard this as an example deserving of emulation, since it clearly implies disregarding the interior as a source of political leadership, is strong. Under José Batlle it served as a political vehicle, and his successors in Colorado leadership continued its use until 1958. Its only fundamental rationale rested on a static interior; *estancieros* were generally willing to accept this concept themselves.[36] But the syndrome cannot continue to be relevant if migration to the cities, and a change of mind on the part of the city professionals and middle classes, place power in Blanco hands. Either *estancieros* must become responsible so that they can play the more important roles now to be assigned them, or Colorados must pay attention to rural needs.

The problem of the study of comparative politics is clarified only in part by the formulation of sophisticated conceptualizations. In the present stage of the political art, in which demands for prescriptions for action will not wait for precise definition and prediction, plans may be only slightly above the curbstone level. Uruguay is sufficiently atypical of its area to limit the guidelines that can be deduced from studying it. Its diminutiveness and homogeneity have perhaps been of short-run benefit and medium-run detriment. It falls among the most "westernized" of the world's political systems, and thus has more in common with the *politically* advanced European States than with the Central American or Andean. Therefore, some of its solutions to socio-economic

[36] It is clear that the productive capacity of the rural areas is limited sharply in the absence of intense capitalization of agricultural activities. Nevertheless, data show that neither ranchers nor farmers take maximum advantage of the currently available possibilities through more active attention to breeding, cultivation, etc. SOFRERAIL, *op. cit.*, pp. 310–316, suggests that productive capacity could be increased 30% over figures for 1950–57; it also suggests that 1970 would be the year in which productivity would flatten out if available opportunities were used.

problems may not be appropriate to other countries. Certainly the commitment of the country to socialism would make support of it by some ethnocentric United States policy-makers difficult.

One must conclude with the question, must freedoms and political functions be enjoyed for their own sakes in their own unique milieu? In part, Uruguayan experience suggests that they must. In the degree that this experience is unique in Latin America, the warning to international planners is evident. The "progress" which will result from the Alliance must meet Latin American criteria, principally, if it is to meet our own, for only then will these countries find in association with the United States the kind of political change which will appear worthwhile.